GUIDE TO WORLD COMMODITY MARKETS

Physical, Futures and Options Trading

Seventh edition

Consultant Editor
JOHN BUCKLEY

KOGAN PAGE

Publisher's note

Every possible effort has been made to ensure that the information contained in this publication is accurate at the time of going to press, and the publishers cannot accept responsibility for any errors or omissions, however caused. All liability for loss, disappointment, negligence or other damage caused by the reliance on the information contained in this publication, or in the event of bankruptcy or liquidation or cessation of trade of any company, individual or firm mentioned, is hereby excluded.

This seventh edition published in Great Britain in 1996
First published in Great Britain and the United States of America in 1977; second edition in 1979; third edition in 1982; fourth edition in 1985; fifth edition in 1986; sixth edition in 1989.

Kogan Page Ltd
120 Pentonville Road
London N1 9JN

British Library Cataloguing in Publication Data

A CIP record for this book is available from the British Library.

ISBN 0 7494 2003 0

Typeset by Northern Phototypesetting Co Ltd, Bolton
Printed and bound in Great Britain
by Clays Ltd, St Ives plc

Contents

List of Figures and Tables in Part 2

Metals

Softs

Acknowledgements

We would like to thank the many organizations who have been so ready, not only to provide the statistical and contract information for this book, but who have conscientiously continued to update material and cater for all the checks and queries necessary to produce a guide to this detail. Among these, we are grateful to all the listed exchanges (with special thanks to the London Metal Exchange for its series of price data); the Association of International Rubber Trade; British Petroleum; C Czarnikow Ltd; Cotton Outlook; Gold Fields Mineral Services; the International Cocoa Organization; the International Coffee Organization; the International Cotton Advisory Committee; the International Grains Council; the International Rubber Study Group; the International Sugar Organization; the International Tea Committee; the International Wool Secretariat; Johnson Mathey; the Meat and Livestock Commission; the Tea Brokers' Association of London; the UN Food and Agriculture Organisation; the World Bureau of Metal Statistics.

Introduction

John Buckley

Commodity markets

For the public at large, commodity markets summon up various media clichés – like the Colonial plantation owner who crops up from time to time in TV coffee commercials; or the City whizz-kid, faced by a battery of computer trading screens or barking orders into his mobile phone over an expense account lunch.

While examples like these still exist after a fashion, for the most part they might be considered somewhat larger than life and, as archetypes, certainly far narrower than the truth. Nowadays, as production and user industries become every more closely integrated, both vertically and horizontally, the commodity trader occurs in as many guises as the multiple links of the supply–demand chain, buying and selling and planning strategies from the offices of producer, merchant, broker, shipper, importer, wholesaler or consumer. In some organizations – like the big farm to supermarket agri-business conglomerates – he or she will represent both 'sides' of the market. In many cases, the commodity trader will be highly specialized, not only in a single commodity or group of items but in aspects of trading that raw material, its documentation, transport, storage, insurance, contractual law, etc.

Examples also still exist of another type of classic entrepreneurial commodity merchant – especially in the smaller physical markets of the Near East and the Indian subcontinent. This type of trader will use exclusive information sources and suppliers, intuition and experience to spot and exploit opportunities to bring producer and consumer together. Often he will be working in the minor commodities like nuts, raisins or spices but sometimes in metals or grains too, often acting as a middleman to fill difficult or unusual orders.

All commodities ultimately have a market – the point where buyers and sellers converge to make a price. But sometimes this is not clearly defined by a single or central exchange or trading base. Some commodities have 'telephone markets' where prices are realized, tested and proved by bids and offers from interested parties and very little of the detail may ever be published. Sometimes traders will meet physically in an exchange where trade takes place in real goods based on samples provided – like the tea and coffee auctions of London and Asia or the corn exchanges which sprang up all over Europe prior to the industrial revolution (and still exist in many countries). Some of these institutions have been superseded by modern telecommunications and become 'telephone markets', yet others still work surprisingly well in their traditional format.

The biggest commodity markets are generally the large futures exchanges upon which our own listings mainly concentrate. Here the principal raw materials are traded in large enough volumes to realize true price 'transparency' – clearly visible indicators of how buying and selling pressures are creating day-to-day and minute-by-minute quotations. These markets are also generally considered 'deep' – that is liquid enough for buyers and sellers to get in and out of their positions without causing undue price disruption.

Trade in some raw materials operates through more structured and less market oriented routes, through intergovernmental deals, multinational links and cartel-like operations of price control or regulation (e.g. steel and coal, some forest products, diamonds, some precious metals and 'rare earths'). Because of the lack of free and open trading, we have avoided digression into these areas. We have also avoided the host of small commodity markets that operates at country or district level, mainly because foreign operators are unlikely to get involved in them – either because of regulatory barriers or simply because they are relevant only at the parochial level.

While many of the mechanisms, structures and actual workings of commodity markets are complex and sometimes highly esoteric, their relevance to us all is beyond question. The clothes on our backs, the food in our stomachs, the roofs over our heads and the machines that support twentieth-century life all owe their existence in our lives ultimately to the efficient action of raw materials markets.

What is a commodity?

Two or three decades ago this question was much easier to answer than it is today. Then we might have concentrated solely on the true raw materials markets, grains, oilseeds, coffee, cocoa and sugar, industrial commodities like the metals, wool, cotton and rubber, etc. At this time, these were the prime reason for the existence of most commodity trading centres and their member companies. Trade was dominated by the Chicago agricultural futures exchanges, the New York and London metal, coffee, cocoa and sugar markets and a few smaller and more diverse centres trading items like coffee, tea and cotton.

In the interim period, new commodities have sprouted at a truly astonishing pace, forcing the raw material commodities to take first shared, then second billing on many of the world's major exchanges. At the same time, new trading centres have blossomed from the Pacific Rim to South America and, latterly, in the former controlled economies of the former Soviet Union, Eastern and Central Europe – although how many of these (already diminished in number) will survive in the next five years is highly questionable.

Futures trading, once the domain of the giant multinational commodity firms and corporate investors in Europe, USA and other wealthy regions, has meanwhile expanded to embrace whole new generic areas of the global business community. Like their American counterparts in the post-war years, more and more smaller investors in other countries are learning how commodity markets work, why they move in a given direction, what opportunities and risks they present for calculated investment, outright speculation or simply hedging of trade and financial risks.

One result has been the growth of interest in commodity funds, either as a straight investment in their own right or as part of a broader based portfolio. For the small/medium-size investor, funds can be a ground floor – and less risky – entry into these sometimes volatile markets. Their attraction as part of a basket investment is considerable. Not just metals and softs but items like oil, interest rates, currencies and stock indices can all find their way into investment baskets to perform two key functions. One is to level overall risk (with currencies and stocks nowadays attracting just as much adverse publicity as the 'high risk' commodity markets) and the other is to expand trading opportunities beyond that of the more traditionally-based stock/bond portfolios. Many household names in the commodity and investment fund world have launched such instruments and some offer tailored products for the individual investor.

Although major bull or bear markets are relatively rare, it is widely held that there is always one going on somewhere. The rationale is that including varying performance of commodities like wheat, silver, coffee, etc, the investor can benefit from exposure to a much wider range of economic conditions than that offered by the often fairly homogeneous movement of stock and bond markets.

In this area, the computer-driven programme is all, usually ignoring the fundamentals of known or perceived supply and demand in favour of buy and sell predictions based on charts of past price performance. Global futures funds under management have grown at a fantastic pace in the last 10 to 15 years and the services of their ancillary industries – the technical analysts – have never been in greater demand. In the last 15 years alone, the number of CTAs or commodity trading advisers, has risen more than fivefold.

To some extent this movement has run away with itself. With the growth of new market centres has bloomed a whole raft of new exotic contracts, tailored to suit almost anything that can be defined, standardized into a contract, indexed, hedged and bet upon. Thus the once clearly defined commodity markets (which have long included items like currencies) have come to mean many things, including electricity prices, mortgages and property futures and options, debt and insurance. Indeed the only point of convergence among this disparate band is their answering to one of my original dictionary definitions of a commodity – 'an article of commerce, that which can be bought and sold.'

Active contracts

Heading the list of the most successful new 'commodities' have been government bonds/interest rates and currencies, which have encountered continued turbulence since futures in them were launched in the wake of the economic shocks caused by the oil crisis of the 1970s. At one time, the most actively traded contract was the US treasury bond future quoted on the Chicago Board of Trade but this has been overtaken now by the Chicago Mercantile exchange's Eurodollar which traded almost 107m lots in 1995 compared with T Bond's 86m. Behind that comes Brazil's BM&F dollar futures (74.2m), Tokyo TIFFE's Euroyen (36.3m) and its one-day interest rate swap (35.2m), the Paris MATIF's 'notional' 10-year futures (33.6m), and London's LIFFE futures German Bund (government bond) with 32.2m.

Then, some way behind several other currency, bond and NYMEX's crude oil contract, comes the CBOT's best-selling agricultural futures in maize (15m), soyabeans (10.6m) and wheat (around 5m).

Where next?

Despite the proliferation of new financial instruments in the last ten years, there is evidence that growth in this sector is now slowing and that commodities are experiencing something of a renaissance in the eyes of investors.

On the one hand, some analysts feel it may become more difficult to invent many new financial instruments that will appeal on a large enough scale – or deliver the same profit margins – to operators as during the 1980s and early 1990s. On the other hand, many of the traditional commodity markets have shown strong price volatility in the last three years, leading many CTAs to view their investment potential more favourably.

Commodities have also begun to achieve a new respectability with institutional investors, especially from 1993–4 onward when bond markets – investors' traditional 'first love' – suffered a considerable loss of confidence while raw material prices boomed.

The recovery in commodity prices that took place from that point has faded in some sectors but reappeared in others and there is still evidence that a long-term economic cycle in this sector has yet to run its course. At the root of the movement was a long period of underpriced commodities, many at or below cost of production, sometimes for as long as 10 to 20 years in real terms. With production already starting to suffer from the poor producer return, stocks of some items gradually running down and demand for others rapidly catching up and overtaking consumption, the stage was set for some spectacular price gains in markets including copper, aluminium, coffee, cocoa, palm oil, rubber, cotton and latterly grains.

Commodities have long been considered safe havens for 'hot' money in times of economic, financial or political uncertainty. When stock markets crashed in 1987, the commodity markets were robbed of investment benefit by the sheer speed and scale of the equity slump and the ensuing loss of many investors' funds and liquidity. In the 1993–4 period, however, hedge funds and other speculators had far more time to adjust to bond jitters and make decisions and portfolio adjustments to include greater commodity weightings. So fund influence became much more marked in several markets – especially from the big hedge funds which were able to take very large positions and weather out short-term profit taking in these markets in the pursuit of their long-term strategies.

A return of high inflation was also a big worry at the time, along with economic instability in the Third World and violent fluctuations in currencies as Mr George Soros reminded governments that they couldn't 'buck' the markets with his spectacular coups in currencies and gold. In the event inflation and interest rates appear to have peaked earlier than expected, generating some profit-taking selling of commodities in 1995 and a partial flow of funds back to equities and bonds. However, many of the individual commodity markets are still strong and the case certainly seems to have been strengthened for more regular involvement in them by the so-called 'wall of money' investors who switch their speculative activity between these market sectors.

The last ten years have seen not only more globalization of markets but more liberalization. This has made cross-border trading easier and more efficient between exchanges and other institutions and may also encourage rapid inflow of investment to commodities when boom opportunities are presented. The increasing influence of screen trading in the commodity sector is another factor in the level of investment. The extraordinary growth of home and portable PCs is meanwhile transforming the ease with which markets can be downloaded to ever-widening audiences with trading 'on the hoof'. The German DTB exchange is a good example of this – a fully electronic 'global village' of individual firms using hundreds of computers to make buy and sell orders and exchange information with no central market.

Long before this revolution the arrival of 24-hour trading became reality in financial markets whose hours overlap across the world's time zones. We can expect the same pattern to be repeated in the next decade in the commodity arena.

Liberalization of physical commodity markets is meanwhile occurring at an unprecedented pace. On the one hand, the GATT Uruguay Round is dictating a lowering of tariffs and enlarged market access as well as a reduction of output and export subsidies. However, quite aside from the GATT, a great many countries have begun to liberalize and privatize their domestic and import export trading systems, encouraging more free trade. Along with burgeoning world population and the impact of economic growth on very low per capita offtake in some developing countries, this is expected to have a major positive effect on both commodity consumption and on prices – well into the twenty-first century.

Recent trends in commodity prices and earnings

Several developing countries have already benefited from the commodity boom in recent years. Up to 1994, the latest year for which any consolidated data is reliably available, the World Bank's data show agricultural exports accounted for 70 per cent of the total increase in export revenues by all low/middle income developing countries. Coffee alone accounted for half the increase in ag export earnings – totalling $10.6bn in 1994 compared with only half that in the preceding two years.

Early pointers for 1995 and 1996 indicate coffee prices held most of their gain in terms of the 1995 annual average price but will dip by around a third in 1996. Cocoa held up better, averaging 143c/kg in 1995 – slightly better than 1994 – and is expected to hold that in 1996 before advancing to 153c in 1997 and progressing towards 200c within the next ten years, the WB's data shows.

Gains from the boom were surprisingly widespread regionally, although the emphasis on coffee – along with gains in aluminium and copper – saw Latin America move way ahead with earnings of $17.8bn in 1994 against $12.2bn in 1993. Next was Asia/Pacific with earnings rising from $9.1bn to $13.4bn, thanks to strong rubber, coffee and palm oil prices. Even sub-Saharan Africa shared in the bonanza with a rise in earnings from $5.4bn to $7.2bn, based largely on gains from coffee and cocoa exports.

In dollar terms, the biggest winner was Malaysia which saw primary commodity earnings rise to $5.2bn from $3.4bn, led by palm oil (up $1.36bn) and rubber (plus $340m). Other top earners from raw material exports were Brazil, FSU, Indonesia and Colombia.

Palm oil prices were expected to average $628 per tonne in 1995, up from $528 in 1994 and only $378 in 1993. However, a gradual descent is foreseen for the next decade, starting this year.

Among the industrials, a period of plateauing or easing is expected for the next few years before items like the metals, rubber and cotton start to pull up again towards 2000 and beyond.

Developing countries should use the revenue from boom periods wisely, the WB says. Busts follow booms and there is no point in frittering away windfall revenue or even in investing it all in monoculture crops that might be booming for a year or two but be back into slump in the future.

Diversification is encouraged by the WB – spreading revenue into other sectors to prepare for the day when the big export earning commodity might run out of luck. Also important is the need to smooth the influx of foreign exchange which can, for example, strengthen a country's currency and make its exports from other commodity – or manufacture – sectors, uncompetitive on the world markets.

An eight-point outline given by the Bank starts with the exhortation not to overspend – or overcommit new resources from commodity booms to unsustainable programmes. Next is the need for fiscal prudence – non-expansionary policies and maybe an emphasis on using some of the revenues for reducing foreign debt. More favourable trade balances derived from commodity earnings can also be a good platform for liberalization of trade restrictions. This can improve economic efficiency and accrue permanent income gains as well as helping trade diversification. Under some circumstances commodity stabilization funds can be used to build up reserves to prepare for harsher economic times. Funds mean foregoing other investments and often need to be large but they can sometimes be made more effective by combining with hedge programmes involving futures, options and swaps.

The Bank also says developing countries should avoid the temptation to overtax exports at times when strong commodity prices make this look more feasible. This can encourage tax evasion and smuggling. Cartels should also be avoided. In the past many commodity exporting countries have entered into such agreements in an attempt to stabilize and – in many cases – raise prices. In anything but the short term, none has succeeded, the Bank points out.

The 1990s' recovery in commodity prices contrasts quite starkly with the supply-led commodity markets of the last twenty years during which we have seen the infamous grain mountains of the USA and Europe, the milk lakes and the beef and butter stockpiles first rise, then melt away. Indeed it may well be that the biggest challenge for the commodity markets in the next decade or two will be meeting this level of demand without runaway prices.

To this cauldron of events must be added the uncertainties over the regeneration of FSU and East European industries and farming systems disrupted by restructuring after the fall of communism, the still hotly debated impact global warming might have on agriculture, pollution and other environmental effects of expansion.

For producers, consumers, investors or for the academic observer, we hope our book will help draw the curtain back a little on what promises to be a fascinating period for the commodity markets.

Part 1: Aspects of Commodity Trading

Commodity indices and allied investments

John Buckley

A number of commodity indices has sprouted in recent years with the resurgence in interest in raw materials as investments. Some, like their stockmarket cousins, are used simply to track performance of a group of commodity markets while others are 'investible' and can be used to speculate or hedge on the movement of commodity prices.

Commodity trading advisers suggest baskets of commodity prices can offer the investor more diverse exposure, lower risk and higher ratio return than traditional equity, bond and currency hedges. Sometimes the basket will be composed solely of true commodities – viz food, industrial raw materials or precious metals; sometimes it may be in the form of a structured note for the investor, designed for his or her specific needs and factoring in elements of commodity, stock, bond and/or currency markets.

The indices may also differ considerably in their components (i.e. whether they are based on industrials or soft commodities) and in the weighting of the individual commodity elements. Generally, however, indices seek a makeup which will offer enhanced performance against other asset classes, especially in seeking so-called 'negative correlation' with bonds and equities (i.e. favourable movement when conditions in the latter are adverse or flat). Commodity indices also expect to exhibit a positive correlation (i.e. exposure) to industrial growth as well as a hedge, or risk insurance, against inflation at times when this looks likely to rise. The investible indices also seek to demonstrate their performance and thus their future prospects by 'backcharting' trends in their commodity baskets to periods long before they came into being and comparing the hypothetical returns with those achieved by competing financial investments.

Some indices use percentage changes in nearby prices to track markets (backcharting then becomes easier as most historical databases until recently tended to record spot/nearby prices). Others claim that fully to compare yields with other assets like stocks and bonds, the index should show 'total return', which is the visible price performance plus the return on 'rolling forward' long futures positions and including full collateralization against treasury bonds.

Leading indices launched in recent years include:

- CRB (Commodity Research Bureau, jointly sponsored by financial news outfit Knight Rydder;
- ENMET (the Energy and Metals Index created by US broker Merrill Lynch);
- BTCF (Bankers Trust Commodity Index);
- ICI (Investible Commodity Index, run by Intermarket);
- GCSI (Goldman Sachs Commodity Index);
- JPMCI (run by investment bank J P Morgan).

Some of these include industrials and softs but others use industrials only on the grounds that softs dilute the positive correlations with growth and inflation and the negative correlations with bond and equity markets. Soft commodity prices also expose the investor to non-cyclical risks – being effectively 'bets against weather' as well as open to risks from crop disease/animal health, changing consumer tastes, etc. For the outside investor softs also require far more specialist knowledge than many of the industrials.

As investments commodities differ against financial assets in several ways. Commodities incur carrying costs which include maintaining a standard quality, freighting, storage and insurance against loss or deterioration in transit, etc. Other than interest paid on money borrowed to fund them, the more traditional investments incur zero costs. Transactions costs on commodity investments also include brokerage fees and market bid/offer spread.

However, against that commodities also offer 'convenience yield', for example, from exploiting a contango to extract a prompt premium from a captive market. In times of shortage – or even fear of shortage – suppliers of crude oil can obtain income from their captive market, refiners short of feedstock, by buying forward and selling spot (whether or not the market is actually rising at the time).

Commodity investors also have to consider tax questions in choosing physicals or futures. Futures can offer investors exposure to price movement (assuming a 'deep' and liquid market) without the risks incurred by physical transactions. Gains on futures are taxable as current income whereas profit and loss is only taxable on physicals when (or if) realized. According to JP Morgan's research, tax-exempt investors tend to prefer futures to physicals since they normally offer higher pretax returns for the same risk.

A claimed advantage in investing in indices is that these can reduce transaction charges and provide lower cost entry into commodity markets.

Some indices have the facility to 'rebalance' their components to reflect changes in weighting of different commodities but generally constant restructuring is avoided. Obviously, an index must be rejigged if a change in a commodity component makes it less relevant (e.g. a commodity market contract might be delisted, a new market could emerge of greater relevance, or a commodity might be substituted by new technology).

At the time of writing, leading indices including CRB and Goldman Sachs are showing a relatively strong performance due to buoyant energy and agricultural markets which have a heavy weighting in both baskets. GSCI believes food and fuel are two commodity items that should be closely watched by investors due to their historically low levels of stocks.

During the last surge of interest in commodity indices in the early 1990s, structured commodity notes quickly gained fervid interest from US mutual and hedge funds but the boom did not appear to last long enough to consolidate interest from pension funds and insurance companies seeking alternatives to flat bond markets.

Risk and return on notes can be highly variable, with their timescale and their structure. Some, for example, guarantee the principal invested but not the interest. If markets go down, the investor gets his money back but earns nothing and forgoes what could have accrued from, say, equity investments. Other notes offer a dividend-type coupon payment after the third or fourth year of an investment while others still have been known to offer an extra 10 per cent on top of any gains in the commodities themselves – provided the investor is happy to risk part of his principal (only 90 per cent of which is guaranteed).

If the commodity markets really are on the verge of a renaissance, we can expect to hear more about indices, futures funds based on them and the legion 'bespoke' sub-indices and structured notes that can be derived from mixing these with more traditional investments.

Growth of funds in commodity markets and price volatility

John Buckley

The growing participation by fund investors in the commodity markets has fuelled considerable debate about the extent to which their activities influence prices – and whether any resultant volatility has possible adverse effects on some market sectors.

The funds fall roughly into three categories – managed accounts operated through commodity trading advisers (CTAs), commodity funds acting as private or public commodity pools (or managed futures funds) and hedge funds.

CTAs are investment managers who do not hold investor money directly but manage accounts (which remain in customers' names) through brokers with the CTAs retaining power of attorney. CTAs attract investment from members of the public or operate accounts for commodity pool operators (CPOs). CPOs operate like mutual funds or unit trusts but hold futures instead of bonds or equities. Private pools are limited to 35 unaccredited investors but may have any number of accredited investors provided their net worth is at least $1m or an annual income in excess of $200,000. Many large funds operate in both CTA and CPO capacities.

The description 'hedge funds' is open to varying interpretations. These tend to hold portfolios comprising a wide range of assets including equities, bonds and real estate and are not restricted to being long. They may use futures either to hedge a position in an underlying asset, to obtain increased leverage or directly as investments in the same way as commodity funds.

In recent years there has been a growth of new public commodity funds taking long positions in a basket of commodities to add diversity to portfolios. There has also been a tendency for the fund investment money in commodity futures to shift more towards larger institutional operators. Because this situation is a new and developing one, it is not yet clear how these more powerful outfits will influence price trends in commodities by their greater ability to finance and sit out trends adverse to their positions.

Since the last edition of *WGCM*, studies have been commissioned into this phenomenon by some of the leading exchanges. In a 1994 study commissioned by the London Commodity Exchange, Christopher Gilbert, professor of applied econometrics at London University's Queen Mary College, looked at the evidence in the London cocoa market where funds built up large positions during a period of price strength.

Gilbert's study found traded volumes on the LCE cocoa contract showed no direct correlation to daily market price volatility. However, he found evidence of a 'direct association between fund activities and the level of the cocoa price over the last 18 months' which strongly suggested the rise was due to fund investment.

Gilbert's methodology measured so-called 'inter-day' volatility – percentage change of prices from one day to the next. However, he also found that using the so-called 'Parkinson' method – charting highs and lows on any given day – much the same result came up.

Chart analysts suggest that whenever funds are attracted into a market *en masse* they can actually have a smoothing effect on inter-day volatility. Because the market is trending more funds will come in and buy/sell large volumes of contracts at certain levels, keeping prices on a line and when no funds are involved, volatility can actually be higher, some analysts point out.

During a period of extreme cocoa volatility in the 1970s, prices shot up from £500 to £3,000/tonne then fell steeply back for a decade. Yet at the peak, average daily turnover on the London market was only 7000 lots compared with up to 11,000 contracts a day in the early 1990s without much increase in volatility. Even during the more recent price rise (since mid-1993) volumes were nowhere near those that would be associated with a real bull market – viz 20,000 or 30,000 lots a day.

Fund managers maintain that the rise in global futures market volume has not boosted volatility which in some cases has even declined. Rather than funds causing trends, they are often seen as anticipating them, based on careful observation of market fundamentals of supply and demand and charts. Traders say the central issue is to what extent funds are driving the market away from an underlying trend and within this context, a case against the increased level of fund activity in cocoa has not been proved.

On the more transparent New York CSCE cocoa market, figures for 'large trader' positions are revealed, enabling a clearer picture of what type of market participant is involved. These show that while some cocoa stocks were effectively transferred from traders to funds during a period of strong prices (so the position held by speculators went up) the actual percentage held by funds did not introduce a relevant change in volatility.

Some areas of fund involvement are thought to merit further analysis, including their impact on switches. When, for example, the delivery month of a futures contract comes to expiry, funds roll forward and those months become more volatile than they might otherwise be. Because funds are typically selling front months and buying the second month, the result can be strengthening pressure on the switch. It would not be surprising if tracking the behaviour of switches over the period during which fund involvement had got bigger showed volatility had gone up. Even then, however, this is thought to be more of a short-term issue, having a relatively small effect during the expiry period and not much long-term impact on prices.

The Gilbert report does acknowledge funds 'can become part of the fundamentals', although he elaborates that cocoa might have been undervalued in relation to fundamentals (before prices rose) with fund money providing the corrective function. 'It is more plausible,' he says, 'to argue that prices were too low 18 months ago than that they are too high now.' In any market like cocoa with a large stock overhang, he points out, it is important who takes on the stockholding role and at what price. In this case, long commodity funds ended up with much of the cocoa stocks, resulting in reduced consumer cover. Funds gained potential risk reduction by extending portfolios with cocoa stock but they also relieved consumers and other physical traders of costs and risks of having to hold those supplies. Effectively, funds simply put a higher value on cocoa than the industry.

Speculative money – be it from traditional trade/independent investors or the newer players, managed accounts, commodity and hedge funds – is vital to provide liquidity, depth and stock-carrying support. Some even suggest funds not only reduce the cost of genuine trade hedging but help smooth volatility.

While he insists it is very unlikely that short-term, trend-following funds can have any sustained effect on commodity prices Gilbert acknowledges the case is less clear with respect to those who invest long term in collateralized commodities for portfolio risk reduction or inflation hedging reasons. His opinion is that funds which take long positions with a long-term horizon 'have been the major factor behind the rise in cocoa prices over the past 15 months'.

The argument that it is only the type of investment that has changed, does not entirely soothe some consumers who argue hedge funds can adopt new strategies because of their size and ability to sit out adverse trends over long timespans. This is why some physical traders say it is not inter-day volatility or long-term trending that necessarily affects their books so much as medium-term exaggeration of price 'spikes'. If fund stockholding, say, as an inflation hedge, can let cocoa prices rise to fundamentally supported levels, then there is sometimes little to stop them pushing prices above those levels for long enough to force consumers into expensive forward cover. This might not have big impact on day-to-day volatility or a lasting effect on exchange quoted prices but it could affect the shop shelf price, profit margins, even consumer demand.

The counter argument is that consumers might end up actually thanking the funds in five years' time for supporting prices, securing investment in cocoa plantations, and thus preventing future squeezes and much higher prices. As funds point out, there are rarely complaints about their involvement from consumers when the market is going down.

The exchanges have generally welcomed fund business which boosts market turnover and adds convincing depth to liquidity for those wanting assurance that there will be matching buyers and sellers when they need to close a position. At the same time, some will be aware that the activities of big operators – like the famous involvement by George Soros in the gold market in the early 1990s

– could be viewed unfavourably by some exchange members. This may be especially true when the exchange has a large physical base in commercial trade hedging (like the LCE).

Recently the London Metal Exchange has published its own study into fund involvement, also by Professor Gilbert. The report again finds no evidence that heavy fund activity since 1993 has caused long-term increases in volatility which it claims is associated more with supply tightness. In the case of aluminium and nickel prices on the exchange, this trending was visible before the funds got involved, he points out.

Gilbert suggests metal price volatility is actually static. While short-term fluctuations in volatility may have been caused by speculative movements, in general volatility was slightly below long-term average levels. He finds no evidence that metals volatility is either high or that it is increasing, rather that the modest rises in volatility in 1994 and 1995 may actually have been due largely to stronger demand growth. 'In general,' he concludes, 'it appears that the speculative funds have been taking the blame for volatility levels which might reasonably have been expected even in their absence.'

With acknowledgements to both studies by Professor Gilbert and to articles by the consultant editor in *Futures & Options World*.

Commodity agreements

Robin Stainer

Treaty-sanctioned intervention in commodity markets to control supplies and prices has moved down the international trade agenda in recent years. International commodity organizations have survived but – with just one exception - their once prime function as regulatory bodies has disappeared.

Today co-operation among commodity trading states is chiefly concerned with ensuring the availability of reliable statistical data and analysis to improve market transparency to facilitate trade. But each commodity treaty also provides for regular intergovernmental meetings that could in the future act as the springboard for renewing price stabilization measures, should the present climate of hostility to interventionism change.

Exploitation of resources available from the Common Fund for Commodities (CFC) is another key role for today's commodity organizations. This Amsterdam-based agency was established in 1989 by the United Nations Conference on Trade and Development (UNCTAD) to provide finance for commodity projects submitted by approved bodies.

As originally conceived in the 1970s, the CFC would have had as much as US$6 billion at its disposal for financing price stabilization operations for at least a dozen commodities. But after the political mood swung against interventionism, what finally emerged was a far more modest operation. The agency still has two accounts, as planned, but the first has never been activated for the intended purpose of helping to finance market intervention. Activity has therefore focused on the second account which was created to fund commodity research and development and measures aimed at encouraging diversification, boosting local processing, raising farm productivity and finding new end uses.

So far the CFC has given its approval for 37 projects costing a total US$81.3 million, of which the second account has contributed US$35.7 million. Since the start of 1996, CFC-approved bodies, which include all the international commodity organizations, have also been allowed to apply to the first account for finance for schemes specifically aimed at helping countries improve commodity marketing. So far US$12 million of the US$28 million held in the account have been made available.

International Natural Rubber Agreement (INRA)

The third INRA, which was finally adopted in February 1995 after negotiations spread over three years, is currently the only international commodity accord with old-fashioned economic clauses. These allow the regulation of supply by a buffer stock mechanism to keep the market price within agreed parameters – something that INRA II failed to do ultimately because it ran out of stocked rubber to sell. Under INRA III, rubber may be bought for the buffer stock, the maximum size of which is set at 550,000 tonnes, if the market indicator price is 15 per cent below the current agreed reference level of 206.68 Malaysian/Singapore cents per kilo, and must be bought if it is 20 per cent below. Stockpiled rubber may be sold at 15 per cent above the reference price and must be at 20 per cent above. The reference price can be revised periodically.

INRA III, which will be administered from Kuala Lumpur (Malaysia), was to have come into force on 28 December 1995. But it failed to do so because the USA – whose participation is deemed essential – was prevented by departmental wrangling over the pact's merits from signing on time. Following assurances from Washington that it was finally ready, the deadline for signatures was on 28 March 1996 extended to 31 July 1996. The expectation in mid-1996 was that, provided the necessary ratifications were received, the pact would begin functioning by early 1997.

International Cocoa Agreement (ICCA)

This accord, which was negotiated in July 1993 at the fifth attempt and entered into force on 22 February 1994 for five years, has, unlike all its four predecessors, no economic clauses, despite attempts by the producers to include them. But it does contain a provision for a voluntary production management programme to be set up to guard against structural oversupply. Output targets have been set both globally and nationally to the end of the century, but there is scant evidence of any serious attempt to meet them. The 35-nation, London-based International Cocoa Organization (ICCO) – which manages the ICCA and has as members all the key cocoa trading nations, except the USA and Indonesia – has accepted that the production programme is flawed and needs reform.

The ICCO's buffer stock, which had been built up under previous ICCAs and stood at 250,000 tonnes when price support buying was indefinitely suspended in 1988, has been in liquidation since October 1993. The agreed monthly disposal rate is 4250 tonnes and the sell-off is scheduled for completion in April 1998, when the final distribution of the proceeds will take place.

International Coffee Agreement (ICA)

The current ICA, which came into force for five years on 1 October 1994, was negotiated after the collapse in March 1993 of efforts to revive the international export quota system that had regulated the market from 1980 to 1989. The new accord is run from London by the International Coffee Organization (ICO), which at the start of 1996 had 53 member states. These included most of the big exporters and all the leading importers, except the USA (which pulled out in September 1993) and Canada.

International Sugar Agreement

The last ISA with market regulatory provisions (export quotas) expired in 1984. The latest pact, which is based in London, was negotiated in 1992 and came into force at the start of 1993 for two years; it was extended until the end of 1997 in November 1995. The ISA's 46 member states account for 62 per cent of world output and 47 per cent of world consumption.

International Grains Agreement (IGA)

The IGA replaced the International Wheat Agreement in mid-1995. Like its predecessor, it has two key elements – a Grains Trade Convention, which sets out the statistical and other services to be provided for members, and a Food Aid Convention. The initial term of the pact, whose name change reflected its wider market coverage, is three years. It is administered by the London-based International Grains Council.

Other international commodity agencies

Unlike all the agreements so far described, none of the others now in existence has ever had economic clauses. They are the International Tropical Timber Agreement (ITTA), International Agreement on Jute and Jute Products and the International Agreement on Olive Oil and Table Olives.

The new ITTA, which was adopted in January 1994 and has its headquarters in Yokohama, Japan, aims to achieve the sustainable management of the world's forests. The objectives of the present olive oil pact, which is run from Madrid and expires at the end of 1998, include the modernization of growing and extraction.

The jute accord, which is based in Dhaka, Bangladesh, seeks an improvement in the market's structural conditions.

The Law of the Sea Convention, which sets rules on (among other things) the exploitation of metals and minerals found on the seabed is another international treaty with relevance to raw materials.

Several well-established intergovernmental bodies concerned with commodities also exist. They include the International Cotton Advisory Committee, the

International Wool Textile Organization, the International Lead and Zinc Study Group, the International Copper Study Group, the International Rubber Study Group and the International Nickel Study Group.

Futures markets

Emma Davey
Managing Editor, Futures & Options World

Much has been written about the history of futures and options, with varying accounts of the source of the first such contracts. Evidence of the preliminary step to futures, forward trading, where two parties agree a price for a product to be delivered at a future date, can be found in the Koran, olive oil trading in Ancient Greece and the seventeenth-century rice exchanges of Japan.

What distinguishes futures and options markets from this more general 'forward' trading is standardization.

A futures contract is one entered into by two parties, to buy and sell a specified quantity and quality of a product at a pre-arranged price, on a pre-arranged date. These contracts are traded under the regulatory oversight of an exchange. They are recognized as providing an efficient price discovery mechanism and provide a vehicle to hedge against price volatility of commodities or financial instruments such as currencies, interest rates and stock indexes. Speculators, taking advantage of movements in price, add to the liquidity of the market, that is the ability to move freely in and out of positions.

When the contract is exchanged, the clearing house, the organization which processes the contracts and settles them, in effect, becomes the counterparty to all contracts registered in the name of its clearing members. It becomes the seller to every buyer and vice versa. This removes the risk of a counterparty not being able to meet its obligation.

On trading a contract, the buyer will place a margin payment with the clearing house as security, the clearing house will maintain adequate levels of margin to cover any shortfall in the market. An initial margin payment is made when the position is opened but variation margin can also be paid to keep the margin levels adequate in volatile markets.

Only a small proportion of futures contracts ever goes through to delivery, the rest changing hands frequently during the period in which they are listed. Contracts are listed by the exchange to cover a certain period of times, usually in cycles of three-monthly expiries.

Those contracts that do go through to delivery are processed by the clearing house. The clearing house, therefore, should be responsible for making sure that commodities being traded, or in storage for future delivery, are of good enough quality to meet contract specifications and reach their destination safely.

Delivery can be in the form of the cash value of the underlying product, which is the case with contracts on financial instruments, such as bonds or currencies, or physical, as is the case with most commodity futures.

The exchange provides the structure and forum through which contracts change hands. Across the globe, the markets have to conform to local laws governing commodity exchanges. The exchanges have a duty to ensure that a fair marketplace operates. An exchange may limit the size of position members can enter into to prevent the likelihood of a squeeze on the market or a failure to meet obligations.

An option bears much of the standardization of a futures contract except that it provides the right but not the obligation to buy or sell a specific quantity and quality of product at a pre-arranged price on a pre-determined date. In some cases, the option can be 'exercised' – taken up – at any point up to its expiry date. When buying an option, an upfront payment, a premium is made, like an insurance premium. Thus any loss is limited to the premium, should the buyer not wish to exercise its option.

By taking a quick overview of the evolution of these markets, it is easy to see how they have progressed from the looser centuries-old commodity trading arrangements mentioned above, to the highly standardized and sophisticated exchange-traded markets of today.

The forerunner to margin payments, for example, was known in the Middle Ages as God's penny. The coffee houses of seventeenth century Holland, an idea subsequently exported to Britain, are the blueprint for today's exchange floors. In much the same way as information is provided on the exchange floor about economic data or commodity news by wire services, the coffee house clubs provided newspapers, shipping lists, information from ports, pricing news and some even created a 'ring' made of sawdust in which trading could take place. The exchanges of today which still trade in the open outcry method, that is traders standing on the exchange floor and make their buy and sell orders by shouting and using clearly defined hand gestures to show the size of position they want, for what month of delivery and at what price, use the same model of a 'ring' or trading pit.

With the rise of the free market and the new more widely available commodities from colonies around the globe came increased trading and growing sophistication of trading methods. The extra risks associated with global shipping and seasonal production brought new hedging requirements. A more advanced use of forwards contracts with greater areas of costs meant the calculation of margins had to take into account the cost of deposit, the insurance to cover the hazards of shipping and the storage costs.

Communications technology was the stimulus for the development of standardized futures markets. The cotton market of Liverpool, for example, was home of the first futures contract in the UK. The trading was subject to the high risks involved in the transatlantic journey from the US producers to the mills of Britain. With telegraph allowing a more accurate prediction of future delivery, trading became more popular.

Technology has advanced to the extent that much of the world's trading now takes place on screen. It is no coincidence that the largest growth in the history of futures came during the 1980s, the decade of greatest development in the field of information technology. The expansion of futures and other derivatives into the next century will only be limited by the abilities of that technology.

These exchange-traded markets are well established but the next generation of derivatives, those traded by banks and brokers outside the standardized framework, provided by an exchange, otherwise known as the over-the-counter market, are less well understood.

The OTC market, like the exchange-traded markets, are now familiar to many large corporations and institutions who use them on an everyday basis to provide greater financial stability in an increasingly volatile economic climate. After the Gulf War in 1991 and its impact on oil prices, for example, the number of airlines hedging the price of their oil through derivatives grew dramatically.

In the US, which pioneered much of the early development in derivatives, these instruments, particularly futures and options have been more widely used than in Europe, but the rest of the world is catching up with even the World Bank recommending hedging on the part of developing countries with a dependence of volatile commodity production.

The use of futures and options, as well as other derivatives, extends across all areas of business: from the grain farmers of the American mid-West who will guarantee the price to be paid for their crops before they are harvested by using futures and options, to utility companies providing electricity and using energy derivatives to stabilize price, or banks hedging their exposure to foreign currency risk.

Part 2: The Commodities

Metals

Further information on non-ferrous metals

British Non-ferrous Metals Federation
10 Greenfield Crescent
Birmingham B15 3AU
UK
Tel: +44 121 456 3322
Fax: +44 121 456 1394

London Metal Exchange Ltd
56 Leadenhall Street
London EC3A 2BJ
UK
Tel: +44 171 264 5555
Fax: +44 171 680 0505

Metal Bulletin
16 Lower Marsh
London SE1 7RJ
UK
Tel: +44 171 827 9977
Fax: +44 171 928 6539

World Bureau of Metal Statistics
27a High Street
Ware
Herts SG12 9BA
UK
Tel: +44 1920 461274
Fax: +44 1920 464258

Aluminium

Alex Standish
Associate Editor (Non-Ferrous), Metal Bulletin

Bauxite, the mineral ore from which alumina is produced, is the most common mineral on the earth's surface; it has been in use for thousands of years. Although the metal itself has a relatively short history, its recyclability has enabled it to catch the popular imagination as the most 'eco-friendly' of the base metals. Its production is, nevertheless, highly energy intensive at the primary smelting stage, when alumina is processed into aluminium, and this has meant that the lowest-cost producers tend to be located in areas of the world where cheap sources of energy, especially hydro-electric power or natural gas, are readily available.

Refining of alumina – which can also be used in a variety of non-metallurgical processes (such as polishing optical lenses) – and its smelting into aluminium was first explored in the mid-eighteenth century. However, it only became a commercial operation in the mid-nineteenth century when French producer Pechiney developed a workable smelter process.

Initially, aluminium was considered an extremely expensive metal and its use was restricted until high-volume production brought down costs. During the course of the twentieth century, however, it has become one of the most important base metals, both in terms of total production and trading, as well as end uses to which it is now put.

The key to aluminium's success is its versatility. It is light, yet strong – especially in its alloy forms – as well as suitable for the production of extruded shapes. This is why aluminium is now well established in the packaging market, especially in the manufacture of drink cans and foil. It is also an essential metal in the aviation sector and is growing in importance in the automotive industry as a means of reducing weight in components such as engine blocks.

Although aluminium smelting remains an international business, its power-intensive nature has favoured Canada and Norway, which both have hydro-electric energy available. The USA is also a major producer with three of the world's largest companies – Alcoa, Kaiser and Reynolds – operating smelters there. Western Europe has seen its primary aluminium production hit by high power and labour costs and some smelters, notably in Austria, France, Italy, Germany and Switzerland, have been shut down in recent years. Some European producers have either relocated their operations to lower-cost regions or entered into partnership with other producers in such areas, including recently-privatized smelters in central and eastern Europe.

In recent years, aluminium smelters have been expanded in South Africa and in the Gulf states such as Dubai and Bahrain, where natural gas and lower labour costs are important attractions. Iran too, is keen to develop its primary aluminium industry for export markets, while Australia, Brazil and Venezuela, which all have the advantage of abundant bauxite and alumina, are also significant metal producers. India, where producers have been forced to cut output in recent years owing to droughts and power shortages, has yet to fulfil its potential.

Both Russia and China are also major producers of aluminium, although China, with its rapid growth is still a net importer of metal and is forecast to remain so for the foreseeable future. Exports of aluminium from the former Soviet Union on the other hand, threatened to flood the international market in the early 1990s, as western traders concluded contracts with state-owned smelters keen to earn higher prices for their products than the domestic market could offer.

Alarmed by the rise in available aluminium, a number of western world producers and their governments concluded a memorandum of understanding (MoU) in 1994 designed to limit production of primary metal for two years. A number of world producers made commitments to idle a proportion of their smelting capacity under the MoU which was a key factor in cutting London Metal Exchange stocks from a peak of 2.4 million tonnes in 1993/94 to around 800,000 tonnes in 1996. Western world production of aluminium is forecast to reach around 15.8 million tonnes in 1996, rising to about 18 million tonnes by 2000.

Both primary and alloy aluminium futures contracts are traded on the London Metal Exchange (LME). Japan's Tokyo Commodity Exchange (Tocom) is planning to launch its own yen-denominated aluminium futures contract during 1997. LME warehouses holding physical aluminium on warrant are located in a variety of countries, including the USA, Japan and Europe.

The future for aluminium is considered bright by most industry analysts, with some predicting that demand will outstrip supply by 1998 unless producers bring additional smelter capacity on stream. One factor which tends to discourage the building of new smelters, however, is the metal's potential for extreme volatility in the international market. Between 1993 and 1995, for example, the LME cash settlement price for aluminium ingot ranged from around \$1,200/tonne to more than \$2,100/tonne. Since an average western world smelter is only able to produce metal at a cost of around \$1,260/tonne (and a very efficient smelter with cheap power at around \$1,000), most producers are wary of committing themselves to costly new smelter projects – especially when the estimated cost of a new 200,000 tonnes capacity smelter is about \$1 billion.

Table 1 Aluminium: world refined production 1991–95 (thousand tonnes)

	1991	*1992*	*1993*	*1994*	*1995*
EUROPE					
Austria	80.4	32.9	–	–	–
France	286.1	417.7	426.2	384.1	364.5
Germany	690.3	602.8	551.9	503.4	575.2
Greece	152.4	152.8	147.7	138.0	130.9
Iceland	89.2	89.9	94.2	98.6	100.2
Italy	217.7	160.7	155.7	175.6	177.9
Netherlands	263.9	235.1	231.8	219.4	215.6
Norway	858.2	838.1	887.5	856.6	846.8
Slovenia	–	–	74.7	74.3	70.2
Spain	355.2	359.0	355.9	338.1	361.9
Sweden	96.9	77.2	82.4	83.9	94.5
Switzerland	65.9	52.6	36.4	24.2	20.7
United Kingdom	293.5	244.2	239.1	231.2	237.9
Yugoslavia	314.0	151.8	36.0	10.6	26.0
Total	3763.7	3414.7	3319.5	3138.0	3222.3
AFRICA					
Cameroon	85.6	82.5	86.5	81.1	79.0
Egypt	177.9	177.8	179.4	181.5	180.3
Ghana	175.4	179.9	175.4	140.7	135.4
South Africa	169.0	173.0	176.0	172.7	233.3
Total	607.9	613.2	617.3	576.0	628.0
ASIA					
Bahrain	213.7	292.5	450.0	451.9	459.0
India	503.9	496.3	466.4	472.0	524.0
Indonesia	173.1	188.8	202.1	221.9	228.1
Iran	70.1	79.3	91.5	116.2	93.4
Japan	32.4	189	18.3	17.0	18.0
South Korea	–	–	–	–	–
Taiwan	–	–	–	–	–
Turkey	55.8	58.6	58.5	59.7	61.5
United Arab Emirates	239.0	244.6	242.3	246.9	239.9
Total	1288.0	1379.0	1529.1	1585.6	1623.9
AMERICAS					
Canada	1821.6	1971.8	2308.9	2254.7	2172.0
USA	4121.2	4042.1	3694.8	3298.5	3375.2
Argentina	169.0	155.6	170.6	175.9	184.1
Brazil	1139.6	1193.3	1172.0	1184.6	1188.2
Mexico	66.9	–	–	–	10.4
Surinam	30.7	32.4	30.1	26.7	28.1
Venezuela	600.5	606.8	567.7	585.4	627.4
Total	7949.5	8002.0	7944.1	7525.8	7585.4
OCEANIA					
Australia	1228.6	1236.1	1376.3	1310.8	1292.7
New Zealand	258.5	242.9	277.4	269.1	273.3
Total	1487.1	1479.0	1653.7	1579.9	1566.0
TOTAL	**15,096.2**	**14,887.9**	**15,063.7**	**14,405.3**	**14,625.6**
Monthly Average	*1258.0*	*1240.6*	*1255.3*	*1200.4*	*1218.8*
OTHER COUNTRIES					
Czechoslovakia	66.3	40.0	–	–	–
Slovakia	–	–	39.7	40.0	39.7
German DR	–	–	–	–	–

Table 1 Aluminium: world refined production 1991–95 (thousand tonnes) contd.

	1991	*1992*	*1993*	*1994*	*1995*
Hungary	63.3	26.8	27.9	29.6	29.6
Poland	45.8	43.6	47.1	49.3	52.0
Romania	168.0	110.0	112.4	119.6	142.9
USSR	3251.0	–	–	–	–
Azerbaijan		25.0	11.0	5.0	6.0
Russia	–	2776.6	2819.0	2670.5	2724.5
Tajikistan		345.0	252.0	236.5	230.0
Ukraine	–	105.0	104.0	102.0	95.1
China	962.0	1096.0	1254.5	1498.4	1657.6
Total	4556.4	4568.0	4667.6	4750.9	4977.4
WORLD TOTAL	**19,652.6**	**19,455.9**	**19,731.3**	**19,156.2**	**19,603.0**

This table shows production of primary aluminium only.

By courtesy of the World Bureau of Metal Statistics

Figure 1 Aluminium: world refined production

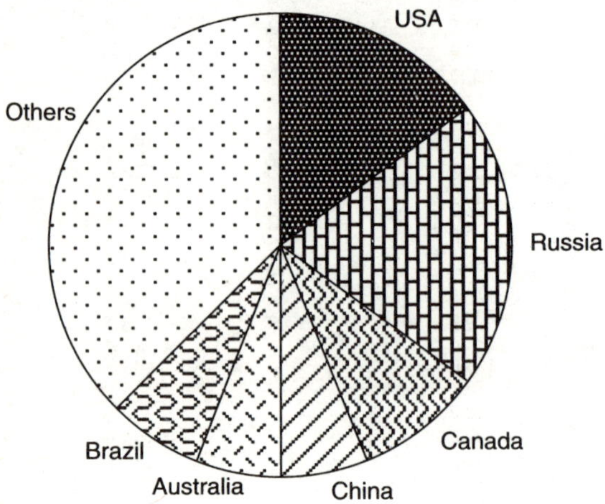

Table 2 Aluminium: world refined consumption 1990–95 (thousand tonnes)

	1990	*1991*	*1992*	*1993*	*1994*	*1995*	*1995*	*1995*	*1995*
						Jan–Dec	Apr–June	July–Sept	Oct–Dec
EUROPE									
Austria	171.0	168.0	165.0	140.0	145.0	150.0	36.3	36.3	36.3
Belgium	317.8	323.0	291.8	275.0	329.0	335.6	94.2	61.1	90.0
Croatia	–	–	–	13.6	24.6	24.0	6.0	6.0	6.0
Denmark	24.1	26.4	24.0	23.0	26.0	28.0	8.7	3.8	7.0
Finland	22.5	15.6	15.0	22.0	19.0	19.0	4.8	4.8	4.8
France	723.0	725.9	722.8	665.0	735.0	720.0	195.5	165.0	172.8
Germany	1295.4	1360.9	1457.1	1150.7	1370.3	1503.9	420.5	371.8	336.9
Greece	110.5	122.8	130.1	105.0	143.0	158.0	39.5	39.5	39.5
Italy	652.0	670.0	660.0	554.0	660.0	651.1	181.5	139.3	150.2
Macedonia	–	–	–	4.0	4.0	2.0	0.5	0.5	0.5
Netherlands	106.6	119.8	123.3	140.0	145.0	150.0	37.5	37.5	37.5
Norway	138.0	156.7	175.4	202.0	212.0	166.0	39.8	54.2	57.7
Portugal	48.9	48.4	58.1	52.0	64.0	74.0	18.5	18.5	18.5
Slovenia	–	–	–	48.0	48.3	48.3	12.1	12.1	12.1
Spain	288.0	297.0	309.0	310.0	352.0	399.9	108.0	101.1	88.5
Sweden	80.1	82.0	89.4	93.0	131.0	116.2	29.4	26.7	28.8
Switzerland	164.1	156.7	145.2	131.0	151.0	143.0	41.9	34.4	31.9
United Kingdom	453.7	412.4	483.3	475.0	500.0	540.0	135.0	135.0	135.0
Yugoslavia	158.2	140.0	75.0	38.0	10.6	26.0	6.5	6.5	6.5
Other Europe	8.6	6.5	6.2	8.8	6.9	6.9	1.7	1.7	1.7
Total	4762.5	4832.1	4930.7	4450.1	5076.7	5261.9	1417.9	1255.8	1262.2
AFRICA									
Cameroon	20.1	20.1	15.5	19.0	16.9	16.9	4.2	4.2	4.2
Egypt	75.7	86.9	65.0	80.4	80.4	77.4	19.4	19.4	19.4
Ghana	10.2	9.8	10.0	10.0	10.0	10.0	2.5	2.5	2.5
South Africa	91.0	86.0	88.0	90.0	120.5	114.7	30.7	25.7	24.8
Other Africa	22.3	17.7	17.9	18.9	10.7	10.7	2.7	2.7	2.7
Total	219.3	220.5	196.4	218.3	238.5	229.7	59.5	54.5	53.6
ASIA									
Bahrain	103.8	105.6	124.7	175.9	132.9	132.9	33.2	33.2	33.2
Hong Kong	28.8	36.7	45.9	45.1	41.5	116.6	52.9	41.5	7.3
India	433.3	430.2	414.3	475.3	536.5	579.2	150.5	144.8	144.8
Indonesia	87.7	89.5	95.7	139.0	179.1	147.7	36.9	36.9	36.9
Iran	120.0	118.8	116.0	110.0	105.0	105.0	26.3	26.3	26.3
Japan	2414.3	2431.6	2271.6	2138.3	2344.8	2335.6	682.9	523.7	574.8
Malaysia	58.8	66.6	75.0	81.7	66.3	66.3	16.6	16.6	16.6
Philippines	14.4	17.4	26.0	22.7	22.9	22.9	5.7	5.7	5.7
Saudi Arabia	21.9	23.9	23.9	25.0	30.0	30.0	7.5	7.5	7.5
Singapore	23.2	13.5	27.5	22.4	30.1	39.9	10.0	10.0	10.0
South Korea	368.9	383.5	397.0	524.8	603.9	692.6	173.5	176.7	170.3
Taiwan	197.7	262.9	265.4	299.1	355.2	362.6	112.1	72.4	76.7
Thailand	128.1	146.5	147.4	180.3	183.4	240.0	67.2	52.9	52.9
Turkey	152.0	114.0	128.6	160.1	115.2	122.1	30.5	30.5	30.5
Other Asia	109.5	111.7	124.9	78.5	72.8	72.8	18.2	18.2	18.2
Total	4262.4	4352.6	4283.9	4478.2	4819.6	5066.2	1424.0	1196.9	1211.7
AMERICAS									
Canada	387.2	408.2	420.4	486.6	532.8	587.0	137.5	162.2	115.5
USA	4330.4	4137.2	4616.9	4877.1	5407.1	5054.8	1314.4	1174.7	1258.9
Argentina	67.9	103.5	108.3	104.5	109.2	109.2	27.3	27.3	27.3
Brazil	341.2	354.2	377.1	378.9	413.8	500.4	148.7	94.8	113.0
Mexico	91.9	94.4	83.4	97.1	80.0	37.8	9.4	9.4	9.4
Venezuela	196.8	170.3	150.0	155.2	132.7	174.1	42.4	42.3	46.5
Other America	33.6	39.0	44.9	54.0	57.9	57.9	14.5	14.5	14.5
Total	5449.0	5306.8	5801.0	6153.4	6734.3	6521.2	1694.2	1525.2	1585.1

Table 2 Aluminium: world refined consumption 1991–95 (thousand tonnes) contd.

	1990	*1991*	*1992*	*1993*	*1994*	*1995*	*1995*	*1995*	*1995*
						Jan–Dec	Apr–June	July–Sept	Oct–Dec
OCEANIA									
Australia	287.8	298.0	308.5	339.5	352.8	344.1	98.9	85.7	87.1
New Zealand	26.9	18.3	22.3	27.1	40.0	38.8	11.2	9.0	6.2
Other Oceania	0.3	–	–	–	–	–	–	–	–
Total	315.0	316.3	330.8	366.6	392.8	382.9	110.1	94.7	93.3
TOTAL	**15,008.2**	**15,028.3**	**15,542.8**	**15,666.6**	**17,261.9**	**17,461.9**	**4705.7**	**4127.1**	**4205.9**
Quarterly Average	*3752.0*	*3757.0*	*3885.7*	*3916.6*	*4315.4*	*4365.4*			
OTHER COUNTRIES									
Bulgaria	35.2	17.7	12.0	11.9	6.5	6.5	1.6	1.6	1.6
Czechoslovakia	150.7	83.0	61.8	–	–	–	–	–	–
Czech Republic	–	–	–	38.9	40.0	40.0	10.0	10.0	10.0
Slovakia	–	–	–	23.7	25.0	25.0	6.3	6.3	6.3
German DR	83.1	–	–	–	–	–	–	–	–
Hungary	155.2	96.4	112.3	140.1	141.1	141.1	35.3	35.3	35.3
Poland	63.4	31.9	54.8	67.7	56.9	56.9	14.2	14.2	14.2
Romania	42.0	94.0	20.6	39.7	20.3	20.3	5.1	5.1	5.1
USSR	2790.0	2409.0	–	–	–	–	–	–	–
Russia	–	–	1242.0	657.0	475.9	480.0	236.9	28.7	28.7
Ukraine	–	–	100.0	100.0	34.3	50.1	12.5	12.5	12.5
Other FSU	–	–	10.0	10.0	10.0	10.0	2.5	2.5	2.5
China	861.0	938.0	1253.8	1318.0	1484.0	1859.9	494.0	515.7	493.4
Cuba	2.5	1.0	1.0	1.0	1.0	1.0	0.3	0.3	0.3
Other	60.5	45.0	38.0	21.0	30.5	30.5	7.6	7.6	7.6
Total	4243.6	3716.0	2906.3	2429.0	2325.5	2721.3	826.3	639.8	617.5
WORLD TOTAL	**19,251.8**	**18,7449.3**	**18,449.1**	**18,095.6**	**19,587.4**	**20,183.2**	**5532.0**	**4766.9**	**4823.4**

This table shows consumption of primary aluminium only.

By courtesy of the World Bureau of Metal Statistics

Figure 2 Aluminium: world refined consumption

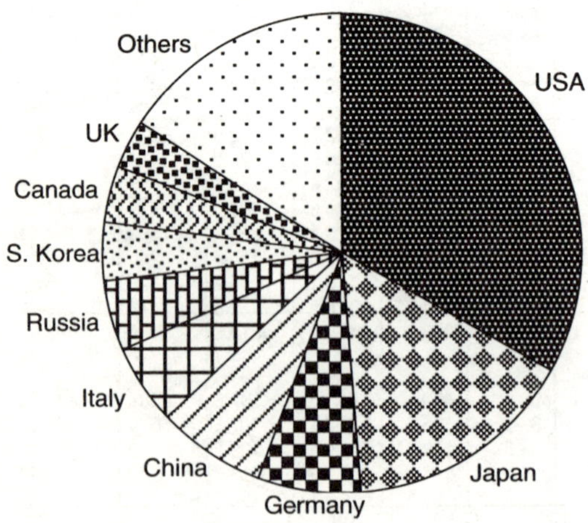

Figure 3 LME primary aluminium: monthly average cash settlement and sellers' prices
All prices quoted in $ per tonne

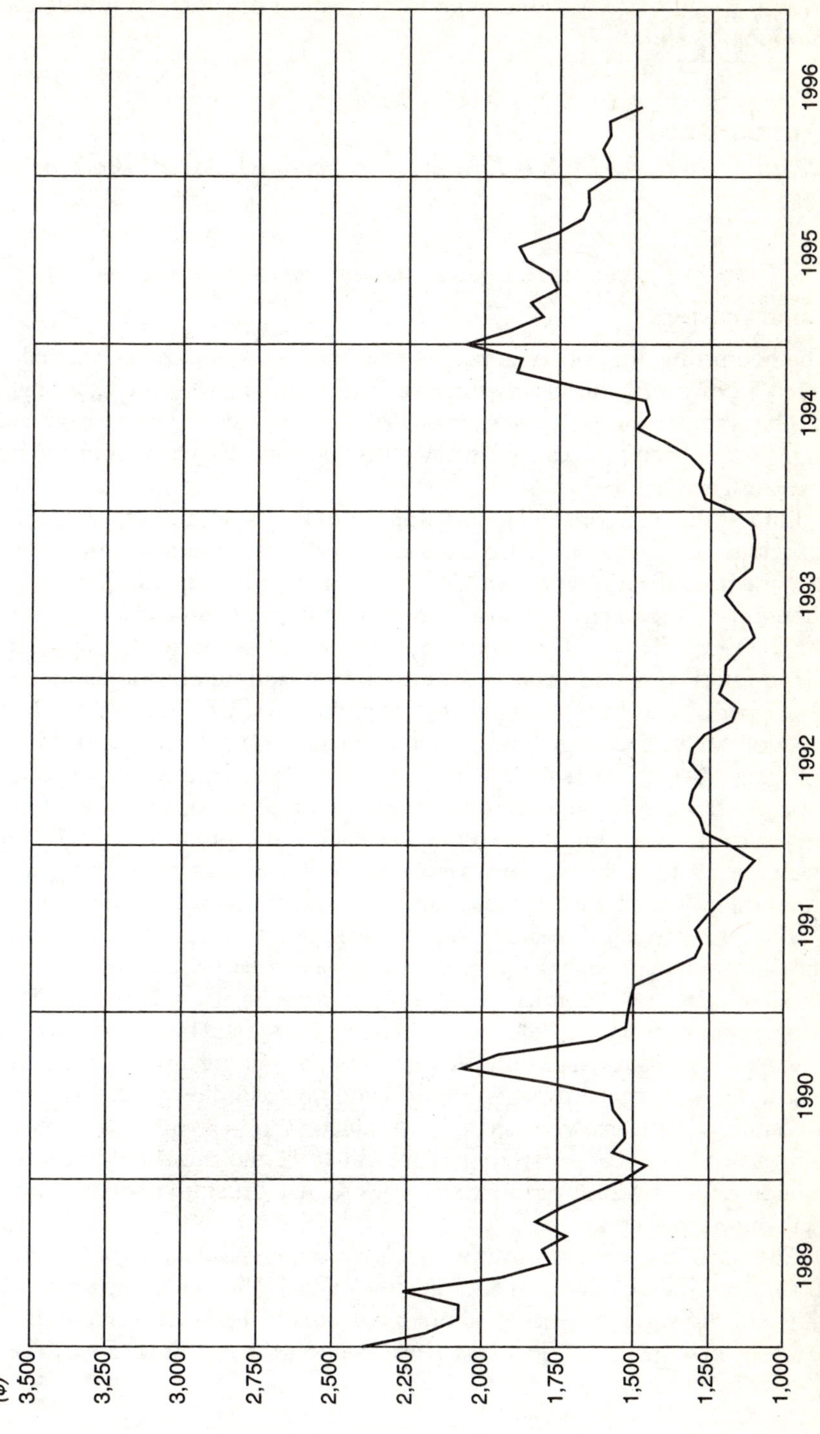

Source: London Metal Exchange

Copper

Camila Reed
Deputy News & Markets Editor (Non-Ferrous), Metal Bulletin

The boom time for copper appears to be drawing to a close as 'the red metal' enters a downturn after nearly three years of phenomenal growth, strong prices and buoyant demand. By the start of 1997, the market will move from a deficit to over-supply and prices are already reflecting this, declining from the historic highs reached in 1995.

But it is not all doom and gloom. Huge offtake by South East Asia, driven by voracious consumption in China and Korea and a predicted turnaround in demand from the former Soviet Union countries (once huge copper consumers) should continue to ensure consumption of at least 11 million tonnes a year for the rest of the decade. The copper industry is meanwhile gearing up to combat the threat of competition and substitution from aluminium and plastics.

Copper is one of the most widely traded commodities, dealt primarily on the London Metal Exchange, and to a lesser degree on the New York Mercantile Exchange. Copper markets were rocked in June 1996 by talk of manipulation as Japanese trading house Sumitomo announced trading losses of over $2 billion on the metal over a ten-year period. The backwash from this is already producing an overhaul of the way the markets function although the investigation into the complexities of the Sumitomo affair is likely to run for several years.

The ease with which a single trader has allegedly manipulated the market and the downturn in prices has also questioned profit-projections for new mining projects and spread a gloomier mood among investors in primary production. If copper prices continue to fall, more mining projects could be postponed or halted.

Copper is produced mainly by conventional mining methods, although in recent years, solvent extraction electrowinning technology (SX-EW) has been accounting for a growing share of production. Approximately 1.08 million tonnes of SX-EW copper were produced in 1994 and this should rise to over 3 million tonnes by 2000 accounting for more than one-fifth of all western world new mine production.

The greatest increases in future SX-EW copper production will come from Latin America – Chile, Peru and Mexico – which already dominate world production. However, the new technology is also being used increasingly in the USA, encouraged by its low cost (it is around 40 per cent cheaper to produce copper by this means).

While developing nations dominate copper production, consumption is strongest in OECD countries, accounting for 75 per cent of the global total. However, the annual growth rate from non-OECD countries is rising rapidly.

Around 75 per cent of all copper ends up in semi-manufactured products such as tube and wire destined for use in the building and construction sector, in air-conditioning units and plumbing, and in electronic products in the telecommunications or power sectors. Copper is also widely used in transportation equipment and military applications.

Building wire accounts for over 35 per cent of all consumption of copper semi-fabricated metal and unlike other sectors – such as automotive and consumer products – this outlet has not yet suffered from substitution. Even the industrial recession in the developed world has been weathered, thanks partly to growth in the DIY consumer market, especially in the USA, where sales of copper-containing products have risen by 50 per cent.

However, it is in the automotive sector where copper has proved most versatile, re-inventing itself for new uses in the face of substitution by aluminium in radiators and other heating appliances. Automotive wire has been a fast-growing market for copper for nearly two decades, mainly because of the increase in electrically operated functions in cars. So, while copper is being replaced in some uses, it maintains a healthy share of this market – one which seems set to continue rising as automatic vehicle functions become more and more sophisticated.

One area where copper is unlikely to reverse the trend of diminishing market share is in telecommunications cables. This sector has not only been the hardest hit but faces yet more erosion of market share in the future as the use of fibre optics continues to grow. The main advantage of fibre optics is in being able to carry far greater numbers of telecommunications in a much smaller space, making it the most economical conduit where call traffic is greatest. However, at this stage, copper appears to be holding its own as the conduit for the residential part of the telephone subscriber loop because it is cheaper to install.

Overall demand in the tube and automotive sectors continues to look healthy, driven in part by economic growth in nations like China and Korea where offtake has been rising by as much as 9 per cent a year. Tubing is the second largest use of copper after wire products with over half of this offtake in plumbing and heating services. The increase in use of air-conditioning world-wide – again linked to increasing prosperity in South East Asia and India – is also expected to provide healthy demand for copper in coming years.

During 1994 and 1995, LME copper prices rode a bullish wave reaching well over $3,000 per tonne in response to a shortage of the metal and fund buying which pushed prompt cash prices to levels $100 per tonne higher than forward copper for months at a time. However, prices of around $1,600–$1,800 per tonne are predicted for 1997 as many new mine projects come on stream and the shockwaves of the Sumitomo affair continue to ricochet through the market. At present, the bulls and the bears are still fighting for dominance of the market, creating huge price fluctuations on the LME and this volatility is expected to continue as prices descend overall.

Further information
Copper Development Association
Orchard House
Mutton Lane
Potters Bar
Hertfordshire EN6 3AP
UK
Tel: +44 1707 650 711
Fax: +44 1707 642 769

International Copper Study Group
6th Floor
Rua Alminante Barroso, 38
1000 Lisbon
Portugal
Tel: +351 1 3534121/3524039
Fax: +351 1 3524035

International Wrought Copper Council
6 Bathurst Street
Sussex Square
London W2 2SD
UK
Tel: +44 171 723 7465
Fax: +44 171 724 0308

Table 1 Copper: world mine production 1991–95 (thousand tonnes)

	1991	*1992*	*1993*	*1994*	*1995*
EUROPE					
Finland	11.7	10.2	11.1	9.5	9.5
France	0.3	0.1	0.1	–	–
Macedonia	–	–	10.0	9.7	6.0
Norway	17.4	12.7	8.7	7.7	6.8
Portugal	157.3	150.5	150.4	130.4	129.7
Spain	10.0	9.8	3.5	4.9	22.4
Sweden	81.7	89.1	88.9	79.4	83.6
United Kingdom	0.2	–	–	–	–
Yugoslavia	113.4	105.0	68.0	84.8	87.6
Total	392.0	377.4	340.7	326.4	345.6
AFRICA					
Botswana	20.6	20.4	21.9	22.8	20.5
Morocco	15.6	13.9	14.3	13.4	13.3
Mozambique	–	–	–	–	–
Namibia	35.0	34.4	33.1	29.4	24.5
South Africa	193.0	197.8	188.6	183.9	198.0
Zaire	291.5	144.0	46.0	30.0	30.0
Zambia	412.4	432.6	431.5	384.4	341.9
Zimbabwe	13.8	10.5	8.2	9.4	7.7
Total	981.9	853.6	743.6	673.3	635.9
ASIA					
Burma	5.0	5.0	5.2	4.8	6.0
Cyprus	0.2	0.2	0.2	–	–
India	50.4	49.0	49.4	45.9	47.0
Indonesia	219.5	290.9	309.7	333.9	459.7
Iran	84.3	105.0	86.6	117.9	102.2
Japan	12.4	12.1	10.3	6.0	2.4
Malaysia	25.6	28.6	25.2	25.3	20.8
Oman	13.5	13.4	8.8	4.3	–
Pakistan	–	–	–	–	4.4
Philippines	148.3	123.5	136.3	116.2	108.1
South Korea	–	–	–	–	–
Turkey	41.8	38.6	39.2	35.0	37.9
Total	601.0	666.3	670.9	689.3	788.5
AMERICAS					
Canada	811.1	768.6	732.6	616.8	728.7
USA	1634.4	1765.1	1801.4	1796.0	1860.0
Argentina	0.4	0.3	–	–	–
Bolivia	–	0.1	0.2	0.1	0.1
Brazil	37.9	39.8	43.6	39.7	30.0
Chile	1814.3	1932.7	2055.4	2219.9	2488.1
Colombia	3.3	2.2	–	2.6	2.8
Mexico	267.0	277.1	301.1	305.5	360.0
Peru	375.3	369.4	374.8	365.5	405.0
Total	4943.7	5155.3	5309.1	5346.1	5874.7
OCEANIA					
Australia	320.0	378.0	402.0	415.6	378.5
Papua New Guinea	204.5	193.4	203.2	206.4	212.7
Total	524.5	571.4	605.2	622.0	591.2
TOTAL	**7443.1**	**7624.0**	**7669.5**	**7657.1**	**8235.9**
Monthly Average	*620.2*	*635.3*	*639.1*	*638.0*	*686.3*

Table 1 Copper: world mine production 1991–95 (thousand tonnes) contd.

	1991	*1992*	*1993*	*1994*	*1995*
OTHER COUNTRIES					
Albania	8.0	1.9	3.5	2.2	4.2
Bulgaria	47.2	47.4	60.4	75.5	75.5
Czechoslovakia	2.6	1.0	–	–	–
Slovakia	–	–	3.0	–	–
German DR	–	–	–	–	–
Poland	320.3	332.0	382.6	376.8	383.6
Romania	27.2	25.0	25.0	25.5	24.0
USSR	840.0	–	–	–	–
Armenia	–	0.5	0.5	0.5	1.2
Georgia	–	3.5	3.5	3.5	3.6
Kazakstan	–	302.0	265.0	202.0	220.0
Russia	–	552.5	460.0	447.9	480.0
Uzbekistan	–	75.0	81.0	80.0	80.0
China	304.0	334.3	345.7	395.6	396.0
Mongolia	91.0	103.0	114.0	119.2	120.2
Cuba	2.0	1.5	2.0	2.0	2.0
Other	14.0	12.0	12.0	12.0	12.0
Total	1656.3	1791.8	1758.2	1742.7	1802.3
WORLD TOTAL	**9099.4**	**9415.8**	**9427.7**	**9399.8**	**10,038.2**

This table shows the recoverable copper content of ores and concentrates produced.

By courtesy of the World Bureau of Metal Statistics

Table 2 Copper: world smelter production 1991–95 (thousand tonnes)

	1991	*1992*	*1993*	*1994*	*1995*
EUROPE					
Austria	44.8	49.0	47.3	49.6	53.2
Belgium	106.0	102.8	141.7	147.6	147.6
Finland	90.1	110.5	107.2	98.2	88.3
France	5.8	5.8	5.9	4.5	4.5
Germany	256.2	234.9	201.3	292.2	304.9
Norway	38.4	39.3	37.2	39.4	34.3
Spain	149.1	150.0	173.0	188.4	160.0
Sweden	97.6	98.4	99.1	102.7	106.5
Yugoslavia	135.5	127.9	57.4	86.6	87.4
Total	923.5	918.6	870.1	1009.2	986.7
AFRICA					
Namibia	33.5	37.5	34.8	30.1	29.8
South Africa	164.7	158.7	156.6	158.3	154.4
Uganda	–	–	–	–	–
Zaire[1]	242.7	118.0	45.9	29.3	28.8
Zambia[1]	300.5	380.2	337.8	265.2	243.2
Zimbabwe	23.8	22.4	18.9	18.2	17.5
Total	765.2	716.8	594.0	501.1	473.7
ASIA					
India	45.5	47.7	37.4	51.2	39.5
Iran	81.1	101.8	85.0	131.8	106.1
Japan	1085.4	1174.9	1184.8	1122.0	1168.5

Table 2 Copper: world smelter production 1991–95 (thousand tonnes) contd.

	1991	*1992*	*1993*	*1994*	*1995*
Oman	15.2	18.7	27.7	31.2	34.2
Pakistan	–	–	–	–	2.0
Philippines	167.5	168.8	212.4	200.3	198.0
South Korea	186.0	174.0	142.0	135.2	151.3
Taiwan	–	–	–	–	–
Turkey	32.4	30.0	39.6	30.4	33.7
Total	1613.1	1715.9	1728.9	1702.1	1733.3
AMERICAS					
Canada	532.2	552.4	562.4	560.5	613.4
USA	1450.3	1573.9	1679.9	1715.0	1630.0
Brazil	145.1	160.0	150.0	150.4	151.2
Chile	1173.6	1201.5	1219.1	1260.4	1293.8
Mexico	182.5	228.9	281.5	276.9	298.1
Peru	313.0	300.7	285.8	315.0	347.3
Total	3796.7	4017.4	4178.7	4278.2	4333.8
OCEANIA					
Australia	205.2	314.3	333.1	325.0	336.7
TOTAL	**7303.7**	**7683.0**	**7704.8**	**7815.6**	**7864.2**
Monthly Average	*608.6*	*640.2*	*642.0*	*651.3*	*655.3*
OTHER COUNTRIES[2]					
Albania	4.8	2.3	2.3	1.5	2.9
Bulgaria	27.8	50.6	71.9	89.4	74.5
Czechoslovakia	8.0	10.0	–	–	–
Slovakia	–	–	22.4	22.0	22.0
German DR	–	–	–	–	–
Hungary	4.9	4.1	–	–	–
Poland	360.0	370.0	411.2	401.9	352.5
Romania	28.0	27.9	26.2	25.3	25.3
USSR	920.0	–	–	–	–
Kazakhstan	–	347.4	322.0	270.0	270.0
Russia	–	690.5	560.2	506.7	540.0
Uzbekistan	–	75.0	81.0	80.0	80.0
China	385.0	418.0	443.7	482.4	444.0
Other	25.0	20.0	23.0	20.0	16.0
Total	1763.5	2015.8	1963.9	1899.2	1827.2
WORLD TOTAL	**9067.2**	**9698.8**	**9668.7**	**9714.8**	**9691.4**

The basis of this table is metal produced in the form of blister and anode copper from ores, concentrates, other primary materials and secondary blister produced from scrap. The figures are in terms of recoverable copper content whenever possible.

Notes [1] Includes leach cathodes. [2] Primary production only.

By courtesy of the World Bureau of Metal Statistics

Figure 1 Copper: world smelter production

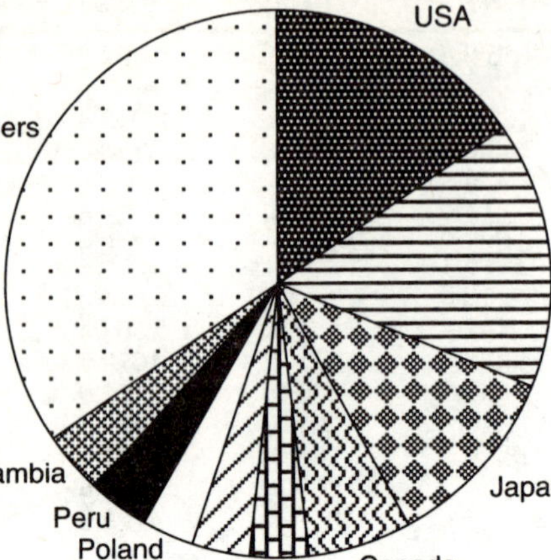

Table 3 Copper: world refined production 1991–1995 (thousand tonnes)

	1991	*1992*	*1993*	*1994*	*1995*
EUROPE					
Austria	52.8	54.7	52.7	52.5	53.5
Belgium[1]	297.6	367.3	378.9	375.0	393.0
Finland	64.5	70.9	73.4	69.2	73.7
France	55.7	56.7	59.3	51.2	42.5
Germany	521.5	581.7	632.1	591.9	616.1
Italy	83.4	76.0	90.3	84.0	98.0
Norway	38.4	39.3	37.2	39.4	34.3
Portugal	0.3	–	–	–	–
Spain	189.9	179.1	179.2	188.3	164.2
Sweden	96.6	101.6	98.8	103.0	111.1
United Kingdom	70.1	42.1	46.6	46.7	55.0
Yugoslavia	134.2	124.8	51.3	72.1	78.5
Total	1605.0	1694.2	1699.8	1673.3	1719.9
AFRICA					
Egypt	4.0	4.0	4.0	4.0	4.0
South Africa	127.0	120.1	127.9	129.6	139.5
Zaire	139.7	57.0	36.0	29.0	33.0
Zambia	423.7	472.0	424.9	369.5	313.8
Zimbabwe	23.8	22.4	18.9	18.2	17.5
Total	718.2	675.5	611.7	550.3	507.8
ASIA					
India	47.2	45.3	36.8	49.0	39.6
Iran	79.7	101.8	85.0	90.2	90.4
Japan	1076.3	1160.9	1188.8	1119.2	1188.0
Oman	11.4	14.2	20.5	24.2	22.0
Philippines	115.5	145.7	166.0	154.7	192.4

Table 3 Copper: world refined production 1991–1995 (thousand tonnes) contd.

	1991	*1992*	*1993*	*1994*	*1995*
South Korea	198.4	209.8	219.5	222.0	233.2
Taiwan	–	–	–	–	–
Turkey	80.0	104.0	92.4	83.0	100.3
Total	1608.5	1781.7	1809.0	1742.3	1865.9
AMERICAS					
Canada	538.3	539.3	561.6	549.9	560.0
USA	1995.1	2143.9	2252.5	2220.0	2250.0
Argentina	15.0	16.0	15.0	16.0	16.0
Brazil	141.4	156.8	162.0	170.0	165.0
Chile	1228.3	1242.3	1268.2	1277.4	1490.9
Mexico	153.9	191.1	171.1	197.0	201.9
Peru	244.1	251.1	261.7	253.0	282.0
Total	4316.1	4540.5	4692.1	4683.3	4965.8
OCEANIA					
Australia	279.0	303.0	309.0	335.9	260.0
TOTAL	**8526.8**	**8994.9**	**9121.6**	**8985.1**	**9319.4**
Monthly Average	*710.5*	*749.5*	*760.1*	*748.7*	*776.6*
OTHER COUNTRIES					
Albania	4.4	2.2	1.9	2.1	3.1
Bulgaria	12.8	18.0	23.8	26.5	26.4
Czechoslovakia	25.3	25.0	–	–	–
Slovakia	–	–	29.2	23.0	23.0
German DR	–	–	–	–	–
Hungary	4.5	4.1	–	–	–
Poland	378.5	387.0	404.2	405.2	406.6
Romania	25.7	26.9	25.2	22.2	22.2
USSR	1120.0	–	–	–	–
Kazakstan	–	337.0	318.0	283.0	256.6
Russia	–	620.7	537.1	551.8	554.6
Uzbekistan	–	75.0	81.0	90.0	80.0
China	560.0	659.0	733.0	736.1	843.7
Other	30.0	28.0	29.0	30.0	30.0
WORLD TOTAL	**10,688.0**	**11,177.8**	**11,304.0**	**11,155.0**	**11,565.6**

This table shows production of refined copper, whether electrolytic or fire refined. It includes production from blister, anodes and other primary materials, together with secondary production from scrap and other similar materials. It does not include copper recovered from secondary materials by simply remelting.

Notes [1] WBMS estimate.

By courtesy of the World Bureau of Metal Statistics

Table 4 Copper: world refined consumption 1991–95 (thousand tonnes)

	1991	*1992*	*1993*	*1994*	*1995*
EUROPE					
Austria	24.0	29.6	21.0	23.3	25.0
Belgium	372.0	385.9	331.6	406.9	362.0
Denmark	0.1	–	–	–	0.2
Finland	87.4	80.0	91.0	82.8	87.4
France	481.2	487.9	473.9	513.3	526.6
Germany	1005.9	1031.6	921.1	999.5	1058.4
Greece	45.5	46.2	65.0	73.0	84.0
Ireland	0.2	–	–	–	–
Italy	470.7	502.4	489.5	480.0	491.3
Netherlands	17.6	18.1	15.4	18.6	31.4
Norway	8.0	5.2	–	–	–
Portugal	26.0	21.4	9.7	7.0	0.1
Spain	156.0	153.4	162.0	178.0	183.7
Sweden	124.6	123.1	139.0	143.4	142.8
Switzerland	4.3	4.7	3.1	5.2	5.2
United Kingdom	269.4	308.3	325.0	377.3	397.9
Yugoslavia	80.0	70.0	50.0	50.0	50.4
Total	3172.9	3267.8	3097.3	3358.3	3446.4
AFRICA					
Egypt	4.0	4.0	4.6	4.3	4.0
South Africa	63.0	63.3	66.5	84.0	81.6
Zaire	2.0	1.4	2.4	1.4	1.4
Zambia	10.7	16.0	18.0	16.0	13.0
Zimbabwe	17.8	17.9	15.9	15.3	15.6
Other Africa	1.1	1.3	1.2	1.9	1.2
Total	98.6	103.9	108.6	122.9	116.8
ASIA					
Hong Kong	6.1	11.5	14.1	3.4	18.6
India	96.3	97.7	110.9	137.0	114.3
Indonesia	49.3	51.7	55.6	60.0	85.0
Iran	52.0	61.0	51.6	43.6	47.5
Japan	1613.2	1411.1	1384.1	1374.9	1414.5
Malaysia	65.4	80.0	91.3	105.8	111.5
Philippines	22.4	17.8	32.0	44.7	54.6
Saudi Arabia	54.0	80.0	93.0	88.7	95.0
Singapore	12.0	12.0	18.8	20.0	20.0
South Korea	343.2	353.5	399.8	476.2	539.6
Taiwan	399.1	415.6	477.2	547.0	563.2
Thailand	67.1	88.8	118.7	173.0	147.5
Turkey	98.1	116.7	109.3	108.0	136.5
Other Asia	23.0	30.0	30.0	25.0	25.2
Total	2901.2	2827.4	2986.4	3207.3	3373.0
AMERICAS					
Canada	159.2	156.1	185.6	199.3	189.7
USA	2057.8	2175.7	2359.4	2678.1	2530.0
Argentina	42.1	56.7	55.1	56.2	47.7
Brazil	170.8	162.2	168.0	183.3	197.6
Chile	47.6	62.8	72.3	86.3	87.3
Mexico	131.3	127.0	137.0	127.0	127.0
Peru	29.0	29.3	35.8	33.6	33.6
Other America	24.6	17.0	20.0	17.3	20.0
Total	2662.4	2786.8	3033.2	3381.1	3232.9

Table 4 Copper: world refined consumption 1991–95 (thousand tonnes) contd.

	1991	*1992*	*1993*	*1994*	*1995*
OCEANIA					
Australia	101.2	122.0	146.0	141.0	160.0
New Zealand	2.6	3.6	4.4	7.0	9.3
Total	103.8	125.6	150.4	148.0	169.3
TOTAL	**8938.9**	**9111.5**	**9375.9**	**10,217.6**	**10,338.4**
Monthly Average	*744.9*	*759.2*	*781.3*	*851.4*	*861.5*
OTHER COUNTRIES					
Albania	3.8	2.0	1.4	1.0	1.0
Bulgaria	18.4	23.8	19.6	17.3	17.3
Czechoslovakia	31.7	31.7	–	–	–
Czech Republic	–	–	8.8	7.2	7.2
Slovakia	–	–	5.1	6.9	6.9
German DR	–	–	–	–	–
Hungary	17.9	14.6	15.9	15.0	15.0
Poland	154.1	125.4	137.6	151.0	213.2
Romania	25.7	26.9	25.2	22.2	22.2
USSR	880.0	–	–	–	–
Kazakhstan	–	115.0	113.0	72.0	43.0
Russia	–	403.1	219.3	191.7	187.0
Ukraine	–	5.0	5.0	6.7	0.9
Uzbekistan	–	33.0	22.0	11.0	10.0
Other FSU	–	5.0	5.0	5.0	4.9
China	590.0	882.0	984.6	797.7	911.6
Other	34.5	34.5	17.0	16.0	16.0
Total	1756.1	1702.0	1579.5	1320.7	1456.2
WORLD TOTAL	**10,695.0**	**10,813.5**	**10,955.4**	**11,538.3**	**11,794.6**

This table shows consumption of unwrought refined copper whether refined from primary or secondary materials. The direct use copper in the form of scrap is excluded.

By courtesy of the World Bureau of Metal Statistics

Figure 2 Copper: world refined consumption

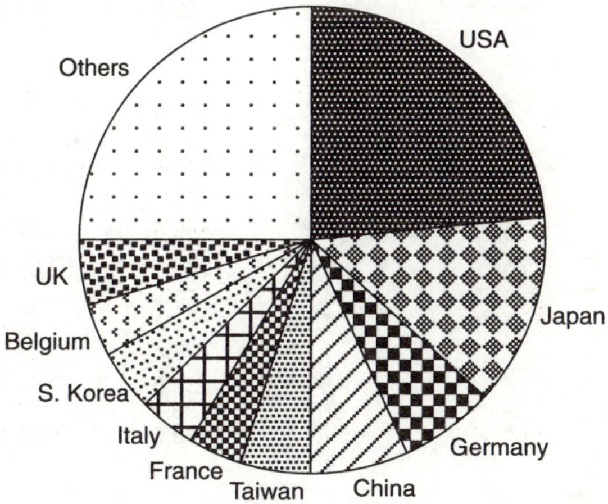

Table 5 Copper: world trade refined copper 1991–95 (thousand tonnes)

	1991	*1992*	*1993*	*1994*	*1995*
EXPORTS					
Austria	41.9	46.8	56.7	59.9	–
Belgium	181.1	161.8	208.1	151.7	104.2[6]
Denmark	–	0.1	–	–	–
Finland	19.8	19.2	21.9	20.7	24.8
France	12.4	15.4	23.4	19.5	11.9
Germany	63.0	59.5	79.5	142.2	130.5
Greece	1.5	1.5	–	–	–[7]
Italy	19.2	3.3	3.5	7.5	12.6
Netherlands	0.7	0.6	1.9	9.6	0.9
Norway	37.7	38.9	35.1	40.0	33.6
Portugal	–	0.1	–	0.1	–
Spain	61.1	53.8	52.8	33.8	15.4
Sweden	32.1	27.8	14.4	12.8	9.7
Switzerland	3.1	0.7	2.0	1.0	1.2
United Kingdom	16.1	4.8	2.9	20.3	5.6
Yugoslavia	56.4	15.2	8.2	19.5	–
South Africa	73.2	61.5	58.6	44.3	47.1
Zaire	118.7[8]	46.2[6]	28.3	13.7	–
Zambia	382.3	411.9	436.5	360.7	269.0
Hong Kong	13.9	44.2	40.7	19.7	32.3
Japan	64.4	100.0	160.0	114.4	158.7
Oman	11.4	11.6	11.8	10.6	–
Philippines	93.9	96.4	136.9	137.4	119.8
Singapore	58.5	94.0	87.7	97.7	197.1
Taiwan	0.7	1.9	3.4	1.6	3.7
Turkey	–	–	–	–	–
Canada[1]	374.6	385.7	404.6	388.6	427.5
USA	271.3	177.1	217.0	157.6	217.4
Brazil	63.1	79.7	76.5	55.9	59.2
Chile	1130.5	1178.0	1189.1	1193.3	1395.6
Mexico	2.1	12.0	13.5	18.0	62.3
Peru	207.5	214.5	217.5	218.3	251.9
Australia	173.9	188.2	156.2	175.9	106.0
Russia[2]	–	47.5	153.0	360.2	281.9
Kazakstan[2]	–	105.7	114.8	122.5	216.6
China	8.7	9.8	1.9	10.7	34.2
TOTAL	**3594.8**	**3715.4**	**4018.4**	**4039.7**	**4230.7**
IMPORTS					
Austria	5.8	8.8	14.1	31.9	–
Belgium	236.0	194.2	152.0	173.0	91.2[6]
Denmark	0.1	–	0.1	0.1	0.2
Finland	19.1	9.7	20.7	34.3	38.6
France	436.7	444.6	437.0	462.7	494.4
Germany	556.5	532.5	466.0	522.7	542.8
Greece[3]	49.0	47.7	66.9	61.6	24.2[7]
Italy	406.6	435.7	402.7	394.3	405.9
Netherlands	18.3	18.7	17.2	25.9	32.3
Norway	0.3	0.1	0.1	0.2	0.1
Philippines	4.2	10.1	20.3	27.4	16.6
Portugal	25.7	21.5	9.7	6.2	0.2
Spain	27.0	28.1	38.1	19.2	25.7
Sweden	60.1	49.3	54.6	53.1	64.4
Switzerland	7.5	5.4	5.2	6.2	6.4

Table 5 Copper: world trade refined copper 1991–95 (thousand tonnes) contd.

	1991	*1992*	*1993*	*1994*	*1995*
Turkey	18.1	12.7	16.9	25.0	38.9[8]
United Kingdom	242.7	278.2	378.5	259.0	273.8
Yugoslavia	8.4	3.8[10]	0.4	0.4	–
South Africa	0.2	0.1	0.2	1.0	3.5[8]
Hong Kong	20.0	55.7	54.8	23.1	50.9
India	49.1	52.5	74.1	87.9	27.7[9]
Indonesia	49.3	51.7	48.4	63.4	86.9
Japan	624.1	366.5	363.6	354.8	389.5
Saudi Arabia	54.0	80.0	93.0	88.7	–
Singapore	83.8	135.9	106.5	93.5	261.5
South Korea	146.4	159.0	183.2	263.4	312.2
Taiwan	397.9	417.5	480.5	548.6	566.9
Thailand	67.0	89.0	90.0	173.0	–
Canada	2.3	8.7	19.3	19.6	24.3
USA	295.1	289.7	348.9	466.8	429.1
Argentina	27.1	40.7	40.1	40.2	–
Brazil	75.9	80.7	57.6	64.1	91.8
Mexico	14.1	6.2	2.5	16.7	2.1
Venezuela	20.9	9.1	13.8	14.1	17.7
Australia	0.1	0.5	0.2	11.9	27.7
New Zealand	2.6	3.6	4.5	7.0	9.3
Russia[2]	–	47.5	0.6	–	–
Kazakstan[2]	–	–	–	–	3.0
Ukraine[2]	–	–	–	6.8	0.9
China[4]	114.0	261.1	253.5	72.3	102.1
Total	**4166.0**	**4256.8**	**4335.8**	**4520.1**	**4462.8**

This table shows principle imports and exports of refined copper.

Notes [1] Includes some blister. [2] Excludes intra – C.I.S. trade before 1995. [3] Primary production only. [4] Includes some alloys. [5] January and February. [6] January to September. [7] January to April. [8] January to November. [9] January to June. [10] January to May.

By courtesy of the World Bureau of Metal Statistics

Figure 3 LME copper grade A: monthly average cash settlement and sellers' prices
Prices prior to July 1993 quoted in £ per tonne. After July 1993 quoted in $ per tonne

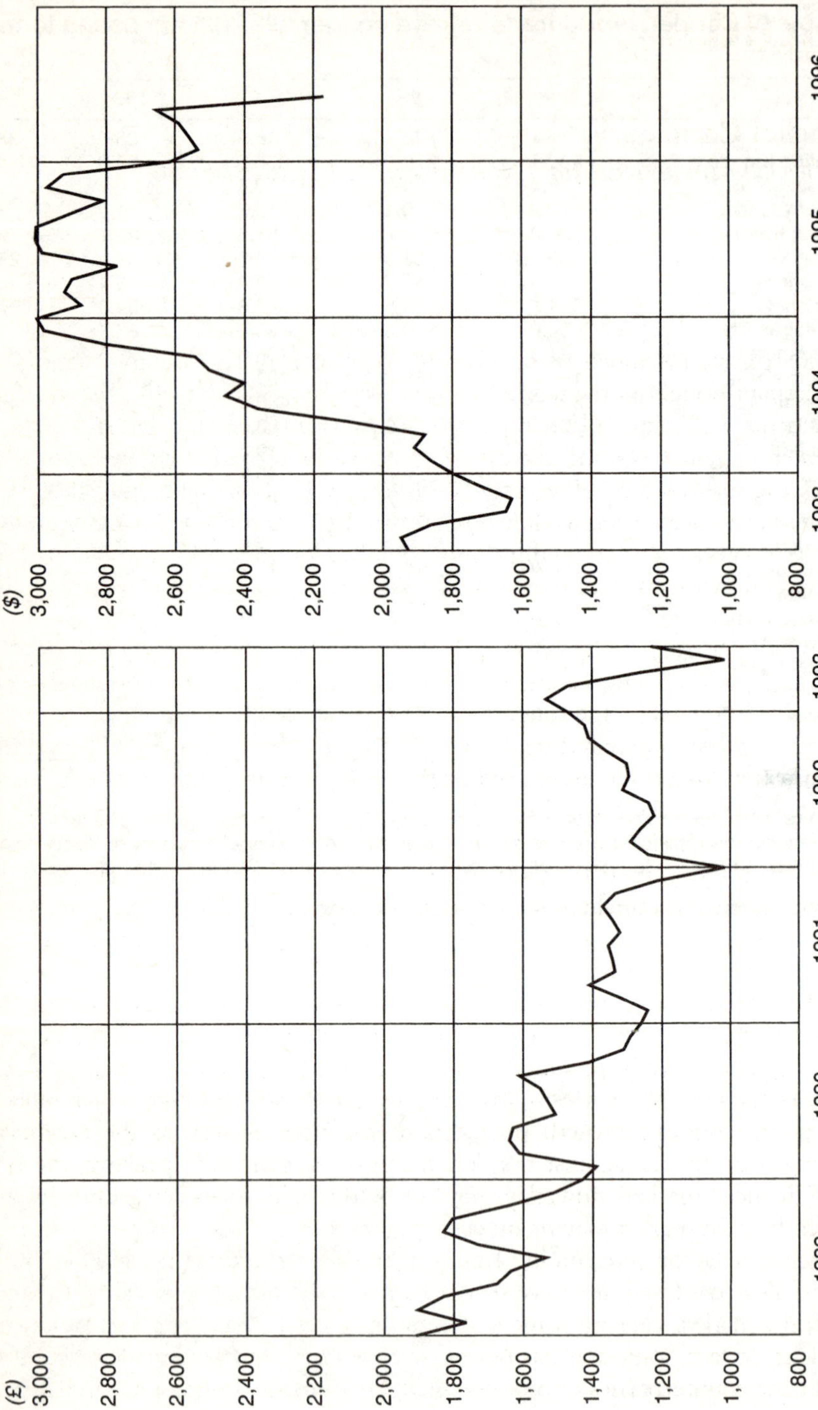

Source: London Metal Exchange

Gold

Rachel Carnac
News & Markets Editor (Non-Ferrous), Metal Bulletin

Gold still retains much of its lustre for exploration and mining 'juniors' are investing throughout the world in prospective mine projects – modern-day 'gold rushes' are still taking place in parts of North and Latin America. However, the market has failed to shine in terms of price. Despite a rally early in 1996, which took the market above the magic $400/oz level for the first time since 1993, prices have since started to slide towards the $370/oz mark again although some analysts forecast a good medium-term outlook for the market through to 1997.

Several factors account for gold's failure to out-perform other major economic indicators.

No longer seen as a barometer of the world economy, the demise of the Gold Standard in 1968 saw the metal becoming just like any other commodity with prices determined by the fundamentals of supply and demand.

While physical demand held up well in 1995, future growth will depend to some extent on purchases of gold jewellery in major consuming regions, particularly India and the Middle East.

Seasonal variations also affect buying patterns, especially before the Chinese New Year and around the Indian wedding season with 15 per cent of annual physical demand bunched into these periods. Gold fabrication levels are, in fact, one of the market's relatively strong sectors, dependent in turn on the buoyancy of the jewellery sector.

While macro-economic factors may play less of a direct role in the gold market, they can still be influential. Concerns over inflation rates, for example, can deter official and private disinvestment in the metal and encourage hoarding. In the first half of 1995 Japan saw a surge in bar hoarding, which reflected its poor economic growth prospects at the time as well as the exceptional strength of the yen against the dollar. However, generally speaking, the bond and financial markets nowadays tend to be the main focus of investor interest, with the gold market playing an ever smaller role.

Another factor determining trends in the gold market is the level of official sales. The past few years have seen a number of central banks selling the metal into the market, causing some softening in prices by balancing out production deficits. In fact, some analysts believe sales of borrowed gold made by commercial bank counterparties of producer-hedgers were the driving force in balancing the market in 1995.

On the supply side of the market, South Africa remains the key gold producer although its production has been falling for the past few years and was last year at its lowest level for 40 years at 523 tonnes. Despite that fall, however, total world output only fell by 1 per cent to 2,102 tonnes.

Much of the decline in South Africa's gold sector has been created by lower grading ores and the problems associated with deep mining. With the end of Apartheid and the success of the multi-party elections in South Africa, the next decade should see some major changes in the country's gold mining industry as mining houses come under pressure to increase workers' wages and conditions. To protect their profitable operations during this period, the gold producing companies will have to increase productivity.

Further gold production deficits are expected this year before output starts to rise again in 1997 and 1998. Finding and developing a successful gold mine is still the dream of many an investor, with exploration work continuing apace throughout the world. It is debatable whether many of these projects will ever come on stream, but the surge in gold prices early in 1996 certainly saw a redoubling of interest from mining juniors.

Much of this interest has been focused on British Columbia and the Yukon, although a number of US and Canadian gold producers have been spreading their wings further afield. This has led to a wave of interest in the former Soviet Union since it broke up in the early 1990s. So far, US gold producer Cyprus-Amax looks as though it will be successful in developing the Kubaka gold project in Russia and is looking at another project in the Urals.

Other mining interest has been directed towards the former Soviet republics of Kazakhstan, Uzbekistan, Tajikistan and Kyrgyzstan. However, the withdrawal of giant mining company RTZ-CRA from Russia has signalled to the market that this is still a very risky region in which to develop a successful gold mine. Development of Kazakhstan's gold projects has also proved difficult.

Other major exploration work is continuing in South East Asia, focusing on Indonesia and the Philippines. So far, though, development of Latin America's gold mining sector seems to be having the most success, in Chile, Peru, Brazil and Venezuela. Production costs remain the key to future mine development, with low-cost miners able to produce at around $200-250/oz.

While mined gold output has been falling, record levels of supply have been created as mining companies increase their forward-selling positions, which were estimated in 1995 to have reached 511 tonnes.

As the pattern of forward sales continues, so gold lease rates have risen as the central banks have been unable to match borrowing demand. If lease rates continue to remain high, this should in turn lend support to gold prices.

Gold is primarily traded on the Comex contract of the New York Mercantile Exchange (NYMEX). The benchmark price for gold is established in London by the major bullion houses. Known as the gold fix, this is arrived at twice a day and published on the major news-wire services, like Reuter. Other major trading centres are in Singapore, Tokyo, Hong Kong and Zurich.

Despite attempts to establish other gold futures contracts outside New York, these have met with little success and several have failed over the past few years.

Further information

Gold Fields Mineral Services Ltd
Greencoat House
Francis Street
London SW1P 1DH
UK
Tel: +44 171 828 8040
Fax: +44 171 233 5096

Johnson Mathey
Precious Metals Marketing
78 Hatton Garden
London EC1N 8JP
UK
Tel: +44 171 269 8000
Fax: +44 171 269 8133

London Bullion Market Association
6 Frederick's Place
London EC2R 8BT
UK
Tel: +44 171 796 3067
Fax: +44 171 796 4345

Samuel Montagu & Co
10 Lower Thames Street
London EC3R 6HB
UK
Tel: +44 171 260 9000
Fax: +44 171 621 0496

Sharp's Pixley
1st Floor
133 Houndsditch
London EC3A 7DX
UK
Tel: +44 171 545 8000
Fax: +44 171 545 1440

World Gold Council
Kings House
10 Haymarket
London SW1Y 4BP
UK
Tel: +44 171 930 5171
Fax: +44 171 839 6561

Table 1 Western world gold supply and demand (tonnes)

	1986	*1987*	*1988*	*1989*	*1990*	*1991*	*1992*	*1993*	*1994*	***1995***
Supply										
Mine production	1296	1384	1551	1683	1755	1790	1872	1904	1897	**1890**
Former communist bloc sales	402	303	263	266	392	230	63	176	109	**102**
Net official sales	–	–	–	366	13	25	624	448	80	**232**
Old gold scrap	513	454	375	372	510	450	448	532	572	**583**
Gold loans	17	55	164	78	5	–	–	–	–	**–**
Forward sales	20	72	126	116	222	96	156	217	163	**461**
Option hedging	8	22	63	–	7	15	103	–	57	**87**
Implied disinvestment	–	–	180	20	–	290	–	–	181	**–**
Total supply	**2255**	**2290**	**2722**	**2901**	**2904**	**2896**	**3266**	**3277**	**3060**	**3355**
Demand										
Fabrication										
Jewellery	1224	1270	1579	1960	2099	2176	2519	2342	2377	**2537**
Electronics	125	126	135	139	148	152	143	155	168	**185**
Other	471	330	263	274	261	289	257	291	261	**285**
Total Fabrication	1819	1725	1976	2373	2508	2617	2919	2788	2806	**3008**
Net official purchases	145	72	285	–	–	–	–	–	–	**–**
Bar hoarding	214	259	461	514	203	233	243	122	203	**281**
Gold loans	–	–	–	–	–	45	85	65	52	**23**
Options hedging	–	–	–	15	–	–	–	31	–	**–**
Implied investment	78	233	–	–	193	–	19	271	–	**44**
Total demand	**2255**	**2290**	**2722**	**2901**	**2904**	**2896**	**3266**	**3277**	**3060**	**3355**
Gold price (London PM, US$/oz)	367.92	446.07	436.77	380.79	383.59	362.26	343.95	359.82	384.15	**384.05**

This table summarizes the gold market on a Western World basis, an artificial sub-division caused by the lack of information on the former communist bloc countries (eg China and the Soviet Union) prior to 1990. The impact of these countries on the World supply/demand balance prior to 1990 appears in a single figure, net sales of bullion to the West.

By courtesy of Gold Fields Mineral Services Ltd, Gold 1996

Table 2 Gold fabrication in industrial and developing countries (including the use of scrap) (tonnes)

	1986	*1987*	*1988*	*1989*	*1990*	*1991*	*1992*	*1993*	*1994*	***1995***
Supply										
Jewellery	590.4	584.6	670.1	814.2	866.6	878.4	921.9	890.9	889.8	**898.1**
Electronics	117.5	116.4	124.5	128.4	136.5	140.6	130.0	139.3	148.2	**161.6**
Dentistry	47.9	44.6	47.1	46.8	48.0	50.4	54.3	53.7	54.9	**56.8**
Other industrial	50.6	51.4	53.5	56.8	56.5	56.5	59.6	59.9	62.3	**65.2**
Medal sales	4.2	6.5	7.6	7.9	8.5	8.9	6.0	4.1	3.9	**2.9**
Coin sales	297.1	170.6	87.7	87.8	89.4	121.1	76.9	97.6	58.1	**75.0**
Sub total	1107.7	974.1	990.5	1142.0	1205.5	1255.9	1248.8	1245.5	1217.3	**1259.6**
Developing countries										
Jewellery	633.5	685.1	909.0	1145.6	1232.4	1298.0	1597.2	1451.2	1486.9	**1639.1**
Electronics	7.1	9.5	10.1	10.9	11.8	11.6	12.8	15.7	19.6	**23.3**
Dentistry	3.9	3.8	4.1	5.0	5.2	5.3	5.6	5.5	5.3	**5.2**
Other industrial	8.0	7.1	8.2	9.3	11.0	11.0	19.7	33.8	35.8	**37.2**
Medal sales	7.6	9.5	12.6	12.6	13.5	17.8	22.8	20.8	22.6	**31.6**
Coin sales	51.2	36.4	41.9	47.4	28.6	17.9	12.6	15.4	18.3	**11.5**
Sub total	711.3	751.4	985.9	1230.8	1302.4	1361.7	1670.7	1542.5	1588.5	**1747.9**
Total	1819.0	1725.4	1976.3	2372.7	2507.9	2617.6	2919.5	2788.0	2805.7	**3007.6**

By courtesy of Gold Fields Mineral Services Ltd, Gold 1996

Table 3 The world's top 10 gold producing countries (tonnes) (1994 figures in brackets)

1	(1)	South Africa	522.4	(583.9)
2	(2)	United States	329.3	(326.0)
3	(3)	Australia	253.5	(254.9)
4	(5)	Canada	150.3	(146.4)
5	(4)	Russia	142.1	(158.1)
6	(6)	China	136.4	(124.1)
7	(10)	Indonesia	74.1	(55.3)
8	(7)	Brazil	67.4	(73.4)
9	(8)	Uzbekistan	63.6	(64.4)
10	(9)	Papua New Guinea	54.8	(60.5)

By courtesy of Gold Fields Mineral Services Ltd, Gold 1996

Table 4 Gold contract volume on world futures exchanges

	Number of contracts		*Total gold equivalent (tonnes)*		
	COMEX (100 oz)	*Tocom (1 kg)*	*Comex +Tocom*	*Others*	*Total*
1986	8,400,175	1,030,438	27,158	146	27,304
1987	10,239,805	2,158,745	34,008	1081	35,089
1988	9,496,402	2,038,400	31,575	391	31,967
1989	9,988,577	2,686,684	33,754	270	34,024
1990	9,730,041	6,873,304	37,137	130	37,267
1991	6,799,917	4,567,630	25,718	44	25,762
1992	6,002,009	4,193,775	22,862	23	22,885
1993	8,916,195	8,764,441	36,497	49	36,546
1994	8,503,366	12,481,095	38,929	53	38,982
1995	7,785,544	10,945,134	35,161	42	35,203

By courtesy of Gold Fields Mineral Services Ltd, Gold 1996

Table 5 Gold options turnovers

	Number of contracts		*Total gold*
Comex (100 oz)	*Comex (5 day)*	*BM&F (250 g)*	*equivalent (tonnes)*
1,646,791	0	96,254	5146
2,080,067	0	177,828	6514
1,698,696	0	1,403,774	5634
1,623,207	0	6,943,310	6785
1,931,804	0	6,000,859	7509
1,398,451	13,464	7,455,129	6255
1,154,497	17,233	7,932,576	5628
1,717,015	418	9,406,163	7693
1,589,065	911	6,164,731	6487
2,006,695	688	1,882,502	6714

By courtesy of Gold Fields Mineral Services Ltd, Gold 1996

Table 6 World gold mine production (tonnes)

	1986	*1987*	*1988*	*1989*	*1990*	*1991*	*1992*	*1993*	*1994*	***1995***
Total Europe	16.7	18.5	21.7	30.2	35.1	32.0	25.2	25.2	26.7	**27.7**
North America										
United States	118.3	154.9	201.0	265.7	294.2	296.0	329.1	332.1	326.0	**329.3**
Canada	105.7	116.5	134.8	159.5	167.4	175.3	160.4	153.1	146.4	**150.3**
Total North America	224.0	271.4	335.8	425.2	461.6	471.3	489.5	485.2	472.4	**479.6**
Latin America										
Brazil	67.4	84.8	102.2	101.2	84.1	78.6	76.5	75.7	73.4	**67.4**
Peru	10.9	10.8	10.0	12.6	14.6	15.1	18.0	27.4	39.3	**51.5**
Chile	24.0	23.3	26.7	29.0	33.3	33.0	39.3	38.5	43.3	**48.5**

Table 6 World gold mine production (tonnes) contd.

	1986	*1987*	*1988*	*1989*	*1990*	*1991*	*1992*	*1993*	*1994*	***1995***
Colombia	27.1	32.5	33.4	31.7	32.5	30.7	29.9	26.4	25.5	**24.1**
Mexico	8.3	9.0	10.4	10.8	9.6	8.5	10.4	11.1	13.9	**20.3**
Venezuela	15.0	16.0	20.0	17.1	14.2	13.2	11.7	11.2	13.7	**17.1**
Bolivia	6.0	6.0	9.0	11.5	10.4	10.0	7.9	12.1	14.7	**16.0**
Other	22.3	23.2	23.0	23.1	21.6	21.0	21.2	26.3	27.8	**29.5**
Total Latin America	181.0	205.6	234.6	236.9	220.3	210.1	214.9	228.7	251.6	**274.4**
Asia										
Indonesia	8.4	12.2	12.3	10.8	17.6	24.4	45.9	52.2	55.3	**74.1**
Papua New Guinea	36.1	33.9	36.6	33.8	33.6	60.8	71.2	61.5	60.5	**54.8**
Philippines	38.7	39.5	39.2	38.0	37.2	30.5	27.2	29.8	31.0	**28.4**
Other	19.1	16.9	18.6	19.8	20.0	22.9	25.1	28.0	29.0	**29.6**
Total Asia	102.3	102.5	106.7	102.4	108.4	138.6	169.4	171.5	175.8	**186.9**
Africa										
South Africa	640.0	607.0	621.0	607.5	605.1	601.1	614.1	619.5	583.9	**522.4**
Ghana	11.5	11.7	12.1	15.3	17.3	27.3	33.3	41.4	44.5	**52.2**
Zimbabwe	15.4	15.2	15.5	16.6	17.9	19.1	19.9	20.7	22.5	**26.1**
Other	26.2	37.0	40.0	35.8	35.3	43.5	48.1	49.2	50.9	**52.1**
Total Africa	693.1	670.9	688.6	675.2	675.6	690.9	715.4	730.8	701.8	**652.8**
Oceania										
Australia	75.1	110.7	157.0	203.6	244.2	236.2	243.5	247.3	254.9	**253.5**
New Zealand	1.4	1.2	2.5	5.0	6.0	7.5	10.5	11.2	10.6	**11.5**
Other	2.7	2.8	4.1	4.4	4.1	2.8	3.8	3.8	3.5	**3.4**
Total Oceania	79.2	114.7	163.6	213.0	254.3	246.5	257.8	262.3	269.0	**268.4**
WESTERN WORLD TOTAL	1296.3	1383.6	1551.0	1682.9	1755.3	1789.3	1872.2	1903.7	1897.3	**1889.8**
Other Countries										
Russia	0.0	0.0	0.0	0.0	0.0	0.0	151.7	164.5	158.1	**142.1**
China	65.0	72.0	78.0	86.0	95.7	104.2	113.1	121.0	124.1	**136.4**
Uzbekistan	0.0	0.0	0.0	0.0	0.0	0.0	64.5	66.6	64.4	**63.6**
North Korea	0.0	0.0	0.0	9.5	13.0	13.0	17.0	15.0	14.0	**14.0**
Other	0.8	1.0	0.9	1.1	1.0	0.8	1.0	1.4	2.1	**4.9**
Other CIS	0.0	0.0	0.0	0.0	0.0	0.0	13.5	17.6	20.0	**21.2**
Sub total other countries (including FSU up to 1991, minus China)	275.0	277.0	280.0	285.0	270.0	252.0	0.0	0.0	0.0	**0.0**
TOTAL OTHER COUNTRIES	340.8	350.0	358.9	381.6	379.7	370.0	360.8	386.1	382.7	**382.2**
WORLD TOTAL	1637.1	1733.6	1909.9	2064.5	2135.0	2159.5	2233.0	2289.8	2280.0	**2272.0**

By courtesy of Gold Fields Mineral Services Ltd, Gold 1996

Figure 1 LME Gold: monthly average cash settlement and sellers' prices
All prices quoted in $ per tonne

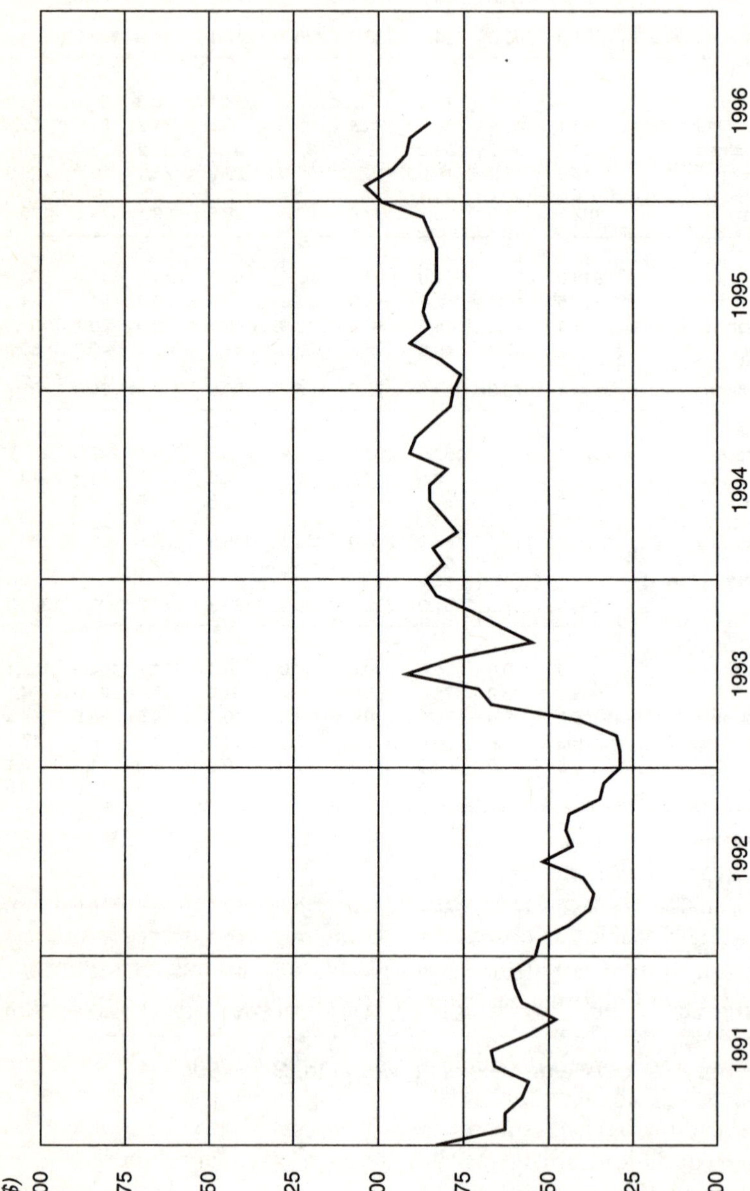

Source: London Metal Exchange

Lead

David Eldridge
Associate Editor, Metal Bulletin

Environmental and health concerns have done much to erode lead's traditional markets, which have been stripped away one by one since the 1960s. However, following the success of the campaign to remove lead from petrol, the metal is now consolidating around one core use for which there is currently no serious alternative – in automotive batteries.

With world demand for lead forecast by most industry observers to continue growing by 1–3 per cent up to 2000, and prices enjoying historical highs, the outlook for lead is now better than it has been for some time.

Storage batteries now account for about 70 per cent of lead's total market, compared with 49 per cent in 1979 but the dominance of one end-use does not necessarily make the metal reliant on the fortunes of the car manufacturers, since the larger market is in replacement batteries for older cars, which is a seasonal rather than cyclical business.

The key to the future of batteries is in vehicle population which is forecast to continue expanding in the long term, fuelled particularly by the Asian countries where vehicle density is a still far lower than in Europe, North America and Japan.

Lead-acid batteries are still proving to be the most commercially effective means of storing power, whether for automotive, traction or stand-by applications. There has been research into alternative battery configurations, such as nickel-cadmium but, so far, none has made serious inroads into lead's market.

This firm position also makes the lead-acid battery a strong contender in the development of electric vehicles. The impetus for low-emission vehicles is coming largely from environmental legislation in the USA, where a number of car manufacturers and research groups are developing their own variants. But a commercially viable car powered by something other than petrol may still be some way off mass production, particularly as the leading environmentally concerned state of California has extended the deadline for a set number of vehicles on the road.

Among lead's other, declining markets, piping, petrol additives, paints and pigments have all fallen out of favour because of health concerns, while use in cable sheathing has been substituted largely by plastics and in solders by tin-lead rather than all-lead amalgams. Lead shot is meanwhile the latest target for environmental substitution.

The lead industry is now very conscious of addressing environmental concerns and an International Lead Management Centre is being set up to extend lead risk-reduction measures. One consequence of being in the environmental spotlight has been that lead producers have invested in new so-called 'clean', technology which limits emissions and slag waste.

Lead is the most recycled of the base metals, with 60–65 per cent of all production in the developed countries coming from scrap sources. European and US companies, including combined battery and lead producers like Exide, have developed integrated battery collection, breaking and recycling systems. Being at the forefront of the trend towards recycling may stand lead producers in good stead as environmental legislation becomes more stringent.

The lead market took a decided turn for the better in March 1996 when London Metal Exchange (LME) cash prices broke through $800/tonne to hit five-and-a-half year highs. The strong price rally had been a long time coming as the physical lead market had been experiencing increasingly tight supply throughout 1995. As that continues, lead producers are optimistic that higher prices will remain for some time.

No significant additions to world lead smelter capacity have been announced for the second half of the 1990s which would imply a continuation of the market deficit of 50,000–100,000 tonnes per year – unless demand suddenly falls away. This deficit is likely to be met by a continuing drawdown of stocks, both in LME warehouses and those held by producers and consumers.

World refined lead production has been steady at 5.4 million tonnes per year in the first half of the 1990s. If there is growth, it is likely to be in secondary production, with primary producers, such as Metaleurop's Nordenham plant in Germany, turning more towards scrap sources.

Primary production is expected to stagnate or even fall, particularly with the closure of Asarco's Omaha refinery in the USA in June 1996. Lead mine production, on the other hand, has started to rise after a decline in 1993 caused by a series of mine closures, and stood at 2.7 million tonnes (in terms of lead content) in 1995.

At present, the major producing countries in the west are Australia, Canada, and the USA, all of which are expected to lift production through new mines and capacity additions. China's mine output started to decline in 1995, caused by financial problems, while the other significant producer, Peru, has embarked on a mine privatization programme which is expected to lead to productivity improvements in the latter half of the 1990s.

Further information

International Lead & Zinc Study Group
2 King Street
London SW1Y 6QP
UK
Tel: +44 171 839 8550
Fax: +44 171 930 4635

Table 1 Lead: world mine production 1991–95 (thousand tonnes)

	1991	*1992*	*1993*	*1994*	*1995*
EUROPE					
Austria	1.1	1.0	1.4	–	–
Denmark	–	–	–	–	–
Finland	1.4	0.6	–	–	–
France	1.7	–	–	–	–
Germany	7.3	2.1	–	–	–
Greece	31.7	28.3	26.4	19.9	20.4
Ireland	39.9	42.9	44.6	53.7	46.1
Italy	14.0	18.0	7.4	13.9	13.6
Macedonia	–	–	24.0	20.0	15.7
Norway	3.5	3.8	1.7	3.2	2.3
Slovenia	–	–	–	–	–
Spain	49.2	31.0	25.3	23.8	30.5
Sweden	87.0	103.8	111.2	112.8	100.1
United Kingdom	1.0	1.0	1.0	1.0	1.0
Yugoslavia	61.0	48.1	12.7	9.3	15.0
Total	298.8	280.6	255.7	257.6	244.7
AFRICA					
Algeria	1.1	0.9	0.9	0.7	0.8
Congo	–	–	–	–	–
Morocco	70.0	72.1	71.3	70.3	67.1
Namibia	16.1	21.2	18.0	21.1	28.7
South Africa	76.3	75.4	100.2	95.8	86.9
Tunisia	0.8	0.8	0.5	2.0	2.8
Zambia	9.8	6.1	7.6	0.6	–
Total	174.1	176.5	198.5	190.5	186.3
ASIA					
Burma	4.8	2.7	1.9	2.4	1.7
India	27.8	30.5	26.0	30.5	28.6
Iran	16.9	12.4	14.7	18.3	15.9
Japan	18.3	18.8	16.5	9.9	9.7
Philippines	–	–	–	–	–
South Korea	12.6	13.6	7.4	2.2	4.1
Thailand	16.5	11.7	6.0	18.7	22.8
Turkey	12.1	9.9	10.9	9.8	10.9
Other Asia	–	–	–	–	–
Total	109.0	99.6	83.4	91.8	93.7
AMERICAS					
Canada	276.5	343.8	183.1	170.9	210.3
USA	476.9	408.5	362.4	372.0	408.2
Argentina	23.7	18.0	11.8	10.0	10.5
Bolivia	20.8	20.0	21.2	19.7	20.4
Brazil	7.3	4.2	4.0	4.0	6.0
Chile	1.1	0.3	0.3	0.5	0.5
Honduras	8.7	9.6	3.8	2.8	2.5
Mexico	167.7	173.0	181.0	175.3	169.5
Peru	199.1	194.2	217.6	216.7	232.5
Other America	2.4	–	–	–	–
Total	1184.2	1171.6	985.2	971.9	1060.4

Table 1 Lead: world mine production 1991–95 (thousand tonnes) contd.

	1991	*1992*	*1993*	*1994*	*1995*
OCEANIA					
Australia	579.0	572.0	514.0	465.0	452.7
TOTAL	**2345.1**	**2300.3**	**2036.8**	**1976.8**	**2037.8**
Monthly Average	*195.4*	*191.6*	*169.7*	*164.7*	*169.8*
OTHER COUNTRIES					
Bulgaria	40.6	39.6	34.4	32.0	32.0
Czechoslovakia	3.4	2.0	–	–	–
Czech Republic	–	–	1.7	1.7	1.7
Hungary	–	–	–	–	–
Poland	47.3	51.0	49.0	51.6	51.6
Romania	16.2	16.8	16.8	21.4	20.5
USSR	230.0	–	–	–	–
Georgia	–	–	–	–	–
Kazakstan	–	184.2	183.8	69.0	53.3
Russia	–	51.9	35.7	26.0	25.0
Tajikistan	–	–	–	–	–
Uzbekistan	–	30.0	30.0	18.0	18.0
China	352.2	330.2	338.1	461.9	369.0
North Korea	80.0	70.0	70.0	55.0	55.0
Total	769.7	775.7	759.5	736.6	653.1
WORLD TOTAL	**3114.8**	**3076.0**	**2796.3**	**2713.4**	**2690.9**

This table shows the content by analysis of lead ores and concentrates plus the lead content of mixed ores.

By courtesy of the World Bureau of Metal Statistics

Figure 1 Lead: world mine production

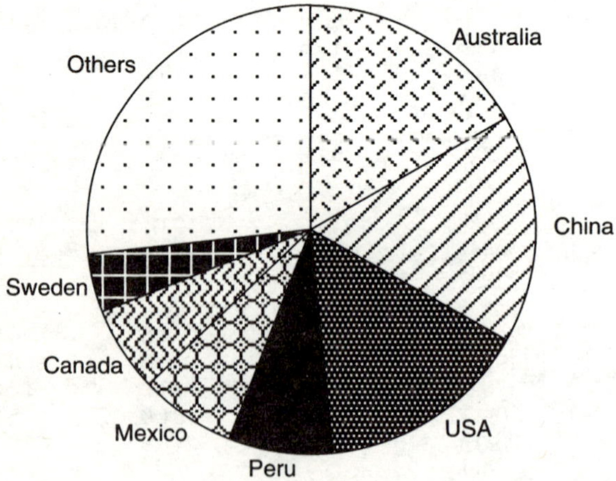

Table 2 Lead: world refined production 1991–95 (thousand tonnes)

	1991	*1992*	*1993*	*1994*	*1995*
EUROPE					
Austria	22.7	23.9	22.6	17.6	21.6
Belgium	99.3	98.9	116.8	123.5	121.7
Denmark	–	–	–	–	–
Finland	–	–	–	–	–
France	283.3	284.1	258.7	260.5	296.7
Germany	362.5	354.3	344.1	331.7	313.9
Greece	–	–	–	–	–
Ireland	11.6	12.0	9.4	10.4	10.4
Italy	207.6	186.3	182.8	203.6	172.0
Macedonia	–	–	21.9	21.0	22.5
Netherlands	33.7	23.5	24.0	24.5	20.2
Norway	–	–	–	–	–
Portugal	4.0	7.4	8.3	13.0	13.2
Slovenia	–	–	12.0	15.0	15.6
Spain	110.4	62.1	62.4	74.6	81.0
Sweden	88.0	91.2	82.5	82.7	91.2
Switzerland	5.2	5.7	5.7	6.0	6.0
United Kingdom	311.0	346.8	363.8	352.5	320.6
Yugoslavia	94.6	54.4	6.0	4.5	11.5
Total	1633.9	1550.6	1521.0	1541.1	1518.1
AFRICA					
Algeria	3.0	3.0	8.6	9.0	8.6
Morocco	72.7	71.4	71.4	63.8	58.0
Namibia	33.4	31.7	31.2	23.8	26.8
Nigeria	4.5	5.0	4.5	5.0	4.8
South Africa	30.5	29.0	31.8	31.6	32.0
Tunisia	–	–	–	–	–
Zambia	3.5	3.4	2.9	0.5	0.5
Other Africa	4.8	4.9	2.8	5.0	4.8
Total	152.4	148.4	153.2	138.7	135.5
ASIA					
Burma	2.2	2.1	1.6	1.8	1.3
India	47.8	63.7	50.7	60.3	62.0
Iran	38.0	42.0	52.0	51.3	46.2
Japan	332.3	330.2	309.5	292.3	286.5
Malaysia	24.0	28.5	29.0	33.2	33.6
Philippines	16.7	19.1	24.3	17.2	17.2
South Korea	74.0	84.0	116.0	129.8	129.8
Taiwan	20.0	20.0	28.4	35.6	36.0
Thailand	15.7	19.6	17.1	16.9	16.9
Turkey	8.5	5.1	5.0	4.0	5.1
Other Asia	39.0	46.4	42.0	39.9	39.9
Total	618.2	660.7	675.6	682.3	674.5
AMERICAS					
Canada	212.4	252.9	217.0	261.6	277.4
USA	1194.6	1157.9	1216.5	1292.3	1262.1
Argentina	25.0	29.7	28.5	25.4	28.7
Brazil	64.0	62.8	66.7	67.0	79.0
Mexico	232.1	288.4	255.5	218.7	216.0
Peru	76.0	83.3	86.3	88.1	89.6
Venezuela	15.0	15.0	15.0	16.0	15.0
Other America	6.0	5.9	7.1	5.8	5.8
Total	1825.1	1895.9	1892.6	1974.9	1973.6

Table 2 Lead: world refined production 1991–95 (thousand tonnes) contd.

	1991	*1992*	*1993*	*1994*	*1995*
OCEANIA					
Australia	239.4	231.8	237.8	231.5	231.6
New Zealand	5.0	5.0	3.0	6.0	6.0
Total	244.4	236.8	240.8	237.5	237.6
TOTAL	**4474.0**	**4492.4**	**4483.2**	**4574.5**	**4539.3**
Monthly Average	*372.8*	*374.3*	*373.6*	*381.2*	*378.2*
OTHER COUNTRIES					
Bulgaria	56.2	53.1	57.0	62.2	62.2
Czechoslovakia	17.8	23.9	–	–	–
Czech Republic	–	–	23.2	19.3	19.3
German DR	–	–	–	–	–
Hungary	–	–	–	–	–
Poland	50.8	53.7	68.0	63.1	66.4
Romania	17.6	16.2	18.1	16.4	15.0
USSR	360.0	–	–	–	–
Kazakstan	–	242.5	255.0	150.3	150.3
Russia	–	37.9	44.9	34.3	34.0
Ukraine	–	38.0	20.0	9.0	9.0
Uzbekistan	–	–	–	–	–
China	320.0	366.0	411.9	384.3	422.1
North Korea	65.0	65.0	65.0	50.0	50.0
Total	887.4	896.3	963.1	788.9	828.3
WORLD TOTAL	**5361.4**	**5388.7**	**5446.3**	**5363.4**	**5367.6**

This table is based on the production of refined lead including the lead content of antimonial lead from primary and secondary materials. Metal recovered from secondary material by remelting alone is excluded.

By courtesy of the World Bureau of Metal Statistics

Table 3 Lead: world refined consumption 1991–95 (thousand tonnes)

	1991	*1992*	*1993*	*1994*	*1995*
EUROPE					
Austria	66.7	66.6	61.8	62.0	66.7
Bosnia	–	–	3.0	3.0	3.0
Croatia	–	–	2.4	0.8	2.6
Belgium	71.7	64.1	74.0	64.9	73.2
Denmark	4.6	4.4	4.0	4.0	3.5
Finland	12.2	7.3	4.3	4.8	4.3
France	252.5	246.0	226.2	236.7	265.2
Germany	413.5	412.2	351.7	356.2	367.5
Greece	11.4	6.7	6.6	7.0	6.5
Ireland	22.1	21.0	21.0	27.4	27.1
Italy	259.0	247.0	223.0	230.2	263.9
Macedonia	–	–	5.0	5.0	5.0
Netherlands	58.6	52.2	48.0	57.5	60.4
Norway	1.5	3.3	2.7	3.7	3.8
Portugal	24.0	31.3	25.7	34.1	27.6
Slovenia	–	–	11.0	8.0	8.0
Spain	121.5	105.0	104.0	119.5	130.2

Table 3 Lead: world refined consumption 1991–95 (thousand tonnes) contd.

	1991	*1992*	*1993*	*1994*	*1995*
Sweden	24.5	26.1	33.6	26.2	26.2
Switzerland	9.8	7.6	5.9	8.3	11.1
United Kingdom	263.8	263.6	263.6	267.6	283.3
Yugoslavia	90.0	40.0	5.0	5.0	5.0
Other Europe	–	0.1	0.2	0.1	0.2
Total	1707.4	1604.5	1482.7	1532.0	1644.4
AFRICA					
Morocco	7.7	6.6	5.8	7.7	7.7
South Africa	52.0	52.5	58.5	58.9	42.3
Tunisia	2.4	4.8	2.9	4.1	4.1
Zambia	2.4	2.9	2.4	2.1	0.9
Other Africa	34.8	33.5	40.7	36.7	36.7
Total	99.3	100.3	110.3	109.5	91.7
ASIA					
Hong Kong	0.6	0.5	0.5	0.9	0.5
India	78.0	60.0	80.0	75.0	80.4
Indonesia	39.9	56.6	75.0	90.9	91.2
Iran	30.0	36.0	36.0	60.0	60.0
Japan	422.2	401.4	370.5	347.7	333.5
Malaysia	45.0	57.0	50.8	56.9	60.0
Philippines	20.3	24.9	31.8	27.0	26.0
Singapore	6.0	8.0	8.0	10.0	8.0
South Korea	163.3	163.9	177.7	220.2	214.3
Taiwan	83.1	104.5	100.7	100.3	133.0
Thailand	41.2	50.2	58.9	61.9	62.4
Turkey	26.9	22.7	33.4	28.2	44.2
Other Asia	33.5	20.7	24.1	22.7	22.7
Total	990.0	1006.4	1047.4	1101.7	1136.2
AMERICAS					
Canada	77.6	88.5	73.7	73.3	71.6
USA	1246.3	1240.7	1357.1	1495.0	1472.2
Argentina	24.5	29.8	32.8	33.2	30.2
Brazil	66.0	70.0	74.5	85.0	98.4
Mexico	91.8	164.5	161.5	162.4	162.0
Peru	14.2	12.4	13.7	13.1	14.3
Other America	36.0	36.8	46.2	39.8	39.8
Total	1556.4	1642.7	1759.5	1901.8	1888.5
OCEANIA					
Australia	56.0	58.6	62.0	78.0	78.0
New Zealand	5.5	4.0	3.9	3.5	3.9
Other Oceania	–	0.4	0.1	0.1	–
Total	61.5	63.0	66.0	81.6	81.9
TOTAL	**4414.6**	**4416.9**	**4465.9**	**4726.6**	**4842.7**
Monthly Average	*367.8*	*368.0*	*372.1*	*393.8*	*403.5*
OTHER COUNTRIES					
Albania	1.0	1.0	1.0	1.0	1.0
Bulgaria	35.2	23.0	28.1	21.0	21.0
Czechoslovakia	29.5	21.3	–	–	–
Czech Republic	–	–	23.0	18.0	17.0
Slovakia	–	–	3.0	3.0	2.0

Table 3 Lead: world refined consumption 1991–95 (thousand tonnes) contd.

	1991	*1992*	*1993*	*1994*	*1995*
German DR	–	–	–	–	–
Hungary	6.5	8.1	7.9	8.0	8.0
Poland	48.9	46.5	58.9	53.0	53.0
Romania	17.6	16.2	18.1	16.4	15.0
USSR	310.0	–	–	–	–
Kazakstan	–	35.0	30.0	30.0	30.0
Russia	–	215.0	181.1	108.5	108.5
Ukraine	–	–	–	7.1	4.5
Uzbekistan	–	–	–	–	–
Other FSU	–	10.0	10.0	10.0	10.0
China	242.0	277.0	314.0	295.1	262.0
North Korea	40.0	40.0	40.0	36.0	36.0
Cuba	1.0	1.6	1.0	1.0	1.0
Other	1.5	3.0	2.0	0.4	0.4
Total	733.2	697.7	718.1	608.5	569.4
WORLD TOTAL	**5147.8**	**5114.6**	**5184.0**	**5335.1**	**5412.1**

By courtesy of the World Bureau of Metal Statistics

Figure 2 Lead: world refined consumption

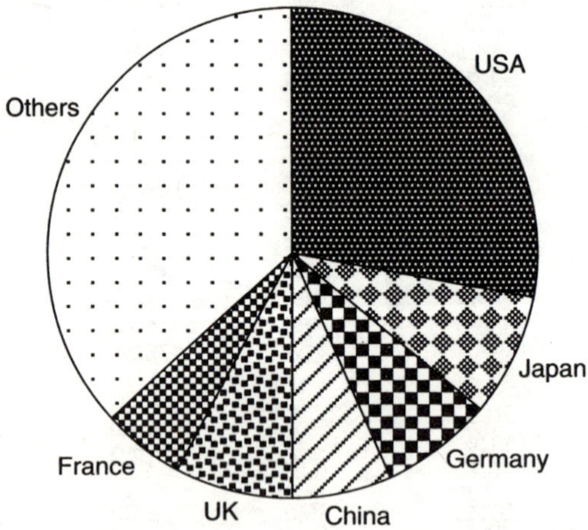

Table 4 Lead: world trade – refined lead 1991–95 (thousand tonnes)

	1991	*1992*	*1993*	*1994*	*1995*
EXPORTS					
Austria	1.7	3.2	2.6	3.9	–[5]
Belgium	47.3	50.3	57.1	87.1	51.0[7]
Denmark[1]	0.2	0.3	0.4	0.6	0.2
Finland	–	0.2	–	–	–
France	55.0	63.0	57.7	74.4	73.0
Germany	62.5	48.6	64.5	79.3	54.0
Greece	–	0.1	2.8	–	0.3[6]
Netherlands	15.7	10.3	8.7	6.2	6.2
Spain	1.2	0.7	3.0	4.8	4.2
Sweden[2]	65.0	66.9	61.6	54.4	47.5
United Kingdom	75.2	79.1	93.9	85.9	79.4
Yugoslavia	29.8	6.6	–	5.4	–
Morocco	60.7	62.0	74.9	55.6	–
Namibia	–	5.1	–	2.9	–
Tunisia	–	–	–	–	–
South Africa	6.0	5.0	7.0	3.0	0.3[7]
Zambia	1.3	0.1	0.2	0.2	–
Japan[3]	–	3.6	7.8	1.0	3.5
Singapore	12.0[7]	6.0	22.4	30.0	15.3
Taiwan	7.9	1.4	0.5	2.8	7.8
Canada[4]	95.1	139.0	128.5	142.3	150.8
USA[3]	65.6	58.0	45.7	45.3	46.8
Argentina	0.5	0.5	0.3	0.3	–
Mexico	92.1	97.5	62.4	54.8	104.0
Peru	59.0	71.5	70.0	74.8	75.4
Australia	176.0	187.0	166.8	176.6	188.6
Total	**929.8**	**966.0**	**938.8**	**991.4**	**908.3**
IMPORTS					
Austria	41.8	40.2	35.9	41.5	–[5]
Belgium	20.3	13.1	17.4	15.5	17.2[7]
Denmark[1]	4.8	4.7	5.2	4.6	3.7
Finland	12.2	7.5	4.3	4.8	3.1
France	36.1	30.5	26.4	49.5	41.5
Germany	117.3	107.5	75.9	85.6	115.2
Greece	9.4	4.9	7.9	5.5	3.2[5]
Ireland[3]	11.0[8]	9.4	18.0	17.4	17.9
Italy	76.7	75.5	62.2	56.3	92.7
Netherlands	39.0	38.1	29.3	39.5	51.5
Norway[3]	1.8	3.3	2.7	3.7	3.8
Poland	2.2[9]	3.0	8.0	9.0	–
Portugal	20.0	27.3	17.5	19.5	18.8
Spain	11.4	45.1	39.0	37.5	53.5
Sweden	0.7	0.5	2.8	2.7	1.1
Switzerland	8.3	5.9	3.6	4.8	5.1
United Kingdom	36.9	28.1	32.3	23.1	47.4
Yugoslavia	–	–	–	1.9	–
South Africa	24.0	23.0	24.0	27.0	21.0
Hong Kong	2.6	6.2	2.2	4.0	4.5
India	24.1	34.4	16.8	26.6	9.2[5]
Japan[3]	103.1	71.0	50.4	62.1	77.2
Philippines	5.4	5.6	12.5	7.5	8.8
Singapore	13.0[7]	39.9	39.7	25.4	16.6
South Korea	94.8	88.5	75.9	106.8	104.8

Table 4 Lead: world trade – refined lead 1991–95 (thousand tonnes) contd.

	1991	*1992*	*1993*	*1994*	*1995*
Taiwan	74.0	89.9	86.2	88.1	104.0
Thailand	25.5	30.6	41.8	45.0	17.9[5]
Canada[4]	6.8	7.6	7.8	4.8	4.0
USA	100.5	162.3	168.6	195.3	211.4
China	–	1.2	1.8	3.4	3.2
Total	**923.7**	**1004.8**	**916.1**	**1018.4**	**1058.3**

This table shows principal imports and exports of refined lead.

Notes [1] Excludes intra – European Union trade from 1993 onwards. [2] May include some bullion. [3] Includes alloy. [4] Includes shot. [5] January to June. [6] January to September. [7] January to November. [8] January and February. [9] January to October.

By courtesy of the World Bureau of Metal Statistics

Figure 3 LME lead: monthly average cash settlement and sellers' price
Prices prior to July 1993 quoted in £ per tonne. After July 1993 quoted in $ per tonne

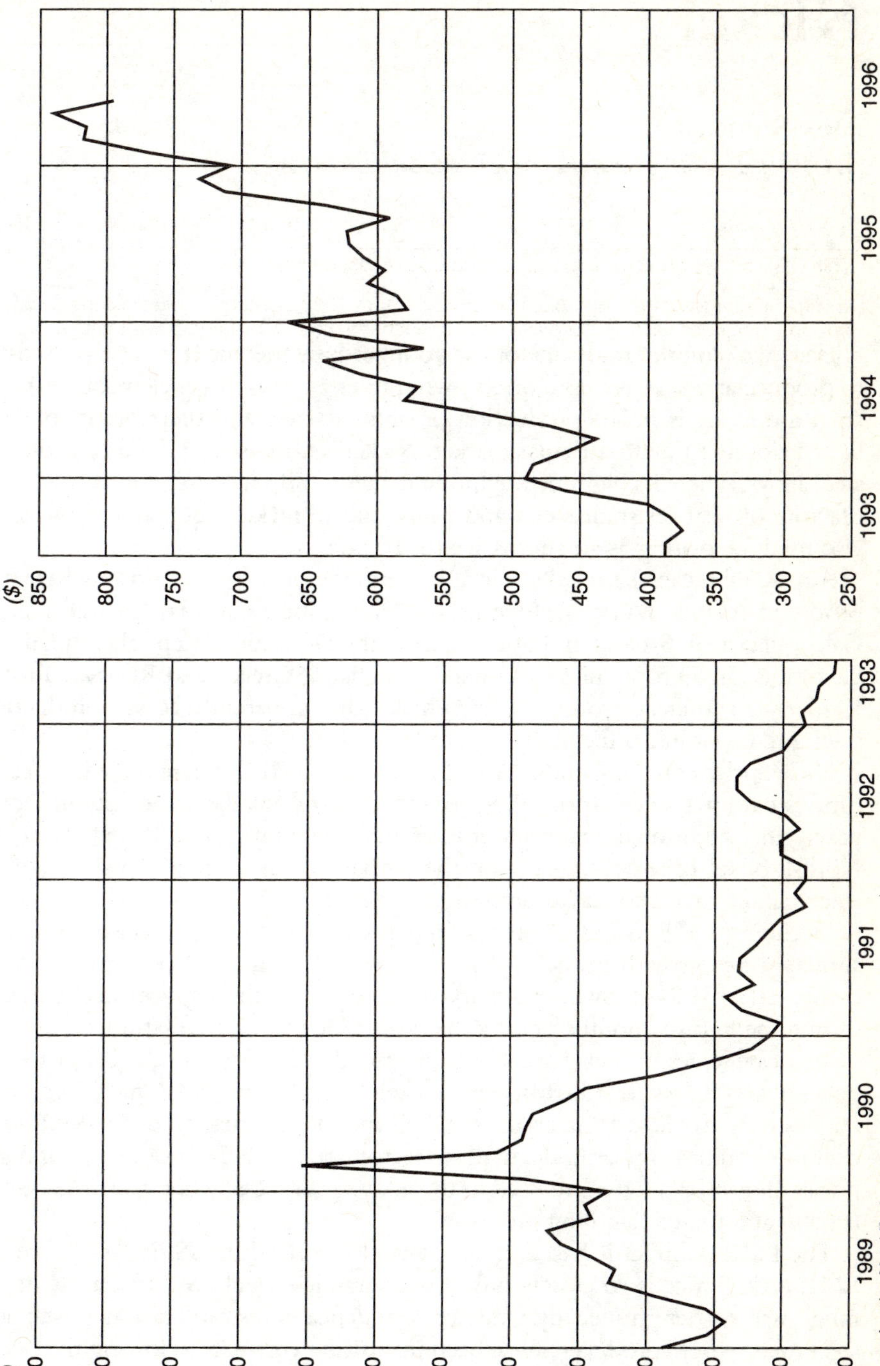

Source: London Metal Exchange

Nickel

Alex Standish
Associate Editor (Non-Ferrous), Metal Bulletin

Nickel, like aluminium, is one of the younger base metals. It is relatively costly to produce and is rarely used on its own, rather as an alloying element. Its principal use today is in the production of stainless steel and therefore its price is linked closely to that particular market. Nickel is also used in the production of steel alloys, where its high melting point makes it especially suitable for the manufacture of heat-resistant steels and irons, and in nickel-based alloys. Nickel is also used for plating as an alternative to chrome.

Almost all nickel is mined as nickel ore and the principal countries where it is produced include Cuba, Indonesia, the Philippines, Canada, Australia, New Caledonia, the USA and, in Latin America, the Dominican Republic, Brazil and Colombia. In Europe, nickel is mined in Finland, Greece and Russia. Albania, formerly a significant source of ferro-nickel, has apparently ceased production owing to economic difficulties.

Nickel prices on the London Metal Exchange (LME), where there has been a futures contract since April 1979, have been very volatile, especially in recent years, since additional quantities of Russian origin material produced mainly by Norilsk Nikel became available on the market. Cyclical trends in the stainless steel market have also had an impact on prices.

Declining LME inventory stocks, in particular, have caused concern for consumers, since growth in nickel demand grew by around 12 per cent in 1995, compared to 1994. However, a marked slowdown in the stainless steel industry during the first six months of 1996 has also added to price volatility.

Two categories of nickel are generally traded: Class I (cathode, briquettes or pellets) and Class II (ferro-nickel, nickel-oxide). The LME nickel contract applies only to Class I material, of which the most widely traded is 99.80 per cent minimum nickel cathode, used in electoplating and the production of high-purity alloys. Briquettes are used in the alloying process, while pellets are often used in automated handling processes.

The LME contract is based on six tonne lots priced in US dollars. Since the LME nickel price is so closely linked with stainless steel production, its future range will be determined by whether confidence is restored amongst stainless steel mills, where producers have been instituting cutbacks following the boom of 1995. The rising availability of nickel scrap may also contribute to a reduction in demand for primary nickel, although potential growth in other uses may offset a decline in overall demand. However, a build-up of stainless steel mill inventories continues to exert a negative effect on prices.

Production of nickel in 1995 rose by nearly 14 per cent to around 675,000 tonnes. Effective mine capacity in 1995 was estimated at 748,000 tonnes. Consumption in 1995 rose to 874,500 tonnes with marked growth in North America (+13 per cent) and Asia (+17.8 per cent). European consumption grew by just over 7 per cent in 1995.

New mining projects currently being evaluated include Diamond Field Resources and INCO's Voisey's Bay (Canada), Dominion Mining's Yakabindi (Western Australia), Inco's Goro (New Caledonia) and Anaconda Nickel's Murrin Murrin mine (Western Australia). However, the high capital costs involved in setting up a nickel mining operation and the need to invest in additional smelting and refining capacity may act as a brake on at least some of the proposed new mining capacity.

One of the major production-side questions is the eventual status of Russia's Norilsk Nikel, which has been the subject of a bitterly disputed privatization during 1996. Finished nickel output at Norilsk totalled 180,100 tonnes in 1995, making it a significant market force, so ongoing instability here is likely to result in price volatility. Expected growth in Russian domestic demand for nickel is another factor which may affect the volume of metal available for export in the future.

The outlook for nickel is so closely linked to conditions in the stainless steel market that while mills are instituting production cutbacks, prices are likely to remain under pressure. The continuing drawdown in LME stocks to below the 78,000 tonnes level, previously regarded as critical, will also be influential. Above all, however, supply-side fundamentals are likely to be highly dependent on the progress made on the development by new mining projects, particularly the giant Voisey's Bay operation which is expected to be in production by 2000.

Further information

International Nickel Study Group
Scheveningseweg 62
2517 KX The Hague
The Netherlands
Tel: +31 70 354 3326
Fax: +31 70 358 4612

Table 1 Nickel: world mine production 1991–95 (thousand tonnes)

	1991	*1992*	*1993*	*1994*	*1995*
EUROPE					
Finland	9.9	9.2	8.3	6.8	3.5
Greece	18.0	15.4	12.6	16.2	17.2
Macedonia	–	–	3.0	4.6	1.5
Norway	2.3	3.4	3.6	3.3	3.6
Yugoslavia	3.2	3.0	0.6	0.8	1.2
Total	33.4	31.0	28.1	31.7	27.0
AFRICA					
Botswana	20.4	18.9	19.7	19.0	18.1
Morocco	–	–	–	–	–
South Africa	29.0	28.4	28.9	30.1	29.8
Zimbabwe	12.4	11.4	12.8	13.8	11.7
Total	61.8	58.7	61.4	62.9	59.6
ASIA					
Burma	0.1	0.1	–	–	–
Indonesia	66.1	78.1	65.8	81.2	86.6
Philippines	13.7	14.0	7.7	14.6	17.2
Total	79.9	92.2	73.5	95.8	103.8
AMERICAS					
Canada	192.3	186.4	188.1	149.9	181.0
USA	5.5	6.7	2.5	2.5	2.5
Brazil	13.8	14.7	15.2	16.5	15.7
Colombia	20.1	20.2	20.2	20.8	25.7
Dominican Republic	29.1	27.5	23.9	30.8	30.9
Guatemala	–	–	–	–	–
Total	260.8	255.5	249.9	220.5	255.8
OCEANIA					
Australia	69.0	57.0	64.7	79.0	98.5
New Caledonia	99.8	99.6	97.1	96.0	133.0
Total	168.8	156.6	161.8	175.0	231.5
TOTAL	**604.7**	**594.0**	**574.7**	**585.9**	**677.7**
Monthly Average	*50.3*	*49.5*	*47.8*	*48.8*	*56.4*
OTHER COUNTRIES					
Albania	4.0	0.2	–	–	–
German DR	–	–	–	–	–
Poland	–	–	–	–	–
USSR	200.0	–	–	–	–
Kazakstan	–	1.0	1.0	1.0	1.2
Russia	–	275.0	209.0	212.0	224.0
Ukraine	–	1.0	1.0	1.0	1.2
China	30.4	32.8	30.7	36.9	31.0
Cuba	33.3	32.2	28.8	31.0	31.0
Other	0.1	–	–	–	–
Total	267.8	342.2	270.5	281.9	288.4
WORLD TOTAL	**872.5**	**936.2**	**845.2**	**867.8**	**966.1**

This table shows the nickel content of ores and concentrates produced.

By courtesy of the World Bureau of Metal Statistics

Figure 1: Nickel: world mine production

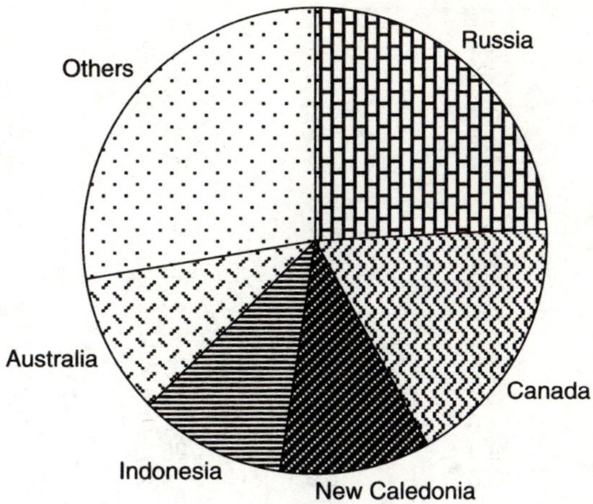

Table 2 Nickel: world refined production 1991–95 (thousand tonnes)

	1991	*1992*	*1993*	*1994*	*1995*
EUROPE					
Finland	14.1	14.8	14.8	15.9	14.8
France	8.6	6.8	9.0	10.0	10.4
Greece	16.0	15.4	10.9	16.2	17.2
Macedonia	–	–	4.5	4.1	2.0
Norway	58.7	54.9	56.8	68.4	53.2
United Kingdom	28.6	28.0	28.0	28.4	35.1
Yugoslavia	3.2	2.7	25.8	6.9	6.9
Total	129.2	122.6	149.8	149.9	139.6
AFRICA					
South Africa	26.9	27.6	29.9	30.1	29.8
Zimbabwe	18.2	17.2	18.2	19.6	16.5
Total	45.1	44.8	48.1	49.7	46.3
ASIA					
Indonesia	5.3	5.5	5.3	5.8	10.7
Japan	116.5	109.4	105.4	112.6	135.0
Philippines	–	–	–	–	–
South Korea	–	–	–	–	–
Taiwan	–	–	–	–	–
Total	121.8	114.9	110.7	118.4	145.7
AMERICAS					
Canada	131.5	135.2	123.1	105.1	121.5
USA	7.1	9.0	4.9	–	8.3
Brazil	13.8	14.7	15.2	16.5	15.7
Colombia	20.2	20.2	20.2	20.8	25.7
Dominican Republic	29.1	27.5	23.9	30.8	30.9
Total	201.7	206.6	187.3	173.2	202.1

Table 2 Nickel: world refined production 1991–95 (thousand tonnes) contd.

	1991	*1992*	*1993*	*1994*	*1995*
OCEANIA					
Australia	49.4	50.6	50.4	66.6	77.3
New Caledonia	34.4	31.9	36.9	39.5	42.2
Total	83.8	82.5	87.3	106.1	119.5
TOTAL	**581.6**	**571.4**	**583.2**	**597.3**	**653.2**
Monthly Average	*48.4*	*47.6*	*48.6*	*49.7*	*54.4*
OTHER COUNTRIES					
Albania	1.1	0.1	–	–	–
Czechoslovakia	2.4	1.5	–	–	–
Czech Republic	–	–	–	–	–
German DR	–	–	–	–	–
Poland	–	–	–	–	–
USSR	210.0	–	–	–	–
Russia	–	247.4	187.8	190.7	201.9
Ukraine	–	1.0	1.0	1.0	1.2
China	28.9	30.8	30.5	31.3	38.1
Cuba	18.8	16.9	16.6	14.1	21.7
Other	–	–	–	–	–
Total	261.2	297.7	235.9	237.1	262.9
WORLD TOTAL	**842.8**	**869.1**	**819.1**	**834.4**	**916.1**

This table shows smelter-refinery production of electrolytic nickel, nickel pellets, briquettes, steel making powder, nickel content of nickel salts, chemical grade nickel oxide, ferro-nickel, nickel oxide sinter and utility nickel.

By courtesy of the World Bureau of Metal Statistics

Table 3 Nickel: world refined consumption 1991–95 (thousand tonnes)

	1991	*1992*	*1993*	*1994*	*1995*
EUROPE					
Austria	6.0	4.6	4.0	3.5	3.6
Belgium	19.6	21.4	22.8	23.0	22.8
Denmark	0.7	0.5	0.5	0.4	0.5
Finland	18.0	23.5	26.8	30.4	35.1
France	36.8	35.0	36.5	44.4	49.4
Germany	77.0	74.0	75.0	87.8	106.1
Greece	0.2	0.2	0.2	0.2	0.2
Ireland	0.1	0.1	0.1	0.1	0.1
Italy	31.5	29.6	38.5	44.0	52.6
Macedonia	–	–	1.0	0.6	1.0
Netherlands	1.8	1.1	1.1	1.1	1.1
Norway	0.2	0.3	0.3	0.4	0.3
Portugal	0.2	0.2	0.2	0.2	0.2
Spain	17.8	13.3	16.8	25.7	29.5
Sweden	16.3	16.3	22.8	24.8	25.6
Switzerland	1.1	1.1	0.7	0.3	1.1
United Kingdom	29.5	28.5	29.8	38.0	41.9
Yugoslavia	1.8	1.0	–	–	–
Total	258.6	250.7	277.1	324.9	371.1

Table 3 Nickel: world refined consumption 1991–95 (thousand tonnes) contd.

	1991	*1992*	*1993*	*1994*	*1995*
AFRICA					
Total	9.3	9.9	9.9	14.9	13.6
ASIA					
India	15.0	13.2	13.2	17.7	13.2
Japan	180.1	148.1	157.2	181.1	195.9
South Korea	23.2	26.0	33.2	41.1	46.1
Taiwan	19.0	19.0	19.0	26.0	26.0
Other Asia	14.1	6.9	–	9.1	9.1
Total	251.4	213.2	222.6	275.0	290.3
AMERICAS					
Canada	10.3	12.5	13.9	16.9	24.2
USA	125.2	119.1	122.1	131.0	147.8
Argentina	0.2	0.6	0.3	0.5	0.2
Brazil	11.4	11.1	12.2	14.2	15.3
Mexico	1.8	1.8	1.4	3.5	1.4
Other America	1.0	1.2	1.2	1.2	1.2
Total	149.9	146.3	151.1	167.3	190.1
OCEANIA					
Australia	1.4	1.5	1.5	1.4	1.5
New Zealand	0.4	0.3	0.3	0.3	0.3
Total	1.8	1.8	1.8	1.7	1.8
TOTAL	**671.0**	**621.9**	**662.5**	**783.8**	**866.9**
Monthly Average	55.9	51.8	55.2	65.3	72.2
OTHER COUNTRIES					
Bulgaria	0.5	0.2	0.2	0.3	0.6
Czechoslovakia	5.2	2.8	–	–	–
Czech Republic	–	–	1.0	1.1	1.2
German DR	–	–	–	–	–
Hungary	3.0	2.0	0.5	0.8	0.8
Poland	0.5	0.1	0.2	1.0	0.8
Romania	0.5	0.3	0.5	0.6	1.0
USSR	85.0	–	–	–	–
Kazakstan	–	–	–	–	–
Russia	–	128.7	95.1	66.7	68.5
Ukraine	–	3.0	3.0	1.6	0.3
Other FSU	–	1.0	1.0	1.0	1.2
China	32.0	35.0	39.0	42.0	37.1
Other	0.8	4.0	0.6	0.6	0.6
Total	127.5	177.1	141.1	115.7	112.1
WORLD TOTAL	**798.5**	**799.0**	**803.6**	**899.5**	**979.0**

This table shows consumption of unwrought nickel, to include refined nickel plus the consumption of nickel contained in other smelter-refinery products.

By courtesy of the World Bureau of Metal Statistics

Figure 2 Nickel: world refined consumption

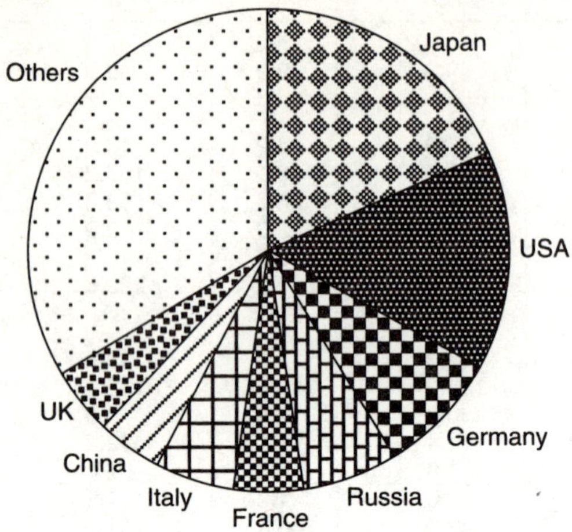

Figure 3 LME nickel: monthly average cash settlement and sellers' prices
All prices quoted in $ per tonne

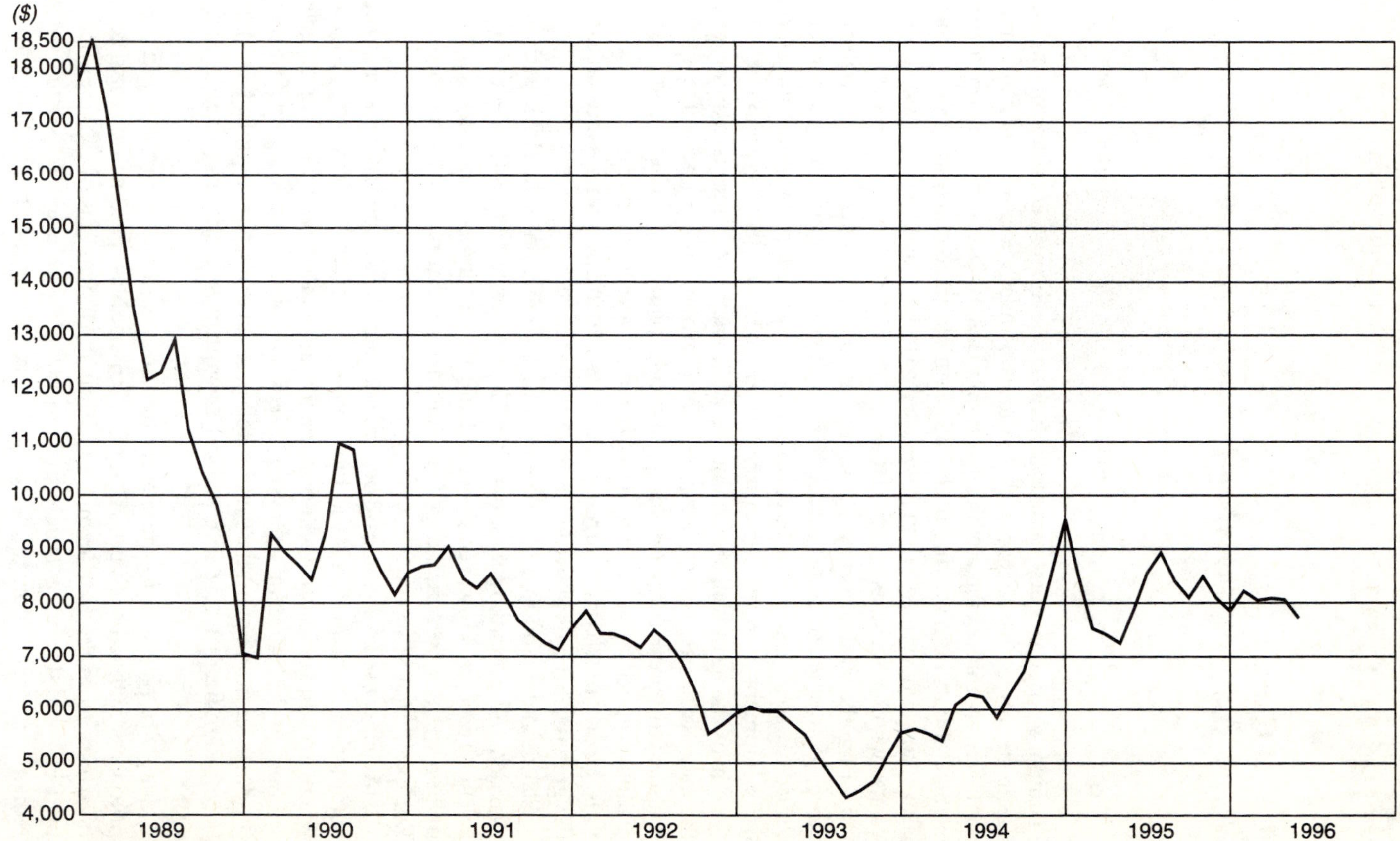

Source: London Metal Exchange

Platinum

Rachel Carnac
News & Markets Editor (Non-Ferrous), Metal Bulletin

Platinum's properties first came to light after the Spanish conquest of the Americas in the fifteenth and sixteenth centuries. While it was seen then as valueless compared to gold, being a white coloured metal, its strengths as a non-corrosive element and its high melting point only brought the metal to prominence in the late seventeenth century when it was used to make crucibles for glass production – a use which continues to this day.

During the 20th century, platinum has grown further in industrial importance, alongside its usage in decorative jewellery, for which it is particularly valued in Japan. Latterly, it has also been widely used in computer and automotive equipment, in drugs for cancer treatment and in dental equipment.

Perhaps the most well known industrial usage for platinum is in autocatalysts: the metal converts harmful emissions into carbon dioxide and water. Platinum is also used by car companies in lightweight plastics for vehicle body parts, in platinum-tipped spark plugs and in oxygen sensors for engine management controls. Hence, much of its current and future demand potential is interlinked with the growth of the worldwide automotive sector.

Platinum demand rose to a new peak of 4.79 million oz in 1995, with industrial demand expanding by a massive 21 per cent to 990,000 oz – the highest level in 16 years. However, demand from the automotive industry fell to 1.85 million oz as lower-than-expected volumes of platinum were needed in the European catalyst sector.

This has caused some unease over the degree of platinum's dependency on the automotive market. While the metal may be susceptible to strong price rises when new auto-catalyst technologies are announced (as when US Engelhard announced the 'PremAir' catalyst), prices can collapse just as easily if those new products do not contain the anticipated high levels of platinum. In fact, this has been a significant factor in a sudden downturn in platinum prices in the past year.

Supply of platinum to the market remains restricted, with the world's major producers confined to South Africa and Russia. New production is also coming on stream from the Hartley mine in Zimbabwe, which is owned and operated by BHP and Delta: a little platinum is also produced in North America. Nonetheless, total world production has been rising, with supplies up 10 per cent in 1995 to 4.98 million oz as South African output rose and Russian shipments reached record levels.

Since the breakup of the Soviet Union, supplies from Russia have become more unsettled as the government has released stockpile material in order to raise much-needed revenue. Shipments from Russia rose to 1.28 million oz in 1995, which was substantially above production levels. It was estimated that around 600,000 oz were released from state stockpiles to achieve this. However, it is difficult to determine just how much material might be stored in the stockpiles and what impact these shipments are likely to have on the market in the future.

Russia's platinum is produced in Siberia at Norilsk Nikel and the plant has suffered a number of financial difficulties over the past few years. The government sold its remaining 38 per cent shareholding in the company to Russian-based Oneximbank in November 1995, which led to several battles over the running of the company, although by mid-1996 the situation appeared to be settling down and the bank was involved in seeking investment capital for the operation.

The political situation in Russia will remain critical to how platinum sales are made and controlled. The Russians are said to understand the price-impact their platinum sales activities have on the international market, but are not averse to making disruptive sales in order to raise hard currency. A toughening of Russia's stance towards exporting metals might mean that supplies could be restricted again in the coming years.

The other main producer, South Africa, produced 3.37 million oz in 1995, returning to previous production highs last seen in 1993. Lonrho, Amplats, Northam and Impala are the main South African producers, with operations centring around the Bushveld Complex.

A proposed merger between Lonrho and Gencor's platinum interests was turned down by the European Commission's anti-competition directorate in 1996, although this looked unlikely to have changed much in the structure of the platinum market.

Platinum futures are traded on the New York Mercantile Exchange (Nymex) and the Tokyo Commodity Exchange (Tocom). Nymex has also introduced platinum options and has introduced the ACCESS trading system which permits longer trading hours.

There is also major speculative interest in platinum, with investment in coinage and bars. Tanaka Kikinzoku Kogo KK, the leading Japanese bullion house, along with Germany's Degussa, Engelhard Corp of the USA and the UK's Johnson Matthey & Co Ltd all produce a number of one and ten ounce platinum bars.

In coinage, Australia's Koala and Canada's Maple Leaf remain the leading platinum coins in terms of annual sales. China, Russia and the Isle of Man have also minted a number of platinum coins.

Despite continuing investor interest in the 'white metal', the platinum market was disappointing throughout 1995 and 1996, largely remaining flat in a

$400–450/oz trading range. However, there are a number of factors which mean that platinum cannot be written off and the market could still return to exciting trading conditions.

On the supply side, for example, South African producers have been running down their concentrate inventories in the past few years and are no longer maintaining stocks of refined platinum. So any industrial action or technical difficulties could provide a swift boost to the market later in 1996 and during 1997.

In the longer term, industry profits will hold the key to levels of platinum production. Margins have already come under pressure from the decline in the dollar platinum price at a time of high inflation and a stable South African rand. A prolonged period of profitability from 1996 onwards will be needed to allow expansion to take place and for the survival of current loss-making operations such as Northam.

Russia will also remain a wild card in determining supply, with little knowledge in the market over the size of its existing stocks or whether shipments will remain at the highs recorded in 1995. Another factor is the potential for US government strategic stockpile sales, which again could unsettle the market over the next few years.

The market outlook from the demand side of the market is also very difficult to forecast. Increased competition from palladium-rich auto-catalysts had already begun to make a dent in platinum offtake by the end of 1995 while future demand patterns will depend on tighter emissions limits being set around the world – and also on continuing high vehicle sales. Over the coming years and into the next century much of this growth is likely to move away from the western world. Clean air legislation in countries such as Argentina, Malaysia, Korea and Brazil may also boost platinum, while there is still enormous potential for vehicles sales to increase in the former Soviet Union, China and India.

The increased importance of auto-catalysts in vehicles since the early 1990s is likely to result in higher levels of recycled platinum throughout the rest of the decade and into the next century. But while this will certainly have some impact on availability, it is difficult to predict whether this will balance out losses in primary supply.

Further information

Johnson Mathey
Precious Metals Marketing
78 Hatton Garden
London EC1N 8JP
UK
Tel: +44 171 269 8000
Fax: +44 171 269 8133

Platinum Guild
25th Floor
150 East 58th Street
New York NY 10022
USA
Tel: +1 212 758 6767
Fax: +1 212 758 3195

Samuel Montagu & Co
10 Lower Thames Street
London EC3R 6HB
UK
Tel: +44 171 260 9000
Fax: +44 171 621 0496

Sharp's Pixley
1st Floor
133 Houndsditch
London EC3A 7DX
UK
Tel: +44 171 545 8000
Fax: +44 171 545 1440

Table 1 Platinum supply and demand: western world

'000 oz	*1986*	*1987*	*1988*	*1989*	*1990*	*1991*	*1992*	*1993*	*1994*	*1995*
Supply										
South Africa	2350	2520	2580	2620	2760	2770	2750	3360	3160	**3370**
Russia	290	400	440	550	720	1100	750	680	1010	**1280**
North America	150	140	210	195	185	220	200	220	220	**230**
Others	40	40	50	60	65	70	120	130	140	**100**
Total supply	**2830**	**3100**	**3280**	**3425**	**3730**	**4160**	**3820**	**4390**	**4530**	**4980**
Demand										
By application										
Autocatalyst:										
gross	1140	1255	1315	1455	1535	1565	1550	1685	1870	**1850**
recovery	(90)	(115)	(160)	(175)	(215)	(215)	(245)	(275)	(310)	**(335)**
Chemical	195	195	160	165	215	240	215	180	190	**215**
Electrical	180	180	185	195	205	175	165	165	185	**205**
Glass	90	120	130	140	135	120	80	80	160	**225**
Investment:										
small	450	215	330	130	100	175	145	125	155	**75**
large	(125)	275	300	30	100	240	110	180	240	**270**
Jewellery	850	990	1180	1300	1365	1470	1510	1615	1740	**1810**
Petroleum	20	55	50	75	140	150	120	105	90	**120**
Other	130	120	120	115	120	140	150	165	190	**225**
	2840	3290	3610	3430	3700	4060	3800	4025	4510	**4660**
* Western sales to China	40	30	40	40	0	(20)	0	20	50	**130**
Total demand	**2880**	**3320**	**3650**	**3470**	**3700**	**4040**	**3800**	**4045**	**4560**	**4790**
Movements in stocks	(50)	(220)	(370)	(45)	30	120	20	345	(30)	**190**
	2830	3100	3280	3425	3730	4160	3820	4390	4530	**4980**
Demand										
By region										
Europe	470	560	545	600	700	775	845	875	915	**885**
Japan	1010	1650	1900	1670	1850	2050	1870	1975	2145	**2220**
North America	1190	900	865	895	790	815	705	760	940	**965**
Rest of western world	170	180	300	265	360	420	380	415	510	**590**
	2840	3290	3610	3430	3700	4060	3800	4025	4510	**4660**
*Western sales to China	40	30	40	40	0	(20)	0	20	50	**130**
Total demand	**2880**	**3320**	**3650**	**3470**	**3700**	**4040**	**3800**	**4045**	**4560**	**4790**

* Before 1993 estimates included Eastern Europe; for 1993 and subsequent years demand in this region is included in our European figures.

By courtesy of John Mathey

Table 2 Platinum demand by application: western world

'000 oz	*1986*	*1987*	*1988*	*1989*	*1990*	*1991*	*1992*	*1993*	*1994*	*1995*
Europe										
Autocatalyst:										
gross	120	225	245	310	375	480	575	610	605	**580**
recovery	0	0	0	0	(5)	(15)	(20)	(25)	(30)	**(30)**
Chemical	75	80	50	50	60	55	50	40	50	**55**
Electrical	40	40	40	40	40	30	30	20	25	**25**
Glass	30	30	30	35	25	20	15	15	30	**35**
Investment:										
small	100	65	55	35	40	40	35	25	45	**10**
Jewellery	55	45	70	75	80	85	85	105	100	**120**
Petroleum	(5)	25	5	10	40	30	20	25	25	**15**
Other	55	50	50	45	45	50	55	60	65	**75**
Total	**470**	**560**	**545**	**600**	**700**	**775**	**845**	**875**	**915**	**885**
Japan										
Autocatalyst:										
gross	255	310	330	360	400	380	350	320	290	**270**
recovery	(5)	(15)	(25)	(25)	(35)	(35)	(45)	(50)	(45)	**(40)**
Chemical	15	15	15	15	25	20	20	15	15	**20**
Electrical	45	45	45	50	50	50	50	45	45	**50**
Glass	30	45	45	40	50	35	20	30	80	**105**
Investment:										
small	35	60	115	35	40	65	40	55	40	**105**
large	(125)	275	300	30	100	240	110	180	240	**270**
Jewellery	740	900	1060	1150	1190	1260	1290	1350	1450	**1480**
Petroleum	0	0	0	0	15	15	10	10	5	**5**
Other	20	15	15	15	15	20	25	20	25	**25**
Total	**1010**	**1650**	**1900**	**1670**	**1850**	**2050**	**1870**	**1975**	**2145**	**2220**
North America										
Autocatalyst:										
gross	745	690	690	725	690	620	525	600	790	**790**
recovery	(85)	(100)	(135)	(150)	(175)	(165)	(180)	(200)	(230)	**(260)**
Chemical	65	55	55	55	50	100	90	75	65	**70**
Electrical	65	65	65	75	80	65	55	65	75	**85**
Glass	25	25	25	30	25	20	15	15	20	**25**
Investment:										
small	300	85	85	50	5	40	65	40	65	**25**
Jewellery	15	15	15	20	20	20	35	45	55	**65**
Petroleum	10	15	15	40	40	50	35	40	5	**50**
Other	50	50	50	50	55	65	65	80	95	**115**
Total	**1190**	**900**	**865**	**895**	**790**	**815**	**705**	**760**	**940**	**965**
Rest of western world										
Autocatalyst:										
gross	20	30	50	60	70	85	100	155	185	**210**
recovery	0	0	0	0	0	0	0	0	(5)	**(5)**
Chemical	40	45	40	45	80	65	55	50	60	**70**
Electrical	30	30	35	30	35	30	30	35	40	**45**
Glass	5	20	30	35	35	45	30	20	30	**60**
Investment:										
small	15	5	75	10	15	30	5	5	5	**5**
Jewellery	40	30	35	55	75	105	100	115	135	**145**
Petroleum	15	15	30	25	45	55	55	30	55	**50**
Other	5	5	5	5	5	5	5	5	5	**10**
Total	**170**	**180**	**300**	**265**	**360**	**420**	**380**	**415**	**510**	**590**

By courtesy of Johnson Mathey

Figure 1 LME platinum: monthly average cash settlement and sellers' prices
All prices quoted in $ per tonne

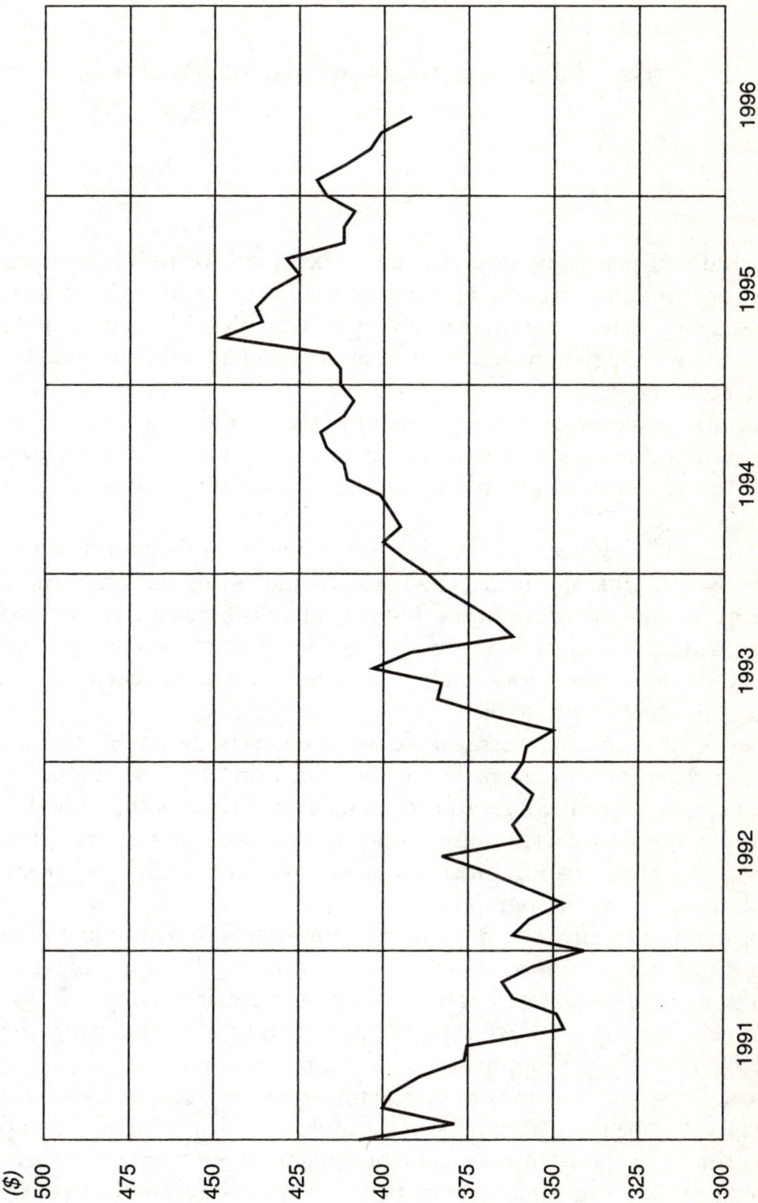

Source: London Metal Exchange

Silver

Rachel Carnac
News & Markets Editor (Non-Ferrous), Metal Bulletin

Like gold and platinum, silver has long been used for decorative/ornamental purposes, including jewellery. However, it has a large number of industrial applications owing to its strength, malleability and ductility, its electrical and thermal conductivity, its high light-reflective properties and its ability to endure extreme temperature ranges.

The most common of all the precious metals, it is also one of the oldest investment commodities. However, silver markets really only started to develop fully in the seventeenth and eighteenth centuries when the Spanish discovered the Americas.

Mexico has long been the major silver producer in the world, although the former Soviet Union, Canada, the USA, Poland, Australia, Chile and Peru are other major producing countries. Usually, silver is obtained as a by-product of copper, zinc and lead mine operations. Indeed, it is rare to find primary silver mines today, such operations tending to open only when prices are high enough to make production profitable.

Uses of silver include electrical sectors in contacts, switches, conductors and fuses; in electronics circuit paths for silk screen printing, in ceramic capacitors and in conductive adhesives. In batteries, silver is used as the cathode element while the metal is also found in brazing and soldering alloys, in catalysts, mirrors and other coating processes, in bearings for aircraft, in rocket engine applications and in photographic film.

For the past seven years, the amount of silver consumed in jewellery and its other major end-use sectors has continued to outstrip the supply of refined metal from primary and secondary sources. To keep the market supplied, stocks built up largely during the 1980s have been sharply eroded during the 1990s although by 1996 the supply deficit had narrowed somewhat.

Stock levels will remain very important to the market over the coming years with investors believed to have been hoarding in anticipation of higher prices. It is difficult to gauge what price is being sought before these stocks are released onto the market, but some analysts believe it could be around $8 per oz. At the end of 1995 world stocks were estimated at around 450 million oz, but this includes a large volume of material which is not for sale or lease.

The silver market is also supplemented by government disposals, with the

Indian government and the US strategic stockpile the most frequent sellers.

Consumption by silver fabricators is greatest in Asia, particularly in India, Thailand, Taiwan and Korea. The USA, Japan and Italy also saw strong demand from their fabrication sectors in 1995. Industrial and decorative fabrication rose to 291 million oz in 1995 (including figures for the former Soviet Union and China) with electrical and electronic demand reaching 203 million oz. Usage in photography is estimated to have reached 222 million oz in 1995, although the metal is losing market share in this sector.

Supply of mined silver to the market has increased over the past two years, rising to just under 470 million oz in 1995. The biggest single contribution was made by the Eskay Creek operation in Canada although other mines have expanded supply too. Analysts forecast a minimal rise in primary production in 1996, with further increases depending on new base mine projects coming on stream by the end of the decade and early into the next century. However, even with increased mine production, if fabrication demand continues its growth trend, further stock drawdowns will be required over coming years.

Secondary sources provide nearly one-third of the market's supply. In 1995, around 171 million oz came from old photographic and electronic materials, jewellery and other ornamental silverware. Scrap and official stock disposals combined contributed 764 million oz to supply last year – marginally down on 1994.

While silver prices have remained stable at around $5.50/oz for the past year or so, some analysts expect a rise in coming years. However, the changing structure of the market over the years and silver's decreasing importance as an economic indicator suggest it may be difficult for the price to sustain a long rally.

Competition in some of the major outlets could also affect silver's future prospects. In photography, the move towards the Advanced Photo System and digital imaging could dent silver offtake, particularly in sectors such as the medical X-ray market.

Silver futures are traded on the Tokyo Commodity Exchange (Tocom), the New York Commodity Exchange (Comex) and at the Chicago Board of Trade (CBoT). Trading volume fell on Nymex-Comex last year, but rose on Tocom and CBoT.

Silver bullion is traded widely throughout the world on a number of stock exchanges, but the main price benchmarks are established in London and New York. The Handy & Harman price is the North American benchmark, providing a daily silver cash quotation accepted by many users. The London spot price is fixed daily, while the Nymex-Comex spot settlement price is also used by the market. There are also investor markets in silver bars and coinage.

Further information

CPM Group
37th Floor
30 Broad Street
New York NY10004
USA
Tel: +1 212 785 8320
Fax: +1 212 785 8325

Johnson Mathey
Precious Metals Marketing
78 Hatton Garden
London EC1N 8JP
UK
Tel: +44 171 269 8000
Fax: +44 171 269 8133

Samuel Montagu & Co
10 Lower Thames Street
London EC3R 6HB
UK
Tel: +44 171 260 9000
Fax: +44 171 621 0496

Sharp's Pixley
1st Floor
133 Houndsditch
London EC3A 7DX
UK
Tel: +44 171 545 8000
Fax: +44 171 545 1440

The Silver Institute
1112 Sixteenth Street
NW Suite 240
Washington DC 20036
USA
Tel: +1 202 835 0185
Fax: +1 202 835 0155

Table 1 Silver: world mine production 1991–95 (thousand tonnes)

	1991	*1992*	*1993*	*1994*	*1995*
EUROPE					
Denmark	–	–	–	–	–
Finland	30.3	27.2	29.3	26.1	27.1
France	23.6	13.3	13.0	2.9	2.9
Germany	7.2	1.8	1.8	1.8	1.8
Greece	70.2	61.0	59.2	44.9	45.0
Ireland	10.5	13.1	13.0	17.3	13.7
Italy	13.6	12.0	5.0	13.7	13.9
Portugal	42.6	38.2	36.0	31.8	38.6
Spain	208.0	160.0	180.0	175.0	175.0
Sweden	239.3	311.1	298.8	275.2	268.2
United Kingdom	–	–	–	–	–
Yugoslavia	92.2	84.0	34.3	31.8	31.8
Other Europe	0.4	0.4	0.4	0.4	0.4
Total	737.9	722.1	670.8	620.9	618.4
AFRICA					
Morocco	228.6	217.1	306.8	332.8	332.8
Namibia	91.9	89.4	71.7	64.0	69.0
South Africa	170.2	178.2	192.6	195.6	174.3
Zaire	50.0	35.0	10.0	1.0	1.0
Zambia	14.2	18.3	18.1	12.1	8.4
Zimbabwe	20.3	16.9	16.8	10.9	10.9
Other Africa	5.3	5.3	5.3	4.3	4.3
Total	580.5	560.2	621.3	620.7	600.7
ASIA					
Burma	6.5	4.8	5.0	5.6	4.4
India	31.9	44.7	51.2	50.3	39.8
Indonesia	79.5	99.9	90.3	106.0	250.4
Japan	170.7	178.3	136.9	133.7	100.1
Malaysia	13.4	15.3	14.0	13.3	11.1
Philippines	34.9	30.9	32.5	31.9	31.1
South Korea	3.1	4.7	2.7	8.6	0.2
Taiwan	–	–	–	–	–
Other Asia	92.4	93.2	81.7	157.9	160.0
Total	432.4	471.8	414.3	507.3	597.1
AMERICAS					
Canada	1338.8	1215.4	895.8	767.8	1245.0
USA	1855.0	1804.0	1640.0	1480.0	1450.0
Argentina	70.0	45.4	42.7	38.1	38.4
Bolivia	337.0	282.4	332.8	352.1	425.0
Brazil	154.0	162.0	160.0	170.0	170.0
Chile	673.6	1042.9	985.0	959.2	1036.4
Colombia	8.0	8.3	7.4	5.8	2.1
Dominican Republic	22.0	14.9	1.7	9.2	–
Honduras	43.0	35.4	24.2	27.6	30.2
Mexico	2295.1	2325.0	2416.0	2325.0	2480.3
Nicaragua	1.0	2.3	2.4	2.6	2.6
Peru	1769.7	1570.0	1621.2	1666.7	1908.3
Other America	0.2	0.2	0.2	0.2	0.4
Total	8567.4	8508.2	8129.4	7804.3	8788.7

Table 1 Silver: world mine production 1991–95 (thousand tonnes) contd.

	1991	*1992*	*1993*	*1994*	*1995*
OCEANIA					
Australia	1180.0	1248.0	1152.0	1045.0	920.0
Papua New Guinea	124.5	95.5	96.1	77.8	65.2
Other Oceania	11.4	22.4	25.8	28.0	30.0
Total	1315.9	1365.9	1273.9	1150.8	1015.2
TOTAL	**11,634.1**	**11,628.2**	**11,109.7**	**10,704.0**	**11,620.1**
Monthly Average	*969.5*	*969.0*	*925.8*	*892.0*	*968.3*
OTHER COUNTRIES					
Bulgaria	37.3	33.0	30.0	29.0	28.9
Czechoslovakia	28.0	20.0	–	–	–
German DR	–	–	–	–	–
Poland	867.3	914.0	767.0	800.0	800.0
Romania	17.0	17.0	18.0	18.0	18.0
USSR	1270.0	–	–	–	–
Kazakstan	–	450.0	450.0	408.4	402.1
Russia	–	300.0	300.0	250.0	250.0
Uzbekistan	–	150.0	150.0	150.0	150.0
China	180.0	200.0	220.0	225.0	225.0
Mongolia	–	–	–	–	–
North Korea	300.0	280.0	250.0	200.0	200.0
Total	2699.6	2364.0	2185.0	2080.4	2074.0
WORLD TOTAL	**14,333.7**	**13,992.4**	**13,294.7**	**12,784.4**	**13,694.1**

This table shows the recoverable silver content of ores and concentrates produced.

By courtesy of the World Bureau of Metal Statistics

Figure 1 Silver: world mine production

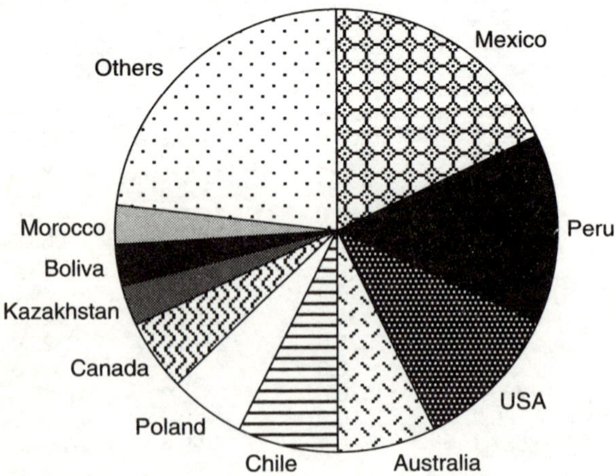

Figure 2 LME silver: monthly average cash settlement and sellers' prices

All prices quoted in US cents per oz

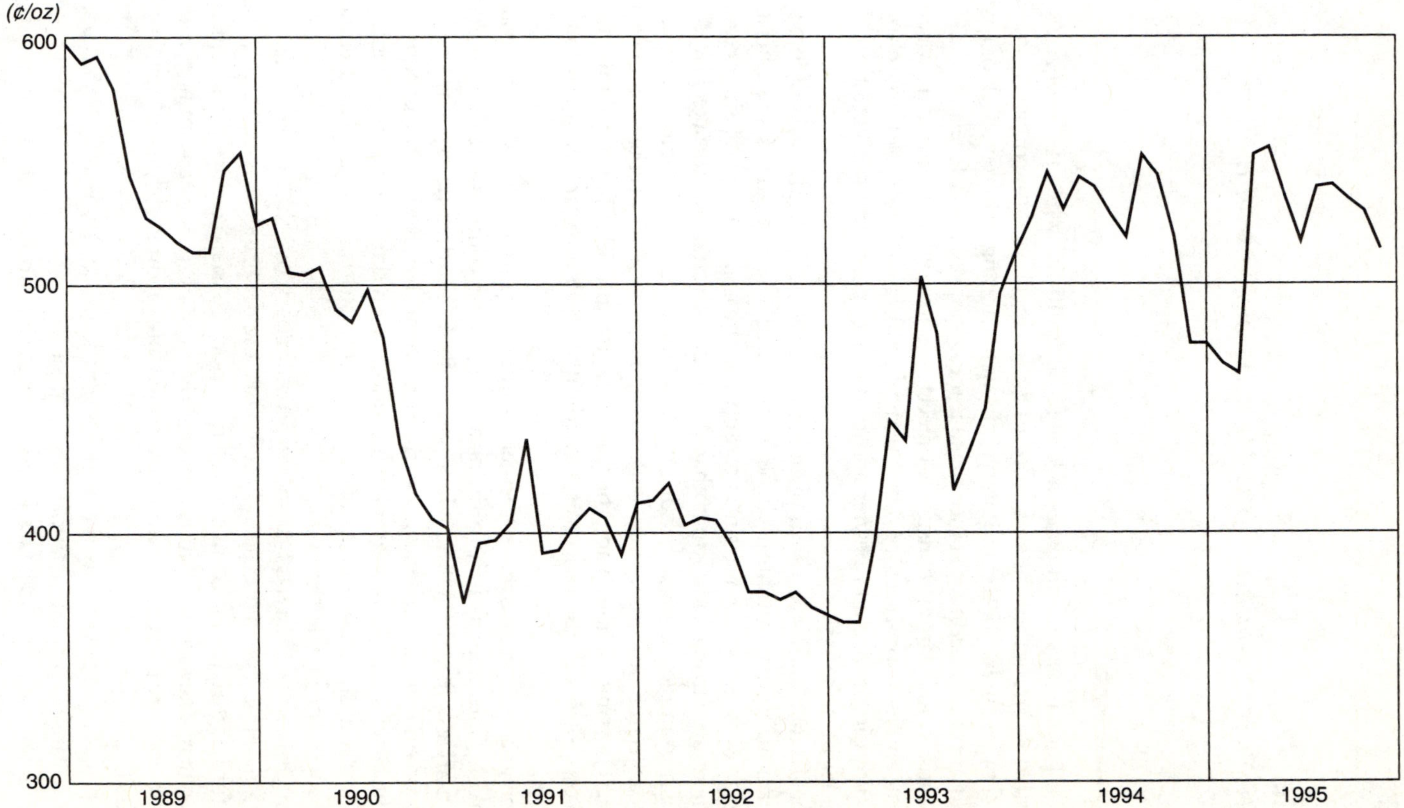

Source: Handy and Harman (through *Metal Bulletin Research*)

Tin

Camila Reed
Deputy News & Markets Editor (Non-Ferrous), Metal Bulletin

The first known uses of tin date back as far as 3500 BC when the Bronze Age discovered its strengthening and protecting uses in alloys with copper. In more modern times tin has become synonymous with canning, where its lack of toxicity and good corrosion resistance make it ideal for preserving foods.

Nowadays, tin's largest consumption sector is in tinplate and solders for the electrical and industrial sectors. The chemical industry is the second largest user, while alloys in bronze and pewter and in coatings continue to account for the remainder of tin's market.

A renaissance in the use of tin-plate in steel cans – after many years of intense competition from aluminium – is being heralded by some analysts as offering strong growth prospects for tin consumption through the rest of the decade. And there are strong indications that this is already starting to take place. In 1995, for example, tin-plate became more dominant than aluminium for use in European beverage canmaking, with the industry body Beverage Canmakers Europe reporting 42 lines using the metal against only 39 still using aluminium. In the previous year, the ratio was 41 dedicated to aluminium versus 34 to tin-plate.

Some analysts predict that a further swathe of up to 15 European beverage canmaking lines may switch to tin-plate in the next couple of years – though other markets, like the USA, where aluminium still dominates, may require more convincing. Nonetheless, the International Tin Research Institute has brought together six major tin-plate producers to discuss technology transfers with three leading European tin-plate producers – British Steel, Sollac of France and Hoogovens in The Netherlands.

In the Far East, Japan has historically accounted for over half the region's consumption of the refined metal. Although Japanese tin-plate use is expected to fall in the future, this may be compensated for by other Asian countries, particularly China where dramatic growth is expected over the next ten years. In fact, more tin-plate lines are currently being installed in China than in the rest of the world combined.

Tin prices have never fully recovered from the market's crisis in 1985 caused by the collapse of the International Tin Agreement (ITA). Losses of $900 million were incurred by the pact's failed attempt to support prices by purchasing metal from the market for its buffer stock and as some ITA member governments refused to honour debts, the bulk had to be borne by the London Metal Exchange which suspended trading in its tin contract between 1985 and 1989.

For much of the period since the LME contract resumed trading, the market has been in a bearish phase. However, 1995 and 1996 have seen prices recover somewhat, aided by investment fund buying on the Exchange and the development of a small supply deficit.

Stocks of tin on the LME during 1996 have declined to around 9,500 tonnes, their lowest level for more than six years. Overshadowing this is the prospect of new capacity waiting to hit the market from Peru and Indonesia. However, for 1996 and 1997 at least, further deficits are predicted of 5–10,000 tonnes and 3–5,000 tonnes respectively.

Western world primary tin production is estimated at around 180,000 tonnes and consumption at about 190,000 tonnes in 1996. World tin production is led by China, followed by Indonesia, Peru, Brazil and Bolivia. Other producers include Mexico, Russia, Malaysia, Portugal and the UK. Since the breakup of the Soviet Union, conditions at Russian mines are reported to have deteriorated with ore grades declining and massive investment needed.

Through a supply rationalization scheme, the Association of Tin Producing Countries (ATPC) has attempted to manage supply through quotas. The ATPC was formed in 1983 but has had relatively little success so far in controlling excess production. Its influence is weakened by the refusal of two of the largest and lowest-cost producers, Brazil and China, to join and with several countries failing to honour quotas the scheme was abolished at the end of June 1996. However, fighting a rearguard action, the ATPC has been urging other countries to join the scheme, including Peru, Vietnam and Myanmar.

Although not a significant producer, the USA has acquired large strategic stocks of tin over the years and from time to time releases these onto the market through sales by the Defense Logistics Agency. The way these disposals are structured has just undergone a review.

Most consumption of tin metal is in developed countries such as the USA, Japan, Germany and the UK. However, up-and-coming economies, such as South Korea, Malaysia, Taiwan and Thailand, are also significant and growing users.

In addition to the LME tin contract, the metal is also traded on the Kuala Lumpur tin market which is also used to price regional business.

Further information

International Tin Research Institute (ITRI Ltd)
Kingston Lane
Uxbridge
Middlesex UB8 3PJ
UK
Tel: +44 1895 272406
Fax: +44 1895 251841

Southeast Asia Tin Research & Development (Seatrade) Centre
Jalan Sultan Azlan Shah
31400 Ipoh
Malaysai
Tel: +60 3 559 1102
Fax: +60 4 559 1159

United Nations Conference on Trade and Development
Palais des Nations
CH – 1211 Geneva 10
Switzerland
Tel: +41 22 719 5506
Fax: +41 22 709 0051

Table 1 Tin: world mine production 1991–95 (thousand tonnes)

	1991	*1992*	*1993*	*1994*	*1995*
EUROPE					
France	–	–	–	–	–
Portugal	3.1	3.0	5.3	4.3	4.6
Spain	–	–	–	–	1.9
United Kingdom	2.3	2.0	2.2	1.9	1.9
Total	5.4	5.0	7.5	6.2	8.4
AFRICA					
Cameroon	–	–	–	–	–
Morocco	–	–	–	–	–
Namibia	0.9	–	–	–	–
Niger	–	–	–	–	–
Nigeria	0.4	0.4	0.3	0.3	0.3
Rwanda[1]	0.7	0.5	0.5	0.2	0.2
South Africa	1.0	0.6	0.5	–	–
Swaziland	–	–	–	–	–
Tanzania	–	–	–	–	–
Uganda	–	–	–	–	–
Zaire	1.2	0.7	0.7	0.5	0.7
Zambia	–	–	–	–	–
Zimbabwe	0.8	0.7	0.7	0.1	–
Total	5.0	2.9	2.7	1.1	1.2

Table 1 Tin: world mine production 1991–95 (thousand tonnes) contd.

	1991	*1992*	*1993*	*1994*	*1995*
ASIA					
Burma	0.5	0.7	0.8	0.4	0.4
Indonesia	37.7	37.0	36.1	38.5	46.1
Japan	–	–	–	–	–
Laos	0.3	0.3	0.3	0.2	0.8
Malaysia	20.7	14.3	10.4	6.5	6.4
South Korea	–	–	–	–	–
Thailand	10.9	8.4	5.1	3.1	1.8
Other Asia[2]	–	–	–	–	–
Total	70.1	60.7	52.7	48.7	55.5
AMERICAS					
Canada	4.5	–	–	–	–
USA	0.1	0.1	0.1	0.1	0.1
Argentina	–	–	–	–	–
Bolivia	16.8	16.5	18.6	16.1	14.4
Brazil	29.3	21.7	25.9	19.7	19.4
Mexico	–	–	–	–	–
Peru	6.6	10.2	13.7	20.0	22.3
Total	57.3	48.5	58.3	55.9	56.2
OCEANIA					
Australia	5.7	6.6	8.0	7.4	6.0
TOTAL	**143.5**	**123.7**	**129.2**	**119.3**	**127.3**
Monthly Average	*11.9*	*10.3*	*10.7*	*9.9*	*10.6*
OTHER COUNTRIES					
Czechoslovakia	–	–	–	–	–
German DR	–	–	–	–	–
USSR	12.0	–	–	–	–
Kazakstan	–	0.5	0.5	0.5	0.5
Russia	–	15.2	13.1	10.5	9.0
China	42.1	43.8	49.1	54.1	54.0
Mongolia	0.3	0.1	0.1	0.1	0.1
Vietnam	0.8	3.4	3.5	4.0	3.6
Total	55.2	63.0	66.3	69.2	67.2
WORLD TOTAL	**198.7**	**186.7**	**195.5**	**188.5**	**194.5**

This table shows the recoverable tin content of ores and concentrates produced.

Notes [1] Includes Burundi prior to 1980. [2] Origin unspecified.

By courtesy of the World Bureau of Metal Statistics

Figure 1 Tin: world mine production

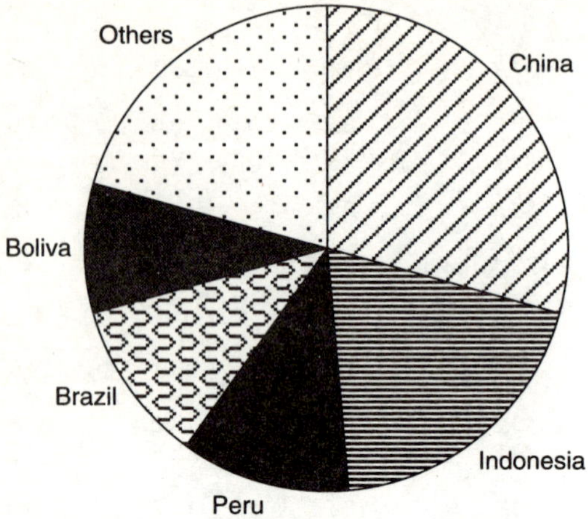

Table 2 Tin: world refined production 1991–95 (thousand tonnes)

	1991	*1992*	*1993*	*1994*	*1995*
EUROPE					
Belgium	0.2	0.2	0.2	0.2	0.2
Denmark	–	–	–	–	–
Germany	0.7	0.1	0.1	–	–
Greece	0.2	0.2	0.2	0.2	0.2
Netherlands	5.0	0.2	0.2	–	–
Norway	–	–	–	–	–
Portugal	0.1	0.1	0.1	0.1	0.1
Spain	1.7	2.4	2.0	2.0	–
United Kingdom	5.2	–	–	–	–
Total	13.1	3.2	2.8	2.5	0.5
AFRICA					
Nigeria	0.4	0.4	0.3	0.3	0.5
Rwanda	–	–	–	–	–
South Africa	1.6	0.6	0.5	–	–
Zaire	–	–	–	–	–
Zimbabwe	0.8	0.7	0.7	0.1	–
Total	2.8	1.7	1.5	0.4	0.5
ASIA					
Burma	0.2	0.1	0.1	0.1	0.1
Hong Kong	–	–	–	–	–
India	0.3	0.2	0.2	0.1	0.1
Indonesia	38.0	35.9	38.3	39.0	44.2
Japan	0.7	0.7	0.8	0.7	0.6
Malaysia	42.7	45.6	40.1	38.0	39.4
Singapore	0.6	–	–	–	–
South Korea	2.3	1.0	1.0	1.1	1.0
Thailand	11.3	10.9	8.3	7.6	8.2
Total	96.1	94.4	88.8	86.6	93.6

Table 2 Tin: world refined production 1991–95 (thousand tonnes) contd.

	1991	1992	1993	1994	1995
AMERICAS					
Canada	0.1	–	–	–	–
USA	0.2	0.2	0.2	0.1	0.2
Argentina	0.2	0.3	0.1	0.1	0.1
Bolivia	14.7	14.4	18.6	19.5	17.7
Brazil	30.9	26.9	26.9	19.4	15.4
Mexico	4.0	2.0	2.5	2.3	2.1
Peru	–	–	–	–	–
Total	50.1	43.8	48.3	41.4	35.5
OCEANIA					
Australia	0.6	0.6	0.2	0.3	0.2
TOTAL	**162.7**	**143.7**	**141.6**	**131.2**	**130.3**
Monthly Average	*13.5*	*11.9*	*11.8*	*10.9*	*10.8*
OTHER COUNTRIES					
Czechoslovakia	0.1	–	–	–	–
Czech Republic	–	–	–	0.1	–
German DR	–	–	–	–	–
USSR	18.0	–	–	–	–
Russia	–	15.0	13.5	12.2	12.0
China	36.0	39.6	52.1	67.8	60.8
Vietnam	1.7	2.4	2.5	2.3	2.4
Total	55.8	57.0	68.1	82.4	75.2
WORLD TOTAL	**218.5**	**200.7**	**209.7**	**213.6**	**205.5**

This table shows total production of refined tin, whether refined from primary or secondary materials.

By courtesy of the World Bureau of Metal Statistics

Table 3 Tin: world refined consumption 1991–95 (thousand tonnes)

	1991	1992	1993	1994	1995
EUROPE					
Austria	0.5	0.7	0.7	0.7	0.8
Belgium	1.5	2.5	2.5	2.0	2.0
Denmark	–	–	–	–	–
Finland	–	–	–	–	–
France	8.2	8.3	7.7	9.2	8.7
Germany	19.2	20.3	18.4	18.2	19.7
Greece	0.8	0.4	0.1	0.1	0.4
Italy	5.2	5.5	5.3	4.7	5.8
Netherlands	6.2	3.4	3.5	3.6	4.7
Norway	0.4	0.4	0.4	0.4	0.5
Portugal	0.8	0.9	0.6	0.7	0.6
Spain	4.9	5.5	6.8	6.7	5.2
Sweden	0.2	0.2	0.3	0.5	0.4
Switzerland	0.8	0.4	0.8	0.6	0.7
United Kingdom	10.3	10.4	10.4	10.4	10.5
Yugoslavia	0.5	0.1	0.1	0.1	–
Other Europe	–	–	–	–	–
Total	59.5	59.0	57.6	57.9	60.0

Table 3 Tin: world refined consumption 1991–95 (thousand tonnes) contd.

	1991	*1992*	*1993*	*1994*	*1995*
AFRICA					
Egypt	0.2	0.2	0.2	0.2	0.2
Morocco	0.1	0.2	0.2	–	–
Nigeria	0.4	0.4	0.3	0.3	0.3
South Africa	1.8	1.2	0.6	0.6	0.6
Other Africa	0.6	1.2	1.2	1.2	1.2
Total	3.1	3.2	2.5	2.3	2.3
ASIA					
Hong Kong	5.8	5.2	–	–	–
India	3.0	1.3	1.4	1.2	1.2
Indonesia	1.3	1.6	1.5	1.8	2.0
Iran	0.5	0.4	0.4	0.4	0.4
Israel	0.1	–	–	–	–
Japan	34.9	31.0	28.6	28.7	28.1
Malaysia	3.4	4.6	5.2	5.6	6.4
Pakistan	0.1	0.1	0.2	0.2	0.2
Philippines	0.3	0.1	0.2	0.1	0.1
Singapore	0.4	–	–	–	–
South Korea	5.9	6.6	9.1	9.8	12.4
Syria	0.1	–	–	–	–
Taiwan	6.2	5.9	8.1	7.9	7.4
Thailand	4.4	3.6	5.0	5.1	5.6
Turkey	1.0	0.8	0.8	0.8	0.8
Other Asia	0.4	0.3	0.3	0.3	0.4
Total	67.8	61.5	60.8	61.9	65.0
AMERICAS					
Canada	3.1	3.0	3.8	3.1	4.3
USA	35.3	35.2	34.8	33.0	34.6
Argentina	0.9	1.0	1.1	1.3	1.3
Bolivia	0.1	0.1	0.2	0.1	0.1
Brazil	6.2	6.2	4.1	3.6	5.5
Chile	0.3	0.4	0.4	0.4	0.4
Mexico	3.0	2.2	2.6	3.5	3.0
Venezuela	0.3	0.7	0.5	0.5	0.5
Other America	0.3	0.6	0.2	0.6	0.8
Total	49.5	49.4	47.7	46.1	50.5
OCEANIA					
Australia	1.3	0.7	0.3	0.3	0.3
New Zealand	0.1	–	–	–	–
Total	1.4	0.7	0.3	0.3	0.3
TOTAL	**181.3**	**173.8**	**168.9**	**168.5**	**178.1**
Quarterly Average	*45.3*	*43.4*	*42.2*	*42.1*	*44.5*
OTHER COUNTRIES					
Bulgaria	–	0.2	0.2	0.1	0.1
Czechoslovakia	1.2	4.3	–	–	–
Czech Reublic	–	–	2.0	2.0	2.0
Slovakia	–	–	2.0	2.0	2.0
German DR	–	–	–	–	–
Hungary	0.4	0.4	0.1	0.1	0.1
Poland	0.6	1.0	0.9	1.0	0.9

Table 3 Tin: world refined consumption 1991–95 (thousand tonnes) contd.

	1991	*1992*	*1993*	*1994*	*1995*
Romania	0.2	0.5	0.5	0.5	0.5
USSR	17.0	–	–	–	–
Russia	–	15.0	12.8	4.7	6.2
Other FSU	–	1.0	1.0	1.0	1.0
China	14.7	12.9	21.1	32.1	36.3
Total	34.1	35.3	40.6	43.5	49.1
WORLD TOTAL	**215.4**	**209.1**	**209.5**	**212.0**	**227.2**

This table shows consumption of unwrought refined tin, whether refined from primary or secondary materials. The direct use of tin in the form of scrap is excluded.

By courtesy of the World Bureau of Metal Statistics

Figure 2 Tin: world refined consumption

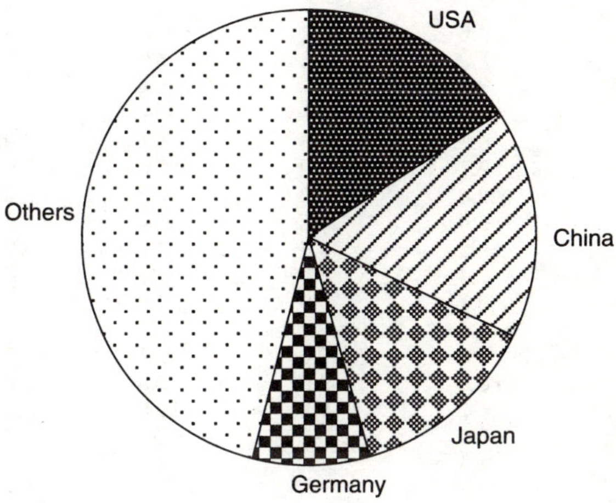

Table 4 Tin: world trade refined tin 1991–95 (thousand tonnes)

	1991	*1992*	*1993*	*1994*	*1995*
EXPORTS					
Belgium	2.8	5.6	6.1	5.2	4.2[4]
Germany	1.1	1.0	0.5	0.4	0.4
Netherlands	1.1	0.3	0.3	0.6	0.9
Spain	0.1	0.2	0.4	0.1	0.1
Sweden	–	–	–	0.1	0.1
Switzerland	–	0.2	–	–	–
United Kingdom	2.9	0.2	0.3	1.2	2.7
Nigeria	–	–	–	–	–
Indonesia	29.2	27.9	18.0	22.3	42.3
Malaysia	42.4	45.2	35.5	35.3	35.2
Singapore	27.0	26.1	27.4	31.9	33.7
Thailand	6.3	7.4	3.4	2.7	2.7
USA	2.6	3.4	3.9	4.4	4.6
Bolivia	14.3	14.3	14.4	15.4	12.9
Brazil	18.1	19.5	22.1	17.6	9.9
Australia	0.3	0.2	0.2	0.2	0.6
China	15.7	24.9	22.4	36.9	25.1
Total	**163.9**	**176.4**	**154.9**	**174.3**	**175.4**
IMPORTS					
Austria	0.5	0.7	0.8	0.7	–
Belgium	2.6	2.5	1.8	1.5	0.5[4]
Denmark[1]	–	–	–	–	–
Finland	–	–	–	–	–
France	8.2	8.5	7.7	9.2	8.7
Germany	19.7	21.9	18.2	19.9	20.6
Greece	0.6	0.2	0.2	0.4	0.1[4]
Italy	5.4	5.5	5.4	5.0	5.8
Netherlands	2.3	3.8	4.2	8.3	9.0
Norway	0.4	0.4	0.4	0.4	0.5
Portugal	0.7	0.9	0.6	0.7	0.6
Spain	3.2	3.1	4.5	4.8	5.3
Sweden	0.3	0.2	0.1	0.5	0.5
Switzerland	0.8	0.6	0.8	0.6	0.7
United Kingdom	4.7	8.9	13.0	13.1	9.8
Hong Kong[2]	5.6	13.0	16.6	11.4	12.2
India	1.2	1.1	1.2	1.5	1.3[4]
Japan	34.3	27.3	27.7	27.6	28.0
Singapore[3]	5.3	5.5	4.0	3.0	4.0
South Korea	6.3	6.5	8.9	10.6	11.2
Taiwan	6.2	5.9	6.9	7.9	7.3
Canada	3.1	3.1	3.8	4.4	4.3
USA	29.7	27.3	34.0	32.1	33.3
Brazil	–	–	–	–	0.1
New Zealand	–	–	–	–	–
Total	**141.1**	**146.9**	**160.8**	**163.6**	**163.8**

This table shows principal imports and exports of refined tin.

Notes [1] Excludes intra-European Union trade from 1993 onwards. [2] Includes some alloy. [3] Excludes imports from Indonesia. [4] January to September

By courtesy of the World Bureau of Metal Statistics

Figure 3 LME tin: monthly average cash settlement and sellers' prices
All prices quoted in $ per tonne

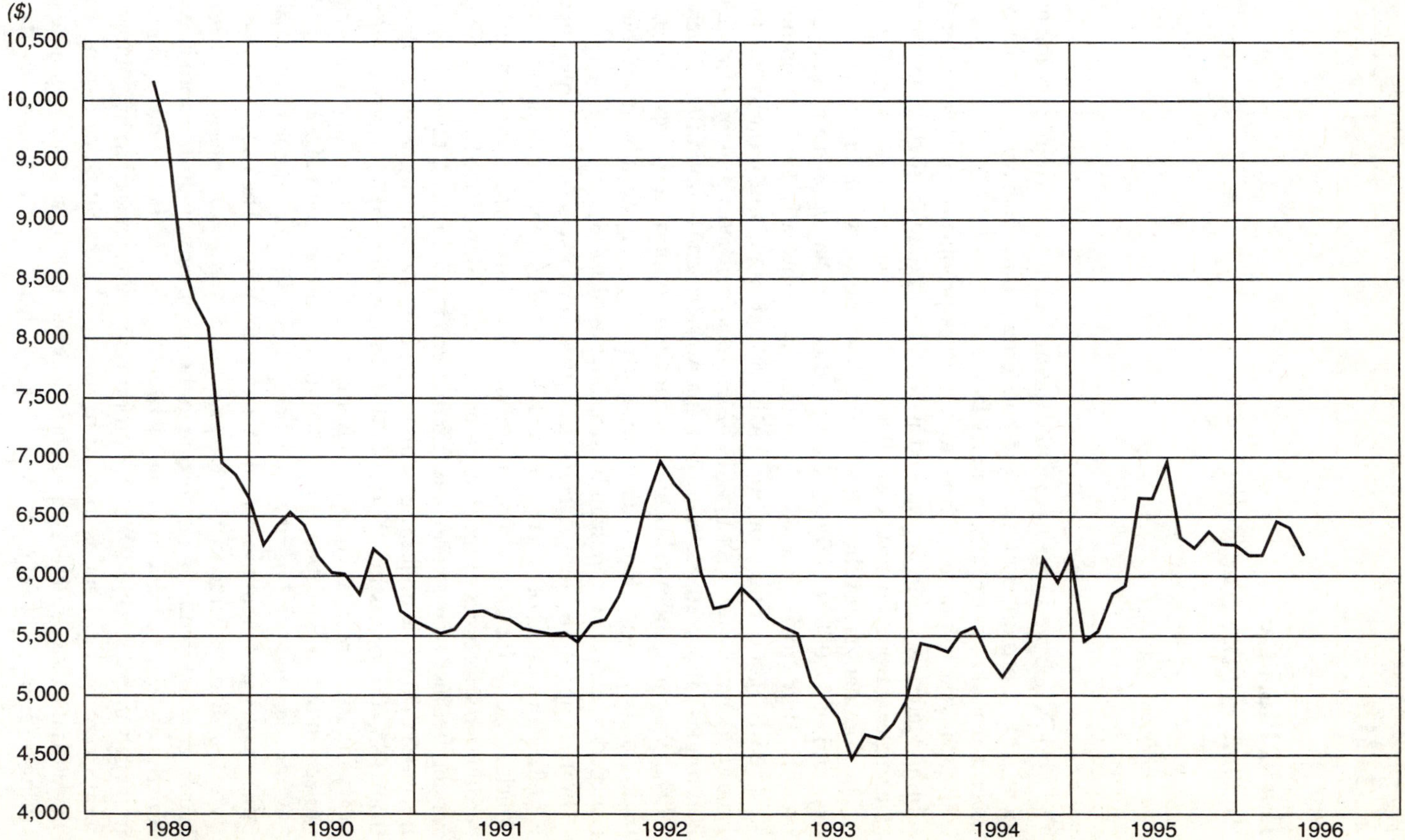

Source: London Metal Exchange

Zinc

David Eldridge
Associate Editor, Metal Bulletin

The world's zinc producers have found themselves in an awkward position in the mid-1990s. Consumption has risen but some producers have suffered a profit squeeze from low prices and currency factors.

In Japan, the response has been to scale back production; one producer, Mitsubishi Materials Corp, announced it would withdraw entirely from primary zinc smelting from the middle of 1996.

The dominant factor that has kept zinc from breaking out of its narrow trading band of $1,000–1,080/tonne on the London Metal Exchange (LME) has been the large stocks. These built up steadily in the early 1990s as producers, attracted by good prices on the LME, placed more and more metal in the Exchange's warehouses. As a result, LME stocks reached a peak of over 1.2 million tonnes (about 20 per cent of annual western consumption) at the end of 1994 before a withdrawal of investment fund support hit prices of all LME-traded metals. Stock levels have since started to fall steadily again, but are nonetheless expected to remain burdensome until 1998.

In the longer term, prospects for zinc generally look good. Its largest market is in the galvanizing of sheet steel and hot-dipped galvanizing of finished items, which accounts for 48 per cent of consumption – up from 41 per cent in 1979. Although the fortunes of the steel industry in the industrialized world have been varying because of recession and faltering economic growth, the Asian market has more than made up for this, with the region's galvanizing sector demand up from 183,300 tonnes in 1979 to 500,200 tonnes in 1994. A proliferation of heavy industry projects requiring galvanized steel, particularly in energy-related projects in South-East Asia, is expected to continue beyond 2000.

While demand for zinc in Asia is being viewed as the engine of the market, other factors are helping to consolidate its position too. The construction industry still provides a large market for galvanized steel in the west, and there has been a growing trend for galvanizing in the automotive industry, both in North America and Europe. From a level of 13 per cent of car bodies made in Europe using galvanized steel in 1985, this proportion was estimated to have jumped to 55 per cent by 1995 and is forecast to rise to 75 per cent. Zinc coating is still viewed as the most durable of anti-corrosion methods in large-scale applications, lasting on average for 20 years. And while advances in galvanizing methods have reduced the thickness of the zinc coating on steel, volumes used have nonetheless been increasing through wider application. Zinc does not have any serious threats of substitution in the steel coating market, its nearest rival – painting – having durability of only about five years.

Use of zinc in die-casting alloys has come under pressure from rival aluminium and magnesium alloys and plastics, and consumption of zinc in this sector slipped by an annual average rate of 0.2 per cent between 1979 and 1994. In the 1960s and 1970s, zinc benefited from a boom in die-cast components as consumer durables took off in western countries. Since then, the manufacturing and casting industries have tried all manner of alternatives such as aluminium and magnesium (because of their lightness) and plastics (because of their cheapness). However, zinc has survived well against its metals rivals because of its relatively cheaper cost and its advantages in precision casting – an important factor as manufacturers demand ever-finer tolerances (zinc also has the edge over plastics in this sector).

Zinc's other main uses, as an alloy in brass and bronze, and in chemicals and oxides, have held fairly steady in recent years.

World zinc mine production, which was depressed in 1993 and 1994, is likely to grow steadily through the rest of the decade. The start-up of the McArthur River mine in Australia in 1995 and increases in Canada, including an expansion at the Red Dog mine, have set the stage for new projects, such as the Galmoy and Lisheen mines in Ireland and the large 450,000 tonnes per year Century mine in Australia.

World mine output could rise to about 8 million tonnes of zinc contained if all projects start up, but there is a large question mark over the Century mine whose construction has been delayed because of a native title claim by an Aboriginal group.

The failure of Century to start production could also spell the end of the road for the 210,000 tonnes per year Budel zinc smelter in The Netherlands, which has an environmental agreement with the government to stop production of jarosite (a waste by-product of zinc smelting) by June 1998, and which was relying on Century's low-iron concentrates to achieve this.

Apart from this, developments in smelting are mostly positive, with capacity additions planned and 'greenfield' smelters scheduled for commissioning at the end of the 1990s. These projects focus mainly on the burgeoning Far East market, including the Padaeng plant in Thailand, Korea Zinc's Onsan plant and a new smelter in Australia. Gencor also plans to locate a 200,000–400,000 tonnes per year smelter on the eastern side of the Cape in South Africa to take advantage of the growth market in Asia.

Further information

International Lead & Zinc Study Group
2 King Street, London SW1Y 6QP
Tel: +44 171 839 8550
Fax: +44 171 930 4635

Table 1 Zinc: world mine production 1991–95 (thousand tonnes)

	1991	*1992*	*1993*	*1994*	*1995*
EUROPE					
Austria	14.8	15.8	19.0	–	–
Denmark	–	–	–	–	–
Finland	55.5	30.8	22.0	16.9	11.2
France	27.1	16.5	13.8	–	–
Germany	54.0	14.3	–	–	–
Greece	30.0	26.2	22.0	17.2	14.5
Ireland	187.5	194.1	193.7	194.5	184.1
Italy	37.0	31.0	7.1	22.9	22.9
Macedonia	–	–	18.0	15.4	16.8
Norway	18.9	21.0	14.4	15.6	11.0
Slovenia	–	–	–	–	–
Spain	264.6	206.3	170.2	170.1	172.2
Sweden	157.5	163.5	167.3	159.9	168.0
United Kingdom	1.0	–	–	–	–
Yugoslavia	74.0	47.2	11.6	8.4	14.7
Total	921.9	766.7	660.8	620.9	615.4
AFRICA					
Algeria	4.2	4.0	3.6	3.0	3.7
Congo	–	–	–	–	–
Morocco	24.5	21.6	60.7	77.0	73.7
Namibia	33.1	36.1	28.4	33.4	29.9
South Africa	64.4	69.8	78.2	76.4	62.5
Tunisia	5.1	2.3	3.1	12.9	17.1
Zaire	42.4	36.0	10.0	0.6	0.8
Zambia	24.8	19.2	19.7	1.0	–
Total	198.5	189.0	203.7	204.3	187.7
ASIA					
Burma	1.7	1.0	0.8	1.3	2.0
Cyprus	–	–	–	–	–
India	104.5	152.8	156.3	147.3	154.5
Iran	31.1	65.0	70.0	72.9	145.1
Japan	133.0	134.5	118.6	100.7	95.3
Philippines	–	–	–	–	–
South Korea	21.6	21.9	13.8	7.1	7.8
Thailand	86.9	68.7	69.5	65.8	66.0
Turkey	32.5	32.5	35.0	35.1	33.1
Total	411.3	476.4	464.0	430.2	503.8
AMERICAS					
Canada	1156.6	1324.7	1004.4	1010.7	1111.5
USA	574.2	551.6	513.1	592.1	609.5
Argentina	39.3	41.0	31.4	26.9	32.1
Bolivia	129.8	143.9	124.6	100.8	146.1
Brazil	103.0	115.2	138.0	140.0	144.0
Colombia	0.2	0.1	–	0.1	0.1
Chile	31.0	29.7	29.6	30.2	34.5
Guatemala	–	–	–	–	–
Honduras	38.3	32.7	24.3	23.6	27.1
Mexico	317.1	340.7	359.8	368.7	346.9
Nicaragua	–	–	–	–	–
Peru	638.1	602.5	664.6	674.2	688.4
Other America	–	–	–	–	–
Total	3027.6	3182.1	2889.8	2967.3	3140.2

Table 1 Zinc: world mine production 1991–95 (thousand tonnes) contd.

	1991	*1992*	*1993*	*1994*	*1995*
OCEANIA					
Australia	1024.0	1008.0	990.0	970.7	903.2
TOTAL	**5583.3**	**5622.2**	**5208.3**	**5193.4**	**5350.3**
Monthly average	*465.2*	*468.5*	*434.0*	*432.7*	*445.8*
OTHER COUNTRIES					
Bulgaria	29.1	31.9	25.0	25.1	25.1
Czechoslovakia	7.8	6.2	–	–	–
Czech Republic	–	–	2.3	2.3	2.3
Slovakia	–	–	–	–	–
Hungary	–	–	–	–	–
Poland	144.7	151.7	151.0	151.0	151.0
Romania	26.8	25.3	27.8	33.2	34.7
USSR	610.0	–	–	–	–
Georgia	–	2.0	2.0	2.0	2.0
Kazakstan	–	221.6	218.8	148.1	148.1
Russia	–	198.0	188.3	145.7	147.0
Tajikistan	–	–	–	–	–
Uzbekistan	–	34.0	33.0	31.0	31.0
China	749.8	758.1	775.4	990.3	1000.0
North Korea	120.0	120.0	120.0	90.0	90.0
Vietnam	15.0	15.0	15.0	11.9	11.9
Total	1703.2	1563.8	1558.6	1630.6	1643.1
WORLD TOTAL	**7286.5**	**7185.0**	**6766.9**	**6824.0**	**6993.4**

This table shows the content by analysis of zinc ores and concentrates plus the zinc content of mixed ores.

By courtesy of the World Bureau of Metal Statistics

Figure 1 Zinc: world mine production

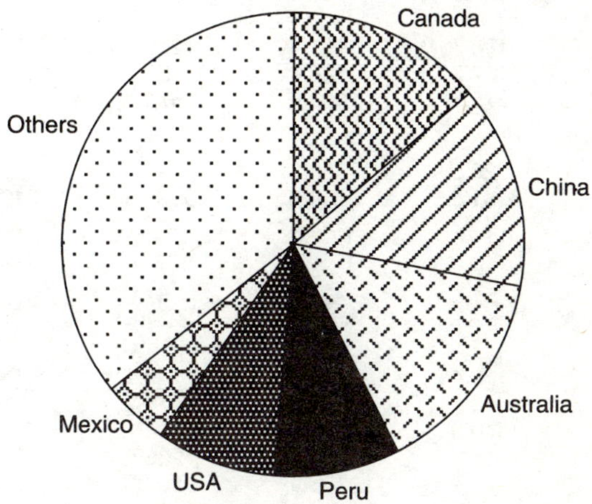

Table 2 Zinc: world slab production 1991–95 (thousand tonnes)

	1991	*1992*	*1993*	*1994*	*1995*
EUROPE					
Austria	16.3	0.6	–	–	–
Belgium	297.6	217.2	209.6	211.2	216.2
Finland	170.4	170.5	170.9	173.2	176.6
France	299.6	304.7	309.8	308.6	290.0
Germany	345.7	383.1	380.9	359.9	322.5
Italy	256.0	252.6	253.6	255.9	229.4
Macedonia	–	–	57.0	49.5	46.7
Netherlands	201.3	218.4	206.0	212.6	206.3
Norway	124.6	127.6	134.2	136.7	129.5
Portugal	2.1	2.2	3.5	4.2	4.2
Slovenia	–	–	–	–	–
Spain	262.2	351.9	327.6	298.7	360.5
United Kingdom	100.7	96.8	102.4	101.3	106.0
Yugoslavia	104.7	74.4	7.0	6.2	7.1
Total	2181.2	2200.0	2162.5	21180.0	2095.0
AFRICA					
Algeria	29.5	31.5	33.4	24.3	24.3
South Africa	91.6	83.2	96.2	93.9	98.8
Zaire	25.0	18.8	4.2	0.6	0.6
Zambia	6.6	7.3	4.7	0.1	–
Total	152.7	140.8	138.5	118.9	123.7
ASIA					
India	83.6	128.1	141.7	156.4	146.5
Japan	730.8	729.5	695.7	665.5	669.7
South Korea	254.1	255.9	276.4	271.9	279.3
Thailand	69.5	70.3	69.4	71.1	70.9
Turkey	17.4	18.8	18.5	18.5	19.6
Total	1155.4	1202.6	1201.7	1183.4	1186.0
AMERICAS					
Canada	660.6	671.7	669.9	691.0	720.1
USA	375.7	399.5	321.8	379.4	357.5
Argentina	35.8	34.5	31.1	35.2	35.8
Brazil	157.5	180.4	183.0	197.6	196.9
Colombia	–	–	–	–	–
Mexico	188.7	151.4	208.7	212.1	212.1
Peru	157.2	126.4	158.7	150.8	127.7
Total	1575.5	1563.9	1573.2	1666.1	1650.1
OCEANIA					
Australia	326.5	333.3	290.0	322.5	316.1
TOTAL	**5391.3**	**5440.6**	**5365.9**	**5408.9**	**5370.9**
Monthly Average	*449.2*	*453.3*	*447.1*	*450.7*	*447.5*
OTHER COUNTRIES					
Bulgaria	51.6	54.7	67.0	76.7	76.7
German DR	–	–	–	–	–
Hungary	–	–	–	–	–
Poland	128.4	134.6	149.1	154.3	165.7
Romania	8.7	13.4	14.7	18.5	18.5
USSR	540.0	–	–	–	–
Kazakstan	–	231.7	238.5	172.5	169.1
Russia	–	186.4	204.0	137.9	167.0

Table 2 Zinc: world slab production 1991–95 (thousand tonnes) contd.

	1991	1992	1993	1994	1995
Ukraine	–	13.0	5.0	14.0	14.0
Uzbekistan	–	80.0	70.0	40.0	40.0
China	612.0	719.0	856.9	1017.0	1015.0
North Korea	130.0	120.0	120.0	100.0	100.0
Vietnam	–	–	–	–	–
Total	1470.7	1552.8	1725.2	1730.9	1766.0
WORLD TOTAL	**6862.0**	**6993.4**	**7091.1**	**7139.8**	**7136.9**

This table is based on the production of slab zinc by smelters and refineries, including production on toll in the reporting country, regardless of the type of source material, i.e. whether ores, concentrates, residues, slag or scrap. Remelted zinc and zinc dust are excluded.

By courtesy of the World Bureau of Metal Statistics

Table 3 Zinc: world slab consumption 1991–95 (thousand tonnes)

	1991	1992	1993	1994	1995
EUROPE					
Austria	44.5	43.0	45.5	46.0	45.6
Belgium	200.0	189.0	210.0	225.0	225.0
Bosnia	–	–	3.0	3.0	3.0
Croatia	–	–	1.2	1.2	2.3
Denmark	13.0	16.3	14.0	11.6	13.2
Finland	26.7	30.6	31.2	32.8	28.0
France	289.1	258.3	225.8	241.1	250.0
Germany	540.1	531.2	514.9	514.1	503.2
Greece	15.5	12.3	12.0	12.0	12.0
Ireland	1.5	0.6	2.0	1.2	1.2
Italy	283.0	300.0	300.0	320.2	341.7
Macedonia	–	–	5.0	5.0	5.0
Netherlands	80.0	86.9	90.0	90.0	88.0
Norway	20.3	21.9	15.2	19.2	15.9
Portugal	4.3	13.9	13.5	14.0	10.6
Slovenia	–	–	20.0	20.0	20.0
Spain	129.0	112.4	119.0	144.9	151.0
Sweden	33.3	29.8	29.1	31.2	33.6
Switzerland	19.4	18.1	17.2	18.2	21.0
United Kingdom	183.7	190.1	195.9	196.5	198.4
Yugoslavia	111.1	60.0	15.0	7.0	7.2
Other Europe	0.2	0.1	0.2	0.2	0.2
Total	1944.7	1914.5	1879.7	1954.4	1976.1
AFRICA					
Nigeria	8.0	8.0	14.6	7.0	7.0
S Africa & Namibia	90.9	85.1	87.2	91.2	87.2
Other Africa	55.4	55.4	39.0	45.0	45.0
Total	154.3	148.5	140.8	143.2	139.2
ASIA					
Hong Kong	10.8	7.3	1.0	6.0	6.0
India	130.0	140.0	150.0	188.0	192.0
Indonesia	48.1	55.8	48.0	84.3	73.2
Japan	845.5	783.7	718.7	721.2	752.2
Malaysia	22.2	20.2	24.0	23.6	24.0

Table 3 Zinc: world slab consumption 1991–95 (thousand tonnes) contd.

	1991	*1992*	*1993*	*1994*	*1995*
Pakistan	14.0	11.0	17.0	17.0	16.8
Philippines	30.6	36.2	38.8	37.8	39.6
Saudi Arabia	8.0	9.3	11.4	11.3	11.4
Singapore	15.0	16.0	30.0	15.0	15.0
South Korea	247.9	265.8	311.2	318.0	296.6
Taiwan	125.7	128.3	170.5	170.3	209.5
Thailand	74.7	78.8	90.1	99.8	99.6
Turkey	47.1	59.1	59.0	41.9	32.2
Other Asia	50.8	53.4	96.6	68.7	68.7
Total	1670.4	1664.9	1766.3	1802.9	1836.8
AMERICAS					
Canada	120.7	126.4	133.9	147.5	151.9
USA	933.0	1035.0	1148.0	1118.3	1202.1
Argentina	28.6	33.9	37.0	33.7	33.6
Brazil	106.5	98.0	124.9	147.9	119.7
Chile	6.0	8.6	7.7	7.7	7.7
Colombia	5.0	10.8	9.9	8.0	9.9
Mexico	107.3	108.0	100.0	108.3	99.6
Peru	70.8	55.2	77.3	69.0	76.8
Venezuela	14.0	15.2	10.5	12.0	17.7
Other America	12.7	12.7	4.6	4.4	4.6
Total	1404.6	1503.8	1653.8	1656.8	1723.6
OCEANIA					
Australia	196.6	191.0	222.4	215.4	174.5
New Zealand	17.2	15.4	17.1	18.7	17.1
Other Oceania	0.1	0.1	0.1	0.1	0.1
Total	213.9	206.5	239.6	234.2	191.7
TOTAL	**5437.9**	**5438.2**	**5680.2**	**5791.5**	**5867.4**
Monthly Average	*453.1*	*453.1*	*473.3*	*482.6*	*488.9*
OTHER COUNTRIES					
Bulgaria	19.9	14.5	13.1	16.6	16.6
Czechoslovakia	36.2	34.1	–	–	–
Czech Republic	–	34.0	11.0	10.0	11.0
Slovakia	–	–	25.0	25.0	25.0
German DR	–	–	–	–	–
Hungary	8.0	10.0	5.0	5.0	5.0
Poland	86.1	84.0	81.1	75.0	75.0
Romania	8.7	14.6	17.1	18.6	18.6
USSR	520.0	–	–	–	–
Kazakstan	–	83.0	83.0	66.0	66.0
Russia	–	260.0	216.1	157.2	154.3
Ukraine	–	75.0	80.0	22.4	20.3
Uzbekistan	–	10.0	10.0	10.0	10.0
Other FSU	–	–	–	–	–
China	392.0	523.0	588.0	611.9	847.8
North Korea	40.0	36.0	35.0	30.0	30.0
Cuba	1.0	0.5	1.0	1.0	1.0
Other	9.0	13.0	16.5	20.0	20.0
Total	1120.9	1191.7	1181.9	1068.7	1300.6
WORLD TOTAL	**6558.8**	**6629.9**	**6862.1**	**6860.2**	**7168.0**

This table shows consumption of slab zinc. Remelted zinc and zinc dust are excluded.

By courtesy of the World Bureau of Metal Statistics

Figure 2 Zinc: world refined consumption

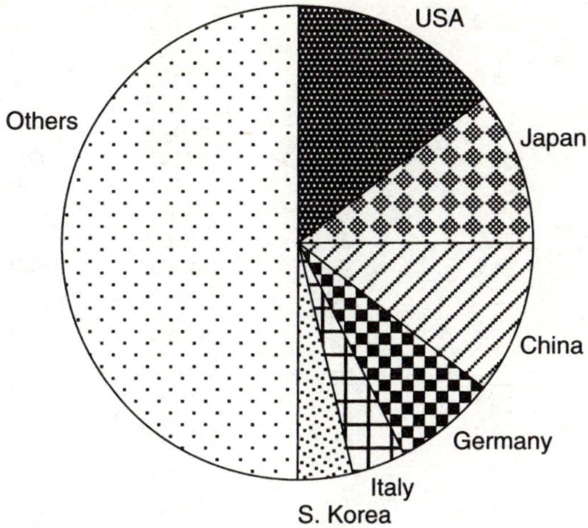

Table 4 Zinc: world trade slab zinc 1991–95 (thousand tonnes)

	1991	*1992*	*1993*	*1994*	*1995*
EXPORTS					
Austria	1.5	2.8	2.7	2.4	–[5]
Belgium[1]	130.7	158.0	182.9	148.4	120.2[6]
Denmark[2]	0.2	–	–	–	0.1
Finland	148.9	138.8	137.5	137.4	125.5
France	81.4	146.8	183.7	129.9	67.4
Germany	73.9	118.0	105.7	103.2	63.4
Ireland	–	–	0.1	–	–
Italy	34.8	34.3	16.4	17.0	13.7
Netherlands	140.3	143.4	124.4	164.1	176.1
Norway	109.3	109.3	122.3	119.7	111.6
Poland	17.9	50.0	69.0	80.0	65.4[7]
Spain[3]	145.7	220.3	204.9	156.8	164.3
United Kingdom	15.5	13.1	19.1	18.2	14.3
Yugoslavia	33.7	10.1	9.9	–	–
South Africa	4.0	3.0	8.0	8.0	3.4[8]
Zaire	27.7[8]	5.4	3.7	–	–
Zambia	6.3	6.1	4.5	4.0	–
Hong Kong	16.4	22.2	38.5	32.8	30.7
Japan	18.1	30.1	32.5	38.6	28.0
South Korea	27.6	58.4	47.5	84.4	35.2
Thailand	–	–	–	–	–[5]
Canada	519.6	509.3	492.8	552.7	536.0
USA	2.1	0.6	1.4	6.4	4.8
Argentina	–	8.0	5.2	9.8	–
Mexico	90.0	55.0	23.6	57.3	59.3
Peru	86.1	97.8	84.9	80.6	94.0
Australia	138.3	153.9	146.3	138.0	108.8
China	6.3	81.9	193.8	269.7	181.2
Total	**1876.3**	**2176.6**	**2261.3**	**2359.4**	**2003.4**

Table 4 Zinc: world trade slab zinc 1991–95 (thousand tonnes) contd.

	1991	1992	1993	1994	1995
IMPORTS					
Austria	20.3	36.5	40.9	42.8	–[5]
Belgium[1]	42.9	147.2	179.9	120.7	108.1[6]
Denmark[2]	13.6	16.3	12.1	11.6	13.5
Finland	–	2.7	0.6	0.4	–
France	82.2	97.9	92.4	115.5	134.7
Germany	269.8	283.1	234.2	247.8	227.5
Greece[4]	15.7	12.3	13.6	15.8	8.6[5]
Ireland[4]	–	0.7	1.2	1.2	1.1
Italy	71.2	82.5	88.7	92.3	113.7
Netherlands	24.8	29.2	138.6	129.3	208.4
Norway	0.3	0.4	1.4	2.0	1.6
Portugal	10.9	11.7	10.0	2.8	9.3
Spain	6.5	1.8	1.3	1.1	3.5
Sweden	33.4	30.0	29.1	31.3	23.5
Switzerland	19.7	18.1	17.7	18.7	21.0
United Kingdom	120.1	122.6	118.7	124.6	145.2
Yugoslavia	–	5.7	6.2	–	–
South Africa	–	–	–	–	7.60
Hong Kong[4]	27.2	29.5	39.0	36.3	32.3
India	37.2	59.1	22.3	15.5	11.2[5]
Indonesia	48.2[8]	55.8[8]	68.1	84.3	99.2
Japan	141.5	103.0	84.3	64.2	117.0
Philippines	29.5	36.0	38.8	39.5	51.2
Singapore	36.0	73.9	134.5	167.1	38.7
South Korea	21.5	25.0	45.7	71.6	52.5
Taiwan	125.9	128.8	170.8	170.2	205.6
Thailand	5.3	8.5	20.7	28.2	25.3[5]
Turkey	19.7	14.8	10.5	22.4	12.6[8]
Canada	0.9	0.4	1.4	5.0	4.0
USA	548.0	683.7	732.7	788.6	847.6
Argentina	4.6	4.6	8.6	5.5	–
Brazil	11.0	8.5	12.0	11.2	37.5
Chile	–	10.1	8.6	–	–
Venezuela	–	16.6	11.0	9.3	–
China	11.7	7.9	3.5	7.3	14.0
Total	**1799.6**	**2164.9**	**2399.1**	**2484.1**	**2576.0**

This table shows principal imports and exports of slab zinc.

Notes [1] Includes remelted zinc. [2] Excludes intra-European Union trade from 1993 onwards. [3] Includes zinc scrap. [4] Includes alloy. [5] January to June [6] January to September [7] January to October. [8] January to November.

By courtesy of the World Bureau of Metal Statistics

Figure 3 LME SHG zinc: monthly average cash settlement and sellers' prices
All prices quoted in $ per tonne

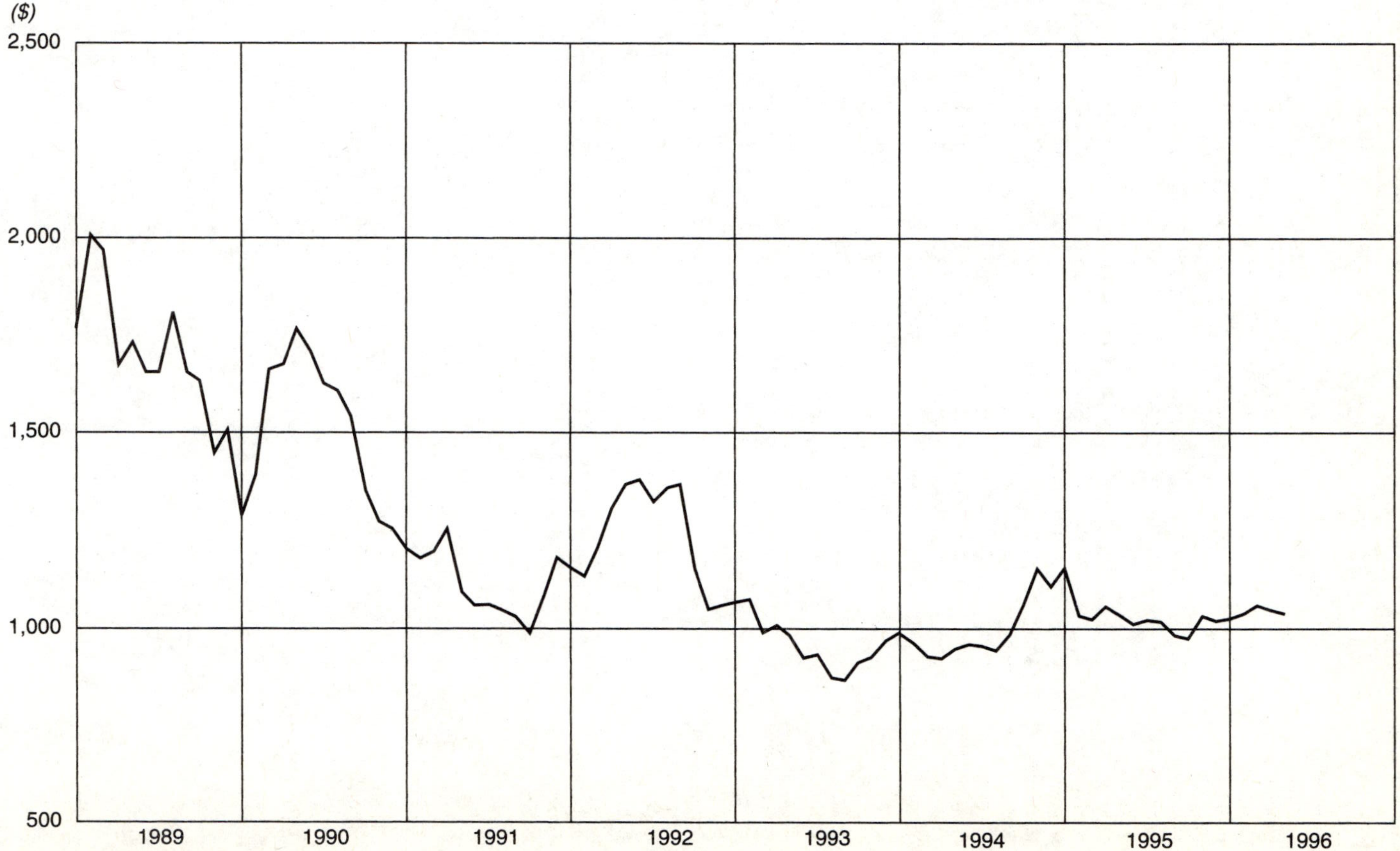

Source: London Metal Exchange

The Commodities

Softs

Further information on soft commodities

The Economist Intelligence Unit
15 Regent Street
London SW1Y 4IR
UK
Tel: +44 171 830 1000
Fax: +44 171 499 9767

US Department of Agriculture
Foreign Agricultural Service
AG Box 1006
Washington DC 20250–1006
USA
Tel: +1 202 720 3448
Fax: +1 202 720 1727

Cocoa

John Buckley

Tropical conditions are essential for growing cocoa, almost all of which is produced in a relatively narrow latitude some 15–20 degrees either side of the equator. Although nearly 50 countries grow marketable quantities, almost 90 per cent of output is concentrated in the hands of just eight large producers. Market shares have shifted considerably among these in recent years.

At the moment, the leading West African cocoa producers are enjoying something of a comeback after several years when output slowed or went into reverse due to weak world prices, reduced export earnings and lack of funds for fertilizer and plantation rehabilitation. Thanks to firmer prices and better weather in recent years, Ivory Coast has done especially well this season and is likely to turn in a new record crop of over 1m tonnes, equal to over a third of world supplies. Ghana could produce as much as 350,000 tonnes this year, compared with a low point of 160,000 in the mid-1980s while Cameroon will also increase production.

Financial constraints have also affected output in the historical second largest supplier, Brazil, leaving the crop heavily exposed to a rampant fungal disease called witches broom which causes massive damage to the cocoa bushes and decimates yields. Brazilian output has already dropped 50 per cent in recent years and efforts to 'ring fence' the disease with more resistant varieties look unlikely to have much impact in the medium term. Brazil also has a large and growing cocoa processing capacity of around 250,000 tonnes. With recent crops of only around 200,000 tonnes, cocoa bean exports have virtually stopped and local processors have even had to import beans to keep running. Unless disease problems are tackled successfully, some traders believe Brazil may become a regular net importer before the end of the century to meet its own consumption of chocolate products – among the fastest growing in the world – and those of its neighbouring Latin American countries.

For much of the 1980s, expansion among cocoa producers was led by Malaysia which boosted output tenfold before coming under the same financial restraints as the West Africans. After peaking at 243,000 tonnes in the late 1980s, output contracted since to around 160,000 tonnes as plantations converted to more lucrative oil-bearing palms. Consumption of chocolate products is growing rapidly here too, recently estimated at 100,000 tonnes of bean equivalent.

Fortunately for consumers, the regional gap is being filled by relentless growth in Indonesian cocoa production and exports. Currently, Indonesia is expected to produce between 250/230,000 tonnes a year compared with less than 100,000 in the late 1980s and under 10,000 only ten years before that. However, Indonesia faces a pest challenge in the form of the pod borer, a moth larva which cuts yields substantially. Originally endemic in Malaysia, this is now spreading through the main Indonesian cocoa regions. Although area is being constantly expanded by clearing virgin lands, some observers believe this pest could thwart Indonesia's dream of overtaking Ivory Coast as the main cocoa supplier in the next century.

Africa too has diseases that affect production, including 'black pod' fungus, capsid beetles and swollen shoot virus. So far (despite dire warnings from some producers), the region has escaped the sort of damage inflicted by witches broom in Brazil and pod bearer in South East Asia.

Although world cocoa production is now rising again, a more vigorous expansion is needed to meet growing consumption. In three out of the last four seasons, world production was under 2.4m tonnes (only 2.28m in 1991–2), compared with 2.51m at the start of the 1990s. Consumption of cocoa on the other hand has been on a steady uptrend, from 1.49m in the late 1970s, to 2.2m in 1989/90, to an estimated 2.55m in 1994/95. Although this represents a slackening in the average annual growth rate from 4.7 per cent to a 3.2 per cent, it has gradually closed the gap between offtake and supply which amassed vast stocks, depressed prices and poor profits for farmers over many prior years. Recent annual deficits have, however, pushed up prices. The ICCO's indicator, for example, bottomed out at around 50 points in 1992 and 1993 before climbing to 65 points in 1995.

With a modest surplus of supply over demand this year suggesting a levelling off in markets some doubt must remain whether optimum levels of inputs can be afforded outside of the lower costed producing countries. Investments in new cocoa ventures are longer-term returns in regions where other plantation crops, like palm oil, rubber – even annual arable crops – can offer more attractive returns. Traditional cocoa trees can take five or six six years to start bearing and about 12 years before they reach full maturity. However, new monohybrid plants now coming into general use will start to bear after about three years and be close to full maturity in eight to ten years. Up and coming Asian producers are also looking at cloning technology to generate stock that will start to bear in its first year and become quite prolific after two years. This should help to raise productivity and bring an earlier return on investments.

Despite the uncertainties over the ability of long-term production to keep pace with demand, there remains a considerable stock overhang in the cocoa market, only partially eroded in recent years of deficit. Global stocks peaked in 1990–91 at a staggering 1.57m tonnes, of which around 1.33m was held in commercial hands and the rest by the International Cocoa Organization (ICCO) buffer stock. Although stocks have been drawn down since to around 1.2m tonnes, they still represent 47 per cent of annual grind. On the plus side, much of it will probably never come to market, or if it does, in a manner that will depress prices. A large part is held in origin countries (some of it for years) and much may now be of questionable quality.

Quality and grading are key issues for the cocoa market due the stringent conditions required to keep the commodity in good order in transit. If moisture content falls below 5 per cent, cocoa beans can dry out, crack and be worth far less. With more than 8 per cent moisture, mould can develop on the beans which have to be fermented at origin to bring out their flavour.

Traditionally, cocoa is shipped in bags and is tendered in this way on the terminal markets. Although there is some pressure from some Dutch companies to introduce a bulk futures contract some traders question whether loose shipments will maintain quality at the desired level.

Indonesia is generally regarded as a lower-grade cocoa producers but some of the top quality beans for speciality outlets like high-grade confectionery come from its island of Java, others from the Central Americas. The main bulk producer of quality cocoas is Ghana while Brazil and Ivory Coast tend to be big in the middle grades.

The International Cocoa Agreement although forced to halt its market intervention, has issued production management guidelines to producers to prevent the return of big structural surpluses in the future. Members of the Cocoa Producers' Alliance based on Lagos, Nigeria, agreed to decide their own production targets but have found it difficult to meet these in recent years and with Indonesia unwilling to join the pact, it is not a real influence on the market yet.

The 1980s saw heaviest growth of cocoa consumption in Western Europe, the USA and Japan. Over the last few years, offtake has been suppressed in the FSU and Eastern Europe by the collapse of communism, subsidised pricing and consumer spending power. There are signs this slump is gradually coming to an end – especially in Eastern/Central Europe.

Cocoa grinding is heavily concentrated within the European Community, led by Netherlands, Germany, UK and France in that order. These four countries alone process more than a third of the world's cocoa beans while other big importing processors include the USA. There is a long-term trend towards increased origin processing of cocoa beans and export in the form of downstream products – cocoa butter, liquor and powder. Ivory Coast is expanding its facilities and recently announced plans to process 50 per cent of its crop by the year 2000. At the moment, processing capacity there is only about 120,000 tonnes or under 15 per cent. Ghana has also doubled its processing capacity in the last three years to over 60,000 tonnes while Malaysia's has increased by around a third to 105,000 tonnes. Even Indonesia is now steadily expanding its own grind. With Brazil's similar moves mentioned above, this could have quite an impact on the volume of cocoa beans available for shipment to importing processor countries in the next few years unless bean production overall grows more.

Like many commodities, cocoa is under threat from substitution, chiefly by alternative vegetable fats which can be processed to mimic its consistency and some of its taste attributes. So far substitutes appear to be growing within the boundaries of the global increase in consumption and many believe its impact will not be too damaging to trade unless cocoa prices become too expensive. Some substitutes are made by blending cocoa butter with oilseed products like shea nut or illipe seed oil. Others are complete replacers, CBRs which tend to go into lower quality outlets and are not generally referred to as 'chocolate'. Within the EU, incorporation of substitutes in chocolate products is capped at 5 per cent in some member states and there have been attempts to harmonise legislation to this effect. Such a move could substitute 200,000 tonnes of annual cocoa imports but so far, with heavy support for the producer view from France, the status quo looks like holding.

In summary, the outlook is bright for cocoa consumption and prices and the challenge may be to keep production coming over the coming decade of growth.

Cocoa statistical and other market information is available from the International Cocoa Organization (ICCO), whose headquarters are at Canada House, Canary Wharf in London.

Most actively traded cocoa futures markets in 1995 were the New York CSCE and London's LCE whose contracts are of international significance. Origin futures markets also exist in Malaysia on the Kuala Lumpur Commodity Exchange and in Brazil (Rio's Bolsa), both based on cocoa for domestic delivery points.

Further information

International Cocoa Organization
22 Berners Street
London W1N 3DD
UK
Tel: +44 171 637 3211
Fax: +44 171 631 0114

Table 1 Production of cocoa beans by country, 1986/87–1995/96

Country		*1986/87*	*1987/88*	*1988/89*	*1989/90*	*1990/91*	*1991/92*	*1992/93*	*1993/94*	*1994/95 (estimate)*	*1995/96 (forecast)*
						(Thousand tonnes)					
Africa											
Angola		0.1	0.1	–	–	–	–	–	–	–	–
Cameroon	m	123.1	132.8	129.4	125.7	115.0	105.0	97.0	98.0	107.9	110.0
Congo		0.9	1.2	0.8	0.4	0.5	0.3	0.3	0.2	0.3	0.3
Côte d'Ivoire	m	619.8	673.9	848.9	724.7	804.4	747.0	697.0	884.0	850.0	1050.0
Equatorial Guinea		6.2	8.3	5.3	7.6	5.2	3.5	5.7	4.0	3.5	4.0
Gabon	m	1.7	1.6	1.9	1.6	1.4	1.4	2.0	1.5	1.1	1.0
Ghana	m	228.0	188.2	301.1	295.1	293.4	242.8	312.1	254.7	309.4	375.0
Guinea		3.0	2.5	3.4	2.0	2.2	3.4	2.2	4.0	3.3	3.5
Liberia		3.1	2.9	3.0	4.5	2.0	0.5	0.1	0.1	–	–
Madagascar		2.9	2.1	2.8	2.5	2.5	3.3	3.0	3.5	3.0	3.5
Nigeria	m	100.0	150.0	165.0	160.0	160.0	110.0	145.0	135.0	142.7	145.0
Sao Tome and Principe	m	2.1	4.7	4.3	2.8	2.6	2.6	3.0	4.0	2.0	3.0
Sierra Leone	m	9.0	9.3	7.6	5.4	13.0	7.5	2.8	2.8	2.8	2.8
Tanzania		1.4	1.5	1.9	2.0	2.5	2.0	2.0	0.8	2.5	2.0
Togo	m	13.5	9.2	9.4	6.1	9.3	4.2	3.2	4.0	4.0	4.0
Uganda		0.3	0.2	0.3	0.3	0.6	0.6	0.8	0.7	0.7	0.7
Zaire		5.0	5.7	4.5	3.6	3.4	3.2	4.0	3.5	3.0	3.0
Other Africa		7.6	1.2	0.1	–	–	–	0.4	–	–	–
Total		**1127.7**	**1195.4**	**1489.7**	**1344.3**	**1418.0**	**1237.3**	**1280.6**	**1400.8**	**1436.2**	**1707.8**
North, Central and South America											
Bolivia		2.5	2.5	2.5	3.5	3.5	3.5	3.5	3.5	3.5	3.5
Brazil	m	357.6	382.6	324.1	347.9	368.1	306.2	308.6	270.0	208.3	200.0
Colombia		52.3	55.0	50.0	50.0	52.0	50.0	50.0	52.0	50.0	50.0
Costa Rica		7.0	4.0	4.5	4.8	4.0	3.0	3.0	3.0	3.0	3.0
Cuba		2.4	2.4	2.2	2.2	2.2	2.2	2.2	2.2	2.2	2.2
Dominican Republic		42.0	53.0	43.0	58.0	42.0	47.5	52.0	60.0	55.5	58.0
Ecuador	m	80.0	83.0	86.7	95.2	111.1	85.0	67.4	80.0	80.0	85.0
Grenada	m	1.6	1.6	1.3	1.0	1.2	0.8	0.9	0.8	0.8	0.8
Guatemala		2.3	1.8	1.1	0.5	0.5	1.0	0.8	0.8	0.9	0.9
Haiti		3.0	3.0	2.8	2.8	1.9	3.2	2.1	2.6	4.5	4.5
Honduras		1.9	2.0	2.2	2.3	3.3	2.7	3.9	3.0	2.4	3.0
Jamaica	m	2.5	2.5	1.3	2.1	1.8	2.3	2.2	2.5	2.5	2.5
Mexico		39.0	44.0	42.0	43.0	43.0	45.0	50.0	38.0	43.0	45.0
Nicaragua		0.2	0.1	0.1	0.3	0.3	0.3	0.3	0.3	0.3	0.3
Panama		1.0	1.0	1.0	1.0	1.0	1.0	1.0	1.0	1.0	1.0
Peru		10.0	12.0	11.5	11.0	11.0	11.0	11.0	11.0	11.0	11.0
Saint Lucia		0.1	0.1	0.1	0.1	0.1	–	–	–	–	–
Trinidad & Tobago	m	1.7	1.8	1.4	2.0	1.8	1.5	1.7	1.5	1.2	1.5
Venezuela		12.2	12.5	10.2	14.4	15.9	15.0	16.0	18.0	17.0	18.0
Other Americas		0.5	0.2	0.2	0.2	0.2	0.2	0.2	0.2	0.2	0.2
Total		**619.8**	**665.1**	**588.2**	**642.3**	**664.9**	**581.4**	**576.8**	**550.4**	**487.3**	**490.4**
Asia and Oceania											
Fiji		0.3	0.3	0.2	0.4	0.3	0.4	0.3	0.3	0.3	0.3
India		6.0	6.0	6.0	6.0	6.0	6.0	6.0	6.0	6.0	6.0
Indonesia		48.0	58.0	93.0	115.0	150.0	180.0	240.0	260.0	240.0	295.0
Malaysia	m	167.0	227.0	225.0	243.0	221.0	220.0	225.0	205.0	120.0	120.0
Papua New Guinea	m	30.6	33.8	48.0	40.8	33.4	40.9	38.8	31.0	29.0	30.0
Philippines		6.0	5.0	8.0	7.0	5.0	5.0	6.0	7.0	7.0	7.0
Samoa		0.5	0.7	0.5	0.5	–	–	–	–	–	–
Solomon Islands		1.2	2.5	2.7	3.6	4.1	3.5	4.5	3.6	3.0	3.5
Sri Lanka		2.5	2.0	2.0	2.0	1.4	1.4	1.4	1.4	1.4	1.4
Thailand		0.3	0.4	0.4	0.4	0.4	0.4	0.4	0.4	0.4	0.4
Vanuatu		1.1	0.8	1.4	2.2	2.2	1.5	1.6	2.0	1.3	2.0
Other Asia and Oceania		0.1	0.1	0.1	0.1	0.1	0.1	0.1	0.1	0.1	0.1
Total		**263.6**	**336.6**	**387.3**	**421.0**	**423.9**	**459.2**	**524.1**	**516.8**	**408.5**	**465.7**
World total		**2011.1**	**2197.1**	**2465.2**	**2407.6**	**2506.8**	**2277.9**	**2381.5**	**2468.0**	**2332.0**	**2663.9**
Total for members		1738.2	1902.0	2155.4	2053.4	2137.5	1877.2	1906.7	1974.8	1861.7	2130.6
Share of members		86.4%	86.6%	87.4%	85.3%	85.3%	82.4%	80.1%	80.0%	79.8%	80.0%

Note: m Member of International Cocoa Agreement, 1986.

By courtesy of the International Cocoa Organization

Figure 1 Cocoa: leading producers

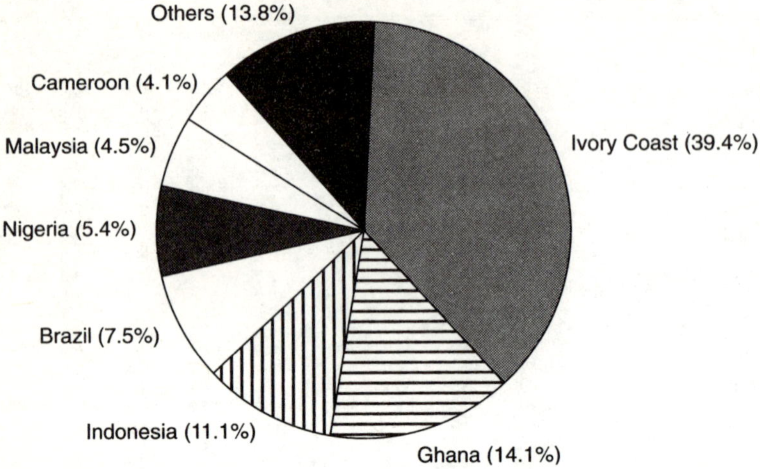

Table 2 Grindings of cocoa beans by country, 1986/87–1995/96

Country		*1986/87*	*1987/88*	*1988/89*	*1989/90*	*1990/91*	*1991/92*	*1992/93*	*1993/94*	*1994/95 (estimate)*	*1995/96 (forecast)*
						(Thousand tonnes)					
Western Europe											
European Community:											
Austria		10.6	12.1	13.9	13.5	14.6	14.1	13.9	14.2	14.0	14.0
Belgium/Luxembourg	m	34.2	35.4	41.1	46.5	44.9	46.4	47.3	52.0	55.0	60.0
Denmark	m	2.4	2.5	2.3	2.4	2.9	2.6	2.5	2.7	3.0	3.0
Finland	m	0.1	0.1	0.2	0.2	0.1	0.1	0.2	0.1	0.1	0.1
France	m	37.8	38.5	46.0	59.2	70.5	66.8	81.9	94.8	109.2	110.0
Germany	m	na	na	na	na	294.2	306.0	304.6	296.7	267.7	260.0
Germany, Fed Rep of		205.0	224.9	243.9	272.6	na	na	na	na	na	na
Greece	m	5.1	5.8	5.4	5.0	4.2	1.6	2.4	1.5	1.5	1.5
Ireland	m	8.3	7.9	10.4	14.1	7.8	8.5	8.7	8.5	6.5	6.5
Italy	m	43.0	46.4	45.5	50.9	55.7	62.0	57.9	66.3	67.2	70.0
Netherlands	m	190.3	214.6	233.9	240.7	267.7	294.2	308.9	331.3	350.0	380.0
Portugal		0.3	0.2	0.2	0.1	0.2	0.2	0.2	0.2	0.2	0.2
Spain	m	32.5	42.9	39.8	41.7	45.4	45.8	43.1	51.0	47.0	48.0
Sweden	m	4.5	4.8	3.3	2.9	0.8	0.4	0.1	–	–	–
United Kingdom	m	93.8	99.1	112.3	120.0	144.7	152.3	168.5	170.1	153.6	170.0
Norway	m	4.4	3.8	2.3	3.2	2.2	3.3	2.0	2.6	2.0	2.0
Switzerland	m	21.5	19.3	21.5	21.9	21.7	22.7	21.3	25.5	24.0	25.0
Yugoslavia*		14.0	12.1	13.2	8.9	12.0	12.0	5.0	5.0	5.0	5.0
Total		**707.8**	**770.4**	**835.2**	**903.7**	**989.6**	**1038.9**	**1068.4**	**1122.5**	**1105.9**	**1155.3**
Eastern Europe											
Bulgaria		6.0	4.9	7.0	5.0	4.0	4.0	4.0	4.0	4.0	4.0
Czechoslovakia*		17.7	13.8	20.4	22.0	20.0	20.0	2.0	na	na	na
Czech Republic	m	na	na	na	na	na	na	12.0	16.0	15.0	15.0
Slovak Republic	m	na	na	na	na	na	na	4.1	6.6	5.8	6.0
German Democratic Rep		19.8	19.9	21.1	14.0	na	na	na	na	na	na
Hungary	m	11.8	12.5	11.9	12.3	9.8	7.3	5.6	3.0	3.2	3.5
Poland		27.5	19.4	26.4	21.3	27.8	32.1	28.4	30.7	31.0	32.0
Romania		4.0	5.0	6.0	6.0	6.0	6.0	3.5	3.7	4.0	4.0
USSR*		164.2	131.7	200.9	106.2	83.3	11.5	na	na	na	na
Russian Federation		na	na	na	na	na	14.6	70.0	75.0	75.0	75.0
Other former USSR		na	na	na	na	na	5.9	25.0	25.0	25.0	25.0
Total		**251.0**	**207.2**	**293.7**	**186.8**	**150.9**	**101.4**	**154.6**	**164.0**	**163.0**	**164.5**

Table 2 Grindings of cocoa beans by country, 1986/87–1995/96 contd.

Country		*1986/87*	*1987/88*	*1988/89*	*1989/90*	*1990/91*	*1991/92*	*1992/93*	*1993/94*	*1994/95 (forecast)*	*1995/96 (estimate)*
						(Thousand tonnes)					
Africa											
Algeria		0.1	0.1	–	–	–	–	–	–	–	–
Cameroon	m	25.0	28.0	26.5	25.0	20.0	17.0	12.3	11.9	15.0	15.0
Côte d'Ivoire	m	99.3	100.0	120.0	112.5	118.1	110.0	95.0	110.0	110.0	140.0
Egypt		1.5	1.5	1.1	0.3	1.0	1.7	0.3	0.3	0.5	0.5
Ghana	m	23.4	25.2	20.0	23.8	29.9	23.4	27.1	35.0	63.7	70.0
Nigeria	m	12.0	15.0	12.8	15.0	13.1	18.0	20.0	20.0	15.0	20.0
Sierra Leone	m	–	–	0.2	0.7	1.6	1.0	0.2	–	–	–
South Africa		2.1	2.9	2.6	5.1	5.3	3.0	3.5	4.8	6.5	6.5
Other Africa		0.9	1.7	2.0	1.2	0.6	1.2	1.8	1.5	1.2	1.2
Total		**164.3**	**174.4**	**185.2**	**183.6**	**189.6**	**175.3**	**160.2**	**183.5**	**211.9**	**253.2**
North, Central and South America											
Argentina		3.0	1.9	1.1	1.4	4.3	3.5	2.0	2.8	3.0	3.0
Bolivia		2.4	2.4	2.2	2.6	2.4	2.4	2.4	2.4	2.4	2.4
Brazil	m	232.8	240.6	210.1	236.3	260.0	225.0	225.0	225.0	195.0	180.0
Canada		19.0	20.5	21.5	23.7	25.0	26.0	29.0	31.5	35.2	35.0
Chile		0.3	0.4	0.4	0.1	0.2	0.3	0.2	0.2	0.2	0.2
Colombia		48.0	46.0	41.0	45.0	47.0	44.0	45.0	42.0	45.0	45.0
Costa Rica		6.0	3.5	3.5	3.5	4.0	4.7	4.7	4.8	4.8	4.8
Cuba		4.4	3.4	4.2	4.1	3.0	2.5	2.2	2.2	2.2	2.2
Dominican Republic		5.3	4.9	5.0	5.5	5.5	5.5	5.5	5.5	5.5	5.5
Ecuador	m	29.3	35.1	38.0	32.4	48.4	45.0	38.0	32.0	35.0	35.0
Guatemala		0.2	0.2	0.3	0.4	0.4	0.4	0.4	0.6	0.6	0.6
Honduras		0.1	0.1	0.1	0.1	0.1	0.1	0.1	0.1	0.1	0.1
Jamaica	m	0.8	0.7	0.4	0.3	0.3	0.4	0.4	0.4	0.4	0.4
Mexico		38.4	40.3	40.0	43.0	43.0	35.0	30.0	29.0	31.0	31.0
Panama		0.9	0.9	1.0	0.9	0.8	0.8	1.0	0.6	0.9	1.0
Peru		10.0	12.0	11.5	13.0	13.5	11.0	11.0	13.0	15.0	15.0
Trinidad and Tobago	m	0.1	0.1	0.1	0.1	0.1	0.1	0.1	0.4	0.3	0.3
United States		227.0	242.0	245.0	273.0	267.9	302.6	324.2	317.1	347.3	350.0
Uruguay		0.2	0.2	0.2	0.2	0.3	0.3	0.3	0.2	0.2	0.2
Venezuela		5.5	6.8	5.6	7.0	7.0	8.0	8.5	8.0	8.0	8.0
Other Americas		0.4	0.4	0.4	0.6	0.6	0.4	0.4	0.4	0.4	0.4
Total		**632.1**	**662.4**	**631.6**	**693.2**	**733.8**	**718.1**	**730.5**	**718.2**	**732.5**	**720.1**
Asia and Oceania											
Australia		1.1	–	–	–	–	–	–	–	–	–
China		14.0	12.9	14.5	17.4	28.4	30.7	32.1	27.7	28.0	30.0
India		5.8	5.8	5.9	5.9	5.9	6.5	6.5	6.2	7.0	7.0
Indonesia		12.0	13.0	18.0	25.0	32.0	35.0	45.0	50.0	52.0	60.0
Israel		1.1	1.4	1.7	1.3	1.5	1.6	1.8	1.8	1.8	1.8
Japan	m	35.8	38.9	40.4	40.0	40.8	42.3	38.9	41.7	41.6	44.0
Korea, Republic of		2.0	1.2	1.5	3.7	3.7	2.9	3.0	2.5	2.3	2.5
Malaysia	m	32.0	39.0	48.0	70.0	78.0	95.0	98.0	100.0	100.0	100.0
New Zealand		1.0	1.6	0.1	0.1	0.1	0.2	0.2	0.2	0.2	0.2
Philippines		4.0	5.0	7.0	15.0	15.0	12.0	11.0	15.0	15.0	15.0
Singapore		38.2	45.1	42.3	50.5	54.5	50.0	45.0	48.0	48.0	50.0
Sri Lanka		1.7	1.7	1.8	1.9	1.2	1.4	1.4	1.4	1.4	1.4
Thailand		0.2	0.3	0.4	1.2	3.6	3.8	2.6	3.0	6.8	7.0
Turkey		6.1	4.2	3.6	4.0	5.9	6.5	7.5	7.2	14.5	15.0
Other Asia and Oceania		0.1	0.1	0.1	0.1	0.1	0.1	0.1	0.1	0.1	0.1
Total		**155.1**	**170.2**	**185.3**	**236.1**	**270.7**	**288.0**	**293.1**	**304.8**	**318.7**	**334.0**
World total		**1910.3**	**1984.6**	**2131.0**	**2203.5**	**2334.6**	**2321.7**	**2406.7**	**2493.0**	**2532.0**	**2627.1**
Total for members		1222.7	1314.8	1377.8	1485.7	1667.1	1636.0	1698.2	1780.3	1761.9	1840.5
Share of members		64.0%	66.3%	64.7%	67.4%	71.4%	70.5%	70.6%	71.4%	69.6%	70.1%
Origin grindings		598.3	631.1	624.9	691.2	754.6	708.9	694.5	719.5	733.0	767.6
Share of origin grindings		31.3%	31.8%	29.3%	31.4%	32.3%	30.5%	28.9%	28.9%	28.9%	29.2%

Note: m Member of International Cocoa Agreement, 1986.

By courtesy of the International Cocoa Organization

Table 3 Consumption of cocoa beans and cocoa products by country, 1984/85–1993/94[a]

Country		*1984/85*	*1985/86*	*1986/87*	*1987/88*	*1988/89*	*1989/90*	*1990/91*	*1991/92*	*1992/93*	*1993/94*
						(Thousand tonnes)					
Western Europe											
European Community:											
Austria		24.2	24.1	23.1	21.8	24.7	27.8	28.1	25.7	26.1	26.3
Belgium/Luxembourg	m	30.9	36.7	35.8	36.3	38.8	47.2	42.9	58.4	54.6	60.0
Denmark	m	7.8	7.7	7.0	9.8	9.9	10.2	11.3	12.9	13.8	14.3
Finland	m	4.1	5.0	5.0	4.4	5.5	6.2	5.6	5.5	4.5	3.7
France	m	106.3	112.4	118.3	126.4	131.0	146.2	156.4	159.8	157.3	157.3
Germany	m	na	na	na	na	na	na	277.6	264.0	261.1	244.1
Germany, Fed Rep of		177.8	158.1	167.0	186.0	199.6	231.4	na	na	na	na
Greece	m	10.1	10.1	10.5	13.1	14.6	13.8	12.6	11.3	11.4	8.4
Italy	m	64.0	65.6	57.6	61.5	62.6	65.0	68.3	71.4	69.2	81.4
Netherlands	m	17.6	20.2	16.5	23.9	25.9	23.0	36.2	37.8	45.7	40.3
Portugal	m	3.7	3.4	4.3	6.7	7.2	6.8	9.3	9.5	9.2	9.5
Spain	m	25.6	30.4	37.4	51.2	50.6	52.0	56.8	60.0	53.2	65.4
Sweden	m	14.1	14.4	15.2	16.2	13.9	14.6	14.6	11.7	12.9	14.4
United Kingdom	m	128.9	136.0	134.6	140.4	156.1	161.8	182.5	180.4	189.2	181.6
Iceland		0.9	0.9	1.0	0.9	0.9	1.1	1.0	1.0	0.9	0.9
Malta		0.3	0.4	0.3	0.3	0.4	0.6	0.5	0.9	0.8	0.8
Norway	m	11.3	12.4	12.5	12.5	11.6	12.8	12.2	12.5	11.3	12.8
Switzerland	m	25.9	28.5	29.3	28.5	33.7	34.2	34.6	33.3	28.9	31.8
Yugoslavia*		16.6	14.7	13.8	17.2	16.5	14.2	20.2	16.5	7.7	8.8
Total		**670**	**681**	**689**	**757**	**803**	**869**	**971**	**972**	**958**	**962**
Eastern Europe											
Bulgaria		9.5	6.1	9.4	7.4	7.1	5.6	5.5	5.3	7.3	9.3
Czechoslovakia*		18.1	19.3	20.4	15.6	21.6	22.3	21.2	24.7	4.3	na
Czech Republic	m	na	na	na	na	na	na	na	na	12.9	17.2
Slovak Republic	m	na	na	na	na	na	na	na	na	6.6	8.0
German Democratic Rep		28.7	24.2	25.8	26.9	28.9	22.2	na	na	na	na
Hungary	m	16.3	16.4	16.4	16.4	18.4	15.4	13.5	10.2	12.5	10.7
Poland		19.9	13.8	23.7	17.6	28.3	20.2	36.6	44.0	43.9	44.5
Romania		4.0	4.7	7.2	7.5	6.2	8.8	8.0	10.0	10.7	14.3
USSR*		216.3	185.6	200.3	159.6	245.3	134.2	93.2	12.3	na	na
Russian Federation	m	na	na	na	na	na	na	na	18.7	112.2	148.0
Other former USSR		na	na	na	na	na	na	na	17.8	33.1	37.2
Total		**313**	**270**	**303**	**251**	**356**	**229**	**178**	**143**	**243**	**289**
Africa											
Cameroon	[b]m	0.5	0.5	0.5	0.5	0.5	0.5	0.5	0.5	0.5	0.5
Côte d'Ivoire	[b]m	4.0	4.0	4.0	4.0	4.0	4.0	4.0	4.0	4.0	4.0
Egypt		4.3	2.4	3.4	2.1	1.5	0.5	4.7	4.4	3.6	5.4
Ghana	[b]m	1.0	1.0	1.0	1.0	1.0	1.0	1.0	1.0	1.0	1.0
Libyan Arab Jamaharia		1.8	1.8	1.5	1.4	0.6	0.4	0.5	0.2	0.3	0.4
Morocco		0.3	0.2	0.3	0.8	0.7	0.9	0.8	1.2	1.4	2.1
Nigeria	[b]m	4.0	4.0	4.0	4.0	4.0	4.0	4.0	4.0	4.0	4.0
South Africa		7.8	8.6	9.8	9.8	10.5	11.3	10.8	9.1	10.1	13.0
Total		**24**	**23**	**25**	**24**	**23**	**23**	**26**	**24**	**25**	**30**
North, Central and South America											
Argentina		14.1	13.3	12.6	11.4	9.1	8.9	26.4	29.1	30.8	30.2
Brazil	m	50.7	43.2	56.2	49.3	62.7	74.1	81.9	68.0	76.0	88.1
Canada		45.8	42.3	51.1	52.0	48.6	51.0	46.9	49.3	55.8	56.9
Colombia		35.4	46.8	44.3	41.6	38.0	39.1	40.1	39.6	41.0	38.3
Dominican Republic		3.6	2.2	2.4	2.5	2.7	3.3	4.2	3.9	3.8	3.8
Ecuador	m	7.4	7.3	5.0	11.4	4.9	3.2	1.5	1.9	2.4	2.8
Mexico		27.7	33.2	28.8	28.1	30.5	39.4	56.0	46.7	41.6	48.9
United States		462.0	483.8	506.0	524.2	488.0	540.0	566.3	593.3	587.4	545.7
Venezuela		7.0	4.6	3.8	5.8	4.6	5.7	5.7	7.3	6.8	6.3
Total		**654**	**677**	**710**	**726**	**689**	**765**	**829**	**839**	**846**	**821**
Asia and Oceania											
Australia		26.4	25.8	27.6	28.7	32.1	32.5	29.9	30.6	32.8	33.4
China		10.8	15.1	22.9	11.2	12.4	11.7	20.8	16.0	13.3	19.4
Cyprus		0.2	0.2	0.3	0.5	0.5	0.6	0.7	0.7	0.9	0.6

Table 3 Consumption of cocoa beans and cocoa products by country, 1984/85–1993/94[a] contd.

Country		1984/85	1985/86	1986/87	1987/88	1988/89	1989/90	1990/91	1991/92	1992/93	1993/94
						(Thousand tonnes)					
Indonesia		4.1	5.9	8.1	8.1	7.6	11.5	15.4	17.3	10.8	15.3
Iran		0.5	0.4	0.4	0.4	0.3	0.8	0.4	1.3	0.7	0.6
Iraq		1.0	0.8	0.7	1.3	0.9	1.3	0.5	0.5	1.3	0.7
Israel		5.9	8.8	7.3	7.7	5.7	5.7	7.6	7.5	9.5	7.9
Japan	m	75.5	79.7	89.1	104.1	113.4	109.5	109.3	110.8	111.6	115.5
Jordan		0.8	0.6	0.7	0.6	0.2	0.6	0.7	0.4	0.7	0.8
Korea, Republic of		4.8	5.4	8.2	1.4	1.3	7.6	9.4	8.1	14.4	11.0
Lebanon		0.7	0.6	0.4	0.8	0.6	0.6	1.2	1.2	1.4	1.8
Malaysia	m	3.8	2.6	2.4	4.7	8.6	11.2	12.4	12.8	3.7	2.5
New Zealand		3.1	5.1	3.2	4.8	2.5	2.9	3.7	4.8	6.6	7.5
Papua New Guinea	m	0.1	0.1	0.1	0.1	0.1	0.1	0.1	0.1	0.1	0.1
Philippines		3.4	1.0	2.4	2.4	3.1	9.8	6.6	6.3	7.7	13.3
Saudi Arabia		3.4	3.3	4.6	6.3	6.3	6.4	6.7	7.4	7.0	7.4
Sri Lanka		1.8	1.7	1.7	1.7	1.8	1.9	1.2	1.0	1.4	1.5
Syria		1.7	0.9	0.8	0.7	1.2	1.0	1.8	2.4	3.5	1.1
Turkey		3.7	3.9	7.3	5.8	5.4	9.0	10.9	10.5	10.2	7.7
Total		**152**	**163**	**188**	**191**	**204**	**225**	**239**	**239**	**238**	**248**
World total (of above)[c]		**1812**	**1813**	**1915**	**1949**	**2075**	**2110**	**2243**	**2218**	**2310**	**2351**

Note: m Member of International Cocoa Agreement, 1986.

[a] Calculated as grindings of cocoa beans plus net imports of cocoa products and of chocolate and chocolate products in beans equivalent, using the following conversion factors: cocoa butter 1.33; cocoa paste/liquor 1.25; cocoa powder and cake 1.18; chocolate and chocolate products 0.40 (0.20 is used in those cases where chocolate products are identified as containing only half the normal quantity of cocoa).

[b] Provisional assumptions for some cocoa-producing countries, including Cameroon, Côte d'Ivoire, Ghana and Nigeria, are ICCO Secretariat estimates relating to domestic consumption. The data are not derived from annual grindings and trade statistics as described in footnote [a] above because of data problems and additional complications associated with changes in stocks and with the appropriateness of conversion factors.

[c] Totals for listed countries only. Some cocoa-producing countries and cocoa-importing countries are not included because of data problems and additional complications associated with changes in stocks and with the appropriateness of conversion factors.

By courtesy of the International Cocoa Organization

Table 4 Monthly and annual averages of daily prices of cocoa beans, January 1971–April 1996

Year	Jan	Feb	Mar	Apr	May	Jun	Jul	Aug	Sep	Oct	Nov	Dec	Average
						US cents/lb[a]							
1971	27.23	25.48	24.47	24.76	23.16	24.04	25.89	26.91	25.00	22.47	21.96	21.79	**24.43**
1972	24.26	24.94	26.12	26.37	27.87	28.19	29.24	31.04	32.85	33.02	32.51	33.37	**29.15**
1973	32.47	33.87	38.30	42.73	53.03	58.02	70.30	64.22	60.25	58.72	51.87	51.74	**51.29**
1974	50.89	58.38	67.39	82.60	82.71	70.28	71.67	73.48	72.35	79.18	75.59	64.36	**70.74**
1975	67.19	67.84	62.64	56.20	48.01	44.90	52.85	53.25	52.47	56.70	55.99	59.83	**56.49**
1976	63.70	65.04	64.17	74.32	80.20	87.26	88.75	96.23	108.41	117.39	132.67	134.92	**92.76**
1977	156.45	173.15	182.92	162.66	171.53	192.84	197.84	180.02	174.65	167.48	157.87	144.87	**171.86**
1978	135.08	128.14	153.35	156.10	142.19	135.68	143.47	152.43	170.09	173.57	182.77	179.03	**154.33**
1979	165.77	158.85	154.02	147.29	152.32	157.82	147.47	142.18	146.13	138.72	136.77	144.52	**149.32**
1980	143.63	146.78	140.18	131.97	117.24	113.27	111.77	104.85	108.20	104.54	98.57	95.70	**118.06**
1981	94.94	92.57	95.97	95.69	87.68	75.31	92.91	101.92	106.01	98.55	93.28	95.46	**94.19**
1982	99.25	94.67	88.35	79.17	77.79	71.29	71.59	70.74	76.48	74.29	69.91	74.55	**79.01**
1983	80.93	88.10	84.34	85.15	93.67	104.22	104.45	104.46	96.98	95.00	100.68	115.25	**96.10**
1984	118.93	113.28	115.04	115.05	121.45	112.72	100.54	100.41	104.83	102.39	102.29	97.09	**108.67**
1985	100.68	103.12	101.26	101.64	96.57	94.88	100.24	103.21	106.24	107.19	104.22	107.93	**102.27**
1986	105.40	100.63	95.58	90.25	86.44	86.48	91.74	93.79	100.08	94.03	91.65	89.65	**93.81**
1987	89.66	88.83	91.16	93.88	93.82	90.74	95.93	91.70	90.16	86.73	87.91	86.05	**90.55**
1988	89.50	81.60	76.44	74.80	77.42	73.67	72.95	65.67	56.21	59.16	66.96	68.12	**71.88**
1989	65.17	67.23	63.90	58.57	54.78	56.80	61.02	58.29	51.75	48.25	45.79	44.01	**56.30**
1990	45.12	45.56	51.32	60.58	65.61	60.08	61.04	58.53	62.21	59.31	61.32	58.69	**57.53**
1991	56.36	55.10	54.90	51.97	48.18	47.21	46.75	51.66	57.80	58.97	59.68	61.99	**54.21**
1992	58.17	54.10	51.19	47.37	45.15	43.66	50.00	53.43	51.03	48.58	48.80	46.98	**49.87**
1993	46.97	45.22	44.24	45.92	45.24	44.78	48.10	49.76	57.51	58.63	60.29	61.47	**50.68**
1994	57.33	55.74	59.29	56.36	62.50	66.18	70.41	70.37	67.40	65.68	65.18	63.48	**63.33**
1995	66.63	68.51	67.36	66.64	65.56	65.19	61.87	64.09	63.36	63.26	65.16	62.54	**65.01**
1996	61.21	62.14	60.72	66.06									
						SDRs per tonne[b]							
1971	600.3	561.7	539.5	545.9	510.6	530.0	570.8	593.3	551.2	495.4	484.1	463.5	**537.2**
1972	492.6	506.4	530.4	535.5	565.9	572.4	593.7	630.3	667.0	670.5	660.1	677.6	**591.9**
1973	659.3	642.2	699.9	780.9	969.1	1060.3	1284.7	1173.6	1101.1	1073.1	947.9	954.5	**944.8**
1974	930.0	1066.9	1231.5	1509.5	1551.5	1284.4	1308.7	1356.8	1345.7	1464.1	1387.1	1169.1	**1297.1**
1975	1201.6	1201.3	1101.4	997.9	849.3	794.1	960.2	987.6	982.2	1060.5	1046.8	1126.2	**1025.8**
1976	1198.4	1225.9	1222.0	1422.9	1540.0	1681.9	1708.6	1847.2	2071.7	2241.1	2534.4	2573.3	**1772.3**
1977	2980.6	3304.0	3483.8	3090.1	3254.9	3658.0	3718.6	3402.1	3315.7	3149.3	2943.4	2659.4	**3246.7**
1978	2453.4	2318.9	2749.0	2791.8	2576.1	2432.3	2531.9	2645.0	2944.1	2886.7	3135.7	3073.1	**2711.5**
1979	2827.3	2720.0	2638.5	2541.2	2642.7	2724.5	2495.1	2410.9	2469.6	2355.2	2330.4	2428.1	**2548.6**
1980	2398.2	2464.4	2419.8	2295.8	1981.3	1891.1	1856.1	1760.3	1809.4	1761.7	1693.8	1664.9	**1999.7**
1881	1650.8	1656.2	1722.5	1743.1	1639.9	1435.8	1803.6	2002.0	2044.0	1882.7	1763.7	1808.2	**1762.7**
1982	1897.2	1842.3	1733.7	1565.3	1511.3	1426.1	1446.0	1435.3	1561.5	1528.8	1444.4	1502.2	**1574.5**
1983	1621.9	1781.8	1713.0	1734.6	1907.5	2149.5	2166.4	2193.4	2034.5	1971.6	2110.3	2436.7	**1985.1**
1984	2531.3	2385.9	2383.7	2399.3	2572.0	2390.2	2172.9	2178.1	2310.9	2273.7	2249.3	2167.6	**2334.6**
1985	2275.2	2363.8	2316.6	2262.6	2151.4	2098.0	2166.7	2201.8	2277.7	2218.6	2127.4	2183.5	**2220.3**
1986	2116.67	1965.21	1833.83	1729.81	1629.78	1636.95	1700.28	1710.97	1823.30	1710.66	1686.01	1637.44	**1765.08**
1987	1578.81	1551.68	1583.25	1602.32	1585.42	1555.12	1666.16	1592.50	1539.23	1476.22	1436.24	1371.68	**1544.89**
1988	1432.78	1327.07	1228.86	1193.58	1240.03	1206.10	1232.26	1120.45	957.85	988.18	1088.31	1107.75	**1176.94**
1989	1084.77	1125.82	1079.40	993.44	953.51	1009.37	1057.99	1018.03	915.07	836.12	790.40	745.39	**967.44**
1990	754.41	773.83	869.31	1026.43	1097.13	1007.69	1001.36	936.66	986.34	915.55	935.59	906.10	**934.20**
1991	873.57	843.28	875.36	847.83	790.64	788.91	779.73	852.69	941.27	954.45	950.07	970.55	**872.36**
1992	909.96	857.80	826.20	761.76	717.22	681.72	763.53	808.71	771.52	746.27	775.74	745.81	**780.52**
1993	752.03	726.65	706.46	716.39	704.54	700.44	762.78	782.63	894.39	918.33	956.89	978.97	**800.04**
1994	920.06	885.47	932.44	884.83	973.96	1022.21	1065.36	1066.57	1015.37	979.96	976.37	963.77	**973.86**
1995	1001.95	1021.73	967.01	931.98	927.97	919.10	875.66	935.64	941.45	930.80	961.10	928.39	**945.23**
1996	919.34	934.46	915.72	1003.98	–	–	–	–	–	–	–	–	–

Note:

[a] The daily price for cocoa beans is the average of the quotations of the nearest three active future trading months on the London Cocoa Terminal Market and on the New York Coffee, Sugar and Cocoa Exchange at the time of the London close. The London prices are converted into United States dollars per tonne by using the current six-month forward rate of exchange in London at closing time. The time of shift to the next three-month period is the fifteenth of the month preceding the nearest active maturing month.

[b] The United States dollar-denominated average of the London and New York prices is converted into SDR equivalent at the appropriate daily official United States dollar/SDR exchange rate published by the International Monetary Fund. Estimates for the years 1971 to 1985, shown in italics, are calculated using the monthly averages of United States dollar/SDR exchange rate.

By courtesy of the International Cocoa Organization

Figure 2 Cocoa: annual average prices

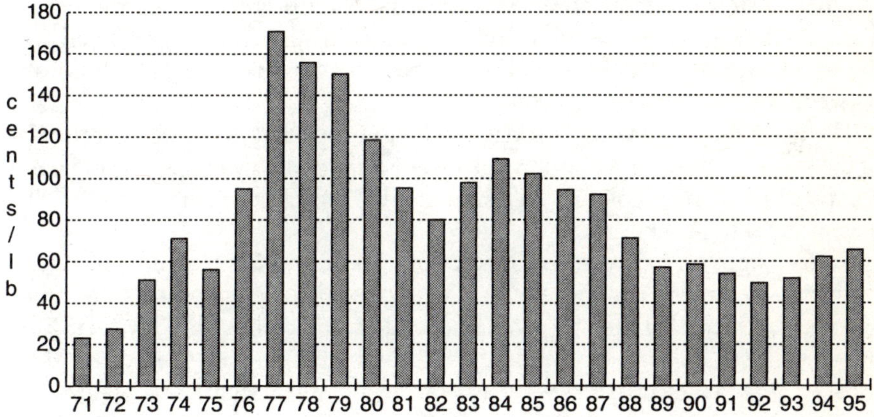

Coffee

Robin Stainer

Perhaps it was an Arabian sheikh two thousand or more years ago who brewed the first coffee, or it may have been a goatherd in third-century Ethiopia. These are the characters favoured by legend, but the truth is that the origins of the world's most popular beverage are now lost.

What is pretty certain, however, is that the plant originated in Ethiopia and Sudan, where it still grows wild, and was first cultivated in the Yemen perhaps a thousand years ago. But it may well have been the leaves that the local dervishes brewed, not the roasted and ground beans.

The beverage as we know it today reached Europe through Turkey at the start of the seventeenth century and by the end of it the Dutch were producing coffee commercially in their colonies and trading it in Amsterdam. Since then there has been no looking back.

Coffee is grown between the Tropics of Cancer and Capricorn in at least 80 countries in America, Asia, Africa and Oceania, just over 50 of which are exporters. At least 20 million people depend on the commodity for their livelihood, while it is drunk by hundreds of millions more. The value of its global trade – US$6.6 billion in 1993 – is usually second only to that of oil, while about a dozen countries rely on it for at least a third of their export earnings. In Uganda's case it is around 90 per cent.

The two varieties of coffee important in world trade are the arabica, which accounts for about 70 per cent of world production and is produced principally in Latin America, and the robusta. Both types of tree do best in deep, well-drained soil and need plentiful rainfall; they begin yielding after three to four years and have a commercially productive life of 20 to 30 years. Both varieties are pretty robust, but disease (particularly coffee rust) and pests (mainly the coffee borer) can cause problems. Neither, moreover, can withstand frosts, although arabica coffee – which is mostly grown at much higher altitudes – is more resilient.

There are two main processing methods for turning the harvested red fruit (cherries) into the green beans that are the basis of about 95 per cent of all coffee traded internationally: the dry (unwashed) and the wet (washed). The beans produced by the former, which is a sun-drying process used for Brazilian and Ethiopian arabicas and for nearly all robusta production, gives a harsher taste (or 'cup quality') when brewed. They are typically used in blends and for soluble (instant) manufacture, which satisfies nearly 30 per cent of world coffee demand although accounting for under 5 per cent of world trade in the commodity.

The wet process, whereby the cherries are soaked and pulped before drying, is considerably more complex. The beans that finally emerge give a milder brew and are more highly prized commercially.

In recent years, washed mild arabica coffee has become increasingly popular because of the growing consumer preference for products with a cachet of quality. This is shown by rising sales of premium arabica-based soluble brands and of 'specialty' roasted coffee beans, which are marketed a little like *appellation controllée* wines. A growing taste for 'lighter' and supposedly healthier foods and drinks has also helped arabicas at the expense of robustas, which, as well as their stronger flavour, have considerably more caffeine.

Colombia, Mexico, Central America, Ecuador, Kenya and Tanzania are among the main producers of mild arabica coffee, which has increased its share of world exportable production (itself roughly 70–75 per cent of the global crop) from around 45 per cent at the end of the 1980s to 50–55 per cent in recent seasons. The world's biggest grower of unwashed arabicas is Brazil, which has also rapidly expanded robusta output to about 20 per cent of the national crop and now ranks alongside Indonesia, Uganda, Côte d'Ivoire and Vietnam as a top producer of the type.

Expansion of robusta production in Brazil and Asia (first Indonesia, then Thailand and now Vietnam) has been one of the biggest structural changes in the coffee market over the past 10 to 20 years. Africa's producers, which are often high cost, inefficient and disaster prone, have been squeezed in the process and now account for only 30 per cent of world robusta output and trade against 50 per cent just ten years ago.

These African states were also hit hardest by the collapse in 1989 of the international export quota system that had artificially preserved their historic market shares. Its removal not only gave buyers complete freedom of choice, but led to a free-for-all as exporters fought for new markets. The result was a huge transfer of stocks from producers to consumers, giving the latter the power to dictate prices for years afterwards. It is only over the past year that consumer controlled stocks have been brought down to more traditional levels.

Another big recent structural change in the market has been Brazil's diminishing role, largely because of stagnating output. It remains the leading producer, but its average share of the world crop in the first five years of this decade fell to 25 per cent from 30 per cent in the second half of the 1980s. Its slice of exports, meanwhile, dropped to 20 per cent from 25 per cent, eroded by rising domestic use, which today absorbs at least 40 per cent of the harvest.

A move to more profitable crops and government neglect have played a part in Brazil's loss of stature, as has the weather. Frosts remain a perennial problem, despite the shift in production northwards to less vulnerable areas after the catastrophic damage caused by 1975's freeze. The last one was in mid-1994, which combined with a drought to cut severely the 1995 crop's potential. The massive jump in wholesale and retail prices that followed led to a drop in global coffee consumption, which traditionally is not particularly price sensitive.

Even before this setback to demand, use had been growing more slowly in the 1990s than in the 1980s, partly because of saturation in some markets and competition from soft drinks. Coffee drinking in the USA – still, with its near 25 per cent share, the world's single biggest consumer of the beverage – has been in steady decline for years, both in absolute volume and per capita terms.

The European Union, whose biggest user is Germany, takes nearly 50 per cent of the world's coffee, and annual growth was averaging an unspectacular 2 per cent until 1995's drop. Strongly rising Japanese consumption had until then also been a feature, providing a growing market for Asia's expanding producers.

The principal trading centres for coffee are in Europe and the USA. For futures transactions, the London Commodity Exchange provides a dollar-based robusta contract and the New York Coffee, Cocoa and Sugar Exchange an arabica. The main places for physical trading of green coffee are Le Havre, Marseilles, Hamburg, Bremen and New York.

E.D. & F. Man, which is one of the big players in the market, also publish regular reports on the coffee market; its address is Sugar Quay, Lower Thames Street, London EC3R 6DU, UK. Another big trader is Rothfos and Cargill.

The longer-term outlook for coffee is one of rising production, stimulated by the much higher prices of the mid-1990s, and relatively sluggish growth in consumption, except where per capita use is low, such as Japan and Russia. The Association of Coffee Producing Countries (ACPC), which was formed in 1993 to end years of price warfare and whose 12 member states account for 80 per cent of world supply, can be expected to try to limit the adverse impact on prices implied by such a scenario through continuing co-ordinated restraints on exports. But internal divisions could sink this strategy.

The liberalization of coffee marketing being forced on producers as a condition for international loans is a potentially bearish future factor for the market, because it promises to increase competition among exporting companies. Also auguring ill for prices is the prospect of a continuing decline in Brazil's share of the world coffee trade, which would therefore leave supply lines less vulnerable to the vagaries of the country's weather. Further expansion of Asian output – especially if Cambodia and Laos join in – could also hold back prices, while other negative long-term pointers are the ability of processors to live with much lower stock cover than once thought safe and coffee's falling popularity among younger drinkers.

Further information

International Coffee Organization
22 Berners Street
London W1P 4DD
UK
Tel: +44 171 580 8591
Fax: +44 171 580 6129

UN Food and Agriculture Organization (FAO)
Viale della Terme di Caracalla
00100 Rome
Italy
Tel: +39 6 522 51
Fax: +39 6 522 53152

World Bank
1818 H Street NW
Washington DC 20433
USA
Tel: +1 202 477 1234
Fax: +1 202 477 6391

FO Licht
Am Muchlengraben 22
Postfach 1220
23902 Ratzeburg
Germany
Tel: +49 4541 889 20
Fax: +49 4541 821 45

Table 1 Imports by importing members from all sources July–June 1989/90 to 1994/95

	June–July					
Importing Member	**1989/90**	**1990/91**	**1991/92**	**1992/93**	**1993/94**	**1994/95**
			(Thousand bags)			
USA	**23 933**	**19 359**	**21 467**	**21 412**	**16 832**	**16 885**
European Community	**41 841**	**43 074**	**42 097**	**43 921**	**44 586**	**41 915**
Austria	1 591	2 063	2 226	2 287	1 265	1 702[1]
Belgium/Luxembourg	2 104	1 813	1 721	1 924	2 257	2 165[1]
Denmark	1 009	994	994	1 003	1 029	927
Finland	1 109	1 010	1 068	1 126	1 321	1 078[2]
France	6 189	6 606	6 422	6 395	6 432	6 250
Germany	13 334	13 706	13 187	13 820	13 968	13 300
Greece	647	556	352	322	458	461[1]
Ireland	117	126	106	98	119	125[3]
Italy	4 659	4 951	4 735	5 277	5 585	5 454
Netherlands	2 993	3 144	3 077	2 958	3 216	1 886
Portugal	554	540	572	627	640	650
Spain	3 005	2 921	3 085	3 170	3 131	2 967
Sweden	1 773	1 777	1 673	1 768	1 804	1 869[1]
United Kingdom	2 756	2 868	2 880	3 144	3 361	3 080
Other Importing Members	**8 653**	**8 260**	**8 838**	**9 219**	**9 761**	**9 164**
Cyprus	51	41	56	41	78	47
Fiji	2	2	2	2	2	2[1]
Japan	5 841	5 271	5 598	5 735	6 024	6 039
Norway	749	752	720	730	730	704
Singapore[4]	821	1 072	1 326	1 644	1 870	1 341
Switzerland	1 189	1 121	1 137	1 067	1 057	1 032
Total	**74 427**	**70 693**	**72 403**	**74 552**	**71 179**	**67 954***

Notes:

Due to rounding the totals may not always reflect the sum of the relevant components.

* Preliminary

1 Includes estimates for January–June 1995.

2 Includes estimates for April–June 1995.

3 Includes estimates for June 1995.

4 Includes estimated imports from Indonesia.

By courtesy of the International Coffee Organization

Figure 1 Coffee: leading importers

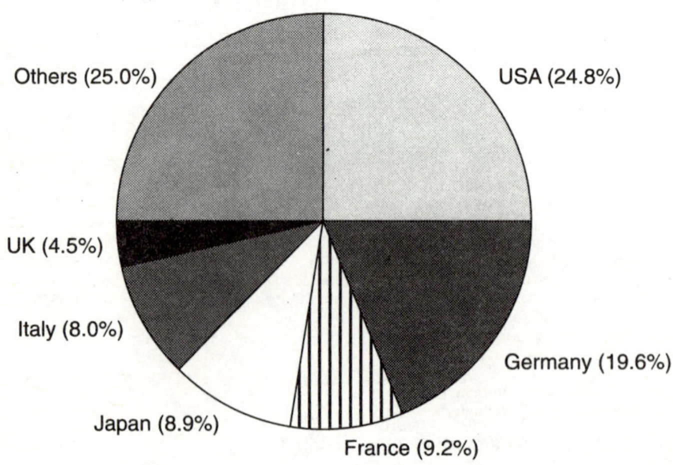

Table 2 Total production crop years 1988/89–1995/96

Crop year commencing		*1988* (1)	*1989* (2)	*1990* (3)	*1991* (4)	*1992* (5)	*1993* (6)	*1994* (7)	*1995* (8)
					(Thousand bags)				
1 April		**37 747**	**40 570**	**39 099**	**43 056**	**35 662**	**42 171**	**33 943**	**27 123**
Angola	(R)	184	120	50	79	79	31	78	110
Bolivia	(A)	152	184	123	107	122	223	122	145
Brazil	(A/R)	22 939	25 341	25 520	27 889	23 417	29 652	21 092	12 500
Burundi	(A/R)	593	535	489	667	620	394	665	421
Ecuador	(A/R)	2 205	2 185	1 504	2 123	1 187	2 068	2 375	2 350
Indonesia	(R/A)	6 768	6 884	7 441	8 464	5 577	7 300	6 418	6 200
Madagascar*	(R/A)	1 120	1 334	982	933	1 122	442	639	1 483
Malawi	(A)	71	113	103	125	136	63	83	90
Papua New Guinea	(A/R)	1 182	1 102	962	747	902	1 019	1 141	1 300
Paraguay	(A)	261	371	202	36	60	69	52	600
Peru	(A)	1 428	1 547	937	1 200	1 723	455	1 150	1 450
Rwanda	(A)	679	625	534	484	639	444	22	333
Zimbabwe	(A)	165	229	252	202	78	11	106	141
1 July		**4 165**	**3 736**	**3 616**	**3 011**	**3 205**	**3 073**	**3 015**	**3 836**
Congo*	(R)	46	25	3	3	4	3	18	25
Cuba	(A)	479	515	415	310	312	370	322	500
Dominican Republic	(A)	853	737	877	321	638	606	729	1 050
Haiti	(A)	453	420	393	540	515	459	369	530
Philippines (R/A)	(R/A)	1 395	1 151	972	1 019	920	875	878	890
Tanzania	(A/R)	931	863	933	789	788	734	676	818
Zambia	(A)	8	25	23	29	28	26	23	23
1 October		**49 259**	**49 997**	**49 897**	**55 918**	**46 373**	**48 447**	**50 348**	**53 392**
Benin*	(R)	46	0	0	0	2	0	0	35
Cameroon*	(R/A)	1 990	1 928	1 682	1 725	259	681	390	1 165
Central African Rep*	(R)	357	226	175	125	134	165	256	300
Colombia	(A)	10 543	12 920	14 231	18 222	13 823	11 320	12 973	12 000
Costa Rica	(A)	2 374	2 300	2 562	2 759	2 999	2 259	2 431	2 300
Côte d'Ivoire*	(R)	3 846	4 799	2 940	4 129	2 245	2 293	2 976	2 833
El Salvador	(A)	1 512	2 788	2 564	2 298	3 002	2 379	2 242	2 454
Equatorial Guinea*	(R)	4	4	4	3	2	0	0	15
Ethiopia	(A)	2 699	3 439	2 910	3 061	1 794	2 865	2 536	3 833
Gabon*	(R)	33	6	4	2	3	4	8	25
Ghana	(R)	9	16	38	76	36	108	80	85
Guatemala	(A/R)	2 991	3 473	3 271	3 496	4 318	3 536	3 671	3 300
Guinea	(R)	91	181	45	90	77	65	71	100
Honduras	(A)	1 680	1 767	1 568	2 321	1 919	1 830	2 181	2 300
India	(A/R)	3 033	1 785	3 166	2 866	2 152	3 145	4 223	3 700
Jamaica	(A)	17	21	22	39	26	35	50	45
Kenya	(A)	2 086	746	1 995	1 133	1 481	2 301	869	1 583
Liberia	(R)	89	21	3	3	3	5	5	10
Mexico	(A)	6 001	5 050	4 675	4 727	3 723	4 284	4 158	4 770
Nicaragua	(A)	645	689	461	711	528	769	676	921
Nigeria	(R)	34	28	30	45	49	45	40	55
Panama	(A)	134	177	215	194	196	142	225	200
Sierra Leone	(R)	101	252	43	54	39	37	64	70
Sri Lanka	(R/A)	80	60	97	82	39	68	33	60
Thailand	(R)	1 077	1 147	749	1 337	1 228	1 242	1 523	1 368
Togo*	(R)	318	165	162	432	86	195	183	250
Trinidad and Tobago	(R)	17	41	15	18	15	16	18	20
Uganda	(R/A)	3 259	1 935	1 955	2 088	2 185	3 149	2 637	3 300
Venezuela	(A)	957	1 248	1 230	1 075	1 115	1 307	1 025	1 395
Vietnam	(R)	1 040	1 006	1 390	1 307	2 341	3 020	3 513	3 500
Zaire	(R/A)	2 196	1 779	1 695	1 500	554	1 182	1 291	1 400
Total		**91 171**	**94 303**	**92 612**	**101 985**	**85 240**	**93 691**	**87 306**	**84 351**

Notes: Total production has been derived on the basis of the verification of stocks for crop years commencing 1988 and 1989. For those Members whose crop year runs from October to September the figures for crop year commencing 1988 are derived on the basis of the Member's estimate of closing stocks. From 1989 onwards figures have been derived on the basis of the Member's or the ICO's estimate of closing stocks.

* Member of the OAMCAF group
(A) Arabica
(R) Robusta
(A/R) Both types. Predominantly Arabica
(R/A) Both types. Predominantly Robusta

By courtesy of the International Coffee Organization

Table 3 Exportable production crop years 1988/89–1995/96

Crop year commencing		*1988* (1)	*1989* (2)	*1990* (3)	*1991* (4)	*1992* (5)	*1993* (6)	*1994* (7)	*1995* (8)
					(Thousand bags)				
1 April		**27 698**	**29 432**	**27 891**	**31 875**	**24 289**	**30 254**	**21 819**	**15 999**
Angola	(R)	166	100	30	49	44	11	53	100
Bolivia	(A)	127	159	98	77	92	188	87	110
Brazil	(A/R)	14 939	16 341	16 520	18 889	14 417	20 652	12 092	3 500
Burundi	(A/R)	592	532	487	665	618	392	663	419
Ecuador	(A/R)	1 865	1 835	1 154	1 773	837	1 718	2 025	2 000
Indonesia	(R/A)	5 576	5 667	6 199	7 214	4 250	5 383	4 106	4 873
Madagascar*	(R/A)	870	1 034	632	633	772	82	472	1 316
Malawi	(A)	69	111	101	123	134	61	81	88
Papua New Guinea	(A/R)	1 177	1 098	959	744	899	1 017	1 139	1 297
Paraguay	(A)	246	356	187	21	45	49	32	580
Peru	(A)	1 238	1 357	747	1 010	1 473	255	950	1 250
Rwanda	(A)	678	624	533	483	638	443	21	332
Zimbabwe	(A)	155	218	244	194	70	3	98	134
1 July		**2 845**	**2 263**	**2 135**	**1 391**	**1 587**	**1 438**	**1 347**	**2 173**
Congo*	(R)	38	17	0	0	1	0	15	22
Cuba	(A)	265	300	202	97	117	176	125	305
Dominican Republic	(A)	535	415	557	1	318	286	399	700
Haiti	(A)	233	200	173	210	185	129	39	200
Philippines	(R/A)	845	451	252	269	170	105	88	120
Tanzania	(A/R)	921	856	929	786	769	717	659	804
Zambia	(A)	8	24	22	28	27	25	22	22
1 October		**40 758**	**42 179**	**42 019**	**47 624**	**38 547**	**40 286**	**42 466**	**45 606**
Benin*	(R)	46	0	0	0	2	0	0	35
Cameroon*	(R/A)	1 907	1 845	1 599	1 642	176	581	290	1 065
Central African Rep*	(R)	328	197	147	97	106	140	236	280
Colombia	(A)	8 843	11 720	12 996	16 822	12 523	9 920	11 598	10 500
Costa Rica	(A)	1 999	1 925	2 187	2 384	2 624	1 884	2 056	1 975
Côte d'Ivoire*	(R)	3 796	4 749	2 890	4 079	2 195	2 243	2 926	2 783
El Salvador	(A)	1 332	2 608	2 284	2 018	2 772	2 149	2 042	2 254
Equatorial Guinea*	(R)	4	4	4	3	2	0	0	15
Ethiopia	(A)	1 532	2 239	1 710	1 661	494	1 565	1 286	2 583
Gabon*	(R)	32	4	2	1	2	3	7	24
Ghana	(R)	7	13	21	59	19	91	52	57
Guatemala	(A/R)	2 691	3 173	2 971	3 196	4 018	3 226	3 361	2 990
Guinea	(R)	70	156	20	65	15	32	21	36
Honduras	(A)	1 506	1 575	1 380	2 064	1 679	1 600	1 928	2 024
India	(A/R)	1 966	1 118	2 299	1 866	1 377	2 145	3 223	2 925
Jamaica	(A)	13	15	15	28	20	25	29	27
Kenya	(A)	1 986	646	1 945	1 083	1 431	2 251	819	1 533
Liberia	(R)	86	18	0	0	0	0	0	5
Mexico	(A)	4 301	3 450	3 301	3 527	2 423	3 214	3 208	3 750
Nicaragua	(A)	577	619	427	573	473	626	571	758
Nigeria	(R)	10	3	3	9	13	5	0	15
Panama	(A)	92	114	152	127	129	75	148	123
Sierra Leone	(R)	93	244	34	45	30	32	59	62
Sri Lanka	(R/A)	45	10	30	15	11	48	13	40
Thailand	(R)	927	980	554	1 177	1 003	975	1 248	1 200
Togo*	(R)	317	164	161	431	85	194	182	249
Trinidad and Tobago	(R)	1	34	7	7	5	6	4	10
Uganda	(R/A)	3 189	1 865	1 885	2 013	2 110	3 074	2 557	3 220
Venezuela	(A)	124	206	340	125	365	447	165	535
Vietnam	(R)	942	906	1 160	1 207	2 091	2 753	3 346	3 333
Zaire	(R/A)	1 996	1 579	1 495	1 300	354	982	1 091	1 200
Total		**71 301**	**73 874**	**72 045**	**80 890**	**64 423**	**71 978**	**65 632**	**63 778**

Notes: Exportable production has been derived on the basis of the verification of stocks for crop years commencing 1988 and 1989. For those Members whose crop year runs from October to September the figures for crop year commencing 1988 are derived on the basis of the Member's estimate of closing stocks. From 1989 onwards figures have been derived on the basis of the ICO's estimate of closing stocks.

* Member of the OAMCAF group
(A) Arabica
(R) Robusta
(A/R) Both types. Predominantly Arabica
(R/A) Both types. Predominantly Robusta

By courtesy of the International Coffee Organization

Figure 2 Coffee: leading producers

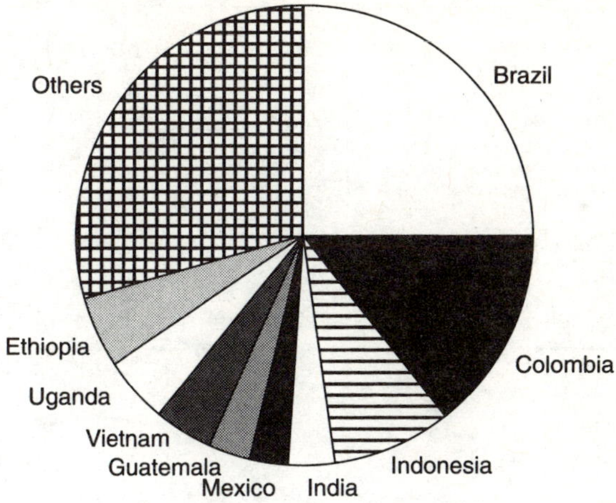

Figure 3 Composite indicator prices: monthly averages in current and constant (April–June 1989) terms, 1980–1992
(US cents per lb)

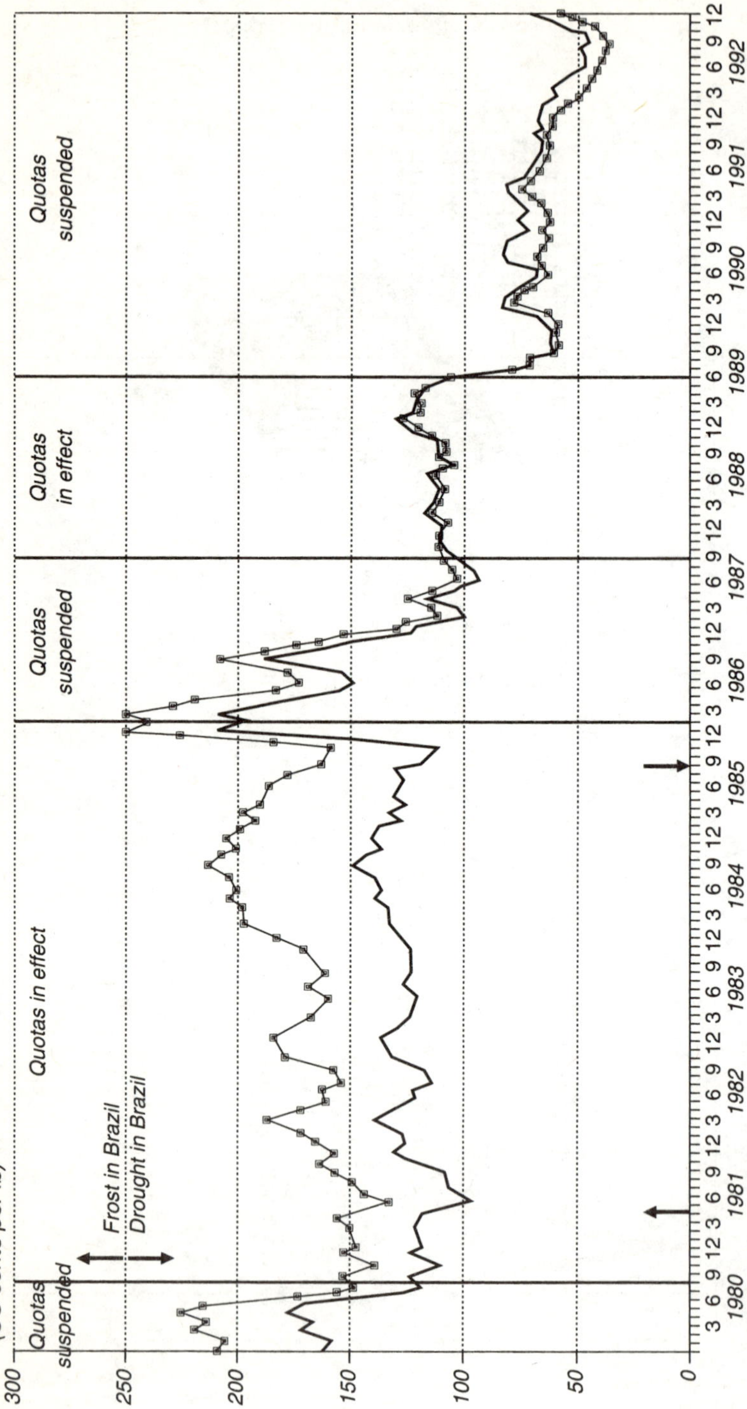

Prices refer to Composite Indicator Price 1976 up to September 1981; and Composite Indicator Price 1979 thereafter. Information up to December 1992

Prices in constant terms refer to prices in current terms deflated by the UN index of unit value of exports of manufactured goods from developed market economies.

Figure 4 Annual averages of ICO indicator prices, 1976–95

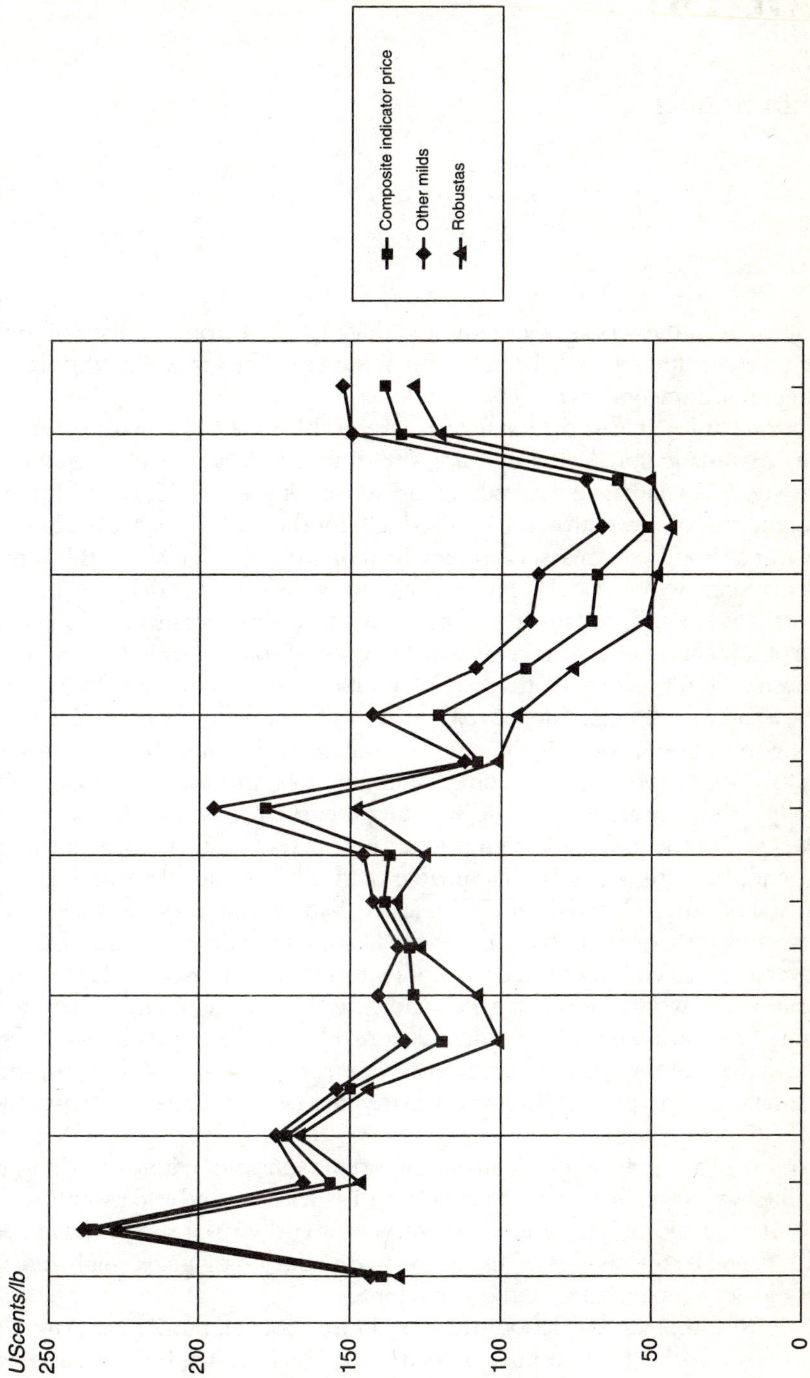

Source: International Coffee Organization

Cotton

Robin Stainer

Image is all in the world of fashion and, luckily for cotton, the natural look – once thought dowdy – has been 'in' for some years. It sits well with this age's greater environmental awareness.

Cotton has for at least the last ten years been able to hold its own against competing manmade fibres, although use – traditionally fairly price inelastic – was unquestionably damaged by the huge price rises of early 1995, when shortages drove the cost of raw cotton above US$1 a lb for the first time since the US Civil War. But although the market has remained historically high since, this setback to demand growth is widely seen by the industry as no more than a blip.

Cotton is still indisputably the world's favourite fibre, yet its near 50 per cent share of total fibre use is a far cry from its heyday up to the 1950s. Cotton, which has been used for making cloth for at least 5000 years, then had a 80–90 per cent slice – a commanding lead destroyed by the mmf production boom of the 1960s. During this period, cotton's competitors really ate into some of its key markets, such as waterproofs and other outer clothing, soft furnishings and car upholstery. It is these, moreover, that it is finding it hardest to win back.

But even in the bad years, cotton never lost its traditional markets for underwear and, because it is less inflammable than mmf, protective clothing. Then came the boom in demand for denim jeans, T-shirts and, more recently, cotton knitwear. Another shot in the arm for the fibre was the development of an easy-care version, which has boosted sales of cotton sheets, trousers and skirts.

Around the world, labels on goods showing '100 per cent cotton' have indisputably become a big selling point and from a low of 30 per cent 25 years ago, cotton's share of the total US fibre market has risen to nearer 40 per cent today. Per capita use there is up 80 per cent over the last ten years, compared with mmf's 25 per cent rise.

Cotton – the seeds of which are an important source of edible oil – is a plant that likes warm weather, growing as far north as Ukraine and as far south as Australia. It is susceptible to diseases, with the leaf curl virus a serious problem in Pakistan, and to the ravages of insects, which are becoming increasingly resistant to pesticides – a particular bugbear in China.

Over 90 countries throughout the world grow cotton, but 70 per cent of the world's crop comes from just five of them – the USA, China, India, Pakistan and

Uzbekistan. The first four are also the main users, accounting for around 60 per cent of the world total. This means that no more than 30 per cent of the world crop is actually traded internationally and that developments in any one of these four countries – but particularly China, the world's biggest producer and consumer – can have a marked market impact.

Chinese mills absorb almost a quarter of the world's cotton and when heavy imports are needed to keep them satisfied – as in 1994–5 – the upward impact on prices is invariably dramatic. The bulk of China's overseas purchases are made in the USA, which is by far the biggest exporter of cotton with its one-third share of world sales on average.

China's status in the 1990s has changed regularly from net importer to net exporter, while India and Pakistan traditionally fall into the latter category. But both were forced by poor local crops into banning exports and making substantial imports in 1993–4, which tightened supply lines appreciably. The squeeze then worsened when China began buying the following season and would have been even worse had it not been for the USA's record 1994–5 crop. The supply picture has since improved, thanks to increased plantings worldwide stimulated by the recent peak prices.

Asia is the powerhouse of world cotton consumption, which correlates closely to economic performance generally. Use in the region has risen by 30 per cent over the past ten years, compared with a global average of under 20 per cent and a fall in Europe. But consumption has also grown strongly in the USA, where textile manufacturers are among the world's most competitive, thanks to heavy investment in ultramodern spinning techniques.

The New York Cotton Exchange, the world's only futures market in the fibre, plays a key role in providing a guide price for contracts domestically and worldwide, while big ports in exporting and importing countries are centres for spot physical trading. They include Bombay, Bremen, Karachi, São Paulo and Shanghai. Liverpool and Geneva are important for secondhand trading, while the Liverpool Cotton Association plays a role in setting contract terms worldwide and arbitrating in disputes.

Further information

International Cotton Advisory Committee
1629 K Street NW, Suite 702
Washington DC, 20006 USA
Tel: +1 202 463 6660
Fax: +1 202 463 6950

Cotton Outlook
458 New Chester Road
Rock Ferry, Birkenhead L42 2AE
UK
Tel: +44 151 644 6400
Fax: +44 151 644 8550

Table 1 Cotton supply and distribution, 29 March 1996 (years beginning 1 August)

	1991	1992	1993	1994 Est	1995 Proj	1996 Proj
			Million metric tons			
Beginning stocks						
World total	**6.649**	**9.260**	**8.669**	**7.034**	**7.56**	**8.01**
China (mainland)	1.550	3.204	2.964	2.126	2.97	3.39
USA	0.510	0.807	1.015	0.769	0.58	0.67
Net exporters	3.117	4.042	3.974	3.342	3.05	3.05
Net importers[1]	3.532	5.217	4.695	3.691	4.51	4.95
Production						
World total	**20.699**	**17.985**	**16.891**	**18.690**	**19.23**	**19.77**
China (mainland)	5.672	4.510	3.739	4.342	4.50	4.10
USA	3.835	3.531	3.513	4.281	3.90	4.30
India	2.053	2.380	2.095	2.361	2.35	2.46
Pakistan	2.180	1.539	1.368	1.478	1.73	1.76
Uzbekistan	1.443	1.306	1.358	1.254	1.27	1.22
Turkey	0.561	0.574	0.602	0.628	0.84	0.79
Others	4.955	4.145	4.216	4.346	4.63	5.15
Consumption						
World total	**18.402**	**18.733**	**18.461**	**18.480**	**18.78**	**19.24**
China (mainland)	4.250	4.589	4.587	4.341	4.60	4.50
USA	2.093	2.232	2.268	2.438	2.26	2.50
India	1.903	2.104	2.160	2.265	2.38	2.47
EU & Turkey	1.764	1.795	1.902	2.058	2.07	2.10
East Asia	2.508	2.365	2.299	2.198	2.19	2.18
Pakistan	1.434	1.514	1.510	1.506	1.52	1.56
Former COMECON	1.910	1.521	1.133	1.005	1.01	1.04
Brazil	0.732	0.793	0.834	0.844	0.87	0.89
Others	1.808	1.821	1.768	1.825	1.88	1.99
Exports						
World total	**6.097**	**5.520**	**5.907**	**6.281**	**6.31**	**5.70**
USA	1.447	1.132	1.494	2.052	1.65	1.65
Uzbekistan	1.052	1.300	1.288	1.150	1.03	0.98
Francophone Africa	0.527	0.506	0.523	0.593	0.61	0.67
Australia	0.459	0.371	0.367	0.285	0.31	0.45
China (mainland)	0.131	0.149	0.166	0.040	0.08	0.05
Pakistan	0.448	0.256	0.069	0.032	0.38	0.07
India	0.000	0.243	0.071	0.017	0.10	0.00
Imports						
World total	**6.312**	**5.791**	**5.773**	**6.635**	**6.31**	**5.70**
East Asia	2.484	2.245	2.225	2.147	2.22	2.15
EU & Turkey	1.112	1.189	1.234	1.281	1.17	1.28
Former COMECON	1.552	1.155	0.853	0.929	0.93	0.93
China (mainland)	0.362	0.053	0.176	0.884	0.60	0.20
South America	0.225	0.503	0.536	0.473	0.63	0.51
Trade imbalance[2]	**0.215**	**0.272**	**–0.134**	**0.353**	**0.00**	**–0.00**
Stocks adjustment[3]	**0.100**	**–0.115**	**0.069**	**–0.035**	**–0.00**	**–0.00**
Ending stocks						
World total	**9.260**	**8.669**	**7.034**	**7.563**	**8.01**	**8.54**
China (mainland)	3.204	2.964	2.126	2.971	3.39	3.14
USA	0.807	1.015	0.769	0.577	0.67	0.83
Net exporters	4.042	3.974	3.342	3.052	3.05	3.66
Net importers[1]	5.217	4.695	3.691	4.511	4.95	4.87
Ending stocks/use[4]	**0.44**	**0.40**	**0.35**	**0.38**	**0.36**	**0.38**
Cotlook A index[5]	**63.05**	**57.70**	**70.60**	**94.30**	**87***	**76***

1 Includes Brazil, China (mainland), Colombia, Mexico, Turkey and traditional importers except Greece.
2 The inclusion of linters and waste, changes in weight during transit, differences in reporting periods and measurement error account for differences between world imports and exports.
3 Difference between calculated stocks and actual; amounts for forward seasons are anticipated.
4 World-less-China (mainland) ending stocks minus China net exports, quantity divided by world-less-China consumption.
5 US cents per pound. Model results for 1995/96 and 1996/97 are based on net China (mainland) trade, ratios of world-less-China (mainland) ending stocks to use, barter sales from Central Asia, and futures prices. The estimate for 1994/95 is adjusted for quotes during June and July.
* 95 per cent confidence intervals extend 9 cents per pound above and below each point estimate.

Source: International Cotton Advisory Committee

Figure 1 Cotton: world production

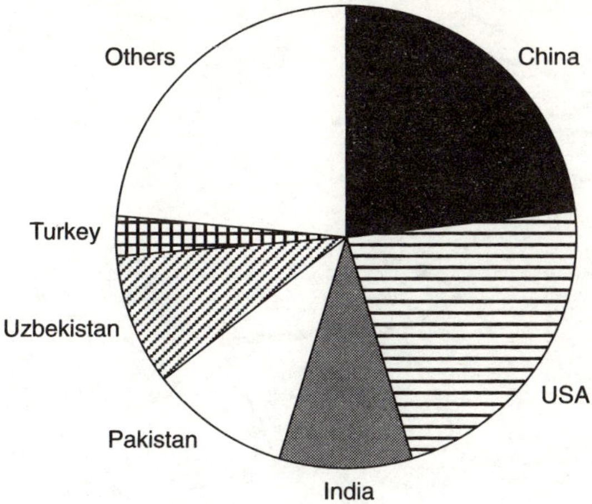

Figure 2 Cotton: world exports

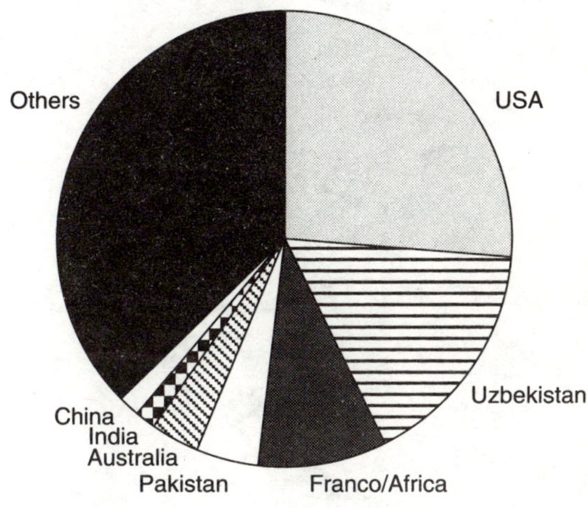

Figure 3 Cotlook A and B indices (monthly average, CIF N. Europe)

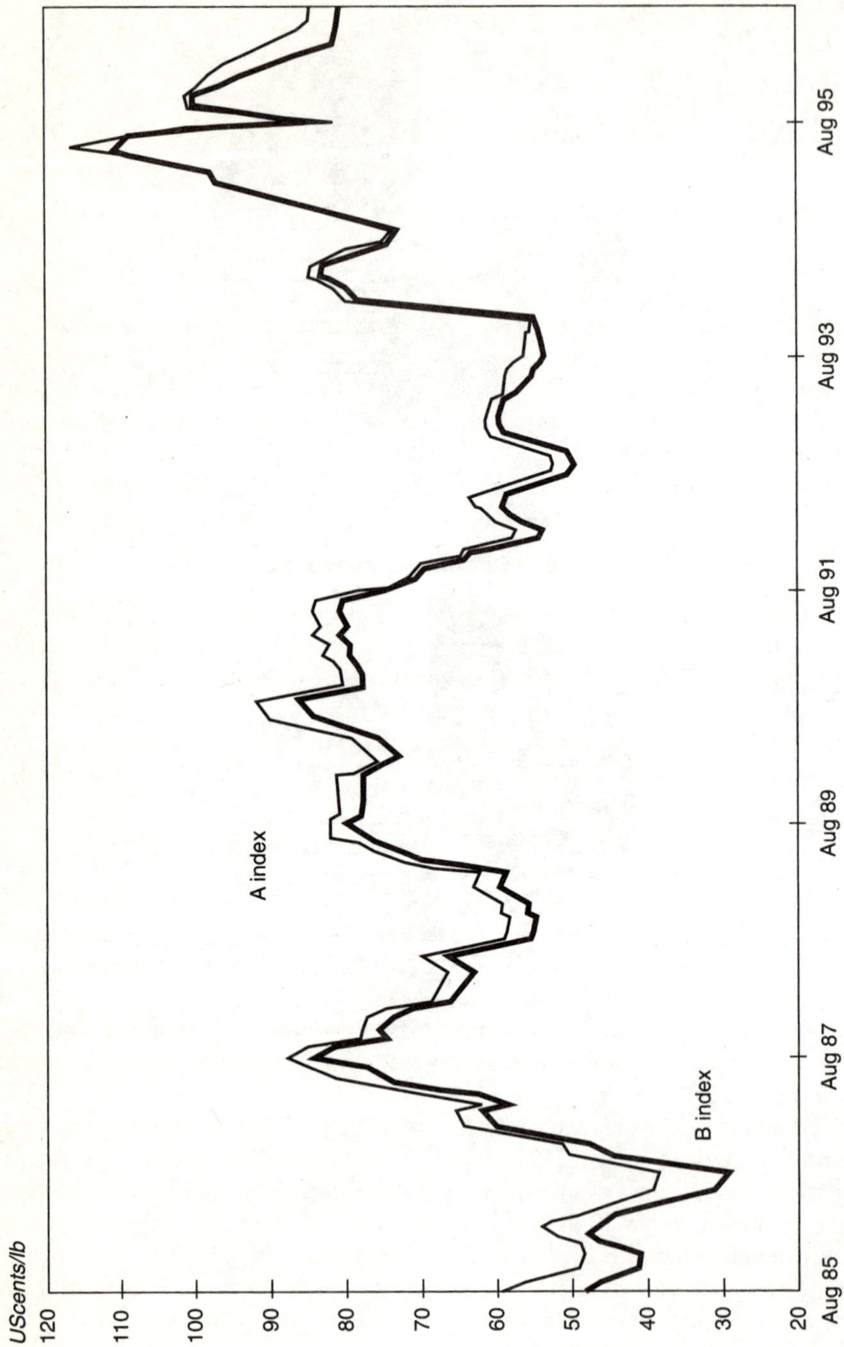

Source: Cotton Outlook

Grains

A. W. De Maria
International Grains Council

Cereals constitute mankind's major food source. They are consumed in processed forms of varying complexity, such as tortillas, couscous or bread, and also serve as an important feed for livestock. With regard to production, some dozen countries account for around 80 per cent of world output of wheat and coarse grains (see *Tables 1 and 2*).

Supplies of wheat entering the international market originate mainly in five major exporters: Argentina, Australia, Canada, EU and the USA (see *Table 1*). However, as many as a dozen other countries have emerged as regular small exporters.

The USA ranks first as a source of coarse grains because of its huge output of maize (corn). Russia, Canada and the EU are the main producers of barley. Output of rice is concentrated in Asia, especially China and India. Only small amounts enter world trade since most is consumed domestically. Thailand and the USA are the main exporters (see *Table 3*). Maize and sorghum account for the greater proportion of total output of cereals in Africa, but wheat predominates in the north of the continent.

While wheat is primarily a food grain, large quantities are used as animal feed in economically advanced countries. Feed use is also rising in newly industrialized countries with expanding livestock industries, such as the Republic of Korea. Coarse grains serve a variety of purposes. Most are traded as animal feed, although they are imported as staple foods in some developing countries. Other uses include brewing, starch extraction and ethanol production. For reasons of price, and because of lower tariffs and levies, imports of coarse grains into the EU may compete with non-cereal feed ingredients such as manioc, corn gluten feed and citrus pulp.

World grain prices are determined largely by the movement of futures on commodity markets in the USA. Options trading is also gaining popularity. Quotations at Chicago, Kansas City and Minneapolis are based on different classes of wheat (Soft Red Winter, Hard Red Winter and Dark Northern Spring), while maize is traded at Chicago. Prices may be set for forward delivery by quoting a price in relation to a particular contract month. Sales may be covered by hedging on other markets or for other delivery months.

The US markets are open to all who wish to participate. Countries competing with the USA also trade in futures, even though they operate different systems in their own markets. In Australia and Canada, for example, wheat exports remain the responsibility of wheat boards, but both may deal with approved private traders who then act as sellers. Despite recent reforms of the Common Agricultural Policy (CAP) the EU exporting system is still based on export refunds or taxes, designed to match internal prices with world market levels. Changes in market conditions for a particular grain can influence prices for others. These inter-relationships are especially evident when grains are readily substitutable. A good example is the competition between wheat and maize for use in livestock rations.

The international grain market is subject to a whole range of political, financial and economic influences. At times these can function in direct opposition to the underlying trends of supply and demand, known as 'fundamental factors'. Such speculative intervention is especially prominent when grain prices are locked into a rising trend. At such times computer driven chart and technical trading may be countered by the safeguards of daily limit price movements specified by the relevant exchange.

World grain supply and demand have witnessed many changes over the past decade. Generous support policies and increasing productivity drove carryover stocks of grain to record levels in the mid-1980s. The so-called 'grain mountains' depressed international market prices, and led major exporters to implement inventive forms of export subsidies. The USA introduced the Export Enhancement Program. Grain, but excluding maize (corn), from government stocks was used to subsidise exports to targeted markets. As stocks declined, cash payments were made. The EU responded via export refunds; other exporters with smaller exchequers competed through lower prices. The international grain market was characterized by quoted prices which were mostly much higher than those actually traded.

The Uruguay Round of trade negotiations held under the General Agreement on Tariffs and Trade (GATT) succeeded, for the first time, in subjecting agriculture to international disciplines already applying to other sectors. Limits were placed on some forms of official support measures, and a schedule was agreed for the reduction of export subsidies. However, when the latter was due for implementation in July 1995, the international market had changed direction. The efforts of governments to reduce carryover stocks and curb excess production, especially in the EU and the USA, sharply reduced total supplies. In addition, unfavourable weather curtailed production in most parts of the world. By mid-1996, stocks of grain were the lowest for 20 years, and prices set new records.

These events served to emphasise the close and often contradictory interaction of government policies and changing weather patterns. But with both grain exporting and importing countries gradually reducing government participation in grain markets, it was hoped that rising prices would encourage producers to expand output.

The tightening balance between grain supply and demand is usually offset by a reduction in feed use. At times of excessive shortage or high prices, extensive liquidation of breeding herds may occur. The most noteworthy example was seen in the former Soviet Union, where livestock slaughter resulted in that region changing status from a predominant to a minor importer of grain.

With the decline of former Soviet Union requirements, demand is fuelled mainly by rising population in the developing world, especially in Far East Asia. The overriding factor influencing world grain trade is the likely level of China's imports. While great progress has been made in expanding domestic production, rapid industrialization could limit the availability of arable land and divert labour to manufacturing activity. Many grain exporting countries therefore look to substantial growth in China's import demand.

Concern is frequently expressed over the world's ability to meet the inexorable rise in demand for grain. There is evidence that average yields could be peaking, and could progress further only at the cost of severe environmental degradation. However, it must be recognized that, thanks mostly to the activities of 'green' activists, there is now enhanced awareness of such limitation throughout the agricultural industry. On balance it would appear that the implementation of suitable technology should be able to meet rising demand for grain. Some parts of the world, such as Eastern Europe, Argentina and the former Soviet Union could greatly increase production, even using existing levels of technology.

It should be recognized that the major increase in grain demand will come from developing countries. Some are successfully meeting higher consumption by expanding both domestic production and imports. However many, especially in Africa, are likely to depend to a large extent on food aid shipments. Financial and logistical constraints will remain their major problems for several years. Commercial purchases of grain will rise as developing countries improve their export income.

The switch from traditional foods to grains, especially wheat, is seldom reversed and can therefore result in transfers of finance from other sectors of the economy.

The fluctuating trend of grain supply and demand over recent years highlights the need for the regular availability of relevant information. The grain trade is less than ideal as a source, since the greater proportion of international activity is conducted by a limited number of private companies. For reasons of commercial advantage, in a highly competitive industry, they publish little information of current value.

The 'information gap' is to some extent bridged by specialized national, intergovernmental, and trade bodies. The US Department of Agriculture (USDA) gives regular reports on most aspects of grain production and trade. The International Grains Council (IGC) specializes in assessing the short-term market outlook and developments in food aid. The Food and Agriculture Organisation (FAO) and the Organisation of Economic Co-operation and Development (OECD) provide long-term forecasts.

Further information

International Grains Council
1 Canada Square
Canary Wharf
London E14 5AE
UK
Tel: +44 171 513 1122
Fax: +44 171 513 0631

Food and Agriculture Organisation
of the United Nations
Viale delle Terme di Caracalla
00100 Rome
Italy
Tel: +39 6 522 51
Fax: +39 6 522 53152

London Rice Brokers' Association
4 St George's Yard
Farnham
Surrey GU9 7LW
UK
Tel: +44 1252 741 400
Fax: +44 1252 727 677

Organisation of Economic Co-operation
and Development
2 rue André-Pascal
75775 Paris Cedex 16
France
Tel: +33 1 45 24 82 00
Fax: +33 1 45 24 85 00

Table 1 Wheat: world production, imports and exports (million tonnes)

	1992/3	*1993/4*	*1994/5*	*1995/6*
		PRODUCTION		
China	101	106	101	103
EU	85	81	86	87
India	56	57	59	64
USA	67	65	63	60
Russia	46	44	32	30
Canada	30	27	23	25
Pakistan	16	16	15	17
Australia	16	17	9	17
Turkey	17	17	15	16
Ukraine	20	21	14	16
Argentina	10	9	11	9
Iran	10	11	11	11
Poland	7	8	8	9
Kazakstan	18	12	9	7
World	**562**	**557**	**524**	**537**
		IMPORTS		
China	6.7	4.5	10.3	12.7
Japan	5.9	6.0	5.9	6.1
Brazil	5.8	5.8	6.5	6.2
Egypt	6.2	5.9	6.3	6.3
FSU	19.3	6.3	4.6	4.4
Algeria	4.0	4.9	5.2	3.5
Indonesia	2.6	2.9	3.2	3.7
Iran	3.0	3.5	3.3	3.5
Morocco	2.9	2.4	1.2	2.8
S Korea	4.0	5.9	4.1	2.7
Philippines	2.0	2.2	2.2	2.3
Pakistan	2.6	2.1	2.2	2.0
World	**105.4**	**92.6**	**95.1**	**94.5**
		EXPORTS		
USA	37.1	32.9	32.4	35.0
Canada	21.6	18.2	21.3	18.6
EU	22.7	19.1	17.1	12.8
Australia	9.5	12.8	7.9	12.1
Argentina	7.3	4.5	7.9	4.5
Hungary	0.5	0.1	1.0	2.0
Turkey	2.0	1.2	1.7	0.9
World	**105.4**	**92.6**	**95.1**	**94.5**

Source: IWC

Figure 1 Wheat: leading producers 1995–96

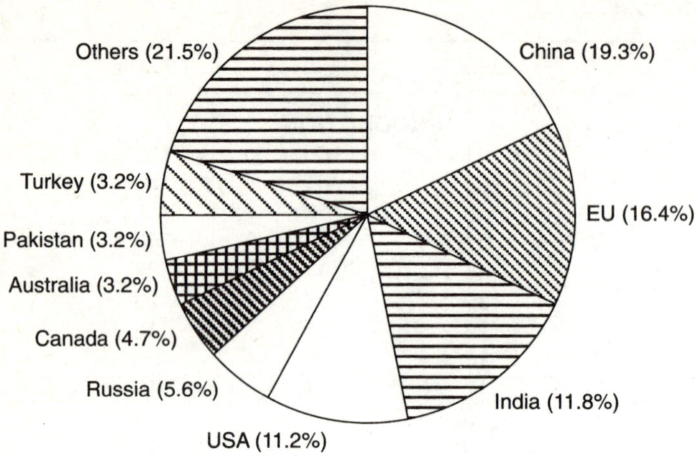

Figure 2 Wheat: regional consumption

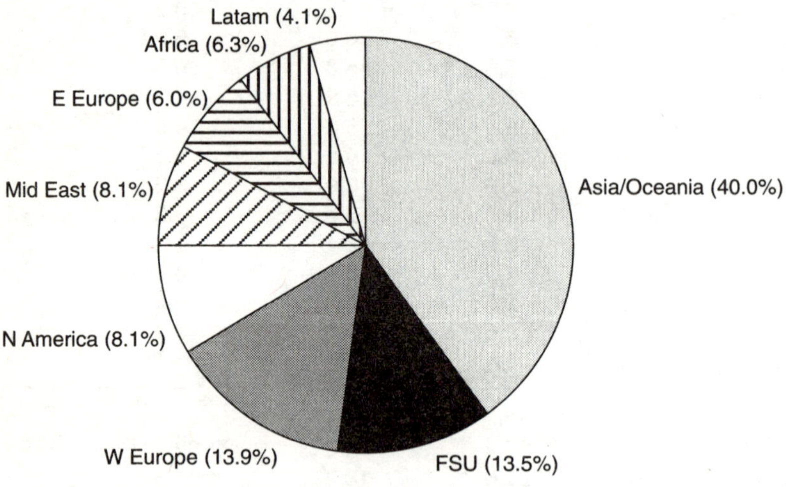

Figure 3 Chicago wheat futures prices 1993–96

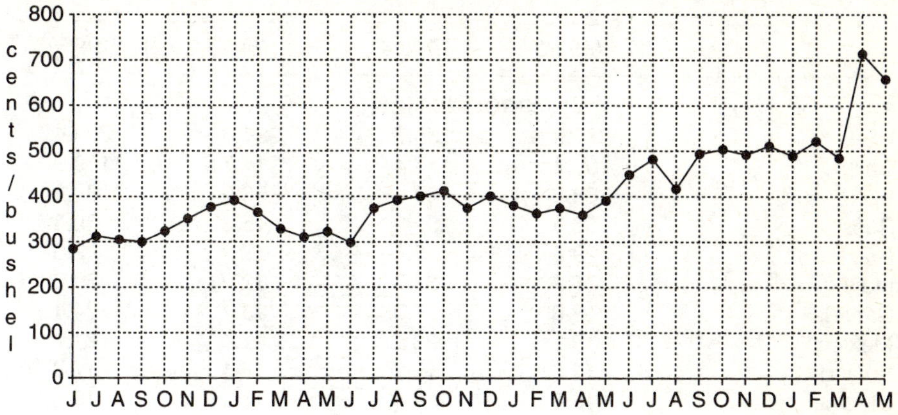

Figure 4 Wheat: world's main importers

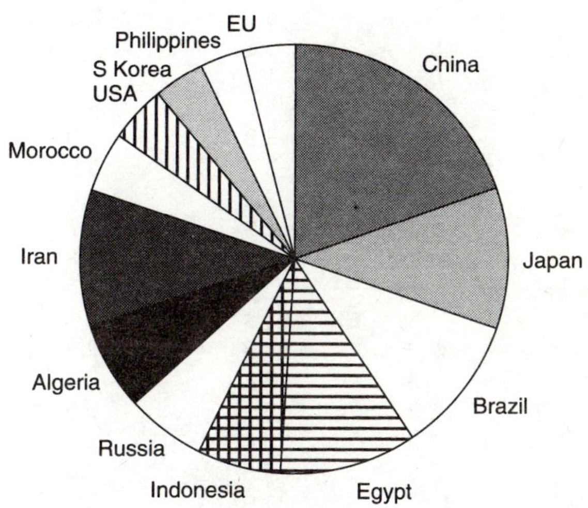

Table 2 Coarse grains: world production, imports and exports (million tonnes)

	1992/3	*1993/4*	*1994/5*	*1995/6*
		PRODUCTION		
USA	277.9	186.7	284.8	209.4
China	109.4	117.4	114.7	119.3
EU	83.6	84.8	88.0	89.2
Russia	56.9	52.9	45.2	38.3
Brazil	29.6	32.8	37.2	29.6
India	37.2	33.7	32.8	29.6
Canada	19.6	24.0	23.4	24.1
Mexico	19.9	23.2	21.4	21.7
Poland	12.6	15.2	14.1	17.3
Ukraine	15.8	19.8	16.2	15.8
Argentina	15.0	13.7	13.4	13.3
S Africa	10.5	13.6	5.3	10.2
World	**866.1**	**799.0**	**868.3**	**796.7**
		IMPORTS		
Japan	21.6	21.3	20.4	20.0
S Korea	5.7	5.0	8.8	9.9
Taiwan	5.8	6.0	6.1	6.0
China	0.6	1.1	4.3	5.1
Saudi Arabia	5.3	5.3	5.2	4.8
Mexico	5.0	3.9	5.9	6.8
EU	2.4	2.9	3.8	4.8
Egypt	1.7	2.2	3.0	2.7
Algeria	1.3	1.9	1.7	0.9
World	**88.7**	**81.4**	**91.3**	**93.7**
		EXPORTS		
USA	53.2	39.6	57.4	64.6
EU	9.3	8.4	8.1	5.5
Argentina	6.3	5.2	5.9	6.0
Canada	3.3	5.6	5.7	4.2
Australia	3.0	4.6	2.3	3.8
China	10.7	11.6	3.9	0.6
S Africa	–	1.7	3.4	0.5
World	**88.7**	**81.4**	**91.3**	**93.7**

Source: IGC

Figure 5 World coarse grain consumption

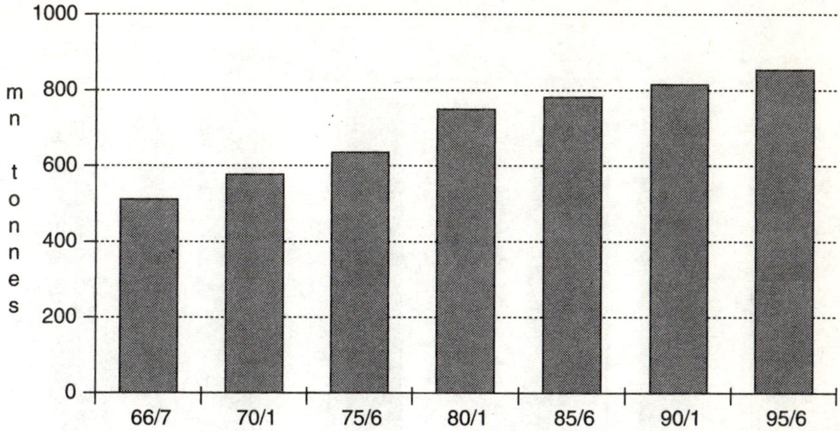

Figure 6 Maize: world exports heavily dependent on USA

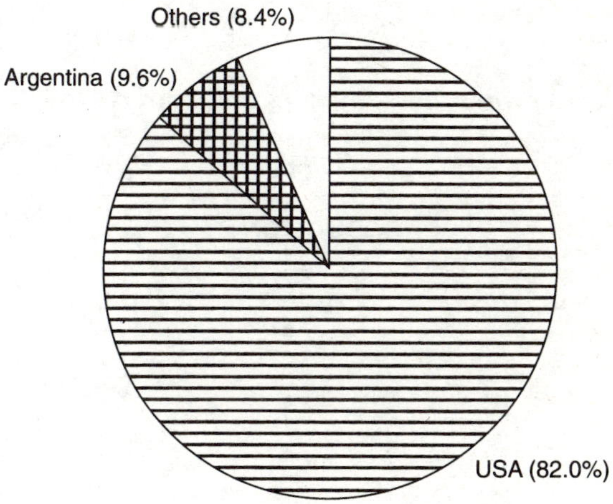

Figure 7 Corn: world balance

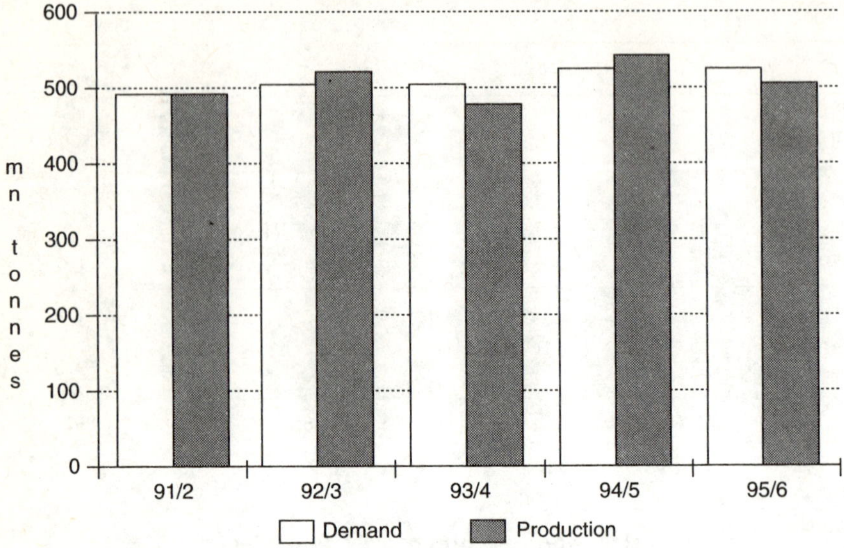

Table 3 Rice: world production, imports and exports (million tonnes)

	1992/3	*1993/4*	*1994/5*	*1995/6*
		PRODUCTION		
China	186	178	176	190
India	109	121	122	119
Indonesia	48	47	49	50
Bangladesh	28	27	25	27
Vietnam	22	24	24	25
Thailand	20	19	21	22
Burma	13	15	16	17
Japan	13	8	15	13
Philippines	10	10	11	11
Brazil	10	11	11	10
S Korea	7	6	7	6
Pakistan	5	6	5	6
World	**521**	**524**	**536**	**548**
		EXPORTS		
Thailand	4.8	4.7	5.9	5.5
USA	2.6	2.8	3.1	2.9
India	0.6	0.6	4.2	2.5
Vietnam	1.8	2.2	2.0	2.0

Table 3 Rice: world production, imports and exports (million tonnes) contd.

	1992/3	*1993/4*	*1994/5*	*1995/6*
Pakistan	0.0	1.4	1.5	1.4
Burma	0.2	0.6	0.7	0.7
Australia	0.5	0.6	0.6	0.6
Argentina	0.3	0.2	0.4	0.4
Uruguay	0.5	0.4	0.5	0.5
World	**14.9**	**16.3**	**20.4**	**17.8**
		IMPORTS		
Brazil	0.7	1.0	0.9	1.3
Indonesia	–	1.0	3.0	1.5
Philippines	0.2	–	0.3	1.0
Bangladesh	–	0.2	1.5	0.8
China	0.1	0.7	1.7	0.8
Iran	1.2	0.7	1.7	0.8
Saudi Arabia	0.9	0.8	0.6	0.8
World	**14.9**	**16.3**	**20.4**	**17.8**

Source: USDA

Figure 8 Rice: leading producers

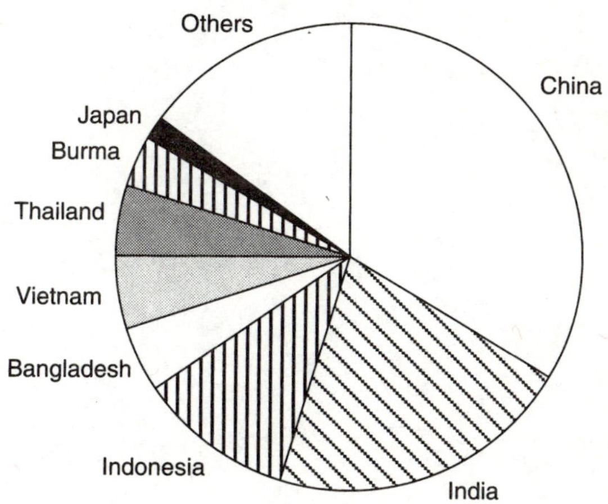

Figure 9 Rice: regional imports

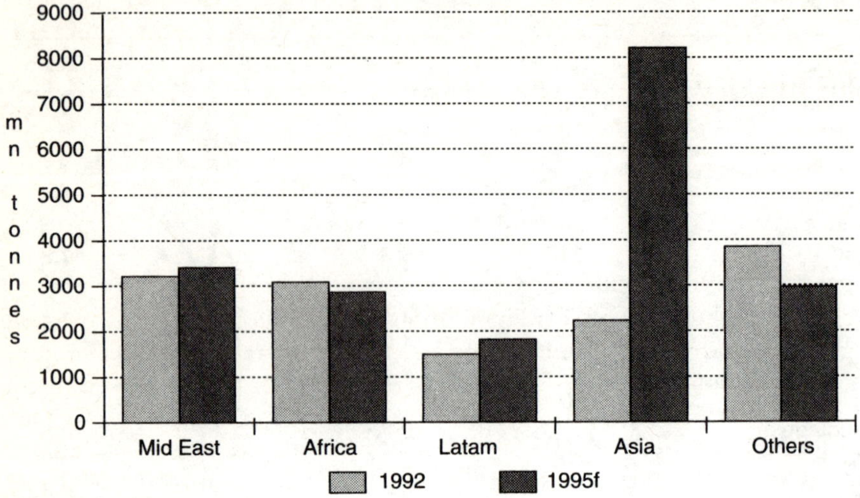

Meat

John Buckley

A relatively high degree of volatility in meat pricing reflects the many overlapping risks and variables between farmgate and supermarket shelf. Meat output is not only seasonal, in terms of when livestock breed or can best be pastured, but also subject to longer-term cyclical trends. These can range from over ten years for beef cattle to four years for hogs and are influenced not only by animal maturity cycles but producer tendencies to sell herds into market troughs or reduce slaughter into price peaks – practices which can exaggerate fluctuations in supply and lead to windows of considerable speculative opportunity.

Profitability of meat production also depends on variables like the price of grain, soyabean meal and other feedstuffs, the effect of weather on the length of the grazing season or upon the mortality of out-wintered stock.

On the consumption side, though custom for certain types of meat is often loyal in the richer developed countries, there is still a high degree of elasticity of demand and substitution of one meat for another, when price differentials between them vary beyond considered norms. Beef for example, is reckoned in Western Europe to carry an approximate 100 per cent premium to pork and if it goes too far above that the threat of substitution emerges. The level of disposable income is another important factor and can turn consumers from meat to other protein sources. This was graphically demonstrated in the FSU and other Eastern bloc countries in the aftermath of the soviet breakup when consumer spending power slumped. As demand for meat fell and producers were unable to support the higher costs of feedstuffs, massive livestock herd reduction has taken place in every year since the 1990s began. Conversely, as consumer spending power has risen with double-digit economic growth figures, so demand for meat has rocketed throughout Far East Asia and the Pacific Rim. Consumption can also be affected by seasonal factors that reduce or expand supply, for example spring lambing.

Currency market movements and interest rates also have considerable impact on meat markets, especially when these are export linked. Markets are also affected by government intervention, financial support for production or trade – like the EU's beef intervention system which built up a vast mountain of frozen beef and spent several years selling it off with subsidies into an increasingly depressed world market. Profit margins in the industry also vary between links of the supply chain, between carcass value, meat packers and retail outlets and the ratio between these can affect the farmers' decision as to whether to keep cattle on feed or sell into a decline.

This complex mesh of supply and demand variables explains why futures markets have sprung up within major meat production and trading centres including the USA, Brazil, Australia and Europe. The price volatility also attracts considerable speculator interest, especially in the USA.

Compared with the 1970s and 1980s, the US futures markets tend to trade rather lower volumes as much of the speculative business has moved into financial futures where risks and rewards are much larger. The most heavily traded of these is the CME live cattle futures contract.

The US cattle industry has a 'feedlot' system, cattle fattening by intensive rearing over a relatively short term for high profits and a valuable aid to standardization and centralization of marketing. Ultimately dependent on a peak, but sometimes uncertain revenue, the feedlot system embodies considerable unhedged risk, for example, between the perceived value of the finished feeder steer and the cost of the grain and other feedstuffs used to put weight on. CME's feeder cattle futures are designed to hedge that risk and are often used against the CME standard live cattle contract to gauge the moving profit farmers can expect from the feedlot operation.

Most exchanges favour on the hoof or live contracts for cattle with several contracts failing in the past based on meat (New York frozen beef, Sydney export beef, etc.) Other exchanges trading cattle include the Sydney Futures Exchange, and the São Paulo Bolsa de Mercadorias.

CME also trades its famous 'pork belly' contract which became synonymous with quick profits (and losses) in the American post-war commodity trade – especially its Hollywood image. It also trades live hogs. Brazil's Bolsa meanwhile has contracts in both live and feeder cattle and in frozen chickens. Amsterdam's Futures Exchange meanwhile offers a futures contract in 'porkers' or live pigs for the European trade.

Cattle herds in the main producing and trading countries have shown diverse trends so far this decade. In Europe numbers of fat cattle ready for market have fallen steeply from their 1992 peak of around 33.9m head to a low of 29.9m in 1994 before recovering partially to just under 30m over last year. The main declines have occurred in Germany, with rationalization of the inefficient East German livestock industry following reunification. On the world market, this has been offset by a rising trend in US beef output with slaughterings up from around 34m head in 1991 to over 37m last year and forecast well in excess of 38m this year. Australian herds dipped a little with a severe drought in 1994–5 but have recovered somewhat since. The other major change has been in FSU livestock numbers which have fallen steeply with restructuring and financial problems following the soviet breakup.

With world population and rising and consumer spending power increasing, demand for meat is rising throughout the world. In the past the EU increased its share of beef trade with subsidies but over the next decade the most successful countries are likely to be those with lowest production costs and those willing to adopt the technology to provide processed and convenience foods demanded by many growing markets. The USA in particular is expected to gain market share at the expense of the EU, whose industry has relatively high costs as well as increasing restraints from animal welfare and environmental lobbies and frequent problems with currency fluctuations between member states. Although EU beef output showed a partial recovery in 1995 after a steep decline in 1993 and 1994, Uruguay Round constraints and decline in consumption in some member states are expected to force output gradually down to the year 2000, according to some experts.

The USA is expected to be one of the main beneficiaries in terms of meat exports from world trade liberalization under the Uruguay Round and structural changes in its industry. A high degree of vertical integration has taken place over recent years and technology introduced to supply a wide range of consumer products to specific markets. Sales prospects are especially promising to Japan and other Asian customers where robust economic growth is occurring to a backdrop of small-scale local production with limited scope to grow fast with consumption. Although it is also a major importer, the USA is expected to become a net pigmeat exporter by the end of this year with sales to Japan already up 40 per cent in volume and 70 per cent in value compared with the mid-1980s. While the EU and Canada export mainly frozen pigmeat, the USA expects to supply 50 per cent of Japan's fresh meat market by the year 2000. Russia is also emerging as low value pigmeat product buyer.

Poultry consumption is also rising globally with economic expansion in the developing world. The tremendous scope is illustrated by the low per capita off-take rates in Asia and Africa – only around 5kg per annum, compared with 43kg in the USA and 19kg averages in the EU and elsewhere in West Europe. With world population expected to rise by 1bn in the current decade, the increase in Asian and other growing countries' incomes spells a sustained and steep rise in demand. Some reports expect world poultry consumption to grow at 4–5 per cent annually or by 2 to 3m tonnes. International trade will supply much of this and has already risen from 2.4m tonnes in 1990 to almost 4m in 1994 with an estimated 6 per cent annual growth rate for the past decade. Most analysts expect this pace to continue for at least the next five years approaching 5.4m by 2000.

US poultry exports are already benefiting from the boom – to China, other Far East countries and Russia, where a huge trade has erupted in chicken legs and wings. Total US poultry exports this year are expected to account for 14 per cent of US production compared with only 3 per cent ten years ago. Because of high production costs, the EU and Japan are less likely to grow into these emerging import markets although China and Brazil are both expected eventually to compete more heavily with the USA as important poultry suppliers to the world market.

Further information

Food and Agriculture Organisation of the United Nations
Viale delle Terme di Caracalla
00100 Rome
Italy
Tel: +39 6 522 51
Fax: +39 6 522 53152

Meat and Livestock Commission
PO Box 44
Winterhill House
Snowdon Drive
Milton Keynesw MK6 1AX
UK
Tel: +44 1908 677577
Fax: +44 1908 609221

Table 1 World beef* production

('000 tonnes)	*1993*	*1994*	*1995*
USA	10,580	11,200	11,380
Brazil	4600	4500	4620
China	2341	3275	4255
Russia	3359	3071	3071
Argentina	2508	2590	2590
India	2458	2496	2496
France	1909	1821	1810
Australia	1826	1825	1780
Germany	1681	1470	1470
Ukraine	1379	1421	1421
Mexico	1256	1365	1234
Italy	1188	1171	1171
Pakistan	768	807	847
Kazakstan	630	615	615
Colombia	573	609	609
Japan	593	602	600
Regional			
N./Central America	13,273	14,058	14,160
Asia	8701	9774	10,816
Europe	10,260	9805	9847
S. America	9200	9294	9503
Africa	3615	3391	3561
Oceania	2402	2416	2370
World	54,116	55,114	56,563

*Some countries include buffalo meat production
Source: FAO

Table 2 World pigmeat production

('000 tonnes)	*1993*	*1994*	*1995*
China	29,710	33,235	38,035
USA	7751	8027	8199
Germany	3747	3606	3606
Russia	2432	2260	2260
France	2017	2116	2156
Spain	2089	2108	2084
Poland	1903	1609	1770
Netherlands	1747	1677	1755
Denmark	1504	1521	1540
Brazil	1250	1300	1400
Italy	1371	1369	1369
Japan	1433	1390	1360
Canada	1195	1234	1265
UK	998	1035	1016
Belgo/Lux	1001	996	997
Vietnam	878	918	957
Ukraine	1013	910	910
S. Korea	796	854	854
Mexico	822	873	880
Philippines	690	720	745
Rumania	836	738	738
Indonesia	621	649	671
Hungary	710	600	580
Austria	538	534	534
Czech Rep.	615	533	530
Regional			
Asia	35,749	39,424	44,291
Europe	21,641	20,911	21,102
N./Central America	10,028	10,395	10,613
S. America	2267	2372	2502
Africa	742	750	763
Oceania	423	439	444
World	75,300	78,483	83,881

Source: FAO

Table 3 World poultry meat production

('000 tonnes)	*1993*	*1994*	*1995*
USA	2063	2122	2223
China	2097	2309	2568
Brazil	973	996	1042
India	489	496	496
France	491	487	493
Argentina	410	420	420
Austria	397	398	395
Germany	358	337	337
Mexico	305	322	318
Pakistan	244	260	276
Japan	282	276	272
Italy	222	220	220
New Zealand	184	185	185
S. Africa	184	152	166
UK	151	159	159
Spain	159	157	157
Vietnam	154	153	153
Regional			
Asia	4357	4609	4889
N./Central America	2592	2679	2779
Europe	2512	2444	2445
S. America	1867	1916	1975
Africa	1051	1061	1102
Oceania	588	590	587
World	12,967	13,300	13,777

Source: FAO

Figure 1 Production trends in some leading cattle supplying countries

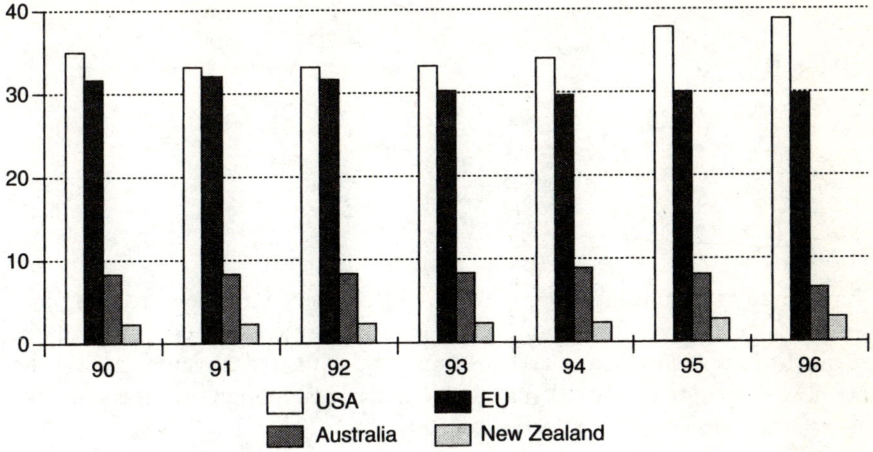

Oil

Sally Clubley
Oil Analyst

Oil trading has been transformed in the past ten years with the introduction of a wide range of over-the-counter derivative instruments to complement the existing futures and options markets. Many producing and consuming countries have now entered the price risk management markets, though the Opec member countries remain generally reluctant to participate.

Non-Opec production has continued to increase and Opec has found it increasingly difficult to maintain prices at a level it feels to be adequate. Prices have spent most of the last five years or so in a narrow range, with the exception of the period following the Iraqi invasion of Kuwait and the consequent Gulf War. Until early 1996, when low stocks and a prolonged cold winter in Europe and the USA took prices higher, the price of the international benchmark West Texas Intermediate crude had remained below $21 for more than three years. At the lower end of the market, prices had a few dips below the $16.00 level, but most of the time support was found in this area.

In 1994, Opec accounted for 40.9 per cent of total world oil production, a higher proportion than in some recent years but not as great as had been expected a few years earlier. Non-Opec producers tend to keep output at the maximum sustainable level, while Opec tries to keep output down to prevent a slide in prices. They have achieved a modicum of success, with discipline a lot better than it was in the late 1980s, but this has been helped by the absence of Iraq from the market for the past five years. When that country returns the cartel will find it difficult to re-allocate quotas.

Consumption has grown little in the major markets of the USA and Europe, but South East Asia has grown sufficiently to generate an overall increase in world consumption of 1.7 per cent in 1994. The countries of South and South East Asia now account for almost 11 per cent of world consumption, compared with 5.8 per cent ten years ago. This trend is likely to continue and is the reason behind the steady growth in the Singapore spot market which has become increasingly active in recent years and is now in the same league as the other major markets such as North West Europe (sometimes called the Rotterdam market) and the US Gulf and East coasts.

Economic growth in North America and Western Europe has boosted total energy consumption, but the share taken by non-oil sources has increased. Natural gas has seen particularly strong growth, taking 26 per cent of the US market in 1994 and increasing its share slightly year by year. A similar pattern is seen in Western Europe.

The opening up of the former Soviet Union is already having an effect on the oil market and as investment increases and markets open up the changes are likely to be more dramatic. The Russian Federation has seen output decline sharply to less than 6.5 million barrels/day (mbd) in 1994 compared with more than 11 million at the end of the 1980s. Legal problems are delaying much of the expected Western investment and preventing the necessary technological improvement, but in time the country could become a significant force in the market. It continues to supply its former satellites, but they are increasingly looking outside for alternative sources.

Deregulation of oil markets is occurring all over the world, with Japan the latest major consuming nation to open up. This is bringing new players to all parts of the market, from the spot physical markets through exchange-traded futures and options to the more complex derivatives. Many new entrants are going straight into derivatives, making swap agreements with the investment banks and others to put ceiling and floor prices in place. Most then begin to look at other hedging instruments.

All these instruments are beginning to spread into the other energy markets, particularly natural gas and electricity. The New York Mercantile Exchange (NYMEX) already has contracts in natural gas and electricity and is actively considering a coal contract. The International Petroleum Exchange (IPE) is planning a natural gas contract and there is an electricity futures market in Norway. Growth in these areas is restricted because they are strictly regulated in many countries and are not international markets. There are also practical problems with storage and transport which can make free markets difficult to operate.

NYMEX is the largest futures market operating in the energy field, with the contracts mentioned above adding to the crude oil, heating oil, gasoline and propane contracts (as well as various non-energy instruments). Its light sweet crude oil contract, based on West Texas Intermediate, is the busiest energy futures contract in the world, trading an average of 100,000 contracts per day, or 100 million barrels. This is equivalent to around 150 per cent of total world oil consumption. The IPE's Brent contract contributes a further 45 million barrels to total crude oil trading. The IPE also has an active gas oil contract.

Looking to the future, the main imponderable in the oil market is the return of Iraqi crude. This has been a cloud hanging over the market for the last five years and each month that passes must bring it closer. In 1989, its last full year of production, Iraq produced 2.8 mbd. An increase of this magnitude in supply will have a devastating effect on prices, at least in the short term, and could have long-term effects unless consumption rises sharply or Opec is able to bring Iraq back within its ceiling. The threat of Iraqi crude returning has been a major factor in the heavy backwardation in the oil market which has made it difficult for producers particularly to hedge forward output.

Short-term price spikes caused by unusual demand are likely to continue, but there seems little reason to believe oil prices will rise significantly over the next few years. Planned new fields and existing spare capacity should more than compensate for any increase in demand. A further period within the recent $16–$21 range for WTI seems likely.

Further information

BP International Ltd
Britannic House
1 Finsbury Circus
London EC2M 7BA
UK
Tel: +44 171 496 4000
Fax: +44 171 496 4630

Table 1 Oil production* (thousand barrels daily)

	1985	1986	1987	1988	1989	1990	1991	1992	1993	1994	1995	Change 1995 over 1994	1995 share of total
USA	10580	10230	9945	9765	9160	8915	9075	8870	8585	8390	**8290**	–1.4%	11.8%
Canada	1810	1805	1905	2000	1960	1965	1980	2060	2185	2275	**2390**	+4.6%	3.4%
Mexico	2910	2760	2880	2875	2895	2975	3125	3120	3130	3140	**3065**	–2.5%	4.7%
Total North America	15300	14795	14730	14640	14015	13855	14180	14050	13900	13805	**13745**	–0.7%	19.8%
Argentina	490	465	460	480	490	515	525	585	625	700	**750**	+7.0%	1.2%
Brazil	560	590	590	575	615	650	645	650	665	690	**715**	+3.3%	1.1%
Colombia	185	305	390	380	405	445	430	440	455	460	**590**	+28.7%	0.9%
Ecuador	285	300	175	310	285	290	305	330	355	390	**395**	+1.7%	0.6%
Peru	190	180	165	140	130	130	115	115	125	125	**125**	–3.1%	0.2%
Trinidad & Tobago	175	170	155	150	150	150	150	145	135	140	**145**	+2.0%	0.2%
Venezuela	1745	1885	1910	2000	2010	2240	2490	2500	2590	2675	**2840**	+6.1%	4.5%
Other S & Cent America	90	90	85	75	75	80	80	75	85	85	**90**	+4.9%	0.1%
Total S & Cent America	3720	3985	3930	4110	4160	4500	4740	4840	5035	5265	**5650**	+7.1%	8.9%
Denmark	60	75	95	100	115	125	145	160	170	190	**190**	+0.6%	0.3%
Norway	815	905	1055	1195	1585	1740	1985	2265	2430	2765	**2995**	+8.2%	4.3%
Romania	230	220	205	200	195	165	145	140	140	140	**140**	–0.4%	0.2%
UK	2670	2665	2585	2390	1925	1915	1915	1975	2115	2680	**2755**	+2.6%	4.0%
Other Europe	600	620	630	635	610	605	585	580	550	570	**535**	–6.2%	0.8%
Total Europe	4375	4485	4570	4520	4430	4550	4775	5120	5405	6345	**6615**	+4.1%	9.6%
Azerbaijan	275	270	285	280	270	255	240	225	215	195	**185**	–4.2%	0.3%
Kazakstan	465	485	505	525	535	550	570	550	490	435	**440**	–1.0%	0.6%
Russian Federation	10900	11295	11480	11440	11190	10405	9320	8035	7155	6420	**6200**	–3.5%	9.4%
Uzbekistan	55	60	65	60	65	70	70	80	95	125	**175**	+43.6%	0.2%
Other Former Soviet Union	340	325	320	290	295	285	270	255	230	220	**230**	+4.1%	0.3%
Total Former Soviet Union	12035	12435	12655	12595	12355	11565	10470	9145	8185	7395	**7230**	–2.3%	10.9%
Iran	2220	2060	2330	2335	2870	3255	3500	3525	3700	3710	**3705**	–0.2%	5.6%
Iraq	1415	1895	2390	2775	2840	2155	280	525	465	515	**545**	+5.1%	0.8%
Kuwait	1125	1365	1070	1490	1590	1265	200	1095	1930	2095	**2105**	+0.4%	3.2%
Oman	500	565	590	625	650	695	715	750	785	820	**870**	+6.4%	1.3%
Qatar	315	355	315	360	405	435	420	495	460	450	**460**	+2.2%	0.7%
Saudi Arabia	3600	5210	4600	5720	5635	7105	8820	9100	8960	8875	**8885**	+0.1%	13.1%
Syria	160	200	230	270	340	405	470	520	570	565	**610**	+8.1%	1.0%
United Arab Emirates	1260	1595	1605	1620	2025	2285	2640	2510	2455	2485	**2485**	–0.4%	3.5%
Yemen	–	10	25	170	180	180	195	185	220	335	**335**	–0.3%	0.5%
Other Middle East	50	50	50	55	55	50	55	55	55	55	**55**	–	0.1%
Total Middle East	10645	13305	13205	15420	16590	17830	17295	18760	19600	19905	**20055**	+0.7%	29.7%
Algeria	1145	1195	1230	1250	1275	1345	1340	1310	1325	1310	**1325**	+1.4%	1.8%
Angola	230	280	355	450	460	480	500	535	505	530	**630**	+18.7%	1.0%
Cameroon	180	175	165	165	160	155	145	135	130	115	**105**	–8.6%	0.2%
Congo	120	120	125	140	160	160	160	175	190	195	**185**	–4.8%	0.3%
Egypt	890	810	915	875	885	905	900	910	945	930	**920**	–1.0%	1.4%

Table 1 Oil production* (thousand barrels daily) contd.

	1985	*1986*	*1987*	*1988*	*1989*	*1990*	*1991*	*1992*	*1993*	*1994*	*1995*	*Change 1995 over 1994*	*1995 share of total*
Gabon	175	165	155	175	205	270	295	290	305	335	**355**	+5.7%	0.6%
Libya	1060	1065	1005	1060	1165	1430	1540	1475	1400	1420	**1415**	–0.4%	2.1%
Nigeria	1500	1465	1325	1445	1715	1810	1890	1945	1910	1880	**1890**	+0.7%	2.9%
Tunisia	115	110	105	105	105	95	110	110	100	95	**90**	–3.3%	0.1%
Other Africa	60	60	55	45	35	35	35	30	40	45	**55**	+32.9%	0.1%
Total Africa	5475	5445	5435	5710	6165	6685	6915	6915	6850	6855	**6970**	+1.9%	10.3%
Australia	645	580	615	585	555	640	605	600	565	610	**575**	–6.8%	0.8%
Brunei	170	165	155	150	150	150	160	180	175	180	**175**	–2.5%	0.3%
China	2505	2620	2690	2740	2760	2775	2830	2840	2890	2930	**2990**	+2.0%	4.6%
India	625	660	645	680	730	730	700	640	620	705	**785**	+11.7%	1.1%
Indonesia	1340	1430	1420	1375	1480	1540	1670	1580	1590	1590	**1575**	–0.7%	2.3%
Malaysia	445	500	495	540	590	620	650	660	645	660	**735**	+12.1%	1.1%
Papua New Guinea	–	–	–	–	–	–	–	55	125	120	**100**	–17.4%	0.1%
Vietnam	–	–	5	15	30	55	80	110	125	135	**150**	+10.9%	0.2%
Other Asia & Australasia	160	155	150	160	170	185	190	205	205	195	**185**	–3.3%	0.3%
Total Asia & Australasia	5890	6110	6175	6245	6465	6695	6885	6870	6940	7125	**7270**	+2.2%	10.8%
TOTAL WORLD	**57440**	**60560**	**60700**	**63240**	**64180**	**65680**	**65260**	**65700**	**65915**	**66695**	**67535**	**+1.2%**	**100.0%**
of which: OECD	19955	19500	19580	19425	18695	18780	19350	19550	19655	20540	**20720**	+0.6%	29.9%
OPEC	16895	19680	19345	21605	23215	25135	25075	26340	27090	27330	**27590**	+0.9%	40.9%
Non-OPEC**	28510	28445	28695	29045	28615	28985	29705	30200	30640	31955	**32720**	+2.3%	48.2%

Notes:

* Includes crude oil, shale oil, oil sands and NGLs (natural gas liquids – the liquid content of natural gas where this is recovered separately) Excludes liquid fuels from other sources, such as coal derivatives

** Excludes Former Soviet Union

Annual changes and shares of total are on a weight basis

Source: BP Statistical Review of World Energy 1996

Table 2 Oil consumption* (thousand barrels daily)

	1985	*1986*	*1987*	*1988*	*1989*	*1990*	*1991*	*1992*	*1993*	*1994*	*1995*	*Change 1995 over 1994*	*1995 share of total*
USA•	15170	15665	16025	16630	16665	16305	16000	16260	16470	16950	**16935**	–0.4%	25.0%
Canada	1490	1540	1580	1665	1740	1690	1630	1625	1680	1720	**1750**	+1.6%	2.5%
Mexico	1240	1230	1290	1295	1390	1455	1520	1545	1555	1680	**1560**	–7.8%	2.2%
Total North America	17900	18435	18895	19590	19795	19450	19150	19430	19705	20350	**20245**	–0.8%	29.7%
Argentina	400	430	455	455	415	390	410	420	420	435	**440**	+1.2%	0.6%
Brazil	1115	1210	1240	1270	1290	1275	1290	1330	1355	1420	**1510**	+6.4%	2.2%
Chile	95	100	105	120	135	140	150	160	175	190	**210**	+10.2%	0.3%
Colombia	170	175	190	195	200	210	215	235	245	255	**265**	+6.2%	0.4%
Venezuela	370	385	390	405	385	395	405	430	430	440	**430**	–2.8%	0.6%
Other S & Cent America	995	1010	1040	1075	1140	1135	1140	1170	1200	1245	**1285**	+3.1%	1.9%
Total S & Cent America	3145	3310	3420	3520	3565	3545	3610	3745	3825	3985	**4140**	+3.9%	6.0%
Austria	200	215	220	215	215	225	240	235	235	235	**230**	–1.2%	0.3%
Belgium & Luxembourg	430	485	490	500	500	510	545	560	545	555	**535**	–4.0%	0.8%
Czech Republic	215	210	210	200	190	175	145	140	140	145	**155**	+8.7%	0.2%
Denmark	220	215	200	195	190	185	185	185	195	210	**220**	+4.4%	0.3%
Finland	220	230	230	230	230	230	220	215	205	215	**210**	–3.8%	0.3%
France	1790	1830	1845	1830	1880	1910	2020	2010	1940	1880	**1895**	+0.9%	2.8%
Germany	2670	2810	2745	2745	2595	2710	2835	2850	2905	2880	**2880**	†	4.2%
Greece	245	250	270	280	305	320	325	330	340	345	**350**	+0.7%	0.5%
Hungary	215	200	210	195	190	200	170	170	160	175	**170**	–3.6%	0.3%
Iceland	10	10	10	10	15	15	15	15	15	15	**15**	+3.4%	†
Republic of Ireland	80	100	90	80	85	90	100	105	105	115	**120**	+3.3%	0.2%
Italy	1730	1770	1850	1880	1930	1930	1920	1925	1910	1915	**1975**	+2.8%	2.9%
Netherlands	635	700	705	740	735	765	765	795	790	790	**830**	+4.4%	1.2%
Norway	200	200	215	205	200	205	195	195	210	210	**210**	+0.2%	0.3%
Poland	335	350	355	365	360	330	315	290	295	315	**330**	+4.3%	0.5%
Portugal	180	195	190	185	230	230	240	265	250	255	**270**	+7.4%	0.4%
Romania	300	320	355	335	345	375	310	260	240	225	**260**	+15.3%	0.4%
Slovakia	125	120	120	115	110	100	85	80	80	85	**90**	+7.5%	0.1%
Spain	925	925	960	990	1040	1040	1055	1115	1080	1120	**1170**	+5.0%	1.7%
Sweden	375	385	355	340	345	340	325	345	335	355	**355**	+0.4%	0.5%
Switzerland	255	280	265	265	255	275	275	280	265	270	**255**	–7.3%	0.4%
Turkey	345	375	435	465	440	470	470	500	575	555	**610**	+10.0%	0.9%
UK	1630	1645	1610	1705	1745	1760	1765	1775	1790	1785	**1750**	–2.0%	2.5%
Other Europe	545	595	600	650	630	585	475	385	395	395	**440**	+11.2%	0.7%
Total Europe	13875	14415	14535	14720	14760	14975	14995	15025	15000	15045	**15325**	+1.8%	22.4%
Azerbaijan	165	175	165	165	165	170	165	165	165	165	**170**	+4.9%	0.3%
Belarus	505	600	590	575	540	500	480	425	280	255	**245**	–4.0%	0.4%
Kazakstan	410	375	365	365	375	430	435	410	315	245	**240**	–2.2%	0.4%
Russian Federation	4910	4970	5015	4980	5075	5015	4890	4505	3790	3265	**2935**	–10.2%	4.5%
Turkmenistan	95	70	70	70	70	90	100	100	65	75	**80**	+5.1%	0.1%

Table 2 Oil consumption* (thousand barrels daily) contd.

	1985	1986	1987	1988	1989	1990	1991	1992	1993	1994	1995	Change 1995 over 1994	1995 share of total
Ukraine	1265	1270	1325	1215	1165	1265	1155	855	500	400	**380**	–4.5%	0.6%
Uzbekistan	230	235	225	275	265	255	220	185	165	145	**135**	–7.1%	0.2%
Other Former Soviet Union	780	705	685	675	655	715	540	250	190	120	**125**	+5.3%	0.2%
Total Former Soviet Union	8360	8400	8440	8320	8310	8440	7985	6895	5470	4670	**4310**	–7.7%	6.7%
Iran	895	855	890	770	865	950	995	1040	1075	1135	**1190**	+4.9%	1.8%
Saudi Arabia	985	975	1015	1035	1030	1090	1175	1095	1115	1160	**1120**	–3.5%	1.6%
United Arab Emirates	145	175	185	220	225	235	305	310	315	320	**320**	+0.7%	0.5%
Other Middle East	955	1000	1010	1050	1080	1110	990	1100	1130	1180	**1245**	+5.3%	1.9%
Total Middle East	2980	3005	3100	3075	3200	3385	3465	3545	3635	3795	**3875**	+2.2%	5.8%
Egypt	415	420	435	440	460	475	470	455	440	435	**445**	+1.3%	0.7%
South Africa	300	290	310	340	350	355	360	370	385	400	**425**	+6.3%	0.6%
Other Africa	1000	980	1030	1075	1125	1170	1170	1225	1250	1275	**1300**	+1.8%	1.9%
Total Africa	1715	1690	1775	1855	1935	2000	2000	2050	2075	2110	**2170**	+2.6%	3.2%
Australia	590	610	625	650	680	695	675	680	720	755	**780**	+3.4%	1.1%
Bangladesh	35	35	35	40	40	45	35	40	40	45	**50**	+5.7%	0.1%
China	1810	2010	2110	2210	2260	2255	2410	2660	2915	3145	**3310**	+5.3%	4.9%
India	885	935	965	1060	1155	1200	1220	1285	1300	1400	**1510**	+7.6%	2.3%
Indonesia	460	465	500	525	560	645	675	730	785	775	**810**	+4.5%	1.2%
Japan	4435	4495	4500	4805	5005	5305	5410	5540	5455	5765	**5780**	–0.4%	8.3%
Malaysia	195	195	200	210	230	270	290	295	330	370	**430**	+15.5%	0.6%
New Zealand	80	85	95	95	95	105	110	110	110	115	**120**	+3.1%	0.2%
Pakistan	155	165	180	195	210	220	230	250	270	295	**305**	+3.8%	0.5%
Philippines	150	160	185	200	225	235	225	280	290	305	**345**	+12.8%	0.5%
Singapore	225	265	270	315	360	370	380	400	425	495	**510**	+3.4%	0.8%
South Korea	535	590	620	740	855	1040	1255	1520	1675	1840	**2010**	+9.0%	2.9%
Taiwan	355	395	415	485	535	550	570	585	625	665	**725**	+9.3%	1.1%
Thailand	235	240	270	305	360	410	445	490	555	615	**690**	+11.9%	1.0%
Other Asia	305	325	325	325	330	355	355	410	435	465	**490**	+6.4%	0.7%
Total Asia & Australasia	10450	10970	11295	12160	12900	13700	14285	15275	15930	17050	**17865**	+4.6%	26.2%
TOTAL WORLD	**58425**	**60225**	**61460**	**63240**	**64465**	**65495**	**65490**	**65965**	**65640**	**67005**	**67930**	**+1.2%**	**100.0%**
of which: OECD	35145	36245	36800	38000	38510	38765	38840	39460	39690	40690	**40805**	†	59.6%
European Union 15	11330	11755	11760	11915	12025	12245	12540	12710	12625	12655	**12790**	+1.0%	18.8%
Other EMEs ◊	13190	13790	14385	15055	15820	16525	17155	18270	19175	20300	**21375**	+5.2%	31.6%

Notes:
- * Inland demand plus international aviation and marine bunkers and refinery fuel and loss
- • US processing gain – 767,000 b/d in 1995 – has been deducted
- † Less than 0.05
- ◊ Excludes Central Europe and Former Soviet Union

Source: BP Statistical Review of the Year 1996

Figure 1 Oil: leading producers

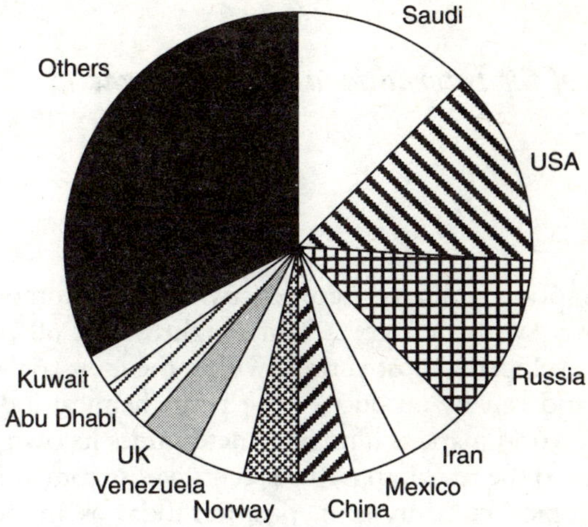

Figure 2 Oil: world consumption

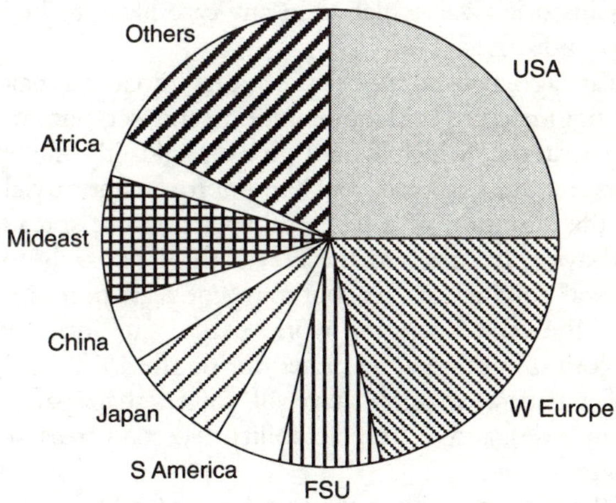

Rubber

J. M. Hobbs
The Association of the International Rubber Trade

Elastomer consumption is shared between two quite commodities, synthetic and natural rubber. Synthetic (representing slightly over 60 per cent of total usage) has been developed almost entirely within the industrial countries of the temperate zone, and is a by-product of the petrochemical industry, where its feedstock value in world markets ultimately determines its own price. This is in surprising contrast to the remaining 40 per cent, whose romantic story, from its beginnings as a tropical curiosity to its position today as an indispensable raw material, is well known. Despite still being collected by the cupful under widely varying conditions, the agricultural product has more than held its own in the modern world, and is nearing a position where demand could well outrun supply. Thus the major growing countries are being forced to examine the possibility of supplementing their production by installing facilities for the manufacture of its historic rival, which is in any case likely to be required for their own emergent industries.

More than 30 years ago, natural rubber producers initiated a major change in their methods of manufacture and presentation, and set out to develop an improved planting material, which would give significantly higher yields per acre. The change is not yet complete, but the improvement in yields has been phenomenal, and the adoption of a technical specification, spreading steadily outwards from Malaysia, has assisted the Hevea three not only to maintain a large share of the total polymer market, but in recent years to recapture a significant percentage of the ever-expanding world usage. The introduction of the radial tyre, the explosion in mineral oil prices during the 1970s and the ecological advantages of a natural material have all played their part; but natural rubber's unique properties, and its irreplaceability in certain areas, have been the deciding factors in its success.

The division of the market between the two types of rubber is tending today towards a non-tyre sector which relies increasingly upon synthetic, and a fast-growing tyre industry which dominates the consumption of natural. This division is very marked in the more industrialized parts of the world, and it seems likely that, as developing countries move towards industrialization, their consumption ratios will show a similar trend. Outside the tyre sector, natural latex continues to command the loyalty of buyers in the important dipped goods area, where Malaysia itself is the leading manufacturer. This sector has received an enormous boost from the AIDS scare which reached hysterical proportions eight years ago, and the offtake for examination gloves and condoms has remained at a high level.

During the present decade, there have been significant changes in the supply pattern of natural rubber, as Thailand and Indonesia have moved some distance ahead of Malaysia in terms of annual tonnages produced. Within the next two years, it appears probable that Thailand will be responsible for one ton in every three grown worldwide, and the possibility of Indonesia overtaking Thailand early next century is quite high. The two new leaders have adopted different courses in their production pattern, with Thailand continuing to export very large tonnages of Smoked Sheet to Japan and elsewhere, and now becoming an important producer of latex, while Indonesia has concentrated its main effort on crumb rubber, especially TSR 20 for the huge market in the USA. Elsewhere, China and India are both advancing strongly, and there are good hopes of an improvement in Vietnam. West Africa, however, has been disappointing, especially Liberia, where the political turmoil has crippled what was once the continent's largest producer.

On the consumption side perhaps the most significant feature of the past five years has been a 33 per cent growth in the usage of natural rubber in the USA since 1991, which owes much to the radialization of tyres. Other notable developments have included the steady progress in Korea, India and China; the emergence of Thailand as a significant user of both types; and the declining role of Russia, both as a consumer and as a producer of synthetic rubber, following the break-up of the USSR. Despite a temporary reversal of the long-term trend in the early nineties caused by the deep recession in Western Europe and Japan and the events in Eastern Europe, current estimates are that overall rubber consumption will continue to grow steadily over the next decade, and that natural rubber will retain its market share provided that production levels can be assured.

The varying economic fortunes of the major countries have had their effect upon the price of natural rubber in the past few years, and there have been wide fluctuations. The latex-based boom of the first half of 1988 was followed by a prolonged bear market lasting until late in 1993, during which the resources of the International Natural Rubber Organisation (INRO) had again to be utilized in an effort to assist the producing countries. The accumulation of a second buffer stock of some 220,000 tonnes achieved little more than to stabilize prices at an unattractively low level, but a significant improvement in demand during 1994 led to its rapid liquidation, which was followed in early 1995 by an upward surge which in some areas of the market exceeded that of 1988. Both the INRO daily indicator price and the tyre grade TSR 20 reached record levels, fuelled by reports of heavy buying by China and a perceived shortage of synthetic. As in 1988, the pace was too hot to last, but the price appears to be settling at a level which is relatively attractive to producers.

Currently, there are many who believe that the recent sharp movements in the natural rubber price have been due in part to the excessively high proportion of business transacted direct between producer and consumer, and that a return to a more widespread use of the market could be beneficial to all concerned. In addition, the differences in price have led to a spate of contractual defaults which have caused much concern. Whether these apparent weaknesses in the natural rubber marketing system can be corrected remains to be seen, but despite the example of synthetic, any type of 'costplus' pricing system for natural rubber has so far found little favour. Advocates of such a system have been unable to answer the argument that, despite its importance as an industrial raw material, it remains primarily a smallholder commodity, and must be marketed accordingly.

There are however obvious problems, of which perhaps the most intransigent is the fact that the number of ultimate buyers has been greatly reduced by the globalization of the tyre industry, and corresponding amalgamations in the non-tyre sector. This in turn has led to a steady reduction in the number of dealers, most of whom now operate as sophisticated distributors rather than as takers of large market positions. The decline in outside speculative interest in the commodity, which has been both the cause and the effect of the current absence of any successful terminal market outside Japan, has not helped liquidity; and even Singapore, with its favourable location at the heart of the main producing area, has not found it easy to maintain adequate facilities for worldwide hedging operations. Thus any attempt to turn the clock back towards greater usage of the market, however desirable, is likely to be a slow and hesitant process.

Further information

The Association of the International Rubber Trade
1st Floor
Wigham House
16–30 Wakering Road
Barking IG11 8PG
UK
Tel: +44 181 594 5346
Fax: +44 181 507 8017

The Association of Natural Rubber Producing Countries
7th Floor
Wisma Getah Asli 2
148 Jalan Ampang
50450 Kuala Lumpur
Malaysia
Tel: +603 261 1900
Fax: +603 261 3014

International Natural Rubber Organisation
4th Floor
Wisma SPK
Jalan Sultan Ismail
50250 Kuala Lumpur
Malaysia
Tel: +603 248 6466
Fax: +603 248 6485

International Rubber Association
c/o Malaysian Rubber Exchange & Licensing Boare
3rd & 4th Floor
Bangunan Getah Asli (Menara)
148 Jalan Ampang
40450 Kuala Lumput
Malaysia
Tel: +603 261 5566
Fax: +603 261 3179

International Rubber Study Group
8th Floor
York House
Empire Way
Wembley
Middlesex HA9 0PA
UK
Tel: +44 181 903 7727
Fax: +44 181 903 2848

Table 1 Natural rubber production in 1995, with estimates for 1996 and forecasts for 1997 (thousand tonnes)

	1995	*1996*	*1997*
Brazil	31	34	35
Guatemala	28	30	32
Other Latin America	14	14	14
Cameroon	55	55	56
Côte d'Ivorie	77	82	87
Ghana	9	11	12
Liberia	13	20	25
Nigeria	93	92	90
Zaire	11	12	13
Gabon	5	7	9
Bangladesh	2	3	4
Cambodia	44	47	49
China	360	380	400
India	500	535	570
Indonesia	1420	1470	1530
Malaysia	1085	1095	1070
Myanmar	18	20	21
Papua New Guinea	5	7	10
Philippines	60	60	60
Sri Lanka	106	110	113
Thailand	1790	1860	1934
Vietnam	95	103	110
Total World[a] (rounded)	**5850**	**6050**	**6240**

Notes: [a] Including statistical discrepancies
By courtesy of the International Rubber Study Group

Table 2 Synthetic rubber production in 1995, with estimates for 1996 and forecasts for 1997 (thousand tonnes)

	1995	*1996*	*1997*
Canada	175	177	185
USA	2440	2389	2412
Argentina	54	55	58
Brazil	295	300	310
Mexico	111	115	120
Austria	5	5	5
Belgium	133	131	135
Finland	36	37	38
France	618	630	650
Germany	488	500	510
Italy	310	315	320
Netherlands	185	180	190
Spain	86	89	95
Sweden	32	32	32
UK	320	325	340
Bulgaria	23	28	30
Czech Rep.	78	80	85
Poland	105	110	115
Romania	42	50	60
Russian Federation	830	860	900
Turkey	49	52	53
Federal Republic of Yugoslavia	0	2	10
Other Europe (former CIS states)	47	50	55
South Africa	57	58	60
Australia	48	49	50
China	493	520	550
India	65	70	90
Japan	1498	1420	1440
Republic of Korea	368	405	455
Taiwan	293	300	330
Total World (rounded)	**9280**	**9330**	**9680**

By courtesy of the International Rubber Study Group

Table 3 Natural and synthetic rubber consumption in 1995, with estimates for 1996 and forecasts for 1997

	1995 NR	*1995 SR*	*1995 Total*	*1995 %SR*	*1996 NR*	*1996 SR*	*1996 Total*	*1996 %SR*	*1997 NR*	*1997 SR*	*1997 Total*	*1997 %SR*
					Thousand tonnes							
Canada	121	198	319	62	119	198	317	62	110	198	308	64
USA	1004	2189	3193	69	1004	2195	3199	69	1010	2207	3217	69
Brazil	140	300	440	68	145	310	455	68	147	320	467	69
Mexico	67	83	150	55	70	85	155	55	75	88	163	54
Other Latin America	115	185	300	62	116	189	305	62	120	192	312	62
Belgium/Luxembourg	40	103	143	72	46	103	149	69	48	110	158	70
France	179	420	599	70	183	431	614	70	190	445	635	70
Germany	208	421	629	67	210	430	640	67	215	440	655	67
Italy	102	293	395	74	104	299	403	74	106	306	412	74
Spain	128	194	322	60	132	200	332	60	136	206	342	60
UK	122	219	341	64	127	222	349	64	130	230	360	64
Other EU	74	316	390	81	77	324	401	81	83	337	420	80
Belarus	10	24	34	71	11	26	37	70	12	28	40	70
Czech Rep	26	56	82	68	30	65	95	68	33	70	103	68
Poland	28	85	113	75	32	95	127	75	35	100	135	74
Romania	15	55	70	79	16	60	76	79	17	65	82	79
Russian Federation	13	424	437	97	18	460	478	96	25	500	525	95
Turkey	75	84	159	53	78	88	166	53	80	93	173	54
Ukraine	4	72	76	95	4	77	81	95	6	85	91	93
Other Europe	34	117	151	77	42	138	180	77	47	154	201	77
South Africa	53	70	123	57	54	72	126	57	56	74	130	57
Other Africa	93	65	158	41	93	66	159	42	95	66	161	41
Australia	49	70	119	59	50	71	121	59	51	74	125	59
China	732	805	1537	52	775	850	1625	52	820	900	1720	52
India	516	133	649	20	566	144	710	20	617	157	774	20
Indonesia	133	45	178	25	142	49	191	26	151	51	202	25
Japan	692	1085	1777	61	687	1080	1767	61	694	1091	1785	61
Republic of Korea	307	380	687	55	320	400	720	56	330	425	755	56
Malaysia	327	87	414	21	350	95	445	21	365	104	469	22
Taiwan	104	242	346	70	106	252	358	70	109	269	378	71
Thailand	150	79	229	34	165	89	254	35	180	98	278	35
Other Asia	222	187	409	46	239	194	433	45	249	202	451	45
Total (rounded)	**5880**	**9090**	**14970**	**61**	**6110**	**9360**	**15470**	**61**	**6340**	**9690**	**16030**	**60**

By courtesy of the International Rubber Study Group

Table 4 World elastomer consumption trends (thousand tonnes)

	1995	*1996*	*% change*	*1997*	*% change*
NR consumption	5880	6110	3.9	6340	3.8
SR consumption	9090	9360	3.0	9690	3.5
Total consumption	14,970	15,470	3.3	16,030	3.6
% SR	61	61	–	60	–

Notes: NR Natural Rubber
SR Synthetic Rubber

By courtesy of the International Rubber Study Group

Table 5 Natural rubber prices (per metric ton)

Year	INRO DMIP Malaysia/Singapore cents per kilo Monthly average	Daily highest	Daily lowest	New York ($) RSS 1 (cif)	New York ($) TSR 20 (cif)	London (£) RSS 1 (cif)	London (£) RSS 3 (cif)	London (£) SMR 20 (cif)	Tokyo 000 Yen RSS 3 (cif)	Kuala Lumpur (Ringgit)[a] RSS 1	RSS 3	SMR L (1 tonne pallets)	SMR 10 (1 tonne pallets)	SMR 20 (1 tonne pallets)	Singapore S'pore $ RSS 1	Singapore S'pore $ TSR 20
1990	181.6	192.6	176.1	1020.8	849.9	536.9	512.4	482.5	115.8	2334	2206	2661	2063	1963	1567	–
1991	176.2	184.8	165.4	1007.5	872.1	519.0	500.0	493.2	111.8	2267	2169	2515	2141	2131	1420	–
1992	174.0	181.6	165.7	1019.6	931.4	545.8	527.2	522.5	109.4	2189	2126	2477	2098	2087	1403	1347
1993	168.2	190.7	155.7	992.9	886.4	608.6	589.2	581.8	89.1	2135	2075	2610	2046	2033	1341	1292
1994	229.1	319.3	171.2	1316.9	1250.8	797.0	784.9	789.6	118.2	2933	2886	3311	2941	2926	1754	1735
1995 Jan	345.6	365.3	319.6	1890.5	2000.7	1141.9	1122.9	1227.5	171.3	4177	4136	5073	4608	4594	2455	2693
Feb	356.7	371.9	344.8	2041.6	2012.0	1170.8	1157.0	1228.8	178.6	4508	4463	5073	5227	4654	2571	2649
Mar	359.8	364.8	353.3	2075.5	1977.5	1209.6	1188.2	1151.5	169.3	4598	4553	5159	4461	4442	2650	2627
Apr	348.1	361.5	329.3	2062.5	1929.0	1189.2	1174.2	1116.9	163.8	4576	4531	4978	4277	4267	2590	2421
May	326.5	335.7	306.5	1973.6	1755.9	1174.9	1161.0	1053.0	162.3	4227	4182	4730	3966	3953	2453	2224
Jun	285.9	305.5	269.1	1780.0	1579.5	1004.9	988.2	926.3	137.3	3753	3703	4290	3521	3501	2146	2006
Jul	249.7	266.6	232.5	1583.6	1319.9	894.9	882.7	796.9	119.9	3294	3244	3732	3029	3000	1884	1771
Aug	247.7	271.7	232.1	1511.1	1360.6	886.0	859.2	839.1	120.5	3201	3151	3609	3063	3039	1861	1763
Sep	263.0	270.7	252.6	1558.9	1414.8	921.4	911.3	871.2	147.5	3374	3328	3737	3266	3251	1964	1831
Oct	275.8	290.4	259.1	1624.6	1444.8	946.7	941.4	887.5	148.4	3561	3516	3790	3373	3363	2083	1899
Nov	318.4	333.8	290.8	1832.0	1730.6	1082.6	1074.2	1066.5	170.2	4086	4037	4340	4044	4030	2308	2253
Dec	317.2	333.4	304.8	1845.8	1706.8	1099.7	1093.6	1065.0	170.5	4112	4009	4496	4136	4104	2263	2290
1995 total	**307.9**	**371.9**	**232.1**	**1815.0**	**1686.0**	**1060.2**	**1046.2**	**1019.2**	**154.9**	**3956**	**3904**	**4430**	**3868**	**3850**	**2269**	**2202**
1996 Jan	308.3	324.7	295.6	1765.8	1668.7	1063.1	1057.3	1059.5	160.4	3957	3847	4395	4028	3992	2197	2146
Feb	306.8	318.8	295.5	1762.3	1613.0	1066.1	1058.6	1019.4	164.2	3947	3837	4260	3876	3837	2252	2169
Mar	298.8	311.6	287.6	1758.4	1539.3	–	–	–	–	–	–	–	–	–	2207	2066

Notes:
DMIP is the Daily Market Indicator Price of the International Natural Rubber Organisation (INRO)
New York quotations refer to sellers' asking prices for delivery during the current month; those for Kuala Lumpur and Singapore are buyers' midday prices f.o.b. in bales
London prices are buyers' prices except for SMR 20 which are sellers' prices
Tokyo prices are contract prices for delivery in current month
[a] Prices for the following grades from 1984 onwards are now available on request: RSS 2, RSS 4, RSS 5, SMR CV, SMR 5, SMR 50 and SMR GP
By courtesy of the International Rubber Study Group

Figure 1 Elastomer: leading producers

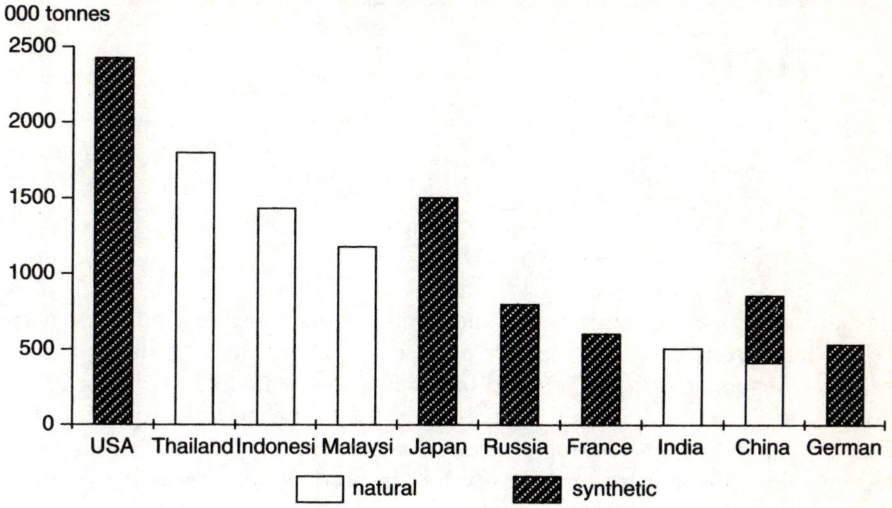

Figure 2 Elastomer consumption

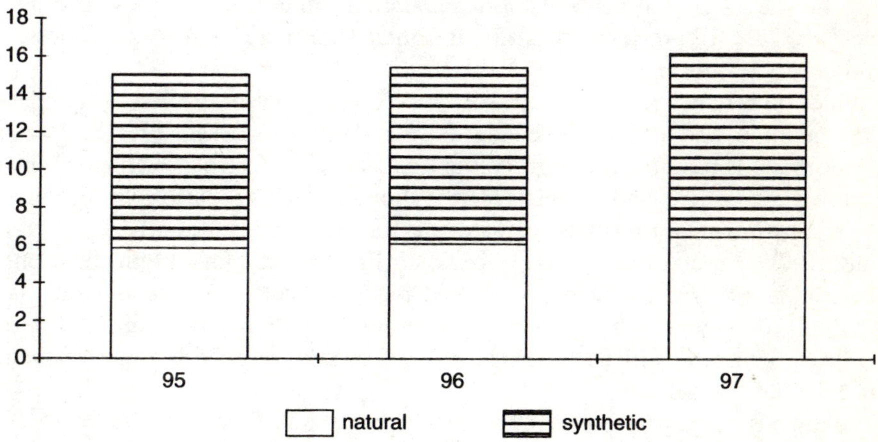

Soyabeans and the Oilseed complex

John Buckley

The great majority of foods on the modern supermarket shelf (and many non-edible items too) owe at least part of their origin to products derived from oilseeds. Vegetable oils/fats are used not only as bottled cooking oils for direct consumption and components for margarine, ice cream and other spreads but in bulking, binding and cooking a host of commercially prepared foods from frozen/'chill-cook' meals to cakes as well as in bottling and canning as preserving agents.

Oils like palm oil have also long been used both for food and industrial purposes like soapmaking while linseed oil is still widely used as a finishing agent and to make linoleum. Rapeseed, sunflower and soyabean oils also find their way into bio-diesel and specialized lubricant outlets while some of these oils also make the base for pesticides, printing ink and a legion of pharmaceutical outlets and beauty products.

Once oil is removed from the oilseed by crushing/solvent extraction it undergoes refining and other processing for its eventual market. Bleaching and deodorizing is used to turn high-colour oils like palm or strong tasting oils like rapeseed into pale, bland products for the shop shelf. Oils are also split into their olein constituents for food use and stearins for soapmaking and other industrial outlets. Over the last few years, processing has also developed 'mid-fractions' that can extract the constituents tailored for a particular end use and this has encouraged a much higher degree of substitution between various oils that once had clearly limited outlets. Hydrogenation is used to aerate oils and turn them into denser or solid fats.

Many oilseeds – soya especially – are not processed primarily for their oil but for the 'meal' residue left after behind after crushing. Rich in protein (often up to half), oilseed meals are a valuable ingredient for livestock feed supplying the nutritional building blocks that help animals grow rapidly and profitably for slaughter weight.

Soyabeans supply around half the world's total consumption of oilseeds. They are also one of the oldest foods known to man – cultivated in China and Japan long before written history (the first Chinese reference dates back to 2207 BC). In the seventeenth century, explorers brought soyabeans back to Europe where they were grown on a limited basis but by the nineteenth century soya was becoming established in the USA as an animal feed. After the high protein content of beans was discovered in the early 1900s the USA began commercial production and processing on a large scale.

For the first half of the twentieth century, China was the main soya producer but between the wars US production mushroomed in response to a global edible oil shortage. After the second world war output again grew rapidly as traditional sources of protein like meat, eggs and cheese ran into short supply. By the 1950s the USA had overtaken China and nowadays produces around half the world's supply. Latin America also became a dominant force in the market over the last three decades, as aggregate production in Brazil, Argentina and Paraguay quadrupled to some 40m tonnes. This has conveniently spread production more evenly over the calendar year with the Latin crops coming to market in the spring and the US supply starting each autumn. It has also ironed out some of the steep price fluctuations which used to occur when the US crop ran into weather problems, although in some years the competition between North and South America for market has resulted in long periods of depressed prices.

The USA is far and away the largest crusher of soyabeans, processing up to 65 per cent of its crop. It is also the largest consumer of soyabean meal, accounting for about 28 per cent of world offtake, closely followed by the EU. The USA also accounts for over 30 per cent of world soyabean oil consumption compared with only 13 per cent by Brazil which tends to concentrate on exporting this product. In terms of world trade, the USA also dominates the soyabean market, shipping over 70 per cent of world exports, with the rest supplied mainly by Latin America. However, in terms of soya product trade, the market shares are somewhat different. Brazil is the largest exporter of soyabean meal (36 per cent of world exports), with Argentina in second place and the USA shipping less than half as much as Brazil. Argentina is the world's largest soyabean oil exporter, followed by Brazil and the USA.

Other important crops – in terms of world trade and markets – include rapeseed, sunflower and the oil-bearing palm. Rising output of all three oilseeds over the last two decades has played a key part in reducing soya's dominance of the oilseed complex, helped by the growing attractiveness of oilseeds more suited for oil than meal production. Soyabeans, for example, only yield about 18–20 per cent of their mass as oil and while worth more per tonne than meal, this is normally regarded as the byproduct of crushing, sometimes accumulating as price depressing stocks (especially in the USA). Rapeseed and sunflowers, however, have oil content in excess of 40 per cent, making these seeds especially valuable in times of firm world oil and fat prices. For palm, virtually the entire fruit is crushed for oil, leaving almost negligible byproducts to market.

Over the 1980s, the demand for oil-rich seeds saw a sharp expansion in output and market shares held by these oilseeds, especially in the European Union (rapeoil and sunoil) and in the Far East (palm oil). Last year, for example, Malaysia was responsible for a quarter of all vegetable oil exports – around 6.5m tonnes. In the late 1970s production was only 1.4m tonnes. As the GATT

Uruguay Round demanded controls on EU oilseed expansion (which required heavy subsidies), other producers have started to resume production growth. Canada recently doubled rapeseed output and is exporting heavily to the EU while the former Eastern bloc countries are gradually employing Western farming methods to grow more rapeseed and sunflowerseed.

Over the last year, oilseeds have been coming out of a period of shortage caused by crop setbacks in the USA, Malaysia and several smaller producers and by a huge and unexpected growth in demand from China which tripled imports to 3.7m tonnes in just two years.

Strong economic growth and present low per capita offtake levels are expected to fuel continued rapid expansion in world vegetable oil trade well into the next century. Consumption has been on a long-term uptrend for some years and has grown by 14 per cent or 8m tonnes in the last four years alone (of which 6m has been in the last two years). Soyabean and palm oil offtake have grown most rapidly – by 21 per cent and 25 per cent respectively. Until recently, much of this increase was fed by larger crops in consuming countries but imports have grown faster than consumption over the last two years (In the last year alone soya oil trade grew 16 per cent and sunflower by a remarkable 28 per cent).

Another favourable development for oilseed producers has been a simultaneous growth in demand for oilmeal with global offtake up by 19m to 139m tonnes in the 1990s alone. Around the world, but especially in Far East Asia and parts of Latin America, economic growth and spending power is being translated into better diets, increasing consumption of meat and poultry. World demand for soyabean meal has grown 22 per cent or by nearly 16m tonnes in the 1990s to 85.5m. In the USA consumption has rocketed by 16 per cent to over 24m tonnes, fuelled by a boom in US meat production for export. Latin American meal consumption has grown over 40 per cent since 1992–3 when it used less than 7m tonnes, to feed an explosion in poultry production, much of it destined for export. However, the most significant growth is in the Asia/Pacific region, where offtake of almost 18m tonnes has risen 67 per cent in just two years. The biggest single factor, once again, is China, whose consumption is up fivefold and now accounts for a third of the region's consumption compared with less than a tenth at the start of the 1990s. World imports of beans and meal have made up three-quarters of the total rise in global oilseed and oilmeal import trade, so this has been something of a comeback period for the soyabean.

In the next decade, oilseed production growth will centre on Asian palm oil, with new plantations still to come on stream and a strong regional demand. East Europe will also continue to expand as it raises yields and responds to still growing demand in West Europe. The Americas, north and south, may also resume their historical expansion as world demand grows although here there will be heavy competition for limited farmland from grains, also in rising demand. The Indian sub-Continent may also be able to lift its oilseed output further having already made huge strides since the 1970s. The former Soviet Union is another area where expansion will ultimately occur when economic growth resumes.

Although this suggests plenty of supply in the future, the very low levels of global demand and the impact of economic growth and population suggest crops may sometimes have difficulty keeping up with consumption. China, for example, is the second largest oilseed producer in the world, after the USA, turning out over 41m tonnes but has turned into the largest importer in just one year because of demand growth. If it adds a mere 1kg per annum to per capita offtake of vegetable oil, the world market will have to find another 1.2m tonnes in supply and an approach to Western consumption levels could easily add four or five mn tonnes to global import needs.

Key trading centres for oilseeds include Rotterdam, Hamburg and London and principal benchmarks include the Chicago soyabean and products futures market, the Dutch, guilder-quoted price of soyabean oil and the Malaysian export market for refined palm oil.

In addition the Chicago Board of Trade, which offers soyabean, meal and oil futures and options, there are thriving oilseed/product futures markets in Paris (MATIF rapeseed futures); Kuala Lumpur (palm oil and products); Winnipeg (rapeseed and linseed); Brazil (the São Paulo Bolsa, soyabeans, meal and oil). Principal international bodies involved in the oilseed industry include the Federation of Oils, Seeds and Fats Associations (FOSFA) and the International Association of Seed Crushers (IASC), both based in London.

Further information

Federation of Oils Seeds and Fats Association
20 St Dunstans Hill
London EC3R 8HL
UK
Tel: +44 171 283 2707
Fax: +44 171 623 1310

International Association of Oil Seed Crushers
PO Box 252
Haywards Heath
West Sussex
RH16 2YG
UK
Tel: +44 1444 483786
Fax: +44 1444 484068

Table 1 World soyabean market (mn tonnes)

	1991–2	*1992–3*	*1993–4*	*1994–5*	*1995–6*
Production					
USA	54.07	59.61	50.92	68.49	58.56
Brazil	19.30	22.50	24.70	26.00	23.00
China	9.71	10.30	15.31	16.00	14.50
Argentina	11.15	11.35	12.30	12.20	12.30
Paraguay	1.30	1.75	1.80	2.20	2.00
EU	1.54	1.27	0.81	1.03	0.97
WORLD	107.38	117.30	117.40	137.09	123.37
Exports					
USA	18.61	20.94	16.03	22.81	22.05
Brazil	3.87	4.06	5.43	3.54	3.40
Argentina	3.20	2.42	3.07	2.90	2.70
Paraguay	0.83	1.25	1.20	1.30	1.20
China	1.09	0.30	1.10	0.39	0.30
WORLD	28.45	29.83	28.04	31.73	30.92
Imports					
EU	13.94	15.17	13.11	15.31	14.83
Netherlands	4.05	4.26	4.14	4.61	4.45
Germany	3.03	3.31	2.79	3.00	2.82
Spain	2.48	2.48	1.72	2.70	2.68
Bel/Lux	1.21	1.31	1.22	1.30	1.26
Italy	1.10	1.33	1.17	1.20	1.16
Portugal	0.64	0.56	0.53	0.78	0.81
Japan	4.67	4.87	4.86	4.84	4.75
Taiwan	2.45	2.51	2.50	2.60	2.55
Mexico	2.10	2.14	2.20	1.95	2.20
Rep Korea	1.33	1.13	1.16	1.40	1.40
Indonesia	0.49	0.53	0.71	0.60	0.52
E Europe	0.31	0.30	0.28	0.32	0.28
FSU	0.63	0.12	0.13	0.13	0.11
WORLD	29.17	30.31	28.41	32.23	31.01
Crush					
USA	34.13	34.81	34.72	38.24	37.56
Brazil	14.94	15.55	18.44	20.47	20.20
EU	13.13	14.09	12.24	14.35	13.93
Argentina	7.70	8.49	8.77	8.68	9.10
China	3.39	4.30	7.20	8.09	7.25
Japan	3.55	3.79	3.70	3.71	3.66
Mexico	2.60	2.67	2.64	2.41	2.41
Taiwan	2.23	2.32	2.24	2.34	2.25
FSU	1.29	0.58	0.65	0.57	0.48
E Europe	0.61	0.53	0.42	0.49	0.45
WORLD	92.62	96.40	101.48	108.84	109.86
Stocks					
USA	7.58	7.96	5.69	9.11	5.16
Brazil	4.39	6.07	5.31	6.69	4.71
Argentina	3.64	3.58	3.40	3.84	3.77
WORLD	18.38	20.03	16.70	22.00	15.76

Table 2 World soyabean meal market (mn tonnes)

	1991–2	*1992–3*	*1993–4*	*1994–5*	*1995–6*
Production					
USA	7.06	27.55	27.68	30.18	29.82
EU	10.53	10.98	9.85	11.43	11.13
Brazil	1.74	12.17	14.49	16.09	15.88
Argentina	6.22	6.86	7.08	7.02	7.35
China	2.75	3.48	5.83	6.55	5.87
India	1.79	2.25	2.88	2.20	3.00
Japan	2.76	2.94	2.85	2.86	2.88
Mexico	2.03	2.08	2.06	1.88	1.88
Taiwan	1.73	1.78	1.75	1.80	1.76
FSU	1.03	0.46	0.51	0.45	0.38
E Eur	0.49	0.42	0.33	0.39	0.37
WORLD	73.20	76.15	80.77	87.20	86.89
Exports					
Brazil	8.78	8.17	10.31	10.45	11.30
Argentina	6.24	6.54	6.76	6.86	7.17
USA	6.30	5.65	4.86	6.09	5.26
EU	3.97	4.04	3.85	4.13	4.02
India	1.18	2.01	2.20	1.50	2.30
China	1.40	0.40	1.05	1.28	0.40
WORLD	28.62	27.60	29.93	31.55	31.57
Imports					
EU	14.51	15.49	16.44	16.85	16.57
France	3.55	3.50	3.80	4.03	3.84
Germany	2.19	2.22	2.12	2.23	2.08
Italy	1.39	1.62	1.75	1.88	1.87
Netherlands	1.21	1.40	1.37	1.55	1.55
Asia/Oceania	3.68	4.16	4.61	5.15	5.54
Mid East/N Afr	2.31	2.30	2.76	3.13	3.17
Latam	1.73	1.96	2.28	2.55	2.62
E Europe	1.82	1.57	1.63	1.92	1.78
FSU	3.00	1.05	1.02	0.45	0.55
WORLD	28.25	27.61	29.89	31.37	31.52
Consumption					
USA	20.87	22.00	22.94	24.08	24.63
EU	21.17	22.24	22.65	24.28	23.62
France	3.65	3.81	4.03	4.41	4.23
Germany	3.54	3.49	3.37	3.66	3.46
Netherlands	1.98	2.51	2.52	2.65	2.57
Italy	3.02	3.15	3.16	3.21	3.19
Spain	3.31	3.32	3.30	3.53	3.45
China	1.49	3.12	4.78	5.33	5.67
Brazil	3.30	3.92	4.19	5.00	5.25
Mid East/N Afr	2.87	2.94	3.42	3.92	4.03
Japan	3.66	3.79	3.73	3.76	3.72
E Europe	2.30	1.98	1.92	2.29	2.16
Mexico	2.35	2.48	2.41	2.28	2.21
Taiwan	1.90	1.94	1.88	1.86	1.81
Rep Korea	1.34	1.45	1.49	1.70	1.76
FSU	4.03	1.51	1.53	0.90	0.93
WORLD	73.36	75.57	80.77	86.40	87.50
STOCKS	3.14	3.74	3.69	3.72	3.65

Figure 1 Chicago soyabean futures 1992–3/1995–6

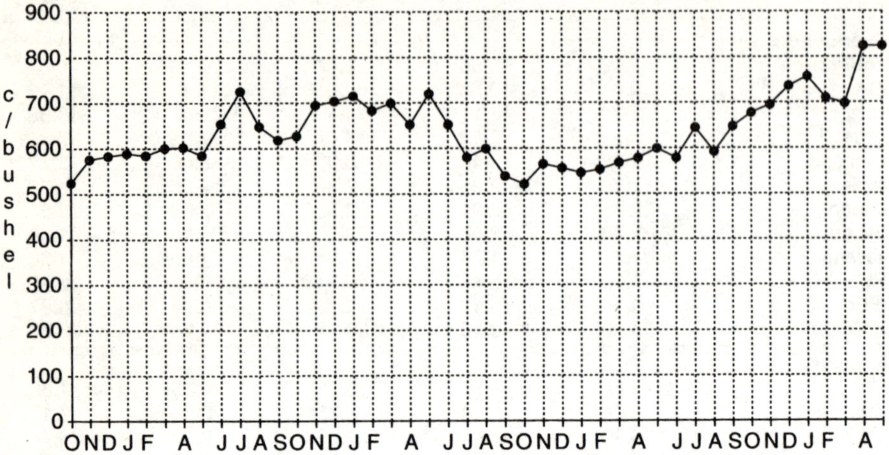

Figure 2 Soyabean: leading suppliers

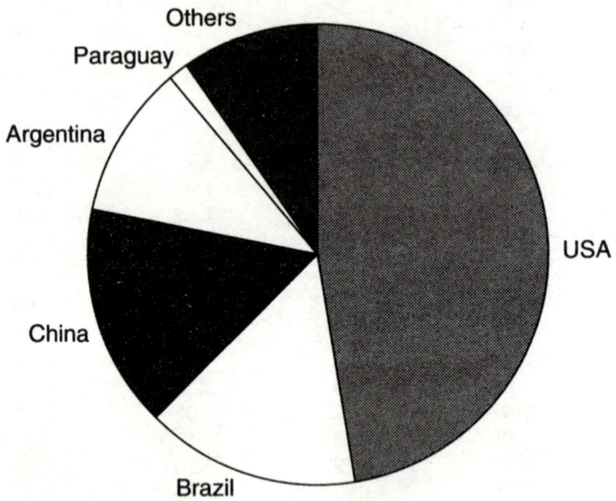

Table 3 World soyabean oil market (mn tonnes)

	1991–2	*1992–3*	*1993–4*	*1994–5*	*1995–6*
Production					
USA	6.51	6.25	6.33	7.08	7.04
Brazil	2.81	2.91	3.47	3.85	3.80
EU	2.35	2.54	2.24	2.62	2.54
Argentina	1.32	1.44	1.52	1.50	1.57
China	0.52	0.65	1.09	1.22	1.09
Japan	0.66	0.69	0.66	0.68	0.66
Mexico	0.44	0.442	0.45	0.41	0.41
Taiwan	0.42	0.42	0.39	0.40	0.40
FSU	0.23	0.11	0.09	0.08	0.07
E Eur	0.11	0.09	0.07	0.09	0.08
WORLD	16.90	17.18	18.17	19.82	19.77
Exports					
Argentina	1.13	1.45	1.45	1.49	1.41
Brazil	0.66	0.69	1.35	1.57	1.30
USA	0.75	0.64	0.69	1.22	0.82
EU	1.43	1.06	0.91	1.22	1.20
WORLD	4.29	4.20	4.84	6.04	5.24
Imports					
China	0.22	0.10	0.64	1.45	1.15
Latin America	0.71	0.78	0.93	1.01	0.87
EU	0.66	0.53	0.50	0.53	0.54
Iran	0.49	0.43	0.49	0.50	0.44
Pakistan	0.20	0.25	0.17	0.15	0.20
Morocco	0.12	0.17	0.18	0.18	0.17
Turkey	0.15	0.21	0.17	0.15	0.15
Tunisia	0.11	0.12	0.11	0.14	0.13
E Europe	0.11	0.11	0.13	0.12	0.11
FSU	0.24	0.24	0.08	0.09	0.10
WORLD	3.97	4.07	4.74	5.87	5.29
Consumption					
USA	5.55	5.92	5.87	5.86	5.92
Brazil	2.18	2.28	2.32	2.47	2.56
China	0.74	0.74	1.69	2.61	2.19
EU	1.59	1.98	1.85	1.97	1.90
India	0.43	0.56	0.71	0.65	0.79
Japan	0.65	0.69	0.67	0.68	0.67
Mexico	0.57	0.53	0.52	0.49	0.46
Iran	0.51	0.45	0.51	0.51	0.45
Taiwan	0.42	0.38	0.39	0.39	0.40
Bangladesh	0.25	0.31	0.32	0.39	0.37
Korea	0.19	0.19	0.22	0.24	0.24
E Europe	0.22	0.22	0.20	0.21	0.19
Pakistan	0.19	0.28	0.18	0.19	0.18
Morocco	0.12	0.18	0.18	0.19	0.18
Turkey	0.16	0.22	0.18	0.16	0.17
FSU	0.47	0.35	0.18	0.17	0.17
WORLD	16.13	17.36	18.34	19.68	19.41
STOCKS	2.32	2.01	1.73	1.71	2.13

Table 4 World oilseed market (mn tonnes)

	1991–2	*1992–3*	*1993–4*	*1994–5*	*1995–6*
Production					
Soyabeans	107.4	117.3	117.4	137.1	123.4
Cottonseed	36.5	31.6	29.7	33.0	34.3
Groundnuts	22.2	23.1	24.0	26.6	25.3
Sunflower	21.8	21.3	20.8	23.6	25.9
Rapeseed	28.3	25.3	26.8	31.0	33.9
Copra	4.7	4.9	5.0	5.4	5.1
TOTAL	24.3	227.5	227.8	261.2	252.5
World oilseed meal consumption					
Soyabean	73.4	75.6	80.8	86.4	87.5
Rapeseed	15.6	14.1	15.0	16.7	18.5
Cottonseed	13.4	11.4	10.8	11.8	12.3
Sunflowerseed	8.6	8.2	8.1	9.5	10.4
Fishmeal	6.3	6.0	6.3	6.6	6.6
Groundnut	4.8	5.1	5.2	6.0	5.5
Palm kernel	1.8	2.1	2.2	2.4	2.5
Copra	1.5	1.7	1.6	1.7	1.7
WORLD	125.3	124.1	129.9	141.1	145.0
World oil and fat consumption					
Soyabean	16.1	17.4	18.3	19.7	19.4
Palm	11.4	12.4	14.0	14.5	14.8
Rapeseed	9.3	8.6	9.0	10.0	11.1
Sunflowerseed	7.7	7.4	7.1	7.9	8.9
Cottonseed	4.3	3.8	3.4	3.7	3.8
Groundnut	3.3	3.7	3.6	4.1	3.8
Coconut	2.9	2.8	2.9	3.4	3.2
Olive	1.9	1.9	1.9	1.9	1.8
Fish	1.1	1.1	1.3	1.3	1.3
Palm kernel	1.5	1.7	1.9	2.0	2.1
WORLD	59.5	60.7	63.6	68.5	70.2

Source: US Department of Agriculture

Figure 3 Oilseed market shares

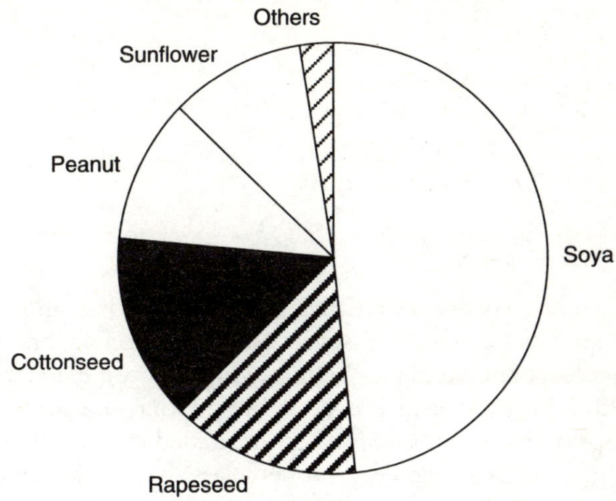

Sugar

John Buckley

Sugar – as a sweetener, energy source and preservative – has, in one form or another, been around as long as man's sweet tooth. In recent years, the sort of refined white sugar best known in the Western world has come under increasing attack from health lobbyists for its less desirable calorific and dental attributes while its consumption base has been further threatened by a whole raft of substitutes, including artificial sweeteners. Nonetheless, global demand for sugar continues to grow each year to new record levels and production with it.

Geographically, demand for sugar has been changing radically over the last two or three decades. In the industrialized world, consumption has tended to plateau, due partly to saturation, partly to negative health concerns and in tandem with the latter, the increasing appeal of low calorific alternative sweeteners.

Demand in the developed world also took a mighty knock from the breakup of the Soviet Union and its Eastern bloc sphere which ended consumption subsidies and reduced both demand and production across a region that had previously boasted some of the highest per capita offtake rates in the world. Against that, however, consumption is growing very rapidly in developing countries where strong economic growth is starting to boost very low per capita offtake rates, ranging from 1kg to 3kg in poor parts of Asia and Africa compared with the mid-30kg in Europe.

Most countries grow sugar crops to a greater or lesser extent. The temperate regions of the world – North America, Europe and FSU – produce beet crops marketed mainly as white sugars which account for about 30 per cent of production. The remaining 70 per cent is produced in tropical zones from sugarcane, generally marketed as raw sugar grown for further refining. The variety of sources tends to ensure a flow of sugar supply throughout the calendar year although there is a seasonal production rise in beet liftings in the northern hemisphere in October to December. Cane cutting in contrast peaks around January to March in Asia and in June to December across the southern hemisphere (Central America, Africa, Australia). Cane is cut 12–18 months after planting each year for up to seven years before it has to be replanted but beets are sown in spring and harvested from October onward. The USA and China produce both types.

Sugar has historically been one of the most subsidized commodities, resulting in a heavy build-up of stocks in the last few decades, frequently to a level equal to a third of annual consumption needs. The last two years have seen a draw-down of stocks due to crop shortfalls at a time of growing demand but this year and next are likely to see considerable return to stock growth as production increases more rapidly than demand.

Two major shifts are taking place in world sugar trade. One is an increasing trend towards exporting in white refined form, shipments of which increased to almost 50 per cent of trade last year compared with only 32 per cent in 1988. China, South Korea and others also 'toll refine' sugar – importing raws to refine and re-export to profit from high margins on white sugar sales. White exports are growing most from the expanding producers of the Asia/Pacific Region. However, there has also been a trend to open new mega-refineries in former leading white importer countries, Saudi Arabia and Dubai, which plan to drag in huge quantities of raws from countries like Australia to export to other Near East markets. This could cause a radical shift in regional demand away from traditional EU white sugar supplies although West European production is being curbed anyway by GATT and CAP reforms.

The lion's share of world sugar output is consumed in the country of origin and only 18–21 per cent is freely traded on global markets (although this is up from the 17–18 per cent average of the 1980s). Around 8m tonnes were once traded outside the free market through intergovernmental deals but in recent years this trade has declined sharply, led by the collapse of pacts between Russia and Cuba (covering 4.5m tonnes at one time). This trade is likely to remain restricted although China has recently emerged as a growing market for Cuban raws. Other controlled trade includes EU and US preferential import quotas for Afro-Caribbean and Asian countries.

Five major players, Cuba, EU, Thailand, Australia and Brazil, account for almost two-thirds of world sugar exports, somewhat down on the last decade, due to Cuba's partial demise. Asia/Pacific (India, Thailand, Australia, Pakistan) and Latin American (Brazil, Argentina) producers are still in an expansionary phase. Some big producers – notably China and India – veer either side of self-sufficiency with dramatic impact on world prices. China is currently a huge net importer but India has moved into huge exportable surplus. Many medium and small producers also supply the export markets on an erratic basis. Most are cane producers and vulnerable to weather.

FSU, the USA, Japan, the Middle East, Western Europe and China account for the bulk of raw imports while Middle East/North African countries are influential importers of white sugar. Many Asian and Latin American producers have been approaching self-sufficiency but some are now finding it more difficult to match supply with demand that is accelerating with economic growth. In much of sub-Saharan Africa, apart from South Africa and its immediate neighbours, supply falls short of demand and funds for imports remain scarce.

Many developing countries and some of the emergent East and Central European economies are making radical attempts to reduce state participation and price control. Deregulation and privatization of both domestic and import/export trade is opening up import markets to new sources of supply as those who formerly had to purchase strict EU contract quality white sugars through state trading bodies are able to buy cheaper alternatives.

This liberalization has helped a rising volume of trade in partly refined sugar, mainly Brazilian crystals, and is stimulating Brazil to expand production of this type. As deregulation progresses, it should make a significant contribution to recovery in the total volume of world sugar export trade which had contracted sharply from its peak in the late 1980s when the Comecon block reduced its protocol deals with Cuba. Liberalization will also expose sugar producers and consumers to world market conditions – suggesting that supply and demand will become more responsive to real rather than subsidized market prices which in turn, could increase long-term prospects for price volatility in this once highly controlled sector.

Sugar substitutes are making their biggest dent in outlets in the manufactured food and soft drink sector – so-called 'indirect' consumption which accounts for about half sugar's use in the developing world and up to 65 per cent in the USA and Western Europe. Traditionally, the main competitor was saccharin but latterly the market has been swamped by organic alternatives like high fructose corn syrup, a byproduct of maize processing and more recently by compounds like aspartame. Some of these are literally thousands of times stronger than sugar but they do not have it all their own way. Some have an undesirable aftertaste, others cannot be baked or stored for long without breaking down and very few have sugar's all round versatility at an affordable price. At present it seems there is room in an expanding sweetener market for both sugar and its rivals.

Key international markets trading sugar futures and options include London's LCE, New York's CSCE, the Paris MATIF, Brazil's Bolsa, and Tokyo's commodity exchange. The International Sugar Organisation, based in London, represents most of the important sugar trading countries and issues diverse and comprehensive information on a regular basis on production, consumption, trade, markets and policy.

Further information

C Czarnokow Sugar Ltd
24 Chiswell Street
London EC1Y 4SG
UK
Tel: +44 171 972 6600
Fax: +44 171 972 6699

International Sugar Organisation
1 Canada Square
Canary Wharf
London E14 5AA
UK
Tel: +44 171 513 1144
Fax: +44 171 513 1146

FO Licht
AM Muchlengraben 22
Postfach 1220
23902 Ratzeburg
Germany
Tel: +49 4541 88920
Fax: +49 4541 82145

Table 1 World beet production estimates – all figures in thousands tonnes, raw value

	1995/96 (estimated)	1994/95	1993/94	1992/93	1991/92	1990/91	1989/90	1988/89
Europe								
Austria	470	438	516	437	466	451	458	357
Belgium	964	942	1134	966	967	1120	1038	1005
Denmark	471	487	566	447	508	591	529	550
Finland	167	168	154	153	163	169	173	147
France	4529	4367	4725	4722	4413	4736	4198	4397
Germany	4149	3991	4732	4400	4249	4674	4004	3513
Greece	312	272	333	385	297	312	421	235
Irish Republic	233	232	192	242	232	245	234	212
Italy	1621	1622	1542	2032	1640	1585	1880	1609
Netherlands	1074	1050	1232	1295	1137	1304	1240	1075
Portugal	8	6	3	2	2	2	2	2
Spain (see also cane)	1174	1205	1325	1026	924	1021	1023	1274
Sweden	387	370	413	333	266	445	421	394
UK	1360	1373	1561	1603	1325	1349	1377	1421
Total EU (beet)	**16,955**	**16,523**	**18,428**	**18,043**	**16,589**	**18,004**	**16,998**	**16,191**
FSU (Former Soviet Union members)								
Russia	2150	1695	2720	2440	2250	2625	3475	3375
Ukraine	3800	3635	4130	3760	4075	5675	5465	4805
Moldova	175	150	210	200	225	309	337	233
Belarus	130	107	139	117	150	174	172	165
Kazakhstan	60	55	107	137	125	95	115	140
Baltic States	110	80	100	100	100	118	132	163
Other FSU	25	20	23	17	15	4	4	19
Total FSU	**6450**	**5742**	**7429**	**6771**	**6940**	**9000**	**9700**	**8900**
Rest of Europe								
Albania	7	5	4	5	15	17	25	30
Bulgaria	30	12	10	25	65	40	70	30
Czech Republic	500	412	625	592	620	580	593	507
Slovakia	140	130	152	165	180	165	167	143
Hungary	525	462	282	375	625	575	612	520
Poland	1700	1490	2175	1565	1635	2200	1860	1825
Romania	215	200	135	243	430	335	525	450
Switzerland	140	128	152	137	136	160	152	150
Turkey	1520	1695	2192	2124	2052	1944	1378	1414
Yugoslavia	250	315	185	460	800	930	920	655
Total Europe	**28,432**	**27,114**	**31,769**	**30,505**	**30,087**	**33,950**	**33,000**	**30,815**
Other Beet								
Canada	166	182	124	122	152	148	117	113
Chile	585	582	505	490	525	360	371	445
China (see also cane)	1400	1045	1090	1800	1815	1650	900	1315
Iran (see also cane)	710	678	710	791	645	455	475	500
Japan (see also cane)	682	634	654	680	781	700	668	705
Morocco (see also cane)	370	410	445	390	433	409	390	405
USA (see also cane)	3675	4076	3710	3984	3381	3485	3123	3182
Uruguay (see also cane)	0	0	0	4	17	10	25	30
Other beet	355	313	281	276	273	201	197	177
World total beet	**36,375**	**35,034**	**39,288**	**39,042**	**38,109**	**41,368**	**39,266**	**37,687**

By courtesy of C Czarnikow Ltd

Table 2 World cane production estimates – all figures in thousands tonnes, raw value

	1995/96 (estimated)	*1994/95*	*1993/94*	*1992/93*	*1991/92*	*1990/91*	*1989/90*	*1988/89*
Spain (see also beet)	9	9	16	12	15	15	15	15
Argentina	1500	1202	1093	1379	1560	1351	1017	1283
Barbados	57	38	51	48	55	67	70	67
Belize	110	118	112	106	107	108	106	96
Bolivia	270	277	223	226	303	235	225	155
Brazil	13,650	12,618	10,038	9986	9348	7935	7793	8683
Colombia	2200	2065	1964	1833	1813	1633	1593	1523
Costa Rica	365	339	329	309	302	265	245	220
Cuba	3800	3400	4024	4365	7000	7729	8156	8188
Dominican Republic	500	520	628	632	568	592	632	735
Ecuador	390	340	362	383	348	355	330	315
El Salvador	350	312	323	329	346	270	211	189
French West Indies	38	43	72	78	47	63	28	85
Guatemala	1250	1275	1118	1105	1118	1015	875	705
Guyana	300	265	265	255	255	168	134	170
Haiti	30	30	30	30	30	35	40	30
Hawaii	415	455	640	614	591	657	744	784
Honduras	235	214	195	186	188	191	200	184
Jamaica	240	220	220	224	223	228	228	185
Mexico	4600	4627	3835	4398	3531	3943	3408	3675
Nicaragua	230	220	185	177	195	217	212	160
Panama	125	125	125	120	127	130	121	108
Paraguay	110	110	110	105	90	106	105	95
Peru	650	698	589	415	454	575	612	674
Puerto Rico	35	40	65	90	90	90	90	90
St. Kitts	20	20	25	20	21	20	16	25
Trinidad	120	116	128	108	114	104	122	97
USA Mainland	2695	2665	2568	2468	2455	2116	2097	2241
Uruguay (cane only)	20	22	30	58	57	63	65	45
Venezuela	545	527	505	525	540	542	569	521
Total Americas	**34,850**	**32,901**	**29,852**	**30,572**	**31,876**	**30,803**	**30,044**	**31,328**
Angola	30	25	35	20	30	25	20	13
Egypt (cane only)	1085	990	965	920	945	940	887	875
Ethiopia	165	165	185	185	165	155	190	183
Ivory Coast	135	129	137	141	170	155	162	159
Kenya	415	328	414	404	472	467	480	447
Malagasy	95	83	104	97	96	118	120	122
Malawi	237	211	139	209	210	204	173	187
Mauritius	570	530	599	681	648	661	602	672
Morocco (cane only)	110	89	94	102	110	110	105	115
Mozambique	31	20	16	14	25	35	30	25
Nigeria	50	45	50	45	45	60	53	55
Reunion	200	190	192	241	227	203	180	266
South Africa	1778	1780	1258	1654	2461	2174	2284	2321
Sudan	505	465	445	511	513	471	421	384
Swaziland	420	478	458	495	517	527	504	464
Tanzania	135	110	123	120	115	110	105	100
Zaire	92	90	71	74	72	75	83	80
Zambia	160	160	147	155	134	135	147	146
Zimbabwe	512	524	51	9	346	493	502	453
Other Africa	434	414	383	401	413	379	405	361
Total Africa	**7159**	**6826**	**5866**	**6478**	**7714**	**7497**	**7453**	**7428**

Table 2 World cane production estimates – all figures in thousands tonnes, raw value contd.

	1995/96 (estimated)	*1994/95*	*1993/94*	*1992/93*	*1991/92*	*1990/91*	*1989/90*	*1988/89*
Bangladesh	260	292	240	203	215	265	196	117
China (see also beet)	5550	4825	5450	6600	6760	5230	4750	3985
China (Taiwan)	410	435	500	426	510	445	511	664
India	16,500	15,850	10,650	11,525	14,570	13,093	11,943	9513
Indonesia	2575	2460	2483	2300	2445	2305	2225	2152
Iran (cane only)	215	220	210	158	150	173	150	150
Japan (see also beet)	202	157	203	234	226	251	362	314
Malaysia	105	107	114	105	104	95	113	110
Pakistan	2770	3243	3153	2582	2496	2064	1990	1976
Philippines	1650	1705	1873	2130	2060	1736	1810	1645
Thailand	6175	5513	4009	3792	5106	4055	3506	4052
Vietnam	475	495	435	500	485	475	450	450
Other Asia	211	178	147	163	160	130	99	91
Total Asia	**37,098**	**35,480**	**29,467**	**30,718**	**35,287**	**30,317**	**28,105**	**25,209**
Australia	5133	5215	4493	4365	3195	3612	3887	3755
Fiji	473	538	460	444	404	424	479	376
Papua New Guinea	38	43	33	37	30	32	33	54
Total Oceania	**5644**	**5796**	**4986**	**4846**	**3629**	**4068**	**4399**	**4,185**
Total cane	**84,760**	**81,012**	**70,187**	**72,626**	**78,521**	**72,700**	**70,016**	**68,165**
WORLD TOTAL CANE & BEET	**121,135**	**116,046**	**109,475**	**111,668**	**116,630**	**114,068**	**109,282**	**105,852**

By courtesy of C Czarnikow Ltd

Table 3 World consumption estimates 1993–96 – all figures in thousands of tonnes, raw value

	1996	*1995*	*1994*	*1993*
Asia				
Afghanistan	50	50	50	48
Bangladesh	350	345	340	315
China	8350	8200	7950	7700
China (Taiwan)	545	540	535	545
Hong Kong	160	157	155	150
India	14,050	13,700	13,250	13,075
Indonesia	2988	2916	2844	2772
Iran	1850	1750	1700	1675
Iraq	450	425	450	475
Israel	310	300	290	285
Japan	2507	2573	2657	2678
Jordan	185	182	183	171
Korea (North)	123	123	122	122
Korea (South)	925	900	864	852
Kuwait	31	32	30	30
Lebanon	92	90	92	93
Malaysia	840	825	815	797
Mongolia	62	62	61	59
Myanmar	65	65	65	64
Pakistan	2825	2750	2725	2700
Persian Gulf	75	75	75	75
Philippines	1925	1875	1825	1739
Saudi Arabia	430	425	425	420
Singapore	185	185	185	185
Sri Lanka	430	410	400	395
Syria	625	625	610	592
Thailand	1750	1630	1480	1368
Vietnam	625	610	600	575
Yemen	330	330	330	330
Other Asia	104	109	106	103
Total Asia	**43, 237**	**42,259**	**41,214**	**40,388**
North and Central America				
Bahamas	9	9	9	9
Barbados	12	12	11	11
Belize	15	18	13	11
Canada	1200	1175	1150	1125
Costa Rica	200	196	193	189
Cuba	625	650	664	796
Dominican Republic	305	300	295	290
El Salvador	200	185	180	175
Guatemala	430	185	416	391
Haiti	62	62	61	61
Honduras	195	190	182	177
Jamaica	122	121	120	123
Mexico	4500	4455	4350	4550
Netherlands Antilles	7	7	7	7
Nicaragua	145	140	135	130
Panama	88	85	85	82
St Kitts	2	2	2	2
Trinidad	65	65	63	59
USA	8650	8550	8454	8192
Others	150	150	150	150
Total North and Central America	**16,982**	**16,792**	**16,540**	**16,530**

Table 3 World consumption estimates 1993–96 – all figures in thousands of tonnes, raw value contd.

	1996	*1995*	*1994*	*1993*
South America				
Argentina	1300	1250	1296	1200
Bolivia	216	214	211	209
Brazil	8300	8250	8000	7650
Chile	625	620	615	598
Colombia	1215	1200	1140	1158
Ecuador	408	406	405	375
Guyana	24	24	23	22
Paraguay	110	107	105	102
Peru	850	820	790	690
Surinam	15	15	15	15
Uruguay	100	95	100	95
Venezuela	870	850	775	700
Total South America	**14,033**	**13,851**	**13,475**	**12,814**
Europe				
Albania	55	50	55	50
Bulgaria	305	285	265	255
FSU				
Russia	5550	5450	5250	5850
Ukraine	2500	2400	2492	2575
Belarus	350	365	385	425
Moldova	205	195	175	205
Kazakstan	525	520	525	558
Other CIS	1254	1240	1220	1294
Baltic States	306	312	317	324
Total FSU	**10,690**	**10,482**	**10,364**	**11,231**
Czech Republic	435	450	475	490
EU-15	14,405	14,345	14,432	14,392
Hungary	450	440	398	382
Norway	190	184	184	177
Poland	1600	1600	1750	1691
Romania	475	450	500	525
Slovakia	215	210	215	200
Switzerland	320	317	310	315
Turkey	2050	1950	1900	1850
Ex-Yugoslavia	400	375	350	400
Other Europe	75	73	73	70
Total Europe	**31,665**	**31,211**	**31,271**	**32,028**
Africa				
Algeria	870	875	885	871
Angola	125	120	120	120
Cameroon	95	94	93	90
Egypt	1960	1850	1750	1675
Ethiopia	145	140	155	152
Ghana	105	108	101	93
Ivory Coast	140	140	140	145
Kenya	625	625	620	609
Libya	210	200	200	200
Malagasy	93	90	90	85
Malawi	158	153	146	162
Mauritius	40	40	39	39

Table 3 World consumption estimates 1993–96 – all figures in thousands of tonnes, raw value contd.

	1996	*1995*	*1994*	*1993*
Morocco	900	875	854	830
Mozambique	90	100	90	80
Nigeria	460	465	470	550
Senegal	110	105	100	102
Somalia	60	65	65	65
South Africa	1400	1390	1480	1303
Sudan	490	490	480	490
Swaziland	180	175	141	103
Tanzania	160	150	178	127
Togo	36	36	35	35
Tunisia	271	262	258	250
Zaire	120	118	117	115
Zambia	110	105	95	86
Zimbabwe	285	265	253	229
Other Africa	627	610	585	568
Total Africa	**9865**	**9646**	**9490**	**9174**
Oceania				
Australia	930	918	927	909
Fiji	49	47	43	46
New Zealand	176	175	172	170
Papua New Guinea	29	29	29	29
Other Oceania	21	21	21	20
Total Oceania	**1205**	**1190**	**1192**	**1174**
WORLD TOTAL	**116,987**	**114,949**	**113,182**	**112,108**

By courtesy of C Czarnikow Ltd

Figure 1 Sugar: world's leading producers

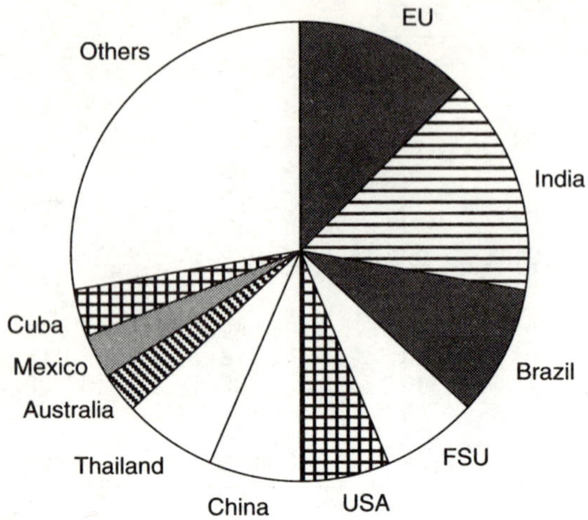

Figure 2 Sugar: ISA indicator monthly averages, 1991–6

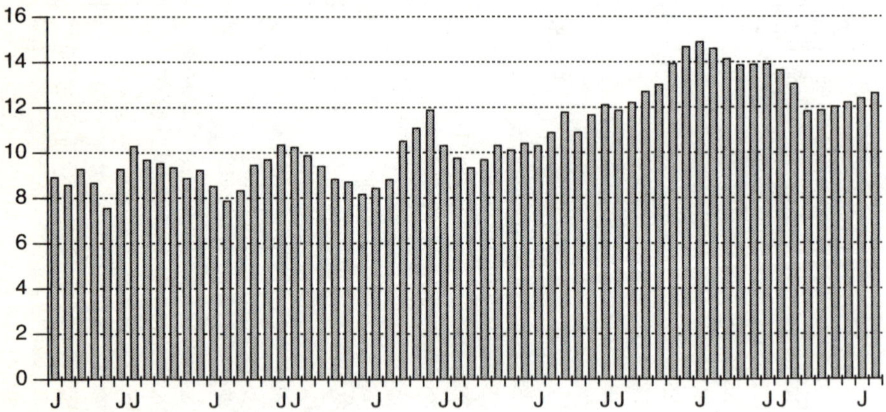

Figure 3 Sugar: per capita consumption

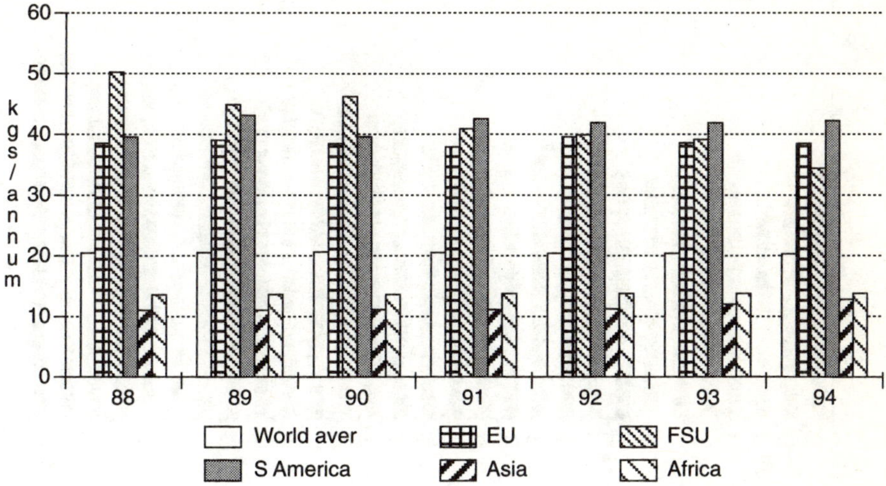

Figure 4 Sugar: world exports

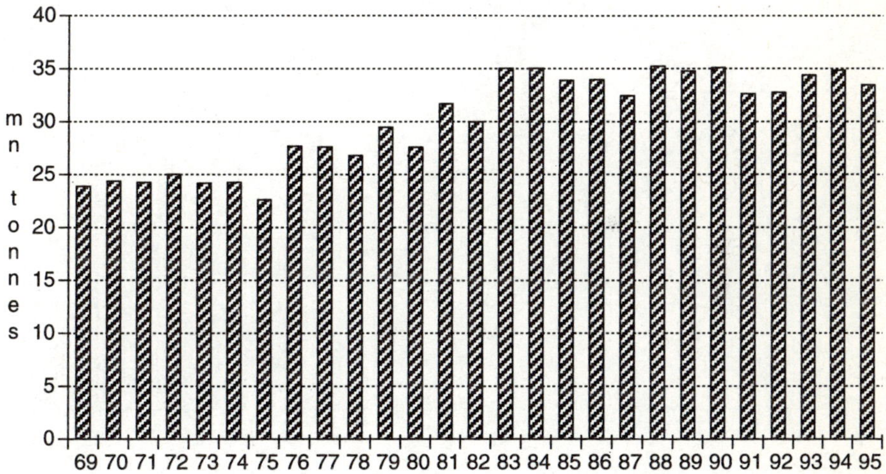

Figure 5 Sugar: world consumption, past and projected

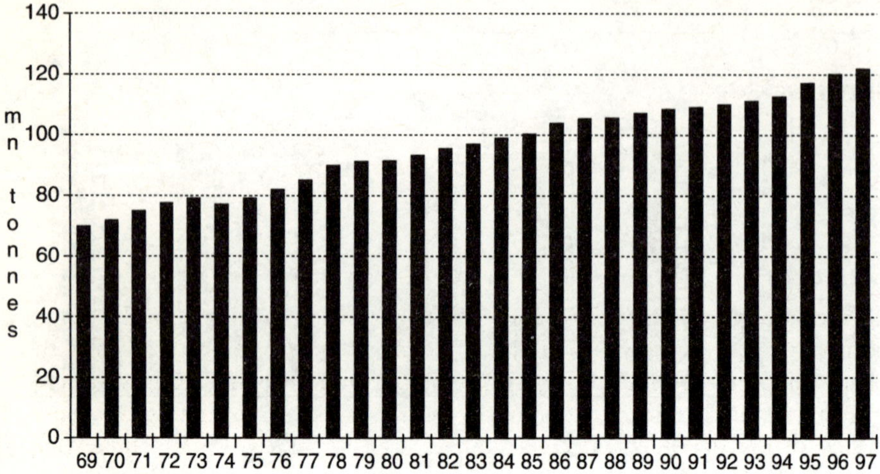

Tea

John Buckley

Cultivation requirements of soil and climate limit the bulk of tea production to a relatively small number of countries. The highlands of East Africa and the Indian sub-Continent are among the most important growing regions, benefiting from plentiful sunshine, rain, moderate temperatures and high soil fertility.

Many of the major producing countries are historically among the leading consumers and some of these – especially India and some of the South East Asian nations – are raising consumption as economic growth increases spending power and per capita offtake.

This concentration of supply and demand has long been a recipe for extreme volatility in tea prices. During the early 1980s for example, the price of medium-grade teas rocketed from 130p to over 300p per kg as supplies ran short, only to collapse back to where it started by the middle of the decade. So far over the 1990s, prices have fluctuated less violently, easing gradually down to just above 100p for mediums in the last year – which is almost as low as they were 20 years ago. However, as demand has grown for speciality teas, the price of higher quality types has tended to fluctuate more.

Production of tea by the main producer countries had been on a more or less steady uptrend over the 1970s and 1980s but plateaued and began to sink in the early 1990s. Although the promise of better prices and good weather in several key producing regions enabled a steep recovery in 1993 the output went into reverse again in 1994 and staged only a partial recovery last year. For 1996 output is expected to do rather better and may just scrape in a new record level next year.

About four-fifths of tea output is in 'black' or fermented form and the remainder is green and partly fermented. Black tea accounts for an even larger proportion of world production – around 90 per cent – although interest in green and other speciality teas has grown in recent years in the West.

In a market subject to a relatively high degree of competing products such as coffee, soft drinks, etc., tea has retained a high degree of consumer loyalty. India is far and away the largest consumer, accounting for 600,000 tonnes in 1995 – about 75 per cent of its own production. Offtake here has grown by 100,000 tonnes this decade alone and has sometimes restricted exports, causing price spikes like that seen in the early eighties. Despite that, India's per capita consumption is still at a very low 0.7kg per annum compared with over 2.5kg in the UK, suggesting vast room for further growth as economic growth boosts consumer spending power. India's production stagnated in the first half of the 1990s due to declining profitability and tangled state taxation laws. Reforms that will offer more grower incentives will be required to prevent the balance tightening further in the next decade.

For many years, the largest importing market for tea was the UK, consuming as much as 208,000 tonnes a year in the early 1970s. Imports have since dropped back to around 150,000 tonnes, to a large extent due to the rising use of tea bags which require a lower volume of tea leaves to achieve the same strength as traditional pot-brewed tea.

The rising international consumption of tea in bag form has also tended to shift more demand into the lower varieties and cheaper qualities of tea leaves/dusts whose price tends to fluctuate in recent years at a discount of 40/50p per kg under medium qualities.

As the UK has consumed less, it has been overtaken by Pakistan as the main importer. Pakistan's offtake has risen from around 60,000 to between 110–120,000 tonnes in the same period.

Another huge market for tea historically has been the former Soviet Union, consuming over 200,000 tonnes at one time but cutting offtake back to under 80,000 in the early 1990s as consumer spending power was reduced by the country's economic troubles. The FSU's own production of tea was also cut sharply after fall-out from the Chernobyl nuclear disaster polluted large areas of its plantations in Georgia.

The USA is also an important tea consumer and demand there has risen steadily from around 70,000 tonnes in the late 1970s to a record 96,000 in 1994. Other large customers include a number of Middle East markets including Egypt, Iran, Morocco, Iraq and Syria.

China is also one of the largest consumers of tea, producing around 400,000 tonnes of black and green teas per annum. The bulk of green tea is consumed internally but some black and green teas are also exported.

Other important producers include Sri Lanka, which has emerged as the largest exporting country since Indian domestic consumption reduced the surplus there. Sri Lankan output has levelled off in recent years around the 240,000 level and a higher figure may be needed in coming years to replace more exports lost from India. With a privatization programme offering greater efficiencies, foreign investment is starting to return to this country and could help boost exports.

The East African countries have been more successful in raising their production in recent years in response to the growing world market (most production in this region is exported). Kenya leads the East African producers and its productivity is starting to respond to renewed investment in recent years with output growing from under 200,000 tonnes to an estimated 240,000. In the mid-1970s, production was under 90,000 tonnes.

World demand for tea is expected to continue to grow as more developing countries can afford to raise their per capita offtake consumption.

Main bodies in the tea trade include the International Tea Brokers Association which meets weekly in London for auctions and publishes the prices obtained. Over the last two decades the world market has increasingly looked to origin and other auction centres for market guidance. In India, these are held in Calcutta, Gauhati, Siliguri, Cochin, Coimbatore and Coonoor; in Bangladesh at Chittagong; in Sri Lanka in Colombo. Auctions are also held in Indonesia (Djakarta); Kenya in Mombasa and Malawi in Limbe.

The International Tea Committee (ITC) is the main disseminator of market data. Prior to the collapse of trade support for international agreements, the ITC oversaw the export quota system administered by the International Tea Agreement. Tea producers created a trade association in 1995 to exchange information. It is not yet clear whether will develop into co-operation on trade policy.

Further information

Food and Agriculture Organisation of the United Nations
Viale delle Terme di Caracalla
00100 Rome
Italy
Tel: +39 6 522 51
Fax: +39 6 522 53152

International Tea Committee Ltd
Sir John Lyon House
5 High Timber Street
London EC4V 3NH
UK
Tel: +44 171 248 4672
Fax: +44 171 329 6955

Tea Brokers' Association of London
Sir John Lyon House
5 High Timber Street
London EC4V 3LU
UK
Tel: +44 171 236 3368
Fax: +44 171 248 3011

Tea Council
5 High Timber Street
London EC4V 3NJ
UK
Tel: +44 171 248 1024
Fax: +44 171 329 4568

Table 1 Tea world production

('000 tonnes)	*1992*	*1993*	*1994*	*1995*
India	704	757	720	720
China	580	621	600	600
Sri Lanka	179	232	242	242
Indonesia	163	169	169	169
Turkey	144	117	134	135
Japan	92	92	86	86
Iran	55	57	75	78
Georgia	50	77	75	74
Bangladesh	46	49	51	51
Malaysia	6	6	6	6
Azerbaijan	7	4	4	4
Russia	2	2	2	2
Total Asia	**2015**	**2145**	**2129**	**2137**
Kenya	188	211	207	230
Malawi	28	39	42	39
Tanzania	18	21	22	22
Uganda	10	12	13	25
Mauritius	6	6	5	5
Rwanda	13	10	5	5
Burundi	6	6	4	4
Cameroon	4	3	3	3
Zaire	3	3	3	3
Mozambique	1	1	1	1
Ethiopia	1	1	1	1
Total Africa	**298**	**340**	**333**	**356**
Argentina	43	55	55	55
Brazil	10	10	10	10
Bolivia	3	3	3	3
Ecuador	2	2	2	2
Peru	2	2	2	2
Total LATAM	**59**	**71**	**71**	**71**
Oceania	9	9	9	9
Papua/NG	9	9	9	9
World	**2439**	**2648**	**2624**	**2653**

Source: FAO

Table 2 Leading tea consumers

('000 tonnes)	*1992*	*1993*	*1994*	*1995*
India	540	560	580	605
UK	147	158	149	140
Pakistan	119	125	107	115
FSU	76	192	127	150
USA	91	85	96	85
World	**1628**	**1753**	**1701**	**1735**

Source: FAO

Figure 1 Tea: monthly average prices

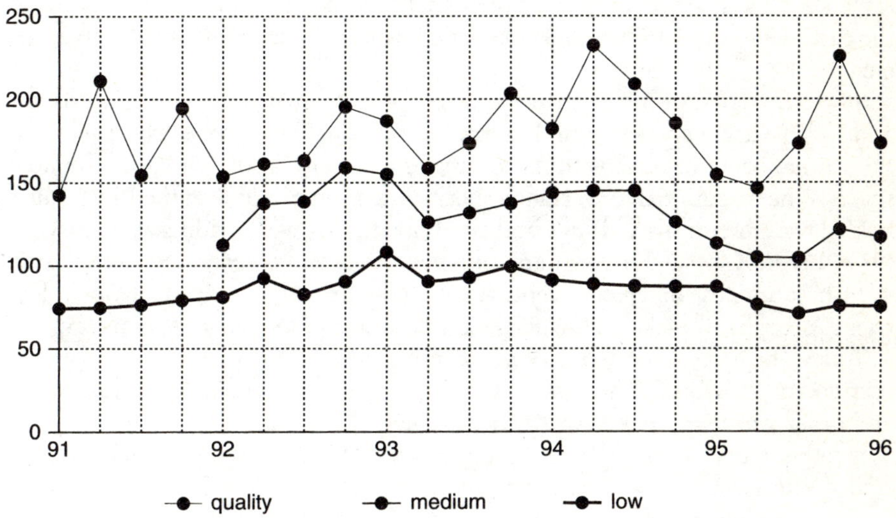

Wool

Robin Stainer

What the wool market does today, especially if natural rubber is doing the same, the rest of the commodity world will copy tomorrow. At least this is the old adage, which owes its origins to the fact that the fibre can be seen as typical of the sector generally by straddling the divide between agricultural and industrial raw materials. The big jump in its price that preceded the commodity booms of the early 1950s and 1970s undoubtedly consolidated its reputation as a barometer.

Since the dawn of history, wool's virtues – its hygroscopic, wrinkle resistant and long-wearing properties and its low heat conductivity – have been esteemed. Babylonia, some historians think, means 'the land of wool', while the humble sheep is the first animal to warrant a specific mention by name in the Bible. Pliny lauded the fibre in his writings and the Phoenicians were trading it many centuries before Christ's birth. International commerce, however, did not take off in earnest until the nineteenth century, when the British developed a wool industry in Australia to make its financially burdensome colony pay its own way.

Today the two basic wool types entering international trade channels are merino and crossbred. The former, which is produced in Australia, South Africa and other warm and dry parts of the Southern Hemisphere, is the finer and is, as its other name – 'apparel' wool – suggests used for clothing. It is the main type traded internationally and sells at a premium.

The principal markets for the coarser crossbred wool, which comes from wetter, cooler regions, such as New Zealand and Europe, are carpets, soft furnishings and blankets. Unlike the merino sheep, which are bred principally for their fleece, the crossbreds are usually just as valuable to farmers for their meat.

Wool production responds slowly to price changes, with climate and the state of the pastureland the key immediate determinants of the fleece yield per sheep, the basic level of which has been boosted over the years by selective breeding. Sheep farming faces competition in some areas from cereals (Australia) and cattle (New Zealand and South America).

Australia, New Zealand, South Africa, Uruguay, Argentina and the UK account for about 50 per cent of world wool production, but nearer 80 per cent of all exports. Some 50 to 60 per cent of the world wool clip is traded internationally and about half of this in its basic greasy (i.e. uncleaned) state.

In recent years the production trend has been downward, underlined by the 12 per cent fall in world woolled sheep numbers since 1990 to an estimated one billion head in 1995. The decline has been mostly in Australia, where falling profits from wool and drought have been problems. In contrast, sheep numbers and wool production have risen in China – traditionally a big player in the international wool market. As a result, its import needs, which are mostly met by Australia, have fallen and prices along with them.

The market has also been undermined in recent years by the switch by the former Soviet Union from a net importer of wool to a net exporter, partly because of a big fall in military spending on uniforms. A further depressant has been the sale by producing countries of stocks built up before price support measures for growers were abandoned earlier this decade. Wool International, which manages Australia's stockpile, has to make regular disposals no matter what is happening to prices – a policy confirmed by the new government at the end of March 1996. It is expected that Australian stocks, which have already been halved, will be exhausted by the end of the century.

The trend in wool consumption follows closely that of the global economy generally. In its core apparel market (which absorbs at least 60 per cent of supply), wool's share of total fibre use has held at around 17 to 18 per cent so far this decade.

Following the expansion that began there in the 1960s fuelled by cheap labour, Asia is today both the main consumer of raw wool and exporter of finished products – mainly to Europe and North America, which were once the dominant wool manufacturing centres. Asia now accounts for at least 40 per cent of world raw wool use (30 per cent ten years ago) and takes about 45 per cent of global imports, with demand growing particularly strongly in Taiwan, Korea and Malaysia.

Most wool traded internationally is first sold by auction in the main exporting countries. Among the leading sales centres are Sydney, Melbourne, Adelaide, Launceston and Fremantle (Australia); Christchurch, Napier and Dunedin (New Zealand); Bradford (UK); and Port Elizabeth (South Africa). The Sydney Futures Exchange has a contract for trading greasy wool, which started in March 1995, while important international trading centres include Osaka (Japan), Roubaix-Tourcoing (Belgium), Bremen (Germany) and London.

The International Wool Secretariat (IWS), which brings together the national bodies promoting and marketing the fibre in the main exporting countries, and the International Wool Textile Organization (IWTO), which links processing and textile agencies in 28 countries, are the key sources of information on all aspects of the wool industry. The IWS is based at Valley Drive, Ilkley, Yorkshire LS29 8PB. The Brussels-based IWTO publishes its regular *International Wool Textile Overview* from 63 Albert Drive, London SW19 6LB. Big players in the wool trade include Chargeurs (France) and Itochu (Japan).

Over the longer term, wool prices are expected to remain relatively stable, which thus indicates a continuing decline in real terms. Output is forecast to rise gradually, helped by some recovery in Australia, but demand may not increase as quickly, although the wool textile industry is working hard to develop new fabrics in an effort to shed the fibre's staid image – a factor limiting growth potential.

Further information

International Wool Textile Organisation
Rue du l'Ouxembourg
19–21 Bte. 13
B–1000 Brussels
Belgium
Tel: +32 2 513 0620
Fax: +32 2 514 0665

International Wool Secretariat
Valley Drive
Ilkley
West Yorkshire OS29 8PB
UK
Tel: +44 1943 601555
Fax: +44 1943 601521

Table 1 World wool production – greasy (Units mkg)

	1980	*1989*	*1990*	*1991*	*1992*	*1993*	*1994*
Afghanistan	23	15	17	17	17	17	15
Algeria	38	46	48	49	49	49	50
Argentina [(a)]	171	164	149	136	121	114	98
Australia[(a)]	709	959	1100	1066	875	869	828
Brazil	31	26	26	27	25	25	18
Bulgaria	35	29	28	23	19	12	15
Chile	20	20	20	20	19	19	19
China	176	237	240	240	238	240	255
France	25	23	23	22	22	22	20
India	35	35	35	35	33	33	33
Iran	34	32	32	32	34	34	32
Iraq	18	17	17	17	18	18	19
Ireland	14	24	26	26	27	29	27
Mongolia	20	19	20	21	21	21	20
Morocco	37	37	37	37	36	35	35
New Zealand[(a)]	357	339	311	305	296	256	284
Pakistan	39	59	63	64	66	67	70
Poland	13	16	15	11	7	5	8
Romania	37	35	33	30	32	34	30
South Africa[(a)]	103	95	97	102	82	78	77
Former USSR	443	479	474	441	401	375	312
Russian Federation	na	na	227	204	179	158	124
Kazakstan	na	na	108	104	97	95	79
Spain	28	37	37	36	36	36	36
Sudan	15	17	18	18	20	20	21
Turkey	80	85	83	77	75	75	75
UK	51	70	72	69	69	69	67
USA	55	48	47	47	45	42	37
Uruguay[(a)]	67	83	94	94	84	88	90
Other	206	239	249	241	235	229	224
TOTAL	2879	3284	3410	3303	3001	2910	2814

Note:
[(a)] Production on a seasonal basis (i.e. 1980 = 1979/80)

Sources: IWTO, IWS

Figure 1 Wool: world production

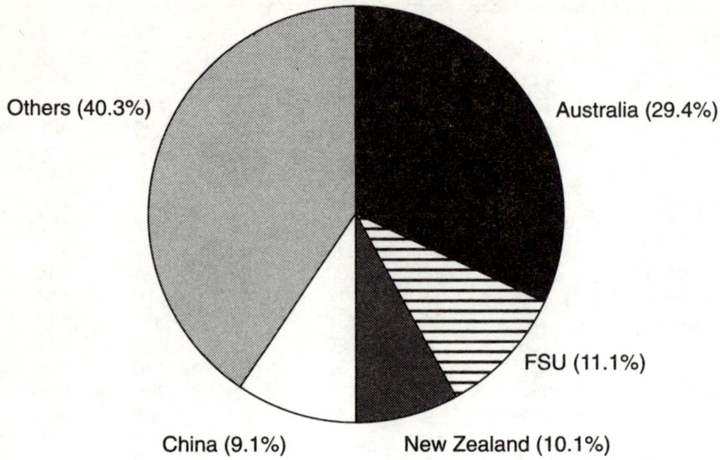

Table 2 Exports of raw wool – actual weight (Units mkg)

	1980	*1990*	*1991*	*1992*	*1993*	*1994*
Afghanistan[(a)]	4.1	3.2	4.5	2.0	2.0	–
Argentina	80.8	55.9	40.8	35.5	45.8	53.7
Australia	555.6	513.2	748.7	705.8	676.1	661.4
Belgium	8.0	9.2	8.3	7.0	7.6	6.6
Brazil	3.2	1.3	5.4	5.2	4.0	4.3
Chile	10.9	6.4	6.0	4.2	4.2	5.6
China[(c)]	3.4	2.7	1.9	5.2	5.6	4.2
Falkland Islands	2.2	2.6	2.6	2.9	2.6	2.6
France	44.3	25.3	30.3	24.8	21.6	24.4
Germany[(b)]	9.2	8.6	11.1	14.6	9.2	10.5
Greece	0.3	2.7	2.5	6.5	7.9	4.9
Hong Kong	2.3	4.0	7.2	21.2	21.7	22.6
Hungary	0.7	2.0	3.2	3.1	3.9	3.7
Iceland	0.3	1.2	0.9	1.2	1.1	1.0
Iraq	1.0	10.1	5.0	5.8	5.0	–
Eire	7.3	11.7	14.1	14.2	16.8	17.6
Italy	3.4	3.9	4.7	5.7	8.5	8.1
Mongolia	17.4	11.0	10.0	8.7	14.5	18.5
Netherlands	5.2	6.0	5.7	3.8	4.7	5.1
New Zealand	273.7	201.5	234.7	214.7	212.7	246.1
Norway	2.2	3.4	3.9	2.7	3.5	3.6
Pakistan[(a)]	3.0	6.7	4.3	5.5	4.8	3.9
South Africa	62.0	49.7	49.1	33.8	29.7	31.4
Former USSR[(c)]	3.6	11.9	7.6	1.4	5.5	69.1
Spain	10.5	9.6	12.2	11.5	12.2	12.3
Syria	5.9	1.8	3.2	4.3	1.5	3.2
Taiwan	3.9	8.9	10.6	13.1	10.6	9.1
UK	17.3	39.6	31.6	34.5	37.8	43.6
Uruguay	41.2	36.9	26.0	24.8	26.1	25.0
Others	12.5	15.6	14.6	20.5	30.4	38.7
TOTAL#	1195	1067	1311	1244	1238	1341

Notes:
[(a)] Fiscal year ending in year shown
[(b)] United Germany after 1990
[(c)] Clean content
Including re-exports

Source: Foreign Trade Statistics

Figure 2 Wool: main exporters

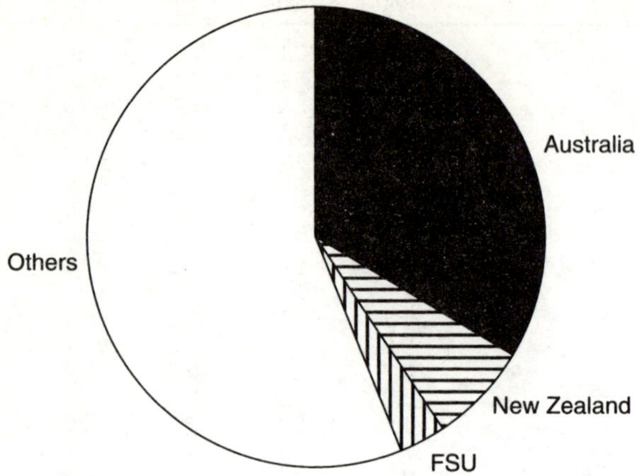

Figure 3 Australian wool prices, seasonal averages

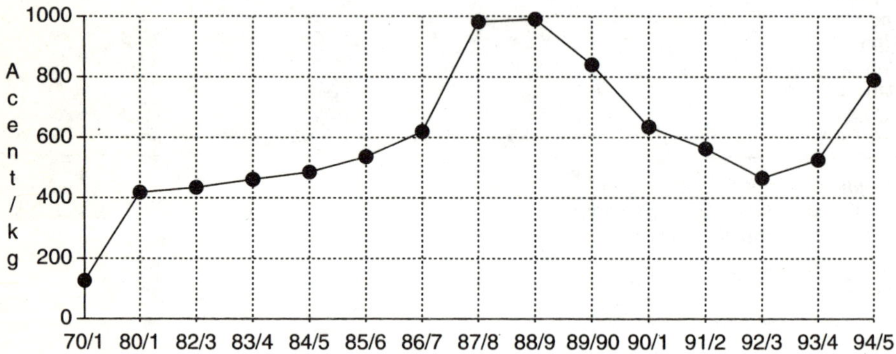

Table 3 Imports of raw wool – actual weight (Units mkg)

	1980	1990	1991	1992	1993	1994
Australia[a]	9.9	9.5	9.6	11.2	11.3	13.9
Austria	5.0	1.9	2.2	2.0	2.2	2.0
Belgium	42.2	54.3	52.3	54.6	37.6	29.3
Brazil	2.4	0.2	0.2	1.7	0.8	0.8
Canada	4.3	1.3	1.0	1.0	1.2	1.6
China[c]	29.1	31.2	101.6	149.2	172.7	201.9
Former Czechoslavakia	26.0	18.0	13.6	7.8	9.3	8.0
Denmark	3.9	3.0	3.2	3.7	3.2	4.2
France	117.2	99.3	127.1	122.0	91.7	113.2
Germany[b]	92.7	77.0	86.5	97.3	82.1	92.0
Greece	10.2	10.0	7.7	7.9	3.2	2.8
Hong Kong	5.0	4.6	7.6	23.7	21.1	25.2
India[a]	13.1	20.4	29.1	27.7	38.5	57.0
Iran[a]	10.5	4.0	4.1	6.9	5.5	5.4
Italy	117.7	118.8	137.5	144.5	121.6	147.6
Japan	175.6	142.7	152.9	145.7	109.1	108.1
Korea, South[c]	22.8	34.3	36.6	38.4	35.1	40.3
Malaysia	5.4	12.5	12.9	11.4	16.5	18.0
Nepal[c]	0.2	7.9	13.9	15.4	19.9	9.3
Netherlands	7.5	4.8	5.5	2.8	2.6	4.0
Pakistan[a]	3.2	8.0	8.3	9.3	2.8	2.0
Portugal	7.6	8.3	9.0	8.9	6.1	9.7
Former USSR[c]	124.2	52.4	49.0	2.7	5.5	3.3
Spain	15.6	12.6	20.9	20.9	14.1	20.4
Taiwan	27.8	31.2	61.2	53.4	55.2	50.2
Turkey	5.7	31.4	31.0	32.3	42.2	24.5
UK	95.5	87.8	92.6	102.2	95.6	127.2
USA[c]	33.0	32.5	39.2	40.5	45.5	41.6
Former Yugoslavia	23.4	9.4	7.8	10.0	1.1	0.3
Others	111.6	63.4	59.8	55.5	55.2	87.5
TOTAL	1148	993	1184	1211	1108	1251

Note:
(a) Fiscal year ending in year shown
(b) United Germany after 1990
(c) Clean content

Source: Foreign Trade Statistics

Part 3: World Directory of Commodity Markets

AUSTRALIA

SYDNEY

Sydney Futures Exchange

30–32 Grosvenor Street, Sydney, New South Wales 2000
Tel: +61 2 256 0555
Fax: +61 2 256 0666
Web site: http://www.sfe.com.au/
Chairman: Bruce Hudson
Chief Executive Officer: Les Hosking
Divisional Manager, Marketing: David Chin

Hours of trading (Sydney time):	*Floor*	*Sycom*
All Ordinaries Share Price Index*:	09.50–12.30 and 14.00–16.10	16.40–06.00
Share Futures: ANZ, BHP, CRA, FBG, MIM, NAB, NCP, PDP, WBC, WMC:	09.50–12.30 and 14.00–16.10	16.40–06.00
90-day bank accepted bills*:	08.30–12.30 and 14.00–16.30	16.40–06.00
3- and 10-year Commonwealth Treasury bonds*:	08.30–12.30 and 14.00–16.30	16.40–06.00
Wool Futures:	10.30–12.30 and 14.00–16.00	16.40–06.00

* Trading hours also apply to options in these contracts

Contract details:
Commodities: All Ordinaries Share Price Index, 90-day bank accepted bills, 3- and 10-year Commonwealth Treasury bonds, wool, Individual Share Futures ANZ, BHP, CRA, FBG, MIM, NAB, NCP, PDP, WBC, WMC

Trading units (minimum lot size):

All Ordinaries Share Price Index	– a sum of money equal to 25 times the Australian Stock Exchange's All Ordinaries Price Index expressed as Australian dollars
90-day bank accepted bills	– A$1,000,000* face value of 90-day bank accepted bills of exchange
3- and 10-year Commonwealth Treasury bonds	– A$100,000 face value, 12% pa

		coupon and a term to maturity of three and ten years – no tax rebate allowed
Wool	–	2,500 kg of merino combing fleece
ANZ Bank (ANZ)	–	1,000 ANZ Bank shares
Broken Hill Proprietary Co (BHP)	–	1,000 BHP shares
CRA Ltd (CRA)	–	1,075 CRA Ltd shares
Fosters Brewing Group (FBG)	–	600 FBG shares
MIM Holdings (MIM)	–	1,000 MIM shares
National Australia Bank (NAB)	–	1,000 NAB shares
News Corporation (NCP)	–	1,000 NCP shares
Pacific Dunlop (PDP)	–	1,000 PDP shares
Western Mining Corporation (WMC)	–	1,000 WMC shares
Westpac Banking Corporation (WBC)	–	1,000 WBC shares

* 90-day bank bill doubled in size from $500,000 to $1,000,000 on 28 April 1995.

Initial margin†:

Share Price Index	–	$2,000
90-day bank bills	–	$800
10-year Commonwealth Treasury bonds	–	$2,800
3-year Commonwealth Treasury bonds	–	$1,200
Wool	–	$1,000
ANZ	–	$200
BHP	–	$750
CRA	–	$900
FBG	–	$50
MIM	–	$150
NAB	–	$400
NCP	–	$450
WBC	–	$200
WMC	–	$400

† Initial margin rates as at 13 March 1995. These are determined by SFECH and are subject to change.

Delivery months:
Share Price Index – March, June, September, December up to six quarter months ahead
90-day bank bills – March, June, September, December up to twelve quarter months ahead
10-year Commonwealth Treasury bonds – March, June, September, December up to two quarter months ahead
3-year Commonwealth Treasury bonds – March, June, September, December up to two quarter months ahead
Wool – February, April, June, August, October, December up to 18 months ahead
ANZ – January, April, July, October up to two quarter months ahead
BHP – March, June, September, December up to two quarter months ahead
CRA – March, June, September, December up to two quarter months ahead
FBG – January, April, July, October up to two quarter months ahead

MIM – January, April, July, October up to two quarter months ahead
NAB – January, April, July, October up to two quarter months ahead
NCP – February, May, August, November up to two quarter months ahead
PDP – February, May, August, November up to two quarter months ahead
WBC – January, April, July, October up to two quarter months ahead
WMC – March, June, September, December up to two quarter months ahead

Termination of trading:
Share Price Index – the last business day of the contract month. On this day, trading terminates at 16.10 or such other time as determined by the Board of SFE
90-day bank bills – 12.00 noon on the business day immediately prior to settlement day
10-year Commonwealth Treasury bonds – the 15th day of the contract month (or the next succeeding business day where the 15th day is not a business day). Trading ceases at 12.00
3-year Commonwealth Treasury bonds – the 15th day of the contract month (or the next succeeding business day where the 15th day is not a business day). Trading ceases at 12.00
Wool – the last day of trading shall be the third Thursday of the contract month. Trading ceases at 12.00 noon
ANZ, BHP, CRA, FBG, MIM, NAB, NCP, PDP, WBC, WMC – trading ceases at 16.10 on the Thursday immediately preceding the last Friday of the settlement month (refer to by-laws). (Timed to coincide with equity options expiry at AOM)

Settlement day:
Share Price Index – the second business day following the last permitted day of trading
90-day bank bills – the second Friday of the delivery month
10-year Commonwealth Treasury bonds – the business day following the last permitted day of trading
3-year Commonwealth Treasury bonds – the business day following the last permitted day of trading
ANZ, BHP, CRA, FBG, MIM, NAB, NCP, PDP, WBC, WMC – the business day following the last day of trading

Volume of trade:

	1993	*1994*
All Ordinary Share Price Index	980,866	2,552,546
90-day bank bills	6,415,394	9,369,008
10-year Commonwealth Treasury bonds	4,781,905	6,814,733
3-year Commonwealth Treasury bonds	6,939,811	9,709,791
Wool	3,271	4,833
BHP	0	17,475
MIM	0	7,909
NAB	0	9,282
NCP	0	20,096
WBC	0	1,874
WMC	0	5,859

Date of establishment of contracts:

All Ordinaries Share Price Index Futures	– 16 February 1983
BHP	– 16 May 1994
MIM	– 26 September 1994
NAB	– 16 May 1994
NCP	– 16 May 1994
WBC	– 26 September 1994
WMC	– 26 September 1994
90-day bank accepted bills	– 17 October 1979
3-year Commonwealth Treasury bonds	– 17 May 1988
10-year Commonwealth Treasury bonds	– 5 December 1984
Wool	– 22 July 1986

Clearing house: Sydney Futures Exchange Clearing House (SFECH) – a wholly-owned subsidiary of the Sydney Futures Exchange (SFE).

Membership: There are three classes of membership: Floor, Associate and Local.

Floor Membership
Floor members have direct access to the trading floor, have full voting rights, are eligible to accept and transact client orders for all SFE contracts if licensed. They are eligible to become Clearing Members.

Associate Membership
There are three classes of Associate Membership (i) Full: full members are eligible to become clearing members, have direct association with the Exchange, are eligible to accept and transfer client orders if licensed, and do not have access to the trading floor; (ii) Introducing broker: these members are eligible to advise clients and accept client orders (but not to hold client funds). They have no access to the trading floor; (iii) Market members: market members have direct association with the Exchange, are eligible to become clearing members and have no access to the trading floor.

Local Members
Local members have direct access to the trading floor, can transact 'give up' business for floor members and have unrestricted access to trade all SFE contracts.

Membership of other organizations: Futures Industry Association; Australian Financial Markets Association; Asia Pacific Managed Futures Association.

Further information: SFE/NYMEX link – SFE now trades some NYMEX energy products on SYCOM/ACCESS link, including light, sweet crude oil, heating oil, unleaded gasoline, natural gas and propane and soon to link with COMEX and trade gold, silver and copper.

SFE now own NZFOE(New Zealand Futures and Options Exchange) and all NZFOE products are traded on SYCOM.

BRAZIL

RIO DE JANEIRO

Bolsa Brasileira de Futuros (Brazilian Futures Exchange)

6th Floor, 20 Pracça XV de Novembro, Rio de Janeiro 20010–010
Tel: +55 21 271 1086
Fax: +55 21 224 5718
CEO: Orestes Mauro Silingardi
Market Relations: Helio Sirimarco
President: Alvaro Bandeira
Operations Manager: Rubem Doherty

Hours of trading (Rio de Janeiro time):

SWAPS, futures and options	–	10.00–16.45
Stock price index future returns index	–	10.00–16.00
Real/Swiss franc exchange rate options	–	11.00–16.30

Contract details:

Commodities: SWAPS interbank deposits, treasury notes, Central Bank bonus, US dollar, Deutschmark, Japanese yen, gold, Rio de Janeiro Stock Exchange indexes; futures – average interest rate on interbank deposits, US dollar denominated arabica coffee, Real/US dollar exchange rate, Real/Deutschmark exchange rate, Real/Japanese yen exchange rate, Real/Swiss franc future exchange rate, long-term interest rate, stock price future returns index; options – average interest rate on interbank deposits index, US dollar denominated arabica coffee, Real/US dollar exchange rate, Real/Deutschmark exchange rate, Real/Japanese yen exchange rate, Real/Swiss franc future exchange rate

Trading units (minimum lot size):

SWAPS interbank deposits, treasury notes, Central Bank bonus, US dollar, Deutschmark, Japanese yen, gold, Rio de Janeiro Stock Exchange indexes	–	R$1,000,000 minimum*

* R$1.00 = US$1.00

Futures

Average interest rate on interbank deposit	–	R$50,000
US dollar denominated arabica coffee	–	100 bags of 60 kg
Real/US dollar exchange rate	–	US$10,000

Real/Deutschmark exchange rate – DM$10,000
Real/Japanese yen exchange rate – ¥$1,000,000
Real/Swiss franc future exchange rate – SF$10,000
Long-term interest rate – R$10,000
Stock price future returns index – the index multiplied by the point value in Reals

Options

Average interest rate on interbank deposits – index option – R$0.50 times the index value†
US dollar denominated arabica coffee option – 100 bags of 60 kg
Real/US dollar exchange rate option – US$10,000
Real/Deutschmark exchange rate option – DM$10,000
Real/Japanese yen exchange rate option – ¥$1,000,000
Real/Swiss franc future exchange rate option – SF$10,000

Trading limits:

Average interest rate on interbank deposits – R$0.50
US dollar denominated arabica coffee – 100 times the Real/US dollar exchange rate
Real/US dollar exchange rate – R$0.010
Real/Deutschmark exchange rate – R$0.00010
Real/Japanese yen exchange rate – R$0.0000010
Real/Swiss franc future exchange rate – R$0.00010
Long-term interest rate – R$0.10
Stock price future returns index – R$ 0.01 per index point

Average interest rate on interbank deposits index option – R$0.50
US dollar denominated arabica coffee option – 100 times the Real/US dollar exchange rate
Real/US dollar exchange rate option – R$0.010
Real/Deutschmark exchange rate option – R$0.00010
Real/Japanese yen exchange rate option – R$0.0000010
Real/Swiss franc future exchange rate option – R$0.00010

Trading months:

Average interest rate on interbank deposits, Real/US dollar exchange rate, Real/Deutschmark exchange rate, Real/Japanese yen exchange rate, Real/Swiss franc future exchange rate – all months

US dollar denominated arabica coffee	– March, May, July, September, December
Long-term interest rate	– December, March, June, September
Stock price future returns index	– all months‡
Average interest rate on interbank deposits index option, Real/US dollar exchange rate option, Real/Deutschmark exchange rate option, Real/Japanese yen exchange rate option, Real/Swiss franc future exchange rate option	– all months
US dollar denominated arabica coffee option	– February, April, June, August, November

† Index value at 29 July 1996 equalled 24,208.08 points

‡ Expiration date: every Wednesday

SÃO PAULO

Bolsa de Mercadorias & Futuros (BM&F)

48, Praça Antonio Prado, São Paulo, Brazil
Tel: +55 11 232 5454
Fax: +55 11 232 7565
Telex: 26928
Chief Executive Officer: Dorival Rodrigues Alves
Clearing & Settlement Director: Edemir Pinto
Market Development Director: Marco Aurelio Teixeira
Trading Director: Paulo Roberto Garbato

Hours of trading (local time):

Gold	– 09.45-16.00
Gold (US dollar denominated)	– 09.45-16.00
1-day interbank deposits	– 09.45-13.00 and 15.00-16.30
30-day interbank deposits	– 09.45-13.00 and 15.00-16.30
C-bond	– 09.45-16.30
Bovespa Stock Index	– 10.00-16.00
Feeder cattle	– 09.45-10.30
Live cattle	– 09.45-10.30
Cotton	– 11.00-11.45
Commercial US dollar	– 09.45-16.30
Floating US dollar	– 09.45-16.30
Arabica coffee	– 10.00-15.30
Robusta coffee	– 10.00-15.30
Soybeans	– 11.30-15.00

Crystal sugar	– 11.15-12.00
Gold options	– 09.45-16.00
1-day interbank deposits options	– 09.45-13.00 and 15.00-16.30
Bovespa Stock Index options	– 10.00-16.00
Live cattle options	– 09.45-10.30
Commercial US dollar options	– 09.45-16.30
Floating US dollar options	– 09.45-16.30
Arabica coffee options	– 10.00-15.30

Contract details:

Commodities: futures – gold, gold (US dollar-denominated), 1-day interbank deposits, 30-day interbank deposits, C-bond, Bovespa Stock Index, feeder cattle, live cattle, cotton, commercial US dollar, floating US dollar, arabica coffee, robusta coffee, soybeans, crystal sugar; options – gold, 1-day interbank deposits, Bovespa Stock Index, live cattle, commercial US dollar, floating US dollar, arabica coffee

Trading currency and unit (manner of price quotation):

Gold	– R$ per gram
Gold (US dollar denominated)	– points per gram (1 point = US$1)
1-day interbank deposits	– points per face value (1 point = R$0.50)
30-day interbank deposits	– points per face value (1 point = R$0.50)
C-bond	– points per US$100 of face value
Bovespa Stock Index	– points
Feeder cattle	– points per feeder steer
Live cattle	– points per net arroba
Cotton	– points per pound
Commercial US dollar	– R$ per US$1,000
Floating US dollar	– R$ per US$1,000
Arabica coffee	– points per bag
Robusta coffee	– points per bag
Soybeans	– points per 60 kg
Crystal sugar	– points per bag
Gold options	– R$ per gram
1-day interbank deposits options	– points per face value (1 point = R$0.50)
Bovespa Stock Index options	– points
Live cattle options	– points per net arroba
Commercial US dollar options	– R$ per US$1,000
Floating US dollar options	– R$ per US$1,000
Arabica coffee options	– points per bag

Trading unit (minimum lot size):

Gold	– 250 grams
Gold (US dollar denominated)	– 1 kg
1-day interbank deposits	– R$50,000*
30-day interbank deposits	– R$50,000*
C-bond	– US$100,000 of face value
Bovespa Stock Index	– index times R$0.30
Feeder cattle	– 33 feeder steers
Live cattle	– 330 net arrobas
Cotton	– 28,108.65 pounds

Commercial US dollar	– US$50,000
Floating US dollar	– US$50,000
Arabica coffee	– 100 60 kg bags
Robusta coffee	– 100 60 kg bags
Soybeans	– 27 metric tons
Crystal sugar	– 270 50 kg bags
Gold options	– 250 grams
1-day interbank deposits options	– R$50,000*
Bovespa Stock Index options	– index times R$0.30
Live cattle options	– 330 net arrobas
Commercial US dollar options	– US$50,000
Floating US dollar options	– minimum of Us$20,000
Arabica coffee options	– 100 60 kg bags

* As of 1 February 1997, contract size of US$100,000 and 1 point = R$1.00

Trading limits:
Minimum price fluctuation:

Gold	– R$0.001 per gram
Gold (US dollar denominated)	– 0.001 of a point/gram
1-day interbank deposits	– R$0.05
30-day interbank deposits	– R$0.05
C-bond	– US$31.25
Bovespa Stock Index	– 50 points
Feeder cattle	– 0.10 of a point/feeder steer
Live cattle	– 0.01 of a point/arroba
Cotton	– 0.01 of a point/pound
Commercial US dollar	– R$0.001/US$1,000
Floating US dollar	– R$0.001/US$1,000
Arabica coffee	– 0.01 of a point/bag
Robusta coffee	– 0.05 of a point/bag
Soybeans	– 0.01 of a point/60 kg
Crystal sugar	– 0.01 of a point/bag
Gold options	– R$0.001 per gram
1-day interbank deposits options	– R$0.005
Bovespa Stock Index options	– 1 index point
Live cattle options	– 0.01 of a point/arroba
Commercial US dollar options	– R$0.001/US$1,000
Floating US dollar options	– R$0.001/US$1,000
Arabica coffee options	– 0.01 of a point/bag

Maximum daily price movement:

Gold	– 5% on third delivery month
Gold (US dollar denominated)	– 5% on third delivery month
1-day interbank deposits	– none
30-day interbank deposits	– 5% on first contract month
C-bond	– 5% on first contract month
Bovespa Stock Index	– none
Feeder cattle	– 5 points/feeder steer for all months, except

spot month
Live cattle – 1 point/arroba for all months, except spot month
Cotton – 0.03 of a point/pound for all months, except spot month
Commercial US dollar – 5% on the traded month, except the first two
Floating US dollar – 5% on the traded month, except the first two
Arabica coffee – 8 points/bag for all months, except spot and first month
Robusta coffee – 3 points/bag for all months, except spot month
Soybeans – 0.50 of a point/60 kg for all months, except spot month
Crystal sugar – 1 point/bag for all months, except for the spot month

Quality:

Gold – gold in bars, cast by a refiner and kept in a depository institution, both formally accredited by the BM&F
Feeder cattle – Nellore crossbreeding
Live cattle – ready for slaughter
Cotton – Brazilian raw cotton basis type 6, 30/32mm, produced in the states of São Paulo and Parana
Arabica coffee – Brazilian 'coffee arabica', grade 6 or better, hard cup or better
Robusta coffee – Brazilian 'robusta conillion' coffee, grade 7 or better
Soybeans – in bulk, export type, in accordance with CONCEX standard
Crystal sugar – minimum 99.70° polarization, maximum 0.10% moisture, maximum 0.07% ashes

Deliverable tolerances:

Gold – refined gold cast in bars of 250 or 1,000 grams, assaying not less than 0.999 fineness, or of 100 or 400 troy ounces, assaying not less than 0.995 fineness
Feeder cattle – minimum weight of 140 kg per feeder steer
Live cattle – 330 net arrobas plus or minus 5%; individual animal weight between minimum 450 kg and maximum 550 kg; maximum 50 months old
Cotton – 850 net arrobas plus or minus 10%; individual bales between 170 kg to 220 kg

Arabica coffee	–	100 60 net kg bags plus or minus 0.5%
Robusta coffee	–	100 60 net kg bags plus or minus 1%
Soybeans	–	maximum 14% moisture, foreign matter basis 1%, maximum 2%, damaged beans maximum 8%; maximum 10% green beans and 30% broken beans
Crystal sugar	–	270 50 kg bags plus or minus 0.5%

Delivery points:

Gold	–	accredited depository institutions
Feeder cattle	–	Aracatuba, Barretos, and Presidente Prudente
Live cattle	–	Aracatuba
Cotton	–	São Paulo
Arabica coffee	–	São Paulo
Robusta coffee	–	Vitoria, Rio de Janeiro, Santos, and Paranagua
Soybeans	–	Paranagua and Rio Grande
Crystal sugar	–	São Paulo

Contract months:

1-day interbank deposits	–	all months
30-day interbank deposits	–	all months
C-bond	–	all months
Bovespa Stock Index	–	even months
Commercial US dollar	–	all months
Floating US dollar	–	all months
1-day interbank deposits options	–	all months
Bovespa Stock Index options	–	even months
Commercial US dollar options	–	all months
Floating US dollar options	–	all months

Delivery months:

Gold	–	all months
Gold (US dollar denominated)	–	all months
Feeder cattle	–	all months
Live cattle	–	February, April, June, August, September, October, November, December
Cotton	–	March, April, May, July, October, December
Arabica coffee	–	March, May, July, September, December
Robusta coffee	–	January, March, May, July, September, November
Soybeans	–	February, March, May, July, September, November
Crystal sugar	–	March, May, August, October, December
Gold options	–	odd months
Live cattle options	–	February, April, June, August, September, October, November, December

Arabica coffee options	– February, April, June, August, November

Termination of trading:

Gold	– last business day of previous month
Gold (US dollar denominated)	– last business day of delivery month
1-day interbank deposits	– last business day of previous contract month
30-day interbank deposits	– first business day of contract month
C-bond	– business day preceding business month
Bovespa Stock Index	– Wednesday closest to the 15th calendar day of contract month
Feeder cattle	– sixth-to-last business day of delivery month
Live cattle	– last business day of delivery month
Cotton	– sixth-to-last business day of delivery month
Commercial US dollar	– last business day of previous month
Floating US dollar	– last business day of previous month
Arabica coffee	– sixth-to-last business day of delivery month
Robusta coffee	– sixth-to-last business day of delivery month
Soybeans	– last business day of delivery month
Crystal sugar	– last business day of month preceding delivery month
Gold options	– third Friday of delivery month or previous business day
1-day interbank deposits options	– first business day of the month preceding underlying futures contract month
Bovespa Stock Index options	– business day following exercise
Live cattle options	– 15th calendar day of contract month or following business day
Commercial US dollar options	– last business day of previous month
Floating US dollar options	– last business day of previous month
Arabica coffee options	– first Friday of contract month or following business day

Settlement date:

Gold	– business day following last trading day
Gold (US dollar denominated)	– business day following last trading day
1-day interbank deposits	– second business day following last trading day
30-day interbank deposits	– second business day following last trading day
C-bond	– first business day of contract month
Bovespa Stock Index	– business day following last trading day
Feeder cattle	– up until the fifth business day following notice day
Live cattle	– between first and seventh business days following last trading day
Cotton	– up until the third business day following notice day
Commercial US dollar	– business day following last trading day
Floating US dollar	– business day following last trading day

Arabica coffee	–	third business day following notice day
Robusta coffee	–	third business day following notice day
Soybeans	–	between sixth business day preceding last trading day and the business day following last trading day
Crystal sugar	–	between the first and fifth business days following delivery notice day
Gold options	–	business day following exercise
1-day interbank deposits options	–	business day following exercise
Bovespa Stock Index options	–	business day following exercise
Live cattle options	–	business day following exercise
Commercial US dollar options	–	business day following exercise
Floating US dollar options	–	business day following exercise
Arabica coffee options	–	business day following exercise

Commission rates and margins:

Commission:	*Regular (%)*	*Day trade (%)*
Gold (250 grams)	0.25	0.10
Gold (1 kg)	0.20	0.07
1-day interbank deposits	3.00	1.50
30-day interbank deposits	3.00	1.50
C-bond	0.20	0.10
Feeder cattle	0.30	0.07
Live cattle	–	–
Cotton	0.30	0.07
Commercial US dollar	0.12	0.06
Floating US dollar	0.12	0.06
Stock index	0.25	0.15
Arabica coffee	0.30	0.07
Robusta coffee	0.30	0.07
Soybeans	0.30	0.07
Crystal sugar	0.30	0.07
Gold options (250 grams)	0.40	0.20
1-day interest rate options	1.50	0.75
Live cattle options	50% of the BCR for the live cattle futures	
Commercial US dollar options	0.40	0.20
Floating US dollar options	0.40	0.20
Arabica coffee options	50% of the BCR for the arabica coffee futures	

Margins:	*Contract month*	*Common (R$)*	*Hedger*
Gold (250 grams)	All	40.00	32.00
Gold (1 kg)	All	160.00	128.00
1-day interest rate	Jul	25.00	20.00
	Aug	120.00	96.00
	Sept	265.00	2,120.00
	Oct	450.00	360.00

Margins:	*Contract month*	*Common (R$)*	*Hedger*
	Nov	690.00	552.00
	Dec	840.00	672.00
	Jan '97	1,130.00	904.00
	As of Feb	3,000.00	2,400.00
30-day interest rate	Jul to Jan '97	750.00	600.00
	As of Feb '97	1,500.00	1,200.00
C-bond	Jul & Aug	3,600.00	2,880.00
	As of Sept	4,000.00	3,200.00
Feeder cattle	All	500.00	400.00
Live cattle	Aug	350.00	280.00
	As of Sept	400.00	320.00
Cotton	All	1,500.00	1,200.00
Commercial US dollar	Jul	500.00	400.00
	Aug	1,000.00	800.00
	Sept & Oct	1,250.00	1,000.00
	As of Nov	5,000.00	4,000.00
Floating US dollar	Jul	500.00	400.00
	Aug	1,000.00	800.00
	Sept & Oct	1,250.00	1,000.00
	As of Nov	5,000.00	4,000.00
Stock index	All	1,200.00	960.00
Arabica coffee	All	1,100.00	880.00
Robusta coffee	All	2,000.00	1,600.00
Soybeans	All	450.00	360.00
Crystal sugar	All	200.00	160.00

Gold options (250 grams)	Two times the average premium or 15% of the cash price, whichever is the larger
1-day interest rate options	Two times the average premium or the difference between the margins for the second and first months of the 1-day interest rate futures, whichever is the larger
Live cattle options	Two times the average premium or the margin for live cattle futures contract, whichever is the larger
Commercial US dollar options	Two times the average premium or the margin basis, whichever is the larger
Floating US dollar options	Two times the average premium or the margin basis, whichever is the larger
Arabica coffee options	Two times the average premium or the margin for the arabica coffee futures contract, whichever is the larger

Volume of trade:

	1993	*1994*	*1995*
Gold spot (250 grams)	5,160,851	2,208,361	441,336
calls (250 grams)	6,641,360	3,455,190	915,032
exercise	826,918	941,690	494,287
puts	2,764,803	3,317,690	967,470

	1993	*1994*	*1995*
exercise	574,452	1,304,984	630,505
futures	11,720	134,240	607,288
Total gold	15, 980,464	11,362,169	4,055,918
Comm USD futures	7,456,986	39,124,825	73,930,297
calls	345,781	331,003	2,898,339
exercise	49,990	45,627	253,151
puts	13,630	256,908	435,381
exercise	200	35,076	145,805
Floating USD futures	151,645	106,919	311,070
calls	–	500	4,300
exercise	–	–	4,000
puts	–	500	–
exercise	–	–	500
Total foreign currencies	8,018,232	39,901,358	77,982,843
Bovespa futures	10,374,860	10,583,594	15,304,666
calls	–	12,445	72,769
exercise	–	–	1,515
puts	–	810	1,700
exercise	–	–	250
Total stock index	10,374,860	10,596,849	15,380,900
Interbank deposit futures	18,996,117	28,474,764	35,152,630
calls	–	320	18,450
exercise	–	120	–
puts	–	–	23,750
Inflation index futures	258,352	75,513	–
Central Bank bonds forward	–	10	–
Total interest rates	19,254,469	28,550,727	35,194,830
Crystal sugar futures	–	–	4,301
Live cattle futures	7,438	5,687	39,174
calls	–	44,114	17,120
exercise	–	–	19,252
puts	–	44,314	17,120
exercise	–	–	19,252
Arabica coffee futures	87,753	79,220	76,206
calls	749,935	1,646,506	1,382,241
exercise	131,757	1,140,794	821,912
puts	754,841	1,644,161	1,428,081
exercise	136,402	218,334	553,844
Robusta coffee futures	36	–	–
Soybeans futures	375	11	3,750
Total agricultural commodities	1,868,537	4,823,141	4,382,253
Total (BM&F)	55,496,562	95,234,244	136,996,744

Date of establishment of markets:

Gold spot (250 grams)	– 31 January 1986
Gold call options (250 grams)	– 31 January 1986
Gold put options (250 grams)	– 27 November 1987
Gold futures (250 grams)	– 14 March 1986
Gold futures (1 kg)	– 27 August 1993
Gold forward (250 grams)	– 31 January 1986
Bovespa futures	– 14 February 1986
Bovespa options	– 21 October 1994
Interbank deposits futures	– 5 June 1991
Interbank deposits options	– 21 October 1994
Commercial US dollar futures	– 23 April 1987
Commercial US dollar options	– 16 August 1991
Floating US dollar futures	– 16 August 1991
Floating US dollar options	– 16 August 1991
C bond futures	– 29 March 1996
Arabica coffee futures	– 3 August 1989
Arabica coffee options	– 20 September 1991
Robusta coffee futures	– 20 March 1992
Live cattle futures	– 7 June 1991
Live cattle options	– 22 July 1993
Feeder cattle futures	– 12 June 1992
Soybeans futures	– 16 July 1993
Crystal sugar futures	– 29 September 1995
Cotton futures	– 27 September 1991
Flexible US dollar options	– 2 June 1995
Flexible Bovespa options	– 31 May 1996

Clearing house: this is an internal department of the Exchange.

Membership: The Commodities & Futures Exchange is a non-profit association with the following members:

Honorary member
Assigned to the São Paulo Stock Exchange (Bovespa) which founded the Mercantile & Futures Exchange. Such members are allowed to nominate four members to the Board of Governors of the BM&F.

Commodity brokerage house
Guarantees its holders the right to trade on their own behalf and on behalf of their customers in all markets of the BM&F.

Clearing member
The holder of such a title is held accountable before the BM&F for the clearing and settlement of all trades either performed on the trading floor or registered through the BM&F's guarantee system. The commodities brokerage houses which do not hold a clearing member title, as well as all local traders, agricultural commodities' local traders and agricultural commodities' trading houses, are obliged to contract one or more clearing members for the registration of their operations. The clearing member must be a brokerage house.

Local trader
Individuals who buy and sell contracts on their own behalf on the BM&F's trading floor, but who are not allowed to trade on behalf of customers. They may, however, carry out orders on behalf of a commodities brokerage house or a non-member authorized to trade.

Agricultural commodities' brokerage house
Although the holder of this title has rights similar to those of a commodities brokerage house, such a member can only trade directly in the agricultural markets.

Agricultural commodities' local trader
Like the local trader, is allowed to trade on his or her own behalf but only with agricultural commodity contracts.

Cotton trader
May operate solely in the physical cotton market which is regulated by the BM&F but not traded within its facilities.

Common member
An individual or company whose titularity grants a reduction on transaction costs.

The titles of a commodities' brokerage house, a clearing member and a common member are granted the right to vote and be voted for in the General Meeting of Members which elects the Board of Governors. There is still the non-member authorized to trade one or more contracts who carries out orders through a membered commodities' brokerage house.

Membership of other organizations: Futures Industry Association; Swiss Commodities, Futures and Options Association (SCFOA); International Organization of Securities Commissions (IOSCO).

Further information: BM&F is among the world's leading derivatives exchanges, trading an average of 500,000 contracts daily.

CANADA

MONTREAL

Montreal Exchange (ME)

Tour de la Bourse, PO Box 61, 4th Floor, 800 Victoria Square, Montreal, Quebec H4Z 1A9
Tel: +1 514 871 2424
Fax: +1 514 871 3514
President and Chief Executive Officer: Gérald A Lacoste (QC)
Senior Vice President, Derivative Products: John S Ballard
Director, Development, Derivative Products: Kevin O'Brien

Hours of trading (EST/EDT):

BAX	– 08.00*–15.00
BAR, OBX, CGB, CGF, OGB	– 08.20–15.00
Stock options and LEAPS	– 09.30–16.00
Bond options	– 08.20–16.00

* Subject to revision in the second quarter of 1996

Contract details:
Commodities: 3-month Canadian Bankers' Acceptance Futures (BAX), Options on 3-month Canadian Bankers' Acceptance Futures (OBX), 1-month Canadian Bankers' Acceptance Futures (BAR), 10-year Government of Canada bond Futures (CGB), options on 10-year Government of Canada bond Futures (OGB), 5-year Government of Canada bond Futures (CGF), Stock options, (29), LEAPS (10), Bond options (3), Dividend Capital Receipts and Secondary Warrants (11)

Trading currency and unit:

BAX	– C$1,000,000 Canadian BAs with a maturity of three months
OBX	– One 3-month Canadian Bankers' Acceptance Futures contract
BAR	– C$3,000,000 Canadian BAs with a maturity of one month
CGF and CGB	– C$100,000 nominal value notional Government of Canada bond with a 9% coupon
OGB	– One 10-year Government of Canada bond Futures contract
Stock options and LEAPS	– 1 contract = 100 shares
Bond options	– C$25,000 face value

Manner of price quotation:

BAX and BAR	– quoted by means of an index system equal to 100 minus the annualized yield of the Canadian Bankers' Acceptances (tick size: 0.01 = C$25 per contract)
OBX	– quoted in points where each 0.01 of a point represents C$25
CGB and CGF	– per C$100 nominal value (tick size 0.01 = C$10 per contract)
OGB	– quoted in points and 1/100 of a point per C$100 nominal value of the underlying futures contract
Stock options and LEAPS	– per C$100 nominal value
Bond options	– minimum fluctuations of 0.01% of C$100 face value. The premium per contract is obtained by multiplying the quote by 250

Minimum lot size:

All contracts	– one contract

Maximum price fluctuation:

BAR, BAX, OBX, OGB, Stock options, LEAPS, Bond options	– no maximum price fluctuation
CGF and CGB	– three points (C$3,000) above or below previous day's settlement

Quality of product – delivery standards

CGB	– Government of Canada bonds which have a remaining time to maturity of between eight years and ten years six months as of the first day of the delivery month, calculated by rounding down to the nearest whole three-month period; have an outstanding amount of at least C$3.5 billion nominal value; have a maximum original maturity of ten years nine months; are issued and delivered on or before the 15th day preceding the first delivery notice day of the contract
CGF	– Government of Canada bonds which have a remaining time to maturity of between three years nine months and five years three months as of the first day of the delivery month, calculated by rounding down to the nearest whole month; have an outstanding amount of at least C$3.5 billion nominal value; have an original maturity of not more than five years nine months; are issued and delivered on or

before the 15th day preceding the first delivery notice day of the contract

Delivery months:

BAX – March, June, September, December, for a total of two years

OBX – four nearest months in the BAX futures quarterly cycle

BAR – first six consecutive months

CGB and CGF – March, June, September, December

OGB – March, June, September, December plus monthly option contracts based on the next quarterly futures contract that is nearest to the option contract

Stock options – a given option is listed in one of five cycles: (1) January, April, July, October (2) February, May, August, November (3) March, June, September, December (4) three near term months with two months from cycle three (5) two near term months with next cycle months

LEAPS – Up to two years and eight months, expiration month of January

Bond options – next three consecutive months plus the following month falling on the March, June, September and December cycle

Termination of trading:

BAX, OBX and BAR – trading ceases at 10.00 (EST/EDT) on the second London (Great Britain) banking day prior to the third Wednesday of the contract month

CGB and CGF – trading ceases at 13.00 (EST/EDT) on the seventh business day preceding the last business day of the delivery month

OGB – options cease trading on the third Friday of the month preceding the option contract month provided, however, that such Friday is a business day and precedes by at least two business days the First Notice Day of the underlying future contract

Stock options, LEAPS and bond options – third Friday of the contract month

Commission rates and margins:

BAX – spec C$1,400; hedge C$1,000; spread: 0–3 months C$375, 6 months C$625, others C$1,000

BAR – spec C$1,600; hedge C$1,000; spread C$375

CGB	– spec C$2,200; hedge C$1,000; spread C$325 five years versus ten years C$725
CGF	– spec C$1,500; hedge C$1,000; spread C$300

Date of establishment of contracts:

BAX	– 22 April 1988
OBX	– 7 April 1994
BAR	– 16 April 1992
CGB	– 15 September 1989
CGF	– 19 January 1995
OGB	– 28 March 1991
Stock options	– 1975
LEAPS	– 21 September 1992
Bond options	– 1982

Clearing house: Canadian Derivatives Clearing Corporation

Further information: The Montreal Exchange offers CFTC approved futures and options on Canadian interest rates as well as options on equities, including LEAPS®, Capital Dividend Receipts and Secondary Warrants

TORONTO

The Toronto Futures Exchange

The Exchange Tower, 2 First Canadian Place, Toronto, Ontario M5X 1J2
Tel: +1 416 947 4487
Fax: +1 416 947 4272
President: Susan Crocker
Marketing: Patrick McDonagh

Hours of trading:

Toronto 35 Index option	– 09.30–16.15 (Eastern time)
Toronto 35 Index participation option	– 09.30–16.00 (Eastern time)
TSE 100 Index future	– 09.15–16.15 (Toronto time)
TSE 100 Index option	– 09.30–16.15 (Toronto time)

Contract details:
Commodities: Toronto 35 Index option (TXO); Toronto 35 Index participation option (TIP); TSE 100 Index future (TOF); TSE 100 Index option (TOP)

Trading unit (minimum lot size):

Toronto 35 Index option	– each option contract represents CAN$100 times the value of the Toronto 35 Index
Toronto 35 Index participation option	– 100 Toronto 35 Index participation units
TSE 100 Index future	– CAN$500 times the TSE 100 Index futures price
TSE 100 Index option	– each option contract represents CAN$100 times the value of the TSE 100 Index

Contract months:

Toronto 35 Index option	– cycle 5(3): the two nearest months and the next two calendar quarterly months from the March, June, September, December cycles
TSE 100 Index future	– the two nearest months and the next two calendar quarterly months from the March, June, September, December cycle

Termination of trading:

Toronto 35 Index option	– Thursday before the third Friday of expiry month
Toronto 35 Index participation option	– third Friday of expiry month
TSE 100 Index future	– Thursday before the third Friday of contract month
TSE 100 Index option	– Thursday before the third Friday of expiry month

Settlement:

Toronto 35 Index option	– cash settlement. European-style option, exercisable only on the day after last trading day. Upon exercise, an option holder will receive the amount equal to the difference between the official opening level of the Toronto 35 Index on the expiration date and the strike price of the option. Settlement is through the facilities of Canadian Derivatives Clearing Corporation two business days after last trading day.
Toronto 35 Index participation option	– American-style exercise. Exercise is automatic for all client positions CAN$0.50 in the money, or pro positions CAN$0.25 in the money versus last trade on last trading day
TSE 100 Index future	– on the third Friday of the month, all open positions will be marked to the market using the official opening level of the TSE 100 Index on Friday and terminated by cash settlement. The value of the TSE 100 Index to two decimal places will be used as the cash settlement price. Settles on the second business day following last trading day
TSE 100 Index option	– European-style. Exercisable only on the day after last trading day. All in-the-money long positions will be automatically exercised. Cash settlement. Upon exercise, an option holder will receive the amount equal to the difference between the official opening level of the TSE 100 Index on

expiration date and the strike price of the option, multiplied by CAN$100, expressed to two decimal places. Delivery will take place two business days after last trading day

Expiry dates:

Toronto 35 Index option – third Friday of expiry month

Toronto 35 Index participation option – the Saturday following the third Friday of expiry month

TSE 100 Index option – calculated using the opening prices for TSE 100 securities on expiry day, generally the third Friday of expiry month

Position limits:

Toronto 35 Index option – 25,000 contracts with no more than 15,000 in the near month

Toronto 35 Index participation option – 3,000 unless the number of outstanding units and trading volume qualifies it for a higher limit; 5,500 where either the most recent six month trading volume has totalled at least 20 million units, or the most recent six month trading volume has totalled at least 15 million units with at least 40 million units currently outstanding; 8,000 where either the most recent six month trading volume has totalled at least 40 million units, or the most recent six month trading volume has totalled at least 30 million units with at least 120 million units currently outstanding

TSE 100 Index future – hedge: 5,000 contracts in total; speculative: 2,500 contracts in total

TSE 100 Index option – 25,000 contracts with no more than 15,000 contracts in the near month

Reporting levels:

Toronto 35 Index option – 1,500 contracts

TSE 100 Index future – 500 contracts in total (speculative and hedge)

TSE 100 Index option – 1,500 contracts. For the purpose of calculating reporting levels, exercise limits, and position limits, all equity index options positions based on the same underlying index and on the same side of the market will be aggregated

Premium quotations:

Toronto 35 Index option – 0.00–0.10 – 0.01 intervals; over 0.10 – 0.05 intervals

Toronto 35 Index participation option – 0.00–0.10 – 0.01 intervals; over 0.10 – 0.05 intervals

TSE 100 Index option – 0.00–0.10 – 0.01 intervals; over 0.10 – 0.05 intervals

Margins:

Toronto 35 Index option – long positions are not margin qualified. Short positions are assessed margin requirements of 10% of the underlying value of the index, plus 100% of the premium, less any out-of-the-money amount

TSE 100 Index future	*Speculative*	*Hedge*	*Spread*
Client:	CAN$	CAN$	CAN$
Initial	6,500	5,500	500
Maintenance	5,500	5,500	500
Firm:			
Initial	5,500		250
Maintenance	5,500		250

A client spread between the Toronto 35 Index futures contracts and the TSE 100 Index futures contract requires an initial margin of CAN$2,000 and a maintenance level of CAN$1,250 per spread. A firm spread requires a margin of CAN$1,250

TSE 100 Index option – long positions are not margin qualified. Short positions are assessed margin requirements of 10% of the underlying value of the index, plus 100% of the premium, less any out-of-the-money amount

WINNIPEG

Winnipeg Commodity Exchange

500 Commodity Exchange Tower, 360 Main Street, Winnipeg, Manitoba R3C 3Z4
Tel: +1 204 925 5000
Fax: +1 204 943 5448
President: Fred Siemens
Director of Finance: Mike Gagne
Director of Marketing: John DePape
Director of Compliance: Stan Casar

Hours of trading (central time):

All futures and options – 09.30–13.15
Canola Cash Call Market – 13.30–13.50

Contract details:

Commodities: futures: (canola, feed oats, feed peas, feed wheat, flaxseed, Western domestic feed barley; options on futures: (canola, feed wheat, flaxseed, Western domestic feed barley; canola cash call.

Trading units:

Job lot – 20 tonnes*
For canola cash call – one railcar lot 66.5 to 73.5 net tonnes

* One contract is 20 tonnes in size (referred to as a job lot). However, for a quote or trade to be shown on the price board or on quote services, a minimum of five contracts (100 tonnes – referred to as a board lot) must be traded.

All commodities are traded in Canadian dollars per metric tonne with the exception of feed peas which are based in US dollars per metric tonne.

	Price fluctuation units (cents per tonne)	*Daily limits up or down from previous close* (dollars per tonne)
Feed wheat	10	5
Feed oats	10	5
Feed peas	10	5
Western domestic feed barley	10	5
Canola	10	10
Flaxseed	10	10
Canola cash call	10	–

Expanded daily limit:
If two of the three nearest contract close limit up or down, the daily limit shall be $15.00 per tonne for the next three successive business days. If two of the three nearest contract months close limit up or down on the third day of that period, the limit shall remain at $15.00 per tonne for another three day period. The daily limit will return to normal if no limit move occurs in two of the three nearest contracts on the third day of any such three day period.

Quality:

Feed wheat	– No. 3 CWRs @ par, or the following with a $5.00/t discount: No. 2CWExSRS, No. 2CPSR (red), No. 2CPSW (white), No. 3 CWRWW, and Canada feed.
Feed oats	– No. 3 CW@ par.
Western domestic feed barley	– 48 lbs/bu (59.9 kg/hl), maximum moisture 14.8%, maximum dockage 2%. All other specifications to meet standards of No. 1CW, or @ $5.00/t discount, 46 lbs/bu, maximum moisture 14.8%, maximum dockage 2%. All other specifications to meet standards of No. 1CW.
Canola	– non-commercially clean Canadian canola with maximum dockage of 8%, all other specifications to meet No. 1 Canada canola, with the privilege of delivering (a) commercially clean No. 1 Canada canola at a premium of $5.00 per net tonne, or (b) commercially clean No. 2 Canada canola at a discount of $8.00 per net tonne, or (c) non-commercially clean Canada canola with maximum of dockage of 8%, all other specifications to meet No. 2 Canada canola, at a discount of $13.00 per tonne.
Flaxseed	– No. 1CW @ par, or No. 2CW @ $2.00/t discount.
Feed peas	– North American origin peas of any variety with a maximum of 8% foreign material, and 17% moisture. Effective with the December 1996 contract, Australian origin peas of any variety, maximum 3% foreign material, 12% moisture, also deliverable.
Canola cash call	– No. 1C, or No. 2C $13.00/t discount (alternative discount may be named in bid or offer for acceptance).

Delivery points:

Feed wheat	– Thunder Bay, Ontario
Feed oats	– Thunder Bay, Ontario
Western domestic feed barley	– Lethbridge, Alberta
Canola	– FOB Buyer's Conveyance, in the Par area (approximately 150 km radius around Saskatoon, Saskatchewan). Effective with September 1996 contract.
Flaxseed	– Thunder Bay, Ontario
Feed peas	– CIF Antwerp / Rotterdam / Amsterdam / Ghent

Delivery months:

Feed wheat, feed oats, and flaxseed	– March, May, July, October, December
Western domestic feed barley	– February, May, August, November (effective for March 1997 and subsequent contracts – March, May, July, October, December)
Canola	– January, March, May, July, August, September, November
Feed peas	– February, May, July, October, December
Canola cash call	– any calendar month named at time and date of sale

Termination of trading: Last trading day is the eighth last business day of the delivery month

Manner of price quotation: Canadian dollars per metric tonne, with the exception of feed peas which are quoted in US dollars per metric tonne.

Commission rates and margins:

Minimum rate per unit of trade (20 tonnes)

	Wheat	*Oats*	*Barley*	*Flax*	*Canola*
A. Regular					
Initial	$100	$100	$100	$250	$250
Maintenance	$70	$70	$70	$175	$175
B. Spreads – regular (both sides)					
Initial	$50	$50	$50	$80	$50
Maintenance	$35	$35	$35	$56	35
C. Hedge					
Initial	$70	$70	$70	$175	$175
Maintenance	$70	$70	$70	$175	$175
D. Spreads – hedge (both sides)					
Initial	$35	$35	$35	$56	$35
Maintenance	$35	$35	$35	$56	$35

Minimum rate per Inter-Commodity Spread (20 tonne unit of trade)

Regular	Initial	Maintenance
Domestic feed wheat-oats	$100	$70
Barley-oats	$100	$70
Domestic feed wheat-barley	$100	$70

Hedge	Initial	Maintenance
Domestic feed wheat-oats	$70	$70
Barley-oats	$70	$70
Domestic feed wheat-barley	$70	$70

Customer margins
Minimum rate per unit of trade (20 metric gross tonnes)
US funds

A. Regular	initial	$100.00 US
	maintenance	$70.00 US
B. Spread – regular	initial	$50.00 US
	maintenance	$35.00 US
C. Hedge	initial	$70.00 US
	maintenance	$70.00 US
D. Spread – hedge	initial	$35.00 US
	maintenance	$35.00 US

Volume of trade:
1994–5: 3,263,047 contracts (total transactions of futures trading), with an estimated gross value of 10.6 billion dollars.

Clearing house: Winnipeg Commodity Clearing Ltd

Membership: the Exchange is a voluntary, non-profit association with 235 members, including terminal elevator companies, domestic merchants, exporters, oilseed crushers, feed manufacturers, malsters, futures commission merchants (brokerage firms), banks and individuals. Each member has one vote. Firms and corporations may be registered annually for trading privileges. The Exchange is a self-regulating institution with an elected Board of Governors.

Membership of other organizations: American Oat Association; Canadian Agri-Marketing Association; Canola Council of America; Flax Growers Western Canada; Futures Industry Association; Manitoba Club; National Grain and Feed Association; The Flax Council of Canada; Western Barley Growers Association; Winnipeg Chamber of Commerce.

Further information: an intensive study is currently underway to determine the feasibility of offering futures on natural gas, hogs and cattle.

FRANCE

PARIS

MATIF (Marché à Terme International de France)

115 Rue Réaumur, 75083 Paris, Cedex 02
Tel: +33 1 40 28 82 82
Fax: +33 1 40 28 80 01
Telex: 218 362
President and CEO: Gérard Pfauwadel

Hours of trading (Paris time):

3-month Pibor (Paris Interbank offered rate) futures	–	08.30–16.00
Notional bond futures	–	09.00–16.30
CAC 40 Stock Index future	–	10.00–17.00
ECU bond futures	–	09.00–16.30
White sugar futures	–	10.45–13.00 and 15.00–19.30
Rapeseed futures	–	11.00–13.00 and 15.30–18.30
Potato futures	–	10.30–12.45 and 14.00–16.00
Option on 3-month Pibor	–	08.30–16.00
Option on Notional bond futures	–	09.00–16.30
Option on ECU bond	–	09.00–16.30
Options on white sugar futures	–	10.45–13.00 and 15.00–19.30
US$/DEM option	–	09.15–17.00
US$/FF	–	09.15–17.00
DEM/FF option	–	09.15–17.00
DEM/ITL option	–	09.15–17.00
£/DEM option	–	09.15–17.00

Contract details:

Commodities: 3-month Pibor futures, Notional bond futures, CAC 40 Stock Index futures, ECU bond futures, white sugar futures, rapeseed futures, potato futures, option on 3-month Pibor, option on Notional bond future, option on ECU bond, option on white sugar futures, US$/FF option, US$/DEM option, DEM/FF option, DEM/ITL option, £/DEM option

Trading currency and unit (manner of price quotation):

3-month Pibor futures	–	0.01% of FF5,000,000 times 90/360, ie FF125

Notional bond futures	– 0.02% of FF500,000, ie FF100
CAC 40 Stock Index futures	– 0.5 index point, ie FF100
ECU bond futures	– two basis points, ie ECU 20
White sugar futures	– US$5
Rapeseed futures	– DEM50
Potato futures	– FF50
Option on 3-month Pibor	– US$10
Option on Notional bond futures	– FF50
Option on ECU bond	– ECU 10
Options on white sugar futures	– US$2.5
US$/FF option	– US$10
US$/DEM option	– US$10
DEM/FF option	– DEM10
DEM/ITL option	– DEM10
£/DEM option	– £5

Trading units (minimum lot size):

3-month Pibor futures	– FF5,000,000
Notional bond futures	– FF500,000
CAC 40 Stock Index futures	– 200 times the futures quoted index
ECU bond futures	– ECU 100,000
White sugar futures	– 50 tonnes in bags of 50 kg
Rapeseed futures	– 50 tonnes
Potato futures	– 20 tonnes in bags of 25 kg
Option on 3-month Pibor	– one 3-month Pibor futures contract
Option on Notional bond futures	– one Notional bond futures contract
Option on ECU bond	– one ECU bond futures contract
Options on white sugar futures	– one white sugar futures contract
US$/FF option	– US$100,000
US$/DEM option	– US$100,000
DEM/FF option	– DEM100,000
DEM/ITL option	– DEM100,000
£/DEM option	– £50,000

Quality:

3-month Pibor futures	– Paris interbank offered rate on 3-month deposits
Notional bond futures	– 7- to 10-year fictitious French Government bond, redeemable at maturity, 10% coupon
CAC 40 Stock Index futures	– CAC 40 index, broadcast with 2 decimals, composed of 40 French stocks listed on the RM, calculated on-line by the SBF, broadcast every 30 seconds
ECU bond futures	– 6- to 10-year fictitious ECU bond, redeemable at maturity, 5.5% coupon
White sugar futures	– white crystal sugar from sugar beet or cane of any origin. Minimum polarization: 99.80°; maximum moisture: 0.06%

Rapeseed futures	– rapeseed of any origin, 00 variety, of sound, loyal and merchantable quality. Oil content: basis 40%; moisture: basis 9%; impurities: basis 2%
Potato futures	– Bintje variety, of 50 mm calibre or more, with a maximum of 8 tubers per kg
Option on 3-month Pibor	– 3-month Pibor futures
Option on Notional bond futures	– 7- to 10-year Notional bond futures
Option on ECU bond	– 6- to 10-year ECU bond futures
Options on white sugar futures	– white sugar futures
US$/FF option	– US$/FF spot transaction
US$/DEM option	– US$/DEM spot transaction
DEM/FF option	– DEM/FF spot transaction
DEM/ITL option	– DEM/ITL spot transaction
£/DEM option	– £/DEM spot transaction

Delivery months:

3-month Pibor futures	– 12 successive quarterly delivery months from March, June, September, December
Notional bond futures	– four successive quarterly delivery months: March, June, September, December
CAC 40 Stock Index futures	– three spot months, three quarterly maturities and two half-yearly delivery months: March, September
ECU bond futures	– two successive quarterly delivery months among March, June, September, December
White sugar futures	– March, May, August, October, December
Rapeseed futures	– August, November, February, May
Potato futures	– February, April, May, November
Option on 3-month Pibor	– four successive quarterly delivery months from March, June, September, December
Option on Notional bond future	– one front month plus three or four successive quarterly delivery months from March, June, September, December
Option on Ecu bond	– two successive quarterly delivery months among March, June, September, December
Options on white sugar futuress	– March, May, August, October, December
US$/FF option	– one fortnightly plus three monthly plus three quarterly delivery months from March, June, September, December
US$/DEM option	– one fortnightly plus three monthly plus three quarterly delivery months from March, June, September, December
DEM/FF option	– three monthly plus three quarterly delivery months from March, June, September, December
DEM/ITL option	– three monthly plus three quarterly delivery months from March, June, September,

December

£/DEM option – three monthly plus three quarterly delivery months from March, June, September, December

Termination of trading:

3-month Pibor futures – second business day preceding the third Wednesday of delivery month at 11.00 (Paris time)

Notional bond futures – second business day preceding the third Wednesday of delivery month at 11.00 (Paris time)

CAC 40 Stock Index futures – last business day of delivery month at 16.00

ECU bond futures – second business day preceding the third Wednesday of delivery month at 11.00 (Paris time)

White sugar futures – 15th of last month preceding delivery month

Rapeseed futures – last business day of the month preceding delivery month

Potato futures – fourth Tuesday of delivery month

Option on 3-month Pibor – second business day preceding the third Wednesday of delivery month at 11.00 (Paris time)

Option on Notional bond futures – last business Thursday of the month preceding Notional option delivery month

Option on ECU bond – last business Thursday of the month preceding ECU bond futures delivery month

Options on white sugar futures – last business day of the month preceding futures expiration closing month

US$/FF option – Thursday following the third Wednesday of expiration month at 09.00 New York time for monthly and quarterly delivery months; Thursday following the first Wednesday of expiration month at 09.00 New York time for fortnightly delivery months

US$/DEM option – Thursday following the third Wednesday of expiration month at 09.00 New York time for monthly and quarterly delivery months; Thursday following the first Wednesday of expiration month at 09.00 New York time for fortnightly delivery months

DEM/FF option – Thursday following the third Wednesday of expiration month at 09.00 New York time

DEM/ITL option – Thursday following the third Wednesday of expiration month at 09.00 New York time

£/DEM option – Thursday following the third Wednesday of expiration month at 09.00 New York time

Volume of trade:

	1993	*1994*	*1995*
3-month Pibor futures	11,863,798	13,176,354	15,488,076
Notional bond futures	36,804,824	50,153,150	33,610,221
CAC 40 Stock Index futures	5,908,739	7,464,449	6,549,953
ECU bond futures	873,002	618,715	657,152
Total financial futures	55,578,836	71,412,731	56,305,402
Option on 3-month Pibor	4,830,198	3,361,277	4,615,434
Option on Notional bond futures	11,572,671	18,024,502	9,517,932
Option on ECU bond	7,797	790	–
US$/FF option	–	75,436	67,286
US$/DEM option	–	225,497	116,127
DEM/FF option	–	–	34,491
DEM/ITL option	–	–	11,249
£/DEM option	–	–	35,734
Total financial options	16,410,666	21,687,502	14,398,253
White sugar futures	262,940	296,416	305,598
Rapeseed futures	–	7,026	51,135
Potato future	11,029	33,302	29,619
Options on white sugar futures	–	–	505
Total commodities	274,459	336,914	386,857
Total MATIF	72,263,961	93,437,147	71,090,512

Date of establishment of contracts:

3-month Pibor futures – 8 September 1988
Notional bond futures – 20 February 1986
CAC 40 Stock Index futures – 9 November 1988
ECU bond futures – 18 October 1990
White sugar futures – 20 May 1994
Rapeseed futures – 28 October 1994
Potato futures – 12 November 1987
Option on 3-month Pibor – 1 March 1990
Option on Notional bond futures – 14 January 1988
Option on ECU bond – 5 May 1992
Options on white sugar futures – 8 December 1995
US$/FF option – 20 May 1994
US$/DEM option – 20 May 1994
DEM/FF option – 23 October 1995
DEM/ITL option – 22 May 1995
£/DEM option – 22 May 1995

Membership: There are three classes of membership: General Clearing Member, Individual Clearing Member, and Negotiating broker.

GERMANY

FRANKFURT

Deutsche Börse AG

Börsenplatz 7–11, Frankfurt am Main 60313
Tel: +49 69 21010
Fax: +49 69 2101–2005
Member of the Executive Board: Dr Jörg Franke
Member of the Executive Board: Dr Reto Francioni

Hours of trading (Frankfurt time):

BOBL future, BUND future, BOBL option, BUND option	– 08.00–17.30
German stock index (DAX) future, DAX option, option on DAX future	– 09.00–17.00

Contract details:
Commodities: futures – 3.5–5 year medium-term notional debt security (BOBL), 8.5–10 year long-term notional debt security (BUND), German stock index (DAX); options – BOBL, BUND, DAX, option on DAX future

Trading unit and currency (manner of price quotation):

BOBL futures, BUND futures	– in a percentage of the par value, with two decimal places
DAX futures, DAX options, options on DAX futures	– in points, with one decimal place
BOBL options, BUND options	– in points with two decimal places

Trading units:

BOBL futures, BUND futures	– DM250,000
DAX futures	– DM100 per DAX index point
BOBL options	– one BOBL futures contract
BUND options	– one BUND futures contract
DAX options	– DM100 per DAX index point
Options on DAX futures	– one DAX futures contract

Trading limits:
Minimum price movement

BOBL futures, BUND futures	– 0.01% (DM25)
DAX futures	– 0.5 point (DM50)
BOBL options, BUND options	– 0.01 point (DM25)
DAX options	– 0.1 point (DM1)
Options on DAX futures	– 0.1 point (DM10)

Delivery months:

BOBL futures, BUND futures, DAX futures	– the three nearest quarter-end months of the cycle March, June, September, December

Delivery day:

BOBL futures, BUND futures	– the delivery day is the tenth calendar day of the respective quarter-end month if this day is an Exchange trading day, otherwise the next succeeding Exchange trading day. Delivery is made through DKV, the clearing organization of the Deutsche Börse AG

Termination of trading:

BOBL futures, BUND futures	– two Exchange trading days prior to the delivery day of the relevant quarter-end month. Trading in the contract for this delivery month ends at 12.30
DAX futures, BUND options	– the Exchange trading day prior to the settlement calculation day
BOBL options	– six Exchange trading days prior to the first calendar day in the expiration month
DAX options	– the third Friday of the expiration month if that is an Exchange trading day, otherwise the exchange trading day immediately preceding this Friday. Trading in the expiring series closes at 13.30 Frankfurt time on the last trading day
Options on DAX futures	– expiration months March, June, September, December: the Exchange trading day preceding the settlement calculation day of the DAX futures contract. The final settlement day is the third Friday of the expiration month if this is an Exchange trading day, otherwise the Exchange trading day preceding the third Friday. Other expiration months: the third Friday of the expiration month if this is an Exchange trading day, otherwise the Exchange trading day preceding the third Friday

Settlement:

BOBL options, BUND options – the exercise of an option on a futures contract results in the creation of a corresponding futures position for the purchaser as well as the seller to whom the exercise is assigned. The position is opened based on the agreed exercise price following the Post-Trading Period of the exercise day

DAX options – cash settlement on the first Exchange trading day after the last trading day

Options on DAX futures – the exercise of an option on a futures contract results in the creation of a corresponding futures position for the purchaser as well as the seller to whom the exercise is assigned. The position is opened based on the agreed exercise price following the Post-Trading Period of the exercise day. If the exercise day falls on the same day as the settlement calculation day of the DAX futures contract, the exercises/assignments will be cash-settled based on the final settlement price of the DAX future

Expiry months:

BOBL options, BUND options – options are available for the three nearest months as well as the next succeeding month of the cycle March, June, September, December, ie options contracts are available with terms of one, two, and three months as well as up to six months. Underlying futures contract: expiration months March, June, September, December – the contract of the underlying futures contract and the expiration month of the option are identical

DAX options – the three nearest months, the following three months from the cycle March, June, September, December as well as the two following months from the June and December cycle, ie terms to maturity of one, two, three, six, nine, 12 as well as 18, and 24 months are available

Options on DAX futures – the three nearest months as well as the next two months of the cycle March, June, September, December, ie options are available with terms of one, two and three as well as up to six and nine months. Underlying futures contract: expiration months March, June, September, December – the contract month of the underlying futures contract and the expiration month of the option are identical. Other expiration months: the contract month of the underlying futures contract is the quarter-end month following the expiration month of the option

Expiry day:

BOBL options, BUND options, DAX options – the expiration day for an option series is the Exchange trading day following the last trading day

Options on DAX futures – expiration months March, June, September, December – the Exchange trading day following the settlement calculation day of the DAX futures contract; other expiration month – the Exchange trading day following the last trading day

Exercise period:

BOBL options, BUND options – American-style, ie an option can be exercised up to the end of the Post-Trading Period on any Exchange trading day during the life of the option

Options on DAX futures – American-style, ie an option can be exercised up to the end of the Post-Trading Period on any Exchange trading day during the life of the option. Expiration months March, June, September, December – the last exercise day is the settlement calculation day of the DAX future, ie exercises are also allowed on the Exchange trading day following the last trading day of the option series; other expiration months – the last exercise day is the last trading day

DAX options – European-style, ie an option can only be exercised up to the end of the Post-Trading Period on the last trading day of the option series

Exercise prices:

BOBL options – option series have exercise prices with price

	graduations of 0.25 points (eg 95.00, 95.25, 95.50, etc). Nine exercise prices are introduced for each contract month
BUND options	– options series have exercise prices with price graduations of 0.50 points (eg 95.00, 95.50, 96.00, etc). Nine exercise prices are introduced for each contract month
DAX options	– at least five exercise prices are introduced for each contract month. For contract months with maturity dates of up to and including six months, the strike prices have price graduations of 25 index points (eg 2125, 2150, 2175, etc). In the case of contract months with a term of nine months the strike prices on principle are graded by 50 index points (eg 2100, 2150, 2200, etc); for contract months with a term of 12 months the strike prices are available in increments of 100 index points (eg 2100, 2200, 2300, etc) and for contract months with maturities of over 12 months, the gradation is by 200 index points (eg, 2100, 2300, 2500, etc)
Options on DAX futures	– exercise price intervals are in increments of 25 index points (eg 2125, 2150, 2175). Five exercise prices are introduced for each expiration month

Margins:

BOBL futures, BUND futures, DAX futures, BOBL options, BUND options, DAX options, options on DAX futures	– DTB determines the daily margin requirement using its Risk-Based Margining method

Date of establishment of contracts:

BOBL futures	– 4 October 1991
BUND futures	– 23 November 1990
DAX futures	– 23 November 1990
BOBL options	– 15 January 1993
BUND options	– 16 August 1991
DAX options	– 16 August 1991
Options on DAX futures	– 24 January 1992

Frankfurt Corn and Produce Exchange

(Frankfurter Getreide- und Produktenbörse), Bösenplatz 6, D 60913 Frankfurt am Main
Tel: +49 69 219 7338
Fax: +49 69 219 7424
Telex: 411255 ihkf d
Chief Executive: Hans Petermann

Hours of trading:

Eggs	– every Tuesday 14.00–14.30
All other products listed below	– every Wednesday 15.15–17.00

Contract details:
Commodities: coarse fodder, eggs, home-grown and foreign fodder, home-grown and foreign grain, milling products, peat, potatoes, specially light fuel oil

Trading units:
Coarse fodder, corn, milling products, peat, potatoes – 100 kg or 1,000 kg
Eggs – 30 cartons of 360 eggs, equivalent to 10,800 eggs
Specially light fuel oil – 100 litres

Quality: qualities traded are determined by the appropriate regulations of the German Republic as well as by EU standards

Delivery points: Frankfurt

Currency dealt in: Deutschmark

Date of establishment of market: 1862

Membership: (a) principals, managers or persons who according to law, statute or contract are appointed to carry out business transactions and are entitled to conclude business transactions independently at the Exchange; (b) employees who are not entitled to conclude business transactions independently.

Membership of other organizations: Study Group of the German Produce Exchanges, Mannheim; Consortium of European Commodity Exchanges.

Branches and affiliates: Quotation Commission for Specially Light Fuel Oil at the Chamber of Industry and Commerce, Wiesbaden.

HONG KONG

The Chinese Gold and Silver Exchange Society

Gold & Silver Commercial Building, 12–18 Mercer Street, Hong Kong
Tel: +852 2544 1945/2543 9158
Fax: +852 2854 0869
President: Henry W C Wu
Manager: Thomas C Y Chan

Hours of trading: Monday to Friday 09.30–12.30 and 14.30–16.30; Saturday 09.30–12.00

Contract details:
Commodities: Gold

Trading currency: Hong Kong dollars

Trading units: 100 taels (1 tael = 37.429 grammes)

Quality: 99% fineness

Delivery points: Hong Kong

Date of establishment of market: 1910

Clearing house: The Chinese Gold and Silver Exchange Society

Membership: Ordinary member (total 191 members)

Hong Kong Futures Exchange Ltd

Suite 605–608, Asia Pacific Finance Tower, Citibank Plaza, 3 Garden Road, Hong Kong 070
Tel: +852 2842 9333
Fax: +852 2845 2043
Telex: 76375 HKFEG HX
Chairman: Frank Wong
Chief Executive Officer: Ivers W Riley
Chief Operations Officer: Steve Chan
Marketing Director: Vincent Wong

Hours of trading (Hong Kong time):

HSI futures and options	– Monday to Friday 10.00–12.30 and 14.30–16.00
Gold futures	– 09.00–12.00 and 14.00–17.30
Stock futures	– Monday to Friday 10.00–12.30 and 14.30–15.55

Rolling Forex	– 08.00–03.00 (early April to early November); 08.00–04.00 (early November to early April)

Contract details:

Commodities: Gold Futures, Hang Seng Index Futures, HIBOR Futures, Hang Seng Properties Sub-index Futures, Hang Seng Commerce and Industries Sub-index Futures, Hang Seng Utilities Sub-index Futures, Hang Seng Finance Sub-index, Hang Seng Index Options, HK Telecom Ltd Futures, HSBC Holdings Plc Futures, Cheung Kong Holdings Ltd Futures, Rolling Forex (Yen and Dem)

Trading currency and unit:

Gold Futures	– US$ per troy ounces
Hang Seng Index Futures	– HK$50 per point
HIBOR	– HK$25 per basis point
Hang Seng Properties	– HK$50 per point
Hang Seng Commerce and Industries	– HK$50 per point
Hang Seng Utilities	– HK$50 per point
Hang Seng Finance	– HK$50 per point
Hang Seng Index Options	– HK$50 per point
HK Telecom Ltd	– HK$100 per point
HSBC Holdings Plc	– HK$20 per point
Cheung Kong Holdings Ltd	– HK$50 per point
Rolling Forex (Yen and Dem)	– US$

Termination of trading:

HSI Futures	– the business day preceding the last business day of the month
HSI Options	– the business day immediately preceding the last business day of contract month
Rolling Forex	– the second FX business day after the day on which open positions are closed. If that day is a bank holiday either in New York or in Germany/Japan, then settlement shall be on the next FX business day which is not a bank holiday in both New York and Germany/Japan

Months/maturities quoted:

Gold Futures	– even month, spot month and the following two months
HSI Futures	– spot month, the next calendar month and the next two calendar quarter months
HSI Options	– current and next calendar month plus next two months from the following cycle: March, June, September, December
HIBOR	– three months

Properties, Commerce and Industries,
Utilities, Finance – spot month and deferred months as notified to all members and commission

Commission rates and margins (as at 1 April 1996):

Market	*Category*	*Initial maintenance spread (/lot/side)*		
HSI Futures	Client	$45,000 (900 points)	$36,000 (720 points)	$3,750 (75 points)
	Member	$35,000 (700 points)	– –	$2,500 (50 points)
HSBC Holdings Plc Futures	Client	$17,000	$13,600	$8,500
	Member	$13,500	–	$6,750
Hong Kong Telecom Ltd Futures	Client	$13,000	$10,400	$6,500
	Member	$10,000	–	$5,000
Cheung Kong (Holdings) Ltd Futures	Client	$20,000	$16,000	$10,000
	Member	$16,000	–	$8,000
Hang Seng Commerce and Industry Sub-index Futures	Client	$27,500 (550 points)	$22,000 (440 points)	$13,750 (275 points)
	Member	$22,000 (440 points)	–	$11,000 (220 points)
Hang Seng Properties Sub-index Futures	Client	$70,000 (1,400 points)	$56,000 (1,120 points)	$35,000 (700 points)
	Member	$56,000 (1,120 points)	–	$28,000 (560 points)
Hang Seng Utilities Sub-index Futures	Client	$32,500 (650 points)	$26,000 (520 points)	$16,250 (325 points)
	Member	$26,000 (520 points)	–	$13,000 (260 points)
Hang Seng Finance Sub-index Futures	Client	($30,000) (600 points)	$24,000 (480 points)	$15,000 (300 points)
	Member	$24,000 (480 points)	–	$12,000 (240 points)
Rolling Yen	Client	US$2,500	US$2,000	–
	Member	US$2,000	–	–

Market	*Category*	*Initial maintenance spread (/lot/side)*		
Rolling Deutsche Mark	Client	US$2,000	US$1,600	–
	Member	US$1,600	–	–

HSI Options – minimum commissions are payable on all trades and are set at the lesser of 1% of the contract value rounded up to the nearest HK dollar with a minimum of HK$30; and HK$100

HIBOR– day trade: minimum HK$10.00 per lot per side

Rolling Forex – maximum commissions HK$150 per contract per side

Volume of trade since 1993 to end 1995 (annual):

	1993	*1994*	*1995*
HSI Futures	2,415,739	4,192,589	4,546,613
HSI Options*	295,220	606,674	645,538

* HSI options launched since 5 March 1993

Date of establishment of market: the current Futures Exchange was established in 1976 as the Hong Kong Commodity Exchange Ltd.

Date of establishment of contracts:

Gold Futures	– August 1980
Hang Seng Index Futures	– 6 May 1986
HIBOR	– February 1990
Hang Seng Properties	– 16 July 1991
Hang Seng Commerce and Industries	– 2 September 1991
Hang Seng Utilities	– 31 October 1991
Hang Seng Finance	– 31 October 1991
Hang Seng Index Options	– 5 March 1993
HK Telecom Ltd	– 31 March 1995
HSBC Holdings Plc	– 31 March 1995
Cheung Kong Holdings Ltd	– 25 September 1995
Rolling Forex (Yen and Dem)	– 3 November 1995

Clearing house: HKFE Clearing Corporation Ltd, which is a wholly-owned subsidiary of Hong Kong Futures Exchange Ltd

Membership: There are three classes of exchanges membership open to ordinarily resident/incorporated in Hong Kong

Trader
A member which only trades for its own account

Broker
A member which trades for its own account and acts as floor agent for transactions for other members

Merchant Trader
A member which trades for its own account and is a merchant in a deliverable commodity traded on the Exchange

HUNGARY

BUDAPEST

Budapest Commodity Exchange

61–65 Róbert Károly krt, Budapest 1134
Tel: +36 1 269 8571
Fax: +36 1 269 8575
Chairman of the Board: Szergej Keresztesi
Vice Chairman of the Board: László Wolf
President & CEO: Dr Andrea Varga Pongrácz

Hours of trading (local time):

Corn, milling wheat, feed wheat, feed barley, black seed, BL-55 wheat flour	– Tuesday, Wednesday, Thursday 10.00–11.30
Live hog No. 1, live hog No. 2, live hog No. 3	– Tuesday and Thursday 09.45–10.15
German mark, US dollar, Japanese yen, ECU, British pound, Italian lire, Swiss franc, interest rate	– weekdays 10.30–12.00

Contract details:

Commodities: corn, milling wheat, feed wheat, barley, black seed, BL-55 wheat flour, live hog No. 1, live hog No. 2, live hog No. 3, German mark, US dollar, ECU, Japanese yen, British pound, Italian lire, Swiss franc, interest rate

Trading currency and unit (manner of price quotation):

Corn, milling wheat, feed wheat, feed barley, black seed	– HUF per ton
BL-55 wheat flour	– HUF per kg
Live hog No. 1, live hog No. 2, live hog No. 3	– HUF per kg, fillér per kg
German mark	– HUF per DM, fillér per DM
US dollar	– HUF per USD, fillér per USD
Japanese yen	– HUF per 100 yen, fillér per 100 Yen
ECU	– HUF per ECU, fillér per ECU
British pound	– HUF per GBP, fillér per GBP
Italian lire	– HUF per ITL, fillér per ITL
Swiss franc	– HUF per CHF, fillér per CHF
Interest rate	– in percentage points

Trading unit (minimum lot size):

Corn, milling wheat, feed wheat, feed barley, black seed – 20 metric tons
BL-55 wheat flour – 5 metric tons
Live hog No. 1, live hog No. 2, live hog No. 3 – 5,000 kg of live hogs
German mark – 1,000 DM
US dollar – 1,000 USD
Japanese yen – 100,000 Yen
ECU – 1,000 ECU
British pound – 1,000 GBP
Italian lire – 1,000,000 ITL
Swiss franc – 1,000 CHF
Interest rate – 3-month, HUF 1,000,000 deposit

Trading limits:

Minimum price fluctuation:

Corn, milling wheat, feed wheat, feed barley, black seed – HUF10 per ton or HUF200 per contract
BL-55 wheat flour, live hog No. 1, live hog No. 2, live hog No. 3 – HUF0.10 per kg or HUF500 per contract
German mark – HUF0.01 per DM or HUF10 per contract
US dollar – HUF0.01 per USD or HUF10 per contract
Japanese yen – HUF0.01 per 100 Yen or HUF10 per contract
ECU – HUF0.01 per ECU or HUF10 per contract
British pound – HUF0.01 per GBP or HUF10 per contract
Italian lire – HUF0.01 per ITL or HUF10 per contract
Swiss franc – HUF0.01 per CHF or HUF10 per contract
Interest rate – 1/16%, HUF 156.25 per contract

Daily price movement limit:

Corn, milling wheat, feed wheat, feed barley, black seed – HUF300 per ton or HUF 6,000 per contract above or below the previous day's settlement. Limits are changed to HUF400 if the market is limit up or limit down for three consecutive sessions. No limit is set if the market is limit up or limit down for three consecutive trading days even by the modified (HUF400) limit and for the nearby delivery month on the last trading day of the month prior to delivery month
BL-55 wheat flour – HUF3 per kg or HUF 15,000 per contract above or below the previous day's

settlement. Limits are changed to HUF4 if the market is limit up or limit down for three consecutive sessions. No limit is set if the market is limit up or limit down for three consecutive trading days even by the modified (HUF4) limit and for the nearby delivery month on the last trading day of the month prior to delivery month

Live hog No. 1, live hog No. 2, live hog No. 3 – HUF4 per kg or HUF 20,000 per contract above or below the previous day's settlement. Limits are changed to HUF6 if the market is limit up or limit down for three consecutive sessions. No limit is set if the market is limit up or limit down for three consecutive trading days even by the modified (HUF6) limit and for the nearby delivery month on the last trading day of the month prior to delivery month

German mark – there is no price movement limit, but at HUF2 per DM or HUF2,000 per contract above or below the previous day's settlement price, intraday clearing is to be ordered by the Exchange while closing down temporarily

US dollar – there is no price movement limit, but at HUF3 per USD or HUF3,000 per contract above or below the previous day's settlement price, intraday clearing is to be ordered by the Exchange while closing down temporarily

Japanese yen – there is no price movement limit, but at HUF3 per Yen or HUF3,000 per contract above or below the previous day's settlement price, intraday clearing is to be ordered by the Exchange while closing down temporarily

ECU – there is no price movement limit, but at HUF3 per ECU or HUF3,000 per contract above or below the previous day's settlement price, intraday clearing is to be ordered by the Exchange while closing down temporarily

British pound – there is no price movement limit, but at HUF3 per GBP or HUF3,000 per contract above or below the previous day's settlement price, intraday clearing is to be ordered by the Exchange while closing down temporarily

Italian lire – there is no price movement limit, but at HUF3 per ITL or HUF3,000 per contract above or below the previous day's settlement price, intraday clearing is to be ordered by the Exchange while closing down temporarily

Swiss franc – there is no price movement limit, but at HUF3 per CHF or HUF3,000 per contract above or below the previous day's settlement price, intraday clearing is to be ordered by the Exchange while closing down temporarily

Interest rate – there is no price movement limit for the spot month; other delivery months have a limit of eight ticks

Quality:

Corn – maximum moisture content 15%; maximum admixture 2% including maximum 0.05% inorganic. In excess of admixture: maximum broken kernels 8%; germinated kernels 2%; heat damaged kernels 3%; small broken 2%. The corn should be sound, sifted, free of foreign smell, living insects and mould. Any other quality aspects not specified here are referred to in the Hungarian Standard under MSZ 12540

Milling wheat – density (hectolitre weight) should be 76–80 kg per hectolitre; maximum moisture 14.5%; maximum admixture 2% including 0.5% inorganic. In excess of admixture: maximum broken kernels 2%; germinated kernels 2%; rye 2%; wheat kernels of inferior quality (falling through the sieve of 2.2 mm) 5%; light weight admixture 0.5%; weevil bitten kernels 4%. Wet gluten minimum 30% can be delivered at minimum 29%, with 1% bonification for 0.5% quality differential tested. Baking quality of the wheat should correspond to the so-called B1 quality group according to the Hungarian Standard. The wheat should be sound, sifted, free of foreign smell, living insects and mould. Any other quality aspects not specified here are referred to in the Hungarian Standard under MSZ

	6383–79
Feed wheat	– density (hectolitre weight) should be a minimum of 70 kg per hectolitre; maximum moisture 14.5%; maximum admixture 2% including 0.5% inorganic; maximum light weight mixture 0.5%. In excess of admixture, maximum broken and germinated kernels 10%. The product should be sound, sifted, free of living insects, foreign smell and toxic substances, and should meet valid veterinary requirements. Any other quality aspects not specified here are referred to in the Hungarian Standard under MSZ 6383–79
Feed barley	– density (hectolitre weight) should be a minimum of 63 kg per hectolitre; maximum moisture 14.5%; maximum admixture 2% including maximum detrimental elements 0.5%; worthless admixture maximum 0.5%. In excess of admixture, maximum broken kernels 5%; maximum rye and oats together 10%. The product should be sound, free of living insects, foreign smell and toxic substances, and should meet valid veterinary requirements
Black seed	– maximum moisture 9%; admixture 2% or maximum 3% including detrimental elements maximum 0.5%; maximum seeds of inferior quality including hulled and/or broken kernels 10%. Oil content in the dry matter of the kernel minimum 45%. The product should be sound, ripened, dry and have a natural smell. It should be free of living insects, moths, foreign smell and toxic substances and should meet valid veterinary requirements. Any other quality aspects not specified here are referred to in the Hungarian Standard under MSZ 6368–81
BL-55 wheat flour	– colour (Pekár value) in minimum two cases 3C; ash maximum 0.55%; moisture content maximum 15.5%; acid degree maximum 2.5%. Foreign substances: foreign grist maximum 0.8%; smut spore content maximum 0.05%; sand maximum 0.03%; no toxic grist, no pests and residuals of pests. Size of flour granules

maximum 250 micrometer; pharinographic baking value group minimum B1; wet gluten content 29%. Packaging: in uniform lead sealed sacks (plastic or jute), 50 kg each with plus or minus 1% difference in weight; or in 0.5 kg, 1 kg, or 5 kg tape sealed retail units

Live hog No. 1 – lean meat 50% or more; gross weight each between 95 and 115 kg; quality class 2; quality deviation plus or minus 2%. In case of quality deficiency, 1% of gross price is discounted at every 1/10 of the quality rating deviation. Animals delivered are to comply with the effective veterinary provisions. Testing and all other costs of other certificates required by the prevailing law is carried by the seller

Live hog No. 2 – lean meat 45–50%; gross weight each between 110 and 125 kg; quality class 2.5; quality deviation plus or minus 2%. In case of quality deficiency, 1% of gross price is discounted at every 1/10 of the quality rating deviation. Animals delivered are to comply with the effective veterinary provisions. Testing and all other costs of other certificates required by the prevailing law is carried by the seller

Live hog No. 3 – lean meat less than 45%

Delivery point:

Corn, milling wheat, feed wheat, feed barley, black seed, BL-55 wheat flour, live hog No. 1, live hog No. 2, live hog No. 3 – Budapest

Contract months:

Corn – March, May, July, October, November, December up to a maximum of 17 months ahead

Milling wheat, feed wheat, – January, March, May, July, August, September, October, December up to a maximum of 17 months ahead

Feed barley – March, May, July, August, September, October, December up to a maximum of 17 months ahead

Black seed – March, May, September, October, November, December up to a maximum of 17 months ahead

BL-55 wheat flour, live hog No. 1, live hog No. 2, live hog No. 3	– any calendar month up to a maximum of 12 months ahead
German mark, US dollar, Japanese yen, ECU, British pound, Italian lire, Swiss franc, interest rate	– every quarterly month (March, June, September, December) up to a maximum of 18 months ahead plus the five consecutive months starting from the prevailing time of trading

Termination of trading:

Corn, milling wheat, feed wheat, feed barley, black seed, BL-55 wheat flour, live hog No. 1, live hog No. 2, live hog No. 3	– the last trading day of the month prior to delivery month
German mark, US dollar, Japanese yen, ECU, British pound, Italian lire, Swiss franc, interest rate	– the third Wednesday of delivery month

Initial margins:

Corn, milling wheat, feed wheat, feed barley, black seed	– HUF8,000 per contract
BL-55 wheat flour	– HUF5,000 per contract
Live hog No. 1, live hog No. 2, live hog No. 3	– HUF20,000 per contract
German mark	– HUF2,000 per contract
US dollar, Japanese yen, ECU, British pound, Italian lire, Swiss franc	– HUF3,000 per contract
Interest rate	– 5,000 per contract

Volume of trade:

	1993	*1994*	*1995*
	(HUF)	(HUF)	(HUF)
Grains	10,693,319,300	8,099,227,500	12,686,281,800
Livestock	190,065,250	217,573,000	511,617,500
Financial	1,447,969,770	26,943,852,125	162,149,515,387
Total	12,331,354,320	35,260,652,625	175,347,414,687

Clearing house: Central Clearing House and Depository Ltd, Budapest

Budapest Stock Exchange

5 u Deak Ferenc, Budapest 1052
Tel: +36 1 117 5226
Fax: +36 1 118 1737
President: Zsigmond Járai
CEO: Jozef Rotyis

Hours of trading (local time):

3-month T-bill	– 10.15–11.00
German mark, US dollar, ECU	– 11.00–11.45
Budapest Stock Index (BUX)	– 12.00–13.00

Contract details:

Commodities: German mark, US dollar, ECU, Budapest Stock Index (BUX), interest rate (3-month Treasury bill)

Trading currency and unit (manner of price quotation):

German mark, US dollar, ECU, BUX, 3-month Treasury bill	– HUF

Trading unit (minimum lot size):

German mark	– DM10,000
US dollar	– USD10,000
ECU	– ECU10,000
BUX	– BUX value times HUF100
3-month Treasury bill	– in the face value of HUF1,000,000

Contract months:

German mark, US dollar, ECU, 3-month Treasury bill	– one year ahead of the March quarterly cycle and the two nearest months
BUX	– one year ahead of the March quarterly cycle

Commission rates and margins:

Commission rates (clearing and transaction fees – HUF):

German mark	– 130 per contract
US dollar	– 190 per contract
ECU	– 240 per contract
BUX	– 133 per contract
3-month Treasury bill	– 150 per contract

Initial margins:

German mark	– 0–6 months HUF15,000; 9–12 months HUF30,000
US dollar, ECU	– 0–6 months HUF20,000; 9–12 months HUF30,000
BUX	– HUF12,000
3-month Treasury bill	– 3,000

Termination of trading:

German mark, US dollar, ECU	– in the expirations listed after 1 February 1996, the third Wednesday of the month
BUX	– the second settlement day after the 14th of the month
3-month Treasury bill	– the second Wednesday of the month

Volume of trade:

	1995 (Apr–Dec)	*1996 (Jan–Jun)*
German mark	1,407	4,785
US dollar	976	7,131
ECU (Nov '95)	494	9,430
BUX	3,207	27,269
3-month Treasury bill	6,333	23,165
Total	12,417	71,780

Date of establishment of markets:

German mark	– 31 March 1995
US dollar	– 31March 1995
Ecu	– 1 November 1995
BUX	– 31 March 1995
3-month treasury bill	– 31 March 1995

Clearing house: Keler, an independent clearing house partly owned by the Exchange (25%).

Membership: full membership with clearing rights – capital requirements HUF50 million; membership requirement – a registered financial company in Hungary (according to the Securities Act 90/6, and the provisions of the State Securities and Exchange Commission).

Membership of other organizations: Federation of European Stock Exchanges correspondent member.

Further information: Budapest Stock Exchange (BSE) was established in 1990 as the first exchange in the Central/Eastern European countries, besides Slovenia, to reopen its doors. Futures trading started in March 1995, for the BUX index, interest rate and currency contracts. Continuity and liquidity of the market is supported by strong market makers (ABN Ambro Hoare Govett Hungary Rt, K&H Broker Co, MKB Securities and Investment Co, Postabank Securities and Investment Co, from November 1995 to October 1996). After the start-up period, average monthly volumes increased eight times and open interest by three times in 1996. The number of actively trading brokerages rose to 25 in 1996. Trading system is open outcry, with semi-automatic opening and closing periods. Futures contracts are settled and cleared by an independent clearing house – Keler – which is owned by the Central Bank (50%), and by the two Hungarian exchanges (25% each). New product launches in 1996 include 12-month Treasury bill, CESI (Central European Stock Index), DEM/USD, BUBOR (Budapest Interbank Offered Rate). The Budapest Stock Exchange has been co-operating with MATIF on introducing standardized options; trading is expected to start at the beginning of 1997.

IRELAND

Irish Futures & Options Exchange (IFOX)

Seagrave House, Earlsfort Terrace, Dublin 2
Tel: +353 1 676 7413
Fax: +353 1 661 4645
Managing Director: Fergus Sheridan
Technical Director: Kieran Luddy

Hours of trading: 08.30–16.15; 16.17–17.15 (late trading)

Contract details:
Commodities: interest rate futures – long gilt futures, medium gilt futures, short gilt futures, 3-month Dibor (Dublin interbank offered rate)

Trading currency and unit (manner of price quotation): Irish pounds

Trading unit:

Long gilt, medium gilt	– IR£50,000
Short gilt	– IR£100,000
3-month Dibor	– IR£500,000

Trading limits:
Minimum price fluctuation:

Long gilt	– 2%
Medium gilt, short gilt	– 1.5%
3-month Dibor	– 1.2%

Trading months:

Long gilt, medium gilt, short gilt	– March, June, September, December
3-month Dibor	– nearest three calendar months and next two quarterly months (eg March, June, September, December)

Termination of trading:

Long gilt, medium gilt, short gilt, 3-month Dibor	– third Monday of delivery month at 11.00

Commission rates and margins:

Short gilt, medium gilt	– IR£2.50 per lot
Long gilt	– IR£5.00 per lot
3-month Dibor	– IR£7.50

Volume of trade:

	1993–95
Short gilt	1,240
Medium gilt	4,300*
Long gilt	23,728
3-month Dibor	7,548
Total	36,816

* Launched March 1995

Date of establishment of contracts:

Long gilt – May 1989
Dibor – May 1989
Short gilt – September 1991
Medium gilt – March 1995

Membership: IFOX is a private company– each member is an ordinary shareholder

Membership of other organizations: Ecofex

JAPAN

KOBE

The Kobe Rubber Exchange

2–5–28 Kyutaro-Machi, Chuo-Ku, Osaka 541
Tel: +81 6 244 2191
Fax: +81 6 243 4427
Chairman: Dick Kitamura
Managing Director: Keiichiro Hayashi

Hours of trading:

Natural rubber index	–	09.20, 10.20, 13.20, 14.20, 15.20
Natural rubber	–	09.30, 10.30, 13.30, 14.30, 15.30, 17.00

Contract details:

Commodities: natural rubber index, natural rubber, international No. 3 ribbed smoked sheet

Trading currency and unit (manner of price quotation):

Natural rubber index	–	yen per 1 kg
Natural rubber	–	point per 1/20,000 of contract unit

Trading units (minimum lot size):

Natural rubber index	–	contract price times 20,000
Natural rubber	–	5,000 kg

Trading limits:

Natural rubber index		Natural rubber	
Average point range	*Price limit*	*Average point range*	*Price limit*
79.99 points and under	2.0 points	¥99.9 and under	¥6.0
80.00–109.00	2.5 points	¥100.0–149.9	¥7.0
110.00–139.99	3.0 points	¥150.0–199.9	¥8.0
140.00 points and above	3.5 points	¥200.0 and above	¥9.0

Quality:
Natural rubber – ribbed smoked sheet RSS No. 3 specified in the international standards of quality and packing for natural rubber grades

Deliverable tolerances:
Natural rubber – deliverable grade is RSS No. 4 which substitutes for RSS No. 3.

Delivery points:
Kobe City and Osaka City

Termination of trading:
Natural rubber index – tenth calendar day of each contract month. If it falls on a holiday, the next day shall be the last trading day of the month.

Natural rubber – fifth business day prior to the end of each contract month.

Commission rates and margins:
Commission:
Natural rubber index – commission is to be charged on the contracts traded at the exchange at the rate of not higher than ¥3,800 per unit. The rate is to be fixed between commission merchants and their clients with the ceiling rate ¥3,800 mentioned above.

Natural rubber:

Contract price	*Commission*	
	Non member	*Member including associate*
¥199.9 and under	¥3,310	¥1,980
¥200–299.9	¥3,480	¥2,080
¥300–399.9	¥3,650	¥2,180
¥400 and above	¥3,650+¥170 per ¥100 up	¥2,180+¥100 per ¥100 up

Margin:
Natural rubber index:

Average price range	*Initial customer margin (per unit)*
79.99 points and under	¥60,000
80.00–109.99	¥75,000
110.00–139.99	¥90,000
140.00 points and above	¥105,000

Natural rubber:

Average price range	*Initial customer margin (per unit)*
¥99.90 and under	¥45,000
¥100.00–149.90	¥52,500
¥150.00–199.90	¥60,000
¥200.00 and above	¥67,500

Date of establishment of contracts:
Natural rubber index – 1995
Natural rubber – 1993

Clearing house: Clearing is one of the functions of the Kobe Rubber Exchange.

Further information: The Kobe Rubber Exchange and Osaka Textile Exchange have agreed to start a discussion on merger plans with its target on 1 October 1997.

MAEBASHI

Maebashi Dried Cocoon Exchange

1–49–1 Fruichi-Machi, Maebashi City, Gumma 371
Tel: +81 272 52 1401
Fax: +81 272 52 1305
President: Saijuro Kaneko
Managing Director: Mitsuo Kodama

Hours of trading:
09.20; 13.20; 11.20; 15.20

Contract details:
Commodities: dried cocoon

Trading currency: yen

Trading unit: 300 kg, 15 bales

Trading limits: the fluctuation in one day is limited to within 5% of the closing price of the preceding day (existing limit 100 yen). Minimum price fluctuation – 1 yen per kg

Deliverable tolerances: 300 kg, 15 bales

Delivery points: warehouses located in Maebashi specified by the Exchange. Approved delivery facilities – Jomo warehouses, Gumma Chuo warehouses and Takasaki warehouses

Delivery months: six months

Commission rates and margins: regardless of contracted price – customer 3650 yen, member 2550 yen, others 2920 yen

Margins:

Level of price	Initial margin
Less than ¥3,000	¥60,000
¥3,000–4,500	¥70,000
¥4,500–6,000	¥80,000
More than ¥6,000	¥90,000

Volume of trade (contracts):

1993	*1994*	*1995*
1,477,293	416,093	656,101

Date of establishment of market: 10 July 1952

Trading members: 50 (commodity commission merchants – 25)

Membership: the members of the Exchange select a fellow trader via an examination set by the Qualification Judging Committee.

TOKYO

The Tokyo Commodity Exchange

Riverside Yomiuri Building, 36–2 Nihonbashi-Hokazakicho, Chuo-ku, Tokyo 103
Tel: +81 3 3661 9191
Fax: +81 3 3661 7568
Chairman: Naozo Mabuchi

Hours of trading:

Gold, silver, platinum, palladium	– 09.00–11.00 and 13.00–15.30
Rubber	– 09.45; 10.45; 13.45; 14.45; 15.30
Cotton yarn	– 08.50; 10.15; 12.50; 15.10
Wool yarn	– traded after the cotton sessions

Contract details:

Commodities: gold, silver, platinum, palladium, rubber, cotton yarn, wool yarn

Trading currency and unit (manner of price quotation):

Gold	– ¥1 per gram
Silver	– ¥0.10 per 10 grams
Platinum	– ¥1 per gram
Palladium	– ¥1 per gram
Rubber	– ¥0.10 per kg
Cotton yarn	– ¥0.10 per 0.45359 kg (1 lb)
Wool yarn	– ¥1 per kg

Trading units (minimum lot size):

Gold	– 1 kg
Silver	– 60 kg
Platinum	– 500 g
Palladium	– 1.5 kg
Rubber	– 5,000 kg
Cotton yarn	– 1,814.36 kg (4,000 lb)
Wool yarn	– 500 kg

Gold

Price fluctuation limits:	Quotation (¥ per gram):	
	below 1,000	30
	1,100 to 1,599	40
	1,600 to 2,099	50
	2,100 or above	60
Initial margin:	Quotation (¥ per contract)	
	below 1,100	45,000
	1,100 to 1,599	60,000
	1,600 to 2,099	75,000
	2,100 or above	90,000

Commission:	Quotation (¥ per contract)	
	below 1,000	4,500
	1,000 to 1,399	5,200
	1,400 to 1,799	5,900
	1,800 to 2,199	6,600
	2,200 to 2,599	7,300
	2,600 to 2,999	8,000
	3,000 or above	plus 700 for each 400

Silver

Price fluctuation limits:	Quotation (¥ per 10 grams)	
	below 150.00	5.0
	150.00 to 199.9	6.0
	200.00 to 249.9	7.0
	250.0 or above	8.0
Initial margin:	Quotation (¥ per contract)	
	below 150.0	45,000
	150.0 to 199.9	54,000
	200.0 to 249.9	63,000
	250.0 or above	72,000
Commission:	Quotation (¥ per contract)	
	below 100.0	2,900
	100.0 to 149.9	3,900
	150.0 to 199.9	4,900
	200.0 to 249.9	5,900
	250.0 to 299.9	6,900
	300.0 to 349.9	7,900
	350.0 or above	plus 1,000 for each 50

Platinum

Price fluctuation limits:	Quotation (¥ per gram)	
	below 1,200	40
	1,200 to 1,799	50
	1,800 to 2,399	60
	2,400 or above	70
Initial margin:	Quotation (¥ per contract)	
	below 1,200	30,000
	1,200 to 1,799	37,500
	1,800 to 2,399	45,000
	2,400 or above	52,500
Commission:	Quotation (¥ per contract)	
	below 1,000	3,100
	1,000 to 1,399	3,400
	1,400 to 1,799	3,700

	1,800 to 2,199	4,000
	2,200 to 2,599	4,300
	2,600 to 2,999	4,600
	3,000 or above	plus 300 for each 400

Palladium

Price fluctuation limits:	Quotation (¥ per gram)	
	below 400	20
	400 to 599	22
	600 to 799	24
	800 or above	26
Initial margin:	Quotation (¥ per contract)	
	below 400	45,000
	400 to 599	49,500
	600 to 799	54,000
	800 or above	58,500
Commission:	¥2,900	

Rubber

Price fluctuation limits:	Quotation (¥ per contract)	
	below 100.0	6.0
	100.0 to 149.0	7.0
	150.0 to 199.9	8.0
	200 or above	9.0
Initial margin:	Quotation (¥ per contract)	
	below 100	45,000
	100.0 to 149.9	52,500
	150.0 to 199.0	60,000
	200.0 or above	67,500
Commission:	Quotation (¥ per contract)	
	below 200.0	3,310
	200.0 to 299.9	3,480
	300.0 to 399.9	3,650
	400.0 or above	plus 170 for each ¥100

Cotton yarn

Price fluctuation limits:	Quotation (¥ per contract)	
	below 150	7.0
	150.0 to 199.9	8.0
	200.0 to 249.9	9.0
	250 or above	10.0
Initial margin:	Quotation (¥ per contract)	
	below 150	42,000
	150.0 to 199.9	48,000
	200.0 to 249.9	54,000
	250.0 or above	60,000

Commision:

Quotation (¥ per contract)	
below 300.0	4,260
300.0 to 399.9	4,460
400.0 or above	4,660

Wool yarn

Price fluctuation limits:

Quotation (¥ per contract)	
below 1,100	50
1,100 to 1,499	60
1,500 to 1,899	70
1,900 or above	80

Initial margin:

Quotation (¥ per contract)	
below 1,100	37,500
1,100 to 1,499	45,000
1,500 to 1,899	52,500
1,900 or above	60,000

Commission:

Quotation (¥ per contract)	
below 2,000	3,300
2,000 to 2,499	3,730
2,500 or above	4,160

Quality:

Gold – fine gold of minimum 99.99% purity
Silver – fine silver of minimum 99.99% purity
Platinum – fine platinum of minimum 99.99% purity
Palladium – fine palladium of minimum 99.99% purity
Rubber – ribbed smoked sheet (RSS) No. 3
Cotton yarn – 40 count single grey weaving yarn, Z twist Murafuji brand
Wool yarn – 48 count double worsted weaving yarn, Z twist AG brand

Delivery points: specified warehouses

Volume of trading:

1993	*1994*	*1995*
21,557,795	30,481,313	35,125,427

Membership: The Tokyo Commodity Exchange membership is divided into two classes: general members and futures commission merchants (FCM). General members trade only for their own accounts, whereas FCMs are authorized to trade both on their accounts and on their customers'. An overseas corporation, if it wishes to become a general member of TOCOM, is required to be qualified as either an FCM in its country or a corporation engaged in the business of such commodities as placed on TOCOM, and then for becoming an FCM of TOCOM, it has to own its office and hold a certain share of its assets or funds in Japan. Membership is also open to corporations which are already members of overseas institutions such as the London Bullion Market Association and the International Rubber Market. An associate member can trade on TOCOM through an FCM with the benefit of reduced commissions and customer margins.

Further information: The Tokyo Commodity Exchange (TOCOM) was established on 1 November 1984 by consolidating the Tokyo Gold Exchange (1982), the Tokyo Rubber Exchange (1952), and the Tokyo Textile Exchange (1951). When TOCOM was established, it listed six commodities futures: gold, silver, platinum, rubber, cotton yarn, and wool yarn. Physical gold was launched on 19 October 1988. Palladium futures was newly placed on the market on 3 August 1992.

TOCOM introduced computerized trading systems into the precious metals market in April 1991 and is now one of the most active precious metals markets in the world, being the largest market for platinum, palladium, and rubber futures.

The Tokyo Grain Exchange

12–5 Nihonbashi Kakigara-cho 1-Chome, Tokyo 103
Tel: +81 3 3668 9321
Fax: +81 3 3661 4496
E-mail: mary-tge@po.iijnet.or.jp
Web site: http://www.toppan.co.jp/tge/

Hours of trading (Tokyo time, session trading):

Azuki beans	– 09.00; 10.00; 11.00; 13.10; 14.10; 15.10. Last trading day: 09.00; 10.00; 11.00
Corn	– 09.00; 11.00; 13.10; 15.10. Last trading day: 09.00; 11.00
Raw sugar	– 09.10; 10.20; 13.00; 14.00; 15.00. Last trading day: 09.10; 10.20
Refined sugar	– 09.05; 10.15; 12.55; 13.55; 14.55. Last trading day: 09.05; 10.15
US soybeans	– 10.00; 11.00; 13.10; 14.10. Last trading day: 10.00; 11.00.
Options on raw sugar	– 09.10–09.30; 09.30–11.30; 13.00–13.15; 13.15–15.00;15.00–15.15
Options on US soybeans	– 10.00–10.20; 10.20–11.30; 13.00–13.15; 13.15–14.30; 14.30–14.45

Contract details:
Commodities:
Futures – azuki beans, corn, raw sugar, refined sugar, US soybeans; options – raw sugar, US soybeans.

Trading units:
Futures:

Azuki beans	– 80 bags (2,400 kg)
Corn	– 100,000 kg
Raw sugar	– 50,000 kg
Refined sugar	– 9,000 kg
US soybeans	– 30,000 kg

Options:

Raw sugar – one TGE raw sugar futures contract (50,000 kg)

US soybeans – one TGE US soybean futures contract (30,000 kg)

Quality:

Azuki beans – No. 2 polished azuki produced in Hokkaido

Corn – No. 3 yellow corn produced in the USA (less than 15% moisture) (CIF Japan)

Raw sugar – Centrifugally separated raw cane sugar syrup polarization of 96% (CIF Japan)

Refined sugar – T1 brand white soft sugar refined within three months by Toyo Seito Co

US soybean – Yellow IOM soybeans produced in USA unscreened (stored in silo)

Deliverable tolerances:

Azuki beans – other grades of azuki produced in Hokkaido and other parts of Japan are deliverable at a premium or a discount. Imported azuki from the People's Republic of China and Japan are deliverable at a discount

Corn – No. 3 yellow corn produced in the USA (less than 15% moisture)

Raw sugar – raw centrifugal cane sugar of a polarization of 96% from Australia, Brazil, Taiwan, Cuba, Fiji, Philippines, Republic of South Africa and Thailand

Refined sugar – T1 brand white soft sugar refined within three months by Toyo Seito Co and those equivalent

US soybeans – non-screened No. 2 yellow soybeans of Indiana, Ohio and Michigan origin, imported from the USA (stored in silo)

Delivery points:

Azuki beans – warehouses in Tokyo, Kanagawa, Chiba, or Saitama designated by the Exchange

Corn – The piers of Kashima, Chiba, Kawasaki or Yokohama port

Raw sugar – Ports of Tokyo, Chiba, Funabashi, Kawasaki, Yokohama, Shimuzu, Kinuura, Nagoya, Izumisano, Sakai, Osaka, Kobe, Uno, Shimonoseki, Hakata and Hosojima

Refined sugar – warehouses in Tokyo designated by the Exchange

US soybeans – warehouses in Tokyo, Kanagawa, Chiba or Saitama designated by the Exchange

Delivery months:
Futures:

Azuki beans – six consecutive months
Corn – January, March, May, July, September, November within a 12-month period
Raw sugar – January, March, May, July, September, November within a 20-month period
Refined sugar – six consecutive months
US soybeans – February, April, June, August, October, December within a 12-month period

Options:

Raw sugar – January, March, May, July, September, November within a 15-month period
US soybeans – February, April, June, August, October, December within a 12-month period

Termination of trading:
Futures:

Azuki beans – 11.00 session of second business day prior to delivery day.
Corn – 11.00 session of 15th* day of the month preceding delivery month
Raw sugar – 10.20 session of the last business day two months prior to delivery month
Refined sugar – 10.15 session of second business day prior to delivery day
US soybeans – 11.00 session of second business day prior to delivery day

Options:

Raw sugar – last business day three months prior to delivery month of the underlying futures contract
US soybeans – 15th† day of the month preceding delivery month of the underlying futures contract

Delivery day:

Azuki beans – first business day prior to the last business day of delivery month
Corn – from the first day to the last day of the delivery month
Raw sugar – from 15th* day of the month preceding the delivery month to the last day of delivery month
Refined sugar – noon of the first business day prior to the last business day of delivery month

US soybeans	–	first business day prior to the last business day of delivery month

* If that day is not a business day, the preceding business day shall apply

† If that day is not a business day, then the last trading day is moved up to the nearest business day

Date of establishment of contracts:

Futures:

Azuki beans	–	October 1952
Corn	–	April 1992
Raw sugar	–	May 1952
Refined sugar	–	May 1952
US soybeans	–	March 1984

Options:

Raw sugar	–	May 1992
US soybeans	–	June 1991

KENYA

MOMBASA

East African Tea Trade Association

PO Box 85174, Mombasa
Tel: +254 11 315245/315687
Fax: +254 11 225823
Chairman: D S F Smyth
Vice Chairman: E Kooyman
Assistant Executive Officer: M Mwangome

Hours of trading: auctions every Monday 08.30 in Mombasa at Tea Trade Centre. Auctions trading conducted by broker members, Africa Tea Brokers Ltd, Anjeli Ltd, Combrok Ltd, Prudential Tea Brokers (East Africa) Ltd, Tea Brokers East Africa Ltd, Union Tea Brokers Ltd, Venus Tea Brokers, and Victory Tea Brokers Ltd. Private contracts conducted five days a week from 08.30 to 16.30

Contract details:
Commodities: black tea

Trading currency and unit (manner of price quotation): US dollars including private treaty. Bidding at auction advances by not less than 1 US cent on all teas

Trading unit (minimum lot size): lots are sold by the kilogram. For Main Grade catalogue the minimum number of packages for a lot is 40 and the minimum weight of each lot is 20 kg. For the Secondary Grade catalogue the minimum lot is 20 packages. A lot may be divided among buyers providing that not more than three buyers participate in the division of any lot and that each of these buyers receives a minimum of 20 kg

Quality: all teas on Estate Account must be offered 'factory bulked' and under estate marks. Second-hand teas may only be offered for sale on condition that they are described as being 'on account of the concerned'. Damaged teas may not be offered for sale unless they are described as 'with all faults and at buyer's risk'

Delivery points: as required by overseas buyer dependent on overseas sale or contract and availability of shipping

Termination of trading: subject to a minimum of US$15,000, brokers shall make payment to sellers of the value less charges on all proceeds received by them by noon on the Friday following the auction. Funds to be credited to seller's bank account by close of business on the following Monday. The value less charges on the balance will be paid to the seller not later than 12.00 noon on Prompt Day. If payment is not made on Prompt Day, the broker so defaulting shall pay the producer interest at the commercial bank rates

Commission rates and margins: brokerage charged 1% to seller, 0.5% to buyer. Buyer at liberty to fix own selling price to overseas buyer

Clearing house: Tea Trade Centre, Nyerere Avenue, Mombasa

Membership:

Buyer member:

Any person, firm or company, actively engaged in buying tea, actively will mean the purchase of at least 50,000 kg of tea in the 12-month period 1 January to 31 December.

Packer member:

Any person, firm or company actively engaged in buying tea in Eastern Africa for retail to the public. For the purpose of this Rule, active will mean purchases through active broker or buyer members of the Association of a minimum of 5,000 kg of tea in a 12-month period 1 January to 31 December.

Producer member:

Any person, firm or company actively engaged in the growing and/or manufacture of tea, or as agents for tea growers and/or tea manufacturers in Eastern Africa.

Broker member:

Any person, firm or company established in Eastern Africa for the purpose of negotiating there the purchase or sale of tea between members of the Association.

Warehouse member:

Any person, firm or company established in Eastern Africa with the object of warehousing teas being sold under the Rules and Regulations of the East Africa Tea Trade Association who is not already a member under another category. A warehouse member will not have the same rights and privileges as full buyer/producer/broker members.

Associate member:

Any person, firm or company not herein before defined connected with the tea industry in Eastern Africa. Associate members will have the same rights and privileges as a warehouse member.

MALAYSIA

KUALA LUMPUR

Kuala Lumpur Commodity Exchange

4th Floor, City Point, Kompleks Dayabumi, Jalan Sultan Hishamuddin, PO Box 11260, 50740 Kuala Lumpur
Tel: +60 3 293 6822
Fax: +60 3 274 2215
Telex: MA 31472 KLCE
Chairman: Tan Sri Ishak Tadin
Chief Executive: Dato' S A J Shahabudin

Hours of trading:

Crude palm oil	–	11.00–12.30 and 15.30–18.00
Tin	–	12.15–13.00 and 16.00–19.00
Rubber	–	10.00–13.00 and 16.00–18.00
Cocoa	–	11.15–12.00 and 16.00–19.00

Contract details:
Commodities: crude palm oil, tin, rubber (SMR 20), cocoa

Trading currency and unit (manner of price quotation):

Crude palm oil	–	M$1.00 per tonne
Tin	–	US$5.00 per tonne
Rubber	–	M$0.0025 per kg
Cocoa	–	US$1.00 per tonne

Trading units (minimum lot size):

Crude palm oil	–	25 tonnes
Tin	–	5 tonnes
Rubber	–	10 tonnes (single delivery month) 30 tonnes (delivery)
Cocoa	–	10 tonnes

Crude palm oil
Trading limits: M$50 above or below the settlement prices of the preceding day for all months, except current month. Limits are expanded when on any one day the settlement prices of all three quoted months following the current month are at the limits listed below:

Day	*Limits (M$)*
First	50
Second	75
Third	100
Fourth	none
Fifth	50

Minimum price fluctuation: M$1.00 per tonne

Quality: of good merchantable quality, in bulk, unbleached and in port tank installations. Free fatty acid (FFA) content of palm oil delivered to port tank installations shall not exceed 4%, and from port tank installations 5%. Moisture and impurities shall not exceed 0.25%.

Deliverable tolerances: 25 tonnes +/– 2%

Delivery points: port tank installations located at the option of the seller at Port Kelang, Butterworth/Prai and Pasir Gudang (Johore).

Termination of trading: 15th of the month, or the preceding business day

Delivery month: current month, the next five succeeding months, and thereafter alternate months up to 12 months forward.

Tin

Trading limits: price limits for all months, except current month, are established at the opening of the market on each day at US$250 above or below the previous day's settlement prices. When prices for the first three months following the current month are being bid or offered at limits, trading in all months except the current month shall cease for 15 minutes. When trading resumes the limits will be adjusted by US$250 up or down to form new limit prices.

In the event of settlement prices for the three consecutive months immediately following the current month reaching the new limit prices, this shall be termed a 'limit day'. In the event of there being three limit days for three consecutive business days, on the fourth business day there shall be no price limits. On the fifth business day the limit price fluctuation shall apply.

Minimum price fluctuations: US$5 per tonne

Quality: refined tin assaying not less than 99.85% Sn and complied with American Society for Testing and Materials (ASTM) specification B 399.86 for Banka, DKS (Escoy), Mentok, MSC and Thaisarco brands.

Deliverable tolerances: 5 tonnes +/– 2% on warrants issued by warehouses approved by the Exchange

Delivery points: at the option of the seller, approved warehouses in Penang, Singapore, Rotterdam, or such places determined by the Exchange

Termination of trading: the business day immediately before the last two business days of the month

Delivery months: current month, the next three successive months, thereafter alternate months up to 12 months forward.

Rubber

Trading limits: price limits, established before the opening of the market each trading day, are set at 105n above and below the settlement prices of the previous day, this applies for all months except the current month.

If trading for the two nearest months excluding the current month is transacted at established limits, trading for all months and quarters ceases for 15 minutes, at which time limit prices are re-established.

Minimum price fluctuation: Mc0.25 per kg

Quality: in accordance with the latest published technical specifications from the Rubber Research Institute of Malaysia for SMR 20

Deliverable tolerances: contract unit: 20 tonnes; tender unit: 19.2 tonnes (one container load)

Delivery points: FOB at the ports of Penang, Port Kelang and Singapore, at the option of the seller.

Termination of trading: the last business day of the month preceding contract month

Delivery months: current month, the next three to five months forward and two distant quarters

Cocoa

Trading limits: US$80 per tonne above or below the settlement prices of the preceding day for all months except current month. Limits are expanded when on any one day the settlement prices of all three quoted months immediately following the current month are at the limits listed below:

Day	*Limits (US$)*
First	80
Second	100
Third	120
Fourth	none
Fifth	80

Minimum price fluctuation: US$1 per tonne

Quality:

Growth – group A: Malaysia, Papua New Guinea – at par; group B: Indonesia, Thailand, Philippines – at a discount of US$45 per tonne

Grade – moisture content – not more than 7.5% by weight; mouldy – not more than 3.0% by count; slaty – not more than 3.0% by count; insect damaged and germinated – not more than 3.0% by count

Bean count: cocoa with a bean count of up to 140 beans per 100 grammes is acceptable subject to the following scale of discounts:

Bean count	*Total discount (US$ per tonne)*
110 and less	none
111 to 120	4.50 to 56.25
121 to 130	63.25 to 137.50
131 to 140	147.25 to 257.50

Deliverable tolerances: 10 tonnes +/– 1% on warehouse warrants

Delivery points: warehouses approved by the KLCE at Tawau, Pasir Gudang (Johore) and Port Kelang.

Termination of trading: 20th of the month or the preceding business day

Delivery months: January, March, May, July, September, November, December

Commission rates and margins:

Commission:

Commodity	*Type of member*	*Day trade* (Roundturn in Ringgit Malaysia (RM))	*Overnight trade*
Crude palm oil	Member	26.50	53.00
	Trade Affiliate	26.50	53.00
	Non-member	51.50	103.00
Rubber	Member	31	62
	Trade Affiliate	41	82
	Non-member	51	102
Cocoa	Member	11	20
	Trade Affiliate	15	30
	Non-member	20	40
		No. of 5-tonne lots transacted per month	
		1–50	Above 50
Tin	Member	40	40
	Trade Affiliate	60	40
	Non-member	90	negotiable (but not less than 40)

Margins: minimum initial margins are set by the clearing house and adjusted from time to time depending on the market volatility. Variation margins are marked market to market.

Volume of trade:

	1994		*1995*	
	lots	*tonnes*	*lots*	*tonnes*
Crude palm oil	569,482	14,237,050	524,665	13,147,225

Date of establishment of market: July 1980

Date of establishment of contracts:

Crude palm oil – October 1980
Tin – October 1980
Rubber – March 1986
Cocoa – August 1988

Clearing house: Malaysian Futures Clearing Corporation Sdn Bhd (MFCC)

Membership: a corporate Member can own multiple memberships, each one entitling the Member to have a trader on the floor of the Exchange to trade in any contract market. The membership of the Exchange is limited to 130, each membership costing M$50,000 and able to be bought or sold. Before a corporate member is allowed to trade on the floor, he or she must first have been qualified and guaranteed by a Clearing member. The Exchange admits local or overseas companies through a restricted form of membership – Trade Affiliates – with no voting rights. A Trade Affiliate can trade for its own account or for the accounts of overseas clients at reduced brokerage. Deals with other Trade Affiliates are not allowed, all business needing to be transacted through a Member. The entrance for this type of membership is M$10,000. Furthermore, the Exchange admits individual residents to trade on the Exchange floor as 'Locals'. A Local is allowed to trade only for his or her own account or for the account of his or her Clearing member.

Membership of other organizations: international member of the US Futures Industry Association (FIA).

Further information: Planned new contracts include plywood futures, lauric oil futures, pepper futures and options on CPO futures.

The Kuala Lumpur Tin Market

4th Floor, City Point, Kompleks Dayabumi, Jalan Sultan Hishamuddin, Kuala Lumpur
Tel: +60 3 293 6822
Fax: +60 3 274 2215
Telex: MA31472
Chairman: Dato' Mohd Ajib Hj. Anuar
Secretary: Ishak Mohd Ali

Hours of trading: 11.45 Monday to Friday

Contract details:
Commodity: refined tin of approved origin, namely DKS (Escoy), MSC, Mentok, Banka and Thaisarco

Trading units (minimum lot size): 1 tonne

Trading currency and unit (manner of price quotation): Malaysian Ringgit per kg

Quality: refined tin ASTM grade A, B 339.86 with minimum tin content of 99.85 Sn of approved brands

Deliverable tolerances: individual weight between 25 kg and 50 kg steel-strapped bundles, self-palleted and one tonne in weight subject to a variation of not more than 2%

Delivery points: approved warehouses in Penang and Singapore.

Delivery: spot trading with prompt delivery by means of warrant within four business days of market contract. Tin for delivery by registered smelters shall be appropriated at seller's option within 45 days from date of contract

Date of establishment of market: 1 October 1984

Membership: ordinary and associate members subject to approval by a Board of Directors. Entrance fee is MR$5,000; annual subscription MR$5,000 and lodge trading guarantee MR$1,000,000

Further information: KLTM was incorporated by the Malaysian Government as a company limited by guarantee on 28 June 1984 to take over from the Penang Tin Market.

THE NETHERLANDS

AMSTERDAM

Agricultural Futures Exchange Amsterdam (ATA Agrarische Termijnmarkt Amsterdam BV)

Damrak 261, 1012 ZJ Amsterdam
Tel: +31 20 638 2258/2239
Fax: +31 20 626 5459
President: R R Muller
Vice President: K Walet
Marketing: B Vermeeren

Hours of trading:

Potatoes	–	10.45–12.45 and 14.00–16.00
Live hogs and piglets	–	10.30–12.00 and 13.30–16.15
Wheat	–	10.00–12.30 and 13.45–16.30

Contract details:
Commodities: Futures – potatoes, live hogs, piglets, wheat

Potato
Trading units: 25,000 kg net

Underlying: potatoes with a tuber size of 50 mm or above

Delivery months: November, February, March, April, May, June

Initial margin: Dfl1,750.00

Tick size: Dfl0.10

Trading limits: no limits

Termination of trading: the last Friday of the month, provided it is at least four working days before the end of the month

Delivery: physical delivery of the commodity

Live hogs
Trading units: 10,000 kg net

Underlying: live hogs

Delivery months: all calendar months and 12 months forward

Initial margin: Dfl2,000.00

Tick size: Dfl0.005

Trading limits: no limits

Termination of trading: with a few exceptions the last Thursday after which remains a minimum of five working days

Delivery: physical delivery of the commodity

Piglets

Trading units: 100 piglets of 23 kg

Underlying: piglets of 23 kgs

Delivery months: all calendar months and 12 months forward

Initial margin: Dfl1,200.00

Tick size: Dfl0.25

Trading limits: no limits

Termination of trading: the last Monday of a calendar month

Delivery: cash settlement

Wheat

Trading units: 125 tonnes

Underlying: wheat in free trade in the EU

Delivery months: August, December 1996, February, April, June 1997

Initial margin: DM 1,500

Tick size: DM 0.25

Trading limits: no limits

Termination of trading: the 23rd calendar day of the month

Delivery: delivery of a bearer warehouse receipt

Volume of trade:

	1993	*1994*	*1995*
Potatoes	155,565	229,070	165,312
Live hogs	44,887	41,379	30,874
Piglets	3,321	3,418	2,522

Date of establishment of contracts:

Potatoes – April 1958
Live hogs – November 1980
Piglets – April 1991
Wheat – May 1996

Clearing house: Amsterdam Futures Clearing (NLKKAS)

NEW ZEALAND

AUCKLAND

New Zealand Options and Futures Exchange Ltd

10th Floor, Stock Exchange Centre, 191 Queen Street, Auckland 1
Postal address: PO Box 6734, Wellesley Street, Auckland
Tel: +64 9 309 8308
Fax: +64 9 309 8817
Chief Executive: Peter Mansell

Hours of trading: 08.00–12.00 and 13.00–17.00

Contract details:
Commodities: futures – 90-day bank bills, NZ 3-year government stock, NZ 10-year government stock, NZSE-10 share index, US dollar, NZ wool; options – 90-day bank bills, NZ 3-year government stock, NZ 10-year government stock, NZSE-10 share index; share options – Brierly Investments Ltd, Carter Holt Harvey Ltd, Fletcher Challenge Ltd: ordinary, Fletcher Challenge Ltd: forestry, Goodman Fielder Ltd, Lion Nathan Ltd, Telecom New Zealand Ltd

Trading currency and unit (manner of price quotation):

90-day bank bills futures, NZ 3-year government stock futures, NZ 10-year government stock futures	– yield per cent per annum quoted as 100% minus price
NZSE-10 share index futures	– index points of the NZSE-10 Capital Share Price Index in whole numbers
US dollar futures	– NZ$ per US$
NZ wool futures	– cents per clean kg
90-day bank bills options, NZ 3-year government stock options, NZ 10-year government stock options, NZSE-10 share index options	– one unit of the underlying security
Brierly Investments Ltd equity options, Carter Holt Harvey Ltd equity options, Fletcher Challenge Ltd: ordinary equity options, Fletcher Challenge Ltd: forestry equity options, Goodman Fielder Ltd equity options, Lion	

Nathan Ltd equity options, Telecom New Zealand Ltd equity options	– NZ cents per share

Trading unit (minimum lot size):

90-day bank bills futures	– NZ$500,000
NZ 3-year government stock futures, NZ 10-year government stock futures	– NZ$100,000
NZSE-10 share index futures	– NZ$25 times index
US dollar futures	– US$50,000
NZ wool futures	– wools of NZ Strong Segment Indicator times 2,500
90-day bank bills options	– one 90-day bank bills futures contract
NZ 3-year government stock options	– one 3-year government stock futures contract
NZ 10-year government stock options	– one 10-year government stock futures contract
NZSE-10 share index options	– one NZSE-10 share index futures contract
Brierly Investments Ltd equity options, Carter Holt Harvey Ltd equity options, Fletcher Challenge Ltd: ordinary equity options, Fletcher Challenge Ltd: forestry equity options, Goodman Fielder Ltd equity options, Lion Nathan Ltd equity options, Telecom New Zealand Ltd equity options	– 1,000 shares

Trading limits:

Minimum fluctuations:

90-day bank bills futures, NZ 3-year government stock futures, NZ 10-year government stock futures	– 0.01% per annum
NZSE-10 share index futures	– 1 index point in whole numbers
US dollar futures	– 0.0001 NZ$
NZ wool futures	– 1 cent
90-day bank bills options, NZ 3-year government stock options, NZ 10-year government stock options	– 0.01 % per annum
Brierly Investments Ltd equity options, Carter Holt Harvey Ltd equity options, Fletcher Challenge Ltd: ordinary equity options, Fletcher Challenge Ltd: forestry equity options, Goodman Fielder Ltd equity options, Lion Nathan Ltd equity options, Telecom New Zealand Ltd equity options	– 0.1 cents

Tick size:

90-day bank bills futures	– approximately NZ$12
NZ 3-year government stock futures,	– approximately NZ$25
NZ 10-year government stock futures	– approximately NZ$60
NZSE-10 share index futures, NZ wool futures	– NZ$25
US dollar futures	– NZ$5
90-day bank bills options	– approximately NZ$12
NZ 3-year government stock options, NZSE-10 share index options	– NZ$25
NZ 10-year government stock options	– approximately NZ$60
Brierly Investments Ltd equity options, Carter Holt Harvey Ltd equity options, Fletcher Challenge Ltd: ordinary equity options, Fletcher Challenge Ltd: forestry equity options, Goodman Fielder Ltd equity options, Lion Nathan Ltd equity options, Telecom New Zealand Ltd equity options	– NZ$1

Delivery:

90-day bank bills options, NZ 3-year government stock options, NZ 10-year government stock options, NZSE-10 share index options, Brierly Investments Ltd equity options, Carter Holt Harvey Ltd equity options, Fletcher Challenge Ltd: ordinary equity options, Fletcher Challenge Ltd: forestry equity options, Goodman Fielder Ltd equity options, Lion Nathan Ltd equity options, Telecom New Zealand Ltd equity options	– for options exercised prior to expiry, the seller will be notified by the clearing house no later than 45 minutes prior to the commencement of the next business day's trading. For options exercised at expiry, the seller will be notified by the clearing house no later than 09.00 hours on the business day following expiration date

Termination of trading:

90-day bank bills futures, NZ 3-year government stock futures, NZ 10-year government stock futures, US dollar futures	– the first Wednesday after the ninth day of relevant settlement month

NZSE-10 share index futures, NZ wool futures	– the second to last business day of relevant settlement month

Settlement months:

90-day bank bills futures, NZ 3-year government stock futures, NZ 10-year government stock futures, NZSE-10 share index futures, US dollar futures	– March, June, September, December
NZ wool futures	– February, April, June, August, October, December
90-day bank bills options, NZ 3-year government stock options, NZ 10-year government stock options, NZSE-10 share index options	– March, June, September, December
Brierly Investments Ltd equity options, Fletcher Challenge Ltd: ordinary equity options, Fletcher Challenge Ltd: forestry equity options	– February, May, August, November
Carter Holt Harvey Ltd equity options, Telecom New Zealand Ltd equity options	– March, June, September, December
Goodman Fielder Ltd equity options, Lion Nathan Ltd equity options	– January, April, July, October

Settlement:

90-day bank bills futures, NZ 3-year government stock futures, NZ 10-year government stock futures, NZSE-10 share index futures, US dollar futures, NZ wool futures	– cash settlement with the parties making payment to or receiving from the clearing house (whichever is applicable) the amount the difference between the contract value and the mandatory settlement value by no later than 14.00 hours on mandatory settlement day

Expiry dates:

90-day bank bills options, NZ 3-year government stock options, NZ 10-year government stock options	– the first Wednesday after the ninth day of relevant settlement month
Brierly Investments Ltd equity options, Carter Holt Harvey Ltd equity options, Fletcher Challenge Ltd: ordinary equity options, Fletcher Challenge Ltd: forestry equity options, Goodman	

Fielder Ltd equity options, Lion Nathan Ltd equity options, Telecom New Zealand Ltd equity options	– the second to last business day of the settlement month. Trading will cease at the close of trading on expiration date

Initial margin:

90-day bank bills futures, NZ wool futures	– NZ$500
NZ 3-year government stock futures	– NZ$800
NZ 10-year government stock futures	– NZ$2,000
NZSE-10 share index futures	– NZ$850
US dollar futures	– NZ$1,500

Clearing house: Sydney Futures Exchange Clearing House

Membership:

New Zealand dealers

There are four classes of membership (i) public brokers (PB) – these dealers are authorized to deal in contracts on behalf of other persons or on their own behalf. They are also authorized to accept and hold client money and property; (ii) introducing brokers (IB) – these dealers may deal in contract on behalf of other persons or on their own behalf but may not hold client money or property. Introducing brokers must direct all client transactions through a trading permit holder; (iii) principal traders – these dealers generally trade only on their own account. They may deal on behalf of other dealers but only on a give-up basis and are not authorized to hold client money or property; (iv) trading permit holders – where a dealer also holds a trading permit they may deal directly on the Automated Trading System of the New Zealand Futures & Options Exchange. Dealers who are not trading permit holders must deal through a dealer who is.

Australian dealers

As well as (i) and (iv) above, there also exists another class of membership for Australian dealers (v) clearing member – authorized as a clearing member of the Sydney Futures Exchange Clearing House Ltd.

PAKISTAN

KARACHI

Karachi Cotton Association

The Cotton Exchange, I. I. Chundrigar Road, Karachi
Tel: +92 21 242 5007
Fax: +92 21 241 3035
Cables: COTEX, Karachi
Chairman: Mr Maqbool Sadiq (Tel: +92 21 241 0336)
Secretary: Mr Fasihuddin (Tel: +92 21 241 2570)

The Karachi Cotton Association is the premier body of the cotton trade in the country and is officially recognized by the Government of Pakistan. It was set up in 1933 to establish just and equitable principles for the cotton trade, to set standards of cotton and provide all necessary facilities for domestic and export trâde in cotton.

The membership of the Association consists of growers, ginners, exporters, textile mills and others. The affairs of the Association are conducted by a 21-man Board of Directors out of which 17 directors are elected annually through a secret ballot and four directors are nominated by the Government of Pakistan.

The by-laws of the Association cover comprehensively the entire field of cotton marketing and have been approved by the Government of Pakistan. Among other things, the by-laws provide for the maintenance of discipline and fair trading practices, running of the futures market, establishment of a clearing house, fixing of daily spot rates, arbitration of disputes, making of ready and forward transactions, standards of different varieties of cotton, etc.

The export trade was nationalised in 1973 and the futures market as closed during 1975–6. Since 1987–8, the private sector has been re-inducted into the export business. The policy of free trading in cotton has been introduced by the Government since 1994–5. Under this policy, the export and import of cotton are free of duty and without any restrictions. The policy of free trading in cotton has been made permanent for another three years.

After three consecutive cotton crop failures, the production of cotton in 1995–6 is estimated at 10.0 million bales (each bale is 375 lbs) against which, mill purchases have aggregated to about 8.0 million bales up to 1 April 1996 and exports of cotton during 1995–6 are estimated at about 1.8 million bales.

The Karachi Cotton Association has urged the Government to allow reopening of hedge trading in cotton which will benefit all sections of the cotton trade by providing a cover against the risk of fluctuations in prices.

RUSSIA

Exchange Saint Petersburg

VO26 Liniya, 15, 199026 Saint Petersburg
Tel: +7 812 355 6867
Fax: +7 812 355 6863
President and CEO: Viktor V. Nikolayev
Vice-President and COO: Anatoly G. Kartashov

Hours of trading: 10.00-14.00

Contract details:
Commodities: (A) – Futures contracts on non-cash US$ index; (B) – Futures contracts on index of federal debentures rates in secondary market (by each kind of debenture); (C) – Futures contracts on price index of federal debentures in primary placement (by each kind of debenture separately). Options (American type) on the futures contracts traded at the exchange.

Trading currency and unit (manner of price quotation):
All the settlements are made in RF Roubles, the prices are fixed in roubles per commodity unit (cash commodity, a security, currency) or in % of the face value of a security. In futures contracts the quotation in index points is allowed.

Delivery points: execution without delivery by means of transfer of the variation margin

Trading months:
Futures contracts (A) and (B) – monthly (11 next months are traded); futures contracts (C) – according to the date of primary placement (six next months are traded); options maturities correspond to the termination of trading in underlying futures (five next months are traded)

Delivery months:
Contracts with monthly maturities – after the last day of trading in the next month's contract, the day after the next contract is introduced for trading (for example, the December contract begins the day after the last day of trading for the January contract). For futures (C) – the next contract begins the day after the notice of the date of primary auction in the appropriate security

Termination of trading:
All futures contracts: the working day before the day of execution; futures (A) – the day before the third day of execution month; futures (B) – the working day before the 15th day of the month; futures (C) – the working day before the day of placement; all options contracts: the last day of trading in underlying futures contracts

Commission rates and margins: vary from 0.01% to 0.1% depending on the contract

Volume of trade:

1993 (*Roubles*)	*1994* (*Roubles*)	*1995* (*Roubles*)
72,432,935,000	166,272,763,000	433,587,651,000

Clearing house: The Exchange Clearing House

SINGAPORE

Singapore Commodity Exchange (SICOM)

111 North Bridge Road #23–04/05 Peninsula Plaza, Singapore 179098
Tel: +65 338 5600
Fax: +65 338 9116/9640/9676
Telex: RS 20554 SICOM
General Manager: Lim Toh Eng
Senior Manager, Clearing House Department: Paul Poh
Manager, Audit, Finance & Surveillance Department: Tabitha Hum
Manager, Marketing & Membership Department: Raymond Chow

Hours of trading (Mondays to Fridays, Singapore local time):

RSS1, RSS3, TSR20 (Award), RCS index	– 10.00–13.00 and 15.30–17.30
Robusta coffee	– 10.00–11.30 and 15.30–19.30 (UK Summer Time)
	– 16.30–20.30 (UK Winter Time)

Ring sessions:	AM*	PM*
RSS1	11.40–11.45	16.40–16.45
RSS3	11.47–11.52	16.47–16.52
TSR20 (Award)	11.54–11.59	16.54–16.59

* Two minutes of interval/extension are provided after each ring session for users to continue trading if they so desire.

Contract details:
Commodities: ribbed smoked sheet 1 (RSS1), RSS3, technically specified rubber 20 (TSR20) (Award), rubber cash settlement (RCS) index, robusta coffee

Trading currency and unit (manner of price quotation):

RSS1	– Singapore cents per kg
RSS3	– US cents per kg
TSR20 (Award)	– Singapore cents per kg
RCS index	– US cents per kg
Robusta coffee	– US dollars per metric tonne

Delivery points:

RSS1	– Singapore, Port Klang, and Penang
RSS3	– Singapore, Bangkok
TSR20 (Award)	– buyers receive Negotiable Award Certificates, representing rubber stored at

SICOM's warehouses which has passed physical and technical quality inspections

RCS index – cash settlement only

Robusta coffee – delivery by warrants, accompanied by valid Certificates of Quality, issued by SICOM's nominated warehouses

Termination of trading:

RSS1, RSS3, TSR20 (Award) – for a single month, the last trading day shall be on the last trading day of the month preceding the contract month. For quarterly periods, the last trading day shall be the last trading day of the fourth month preceding the first month of that quarter

RCS index – at 13.00 hours (Singapore local time) on the first day before KRE/TOCOM's last trading day during which both Singapore and Japan are trading

Robusta coffee – at 11.30 hours (Singapore local time) on the last trading day of delivery month

Months/maturities quoted:

RSS1, RSS3, TSR20 (Award) – may be made for future deliveries as determined by the Board from time to time but generally extending to 15 months forward, beginning with single months and followed by quarters

RCS index – spot month followed by eight consecutive months

Robusta coffee – seven consecutive odd months – January, March, May, July, September, November, January

Margins:

	Outright	*Spread*
RSS1, RSS3, TSR20 (S$ per tonne):		
Initial margin	75	35
Maintenance margin	55	25
RCS index (S$ per lot of 5 tonnes):		
Initial margin	650	250
Maintenance margin	500	200
Robusta coffee (US$ per lot of 5 tonnes):		
Initial margin	1,700	400
Maintenance margin	1,200	300

Volume of trade:

	1993	*1994*	*1995*
RSS1	697,515	557,395	639,020
RSS3	419,900	641,210	795,815
TSR20	598,520	528,640	828,780
RCS index	4,400	0	10
Robusta coffee	–	–	31,180
Total	1,720,335	1,747,245	2,294,805

Date of establishment of contracts:

RSS1, RSS3, TSR20 (Award) – 27 May 1992
RCS index – 20 August 1993
Robusta coffee – 1 March 1995

Clearing house: The Clearing House exists within SICOM as the Clearing House Department. It requires all clearing members to post margins for open positions before the opening of each trading day. At the end of each day, the Clearing House Department marks-to-market all open positions of its clearing members, collecting losses and paying out gains daily to ensure contract performance.

Membership: there are two types of membership (i) clearing membership – market-maker; broker; and dealer; and (ii) non-clearing membership – trade member; non-clearing broker membership; associate membership; and local/individual membership.

Membership of other organizations: International Rubber Association.

Further information:

Background: SICOM provides a centralized and regulated market-place for commodity futures trading in Singapore. It evolved from the rubber futures trade that has been thriving since the 1920s. At that time, facilities were provided by the Rubber Association of Singapore, which was privatized and later renamed the Singapore Commodity Exchange, or SICOM, to reflect its mission to become a broad-based multi-commodity futures trading centre within the Asian time zone.

New developments: in September 1996, a new computerized order-driven trading session for RSS1, RSS3, and TSR20 (Award) rubber futures contracts was introduced. Two sessions, called ring sessions, are held on each trading day. During the rest of the trading day, the traditional market-making system is still available for trading in these contracts. SICOM determines its official noon rubber prices based on trades in the morning ring session, while the settlement prices of its rubber futures contracts are based on trades in the afternoon ring session.

Singapore International Monetary Exchange Ltd (SIMEX)

1 Raffles Place, OUB, Centre #07–00, Singapore 048616
Tel: +65 535 7382
Fax: +65 535 7282
E-mail: simex@pacific.net.sg
Web site: http.//www.simex.com.sg
Chairman: Elizabeth Sam
President: Ang Swee Tian

US office
SIMEX America Ltd, 10 East 40th Street, Suite 4205, New York, NY 10016
Tel: +1 212 481 8080
Fax: +1 212 481 7373

Hours of trading (open outcry):

Eurodollar futures	– 07.45–19.00
Euroyen futures	– 07.58–11.15 and 12.15–19.05
Euromark futures	– 10.00–19.10
JGB futures	– 07.45–10.30 and 11.30–19.10
Nikkei 225 futures	– 07.55–10.15 and 11.15–14.15
Nikkei 300 futures	– 08.00–10.15 and 11.15–14.15
HK MSCI futures	– 10.00–12.30 and 14.30–16.00
Gold futures	– 09.00–17.15
High sulphur fuel oil futures	– 09.30–12.30 and 14.30–19.00
Brent crude futures	– 09.25–12.30 and 14.30–18.00
Deferred spot US$/Yen	– 08.00–19.00
Deferred spot US$/Mark	– 08.05–19.05
Eurodollar options	– 07.45–19.00
Euroyen options	– 07.58–11.15 and 12.15–19.05
Nikkei 225 options	– 07.55–10.15 and 11.15–14.15
Nikkei 300 options	– 08.00–10.15 and 11.15–14.15
JGB options	– 07.45–10.30 and 11.30–19.10

Contract details:
Commodities: futures – Eurodollar, Euroyen, Euromark, Japanese Government bonds, Nikkei 225, Nikkei 300, MSCI Hong Kong Index, gold, high sulphur fuel oil, Brent crude
Deferred spot: US dollar/Japanese yen, US dollar/Deutschmark
Options – Eurodollar, Euroyen, Nikkei 225, Nikkei 300, Japanese Government bonds
Eurodollar futures
Trading unit: US$1,000,000

Minimum price fluctuation: 0.01

Value of one tick: US$25

Daily price limit: none

Termination of trading: second London business day preceding the third Wednesday of contract month

Contract months: two serial months and March, June, September and December contracts on a 10-year cycle

Margins:

Quarterly months	*Initial (US$)*	*Maintenance (US$)*
Month 1	540	400
Month 2–8	945	700
Month 9–40	743	550
Serial months		
Month 1–2	540	400

Euroyen futures
Trading unit: ¥ 100,000,000

Minimum price fluctuation: 0.01

Value of one tick: ¥2,500

Daily price limit: none

Termination of trading: second business day immediately preceding the third Wednesday of contract month

Contract months: March, June, September and December contracts on a 3-year cycle

Margins:

	Initial (¥)	Maintenance (¥)
Month 1	33,750	25,000
Month 2	40,500	30,000
Month 3	47,250	35,000
Months 4–12	67,500	50,000

Euromark futures
Trading unit: DM1,00,000

Minimum price fluctuation: 0.01

Value of one tick: DM25

Daily price limit: none

Termination of trading: second London business day immediately preceding the third Wednesday of contract month

Contract months: March, June, September and December on a 2-year cycle

Margins:

Initial	DM270
Maintenance	DM200

Japanese Government bond futures
Trading unit: ¥50,000,000 face value notional 10-year JGB with 6% coupon

Minimum price fluctuation: ¥0.01 per ¥100 face value

Value of one tick: ¥5,000

Daily price limit: none

Termination of trading: one business day immediately preceding Tokyo Stock Exchange (TSE) JGB futures last trading day. Usually, the last trading day for the TSE's JGB futures is the ninth TSE business day prior to the 20th calendar day of delivery month

Contract months: five quarterly contract months based on March, June, September and December cycle

Margins:

Initial	¥1,215,000
Maintenance	¥900,000

Nikkei 225 futures

Trading unit: ¥500 times Nikkei 225 stock index futures price

Minimum price fluctuation: 5 points

Value of one tick: ¥2,500

Daily price limit: initial price limit of 7.5% followed by a 15-minute cooling-off period. Final price limit of 12.5% comes into effect for the rest of the trading day. On the last trading day for the expiring contract, there are no price limits following the 15-minute cooling-off period after the initial price limit (7.5%) has been reached. No price limits apply during the last 30 minutes before the close of trading on the last day of the expiring contract. However, if the cooling-off period overlaps the last 30 minutes of the trading session, the portion of the cooling-off period which overlaps the last 30 minutes of the trading session continues to be in force

Termination of trading: the day before the second Friday of contract month

Contract months: March, June, September and December on a five quarterly-month cycle

Margins:

Initial	¥906,250
Maintenance	¥725,000

Nikkei 300 futures

Trading unit: ¥10,000 times Nikkei Stock Index 300 futures price

Minimum price fluctuation: 0.1 point of Nikkei 300 Index

Value of one tick: ¥1,000

Daily price limit: initial price limit of 7.5% followed by a 15-minute cooling-off period. Final price limit of 12.5% comes into effect for the rest of the trading day. On the last trading day for the expiring contract, there are no price limits following the 15-minute cooling-off period after the initial price limit (7.5%) has been reached. No price limits apply during the last 30 minutes before the close of trading on the last day of the expiring contract. However, if the cooling-off period overlaps the last 30 minutes of the trading session, the portion of the cooling-off period which overlaps the last 30 minutes of the trading session continues to be in force

Termination of trading: the day before the second Friday of contract month

Contract months: March, June, September, listed on a five quarterly-month cycle

Margins:

Initial	¥150,000
Maintenance	¥120,000

MSCI Hong Kong Index futures
Trading unit: HK$100 times SIMEX MSCI Hong Kong Index futures price

Minimum price fluctuation: 1 index point

Value of one tick: HK$100

Daily price limit: none

Termination of trading: the second last business day of contract month

Contract months: two serial months and March, June, September, December contracts listed on a five quarterly month cycle

Margins:

Initial	HK$18,750
Maintenance	HK$15,000

Gold futures
Trading unit: 100 fine troy ounces of gold

Minimum price fluctuation: US$0.05 per fine troy ounce

Value of one tick: US$5.00

Daily price limits: whenever the price moves by US$25 from the previous day's settlement price, trading within the price limit of US$25 is allowed for the next 30 minutes. Thereafter, the price limit is expanded to S$50. If for two consecutive business days, the expanded price limit of US$50 is reached, there will be no price limits on the third day. On the fourth day, the price limits will be reinstated. There are no price limits on the last trading day for the expiring contract month

Termination of trading: the second last business day of the month preceding the first business day of contract month

Contract months: February, April, June, August, October, December

Margins:

Initial	US$1,080
Maintenance	US$800

High sulphur fuel oil futures
Trading unit: 100 metric tons

Minimum price fluctuation: US$0.10 per metric ton

Daily price limits: (i) for non-spot month contracts: whenever the price moves by US$10 per ton from the previous day's settlement price, trading at or within the normal price limit of US$10 per ton is allowed for the next 30 minutes. Thereafter the price limit is expanded to US$30 per ton. When the expanded limit of US$20 per ton is reached, trading at or within the price limit of US$20 per ton is allowed for the next 30 minutes. Thereafter, there are no price limits for the remainder of the day. (ii) for spot-month contracts – no limits

Termination of trading: trading terminates at 12.30 on the last business day of the month preceding contract month

Contract months: nine consecutive months

Margins:

	Tier 1 (US$)	Tier 2 (US$)	Tier 3 (US$)
Initial	438	563	688
Maintenance	350	450	550

Brent crude futures

Trading unit: 1,000 barrels (42,000 US gallons)

Minimum price fluctuation: 1 cent per barrel

Value of one tick: US$10 per unit

Daily price limit: whenever the price moves by US$15 per barrel from the previous day's settlement price, trading at or within the price limits of US$15 per barrel is allowed for the next 15 minutes. Thereafter, trading is not subject to any price limits for the rest of the day. No price limits apply during the last 30 minutes before the close of trading on any day. There shall be no price limits on the last trading day of the expiring contract

Termination of trading: the IPE business day immediately preceding either the 15th calendar day before the first date of the contract month, if such 15th calendar day is a day (other than a Saturday) on which banks are open in London, or, if such 15th calendar day is a Saturday or a day on which banks are not open in London, the next preceding day (other than a Saturday) on which banks are open in London

Contract months: 12 consecutive months

Margins:

Initial	US$1,250
Maintenance	US$1,000

Deferred spot US dollar/Japanese yen

Trading unit: US$100,00

Minimum price fluctuation: ¥0.01

Value of one tick: ¥1,000

Daily price limit: none

Termination of trading: the second business day immediately preceding the second Wednesday of contract month

Contract months: one quarterly contract (based on the March, June, September, December cycle) shall be listed at a time when the next quarterly contract shall be listed four business days prior to the last trading day of expiring contract

Margins:

Initial	¥202,500
Maintenance	¥150,000

Deferred spot US dollar/Deutschmark
Trading unit: US$100,000

Minimum price fluctuation: DM0.0001 per US$

Value of one tick: DM10

Daily price limit: none

Termination of trading: the second business day immediately preceding the second Wednesday of contract month

Contract month: one quarterly contract (based on the March, June, September, December cycle) shall be listed at a time when the next quarterly contract shall be listed four business days prior to the last trading day of expiring contract

Margins:

Initial	DM2,700
Maintenance	DM2,000

Eurodollar options
Trading unit: one Eurodollar futures contract covering 3-month US$1,00,000 principal

Minimum price fluctuation: 0.01 Eurodollar point (US$25) except that trade may occur at a price of US$1 if such trades result in the liquidation of positions for both parties to the trade

Strike price: intervals of 0.50 index points for Eurodollar levels below 88.00 and intervals of 0.25 index points for Eurodollar levels above 88.00

Termination of trading: the second business day immediately preceding the third Wednesday of contract month

Contract months: March, June, September, December

Margins:
Short option minimum: US$18

Euroyen options
Trading unit: one Euroyen futures contract covering 3-month deposit on ¥100,000,000

Minimum price fluctuation: 0.01 index point

Strike price: intervals of 0.25 index point

Daily price limit: none

Termination of trading: trading terminates at 10.00 on the second day business day immediately preceding the third Wednesday of contract month

Contract months: March, June, September, December contracts listed on a 2-year cycle

Margins:
Short option minimum: ¥1,250

Nikkei 225 options
Trading unit: one SIMEX Nikkei 225 futures contract

Minimum price fluctuation: 5 index points

Strike price: intervals of 500 Nikkei index points

Daily price limits: there shall be no trading in any options contract when the Nikkei 225 futures contract is bid or offered: (i) at its initial daily price limit, or (ii) at its expanded daily price limit except that the above provisions shall not apply on an option's last trading day

Termination of trading: the day before the second Friday of contract month

Contract months: three serial months and March, June, September, December contracts listed on a five quarterly-month cycle

Margins:
Short option minimum: ¥18,200

Nikkei 300 options
Trading unit: one Nikkei 300 Stock Index futures contract

Minimum price fluctuation: 0.1 point of Nikkei 300

Strike price: intervals of 5 points on the Nikkei 300 Index

Daily price limits: there shall be no trading in any options contract when the Nikkei 300 futures contract is bid or offered (i) at its initial daily price limit, or (ii) at its expanded daily price limit except that the above provisions shall not apply on an option's last trading day

Termination of trading: the day before the second Friday of contract month.

Contract months: three serial months and five quarterly months in the March, June, September and December cycle

Margins:
Short options minimum: ¥3,000

Japanese Government bond options
Trading unit: one 10-year JGB futures contract with face value of ¥50,000,000

Minimum price fluctuation: ¥0.01 per ¥100 face value

Strike price: intervals of ¥0.05

Daily price limit: none

Termination of trading: last Tokyo Stock Exchange business day of the calendar month which precedes expiring contract month. Usually, the last trading day for the TSE's JGB futures contract is the ninth TSE business day prior to the 20th calendar day of delivery month

Contract months: the two nearest serial months plus two nearest quarterly months in March, June, September and December cycles

Margins:
Short option minimum: ¥22,500

Note: Euroyen futures, Euromark futures, JGB futures, gold futures, deferred spot US$/yen, deferred spot US$/mark are also traded on the SIMEX Automated Trading System (ATS) from 19.30 to 01.00 (Singapore time).

Date of establishment of contracts:

Eurodollar futures	– 7 September 1984
Euroyen futures	– 27 October 1989
Euromark futures	– 20 September 1990
JGB futures	– 1 October 1993
Nikkei 225 futures	– 3 September 1986
Nikkei 300 futures	– 3 February 1995
HK MSCI futures	– 31 March 1993
Gold futures	– 5 July 1984
High sulphur fuel oil futures	– 22 February 1989
Brent crude futures	– 9 June 1995
Deferred spot US$/Yen	– 1 November 1993
Deferred spot US$/Mark	– 1 November 1993
Eurodollar options	– 25 September 1987
Euroyen options	– 19 June1990
Nikkei 225 options	– 19 March 1992
Nikkei 300 options	– 3 February 1995
JGB options	– 11 May 1994

Clearing house: SIMEX Clearing House

Membership:
Corporate Clearing Members – 37 in number. Entitlements include full trading rights on the trading floor, authority to accept customers' business and to clear trades.

Corporate Non-Clearing Members – 29 in number. Entitlements include full trading rights on the trading floor, authority to accept customers' business, but no authority to clear trades.

Commercial Associate Members – 12 in number. Trading rights limited to energy futures contracts only, may trade only for own account and that of their related and associated companies, no authority to clear trades.

Individual Non-Clearing Members – 588 in number. Full trading rights on the trading floor, may trade only for own account.

SOUTH AFRICA

JOHANNESBURG

South Africa Futures Exchange (SAFEX)

105 Central Street, Houghton Estate, Johannesburg 2000
Postal address: Box 4406, Johannesburg 2000
Tel: +27 11 728 5960
Fax: +27 11 728 5970
E-mail: Webmaster@safex.co.za
Web site: URL: http://www.safex.co.za
Chief Executive: Stuart A Rees
GM Surveillance: Patrick Birley
GM Operations: Ashley Mendelowitz
Marketing Manager: Tilly Smith

Hours of trading:

24 hours daily on Automatic Trading System (ATS). Most active	– office hours 08.30–17.00 Monday to Friday

Contract details:

Commodities: futures – all share index, all gold index, industrial index, financial industrial index, Kruger rand, long bond E168, long bond R150, short-term interest rate; options – all share index, all gold index, industrial index, financial industrial index, Kruger rand, long bond E168, long bond R150, short-term interest rate

Trading currency and unit (manner of price quotation):

All share index futures, all gold index futures, industrial index futures, financial industrial index futures	– index level (no decimal point)
Kruger rand futures	– in whole rand (no decimal point)
Long bond E168 futures, long bond R150 futures	– yield to maturity to four decimal places
Short-term interest rate futures	– discount rate to two decimal points

Trading units (minimum lot size):

All share index futures, all gold index futures, industrial index futures, financial industrial index futures	– R10 times index level
Kruger rand futures	– 10 coins

Long bond E168 futures, long bond R150 futures	– R1,000,000 nominal
Short-term interest rate futures	– R1,000,000 nominal 1
All share index options	– one all share index futures contract
All gold index options	– one all gold index futures contract
Industrial index options	– one industrial index futures contract
Financial industrial index options	– one industrial index futures contract
Kruger rand options	– one Kruger rand futures contract
Long bond E168 options	– one long bond E169 futures contract
Long bond R150 options	– one long bond R150 futures contract
Short-term interest rate options	– one short-term interest rate futures contract

Trading limits:

Minimum price movement:

All share index futures, all gold index futures, industrial index futures, financial industrial index futures	– one index point (R10)
Kruger rand futures	– one rand (R10)
Long bond E168 futures, long bond R150 futures	– one fifth of a point (0.0005%)
Short-term interest rate futures	– one point (0.01%)

Termination of trading:

All share index futures, all gold index futures, industrial index futures, financial industrial index futures, Kruger rand futures	– March, June, September, December
Long bond E168 futures, long bond R150 futures	– first Thursday: February, May, August, November
Short-term interest rate futures	– third Thursday of every month

Commission rates and margins:

Clearing house fees:

All share index futures and options, all gold index futures and options, industrial index futures and options, financial industrial index futures and options	– R1.70 per contract
Kruger rand futures and options	– R0.55 per contract
Long bond E168 futures and options, long bond R150 futures and options	– R5.00 per contract
Short-term interest rate futures and options	– R1.15 per contract

Initial margin:

All share index futures	– approximately R3,500*
All gold index futures	– approximately R2,000*
Industrial index futures	– approximately R4,000*

Financial industrial index	– approximately R4,500*
Kruger rand futures	– approximately R700*
Long bond E168 futures	– approximately R22,500*
Long bond R150 futures	– approximately R22,00*
Short-term interest rate futures	– approximately R2,000*

* Revised periodically by the Risk Committee. Reduced margin for spread positions.

Volume of trade:

Jan 1993 to December 1995	19,767,556
Total (May 1990 to May 1996)	26,526,260

Date of establishment of markets:

All share index, all gold index, industrial index, long bond E168, long bond R150, short-term interest rate	– 1990
Kruger rand	– 1994
Financial industrial index	– 1995

Clearing house: South African Futures Exchange Clearing Company (Pty) Ltd

Membership: there are two classes of membership – clearing members and non-clearing members.

Further information: SAFEX trading commenced in May 1990 and is the only futures exchange in Africa.

SAFEX, Agricultural Markets Division

105 Central Street, Houghton Estate, Johannesburg 2000
Tel: +27 11 728 5960
Fax: +27 11 728 5970/483 2527
General Manager (AMD): John Wixley
Manager, Marketing & Training: Rod Gravelet-Blondin

Hours of trading: 08.00–12.00

Contract details:
Commodities: chilled beef, potatoes, white maize, yellow maize

Trading currency and unit (manner of price quotation):

Chilled beef	– rand per kg
Potatoes	– rand per 10 kg
White maize, yellow maize	– rand per ton

Trading unit (minimum lot size):

Chilled beef	– 2,000 kg
Potatoes	– 100 pockets of 10 kg

White maize, yellow maize	–	100 tons

Trading limits:

Chilled beef , potatoes	–	no limits
White maize, yellow maize	–	R40 per day

Quality:

Chilled beef	–	A2/A3
Potatoes	–	class I medium
White maize	–	South African WMI
Yellow maize	–	South African YMI

Delivery points:

Chilled beef	–	Ganteng Province
Potatoes	–	cash settled at national potato price index White maize, yellow maize 80 silos in maize production area, Par – Randfontein

Trading months:

Chilled beef	–	four near consecutive calendar months
Potatoes	–	February, April, June, August, October, December
White maize, yellow maize	–	March, May, July, September, December

Termination of trading:

Chilled beef	–	second last Wednesday of month
Potatoes	–	last Thursday of month
White maize, yellow maize	–	eighth last business day

Commission rates and margins:

	Initial margin (per contract)	*Fees (per contract)*
Chilled beef	R2,500	R10
Potatoes	R200	R2
White maize, yellow maize	R8,000	R40

Volume of trade (since establishment of contracts):

Chilled beef	1,270
Potatoes	900
White maize	400
Yellow maize	400

Clearing house: SAFCOM

Date of establishment of contracts:

Chilled beef	–	3 July 1995
Potatoes	–	16 October 1995
White maize	–	25 February 1996
Yellow maize	–	25 February 1996

Further information: the agricultural markets division of the South African Futures

Exchange (SAFEX) was established at the end of 1994 following three years of intermittent research and development initiated by the deregulation of the agricultural markets. The financial markets of SAFEX had already been operating successfully for seven years, primarily in share index futures. Approximately half of the 61 members of the new agricultural division who took up seats at an issue price of R50,000 were already members of the financial division. The other half were an assortment of commodity traders. Due to a history of controlled markets, most of the original trading firms had disappeared and those who remained survived on exports and imports rather than domestic trade, due to the Control Boards, which were introduced by the government to set the price of most agricultural commodities.

Trading began in August 1995 with beef futures, the first futures contract in the world on chilled beef. This was followed by potato futures in October 1995 and white and yellow maize in February 1996. Like beef, trade in potatoes had been relatively free, taking place through daily sales on 15 national fresh produce markets with little interference. Maize prices were allowed to fluctuate for the first time since the 1930s in May 1995.

Current users of the market include banks, retailers, individual farmers, co-operatives, international grain traders, maize millers, feedlotters, manufacturers and distributors. Due to its history of controlled markets, South Africa does not have a well-developed pool of individual traders and speculators. Trade tends to be dominated by large corporate and institutional players. However, as exchange controls are relaxed and South Africa increasingly becomes part of international markets, this is changing. Interest has recently been expressed by foreign traders in purchasing seats on the SAFEX agricultural division and set prices have risen from their initial issue price of R50,000 to R65,000.

SPAIN

VALENCIA

FC&M, Sociedad Rectora del Mercado de Futuros de Citros

2 and 4 Calle Libreros, Valencia 46111
Tel: +34 6 387 0188
Fax: +34 6 394 3630
General Manager: J M del Rivero
Marketing Manager: R de Benito
Market Supervisor: Lamberto Samper

Hours of trading: 10.00–13.00

Contract details:
Commodities: navels (oranges) futures, Valencia lates (oranges) futures, clementine futures

Trading currency and unit (manner of price quotation):
Navels, Valencia lates, clementines – pesetas (pts) per kg

Trading unit:
Navels, Valencia lates, clementines – 5,000 kg

Delivery points:
Navels, Valencia lates, clementines – Exchange-licensed warehouses in Spain

Trading months:
Navels – November, December, January, February, March
Valencia lates – April, May, July
Clementines – November, December, January

Termination of trading:
Navels, Valencia lates – third Monday
Clementines – second Monday

Margins:
Navels, clementines – 25%
Valentia lates – 35%

Date of establishment of contracts:
Navels – 8 September 1995
Valencia lates – 8 September 1995
Clementines – 2 September 1996

Clearing house: FC&M

UNITED KINGDOM

LONDON

International Petroleum Exchange (IPE)

International House, 1 St Katharine's Way, London E1 9UN
Tel: +44 171 481 0643
Fax: +44 171 481 8485
Telex: 927679
Chief Executive: Lynton Jones
Divisional Director, Business Development: Richard Ward
Divisional Director, Operations: Mike O'Donnell

Hours of trading:

Brent futures	–	10.02–20.15
Gas oil futures	–	09.15–17.29
Brent options	–	10.02–20.15
Gas oil options	–	09.15–17.27

Contract details:
Commodities: futures and options contracts in Brent crude oil and gas oil

Trading currency and unit (manner of price quotation):

Brent crude oil	–	US$ per barrel
Gas oil	–	US$ per metric ton

Trading units (minimum lot size):

Brent crude futures	–	traded in units of 1,000 barrels
Gas oil futures	–	traded in units of 100 metric tons
Brent crude options	–	traded in units of 1,000 barrels or one underlying futures contract
Gas oil options	–	traded in units of 100 metric tons or one underlying futures contract

Delivery points:

Brent crude futures	–	deliverable contract based on EFP delivery with an option to cash settle against published settlement price
Gas oil futures	–	Amsterdam, Rotterdam, Antwerp (ARA) areas (including Vlissingen and Ghent)

Delivery months:

Brent futures	– 12 consecutive months
Gas oil futures	– up to 18 months
Brent options	– six consecutive months
Gas oil options	– six consecutive months

Termination of trading:

Brent futures	– trading shall cease at the close of business on the business day immediately preceding the 15th day prior to the first day of delivery month, if such 15th day is a banking day in London. If the 15th day is a non-banking day in London (including Saturday), trading shall cease on the business day immediately preceding the next business day prior to the 15th day
Oil futures	– trading shall cease at 12.00 hours, two business days prior to the 14th calendar day of delivery month
Brent options	– trading shall cease at close of business on the third business day prior to cessation of trading in the underlying futures contract
Oil options	– trading shall cease at close of business on the 5th business day prior to cessation of trading in the underlying futures contract

Commission rates and margins:
Initial margin

Brent crude	– US$1,000
Gas oil	– US$1,000
Inter month	– US$1,000
Inter commodity	– 65% saving range

Volume of trade:

	1993	*1994*	*1995*
Brent futures	8,852,549	10,082,741	9,773,488
Gas oil futures	3,608,637	3,779,064	4,491,511
Brent options	1,059,222	531,742	571,308
Gas oil options	217,508	136,859	116,424
Total	13,769,978	14,534,403	14,955,761

Date of establishment of contracts:

Brent futures	– 23 June 1988
Gas oil futures	– 6 April 1981
Brent options	– 11 May 1989
Gas oil options	– 20 July 1987

Clearing house: London Clearing House

Membership: there are three classes of membership – floor members, local members and trade associate members.

London International Financial Futures and Options Exchange (LIFFE)

From 16 September 1996, The London International Financial Futures & Options Exchange (LIFFE) and the London Commodity Exchange (LCE) began operation as a merged market with unified administration, exchange systems and clearing arrangements.

The merger of both exchanges creates the only exchange in the world to offer trading in futures and options on financial, agricultural, soft commodity and equity index products, as well as options on individual equities. Both exchanges expect to draw mutual benefit from the increased liquidity brought about by additional traders on the Exchange Floor – with LIFFE members able to trade in both financial and commodity derivatives.

Cannon Bridge, London EC4R 3XX
Tel: +44 171 623 0444
Fax: +44 171 588 3624
Telex: 893893
Chairman: Jack Wigglesworth
Chief Executive: Daniel Hodson
Deputy Chief Executive: John Foyle

Representative office: One Exchange Plaza, 55 Broadway, Suite 2602, New York, NY 10006-3008
Tel: +1 212 482 3000
Fax: +1 212 482 1100
Vice President, Business Development – USA: George Anagnos

Contract details:
Commodities: futures – 3-month sterling, 3-month Euromark, 3-month Eurolira, 3-month Euroswiss, 3-month ECU, 3-month Euroyen, Government bonds, long gilt, German Government bonds (Bund), Italian Government bond (BTP), Japanese Government bond (JGB), FTSE 100, FTSE Mid 250; options – short-term interest rate futures, 3-month sterling, 3-month Euromark, 3-month Eurolira, 3-month Euroswiss, Government bond futures, long gilt, German Government bond (Bund), Italian Government bond (BTP), FTSE 100 (American-style exercise), FTSE (European-style exercise), FTSE 100 FLEX, equity options

LIFFE Commodity Products: futures – Biffex, Robusta coffee, wheat, barley, potato, No. 5 white sugar; options – Biffex, No. 7 cocoa, Robusta coffee, wheat and barley, No. 5 white sugar

3-month sterling (short sterling) future
Hours of trading: 08.05–16.05

APT trading hours: 16.22–17.57

Trading unit: £500,000

Minimum price fluctuation: 0.01

Tick size: £12.50

Delivery months: March, June, September, December

Delivery day: first business day after last trading day

Termination of trading: 11.00 third Wednesday of delivery month

Quotation: 100.00 minus rate of inflation

3-month Euromark future
Hours of trading: 08.00–16.10

APT trading hours: 16.25–17.59

Trading unit: DM1,000,000

Minimum price fluctuation: 0.01

Tick size: DM25

Delivery months: March, June, September, December

Delivery day: first business day after the last trading day

Termination of trading: 11.00 two business days prior to the third Wednesday of delivery month

Quotation: 100.00 minus rate of interest

3-month Eurolira future
Hours of trading: 07.55–16.10

APT trading hours: 16.23–17.58

Trading unit: ITL1,000,000,000

Minimum price fluctuation: 0.01

Tick size: ITL25,000

Delivery months: March, June, September, December

Delivery day: first business day after the last trading day

Termination of trading: 11.00 two business days prior to the third Wednesday of delivery month

Quotation: 100.00 minus rate of interest

3-month Euroswiss franc future
Hours of trading: 08.10–16.05

APT trading hours: 16.24–17.55

Trading unit: SFr1,000,000

Minimum price fluctuation: 0.01

Tick size: SFr25

Delivery months: March, June, September, December

Delivery day: first business day after the last trading day

Termination of trading: 11.00 two business days prior to the third Wednesday of delivery month

Quotation: 100.00 minus rate of interest

3-month ECU future
Hours of trading: 08.05–16.05

Trading unit: ECU1,000,000

Minimum price fluctuation: 0.01

Tick size: ECU25

Delivery months: March, June, September, December

Delivery day: first business day after the last trading day

Termination of trading: 11.00 two business days prior to the third Wednesday of delivery month

Quotation: 100.00 minus rate of interest

3-month Euroyen future
Trading hours: 09.00–16.00 GMT; 10.00–16.00 British Summer Time

Trading unit: ¥100,000,000

Minimum price fluctuation: 0.01

Tick size: ¥2,500

Delivery months: March, June, September, December on a three-year cycle

Termination of trading: 16.00 two LIFFE business days prior to the TIFFE last trading day for the equivalent TIFFE Euroyen contract month

Quotation: 100.00 minus rate of interest

Long gilt future
Hours of trading: 08.00–16.15

APT trading hours: 16.30–18.00

Trading unit: £50,000 nominal value notional gilt with 9% coupon

Minimum price fluctuation: £1/32

Tick size: £15.625

Delivery months: March, June, September, December

Delivery day: any business day in delivery month (at seller's choice)

Termination of trading: 11.00 two business days prior to the last business day in delivery month

Quotation: per £100 nominal

German Government bond (Bund) future
Hours of trading: 07.30–16.15

APT trading hours: 16.20–17.55

Trading unit: DM250,000 nominal value notional German Government bond with 6% coupon

Minimum price fluctuation: DM0.01

Tick size: DM25

Delivery months: March, June, September, December

Delivery day: tenth calendar day of delivery month. If such a day is not a working day in Frankfurt, then the delivery day will be on the next following Frankfurt working day

Termination of trading: 11.00 Frankfurt time, three Frankfurt working days prior to delivery day

Quotation: per DM100 nominal value

Italian Government bond (BTP) future
Hours of trading: 08.00–16.10

APT trading hours: 16.21–17.58

Trading unit: ITL200,000,000 nominal value notional Italian Government bond with 12% coupon

Minimum price fluctuation: ITL0.01

Tick size: ITL20,000

Delivery months: March, June, September, December

Delivery day: tenth calendar day of delivery month. If such a day is not a working day for the Stanza di Compensazione Titoli in Italy, then the delivery day will be the next following working day for the Stanza di Compensazione Titoli in Italy

Termination of trading: 12.30 Italian time, four Stanza di Compensazione Titoli working days prior to delivery day

Quotation: per ITL100 nominal value

Japanese Government bond (JGB) future
Hours of trading: 07.00–16.00 on APT

Trading unit: ¥100,000,000 face value notional long-term Japanese Government bond with 5 % coupon

Minimum price fluctuation: ¥0.01

Tick size: ¥10,000

Delivery months: March, June, September, December

Delivery day: next business day

Termination of trading: 16.00 one business day prior to Tokyo Stock Exchange last trading day

Quotation: per ¥100 face value

FTSE 100 Index future

Hours of trading: 08.35–16.10

APT trading hours: 16.32–17.30

Trading unit: valued at £25 per index point (eg value £75,000 at 3,000.0)

Minimum price fluctuation: 0.5

Tick size: £12.50

Delivery months: March, June, September, December (nearest three available for trading)

Delivery day: first business day after the last trading day

Termination of trading: 10.30 third Friday of delivery month. In the event of the third Friday not being a business day, the last trading day shall normally be the last business day preceding the third Friday

Quotation: index points

FTSE Mid 250 Index future
Hours of trading: 08.30–16.05

Trading unit: valued at £10 per index point (eg value £30,000 at 3,000.0)

Minimum price fluctuation: 0.5

Tick size: £5

Delivery months: March, June, September, December (nearest two available for trading)

Delivery day: first business day after the last trading day

Termination of trading: 10.30 third Friday in delivery month. In the event of the third Friday not being a business day, the last trading day shall normally be the last business day preceding the third Friday

Quotation: index points

3-month sterling (short sterling) option
Hours of trading: 08.07–16.05

Trading unit: one 3-month sterling futures contract

Minimum price fluctuation: 0.01

Tick size: £12.50

Delivery day: delivery on the first business day after the exercise day

Termination of trading: 11.00 last trading day of the 3-month sterling futures contract

Expiry months: March, June, September, December

Expiry day: expiry at 12.30 on the last trading day

Quotation: multiples of 0.01 (ie 0.01%)

Exercise day: exercise by 17.00 on any business day prior to the last trading day

3-month Euromark option
Hours of trading: 08.02–16.10

Trading unit: one 3-month Eurodeutschmark futures contract

Minimum price fluctuation: 0.01

Tick size: DM25

Delivery day: first business day after the exercise day

Termination of trading: two business days prior to the third Wednesday of the expiry month at: 10.00 for serial expiry dates; 11.00 for quarterly expiry months

Expiry months: March, June, September, December plus additional serial months such that six expiry months, including the three nearest calendar months, are always available for trading

Expiry day: on the last trading day, serial expiry months expire at 11.30 and quarterly expiry months expire at 12.30

Quotation: multiples of 0.01 (ie 0.01%)

Exercise day: exercise by 17.00 on any business day prior to the expiry day

3-month Eurolira
Hours of trading: 07.57–15.10

Trading unit: one 3-month Eurolira futures contract

Minimum price fluctuation: 0.01

Tick size: ITL25,000

Delivery day: delivery on the first business day after the exercise day

Termination of trading: 11.00 last trading day of the 3-month Eurolira futures contract

Expiry months: March, June, September, December

Expiry day: expiry at 12.30 on the last trading day

Quotation: multiples of 0.01 (ie 0.01%)

Exercise day: exercise by 17.00 on any business day prior to the last trading day

3-month Euroswiss option
Hours of trading: 08.12–16.05

Trading unit: one 3-month Euroswiss futures contract

Minimum price fluctuation: 0.01

Tick size: SFr25

Delivery day: delivery on the first business day after the exercise day

Termination of trading: 11.00 last trading day of the 3-month Euroswiss futures contract

Expiry months: March, June, September, December

Expiry day: expiry at 12.30 on the last trading day

Quotation: multiples of 0.01

Exercise day: exercise by 17.00 on any business day prior to the last trading day

Long gilt options
Hours of trading: 08.02–16.15

Trading unit: one long gilt futures contract

Minimum price fluctuation: £1/64

Tick size: £7.8125

Delivery day: delivery on the first business day after the exercise day

Termination of trading: 10.00 six business days prior to the first day of delivery month

Expiry months: March, June, September, December plus additional serial months such that four expiry months, including the three nearest calendar months, are always available for trading

Expiry day: expiry at 11.30 on the last trading day

Quotation: multiples of £1/64

Exercise day: exercise by 17.00 on any business day, brought forward to 11.30 on the last trading day

German Government bond (Bund) option
Hours of trading: 07.32–16.15

Trading unit: one Bund futures contract

Minimum price fluctuation: DM0.01

Tick size: DM25

Delivery day: delivery on the first business day after the exercise day

Termination of trading: 10.00 six business days prior to the first day of delivery month

Expiry months: March, June, September, December plus additional serial months such that four expiry months, including the three nearest calendar months, are always available for trading

Expiry day: expiry at 11.30 on the last trading day

Quotation: multiples of DM0.01

Exercise day: exercise by 17.00 on any business day, brought forward to 11.30 on the last trading day

Italian Government bond (BTP) option
Hours of trading: 08.02–16.10

Trading unit: one BTP futures contract

Minimum price fluctuation: ITL0.01

Tick size: ITL20,000

Delivery day: delivery on the first business day after the exercise day

Termination of trading: 10.00 seven business days prior to the first day of delivery month

Expiry months: March, June, September, December

Expiry day: expiry at 11.30 on the last trading day

Quotation: multiples of ITL0.01

Exercise day: exercise by 17.00 on any business day, brought forward to 11.30 on the last trading day

FTSE 100 Index option (American style exercise)
Hours of trading: 08.35–16.10

Trading unit: valued at £10 per index point (eg value £30,000 at 3,000.0)

Minimum price fluctuation: 0.5

Tick size: £5

Termination of trading: 10.30 third Friday of the expiry month. In the event of the third Friday not being a business day, the last trading day shall normally be the last business day preceding the third Friday

Expiry months: June and December plus additional months so that the nearest four calendar months are always available for trading

Exercise day: exercise by 16.31 on any business day, extended to 18.00 for expiring series on the last trading day. Settlement day is the first business day after the day of exercise/last trading day

Quotation: index points

FTSE 100 Index option (European style exercise)
Hours of trading: 08.35–16.10

Trading unit: valued at £10 per index point (eg value £30,000 at 3,000.0)

Minimum price fluctuation: 0.5

Tick size: £5

Termination of trading: 10.30 third Friday of the expiry month. In the event of the third Friday not being a business day, the last trading day shall normally be the last business day preceding the third Friday

Expiry months: March, June, September, December plus additional months so that the nearest three calendar months are always available for trading

Exercise day: exercise by 18.00 for expiring series on the last trading day. Settlement day is the first business day after the last trading day. (An option can only be exercised on the last trading day)

Quotation: index point

FTSE 100 Index FLEX® option (European style exercise)
Hours of trading: 09.00–15.45

Trading unit: valued at £10 per index point (eg value £30,000 at 3,000.0)

Minimum price fluctuation: 0.5 index points

Tick size: £5

Termination of trading: 10.30 on the expiry date

Expiry date: any business day within two years from the date when the contract is made

Exercise day: exercise by 18.00 on expiry date. Settlement day is the first business day after expiry date (an option can only be exercised on expiry date)

Quotation: index points or percentage of an index figure

Equity options
Hours of trading: 08.35–16.10 (commencement of closing rotation)

Trading units: one option normally equals rights over 1000 shares

Minimum price fluctuation: 0.5 pence/share

Tick size: £5

Termination of trading: 16.10 (commencement of closing rotation)

Expiry months: January cycle (J) means the three nearest expiry months from January, April, July, October cycle; February cycle (F) means the three nearest expiry months from February, May, August, November cycle; March cycle (M) means the three nearest expiry months from March, June, September, December cycle

Exercise day: exercise by 17.20 on any business day, extended to 18.00 for all series on a last trading day. Settlement day is six business days after the day of exercise/last trading day.

Quotation: pence/share

Dates of establishment of contracts:

Futures:

German Government bond (Bund)	– 28 September 1988
3-month ECU	– 26 October 1989
Long gilt	– 18 November 1982
Japanese Government bond	– 13 July 1987
3-month Euroyen	– 11 April 1996
3-month sterling	– 4 November 1982
New Japanese Government bond	– 3 April 1991
3-month Euroswiss	– 7 February 1991
3-month Euromark	– 20 April 1989
3-month Eurolira	– 12 May 1992
Italian Government bond (BTP)	– 19 September 1991
FTSE 100	– 3 May 1984
FTSE Mid 250	– 25 February 1994

Options:

German Government bond (Bund)	– 20 April 1989
Serial options on Bund	– 10 May 1994
Long gilt	– 13 March 1986
Serial options on long gilt	– 14 February 1995
3-month sterling	– 5 November 1987
3-month Euroswiss	– 15 October 1992
3-month Euromark	– 1 March 1990
Serial options on Euromark	– 1 June 1994
3-month Eurolira	– 16 May 1995
Italian Government bond (BTP)	– 24 October 1991

LIFFE Commodity Products (formerly the London Commodity Exchange)

Hours of trading: 09.30–17.30 Monday to Friday

Contract details:

Commodities: futures and options on cocoa, coffee, sugar, wheat, barley, potatoes, biffex (dry cargo freight)

Biffex futures (The Baltic International Freight Futures Market)

Hours of trading (London time): 10.15–12.30 and 14.30–16.30

Trading units: Baltic Freight Index valued at $10 per full index point

Tick size: one full index point, equivalent to $10 per lot

Trading months: the current month, the following two consecutive months and January, April, July, October for up to 18 months forward

Settlement date: the first business day after the last trading day of settlement month

Settlement: each month

Settlement price: the average of the index on the last trading day and the four previous working days of settlement month

Termination of trading: the last business day of settlement month at 12.00 hours with the exception of December which will be 20 December (if that day is not a business day then the immediate preceding business day)

Biffex options
Hours of trading (London time): 10.15–12.30 and 14.30–16.30

Trading months: the same months as the underlying futures contract

Expiry date: the last business day of expiry month at 12.00 hours with the exception of December which will be 20 December. (If not a business day the preceding business day shall be substituted)

No. 7 cocoa futures
Hours of trading (London time): 09.30–12.28 hours call and 14.00–16.45 hours call

Trading units: 10 tonnes

Tick size: £1 per tonne

Delivery: pounds sterling per tonne in nominated warehouse in the UK or in nominated warehouse in, or in the Committee's opinion, sufficiently close to Amsterdam, Antwerp, Bremen, Hamburg or Rotterdam

Origins tenderable: Ghana, Côte d'Ivoire, Nigeria, Sierra Leone, Togo, Cameroon, Equatorial Guinea (Bioko), Zaire, Western Samoa, Grenada Fine Estates, Trinidad & Tobago Plantation, Jamaica at contract price. All other growths at set discounts

Delivery months: March, May, July, September, December – 10 months quoted

Expiry dates: last business day of delivery month at 15.30 London time

No. 7 cocoa traded options
Hours of trading (London time): 09.30–12.28 hours call and 14.00–16.45 hours call

Option type: American type option on the No 7 Cocoa futures contract

Trading units: 10 tonnes

Tick size: £1 per tonne

Strike price: £25 per tonne up to £1,000 and £50 thereafter

Trading months: March, May, July, September, December – 10 months quoted (as for underlying futures subject to the option expiry date)

Expiry dates: close of the morning trading session on the third Wednesday in the preceding month. Declaration (or non-declaration) instructions must be given to the clearing house not later than 30 minutes after this time. All options that expire in-the-money will be automatically exercised.

Robusta coffee futures
Hours of trading (London time): 09.45–12.32 and 14.15–17.00

Trading units: 5 metric tonnes

Tick size: US$1 per tonne

Delivery: US dollars per tonne in an Exchange-nominated warehouse in London, Home Counties, Bristol, Felixstowe, Hull, Amsterdam, Rotterdam, Le Havre, Antwerp, Hamburg, Bremen, Barcelona, Trieste, New York and New Orleans.

Origins tenderable: Angola, Brazilian Conillon, Cameroon, Central African Republic, Ecuador, Ghana, Guinea, India, Indonesia, Côte d'Ivoire, Liberia, Malagasy Republic, Nigeria, Philippines, Republic of Zaire, Sierra Leone, Tanzania, Thailand, Togo, Trinidad, Uganda and Vietnam

Delivery months: January, March, May, July, September, November (seven months quoted)

Tender period: the seller may submit a tender to the clearing house up to 12.00 on any market day in delivery month and, in respect of each sale contract that remains open at cessation of trading for that month, shall be bound to do so no later than 14.30 London time on the last market day in that month

Termination of trading: at 12.32 London time on the last market day of delivery month.

Robusta coffee traded options
Hours of trading (London time): 09.45–12.32 and 14.30–17.00

Option type: American type options on the robusta coffee futures contract

Trading units: 5 metric tonnes

Tick size: US$1 per tonne

Strike price: US$50 dollars per tonne

Trading months: January, March, May, July, September, November (seven months quoted as for the underlying future but subject to the earlier option expiry date)

Expiry dates: at 12.32 London time on the third Wednesday in the month preceding the futures delivery month. Declaration (or non-declaration) instructions must be given to the clearing house no later than one hour after expiry. All options that expire in-the-money will be automatically exercised.

Wheat futures
Hours of trading (London time): 10.00–12.30 and 14.30–16.00

Trading units: 100 tonnes

Tick size: £0.05 per tonne (5 pence)

Quality: EU wheat. Wheat to be sound, sweet, in good condition and to contain not more than 3% heat damage. Natural weight to be not less than 72.5 kg per hectolitre. Moisture content not to exceed 15%. Admixture: (i) seeds and/or total admixture of farinaceous grain (including wild oats) and dirt not to exceed 2%, of which the dirt content not to exceed 1%; (ii) ergot or garlic not to exceed 0.001%. Sprouted grains not to exceed 8%. All the above tests to be applied on a weight basis. Grain shall be delivered from a registered futures store in mainland Great Britain

Delivery: pounds sterling and pence per tonne

Delivery months: September, November, January, March, May, July (six months quoted)

Termination of trading: 23rd day of delivery month (14th day for July) at 12.30 hours. (If not a business day then the first business day immediately prior)

Barley futures
Hours of trading (London time): 10.00–12.30 and 14.30–16.00

Trading units: 100 tonnes

Tick size: £0.05 per tonne (5 pence)

Quality: EU barley. Barley to be sound and sweet and in good condition and to contain not more than 3% heat damage. Natural weight to be not less than 62.5 kg per hectolitre. Moisture content not to exceed 15%. Admixture: seeds and/or total admixture of farinaceous grain (including wild oats) and dirt not to exceed 2%, of which the dirt content not to exceed 1%. Sprouted grains not to exceed 8%. All the above tests to be applied on a weight basis. Grain shall be delivered from a registered futures store in mainland Great Britain

Delivery: pounds sterling and pence per tonne

Delivery months: September, November, January, March, May (five months quoted)

Termination of trading: 23rd day of delivery month at 12.30. (If not a business day then the first business day immediately prior)

Wheat and barley traded options
Hours of trading (London time): 10.00–12.30 and 14.30–16.00

Tick size: £0.05 per tonne (5 pence)

Strike price: £1 per tonne

Delivery: pounds sterling and pence per tonne

Trading months: the same months as the underlying futures

Expiry dates: second Thursday of the month prior to delivery month specified in the contract. Declaration (or non-declaration) instructions must be given to the clearing house not later than one hour after this time. All options that expire in-the-money shall be automatically exercised.

Potato futures
Hours of trading (London time): 11.00–12.30 and 14.30–16.00

Trading units: 20 tonnes

Tick size: £0.10 per tonne

Quality: PMB ware standard, however the seller may deliver up to a maximum of 10%

faults. Where the proportion of faults exceeds 5% the seller shall make an allowance to the buyer of 1% of the settlement price for each 1% or part 1% of such faults. Should any delivery fail to meet the contract quality specification, the seller shall be in default and the goods invoiced back at the futures settlement price plus 20% of such price and £5 per tonne. *Tuber count:* 35 to 70 tubers per 10 kg sample

Varieties: unwashed potatoes in bulk of any variety determined by the Market Committee and listed by the Exchange. To be of EU origin

Delivery: pounds sterling and pence per tonne. Bulk (buyer's option to receive in new 3 ply 25 kg bags at an additional charge), free onto buyer's transport at time determined by seller from a registered Grading Station in mainland Great Britain

Delivery months: November, March, April, May, June (minimum four months quoted)

Termination of trading: fourth calendar day of delivery month at 16.00. (If not a business day then the next business day following)

Potato traded options
Hours of trading (London time): 11.00–12.30 and 14.30–16.00

Tick size: £0.10 per tonne

Strike price: £5 per tonne

Delivery: pounds sterling and pence per tonne

Trading months: November and April

Expiry date: 15th day of the month prior to delivery month. (If not a business day the next business day following). All options that expire in-the-money shall be automatically exercised.

No. 5 white sugar futures
Hours of trading (London time): 09.45–18.30

Trading units: 50 tonnes

Trading medium: FAST (Fast Automated Screen Trading)

Tick size: 10 cents per tonne

Quality: white beet or cane crystal sugar or refined sugar of any origin of the current crop at the time of delivery, free running of regular grain size and fair average of the quality of deliveries made from the declared origin from such crop, with minimum polarisation 99.8°, moisture maximum 0.06%, and colour maximum 60 units ICUMSA attenuation index, all at time of delivery to vessel at port

Delivery: US dollars and cents per tonne FOBS designated ports

Packaging: new sound jute bags with polythene liners of uniform weight of 50 kg net with minimum tare 400 g

Delivery points: sugar to be stowed in vessel's hold at one of the following designated ports: Amsterdam, Antwerp, Bangkok/Kohsichang, Bilbao, Bremen, Buenos Aires, Cadiz, Calais, Delfzijl, Dunkirk, Durban (South Africa), Eernshaven, Flushing, Gdansk,

Gdynia, Gijon, Guangzhou, Hamburg, Huangpu, Imbituba/Itajai, Immingham, Inchon, Laemchabang*, Le Havre, Leixoes, Lisbon, Maceio, Matanzas, New Orleans, Penang, Port Kelang, Recife, Rostock, Rotterdam, Rouen, Santander, Santos, Savannah, Shekou, Singapore, Sri Racha*, Stettin, Ulsan, Xiamen

* Effective from May 1997 delivery onwards

Delivery months: March, May, August, October, December (seven months quoted)

Delivery period: the specified delivery month and the following month

Termination of trading: 16 days prior to the first day of delivery month. If this is not a working day then the first working day preceding the tender date. Trading ceases at 18.30 London time

No. 5 white sugar traded options
Hours of trading (London time): 10.00 to 18.30

Option type: American type options on the No. 5 white sugar futures contract

Trading units: 50 tonnes

Trading medium: FAST

Tick size: $0.05 per tonne (5 cents)

Strike price: $10 per tonne

Trading months: March, May, August, October, December – seven months quoted (as for underlying futures subject to the option expiry date)

Expiry dates: close of the first business day of the month preceding the delivery month. Declaration (or non-declaration) instructions must be given to the clearing house not later than one hour after this time.

Margins:

Contract	*Initial margin*
Barley	£200
Biffex	$800
Cocoa	£300
Potatoes	£200
Robusta coffee	$750
White sugar	$600
Wheat	£200

Volume of trade:

	Jan 95–Dec 95	*Jan 94–Dec 94*	*Jan 93–Dec 93*
Futures			
Cocoa	1,626,560	1,548,712	1,849,126
Robusta coffee dollar	1,043,957	1,247,657	885,940
No. 5 white sugar	556,769	466,587	316,800
No. 7 Premium Raw sugar	25,968	29,420	14,202
Biffex	73,442	47,338	42,724

	Jan 95–Dec 95	*Jan 94–Dec 94*	*Jan 93–Dec 93*
Wheat	98,644	82,907	62,000
Barley	17,751	7,911	13,317
Potato	26,584	36,197	22,759
Total futures	3,469,675	3,466,729	3,206,868
Options			
Cocoa	46,646	81,625	105,424
Robusta coffee dollar	163,575	201,444	276,092
No. 5 white sugar	20,572	7,196	0
Biffex	477	94	10
Wheat	12,532	6,681	1,769
Barley	16	34	110
Potato	0	0	0
Total options	243,818	297,074	383,405
Total LCE	3,713,493	3,763,803	3,590,273

The London Clearing House Ltd (LCH)

Roman Wall House, 1–2 Crutched Friars, London EC3N 2AN
Tel: +44 171 265 2000
Fax: +44 171 481 3462
Chairman: Tom Frost
Managing Director: David Hardy

Contract details:
The LCH clears the following exchanges in London: London Commodity Exchange, International Petroleum Exchange (IPE), London International Financial Futures Exchange (LIFFE), London Metal Exchange (LME), Tradepoint Financial Networks Plc.

Commodities:
IPE – gas oil, unleaded gasoline, Brent crude oil*

LIFFE Commodity Products – cocoa, coffee, white sugar, raw sugar, bulk potatoes, barley, wheat, biffex

LME – aluminium alloy, high grade primary aluminium, copper grade A, primary nickel, standard lead, tin, special high grade zinc

LIFFE – 3-month sterling, 3-month Eurodollar, 3-month Euromark, 3-month ECU, 3-month Eurolira, 3-month Euroswiss, long gilt, German Government bond (Bund), Italian Government bond (BTP), FTSE 100 Index future, FTSE 250 Index future, FTSE 100 Index options, equity options, flex options.

* Contract can be cash settled against the published settlement price – the Brent index price for the last futures trading day.

Trading currency and unit:

Gas oil	– US dollars
Unleaded gasoline	– US dollars
Brent crude oil	– US dollars
Cocoa	– sterling
Coffee	– US dollars
White sugar	– US dollars
Raw sugar	– US dollars
Bulk potatoes	– sterling
Barley	– sterling
Wheat	– sterling
Biffex	– US dollars
Aluminium alloy	– US dollar, sterling, Deutschemark, yen
High grade primary aluminium	– US dollar, sterling, Deutschemark, yen
Copper grade A	– US dollar, sterling, Deutschemark, yen
Primary nickel	– US dollar, sterling, Deutschemark, yen
Standard lead	– US dollar, sterling, Deutschemark, yen
Tin	– US dollar, sterling, Deutschemark, yen
Special high grade zinc	– US dollar, sterling, Deutschemark, yen
3-month sterling	– sterling
3-month Eurodollar	– US dollar
3-month Euromark	– Deutschmark
3-month ECU	– ECU
3-month Eurolira	– lira
3-month Euroswiss	– Swiss franc
Long gilt	– sterling
German Government bond (Bund)	– Deutschmark
Italian Government bond (BTP)	– lira
FTSE 100 Index future	– sterling
FTSE 250 Index future	– sterling
FTSE 100 Index options	– sterling
Equity options	– sterling
Flex option	– sterling

Trading unit:

Gas oil	– 100 tonnes
Unleaded gasoline	– 100 tonnes
Brent crude oil	– 1,000 barrels
Cocoa	– 10 tonnes
Coffee	– 5 tonnes
White sugar	– 50 tonnes
Raw sugar	– 50 long tons
Bulk potatoes	– 20 tonnes
Barley	– 100 tonnes
Wheat	– 100 tonnes
Biffex	– $10 per index point
Aluminium alloy	– 20 tonnes
High grade primary aluminium	– 25 tonnes

Copper grade A	– 25 tonnes
Primary nickel	– 6 tonnes
Standard lead	– 25 tonnes
Tin	– 5 tonnes
Special high grade zinc	– 25 tonnes
3-month sterling	– 500,000
3-month Eurodollar	– 1,000,000
3-month Euromark	– 1,000,000
3-month ECU	– 1,000,000
3-month Eurolira	– 1,000,000,000
3-month Euroswiss	– 1,000,000
Long gilt	– 50,000
German Government bond (Bund)	– 250,000
Italian Government bond (BTP)	– 200,000,000
FTSE 100 Index future	– £25 per Index point
FTSE 250 Index future	– £10 per Index point
FTSE 100 Index options	– £10 per Index point
Equity options	– usually 1,000 shares
Flex option	

Volume of trade:

	1993	*1994*	*1995*
Futures:			
IPE			
Brent crude oil	8,852,549	10,082,761	9,773,146
Gas oil	3,608,637	3,779,064	4,491,463
Unleaded gasoline	32,062	3,977	3,030
Total	12,493,248	13,865,802	14,267,639
LCE			
Barley	13,479	8,072	18,088
Biffex	43,105	47,805	74,696
Cocoa	1,908,136	1,600,746	1,653,790
Coffee	908,963	1,269,477	1,062,744
Potatoes	23,073	36,672	27,268
Raw sugar	4,449	32,063	34,219
Wheat	62,546	84,212	101,025
White sugar	329,414	480,973	575,734
Total	3,293,165	3,560,020	3,547,564
LME			
Aluminium	10,194,792	14,752,903	14,271,030
Copper	14,855,430	17,236,317	17,530,263
Lead	1,020,579	1,942,234	1,758,742
Nickel	2,118,710	3,404,942	3,319,697

	1993	*1994*	*1995*
Tin	613,952	1,192,735	1,275,718
Zinc	4,167,832	5,309,356	5,241,931
Total	32,971,295	43,838,487	43,397,381
LIFFE			
Bond futures:			
Bobl	1,049,640	73,043	–
BTP	6,344,233	11,823,741	9,612,899
Bund	20,440,442	37,335,437	32,231,210
JGB	421,454	610,925	845,329
Long gilt	11,808,998	19,048,097	13,796,555
Total	40,064,767	68,891,243	56,485,993
Index and interest rate futures:			
ECU	720,788	622,457	693,526
Eurodollar	244,728	91,738	2,720
Eurolira	1,479,012	3,456,437	4,005,125
Euromark	21,318,942	29,312,222	25,737,379
Euroswiss	1,846,376	1,698,736	1,749,774
FTSE 100	3,119,971	4,227,490	3,373,259
FTSE 250	–	40,674	35,068
Short sterling	12,135,981	16,603,152	15,314,576
Total	40,865,798	56,052,906	50,911,427

Options:	*1993*	*1994*	*1995*
IPE			
Brent crude oil	1,059,222	531,742	571,308
Gas oil	217,508	136,859	116,424
Total	1,276,730	668,601	687,732

	1993	*1994*	*1995*
Futures:			
LCE			
Barley	110	64	18
Biffex	10	94	532
Cocoa	107,102	87,215	48,196
Coffee	282,263	204,945	169,130
Wheat	1,769	6,866	12,907
White sugar	–	8,196	23,016
Total	391,254	307,380	253,799
LME			
Aluminium	900,266	1,231,794	1,241,692
Copper	1,156,352	2,155,587	2,212,821
Lead	17,299	45,769	22,262

	1993	1994	1995
Nickel	70,607	142,107	83,637
Tin	10,638	26,487	15,532
Zinc	163,475	261,912	177,005
Total	2,318,637	3,863,656	3,752,949
LIFFE			
Bond options:			
BTP	602,096	1,030,672	1,130,762
Bund	4,416,480	8,574,137	6,988,655
Long gilt	2,059,142	2,357,348	1,756,533
Total	7,077,718	11,962,157	9,875,950
Index and interest rate options:			
Eurodollar	20,015	12,400	2
Euromark	2,906,476	2,943,936	3,427,376
Euroswiss	32,163	19,245	33,781
FTSE 100 (SEI)	2,647,304	3,640,668	2,915,214
FTSE 100 (ESX)	792,156	1,145,988	1,518,872
Short sterling	2,666,711	4,057,878	3,348,945
Total	9,064,825	11,820,115	11,244,190

Date of establishment of market: formed in 1888 as the London Produce Clearing House Ltd, by a group of commodity merchants and bankers in the City of London.

Membership: Clearing membership is open to organizations resident in any part of the world and subject to approval by the Board of Directors. LCH is owned by six major UK clearing banks – Barclays, Lloyds, Midland, National Westminster, Royal Bank of Scotland and Standard Chartered.

The London Metal Exchange

56 Leadenhall Street, London EC3A 2 BJ
Tel: +44 171 264 5555
Fax: +44 171 680 0505
Chairman: R K Bagri, CBE
Vice Chairman: R Kestenbaum
Chief Executive: D E King

Hours of trading: 11.45–13.30 and 15.20–17.00
The two floor trading sessions are broken down into two rings made up of five minutes' trading in each contract. Each session is followed by a short period of open outcry dealing in all metals simultaneously (known as kerb trading). After a second ring of the first session the official prices for the day are announced. The trading times for the contracts are as follows:

Copper – 12.00–12.05, 12.30–12.35, 15.30–15.35, 16.10–16.15
Aluminium – 11.55–12.00, 12.55–13.00, 15.35–15.40, 16.15–16.20
Zinc (high special) – 12.10–12.15, 12.50–12.55, 15.25–15.30, 16.05–16.10

Lead	– 12.05–12.10, 12.45–12.50, 15.20–15.25, 16.00–16.05
Nickel	– 12.15–12.20, 13.00–13.05, 15.45–15.50, 16.30–16.35
Tin	– 11.50–11.55, 12.40–12.45, 15.40–15.45, 16.20–16.25
Aluminium alloy	– 11.45–11.50, 13.05–13.10, 15.50–15.55, 16.30–16.35

Contract details:
Commodities: electrolytic copper, high grade primary aluminium, special high grade zinc, lead, primary nickel, refined tin and aluminium alloy futures.

Traded options contracts are also available for the above metals.

Futures:
Trading currency and unit (manner of price quotation):

Copper, lead, aluminium alloy, aluminium, zinc, nickel and tin	– US dollars

Trading unit (minimum lot size):

Copper, aluminium, zinc, lead	– 25 tonnes
Nickel	– 6 tonnes
Tin	– 5 tonnes
Aluminium alloy	– 20 tonnes

Trading limits:

Copper	– 50 cents per tonne
Aluminium	– 50 cents per tonne
Zinc	– 50 cents per tonne
Lead	– US$1.00 per tonne
Nickel	– 50 cents per tonne
Tin	– US$1.00 per tonne
Aluminium alloy	– 50 cents per tonne

Quality:

Copper	– electrolytic, in the form of grade A cathodes; of brands listed in the LME approved list of copper; of British Standard 6017–1981
Aluminium	– high grade primary of minimum 99.70% in the purity in the form of ingots in the range of 12–26kg, T bars not exceeding 5% more than 675kg or sows not exceeding 5% more than 75kg
Zinc	– special high grade of minimum 99.995% purity in the form of slabs, plates or ingots weighing not more than 55kg each; of brands listed in the LME approved list of special high grade zinc brands
Lead	– refined pig assaying not less than 99.97% purity in pigs weighing not more than 55kg each; of brands listed in the LME approved list of lead brands
Nickel	– primary, of minimum 99.80% purity with

chemical analysis conforming to the current ASTM specification; in the form of cathodes, pellets or briquettes; of production of products named in the LME approved nickel list

Tin – refined, of minimum 99.85% purity, conforming to BS 3252–1986 in ingots or slabs weighing not less than 12kg or not more than about 50kg each; of brands listed in the LME approved list of tin brands

Aluminium alloy – produced in association with The Aluminium Association Inc specification (1989); produced in conformity with GBD–A1Si9Cu3 as described in DIN standard1725 (9186); produced in conformity with JIS H2118–1976, Class 12; of brands listed in the LME approved list of aluminium alloy brands

Delivery: cash/spot, two days from the date of contract, then every London working day out to three months, then weekly (every Wednesday) for the next three months, then monthly (every third Wednesday) for the next nine months for lead, tin and aluminium alloy (a total of 15 months forward) and copper, primary aluminium, zinc and nickel (a total of 27 months forward).

Delivery points:
Belgium: Antwerp; France: Dunkirk, Strasbourg; Germany: Bremen, Duisburg, Hamburg; Greece: Piraeus; Italy: Brescia, Genoa, Leghorn, Trieste; Japan: Hakata, Kobe, Moji, Nagoya, Osaka, Yokohama; The Netherlands: Rotterdam, Vlissingen; Singapore; Spain: Barcelona, Bilbao; Sweden: Gothenburg, Helsingborg; UK: Avonmouth, Derby, Felixstowe, Goole, Hull, Liverpool, Newcastle, Sunderland; USA: Baltimore, Bridgeport, Chicago, Detroit, Long Beach/LA, New Haven, New York/New Jersey, Pittsburgh, St Louis, Toledo.

Options:
The LME has seven options contracts, based on the underlying futures contracts. They are available against monthly prompt dates out to a total of 15 months for lead, tin and aluminium alloy and out to 27 months for copper, primary aluminium, zinc and nickel.

Strike price:

Copper and aluminium – US$25 per tonne gradation. Where the strike price is between US$1,750 and US$4,950 the gradation increases to US$50 per tonne, and where the price rises to US$5,000 or above the gradation increases to US$100 per tonne

Zinc – US$25 per tonne. Where strike price is US$1,750 or above the gradation is US$50 per tonne and US$100 gradations

for all strikes over US$3,000
Lead – US$25 over US$25 per tonne
Nickel – US$100 over US$100 per tonne

Delivery: Under LME rules the declaration date (ie the last day that an option can be declared) is the first Wednesday of the prompt month, and the prompt date is the third Wednesday of that month.

Date of establishment of market: established as a company in 1877.

Date of establishment of contracts:

Copper – 1899
Aluminium – 1978
Zinc – 1920
Lead – 1920
Nickel – 1979
Tin – 1899
Aluminium alloy – 1992

Further information: The LME is now subject to the Financial Services Act (FSA) of 1986, and the regulations of the Securities and Investment Board (SIB) created in 1987. In order to qualify as a Recognized Investment Exchange (RIE) the LME had to incorporate a clearing house system with price transparency and audit trails. With the introduction of a clearing system the LME extended its trading period from three to 27 months.

The London Metal Exchange was formed in July 1987, with a new constitution and a single tier Managing Board made up of ten drawn from the membership, one appointee (the chief executive) and up to four invited members.

Clearing house: London Clearing House (LCH).

Membership: there are seven classes of membership, which each have different rights and minimum capital worth requirements. They are authorized and regulated by the LME, the relevant regulatory body and the London Clearing House as appropriate to their trading rights. Applicant members must be proposed and seconded from among the membership and the Board of Directors will take the following points into account when considering an application: whether the applicant has had an active interest in the metals industry for at least one year; whether the applicant has, at the time of applying, sufficient properly qualified staff (both trades and support staff) to support their anticipated level of activity; whether the applicant is owned and/or controlled by a person who is, in the opinion of the Board, suitable to own and/or control a member of the LME of the level of membership for which the applicant is applying, after taking into account all or any of the factors which the Board would take into account in respect of the applicant; any other matter considered appropriate by the Board.

The Tea Broker's Association of London

Sir John Lyon House, Upper Thames Street, London EC4V 3LU
Tel: +44 171 236 3368
Chairman: R H L Harrison
Vice Chairman: T D Clifton
Secretaries: Thompson Lloyd & Ewart Ltd

Hours of trading: auction sales are held each Monday from 10.30

Contract details:
Commodity: tea

Trading currency and unit (manner of price quotation): pence per kilogram

Trading unit: auction lot size may vary, minimum normally 20 packaages, approximately 1,000 kg landed weight

Quality: sales are against sample of each individual lot

Delivery points: landed auctions – ex UK warehouses; CIF auctions – UK ports

Commission rates and margins: landed auctions – 1.75%; CIF auctions – 2%

Volume of trading: 1995 – 30,000,000 kg

Date of establishment of market: 18 April 1890

Clearing house: Tea Auction Services Ltd

Membership: full – auctioneers; associate – others

Useful Trade Associations

Federation of Commodity Associations (FCA)

Gafta House, 6 Chapel Place, Rivington Street, London EC2A 3DQ
Tel: +44 171 814 9666
Fax: +44 171 814 8383
Telex: 886984
E-mail: post@gafta.demon.co.uk
Secretary: Pamela Kirby Johnson
PR Manager: Sandra Black

The Federation of Commodity Associations (FCA) is a non-profit organization, recognized by the Commission of the European Community, whose purpose is to represent European Commodity businesses.

The commodities represented are cocoa, coffee, sugar, oils and fats, energy, general produce (tapioca, rice, spices), cotton, metal and grain.

The FCA has observer status at UNCTAD, an organization set up by the United Nations to promote trade and development, mainly in the production and trade of raw materials.

Objectives: to promote and protect the commercial interests of various European commodity associations, companies and firms; to promote or oppose European legislation and EEC directives affecting the interests of the Federation's members; to act as a link for the exchange of views and information between different European commodity associations and relevant international organizations.

Membership:

Full Members

Trade associations or similar organizations; may be represented on the council and special sub-committee, their representatives having full voting powers.

Associate Members

Companies, firms or individual traders in commodities; may be invited to provide representatives who can be co-opted on to the council or special sub-committee and granted voting rights.

The Grain and Feed Trade Association (GAFTA)

Gafta House, 6 Chapel Place, Rivington Street, London EC2A 3DQ
Tel: +44 171 8114 9666
Fax: +44 171 81114 8383
Director General: Pamela Kirby Johnson
PR Manager: Sandra Black

GAFTA is a unique worldwide organization promoting international trade in grains, animal feedingstuffs, pulses and rice. Serving the interests of over 670 members in 76 countries, GAFTA is recognized worldwide for its expertise in three main areas: contracts and arbitration; trade policy; and training and education.

A very large proportion of the international sales of grain, animal feedingstuffs and pulses are carried out under the terms of GAFTA contracts. Contract disputes are resolved through GAFTA's arbitration and appeal service. GAFTA provides regular information and commentary on trade issues and has also developed a comprehensive Continuing Professional Development Programme for members throughout the world, providing training at three levels from Foundation to Advanced.

GAFTA has about 80 standard contract forms, all for physical goods. These include grains – cereals, legumes, pulses and feedstuffs – oilseed derivatives, cereal by-products, rootcrops, fishmeal.

List of contracts:

1. General feedingstuffs TQ – CIF
2. Chinese (other than wheat) TQ – parcels, CIF
3. Indian pulse or grain (other than wheat) TQ – parcels, CIF
4. Home produced cakes and/or meal
6. Imported feedingstuffs to the UK TQ – bags, CIF
8. Locust beans TQ – CIF
9. Imported feeding meat meal and meat and bone meal TQ – bags, CIF
10. Feeding fish meal TQ – bags, CIF
12. Australian grain TQ – cargoes, CIF
13. Australian offals TQ – parcels, CIF

14. Australian grain TQ – parcels, CIF
14A. Australian and New Zealand peas TQ – bags, parcels, CIF
15. Imported feedingstuffs TQ – bags, CIF
16. Australian seed TQ – parcels, CIF
17. General short form
21 Intra-Asia supply terms for feedingstuffs TQ – bulk/bags, CIF, CRF
22. Rice bran TQ – bags, CIF
23. Pulses for human consumption – bulk/bags, FOB
23A Addendum FAS terms – FAS
24 Pulses for human consumption – TQ – bulk/bags, CIF, C & F
25. Feed pulses TQ – bulk, CIF
27. Canadian and USA grain TQ – cargoes, CIF
28. Canadian and USA grain TQ – parcels, CIF
30 Canadian and USA grain TQ – bulk, parcels, CIF
31. Canadian Pacific Coast TQ – parcels, CIF
32. La Plata grain RT – cargoes, CIF
35. La Plata grain TQ – parcels, CIF
36. La Plata grain RT – parcels, CIF
41. La Plata grain RT – parcels, CIF
43. South American offal RT – parcels, CIF
54A. Baltic grain RT – parcels or cargoes, CIF
59. South African grain TQ – cargoes, CIF
60. South African grain TQ – parcels, CIF
61. Mediterranean and Moroccan TQ – cargoes, CIF
62. Mediterranean and Moroccan TQ – parcels, CIF
64. General grain – bulk, FOB
75. Malagasy beans TQ – bags, parcels, CIF
76. Addendum malting barley terms
77. Brazilian RT – parcels, CIF
78. Grain and pulses by rail RT – bulk
79. UK and Republic of Ireland grain RT – CIF
79A. UK and Republic of Ireland grain – FOB
79B. UK and Republic of Ireland grain – delivery/collection
80. EEC grain RT – cargoes or parcels, CIF
80A. EEC grain TQ – cargoes or parcels, CIF
83. Transhipment/re-shipment of grain TQ – cargoes or parcels, CIF
84. Short form
85. Addendum for transhipments
86. Full container loads for cereals FCLS
86A. Full container loads short form FCLS
93. European quality terms for feedingstuffs contracts – addendum
94. Intra-Community sales for the arrival of grain RT – bulk
94A. Intra-Community sales for the arrival of grain TQ – bulk
95. Arrival of feedingstuffs TQ – bulk
96. Tapioca, manioc and cassava products TQ – bulk, CIF
97. North American soyabean meal and/or pellets TQ – bulk, CIF
98. North American soyabean meal and/or pellets TQ – bulk, CIF
99. North American HIPRO (high protein) soyabean meal and/or pellets TQ – bulk,

CIF
100. Feedingstuffs TQ – bulk, CIF
100A. Feedingstuffs in full lash barge loads – CIF
101. Feedingstuffs RT – bulk, CIF
102. Transhipment of feedingstuffs to the UK TQ – bulk, cargoes or parcels, CIFFO
103. Shipment of feedingstuffs to the UK TQ – bulk, CIF
104. Feeding fishmeal TQ – bulk, CIF
107. Full container loads – feedingstuffs – FCLS
108. Short form for full container loads – feedingstuffs – FCLS
109. Ex store/silo for proteins feedingstuffs – bulk
110. Ex store/silo for cereals – bulk
111. EEC grain – delivered premises
112. Feedingstuffs, freeout alongside buyers berth, to Denmark TQ – bulk
113. UK produced feedingstuffs of marine and animal origin
114. Fertiliser TQ – bulk/bags, parcels or cargoes, CIF/CIFFO
115. Molasses – FOB
117. Model computer contract
118. Feeding fish meal – bulk/bags, FOB
119. General feedingstuffs – bulk/bags, FOB
120. Thai rice – bulk/bags, FOB
200. Euro-supply general terms delivery – despatch, collection, bulk, bags

List of rules:
65. Natural weight rules for wheat and rye, oats and barley
72. Insurance clauses
123. Weighbridge weighing rules
124. Sampling rules
125. Arbitration rules
126. Simple dispute rules
129. Loading port terms for the UK
130. Methods of analysis to be used for testing under GAFTA contracts

Membership: importers, exporters, brokers, dealers, processors of raw materials, millers, brewers, distillers, banks, chemical companies, superintendents, forwarding agents, arbitrators, professional firms and solicitors.

Membership of other organizations: Comité du Commerce des Céréales et des Aliments du Bétail de la CEE (COCERAL) in Brussels, which nominates trade representatives to the EC Commission's Consultative Committee for Cereals; Confédération Internationale du Commerce et des Industries des Légumes Secs (CICILS) in Brussels and Paris, which represents the trade in peas, beans and other pulses; Euromarket Federation of Animal Protein Importers and Traders (EFAPIT) in Hamburg, representing fish meal and meat meal interests; European Commodity Exchanges Association (ECEA), based in Strasbourg, organizer of 'annual trading days' in member countries; London Chamber of Commerce and Industry.

The International General Produce Association (IGPA)

Gafta House, 6 Chapel Place, Rivington Street, London EC2A 3DQ
Tel: +44 171 814 9666
Fax: +44 171 814 8383
Telex: 886984
E-mail: igpa@gafta.demon.co.uk
Secretary: Pamela Kirby Johnson
PR Manager: Sandra Black

Founded in 1876, the International General Produce Association is a contract issuing body for the international trade in herbs, spices, essential oils, aromatic chemicals and general produce. To support the contracts service, an arbitration and appeal service is provided, enabling contract disputes to be settled quickly and efficiently.

Membership: companies, firms sole traders, organizations or individuals engaged in the trade in general produce commodities.

UNITED STATES OF AMERICA

CHICAGO

Chicago Board of Trade

141 West Jackson Boulevard, Chicago, Illinois 60604
Tel: +1 312 435 3500
Fax: +1 312 341 3392
Web site: http://www.cbot.com
Chairman: Patrick H Arbor
President: T R Donovan

European office: 52–54 Gracechurch Street, London EC3V 0EH, UK
Tel: +44 171 929 0021
Fax: +44 171 929 0558
Managing Director: Suzanne Matus

Asia-Pacific office: Shoyu Kaikan Building, 3–3–1 Kasumigaseki, Chiyoda-ku, Tokyo 100, Japan
Tel: +81 3 3595 2251
Fax: +81 3 3595 2244
Managing Director: Akio Shimizu

Hours of trading (Chicago time):
Financial futures
US treasury bonds*, 10-year US treasury notes*, 5-year US treasury notes*, 2-year US treasury notes*, long-term municipal bond index futures*, 30-day federal funds*, Brady Bond Index – 07.20–14.00

Financial options
US treasury bonds*,10-year US treasury notes*, 5-year US treasury notes*, 2-year US treasury notes*, long-term municipal bond index futures*,

Brady Bond Index	– 07.20–14.00
Flexible US treasury bonds, flexible 10-year US treasury notes, flexible 5-year US treasury notes, flexible 2-year US treasury notes	– 07.20–14.00

Insurance options

Quarterly Property Claim Services (PCS) catastrophe insurance, annual Property Claim Services (PCS) catastrophe insurance	– 08.30–12.30

Agricultural futures

Soybean, soybean oil, soybean meal, corn, oats, wheat	– 09.30–13.15
Rough rice	– 09.30–13.30
Anhydrous ammonia (NH_3)	– 09.05–12.20
Diammonium phosphate (DAP)	– 09.00–12.15

Agricultural options

Soybean, soybean oil, soybean meal, corn, oats, wheat	– 09.30–13.15
Rough rice	– 09.15–13.30

Corn yield insurance futures

Iowa corn yield insurance, Nebraska, Illinois, Indiana, Ohio and US corn yield insurance†	– 10.30–12.45

Corn yield insurance options

Iowa corn yield insurance, Nebraska, Illinois, Indiana, Ohio and US corn yield insurance†	– 10.30–12.45

Metals futures

Kilo gold, 100 ounce gold	– 07.20–13.40
1,000 ounce silver, 5,000 ounce silver	– 07.25–13.25

Metals options

1,000 ounce silver	– 07.25–13.25

* Evening trading hours are 17.05–20.05 (CST) or 18.20–21.05 (CDST), Sunday to Thursday. Project A Afternoon session hours are from 14.20–14.30 Chicago time, Monday to Thursday and Project A Overnight session hours are from 22.30–06.00 Sunday to Thursday.

† Pending CFTC approval

Contract details:

Commodities: futures – US treasury bonds, 10-year US treasury notes, 5-year US treasury notes, 2-year US treasury notes, long-term municipal bond index, 30-day federal funds,

Brady Bond Index, soybean, soybean oil, soybean meal, corn, oats, wheat, rough rice, anhydrous ammonia (NH_3), diammonium phosphate (DAP), Iowa corn yield insurance, Nebraska, Illinois, Indiana, Ohio and US corn yield insurance, kilo gold, 100 ounce gold, 1,000 ounce silver, 5,000 ounce silver; options – US treasury bonds, 10-year US treasury notes, 5-year US treasury notes, 2-year US treasury notes, long-term municipal bond index, Brady Bond Index, flexible US treasury bonds, flexible 10-year US treasury notes, flexible 5-year US treasury notes, flexible 2-year US treasury notes, quarterly Property Claim Services (PCS) catastrophe insurance, annual Property Claim Services (PCS) catastrophe insurance, soybean, soybean oil, soybean meal, corn, oats, wheat, rough rice, Iowa corn yield insurance, Nebraska, Illinois, Indiana, Ohio and US corn yield insurance, 1,000 ounce silver

Trading currency and unit (manner of price quotation):

Financial futures

US treasury bonds, 10-year US treasury notes, long-term municipal bond index	– points (US$1,000) and thirty-seconds of a point, eg 80-16 equals 80 16/32
5-year US treasury notes	– points (US$1,000) and one half of 1/32 of a point, eg 84-16 equals 84 16/32
2-year US treasury notes	– points (US$2,000) and one quarter of 1/32 of a point, eg 91-16 equals 91 16/32
30-day federal funds	– 100 minus the monthly average overnight federal effective rate for delivery month
Brady Bond Index	– points; 1 point equals US$1,000

Agricultural futures

Soybean, corn, oats, wheat	– cents and 1/4 cents/bushel
Soybean oil	– cents/pound
Soybean meal, Anhydrous ammonia (NH_3), diammonium phosphate (DAP)	– dollars and cents/ton
Rough rice	– cents/cwt

Metals futures

Kilo gold, 100 ounce gold	– dollars and cents/troy ounce
1,000 ounce silver, 5,000 ounce silver	– dollars and cents to the last 1/10 of a cent/troy ounce

Financial options

US treasury bonds	– 1-point strikes (US$1,000) for the nearby contract month in a band consisting of the at-the-money, four above and four below. 2-point strikes (US$2,000) are listed outside this band. Back months are also listed in 2-point strike price intervals
10-year US treasury notes	– 1 point (US$1,000) to bracket the current T-note futures price
5-year US treasury notes	– 1 half point (US$500/contract) to bracket the current T-note futures price

2-year US treasury notes	– 1 quarter point (US$500/contract) to bracket the current T-note futures price
Long-term municipal bond index	– 1 point (US$1,000) to bracket the current muni-bond futures price
Brady Bond Index	– 1 point (US$1,000)
Flexible US treasury bonds, flexible10-year US treasury notes	– may be expressed (i) in absolute levels, set to any 1/32 of a point; or (ii) in levels relative to the underlying futures contract, set in 1/32 of a point increments
Flexible 5-year US treasury notes, flexible 2-year US treasury notes	– may be expressed (i) in absolute levels, set to any 1/64 of a point; or (ii) in levels relative to the underlying futures contract, set in 1/64 of a point increments

Insurance options

Quarterly Property Claim Services (PCS) catastrophe insurance, annual Property Claim Services (PCS) catastrophe insurance	– listed in multiples of 5 points (US$1,000)

Agricultural options

Soybean	– 25 cents/bushel
Soybean oil	– at the initial listing for all strike prices less than 30 cents, there will be 11 strikes above and below the at-the-money strikes at 1/2 cent intervals plus the next four consecutive strikes above 1 cent intervals. If the underlying is equal to or greater than 30 cents, there will be six strikes above and below at 1 cent intervals, plus the next four consecutive strikes above at 2 cent intervals
Soybean meal	– US$5/ton when futures price is less than US$200/ton; US$10/ton when futures price is US$200/ton or over
Corn, oats, wheat	– 10 cents/bushel
Rough rice	– 11 strike prices will be listed in integral multiples of 20 cents/cwt to bracket the underlying futures contract (ie, the strike price closest to the previous day's futures settlement price and the next five consecutive higher and lower strike prices). Also, four strikes in 40 cent multiples will be listed above the strikes listed in 20 cent multiples

Metals options

1,000 ounce silver	– 25 cents/troy ounce for strike prices less

than US$8; 50 cents/troy ounce for strike prices from US$8 to US$20; US$1/troy ounce for strike prices of US$20 or more

Trading units (minimum lot size):

Financial futures

US treasury bonds	– 1 US treasury bond having a face value at maturity of US$100,000 or multiple thereof
10-year US treasury notes, 5-year US treasury notes	– 1 US treasury note having a face value at maturity of US$10,000 or multiple thereof
2-year US treasury notes	– US treasury notes having a face value at maturity of US$200,000 or multiple thereof
Long-term municipal bond index	– US$1,000 times the closing value of *The Bond Buyer*™ Municipal Bond Index‡. A price of 90-00 reflects a contract size of US$90,000
30-day federal funds	– US$5 million
Brady Bond Index	– US$1,000 times the CBOT Argentina, Brazil, or Mexico Brady Bond Index**

Agricultural futures

Soybean, corn, oats, wheat	– 5,000 bushels
Soybean oil	– 60,000 lbs
Soybean meal	– 100 tons (2,000 lbs/ton)
Rough rice	– 2,000 cwt
Anhydrous ammonia (NH_3), Diammonium phosphate (DAP)	– 100 tons

Corn yield insurance futures

Iowa corn yield insurance	– each monthly contract will reflect the Iowa yield estimate times US$100
Nebraska, Illinois, Indiana, Ohio and US corn yield insurance	– each monthly contract for each underlying futures contract will reflect the corn yield estimate times US$100

Metals futures

Kilo gold	– 1 gross kg (32.15 troy ounces)
100 ounce gold	– 100 fine troy ounces
1,000 ounce silver	– 1,000 troy ounces
5,000 ounce silver	– 5,000 troy ounces

‡ Copyright 1995, *The Bond Buyer*™ and the Board of Trade of the City of Chicago.
** Copyright 1996, Board of Trade of the City of Chicago

Financial options

US treasury bonds – 1 CBOT US treasury bond futures contract (of a specified delivery month) having a face value at maturity of US$100,000 or multiple thereof

10-year US treasury notes – 1 CBOT 10-year US treasury note futures contract (of a specified delivery month) having a face value at maturity of $100,000 or multiple thereof

5-year US treasury notes – 1 CBOT 5-year US treasury note futures contract (for a specified delivery month) having a face value at maturity of US$100,000 or multiple thereof

2-year US treasury notes – 1 CBOT 2-year US treasury note futures contract (of a specified delivery month) having a face value at maturity of US$200,000 or multiple thereof

Long-term municipal bond index – 1 CBOT long-term municipal bond index futures contract (of a specified delivery month)

Brady Bond Index – 1 CBOT Brady Bond Index futures contract

Flexible US treasury bonds – the minimum size to initiate a Request for Quote (RFQ) is 100 contracts, each having a face value at maturity of US$100,000

Flexible 10-year US treasury notes, flexible 5-year US treasury notes – the minimum size to initiate a Request for Quote (RFQ) in an unopened option is 100 contracts, each having a face value at maturity of US$100,000

Flexible 2-year US treasury notes – the minimum size to initiate a Request for Quote (RFQ) is 100 contracts, each having a face value at maturity of US$200,000

Agricultural options

Soybean – 1 CBOT soybean futures contract (of a specified contract month) of 5,000 bushels

Soybean oil – 1 CBOT soybean oil futures contract (of a specified contract month) of 60,000 lbs

Soybean meal – 1 CBOT soybean meal futures contract (of a specified contract month) of 100 tons

Corn – 1 CBOT corn futures contract (of a specified month) of 5,000 bushels

Oats – 1 CBOT oat futures contract (of a specified month) of 5,000 bushels

Wheat – 1 CBOT wheat futures contract (of a

specified month) of 5,000 bushels

Rough rice – 1 CBOT rough rice futures contract (of a specified contract month) of 2,000 cwt

Corn yield insurance options

Iowa corn yield insurance – 1 CBOT Iowa corn yield insurance futures (of a specified contract month)

Nebraska, Illinois, Indiana, Ohio and US corn yield insurance – 1 CBOT corn yield insurance futures for a specific corn growing area for a specified contract month

Metals options

1,000 ounce silver – 1 CBOT silver futures contract (of a specified contract month) of 1,000 troy ounces

Trading limits:

Financial futures

US treasury bonds, 10-year US treasury notes, 5-year US treasury notes – 3 points (US$3,000/contract) above or below the previous day's settlement price (expandable to 4 1/2 points). Limits are lifted the second business day preceding the first day of delivery month

2-year US treasury notes – 1 point (US$2,000/contract) above or below the previous day's settlement price (expandable to 1 1/2 points). Limits are lifted the second business day preceding the first day of delivery month

Long-term municipal bond index – 3 points (US$3,000/contract) above or below the previous day's settlement price (expandable to 4 1/2 points)

30-day federal funds – 150 basis points (variable trading limits of 225 basis points); no limit in the spot month

Brady Bond Index – no trading limits

Agricultural futures

Soybean – 30 cents/bushel (US$1,500/contract) above or below the previous day's settlement price (expandable to 45 cents/bushel)‡‡

Soybean oil – 1 cent/lb (US$600/contract) above or below the previous day's settlement price (expandable to 1 1/2 cents/lb)‡‡

Soybean meal – US$10/ton (US$1,000/contract) above or below the previous day's settlement price (expandable to US$15/ton)‡‡

Corn – 12 cents/bushel (US$600/contract) above or below the previous day's settlement price (expandable to 18 cents/bushel)‡‡

Oats – 10 cents/bushel (US$500/contract) above or below the previous day's settlement price (expandable to 15 cents/bushel)‡‡

Wheat – 20 cents/bushel (US$1,000/contract) above or below the previous day's settlement price (expandable to 30 cents/bushel)‡‡

Rough rice – 30 cents/cwt (US$600/contract) above or below the previous day's settlement price (expandable to 40 cents/cwt)‡‡

Anhydrous ammonia (NH_3), diammonium phosphate (DAP) – US$10/ton (US$1,000/contract) above or below the previous day's settlement price (expandable to US$15/contract)‡‡

Metals futures

Kilo gold – US$50/troy ounce (US$1,607.50/contract) above or below the previous day's settlement price (expandable to US$75/troy ounce)

100 ounce gold – US$50/troy ounce (US$5,000/contract) above or below the previous day's settlement price (expandable to US$75/troy ounce)

1,000 ounce silver – US$1/troy ounce (US$1,000/contract) above or below the previous day's settlement price (expandable to US$1.50/troy ounce)

5,000 ounce silver – US$1/troy ounce (US$5,000/contract) above or below the previous day's settlement price (expandable to US$1.50/troy ounce)

Financial options

US treasury bonds, 10-year US treasury notes, 5-year US treasury notes, flexible US treasury bonds, flexible 10-year US treasury notes, flexible 5-year US treasury notes – 3 points (US$3,000/contract) above or below the previous day's settlement premium (expandable to 4 1/2 points)***

2-year US treasury notes, flexible 2-year US treasury notes – 1 point (US$2,000/contract) above or below the previous day's premium (expandable to 1 1/2 points)***

Long-term municipal bond index	– 3 points (US$3,000/contract) above or below the previous day's settlement premium (expandable to 4 1/2 points)‡‡

Insurance options

Quarterly Property Claim Services (PCS) catastrophe insurance, annual Property Claim Services (PCS) catastrophe insurance	– 10 points for small cap options and 20 points for large cap options

Agricultural options

Soybean	– 30 cents/bushel (US$1,500/contract) above or below the previous day's settlement premium (expandable to 45 cents/bushel)***
Soybean oil	– 1 cent/lb (US$600/contract) above or below the previous day's settlement premium (expandable to 1 1/2 cents/lb)***
Soybean meal	– US$10/ton (US$1,000/contract) above or below the previous day's settlement premium (expandable to US$15/ton)***
Corn	– 12 cents/bushel (US$600/contract) above or below the previous day's settlement premium (expandable to 15 cents/bushel)***
Oats	– 10 cents/bushel (US$500/contract) above or below the previous day's settlement premium (expandable to 15 cents/bushel)***
Wheat	– 20 cents/bushel (US$1,000/contract) above or below the previous day's settlement premium (expandable to 30 cents/bushel)***
Rough rice	– 30 cents above and below the previous day's option premium settlement

Metals options

1,000 ounce silver	– US$/troy ounce (US$1,000/contract) above or below the previous days settlement premium (expandable to US$1.50/troy ounce)***

‡‡ No limit in the spot month (limits are lifted two business days before spot month begins).
*** Limits are lifted on the last trading day.

Tick size:

Financial futures

US treasury bonds, 10-year US treasury notes	– 1/32 of a point (US$31.25/contract); par is on the basis of 100 points
5-year US treasury notes	– one 1/2 of 1/32 of a point (US$15.625/contract) rounded up to the nearest cent/contract; par is on the basis of 100 points
2-year US treasury notes	– one 1/4 of 1/32 of a point (US$15.625/contract) rounded up to the nearest cent/contract; par is on the basis of 100 points
Long-term municipal bond index	– 1/32 of a point (US$31.25/contract)
30-day federal funds	– increments of 1/2 of 1/100 of 1% of US$5 million on a 30-day basis in the spot month only (US$20.84) and 1/100 of 1% of US$5 million on a 30-day basis in all other contract months (US$41.67)
Brady Bond Index	– minimum price fluctuation is 1/32, or US$31.25

Agricultural futures

Soybean, corn, oats, wheat	– 1/4 cent/bushel (US$12.50/contract)
Soybean oil	– 1/100 cent (US$0.0001/lb)(US$6/contract)
Soybean meal	– 10 cents/ton (US$10/contract)
Rough rice	– 1/2 cent/cwt (US$10/contract)
Anhydrous ammonia (NH_3), diammonium phosphate (DAP)	– 10 cents/ton (US$10/contract)

Corn yield insurance futures

Iowa corn yield insurance; Nebraska, Illinois, Indiana, Ohio and US corn yield insurance	– 1/10 bushel/acre harvested (US$10/contract)

Metals futures

Kilo gold	– 10 cents/fine troy ounce (US$3.22/contract) basis Chicago
100 ounce gold	– 10 cents/troy ounce (US$10/contract)
1,000 ounce silver	– 10/100 cents/troy ounce (US$1/contract) basis Chicago
5,000 ounce silver	– 10/100 cents/troy ounce (US$5/contract)

Financial options

US treasury bonds, 10-year US treasury notes, 5-year US treasury notes, long-term municipal bond index,

flexible US treasury bonds, flexible
10-year US treasury notes, flexible
5-year US treasury notes – 1/64 of a point (US$15.625/contract) rounded up to the nearest cent/contract
2-year US treasury notes, flexible
2-year US treasury notes – 1/2 of 1/64 of a point (US$15.62/contract) rounded up to the nearest cent/contract
Brady Bond Index – 1/64 of a point (US$1,000) or US$15.62

Insurance options
Quarterly Property Claim Services (PCS) catastrophe insurance, annual Property Claim Services (PCS) catastrophe insurance – 1/10 of one index point (US$20/contract)

Agricultural options
Soybean, corn, oats, wheat – 1/8 cent/bushel (US$6.25/contract)
Soybean oil – 5/1,000 cent (US$0.00005/lb)(US$3/contract)
Soybean meal – 5 cents/ton (US$5/contract)
Rough rice – 1/4 cent/cwt (US$5/contract)

Corn yield insurance options
Iowa corn yield insurance; Nebraska, Illinois, Indiana, Ohio and US corn yield insurance – 1/10 bushel/acre harvested (US$10/contract)

Metals options
1,000 ounce silver – 10/100 cents/troy ounce (US$1/contract)

Quality:

Financial futures
US treasury bonds – US treasury bonds that, if callable, are not callable for at least 15 years from the first day of delivery month, or if not callable, have a maturity of at least 15 years from the first day of delivery month
10-year US treasury notes – US treasury notes maturing at least six and a half years, but not more than ten years, from the first day of delivery month
5-year US treasury notes – US treasury notes that have an original maturity of not more than five years and three months and a remaining maturity of not less than four years and three months as of the first day of delivery month. The 5-year US treasury note issued after the last trading day of the contract month will not be eligible for delivery into that month's

contract

2-year US treasury notes – US treasury notes that have an original maturity of not more than five years and three months and a remaining maturity of not less than one year and nine months from the first day of delivery month but not more than two years from the last day of delivery month

Agricultural futures

Soybean – No. 2 yellow at par and substitutions at differentials established by the Exchange

Soybean oil – crude soybean oil meeting Exchange-approved grades and standards

Soybean meal – one grade of soybean meal only with minimum protein of 48%

Corn – No. 2 yellow at par and substitutions at differentials established by the Exchange

Oats – No. 2 heavy and No. 1 at par and substitutions at differentials established by the Exchange

Wheat – No. 1 northern spring wheat, No. 2 soft red winter,No. 2 hard red winter and No. 2 dark northern spring at par. Substitutions at differentials established by the Exchange

Rough rice – US No. 2 or better long grain rough rice with a total milling yield of not less than 65% including head rice of not less than 48%. Premiums and discounts are provided for each percent of head rice over or below 55%, and for each percent of broken rice over or below 15%

Anhydrous ammonia (NH_3) – (.5% ammonia (NH_3) minimum by weight; 82% nitrogen (N) minimum by weight; 0.2% moisture (water) minimum by weight; 0.5% moisture (water) maximum by weight; 5 parts per million maximum oil content

Diammonium phosphate (DAP) – 18-46-0 diammonium phosphate with analysis of: 17.5% minimum nitrogen by weight; 45.5% minimum P_2O_5 by weight; 2% maximum moisture as H_2O; 85% minimum of P_2O_3 water soluble; and 90% minimum – 5+14 Tyler mesh content

Metals futures

Kilo gold – one bar of refined gold assaying not less than 995 fineness, weighing at least 1 kg (32.15 troy ounces), and bearing brands and markings approved by the Exchange

100 ounce gold – one bar of refined gold in the form of one 100 ounce bar or three 1 kg gold bars assaying not less than 995 fineness. The total pack cannot vary from a 100 troy ounce weight by more than 5%

1,000 ounce silver – refined silver assaying not less than 999 fineness and made up of one or more brands and markings officially listed by the Exchange. Each bar cannot vary from a 1,000 troy ounce weight by more than 12%

5,000 ounce silver – refined silver in the form of four or five bars and assaying not less than 999 fineness. Each bar must weigh 1,000 or 1,100 troy ounces with a 10% tolerance, and bear brands and markings approved by the Exchange. The total pack cannot vary from a 5,000 troy ounce weight by more than 6%

Delivery:

Financial futures

US treasury bonds, 10-year US treasury notes, 5-year US treasury notes, 2-year US treasury notes – Federal reserve book-entry wire-transfer system

Metals futures

Kilo gold, 100 ounce gold, 1,000 ounce silver, 5,000 ounce silver – by vault receipt drawn on deposits made in Exchange-approved vaults in Chicago or New York

Contract months:

Financial futures

US treasury bonds, 10-year US treasury notes, 5-year US treasury notes, 2-year US treasury notes, long-term municipal bond index, Brady Bond Index – March, June, September, December

30-day federal funds – first 25 calendar months (and the next two months in the March, June, September, December cycle)

Agricultural futures

Soybean – September, November, January, March, May, July, August

Soybean oil, soybean meal	– October, December, January, March, May, July, August, September
Corn	– December, March, May, July, September
Oats, wheat	– July, September, December, March, May
Rough rice	– September, November, January, March, May, July
Anhydrous ammonia (NH_3)	– February, April, June, September, December
Diammonium phosphate (DAP)	– March, June, September, December

Corn yield insurance futures

Iowa corn yield insurance; Nebraska, Illinois, Indiana, Ohio and US corn yield insurance	– September, October, November, January

Metals futures

Kilo gold, 100 ounce gold, 1,000 ounce silver, 5,000 ounce silver	– current month, the next two succeeding months, plus February, April, June, August, October, December

Financial options

US treasury bonds, 10-year US treasury notes, 5-year US treasury notes, 2-year US treasury notes,	– the first month of the current quarter plus the next three contracts of the quarterly cycle (March, June, September, December). If the front month is a quarterly contract month, no monthly contract will be listed. The monthly option contract exercises into the current quarterly futures contract
Long-term municipal bond index	– the first three months plus the next two months in the quarterly cycle
Brady Bond Index	– quarterly and serial

Insurance options

Quarterly Property Claim Services (PCS) catastrophe insurance	– each loss period is tracked by small and large cap quarterly contracts
Annual Property Claim Services (PCS) catastrophe insurance	– listed on an annual basis

Agricultural options

Soybean	– September, November, January, March, May, July, August
Soybean oil, soybean meal	– October, December, January, March, May, July, August, September
Corn	– December, March, May, July, September
Oats, wheat	– July, September, December, March, May

Rough rice – January, March, May, July, September, November

Corn yield insurance options

Iowa corn yield insurance; Nebraska, Illinois, Indiana, Ohio and US corn yield insurance – September, October, November, January

Metals options

1,000 ounce silver – February, April, June, August, October, December

Delivery days:

Financial futures

US treasury bonds, 10-year US treasury notes, 5-year US treasury notes – last business day of delivery month

2-year US treasury notes – third business day following the last trading day

Agricultural futures

Soybean, soybean oil, corn, oats, wheat, rough rice – last business day of delivery month

Soybean meal – second business day preceding the last trading day of delivery month

Anhydrous ammonia (NH_3) – second business day after the last day of trading

Diammonium Phosphate (DAP) – second business day after the last trading day in delivery month

Termination of trading:

Financial futures

US treasury bonds, 10-year US treasury notes, 5-year US treasury notes, long-term municipal bond index – seventh business day preceding the last business day of delivery month

2-year US treasury notes – the earlier of (i) the second business day prior to the issue day of the 2-year note auctioned in the current month, or (ii) the last business day of the calendar month

30-day federal funds – last business day of delivery month

Brady Bond Index – eighth to last business day of contract month

Agricultural futures

Soybean, soybean oil, soybean meal, corn, oats, wheat, rough rice, diammonium phosphate (DAP) – seventh business day preceding the last business day of delivery month

Anhydrous ammonia (NH_3) – fifth business day prior to the 25th calendar day of delivery month

Corn yield insurance futures

Iowa corn yield insurance – last business day of the month prior to USDA's release of corn crops production and yield estimates for Iowa

Nebraska, Illinois, Indiana, Ohio and US corn yield insurance – last business day of the month prior to USDA's release of corn crop production estimate reports for the respective states and the entire USA

Metals futures

Kilo gold, 100 ounce gold, 1,000 ounce silver, 5,000 ounce silver – fourth to last business day of delivery month

Financial options

US treasury bonds, 10-year US treasury notes, 5-year US treasury notes, 2-year US treasury notes – options cease trading in the month prior to the delivery month of the underlying futures contract

Long-term municipal bond index – quarterly options cease trading at 14.00 Chicago time on the last day of trading of the Municipal Bond Index futures of the corresponding delivery month. Options not in the quarterly cycle cease at noon on their last day of trading. The last day of trading for these options is the last Friday, which precedes by at least five business days, the last business day of the expiration month

Brady Bond Index – for quarterly options, the eighth to last business day of the contract month. For serial options, the last Friday preceding by at least five business days the last business day of the contract month

Flexible US treasury bonds, flexible 10-year US treasury notes, flexible 5-year US treasury notes, flexible 2-year US treasury notes – unexercised options expire on the last trading day. On the last trading/expiration day, trading ceases at noon and expiration occurs later that day at 16.30 Chicago time

Insurance options

Quarterly Property Claim Services (PCS) catastrophe insurance, annual Property Claim Services (PCS) catastrophe insurance – same day as expiration

Agricultural options

Soybean, soybean oil, soybean meal, corn, oats, wheat – the last Friday preceding the first notice day of the corresponding futures contract by at least five business days

Rough rice – options expiring in the current month shall cease trading at 12.15 on the last Friday that precedes by at least five business days the first notice day of the underlying futures contract

Corn yield insurance options

Iowa corn yield insurance – last business day of the month prior to USDA's release of corn crop production and yield estimates for Iowa

Nebraska, Illinois, Indiana, Ohio and US corn yield insurance – last business day of the month prior to USDAs release of corn crop production and yield estimates for the respective states and the entire USA

Metals options

1,000 ounce silver – the last Friday preceding the first notice day for the corresponding silver futures contract by at least five business days

Settlement:

Financial futures

Long-term municipal bond index – Municipal Bond Index futures settle in cash on the last day of trading. Settlement price equals *The Bond Buyer*™ municipal bond index value on that day

30-day federal funds – the contract will be cash settled to the nearest half-basis point against the simple average overnight federal funds effective rate for the delivery month. The overnight federal funds effective rate is calculated and reported daily by the Federal Reserve Bank of New York

Corn yield insurance futures

Iowa corn yield insurance – cash settled following the USDA's release of corn crop production and yield estimates for Iowa

Nebraska, Illinois, Indiana, Ohio and US corn yield insurance – cash settled following the USDA's release of corn crop production and yield estimates for the respective states and the entire USA

Expiry dates:

Financial options

US treasury bonds, 10-year US treasury notes, 5-year US treasury notes, 2-year US treasury notes	– unexercised options expire at 10.00 Chicago time on the first Saturday following the last day of trading
Long-term municipal bond index	– unexercised options expire at 18.00 Chicago time on the last day of trading
Brady Bond Index	– 09.15 on the last day of trading
Flexible US treasury bonds, flexible 10-year US treasury notes, flexible 5-year US treasury notes, flexible 2-year US treasury notes	– any Monday to Friday, provided that (i) it is not an Exchange holiday, and (ii) the date does not exceed the expiration date of the standard option whose underlying is the most deferred futures contract to have had trading activity

Insurance options

Quarterly Property Claim Services (PCS) catastrophe insurance, annual Property Claim Services (PCS) catastrophe insurance	– may be specified as the last business day of the sixth month following the loss period or the last business day of the 12 month following the loss period

Agricultural options

Soybean, soybean oil, soybean meal, corn, oats, wheat, rough rice	– unexercised options expire at 10.00 Chicago time on the first Saturday following the last day of trading

Corn yield insurance options

Iowa corn yield insurance; Nebraska, Illinois, Indiana, Ohio and US corn yield insurance	– unexercised options will expire at 18.00 Chicago time on the same day final settlement yield for the underlying futures contract is made publicly available

Metals options

1,000 ounce silver	– unexercised options expire at 10.00 Chicago time on the first Saturday following the last day of trading

Exercise:

Financial options

US treasury bonds, 10-year US treasury notes, 5-year US treasury notes, 2-year US treasury notes – the buyer of a futures option may exercise the option on any business day prior to the expiration by giving notice to the Board of Trade Clearing Corporation by 18.00 Chicago time. Options that expire in-the-money are automatically exercised into a position, unless specific instructions are given to the Board of Trade Clearing Corporation

Long-term municipal bond index – the buyer of a futures option may exercise the option on any business day up to and including the expiration day by giving notice to the Board of Trade Clearing Corporation by 18.00 Chicago time. Options in-the-money on the last day of trading are automatically exercised

Brady Bond Index – any business day that the option is traded

Flexible US treasury bonds, flexible 10-year US treasury notes, flexible 5-year US treasury notes, flexible 2-year US treasury notes – the buyer of an American-style option may exercise the option on any business day prior to expiration by giving notice to the Board of Trade Clearing Corporation by 16.10 Chicago time. For European-style, the option is exercised on the expiration day only, prior tot he 16.10. At expiration, all in-the-money options are automatically exercised

Insurance options

Quarterly Property Claim Services (PCS) catastrophe insurance, annual Property Claim Services (PCS) catastrophe insurance – European-PCS options can be exercised only at expiration. In-the-money options are automatically exercised by 18.00 Chicago time on expiration day

Agricultural options

Soybean, soybean oil, soybean meal, oats, wheat – the buyer of a futures option may exercise the option on any business day prior to expiration by giving notice to the Board of

Trade Clearing Corporation by 18.00 Chicago time. Option exercise results in an underlying futures market position. Options in-the-money on the last day of trading are automatically exercised

Corn – the buyer of a futures option may exercise the option on any business day prior to expiration by giving notice to the Board of Trade Clearing Corporation by 18.00 Chicago time. Option exercise results in an underlying futures market position. Options at least 10 cents/bushel in-the-money on the last day of trading are automatically exercised

Rough rice – option buyers may exercise an option contract on any business day prior to expiration by giving notice to the clearing house by 18.00 Chicago time on such day. Exercised options are randomly assigned to option sellers. Options that are at least 30 cents in-the-money after the close on the last trading day are automatically exercised, unless notice to cancel is given to the clearing house

Metals options

1,000 ounce silver – the buyer of a futures option may exercise the option on any business day prior to expiration by giving notice to the Board of Trade Clearing Corporation by 18.00 Chicago time. Option exercise results in an underlying futures market position. Options in-the-money on the last day of trading are automatically exercised

Margins:

Financial instruments *US$/contract*

	Initial	*Maintenance*	*Hedge*
US treasury bonds	2,700	2,000	2,000
10-year US treasury notes	1,755	1,300	1,300
5-year US treasury notes	1,215	900	900
2-year US treasury notes	1,080	800	800
Long-term municipal bond index	2,295	1,700	1,700
30-day federal funds	338	250	250
Brady Bond Index	3,375	2,500	2,500
Agricultural group			
Soybean	1,890	1,400	1,400

	Initial	*Maintenance*	*Hedge*
Soybean oil	675	500	500
Soybean meal	1,215	900	900
Corn	810	600	600
Oats	675	500	500
Wheat	1,688	1,250	1,250
Rough rice	810	600	600
Anhydrous ammonia (NH_3)	1,013	750	750
Diammonium phosphate (DAP)	540	400	400
Iowa corn yield insurance	405	300	300
Nebraska, Illinois, Indiana, Ohio and US corn yield insurance	405	300	300
Metals group			
Kilo gold	203	150	150
100 ounce gold	608	450	450
1,000 ounce silver	270	200	200
5,000 ounce silver	1,350	1,000	1,000

Volume of trade:

	Jan-Dec 1994	*Jan-Dec 1995*
Financial futures		
US treasury bonds	99,959,881	86,375,916
10-year US treasury notes	24,077,828	22,445,356
5-year US treasury notes	12,462,838	12,637,054
2-year US treasury notes	939,043	744,866
Long-term municipal bond index	1,600,533	1,169,470
30-day federal funds	416,200	643,717
Agricultural futures		
Soybean	10,749,109	10,611,534
Soybean oil	5,063,188	4,611,336
Soybean meal	4,593,814	5,601,242
Corn	11,592,884	15,105,147
Oats	492,504	475,538
Wheat	3,620,631	4,955,067
Rough rice	16,693	121,914
Anhydrous ammonia (NH_3)	2,811	1,060
Diammonium phosphate (DAP)	15,588	6,755
Metals futures		
Kilo gold	22,712	20,245
100 ounce gold	984	647
1,000 ounce silver	88,663	76,667
5,000 ounce silver	10,278	8,617
Financial options		
US treasury bonds	28,142,549	25,639,950
10-year US treasury notes	6,437,215	6,887,102
5-year US treasury notes	2,675,097	3,619,462
2-year US treasury notes	12,862	13,189

	Jan-Dec 1994	Jan-Dec 1995
Financial futures		
Long-term municipal bond index	24,772	13,018
Flexible US treasury bonds	174,295	59,804
Flexible 10-year US treasury notes	46,606	36,425
Flexible 5-year US treasury notes	19,060	14,730
Flexible 2-year US treasury notes	250	100
Agricultural options		
Soybean	2,710,656	3,149,635
Soybean oil	287,905	232,635
Soybean meal	263,734	304,835
Corn	2,144,461	3,783,446
Oats	20,495	35,250
Wheat	827,930	1,243,567
Rough rice	1,750	14,336
Metals options		
1,000 ounce silver	5,952	1,476

Date of establishment of contracts:

Financial futures

US treasury bonds – 22 August 1977
10-year US treasury notes – 3 May 1982
5-year US treasury notes – 20 May 1988
2-year US treasury notes – 22 June 1990
Long-term municipal bond index – 11 June 1985
30-day federal funds – 3 October 1988
Brady Bond Index – 1 March 1996

Agricultural futures

Soybean – 5 October 1936
Soybean oil – 17 July1950
Soybean meal – 19 August 1951
Corn – 2 January 1877
Oats – 2 January 1877
Wheat – 2 January 1877
Rough rice – 3 October 1994
Anhydrous ammonia (NH_3) – 11 November 1992
Diammonium phosphate (DAP) – 18 October 1991

Corn yield insurance futures

Iowa corn yield insurance – 2 June 1995
Nebraska, Illinois, Indiana, Ohio
and US corn yield insurance – 19 January 1996

Metals futures

Kilo gold – 12 April 1983
100 ounce gold – 14 September 1987
1,000 ounce silver – 16 March 1981
5,000 ounce silver – 14 September 1987

Financial options

US treasury bonds – 1 October 1982

10-year US treasury notes	– 1 May 1985
5-year US treasury notes	– 24 May 1990
2-year US treasury notes	– 1 May 1992
Long-term municipal bond index	– 11 June 1987
Brady Bond Index	– 1 March 1996
Flexible US treasury bonds	– 7 January 1994
Flexible 10-year US treasury notes	– 7 January 1994
Flexible 5-year US treasury notes	– 7 January 1994
Flexible 2-year US treasury notes	– 7 January 1994
Agricultural options	
Soybean	– 31 October 1984
Soybean oil	– 19 February 1987
Soybean meal	– 19 February 1987
Corn	– 27 February 1985
Oats	– 1 May 1990
Wheat	– 17 November 1986
Rough rice	– 3 October 1994
Corn yield insurance options	
Iowa corn yield insurance	– 2 June 1995
Nebraska, Illinois, Indiana, Ohio and US corn yield insurance	– 19 January 1996
Metals options	
1,000 ounce silver	– 29 March 1985

Clearing house: Board of Trade Clearing Corporation

Membership:

Full Membership

1,402; provides individual access to all CBOT markets.

Associate membership

760; provides access to financial instruments, and gold futures.

Delegates

Persons who qualify may obtain the trading privileges of full members or associate members through leasing as delegates.

Membership interests

Provides access to the following markets: Government Instrument Market (GIM; 212) – bonds, notes; Index, Debt and Energy Market (IDEM; 642) – gold and stock indexes; Commodity Options Market (COM; 643) – treasury bond options and soybean futures options, corn futures options, treasury note options and silver futures options. Membership interests confer trading privileges on the holders but no voting rights.

Chicago Mercantile Exchange

30 South Wacker Drive, Chicago, Illinois 60606
Tel: +1 312 930 1000
Fax: +1 312 930 3439
President and Chief Executive: William J Brodsky
Chairman, Executive Committee: John F Sandner
PR/Information: Ellen Resnick

Hours of trading:

Agricultural futures and options:

Live cattle futures, feeder cattle futures, feeder cattle options	– 09.05-13.00 (12.00)*
Live cattle options	– 09.05-13.00 (13.00)*
Lean hogs futures, lean hogs options, pork bellies futures	– 09.10-13.00 (12.00)*
Pork bellies options	– 09.10-13.00 (13.00)*
Fluid milk futures	– 08.00-13.10 (12.10)*
Fluid milk options	– 08.00-13.10 (13.10)*

Forest produce futures and options:

Random length lumber futures	– 09.00-13.05 (12.05)*
Random length lumber options	– 09.00-13.05 (13.05)*

Currency futures and options:

Australian dollar futures	– 07.20-14.00 (09.16)*
Australian dollar options	– 07.20-14.00 (14.00)*
British pound futures	– 07.20-14.00 (09.16)*
British pound options	– 07.20-14.00 (14.00)*
Canadian dollar futures	– 07.20-14.00 (09.16)*
Canadian dollar options	– 07.20-14.00 (14.00)*
Deutsche mark futures	– 07.20-14.00 (09.16)*
Deutsche mark options	– 07.20-14.00 (14.00)*
French franc futures	– 07.20-14.00 (09.16)*
French franc options	– 07.20-14.00 (14.00)*
Japanese yen futures	– 07.20-14.00 (09.16)*
Japanese yen options	– 07.20-14.00 (14.00)*
Mexican peso futures	– 08.00-14.00 (09.16)*
Mexican peso options	– 08.00-14.00 (14.00)*
Brazilian real futures	– 08.00-14.00 (14.00)*
Brazilian real options	– 07.20-14.00 (14.00)*
Swiss franc futures	– 07.20-14.00 (09.16)*
Swiss franc options	– 07.20-14.00 (14.00)*
British pound rolling spot futures	– 07.20-14.00 (09.16)*
British pound rolling spot options	– 07.20-14.00 (14.00)*

Foreign currency-denominated futures and options:

Deutsche mark rolling spot futures	– 07.20-14.00 (09.16)*
Deutsche mark rolling spot options	– 07.20-14.00 (14.00)*

Deutsche mark currency forward – 07.20-14.00 (09.16 quarterly months; 14.00 serial months)*
Japanese yen rolling spot futures – 07.20-14.00 (14.00)*
Japanese yen rolling currency forward – 07.20-14.00 (09.16 quarterly months; 14.00 serial months)*

Foreign currency-denominated interest rate futures and options:
EuroYen futures – 07.20-14.00 (14.00)*

Interest rate futures and options:
Eurodollar time deposit futures – 07.20-14.00 (09.30)*
Eurodollar time deposit options – 07.20-14.00 (09.30)*
13-week treasury bills futures – 07.20-14.00 (10.00)*
13-week US treasury bills options – 07.20-14.00 (14.00)*
1-year treasury bills futures – 07.20-14.00 (12.00)*
1-year treasury bills options – 07.20-14.00 (12.00)*
1-month Libor futures – 07.20-14.00 (09.30)*
1-month Libor options – 07.20-14.00 (09.30)*
3-month Euromark futures – 07.20-14.00 (14.00)*
3-month Euromark options – 07.20-14.00 (14.00)*
Federal funds rate – 07.20-14.00 (09.30)*
Mexican par Brady Bond futures – 07.20-14.00 (10.30)*
Mexican par Brady Bond options – 07.20-14.00 (10.30)*
Argentine FRB Bond futures – 07.20-14.00 (10.30)*
Argentine FRB Bond options – 07.20-14.00 (10.30)*
Brazilian C bond futures – 07.20-14.00 (10.30)*
Brazilian C bond options – 07.20-14.00 (10.30)*
Brazilian EI bond futures – 07.20-14.00 (10.30)*
Brazilian EI bond options – 07.20-14.00 (10.30)*

Stock index futures and options:
Standard & Poor's 500 futures – 08.30-15.15 (15.15)*
Standard & Poor's 500 options – 08.30-15.15 (15.15)*
Standard & Poor's MidCap 400 futures – 08.30-15.15 (15.15)*
Standard & Poor's MidCap 400 options – 08.30-15.15 (15.15)*
Nikkei 225 stock average futures – 08.30-15.15 (15.15)*
Nikkei 225 stock average options – 08.30-15.15 (15.15)*
Goldman Sachs commodity index futures – 08.15-14.15 (14.15)*
Goldman Sachs commodity index options – 08.15-14.15 (14.15)*
FTSE share index futures – 08.30-15.15 (15.15)*
FTSE share index options – 08.30-15.15 (15.15)*
Russell 2000 stock price index futures – 08.30-15.15 (15.15)*
Russell 2000 stock price index options – 08.30-15.15 (15.15)*
Major market index futures – 08.30-15.15 (15.15)*
Major market index options – 08.30-15.15 (15.15)*
S&P 500/BARRA growth index futures – 08.30-15.15 (15.15)*
S&P 500/BARRA growth index options – 08.30-15.15 (15.15)*
S&P 500/BARRA value index futures – 08.30-15.15 (15.15)*

S&P 500/BARRA value index options	–	08.30-15.15 (15.15)*
NASDAQ 100 index futures	–	08.30-15.15 (15.15)*
NASDAQ 100 index options	–	08.30-15.15 (15.15)*
IPC index futures	–	08.30-15.15 (15.15)*
IPC index options	–	08.30-15.15 (15.15)*

* Times in parentheses indicate close on last day of trading (Central Time)

Trading units:

Commodity	*Size of contract*	*Min price fluctuation per contract*
Agricultural futures and options:		
Live cattle futures	40,000 lbs	US$10.00
Live cattle options	40,000 lbs	US$10.00
Feeder cattle futures	50,000 lbs	US$12.50
Feeder cattle options	50,000 lbs	US$12.50
Lean hogs futures	40,000 lbs	US$10.00
Lean hogs options	40,000 lbs	US$10.00
Pork bellies futures	40,000 lbs	US$10.00
Pork bellies options	40,000 lbs	US$10.00
Fluid milk futures	50,000 lbs	US$12.50
Fluid milk options	50,000 lbs	US$12.50
Forest produce futures and options:		
Random length lumber futures	80,000 board feet	US$8.00
Random length lumber options	80,000 board feet	US$8.00
Currency futures and options:		
Australian dollar futures	A$100,000	US$10.00
Australian dollar options	A$100,000	US$10.00
British pound futures	£62,500	US$12.50
British pound options	£62,500	US$12.50
Canadian dollar futures	C$100,000	US$10.00
Canadian dollar options	C$100,000	US$10.00
Deutsche mark futures	DM125,000	US$12.50
Deutsche mark options	DM125,000	US$12.50
French franc futures	FFr500,000	US$10.00
French franc options	FFr500,000	US$10.00
Japanese yen futures	¥12,500,000	US$12.50
Japanese yen options	¥12,500,000	US$12.50
Mexican peso futures	Mex pesos500,000	US$12.50
Mexican peso options	Mex pesos500,000	US$12.50
Brazilian real futures	BrReals100,000	US$10.00
Brazilian real options	BrReals100,000	US$10.00
Swiss franc futures	SwFr125,000	US$12.50
Swiss franc options	SwFr125,000	US$12.50
British pound rolling spot futures	£250,000	US$25.00
British pound rolling spot options	£250,000	US$25.00

Commodity	*Size of contract*	*Min price fluctuation per contract*
Foreign currency-denominated futures and options:		
Deutsche mark rolling spot futures	US$250,000	DM25.00
Deutsche mark rolling spot options	US$250,000	DM25.00
Deutsche mark currency forward	US$250,000	DM25.00
Japanese yen rolling spot futures	US$250,000	¥2,500
Japanese yen rolling currency forward	US$250,000	¥2,500
Foreign currency-denominated interest rate futures and options:		
EuroYen futures	¥100,000,000	¥2,500
Interest rate futures and options:		
Eurodollar time deposit futures	US$1,000,000	US$25.00
Eurodollar time deposit options	US$1,000,000	US$25.00
13-week treasury bills futures	US$1,000,000	US$25.00
13-week US treasury bills options	US$1,000,000	US$25.00
1-year treasury bills futures	US$500,000	US$25.00
1-year treasury bills options	US$500,000	US$25.00
1-month Libor futures	US$3,000,000	US$25.00
1-month Libor options	US$3,000,000	US$25.00
3-month Euromark futures	DM1,000,000	DM25.00
3-month Euromark options	DM1,000,000	DM25.00
Federal funds rate	US$3,000,000	US$25.00
Mexican par Brady Bond futures	US$1,000 times price of Mexican par bond	US$10.00
Mexican par Brady Bond options	US$1,000 times price of Mexican par bond	US$10.00
Argentine FRB Bond futures	US$1,000 times price of Argentine FRB Bond	US$10.00
Argentine FRB Bond options	US$1,000 times price of Argentine FRB Bond	US$10.00
Brazilian C bond futures	US$1,000 times price of Brazilian C bond	US$10.00
Brazilian C bond options	US$1,000 times price of Brazilian C bond	US$10.00
Brazilian EI bond futures	US$1,000 times price of Brazilian EI bond	US$10.00
Brazilian EI bond options	US$1,000 times price of Brazilian EI bond	US$10.00
Stock index futures and options:		
Standard & Poor's 500 futures	US$500 times S&P's 500 stock index	US$25.00
Standard & Poor's 500 options	US$500 times S&P's 500 stock index	US$25.00
Standard & Poor's MidCap 400 futures	US$500 times S&P's MidCap 400 stock price index	US$25.00

Commodity	*Size of contract*	*Min price fluctuation per contract*
Standard & Poor's MidCap 400 options	US$500 times S&P's MidCap 400 stock price index	US$25.00
Nikkei 225 stock average futures	US$5 times Nikkei stock index	US$25.00
Nikkei 225 stock average options	US$5 times Nikkei stock index	US$25.00
Goldman Sachs commodity index futures	US$250 times GS com index	US$25.00
Goldman Sachs commodity index options	US$250 times GS com index	US$25.00
FTSE share index futures	US$50 times FTSE	US$25.00
FTSE share index options	US$50 times FTSE	US$25.00
Russell 2000 stock price index futures	US$500 times Russell 2000	US$25.00
Russell 2000 stock price index options	US$500 times Russell 2000	US$25.00
Major market index futures	US$500 times Major market index	US$25.00
Major market index options	US$500 times Major market index	US$25.00
S&P 500/BARRA growth index futures	US$500 times S&P 500/BARRA growth index	US$25.00
S&P 500/BARRA growth index options	US$500 times S&P 500/BARRA growth index	US$25.00
S&P 500/BARRA value index futures	US$500 times S&P 500/BARRA value index	US$25.00
S&P 500/BARRA value index options	US$500 times S&P 500/BARRA value index	US$25.00
NASDAQ 100 index futures	US$100 times index	US$5.00
NASDAQ 100 index options	US$100 times index	US$5.00
IPC index futures	US$25 times index	US$25.00
IPC index options	US$25 times index	US$25.00

Contract months:

Agricultural futures and options:

Live cattle futures – February, April, June, August, October, December

Live cattle options – February, April, June, August, October, December and serial months

Feeder cattle futures	– January, March, April, May, August, September, October, November
Feeder cattle options	– January, March, April, May, August, September, October, November
Lean hogs futures	– February, April, June, July, August, October, December
Lean hogs options	– February, April, June, July, August, October, December and serial months January, March, November
Pork bellies futures	– February, March, May, July, August
Pork bellies options	– February, March, May, July, August, November
Fluid milk futures	– February, April, June, July, September, November
Fluid milk options	– February, April, June, July, September, November

Forest produce futures and options:

Random length lumber futures	– January, March, May, July, September, November
Random length lumber options	– January, March, May, July, September, November

Currency futures and options:

Australian dollar futures	– January, March, April, June, July, September, October, December and spot month
Australian dollar options	– quarterly, serial months and weekly expiration options†
British pound futures	– January, March, April, June, July, September, October, December and spot month
British pound options	– quarterly, serial months and weekly expiration options†
Canadian dollar futures	– January, March, April, June, July, September, October, December and spot month
Canadian dollar options	– quarterly, serial months and weekly expiration options†
Deutsche mark futures	– January, March, April, June, July, September, October, December and spot month
Deutsche mark options	– quarterly, serial months and weekly expiration options†
French franc futures	– January, March, April, June, July, September, October, December and spot month
French franc options	– quarterly, serial months and weekly expiration options†

Japanese yen futures – January, March, April, June, July, September, October, December and spot month
Japanese yen options – quarterly, serial months and weekly expiration options†
Mexican peso futures – March, June, September, December
Mexican peso options – quarterly, serial months and weekly expiration options†
Brazilian real futures – all 12 calendar months
Brazilian real options – all 12 calendar months and weekly expiration options
Swiss franc futures – January, March, April, June, July, September, October, December and spot month
Swiss franc options – quarterly, serial months and weekly expiration options†
British pound rolling spot futures – March, June, September, December
British pound rolling spot options – all 12 calendar months with weekly expirations†

Foreign currency-denominated futures and options:
Deutsche mark rolling spot futures – March, June, September, December
Deutsche mark rolling spot options – all 12 calendar months with weekly expirations
Deutsche mark currency forward – 12 consecutive months plus four additional months in the March quarterly cycle
Japanese yen rolling spot futures – March, June, September, December
Japanese yen rolling currency forward – 12 consecutive months plus four additional months in the March quarterly cycle

Foreign currency-denominated interest rate futures and options:
EuroYen futures – March, June, September, December on a 3-year cycle

Interest rate futures and options:
Eurodollar time deposit futures – March, June, September, December, two serial months and spot month
Eurodollar time deposit options – March, June, September, December, serial, nearest 1-year and 2-year mid-curve quarterly months
13-week treasury bills futures – March, June, September, December
13-week US treasury bills options – March, June, September, December
1-year treasury bills futures – March, June, September, December
1-year treasury bills options – March, June, September, December and serial months
1-month Libor futures – all 12 calendar months
1-month Libor options – all 12 calendar months
3-month Euromark futures – March, June, September, December
3-month Euromark options – March, June, September, December and

	serial months
Federal funds rate	– all 12 calendar months
Mexican par Brady Bond futures	– March, June, September, December
Mexican par Brady Bond options	– March, June, September, December and serial months
Argentine FRB Bond futures	– March, June, September, December
Argentine FRB Bond options	– March, June, September, December and serial months
Brazilian C bond futures	– March, June, September, December
Brazilian C bond options	– March, June, September, December and serial months
Brazilian EI bond futures	– March, June, September, December
Brazilian EI bond options	– March, June, September, December and serial months

Stock index futures and options:

Standard & Poor's 500 futures	– March, June, September, December
Standard & Poor's 500 options	– March, June, September, December, serial months and FLEX options
Standard & Poor's MidCap 400 futures	– March, June, September, December
Standard & Poor's MidCap 400 options	– March, June, September, December, serial months and FLEX options
Nikkei 225 stock average futures	– March, June, September, December
Nikkei 225 stock average options	– March, June, September, December, serial months and FLEX options
Goldman Sachs commodity index futures	– all 12 calendar months
Goldman Sachs commodity index options	– all 12 calendar months
FTSE share index futures	– March, June, September, December
FTSE share index options	– March, June, September, December, serial months and FLEX options
Russell 2000 stock price index futures	– March, June, September, December
Russell 2000 stock price index options	– March, June, September, December, serial months and FLEX options
Major market index futures	– nearest three consecutive months and next three months in March quarterly cycle
Major market index options	– nearest three consecutive months, next three months in March quarterly cycle and FLEX options
S&P 500/BARRA growth index futures	– March, June, September, December
S&P 500/BARRA growth index options	– March, June, September, December, serial months and FLEX options
S&P 500/BARRA value index futures	– March, June, September, December
S&P 500/BARRA value index options	– March, June, September, December, serial months and FLEX options
NASDAQ 100 index futures	– March, June, September, December
NASDAQ 100 index options	– March, June, September, December, serial months and FLEX options

IPC index futures – March, June, September, December
IPC index options – March, June, September, December and nearest serial contract months

† The underlying futures contract for both serial and quarterly options as well as for weekly expiration options is the futures contract with greater than two Exchange business days before its LDT when the options expire. Please note that a weekly option will expire during each week in which no serial or quarterly option is scheduled to expire; however, weekly currency options may be listed up to five weeks prior to their expiration.

Date of establishment of the market: The Chicago Mercantile Exchange (CME) was founded in 1919. The Exchange pioneered trading in livestock futures and financial futures, two of the industry's most active areas.

Membership: The Exchange comprises three membership divisions: (i) a full Chicago Mercantile Exchange seat entitles its owner to execute trades in any contract listed on the Exchange; (ii) the International Monetary Market (IMM) membership, established in 1972, gives its owner the right to trade all of the Exchanges currency, interest rate and stock index futures and options; and (iii) the Index and Option Market (IOM) membership, instituted in 1982, entitles its owner to trade any of the Exchange's index futures contracts, random length lumber contracts and all options listed on the Exchange.

All CME members are approved by the Exchange's Board of Directors. Memberships are purchased from existing members at prevailing market prices, with bids to buy and offers to sell posted by the Exchange.

Further information: The Chicago Mercantile Exchange is one of the world's biggest market-places. In the Exchange's two-floor, 70,000 square foot trading arena, the biggest in the world, some 900,000 futures and options change hands on every business day. At the same time, the pacesetting underlying notional value of the CME's annual trading activity approaches US$200 trillion. In addition, the CME has long led the world's exchanges in open interest – the number of futures contracts and options still open or outstanding at the close of trading. This measure of market liquidity and of the long-term asset and risk management use of CME products is the key to understanding the significant role the CME plays in the world economy. Since 1990, open interest in CME products has grown from 1.8 million positions to nearly 7 million positions in 1994.

KANSAS

Kansas City Board of Trade

Suite 303, 4800 Main Street, Kansas City, Missouri 64112
Tel: +1 816 753 7500
Fax: +1 816 753 3944
President and CEO: Mike Braude
Senior Vice President and CFO: Jeff Borchardt
Vice President, Marketing: Linda Hopwood

Hours of trading (Central time):

Value line stock index futures	– 08.30-15.15
Mini value line stock index futures	– 08.30–15.15
Mini value line options	– 08.30–15.15
Western natural gas options	– 08.30–14.35
Western natural gas futures	– 08.30–14.30
Hard red winter wheat options	– 09.30–13.20
Hard red winter wheat futures	– 09.30–13.15

Contract details:

Commodities: value line stock index futures, mini value line stock index futures, mini value line options, Western natural gas options, Western natural gas futures, hard red winter wheat options, hard red winter wheat futures.

Trading currency and unit (manner of price quotation):

Value line stock index futures	– index points
Mini value line stock index futures	– index points
Mini value line options	– index points
Western natural gas options	– dollars and cents per million British thermal units (MMBtu)
Western natural gas futures	– dollars and cents per MMBtu
Hard red winter wheat options	– dollars, cents and one eighth cents per bushel
Hard red winter wheat futures	– dollars, cents and one quarter cents per bushel

Trading unit (minimum lot size):

Value line stock index futures	– $500 times futures price
Mini value line stock index futures	– $100 times futures price
Mini value line options	– one Kansas City Board of Trade (KCBT) mini value line futures contract
Western natural gas options	– one KCBT Western natural gas futures contract
Western natural gas futures	– 10,000 British thermal units (MMBtu)
Hard red winter wheat options	– one KCBT hard red winter wheat futures contract
Hard red winter wheat futures	– 5,000 bushels

Minimum price fluctuation:

Value line stock index futures	– 0.05 point ($25 per contract)
Mini value line stock index futures	– 0.05 point ($5 per contract)
Mini value line options	– .05 point ($5)
Western natural gas options	– $0.001 per MMBtu
Western natural gas futures	– $0.001 per MMbtu ($10 per contract)
Hard red winter wheat options	– one eighth cent ($6.25 per contract)
Hard red winter wheat futures	– one quarter cent ($12.50 per contract)

Maximum daily price fluctuation:

Value line stock index futures	– in index points, above or below the previous settlement as follows:

	Down Initial	*Intermediate*	*2nd intermediate*	*Total*	*Up*
First day	12	20	30	30	30
Second day	12	20	30	50	50

Mini value line stock index futures – in index points, above or below the previous settlement as follows:

	Down Initial	*Intermediate*	*2nd intermediate*	*Total*	*Up*
First day	12	20	30	30	30
Second day	12	20	30	50	50

Mini value line options – same as the daily trading limit for underlying futures. In index points, above or below the previous settlement as follows:

	Down Initial	*Intermediate*	*2nd intermediate*	*Total*	*Up*
First day	12	20	30	30	30
Second day	12	20	30	50	50

Western natural gas options – none

Western natural gas futures – $.10 per MMBtu ($1,000 per contract) above or below previous day's settlement price. No maximum daily limit in first nearby contract month.

Hard red winter wheat options – 25 cents ($1,250 per contract) above or below previous day's settlement price.

Hard red winter wheat futures – 25 cents ($1,250 per contract) above or below previous day's settlement price.

Speculative position limits:

Value line stock index futures – 5,000 contracts net long or short in all months combined.

Mini value line stock index futures – 5,000 contracts net long or short in all months combined.

Mini value line options – maximum nominal limit in all months combined of 5,000 contracts.

Western natural gas options
- spot month – 250 futures equivalent contracts
- single month – 5,000 futures equivalent contracts
- all months combined – 7,000 futures equivalent contracts

Western natural gas futures
- spot month – 250 futures equivalent contracts
- single month – 5,000 futures equivalent contracts
- all months combined – 7,000 futures equivalent contracts

Hard red winter wheat options – combined with wheat futures for a net long or net short futures-equivalent
– spot month – 3 million bushels (maximum)
– single month – 10.5 million bushels (maximum)
– all months combined – 16 million bushels (maximum)

Hard red winter wheat futures – combined with wheat options for a net long or net short futures-equivalent
– spot month – 3 million bushels (maximum)
– single month – 10.5 million bushels (maximum)
– all months combined – 16 million bushels (maximum)

Delivery months:

Value line stock index futures, mini value line stock index futures, – March, June, September, December

Western natural gas options, Western natural gas futures – 18 consecutive months

Hard red winter wheat options, hard red winter wheat futures – July, September, December, March, May

Delivery mechanism:

Value line stock index futures, mini value line stock index futures – since this is a cash settled contract, the value line arithmetic index value at the close of trading on the last trading day will be used to settle all remaining open positions.

Western natural gas futures – physical: seller is responsible for transport of gas through the hub (hub fee: $.02 per MMBtu)

Hard red winter wheat futures – physical: registered warehouse receipt issued by regular elevators

Termination of trading:

Value line stock index futures, mini value line stock index futures – third Friday of the month

Mini value line options – 15.15 Central time, on the third Friday of contract month. If that day is not a business day, then options trading will end at 15.15 the preceding business day.

Western natural gas options – the business day prior to the last trading day in the underlying futures contract month. All options not exercised by 16.00

	on the last trading day shall expire at such time.
Western natural gas futures	– fourth business day prior to the first day of delivery month
Hard red winter wheat options	– 13.00 Central time, on the Friday at least five business days before the first notice day for wheat futures
Hard red winter wheat futures	– there is no trading during the last seven business days of liquidating month

Exchange minimum margins:

	Initial	*Maintenance*
Hard red winter wheat		
1 Speculative	$800	$650
2 Hedge	$650	$650
3 Omnibus account	$650	$650
4 Member – for own account	$650	$650
5 Intra-market spread	$100	$100
KCBT floor trader	–*	–*
6 Inter-market spread (KCBT side)		
vs CBT wheat	$200	$200
vs MGE red or white wheat	$200	$200
vs CBT corn	$300	$300
Western natural gas		
1 Speculative	$1,400	$1,000
2 Hedge	$1,400	$1,000
3 Omnibus account	$1,000	$1,000
4 Member – for own account	$1,100	$1,000
5 Spot month (add)	$3,000	$3,000
6 Intra-market spread	–*	–*
KCBT floor trader	–*	–*
7 Inter-market spread (KCBT side)		
vs NYMEX natural gas	–*	–*
Value line		
1 Speculative	$7,000	$5,000
2 Hedge	$5,000	$5,000
3 Omnibus account	$5,000	$5,000
4 Member – for own account	$5,000	$5,000
5 Intra-market spread	$400	$200
KCBT floor trader	–*	–*
6 Inter-market spread (KCBT side)		
1 VL vs 1 S&P 500	$1,000	$1,000
3 VL vs 2 S&P 500	$2,500	$2,500
4 VL vs 3 S&P 500	$3,500	$3,500
5 VL vs 4 S&P 500	$4,000	$4,000
6 VL vs 5 S&P 500	$5,000	$5,000
1 VL vs 1 NYSE Composite	$1,000	$1,000
1 VL vs 2 NYSE Composite	$1,000	$1,000
2 VL vs 3 NYSE Composite	$1,500	$1,500

	Initial	*Maintenance*
1 VL vs 1 MMI Maxi	$1,000	$1,000
1 VL vs 1 S&P 400 MidCap	$1,000	$1,000
1 VL vs 2 S&P 400 MidCap	$1,000	$1,000
1 VL vs 1 Wilshire Small Cap	$1,000	$1,000
Mini value line		
1 Speculative	$1,400	$1,000
2 Hedge	$1,000	$1,000
3 Omnibus account	$1,000	$1,000
4 Member – for own account	$1,000	$1,000
5 Intra-market spread	$80	$40
KCBT floor trader	–*	–*
6 Inter-market spread (KCBT side)		
5 MVL vs 1 S&P 500	$1,000	$1,000
5 MVL vs 1 NY Composite	$1,000	$1,000
5 MVL vs 2 NY Composite	$1,000	$1,000
3 MVL vs 1 NY Composite	$1,000	$1,000
5 MVL vs 1 MMI Maxi	$1,000	$1,000
5 MVL vs 1 S&P 400 MidCap	$1,000	$1,000
5 MVL vs 2 S&P 400 MidCap	$1,000	$1,000
5 MVL vs 1 Wilshire Small Cap	$1,000	$1,000

Mini value line versus value line – spread margins

	1 to 1	2 to 1	3 to 1	4 to 1	5 to 1
Speculative:					
Initial	$5,600	$4,200	$2,800	$1,400	–*
Maintenance	$4,000	$3,000	$2,000	$1,000	–*
Hedge:					
Initial	$4,000	$3,000	$2,000	$1,000	–*
Maintenance	$4,000	$3,000	$2,000	$1,000	–*
Omnibus:					
Initial	$4,000	$3,000	$2,000	$1,000	–*
Maintenance	$4,000	$3,000	$2,000	$1,000	–*
Member own account:					
Initial	$4,000	$3,000	$2,000	$1,000	–*
Maintenance	$4,000	$3,000	$2,000	$1,000	–*

* Marked to Market

MidAmerica Commodity Exchange

141 West Jackson Boulevard, Chicago, Illinois 60604
Tel: +1 312 341 3000
Fax: +1 312 341 3203
Chairman: Patrick H Arbor
President: T R Donovan

Hours of trading:

Futures:

Live hogs	–	09.10–13.15
Live cattle	–	09.05–13.15
Corn, wheat, oats, soybeans, soybean meal, soybean oil	–	09.30–13.45
New York gold, platinum	–	07.20–13.40
New York silver	–	07.25–13.20
Treasury bonds	–	07.20–15.15
Treasury bills	–	07.20–14.15
10-year Treasury notes, 5-year Treasury notes	–	07.20–15.15
Eurodollars, Deutschmark, pound sterling, Swiss franc, Japanese yen, Canadian dollar, Australian dollar	–	07.20–14.15

Options:

Soybeans, corn, wheat, soybean oil	–	09.30–13.45
Gold	–	07.20–13.40
Treasury bonds	–	07.20–15.15

Contract details:

Commodities: futures – live hogs, live cattle, corn, wheat, oats, soybeans, soybean meal, soybean oil, New York gold, New York silver, platinum, Treasury bonds, Treasury bills, 10-year Treasury notes, 5-year Treasury notes, Eurodollars, Deutschmark, pound sterling, Swiss franc, Japanese yen, Canadian dollar, Australian dollar; options – soybeans, corn, wheat, soybean oil, gold, Treasury bonds

Live hogs

Trading unit (minimum lot size): 20,000 lbs

Trading limits:

Minimum price fluctuation:	– US$0.00025 (1/4000 cent) per lb (US$5 per contract)
Daily price limit:	– 1 1/2 cent per lb (300 per contract)
Speculative position limits:	– 400 contracts in any one month, 800 in all months combined

Quality: USDA No. 1–3 barrows and gilts. Average weight of delivery unit and at least 75 hogs must fall into the 230–260 lb weight range. Hogs under 220 but not under 215 are deliverable at a US$3 discount per cwt. Hogs under 230 but not under 220 are deliverable at a US$1 discount per cwt. Hogs under 215 or over 280 shall not be deliverable.

Delivery points: stockyards at par: Peoria, Omaha, Sioux City, and Sioux Falls

Stockyards at a discount:	*US$0.25*	*US$0.50*	*US$0.75*
	East St Louis	Kansas City St Joseph	St Paul

Delivery months: February, April, June, July, August, October, December

Live cattle
Trading unit (minimum lot size): 20,000 lbs

Trading limits:

Minimum price fluctuation:	– US$0.00025 cent per lb (US$5 per contract)
Daily price limit:	– 1 1/2 cent per lb (US$300 per contract)
Speculative position limits:	– 600 contracts in any delivery month. Limits do not apply to bona fide hedging transactions

Quality: USDA 55% choice, 45% select quality steers yield Nos 1, 2, 3, 4. A maximum of one head of No. 4 choice steer is deliverable at a discount of US$10 per cwt or 12.5% of the settlement price. Cattle must average between 1,050 and 1,250 lbs. Steers weighing between 100–200 lb over or under the average are deliverable at a 3 cent per lb discount; no animal may weigh more than 200 lb over or under the average, and no animal weighing less than 1,000 lb or more than 1,300 lb is deliverable. Par delivery units containing steers with average weight between 1,050 lb and 1,250 lb must have an estimate average hot yield of 63%. Units with average hot yield over or under par are deliverable at a price computed by dividing the estimated hot yield by 63% (the par hot yield) and multiplying the result by the settlement price. No units with an average hot yield of less than 60% are deliverable

Delivery points: stockyards at Amarillo, Sioux City, Omaha, Dodge City, Norfolk, North Platte, Ogallala, Pratt, Guymon, Clovis

Delivery months: February, April, June, August, September, October, December

Corn
Trading unit (minimum lot size): 1,000 bushels

Trading limits:

Minimum price fluctuation:	– 1/8 cent per bushel (US$1.25 per contract)
Daily price limit:	– US$0.12 per bushel (US$120 per contract)
Speculative position limits:	– 3 million bushels in the spot month, net 6 million in all delivery months combined

Quality: No. 2 yellow corn is deliverable at par; No. 1 yellow corn is deliverable at a 1/2 cent per bushel premium; No. 3 yellow corn is deliverable at a 1 1/2 cent per bushel discount

Delivery points: by warehouse receipt issued by an Exchange-approved elevator in Chicago or Burns Harbor at par, at St Louis-East St Louis and Alton at a 7 cent per bushel premium, and Toledo at a 3 cent per bushel discount

Delivery months: March, May, July, September, December

Wheat
Trading unit (minimum lot size): 1,000 bushels

Trading limits:

Minimum price fluctuation:	– 1/8 cent per bushel (US$1.25 per contract)
Daily price limit:	– US$0.20 per bushel (US$200 per contract)
Speculative position limits:	– 3 million bushels in the spot month, net 6 million in all delivery months combined

Quality: No. 2 soft red winter, No. 2 hard red winter, No. 2 dark northern spring and No. 1 northern spring wheat is deliverable at par; No. 1 soft red, No. 1 hard red winter and No. 1 dark northern spring is deliverable at 3 cent per bushel premium; No. 2 northern spring is deliverable at a 1 cent per bushel discount. Wheat containing moisture in excess of 13.5% is not deliverable

Delivery points: by warehouse receipt issued by an Exchange-approved elevator in Chicago or Burns Harbor at par, and at Toledo at a 2 cent per bushel discount. Only No. 1 soft red winter and No. 2 soft red winter located at St Louis-East St Louis and Alton switching district may be delivered at an 8 cent per bushel premium

Delivery months: March, May, July, September, December

Oats

Trading unit (minimum lot size): 1,000 bushels

Minimum price fluctuation:	– 1/8 cent per bushel (US$1.25 per contract)
Daily price limit:	– US$0.10 per bushel (US$100 per contract)
Speculative position limits:	– 2 million bushels in the spot month, net 2 million in all delivery months combined

Quality: No. 2 heavy and No. 1 at par; No. 1 heavy at 3 cents premium; No. 2 extra heavy at 4 cents premium; No. 1 extra heavy at 7 cents premium; No. 2 34 lb minimum test weight at 6 cent discount; No. 2 36 lb minimum test weight at 3 cent discount

Delivery points: by warehouse receipt issued by an Exchange-approved elevator in Chicago or Burns Harbor at par, and at Minneapolis or St Paul at a 7 1/2 cent per bushel discount

Delivery months: March, May, July, September, December

Soybeans

Trading unit (minimum lot size): 1,000 bushels

Trading limits:

Minimum price fluctuation:	– 1/8 cent per bushel (US$1.25 per contract)
Daily price limit:	– US$0.30 per bushel (US$300 per contract)
Speculative position limits:	– 3 million bushels in the spot month, net 6 million in all delivery months combined

Quality: US No. 2 yellow soybeans are deliverable at par; US No. 2 yellow soybeans are deliverable at a 6 cent per bushel premium; US No. 3 yellow soybeans (all factors equal to No. 2 or better except foreign material) are deliverable at a 4–6 cent per bushel discount

Delivery points: by warehouse receipt issued by an Exchange-approved elevator in Chicago or Burns Harbor at par, at St Louis-East St Louis and Alton switching districts at 8 cent per bushel premium, and at Toledo at an 8 cent per bushel discount

Delivery months: March, May, July, August, September, November

Soybean meal

Trading unit (minimum lot size): 50 tons of 44% protein soybean meal, basis bulk, Decatur

Trading limits:

Minimum price fluctuation:	– prices are quoted in dollars per ton, in multiples of 10 cents per ton (US$5 per contract)
Daily price limits:	– US$10 per ton (US$500 per contract). No daily limits in the spot month
Speculative position limits:	– 800 contracts prior to the spot month. Spot month limits for hedge and speculative accounts – 240 contracts effective one business day prior to the spot month and extending throughout the spot month

Delivery: each contract which is not offset prior to the expiration of trading shall be offset with the clearing house on the day following the last day of trading at a settlement price calculated by averaging the settlement prices from the last three days of the contract

Delivery months: January, March, May, July, August, September, October, December

Termination of trading: no trading in soybean meal, deliverable in the current month, shall be conducted during the last 12 business days of the month

Soybean options

Trading unit (minimum lot size): one MidAmerica 1,000 bushel soybean futures contract

Trading limits:

Minimum price fluctuation:	– 1/8 cent per bushel (US$1.25 per contract)
Daily price limit:	– US$0.30 per bushel (US$300 per contract)
Speculative position limits:	– 15,000 contracts long or short of the same type (put or call), and 6,000 futures-equivalent contracts net on the same sideof the market in all months and all strike prices combined or in any single month in all strike prices combined

Contract months: January, March, May, July, August, September, November

Termination of trading: 12.15 on the last Friday which precedes by at least ten business days the first notice day for the underlying soybean futures contract

Exercise: until 18.00 (central time) on the last trading day

Deep-out-of-the-money option: an option whose strike price is more than two plus the number of calendar months remaining until option expiration strike prices distant from the strike price closest to the underlying futures settlement

Wheat options

Trading unit (minimum lot size): one MidAmerica wheat futures contract

Trading limits:

Minimum price fluctuation:	– 1/8 cent per bushel (US$6.25 per contract)
Strike price increments:	– US$0.10 per bushel and in integral multiples of 20 cents per bushel. Strike prices available for trading shell duplicate all CBOT® strike prices
Price limits:	– US$0.20 per bushel (same as underlying

	futures)
Speculative position limits:	– 15,000 contracts long or short of the same type (put or call) and 6,000 futures-equivalent contracts net on the same side of the market in all months and all strike prices combined or in any single month in all strike prices combined

Contract months: March, May, July, September, December

Termination of trading: the last Friday which precedes by at least ten business days the first notice day for the underlying wheat futures contract

Exercise: until 18.00 (Central time) on the last trading day. Upon exercise, option holders receive the appropriate short or long MidAmerica wheat futures contracts by way of a book entry. Writers of options who receive a notice of exercise are assigned the opposite futures position

New York gold
Trading unit (minimum lot size): 33.2 fine troy ounces

Trading limits:

Minimum price fluctuation:	– US$0.10 per fine troy ounce or US$3.32 per contract
Daily price limit:	– no limit
Speculative position limits:	– 4,000 contracts in any one month, 6,000 in all months combined

Quality: one bar of not less than 0.9995 fineness, bearing brands and markings officially approved by the Exchange

Delivery: by warehouse receipt issued by depositories in New York, as approved by the Exchange

Delivery months: the current month and any subsequent months, generally up to 12 months in the future. The most frequently traded are February, April, June, August, September, October

Gold options
Trading unit (minimum lot size): 33.2 fine troy ounces

Trading limits:

Minimum price fluctuation:	– 10 cents per troy ounce (US$3.32 per contract)
Strike price increments:	– US$10 per ounce for strike prices below US$500; US$20 per ounce for strike prices between US$500–US$1,000; US$50 per ounce apart for strike prices above US$1,000. On the first day of trading for any option the following 13 strike prices will be listed: the striking price closest to the previous day's settlement price of the underlying future, unless this settlement price is precisely midway between two striking prices in which case the higher striking price

	will be chosen, and the next six higher and six lower striking prices
Speculative position limits:	– 10,000 contracts long or short of the same type (put or call) for all months and all strike prices combined, and 4,000 futures-equivalent contracts net on the same side of the market in a single month and 6,000 futures-equivalent contracts net on the same side of the market in all months and all strike prices combined or in any single month in all strike prices combined

Delivery months: current three months and cycle months of February, April, June, August, October, December

New York silver

Trading unit (minimum lot size): 1,000 troy ounces

Trading limits:

Minimum price fluctuation:	– 10/100 cents per troy ounce (US$1 per 1,000 ounce contract)
Daily price limit:	– none
Speculative position limits:	– 1.5 million troy ounces in any one month, 3 million in all months combined

Quality: refined silver in a bar cast in a basic weight of either 1,000 or 1,100 troy ounces (varying in weight no more than plus or minus 10%), assaying in weight not less than 0.999 fineness, and bearing one of the brands and markings officially listed by the Exchange

Delivery: by warehouse receipt issued by depositories in New York as approved by the Exchange

Delivery months: current month and any subsequent months

Platinum futures

Trading unit (minimum lot size): 25 fine troy ounces

Trading limits:

Minimum price fluctuation:	– US$0.10 per fine troy ounce (US$2.50 per contract)
Maximum daily price fluctuation:	– US$25 per ounce (US$625 per contract. No limit in the spot month
Speculative position limits:	– 500 contracts in the spot month, 3,000 in any one month and 3,000 in all months combined

Quality: one ingot or plate of 0.9995 fineness, bearing brands and markings officially approved by the Exchange

Delivery: by warehouse receipt issued by depositories in New York as approved by the Exchange. Delivery notices of intention to deliver must be tendered to the clearing house by 12.00 noon in the day immediately prior to delivery

Delivery months: the spot month and cycle months of January, April, July, October

Termination of trading: there shall be no trading during the last three days of contract month

First notice day: first business day of contract month

Last notice day: second business day prior to the end of contract month

Treasury bonds

Trading unit (minimum lot size): US Treasury bonds with a face value at maturity of US$50,000

Trading limits:

Minimum price fluctuation:	– 1/32 of a percentage point (US$15.62 per contract)
Daily price limit:	– 64/32 of a percentage point (US$1,500 per contract). No limit in the spot month
Speculative position limits:	– US$100 million face value net long or short

Quality: US Treasury bonds maturing at least 15 years from the date of delivery if not callable; if callable, not callable for at least 15 years from date of delivery

Delivery: Federal Reserve book entry wire transfer system. Invoice is adjusted for coupon rates and term to maturity or call

Delivery months: March, June, September, December

Treasury bills

Trading unit (minimum lot size): US$500,000 face value US Treasury bills with 90 days until maturity

Trading limits:

Minimum price fluctuation:	– one basis point (US$12.50 per contract)
Speculative position limits:	– US$200 million face value in any one month, and US$400 million face value in all months combined

Delivery: contracts outstanding as of the expiration of trading shall be settled in cash at the settlement price of the corresponding International Monetary Market T-bill contract

Delivery months: March, June, September, December

10-year Treasury notes

Trading unit (minimum lot size): US$50,000 face value US Treasury note

Trading limits:

Minimum price fluctuation:	– 1/32 of one point (US$15.62 per contract)
Speculative position limits:	– US$100 million face value net long or short

Quality: US Treasury notes maturing not less than 6 1/2 years, not more than 10 years, from first day of delivery month

Delivery: Federal Reserve book entry wire transfer system. Invoice price on delivery is adjusted to a standard 8% and actual term to maturity

Delivery months: March, June, September, December

Deutschmark
Trading unit (minimum lot size): 62,500 Deutschmark

Trading limits:
Minimum price fluctuation: – US$0.0001 per deutschmark (US$6.25 per contract)
Speculative position limits: – net position of 6,000 contracts in one or all months combined

Delivery: the currency shall be deliverable in the country of issue at a bank approved by the exchange

Delivery months: March, June, September, December

Pound sterling
Trading unit (minimum lot size): £12,500

Trading limits:
Minimum price fluctuation: – US$0.0002 per British pound (US$2.50 per contract)
Speculative position limits: – net position of 6,000 contracts in one or all months combined

Delivery: the currency shall be deliverable in the country of issue at a bank approved by the Exchange

Delivery months: March, June, September, December

Swiss franc
Trading unit (minimum lot size): 62,500 Swiss francs

Trading limits:
Minimum price fluctuation: – US$0.0001 per Swiss franc (US$6.25 per contract)
Speculative position limits: – net position of 6,000 contracts on one or all months combined

Delivery: the currency shall be deliverable in the country of issue at a bank approved by the Exchange

Delivery months: March, June, September, December

Japanese yen
Trading unit (minimum lot size): ¥6,250,000

Trading limits:
Minimum price fluctuation: – US$0.000001 per Japanese yen (US$6.25 per contract)
Speculative position limits: – net position of 6,000 contracts in one or all months combined

Delivery: the currency shall be deliverable in the country of issue at a bank approved by the Exchange

Delivery months: March, June, September, December

Canadian dollar
Trading unit (minimum lot size): 50,000 Canadian dollars

Trading limits:
Minimum price fluctuation: – US$0.0001 per Canadian dollar (US$5 per contract)
Speculative position limits: – net position of 6,000 contracts in one or all months combined

Delivery: the currency shall be deliverable in the country of issue at a bank approved by the Exchange

Delivery months: March, June, September, December

Australian dollar
Trading unit (minimum lot size): 50,000 Australian dollars

Trading limits:
Minimum price fluctuation: – US$0.0001 per Australian dollar (US$5 per contract)
Speculative position limits: – 6,000 contracts net long or net short in any one month or in all months combined

Delivery: the currency shall be deliverable in the country of issue at a bank approved by the Exchange

Delivery months: January, March, May, July, August, September, October, December

Soybean oil
Trading unit (minimum lot size): 30,000 lb

Trading limits:
Minimum price fluctuation: – 1/100 of one cent per pound (US$3 per contract)
Daily price limit: – US$0.01 per lb (US$300 per contract) except during spot month when daily price limit is removed
Speculative position limits: – 2,000 contracts net long or net short in any one month when daily price limit is removed
Speculative position limits: – 2,000 contracts net long or net short in any one month or in all months combined; 240 contracts effective one business day prior to the spot month and extending throughout the spot month

Quality: crude soybean oil

Delivery: cash settlement by averaging the settlement price from the day of tender and the following two business days. Any notice tendered during the last three trading days and any contract not offset prior to expiration shall be cash settled on the day following the last day of trading at a settlement price calculated by averaging the settlement prices from the last three trading days of the contract

Delivery months: January, March, May, July, August, September, October, December

Soybean oil options
Trading unit (minimum lot size): one MidAmerica soybean oil futures contract

Trading limits:
Minimum price fluctuation: – 1/100 of a cent per lb (US$3 per contract)

Strike price increments: – listed in integral multiples of 1 half cent per pound and 1 cent per lb in accordance with the CBOT® oil option contract. All strike prices available for trading shall duplicate all CBOT® striking prices available for trading

Delivery months: January, March, May, July, August, September, October

Termination of trading: 12.15 on the Friday which immediately precedes, by at least five business days, the first notice day for the underlying futures contract

Exercise: until 18.00 (Central time) on any business day for which the option is listed for trading. Upon exercise, option holders receive the appropriate short or long MidAmerica soybean oil futures contract(s) by way of a book entry. Writers of options who receive a notice of exercise are assigned the opposite futures position

5-year Treasury notes

Trading unit (minimum lot size): US$50,000 face value

Trading limits:

Minimum price fluctuation: – one half of 1/32 point, or US$7.81 per tick

Daily price limit: – 96/32 per unit of trading (US$1,500 per contract)

Speculative position limit: – 2,000 contracts net long or short in any one month or in all months combined

Quality: US Treasury notes having an original maturity not more than five years and three months and a remaining maturity of not less than four years and three months as of the first day of the delivery month

Delivery: by Federal Reserve book entry wire transfer

Delivery months: March, June, September, December

Bond options

Trading unit (minimum lot size): one MidAmerica US$50,000 face value long-term US Treasury bond futures contract

Trading limits:

Minimum price fluctuation: – 1/64 of 1% or US$7.81 (US$500 per contract)

Strike price increments: – in integral multiples of two points. Initially, the striking price closest to the future's previous day settlement price and the next three consecutive higher and lower striking prices will be listed

Quality: US Treasury bonds futures contract. For options which trade in months in which futures do not trade, the underlying instrument is the nearest available futures contract (eg May, options exercise June futures)

Delivery months: March, June, September, December

Strike prices: listed in multiples of two points. Initially, the striking price closest to the future's previous day settlement price and the next three consecutive higher and lower striking prices will be listed

Volume of trade:

	1994	1995
Agricultural futures		
Wheat	102,145	137,573
Corn	232,855	305,347
Oats	5,208	5,846
Soybeans	797,803	868,577
Soybean meal	3,757	4,060
Soybean oil	–	6,658
Live hogs	19,614	24,059
Live cattle	15,895	18,811
Rice	68,379	–
Agricultural options		
Wheat	3,536	2,425
Corn	5,765	7,296
Soybeans	13,498	11,908
Rough rice	5,588	–
Soybean oil	–	5
Financial futures		
US Treasury bonds	1,385,904	1,342,877
US Treasury bills	826	754
10-year Treasury notes	35,303	38,494
5-year Treasury notes	4	37
Eurodollars	8,997	23,550
Financial options		
US Treasury bonds	3,143	721
Currency options		
Canadian dollar	9,522	11,970
Swiss franc	54,501	50,201
Deutschmark	113,166	95,775
British pound	66,162	23,620
Japanese yen	67,641	55,213
Australian dollar	–	221
Metals futures		
New York gold	24,926	18,964
New York silver	17,170	13,320
Platinum	2,841	3,055
Metals options		
Gold	417	772

	1994	*1995*
Total futures group		
Agricultural	1,245,556	1,370,931
Financial	1,431,024	1,404,712
Currency	320,992	237,000
Metals	44,937	35,339
Total futures group	3,042,509	3,047,982
Total options group		
Agricultural	28,387	21,634
Financial	3,149	721
Metals	417	772
Total options group	31,953	23,127
Total futures and options combined		
Agricultural	1,274,043	1,392,565
Financial	1,434,173	1,405,433
Currency	320,992	237,000
Metals	45,354	36,111
Total Mid America	3,074,562	3,071,109

MINNEAPOLIS

Minneapolis Grain Exchange

400 South 4th Street, 130 Grain Exchange Building, Minneapolis, Hennepin, Minnesota 55415
Tel: +1 612 338 6212
Fax: +1 612 339 1155
President: J L Lindau
Chairman of the Board: G R Gustafson
Vice President, Treasury: G B Wollan
Director, Marketing & PR: K M Newton

Hours of trading:

Spring wheat	– 09.30–13.15
White wheat	– 09.35–13.20
White shrimp	– 09.40–13.30
Spring wheat options	– 09.35–13.25
White wheat options	– 09.35–13.25
White shrimp options	– 09.45–13.40
Black tiger shrimp options	– 09.45–13.40

Contract details:

Commodities: spring and white wheat futures and options, white and black tiger shrimp futures

Trading currency and unit (manner of price quotation):
Grain futures and options – American dollars and cents per bushel; shrimp futures – American dollars and cents per pound

Trading units:
Grain futures and options – 5,000 bushels; shrimp futures – 5,000 pounds

Trading limits:

Spring wheat and white wheat	– US$0.0025 per bushel minimum price fluctuation; US$0.20 maximum
Spring wheat and white wheat options	– US$0.00125 per bushel; US$0.20 maximum
Shrimp	– US$0.0025 per pound minimum price fluctuation; US$0.20 maximum

Quality:

Spring wheat	– No. 2 northern spring, No. 1 dark northern spring or No. 1 northern spring, 13.5% protein or better at par, with scale of discount to 13% protein and premium for above 60 lb test weight
White wheat	– No. 1 soft white at par, with No. 2 soft white deliverable at US$0.02 per bushel discount
Shrimp	– MGE class 1 shrimp (equivalent to US grade A)

Delivery points:

Spring wheat	– Minneapolis/St Paul, Duluth/Superior, Red Wing
White wheat	– delivered to the Columbia River district, as defined in Exchange rules
Shrimp	– Miami, Tampa, Brownsville, New York City area, and Los Angeles, as defined in Exchange rules

Delivery months:

Grain	– March, May, July, September, December
Shrimp	– all 12 months

Termination of trading:

All futures	– maturing futures contracts may not be traded during the last seven business days of delivery month; options trading in an option class shall terminate on the last Friday that precedes by at least five business days the first notice day for the underlying futures contract.

Volume of trade:

	1994	*1995*
Spring wheat futures	3,685,443,000	4,574,410,000

Date of establishment of contracts:

Spring wheat – 3 January 1983
Spring wheat options – 30 October 1984
White wheat – 10 September 1984
White wheat options – 24 June 1991
White shrimp futures and options – 12 July 1993
Black tiger shrimp futures and options – 14 November 1994

Clearing house: Minneapolis Grain Exchange Clearing House
Membership: any person of legal age whose character, credit and reputation for fair dealing are such as to satisfy the directors' membership committee and Board of Directors that the applicant will be a suitable person to entrust with the privileges and responsibilities of membership, and only such persons shall be eligible to membership in this Association.

Membership of other organizations: National Grain and Feed Association, National Grain Trade Council, National Association of Wheat Growers, National Futures Association, National Fisheries Institute.

NEW YORK

Coffee, Sugar and Cocoa Exchange, Inc

4 World Trade Centre, New York, NY 10048
Tel: +1 212 742 6103
Fax: +1 212 748 4321
President: James J Bowe
Chairman of the Board: Brian Kelley
First Vice Chairman: Daniel Rosenblum
Treasurer: W C Hay

Hours of trading (New York time):

Coffee 'C' – 09.45–14.30
Sugar No. 11 – 10.00–13.45
Sugar No. 14 – 09.40–13.35
World white sugar – 09.45–13.45
Cocoa – 09.30–14.15
International market index – 09.30–16.15
Coffee options – 09.45–14.45
Sugar No. 11 options – 10.00–14.00
Cocoa options – 09.30–14.15
Milk futures – 09.00–14.00
Milk options – 09.00–14.00

Contract details:

Commodities: Coffee 'C', sugar No. 11 (world), sugar No. 14 (domestic), world white sugar (refined), cocoa, milk, international market index futures, coffee options, sugar options, cocoa options, milk options.

Trading currency and unit (manner of price quotation):

Coffee 'C'	– cents per pound
Sugar No. 11	– cents per pound
Sugar No. 14	– cents per pound
World white sugar	– cents per pound
Cocoa	– dollars per ton
Milk	– dollars and cents per hundredweight
International market index	– quoted in points and hundredths of a point. One point equals $250
Coffee 'C' options	– cents per pound
Sugar No. 11 options	– cents per pound
Cocoa options	– cents per pound
Milk options	– dollars and cents per hundredweight

Trading limits:

Coffee 'C'	– 37,500 lbs in approximately 250 bags
Sugar No. 11	– 112,000 lbs (50 long tons)
Sugar No. 14	– 112,000 lbs (50 long tons)
World white sugar	– 110,230 lbs (50 tonnes)
Cocoa	– 10 tonnes
International market index	– $250 times the index value
Coffee 'C' options	– one coffee 'C' futures contract
Sugar No. 11 options	– one sugar No. 11 futures contract
Cocoa options	– one cocoa futures contract

Trading limits:

Coffee 'C'	– no daily trading limits. Minimum fluctuation 1/100 cents per pound ($3.75 contract)
Sugar No. 11	– no daily trading limits. Minimum fluctuation 1/100 or 0.01 cents per pound ($11.20 per lot)
Sugar No. 14	– no daily trading limits. Minimum fluctuation 1/100 or 0.01 cents per pound ($11.20 per lot)
World white sugar	– no daily trading limits. Minimum fluctuations are 20 cents per tonne ($10.00 per contract)
Cocoa	– no daily trading limits. Minimum fluctuations are per $1.00 tonne ($10.00 per lot)
International market index	– no daily trading limits. Daily prime limit, initial limit of 30 points below and 50 points above the previous day's settlement

price

Coffee 'C' options – minimum fluctuation same as the future
Sugar No. 11 options – minimum fluctuation same as the future
Cocoa options – minimum fluctuation same as the future

Quality:

Coffee 'C' – determined on the basis of the grade of beans and by dup testing for flavour. If found deliverable, a certificate of Grade and Quality is issued. Since not all coffees are of equal value, the Exchange has established certain differentials when delivery occurs. Certain coffees are used to establish the 'basis'. Coffees judged better than the basis are deliverable at a premium; those judged inferior at a discount.

Sugar No. 11 and Sugar No. 14 – raw centrifugal cane sugar based on 96° average polarization

World white sugar – refined or white, beet cane sugar based on a minimum 99.8° polarization

Cocoa – grades are established by the Exchange-licensed graders in accordance with specified tolerances or defects, bean count and other standards

Deliverable tolerances:

Coffee 'C' – Growths deliverable at basis: Mexico, Salvador, Guatemala, Costa Rica, New Guinea, Nicaragua, Kenya, Tanzania and Uganda.

Growths deliverable plus 200 points: Colombia
Growths deliverable minus 100 points: Honduras, Venezuela
Growths deliverable minus 300 points: Burundi, India, Rwanda
Growths deliverable minus 400 points: Dominican Republic, Ecuador
Growths deliverable minus 500 points: Ethiopia

The delivery must consist of one growth and must be in sound condition, the soundness requirement meaning that the coffee being delivered has not been damaged by any external cause resulting from, but not limited to, improper storage, shipping or handling.

Imperfections: the foregoing is the basis, or standard, deliverable for these growths. Each growth, however, is allowed a maximum of 23 imperfections, with a differential in deliverable price of 10 points for each full imperfection below basis.

Basis: Colombian coffee (13); Ethiopian coffee (50); other growths (8).

Maximum below basis: Colombian coffee (10); Ethiopian coffee (10); other growths (15).

Total imperfections permitted: Colombian coffee (23); Ethiopian coffee (60); other growths (23).

Sugar No. 11 – growths of Argentina, Australia, Barbados, Belize, Brazil, Colombia, Costa Rica, Dominican Republic, El Salvador, Ecuador, Fiji Islands, French Antilles, Guatemala, Honduras, India, Jamaica, Malawi, Mauritius, Mexico, Nicaragua, Peru, Philippines, Republic of South Africa, Swaziland, Taiwan, Trinidad, United States and Zimbabwe delivered FOB and stowed in bulk.

Sugar No. 14 – cane sugars of the United States, duty free, foreign origin, duty paid and delivered in bulk.

World white sugar – sugars manufactured in the country of the delivery port, except EU nations where the sugar may be of any EU manufacturer.

Cocoa – the growth of any country or clime, including new or yet unknown growths. Growths are divided into three classifications: Group A, deliverable at a premium of $160 per ton (includes Ghana, Nigeria, Ivory Coast, among others); Group B, deliverable at a premium of $80 per tonne (includes Bahia, Central America, Venezuela, among others); Group C, deliverable at par (includes Sanchez, Haiti, Malaysia and all others). Deliveries are discounted for subnormal size beans.

Delivery points:

Coffee 'C' – at Exchange-licensed warehouses in Port of New York District, and the Port of New Orleans

Sugar No. 11 – a port in the country of origin in the case of landlocked countries, at the berth or anchorage in the customary port of export, FOB and stowed in bulk.

Sugar No. 14 – New York, Galveston, Baltimore, New Orleans, Savannah

World white sugar – Ports of Rotterdam, Flushing , Antwerp, Hamburg, Dunkirk, Rouen, Immingham, Galveston, New Orleans, Savannah, Baltimore, New York (including Yonkers), Recife/Maceio, Imbituba/Itajai, Santos, Pusan, Inchon, Ulson, Gdansk/Gdynia

Cocoa – at licensed warehouses in the port of New York District, Delaware River Port District,

	or port of Hampton Roads
Milk –	IMS certified plants, receiving stations or transfer stations located in the Madison, Wisconsin District

Delivery months:

Coffee 'C' –	March, May, July, September, December
Sugar No. 11 –	January, March, May, July, October
Sugar No. 14 –	January, March, May, July, September, November
World white sugar –	January, March, May, July, October
Cocoa –	March, May, July, September, December
Milk –	February, April, June, August, October, December
International market index –	the current calendar month, immediately following two calendar months, and every March, June, September and December thereafter in a 14–month period from the current calendar month
Coffee options –	same as future
Sugar No. 11 options –	March, May, July, October and first of these months in next year for which futures trading has begun, as well as an options which futures trading has begun, as well as an option which expires in December and calls for delivery of March futures
Cocoa options –	same as future

Termination of trading:

Coffee 'C' –	the business day that is one day prior to the seven business days prior to the last business day of the business month
Sugar No. 11 –	the last full business day of the month preceding delivery month
Sugar No. 14 –	the eighth calendar day of the month preceding delivery month. If this day is not a business day then the last trading day shall be the next succeeding business day
World white sugar –	15th calendar day of the month preceding delivery month, or next succeeding business day if 15th calendar day is not a business day
Cocoa –	the business day one day prior to the ten business days prior to the last business day of delivery month
Milk –	six Exchange business days prior to the last Exchange business day of the month
International market index –	business day prior to the third Friday of

	contract month
Coffee options –	first Friday of the month preceding contract month
Sugar No. 11 options –	second Friday of the month preceding contract month. The one exception is the December/March option, which expires on the second Friday of December
Cocoa options –	first Friday of the month preceding the contract month

Volume of trade:	*1993*	*1994*	*1995*
	11,304,823	12,664,052	11,315,979

Date of establishment of markets:

Coffee, Sugar of the City of New York	– 1882
New York Coffee & Sugar Exchange, Inc	– 1916
New York Cocoa Exchange	– 1925
Coffee, Sugar & Cocoa Exchange, Inc	– 1979

Clearing house: CSC Clearing Corporation

Membership: *Full Membership* (527)
Eligible to trade all futures and options contracts listed with the Exchange. Minimum financial requirements (net liquid assets) – $25,000 without floor trading privileges; $50,000 with floor trading privileges.

Associate Membership (250)
Eligible to trade options listed with the Exchange. Minimum financial requirements (net liquid assets) – $25,000 without floor trading privileges; $50,000 with floor trading privileges. Member firms must have minimum net liquid assets of $100,000; associate member firms must have minimum net liquid assets of $50,000. Individuals may be guaranteed by the Exchange members in lieu of meeting the above requirements for individuals.

Membership of other organizations: The CSCE is a member of the Futures Industry Association and the National Futures Association.

New York Cotton Exchange

4 World Trade Center, New York, NY 10048
Tel: +1 212 742 5050
Fax: +1 212 748 1241
President: J J O'Neill
Chairman: Stephen J Place
Vice Chairman: Gary N Hoffman
Treasurer: John S Ruffino

Hours of trading (New York time): 10.30–14.40

Contract details:
Commodities: cotton futures and options

Cotton No. 2 futures

Trading currency and unit (manner of price quotation): cents and hundredths of a cent per pound

Trading unit (minimum lot size): 50,000 lb (approximately 100 bales)

Trading limits:

Minimum price fluctuation: – 1/100 cent per lb below 95 cents per lb; 5/100 of a cent per lb at prices of 95 cents or higher

Maximum price fluctuation: – 3 cents above or below previous day's settlement price. However, if any contract month settles at or above US$1.10 per pound, all contract months will trade with 4 cents price limits. Should no month settle at or above US$1.10 per pound, price limits stay (or revert) to 3 cents per pound.

Spot month – no limit on or after first notice day

Quality: strict low middling 1 to 1/16 inch

Delivery points: Galveston, Houston, New Orleans, Memphis, Greenville

Delivery months: March, May, July, October, December

Termination of trading: 17 business days from the end of the spot month

Cotton No. 2 options

Trading currency and unit (manner of price quotation): cents and hundredths of a cent per pound

Trading unit (minimum lot size): one New York Cotton Exchange No. 2 futures contract

Trading limits:

Minimum price fluctuation: – 1/100 of a cent

Delivery points: Galveston, Houston, New Orleans, Memphis, Greenville

Delivery months: March, May, July, October, December

Termination of trading: the last Friday which precedes the first notice day for the underlying future by at least five business days

Exercise: until 17.00, New York time, on any trading day including last trading day. Automatic exercise at one tick or more in-the-money at expiration on last trading day

Margins:

	Initial				*Maintenance*			
	Outright		*Straddle*		*Outright*		*Straddle*	
	S	*H*	*S*	*H*	*S*	*H*	*S*	*H*
Agricultural								
Cotton – old	1,500	750			1,125	750		
Cotton – new	1,000	500			750	500		
FCOJ	1,000	500	250	250	750	375	187.50	187.50

	Initial				Maintenance			
	Outright		Straddle		Outright		Straddle	
	S	H	S	H	S	H	S	H
Indices								
USDX	1,064	532	399	399	800	400	300	300
EMDX	2,660	1,330	133	133	2,000	1,000	100	100
NYSE Composite	3,500	3,000	200	200	3,000	3,000	100	100
PSE Tech 100	3,500	3,000	200	200	3,000	3,000	100	100
KR-CRB Index	2,000	1,750	200	200	1,750	1,750	100	100
Interest rate								
FYTR	1,330	665	399	399	1,000	500	300	300
2YTN	1,330	665	399	399	1,000	500	300	300
Currency, cross rates								
Sterling/mark (DM)	3,325	1,663	226	226	2,500	1,250	170	170
Mark/Paris (FF)	8,246	4,123	765	765	6,200	3,100	575	575
Mark/yen (JY)	133,000	66,500	13,300	13,300	100,000	50,000	10,000	10,000
Mark/lira (IL)	4,522,000	2,261,000	212,800	212,800	3,400,000	1,700,000	160,000	160,000
Mark/Swiss franc (SF)	1,729	865	120	120	1,300	650	90	90
Mark/Swedish krona	9,310	4,655	931	931	7,000	3,500	700	700
US$/mark old ($)	1,330	665	133	133	1,000	500	100	100
US$/mark new (DM)	4,665	2,328	226	226	3,500	1,750	170	170
US$/sterling old ($)	1,330	665	133	133	1,000	500	100	100
US$/sterling new ($)	2,660	1,330	133	133	2,000	1,000	100	100
US$/yen old ($)	1,995	998	133	133	1,500	750	100	100
US$/yen new (JY)	359,100	179,550	133,300	133,300	270,000	135,000	10,000	10,000
US$/Sw franc old ($)	1,862	931	133	133	1,400	700	100	100
US$/Sw franc new (SF)	4,522	2,261	120	120	3,400	1,700	90	90

Volume of trade:

	1993	1994	1995
Futures:			
Cotton	1,603,027	2,289,998	2,525,434
Cotlook World Cotton	3,363	–	–
FCOJ	640,131	653,824	688,932
US dollar index	599,112	558,439	456,859
Mark/pound	–	12,351	32,804
Mark/Paris	–	10,295	36,649
Dollar/mark	–	30,385	29,441
Mark/yen	–	30,566	66,405
Mark/lira	–	3,572	31,604
US dollar/Swiss franc	–	10	1,586
US dollar/Japanese yen	–	2	4,943
US dollar/British pound	–	2	3,021

	1993	*1994*	*1995*
Mark/Swiss franc	–	–	1,209
EMDX	–	–	732
FYTR	50,200	69,858	44,959
2YTN	734	3,233	11,072
NYSE Composite Index	–	–	685,922
CRB Index	–	–	81,413
Options:			
Cotton	372,074	816,031	1,416,054
Cotlook World Cotton	206	–	–
	1993	*1994*	*1995*
Orange juice	101,214	159,365	171,209
US dollar index	67,603	42,268	23,987
NYSE Composite Index	–	–	26,457
CRB Index	–	–	6,384
Mark/pound	–	–	116
Mark/Paris	–	–	570
Mark/yen	–	–	160
Mark/lira	–	–	354
Mark/Swiss franc	–	–	33
Total	3,437,664	4,680,278	6,348,309

Clearing house: Commodity Clearing Corporation

Membership: all seats and licences are bought and sold through a bid/offer system.

New York Futures Exchange*

4 World Trade Centre, New York, NY 10048
Telephone: +1 212 748 1248
Fax: +1 212 742 5026
President: Joseph O'Neill
* NYFE is a wholly owned subsidiary of the New York Cotton Exchange.

NYSE Composite index futures
Trading unit (minimum lot size): $500 x NYSE Composite index.

Trading limits:
Minimum price fluctuation – 0.05, 5 basis points ($25 per contract).
Price limits – 40 points.

Delivery months: March, June, September, December cycle.

Termination of trading: Thursday before the third Friday of the month, unless not an Exchange or NYSE business day when the last trading day shall be the preceding business day.

Settlement: At maturity by cash payment; final settlement is based upon a special calculation of the third Friday's opening prices of all the stocks listed in the NYSE Composite index. Settlement day is the business day following the third Friday of the month.

Option on NYSE Composite Index futures contract
Trading unit (minimum lot size): Call and put options on one NYSE Composite Index futures contract.

Trading limits:
Price fluctuations – 0.05 (five base points); however, if an option transaction liquidates an existing position, the minimum fluctuation can be one point if the price is then than five points.

Strike prices – Integers evenly divisible by two. Minimum of nine exercise prices at all times: four in-the-money, one at-the-money, and four out-of-the-money.

Termination of trading: The last trading day of the underlying NYSE Composite Index futures contract.

Exercise: Open puts and calls in index options may be exercised on any Exchange business day during the life of the contract by notifying the Intermarket Clearing Corporation by 20.00 on that day. Any short position open at the end of a trading day is subject to assignment. A long call (put) that is exercised receives a long (short) position in the underlying futures contract, whereas a short call (put) that is assigned receives a short (long) position in the underlying futures contract. (Exercises on the final day of trading result in cash settlement rather than the assignment of a futures position.) At the close of business on the last trading day, all in-the-money options will be automatically exercised.

CRB futures price index futures contract
Trading unit (minimum lot size): $500 x the CRB Futures Price Index.

Trading limits:
Minimum price fluctuation – 0.05 ($25 per contract).
Position limits – 5000 contracts long or short.

Delivery months: January, February, April, June, August, November (with at least four months trading at all times).

Termination of trading: Second Friday of expiration month.

Settlement: All contracts are marked-to-market daily. Settlement at contract maturity by cash payment.

Option on CRB futures price index futures contract
Trading unit (minimum lot size): Call and put options on one CRB index futures contract.

Trading limits:
Minimum price fluctuation – 0.05 (5 basic points); if an option transaction liquidates an existing position however, the minimum fluctuation can be 1 point if the price is less than 5 points.

Strike prices – Integers evenly divisible by two. Minimum of nine exercise prices at all times: four in the morning, one at the money, four out-of-the-money.
No price limits.

Termination of trading: The last day of trading of the underlying CRB index futures contract.

Exercise: On any NYFE business day the option is traded by notifying the clearing member carrying the account by 18.00 on that day. The clearing member must then notify the Intermarket Clearing Corporation by 20.00 on that day. Upon expiration, all in-the-money options will be automatically exercised, in the absence of written instructions to the contrary.

PSE Technology Index futures
Hours of trading (local time): 09.30–16.15.

Contract size and value: \$500 x PSE Technology Index (eg, \$500 x 220.00 = \$110,000; 220.00 represents recent Index level).

Contract months: March, June, September, December cycle (minimum of 4 months traded at all times).

Price fluctuations: 0.05 (5 basic points) – eg, 220.05, 220.10, 220.15.

Value of minimum move: \$25.00

Termination of trading: The Thursday preceding the third Friday of the month.

Settlement: Cash settlement. Final settlement is based upon a special calculation of the third Friday's opening prices of all the stocks listed in the PSE Technology Index.

PSE Technology Index Options on Futures
Trading unit: Call and put options on PSE Technology Index futures contract.

Trading limits: None

Hours of trading (local time): 09.30–16.15

Strike prices: Integers which are evenly divided by two (eg, 210.00, 212.00); minimum of twenty-nine exercise prices at all times, fourteen in-the-money, one at-the-money, fourteen out-of-the-money. For the most deferred contract only, integers which are evenly divisible by ten (eg, 210.00, 220.00); minimum of seven exercise prices at all times, three in-the-money, one at-the-money, three out-of-the-money.

Premium quotations: Price or premiums are quoted in points, where 0.01 equals \$5. A premium of 1.00 equals \$500. Minimum price fluctuations (tick size) in premiums shall be 5 points or 0.05 (equivalent to \$25.00 per contract); however, if an option transaction liquidates an existing position, the minimum fluctuation can be 1 point (\$5.00) if the price is less than 5 points.

Contract months: The current calendar month, the two months following the current calendar month, and the next three months in the calendar quarterly cycle (six options months traded at all times). The futures contract underlying the non-calendar quarterly cycle months is the next futures contract following the option expiration.

Termination of trading: For the calendar quarterly cycle months (March, June, September, December) the last day of trading is the last trading day of the underlying futures contract (the business day preceding the third Friday of the expiration month). For the non-quarterly cycle months, the last day of trading is the third Friday of the expiration month.

Exercise: American style. Consult rules for details.

Margin: The purchase of long option positions requires the full payment of the premium in cash. Consult your broker for details on margin requirements for short option positions.

Margins:

	Initial	*Maintenance*
	(US dollars)	
NYSE Composite index:		
Speculative	3500	3500
Members and hedgers	3500	3500
Spreads	200	100
CRB futures price index:		
Speculative	2000	1750
Members and hedgers	1750	1750
Spreads	200	100

Volume of trading:

	1991	*1992*	*1993*	*1994*	*1995*
NYSE Composite index	1,486,166	1,315,438	848,522	729,231	685,922
NYSE Utility index			10	11	
Commodity Research Bureau index	61,185	56,255	91,908	109,986	81,413

Date of establishment of the market: 1980.

New York Mercantile Exchange

Four World Trade Center, New York, NY 10048
Tel: +1 212 748 3000
Fax: +1 212 742 5263
Chairman of the Board: Daniel Rappaport
President: R Patrick Thompson
Executive Vice President & General Counsel: Ronald Oppenheimer
Executive Vice President: Neal Wolkoff

Hours of trading (New York time):
Futures:

Light, sweet crude oil – 09.45-15.10[1]
Sour crude oil – 09.35-15.20
Heating oil, New York Harbor unleaded gasoline – 09.50-15.10[1]
Gulf Coast unleaded gasoline – 09.40-15.10
Natural gas – 10.00-15.10[2]
Propane – 09.55-15.00[3]
Gold, platinum – 08.20-14.30[1]
Silver – 08.25-14.25[1]
High-grade copper – 08.10-14.00[1]
Palladium – 08.10-14.20

Eurotop 100 Index	– 05.30-11.30
California Oregon Border electricity	– 10.30-15.30[4]
Palo Verde electricity	– 10.30-15.30[4]

Options:

Light, sweet crude oil	– 09.45-15.10[1]
Heating oil, New York Harbor unleaded gasoline	– 09.50-15.10[1]
Natural gas	– 10.00-15.10[2]
Gold, platinum	– 08.20-14.30[1]
Silver	– 08.25-14.25[1]
High-grade copper	– 08.10-14.00[1]
Palladium	– 08.10-14.20
Eurotop 100 Index	– 05.30-11.30
California Oregon Border electricity	– 10.30-15.30[4]
Palo Verde electricity	– 10.30-15.30[4]

[1] After-hours trading is conducted via the NYMEX ACCESS℠ electronic trading system starting at 16.00 between Monday and Thursday, and concluding at 08.00 the following day. On Sunday, the electronic session begins at 19.00. All times are New York time.

[2] After-hours trading is conducted via the NYMEX ACCESS℠ electronic trading system starting at 16.00 between Monday and Thursday. All times are New York time.

[3] After-hours trading is conducted via the NYMEX ACCESS℠ electronic trading system from 17.00 to 19.00 between Monday and Thursday. All times are New York time.

[4] After-hours trading is conducted via the NYMEX ACCESS℠ electronic trading system from 16.15 to 19.15 between Monday and Thursday. All times are New York time.

Contract details:

Commodities: futures – light, sweet crude oil, New York Harbor gasoline, Gulf Coast gasoline, heating oil, natural gas, propane, Palo Verde electricity, California Oregon Border electricity, sour crude oil, platinum, palladium, gold, silver, copper, Eurotop 100* Index, Permian Basin natural gas; options – light, sweet crude oil, New York Harbor gasoline, heating oil, natural gas, Palo Verde electricity, California Oregon Border electricity, platinum, gold, silver, copper, 5-day gold, 5-day silver, 5-day copper, Eurotop 100 Index, Permian Basin natural gas

* 'Eurotop 100 Index' and 'E100' are proprietary names of the Optiebeurs NV (European Options Exchange) and have been licensed for use by COMEX.

Light, crude sweet oil futures

Trading currency and unit (manner of price quotation): dollars and cents per barrel

Trading units (minimum lot size): 1,000 US barrels (42,000 gallons)

Trading limits:

Minimum price fluctuation – US$0.01 per barrel (US$10 per contract)

Maximum daily price fluctuation – US$15 per barrel (US$15,000 per contract) for the first two contract months. Initial back month limits of US$1.50 per barrel rise to US$3 per barrel if the previous day's settlement price in any back month is at the US$1.50 limit. In the event of a US$7.50 per barrel move in either of the first two contract months, back month limits are expanded to US$7.50 per barrel from the limit in place in the direction of the move

Quality: specific domestic crudes with 0.42% sulfur by weight or less, not less than 37° API gravity or more than 34° API gravity. The following domestic crude streams are deliverable: West Texas Intermediate, Low Sweet Mix, New Mexican Sweet, North Texas Sweet, Oklahoma Sweet, South Texas Sweet. Specific foreign crudes of not less than 34° API nor more than 42° API. The following foreign streams are deliverable: UK Brent and Forties Blends, and Norwegian Oseberg Blend, for which the seller shall receive a 30 cent per barrel discount below the settlement price; and Norwegian Bonny Light, for which the seller shall receive a 60 cent per barrel premium

Delivery points: FOB seller's facility, Cushing, Oklahoma, at any pipeline or storage facility with pipeline access to Arco, Cushing storage, or Texaco Trading and Transportation Inc, by in-tank transfer, in-line transfer, book-out, or inter-facility transfer (pumpover)

Delivery months: all deliveries are rateable over the course of the month and must be initiated on or after the first calendar day and completed by the last calendar day of delivery month

Termination of trading: trading terminates at the close of business on the third business day prior to the 25th calendar day of the month preceding delivery month

Trading months: 30 consecutive months plus two long-dated futures which are initially listed 36 and 48 months prior to delivery. The Exchange has received approval for listing 60, 72, and 84 month contracts and is expected to do so shortly. Additionally, trading can be executed at an average differential to the previous day's settlement prices for periods of two to 30 consecutive months in a single transaction. These calendar strips are executed during open outcry trading hours

Light, sweet crude oil options

Trading currency and unit (manner of price quotation): dollars and cents per barrel

Trading units (minimum lot size): one NYMEX Division light, sweet crude oil futures contract

Trading limits:

Minimum price fluctuation – US$0.01 per barrel (US$10 per contract)

Strike prices: at all times at least 21 strike prices are available. The first nine strike prices are increments of US$0.50 per barrel, and the next three are in increments of US$1 per barrel. Additionally, three strike prices are offered in the nearest US$5 increment above the furthest higher and below the furthest lower existing strike prices. The at-the-money strike price is nearest to the previous day's close of the underlying futures contract. Strike price boundaries are adjusted according to the futures price movements

Termination of trading: expiration day is the Friday immediately preceding the expiration of the underlying futures contract as long as there are three trading days left in the futures contract. In the event there are less than three days to futures expiration, options expiration will be the second Friday prior to futures expiration

Exercise: by a clearing member to the Exchange clearing house not later than 17.30 or 45 minutes after the underlying futures settlement price is posted, whichever is later, on any day up to and including the option's expiration

Sour crude oil futures

Trading currency and unit (manner of price quotation): dollars and cents per barrel

Trading unit (minimum lot size): 1,000 US barrels (42,000 barrels)

Trading limits:

Minimum price fluctuation	–	US$0.01 per barrel (US$10 per contract)
Maximum daily price fluctuation	–	US$15 per barrel (US$15,000 per contract) for the first two contract months. Initial back month limits of US$1.50 per barrel rise to US$3 per barrel if the previous day's settlement price in any back month is at the US$1.50 limit. In the event of a US$7.50 move in either of the first two contract months, back month limits are expanded to US$7.50 per barrel above the limit in place, in the direction of the move

Quality: deliverable grades with a minimum of 0.5% and a maximum of 2.2% sulfur by weight, not less than 26° API gravity are: West Texas Sour/New Mexico Sour, Alaska North Slope Sour, Dubai, Flotta, Iranian Light, Oman, and Oriente. Commingling these crude streams for delivery is not permitted except for pipeline common stream designated as West Texas Sour/New Mexico Sour. A premium 90 cents per barrel will be paid by the receiving party for the delivery of West Texas Sour/New Mexico Sour. The other six deliverable crudes will be valued at the final settlement price

Delivery points: deliveries take place along the Texas US Gulf Coast at one of several qualified marine terminals; by pipeline into designated pipeline connections; or out-of-storage from qualified storage facilities

Trading months: 18 consecutive months

Delivery months: all deliveries must be initiated by the first calendar day and completed no later than the last calendar day of the month

Termination of trading: trading terminates at the close of business on the third business day prior to the 25th calendar day of the month preceding delivery month

Heating oil futures

Trading currency and unit (manner of price quotation): dollars and cents per gallon

Trading units (minimum lot size): 42,000 US gallons (1,000 barrels)

Trading limits:

Minimum price fluctuation	– US$0.0001 per gallon (US$4.20 per contract)
Maximum daily price fluctuation	– US$0.40 per gallon (US$16,800 per contract) for the first two contract months. Initial back month limits of US$0.04 per gallon rise to US$0.06 per gallon if the previous day's settlement price in any back month is at the US$0.04 per gallon limit. In the event of a US$0.20 per gallon move in either of the first two contract months, back month limits are expanded to US$0.20 per gallon from the limit in place in the direction of the move

Quality: generally conforms to industry standards for fungible No. 2 heating oil

Delivery points: FOB seller's facility in New York Harbor, ex-shore. All duties, entitlements, taxes, fees, and other charges paid. Requirements for seller's shore facility: capability to deliver into barges. Buyer may request delivery by truck, if available at the seller's facility, and pays a surcharge for truck delivery. Delivery may also be completed by pipeline, tanker, book transfer, or inter- or intra-facility transfer. Delivery must be made in accordance with applicable federal, state, and local licensing and tax laws

Trading months: trading is conducted in 18 consecutive months commencing with the next calendar month

Delivery months: deliveries may only be initiated the day after the fifth business day and must be completed before the last business day of delivery month

Termination of trading: trading terminates at the close of business on the last business day of the month preceding delivery month

Heating oil options

Trading currency and unit (manner of price quotation): dollars and cents per gallon

Trading units (minimum lot size): one NYMEX Division heating oil futures contract

Trading limits:

Minimum price fluctuation	– US$0.0001 per gallon (US$4.20 per contract)

Strike prices: 1 cent strike prices for the first three months listed at US$0.05 above and below the at-the-money strike price. After that, increments of US$0.02 per gallon, listed only as even numbers. At least 21 strike prices will be listed at all times. 1 cent strike prices will only be listed at levels below US$0.75

Trading months: 12 consecutive months

Termination of trading: expiration day is the Friday immediately preceding the expiration of the underlying futures contract as long as there are three trading days left in the futures contract. In the event there are less than three days to futures expiration, options expiration will be the second Friday prior to futures expiration

Exercise: by a clearing member of the Exchange clearing house not later than 17.30 or 45 minutes after the underlying futures settlement price is posted, whichever is later, on any day up to and including the option's expiration

New York Harbor unleaded gasoline futures

Trading currency and unit (manner of price quotation): dollars and cents per gallon

Trading units (minimum lot size): 42,000 US gallons (1,000 barrels)

Trading limits:

Minimum price fluctuation	– US$0.0001 per gallon (US$4.20 per contract)
Maximum daily price fluctuation	– US$0.40 per gallon (US$16,800 per contract) for the first two contract months. Initial back month limits of US$0.04 per gallon rise to US$0.06 per gallon if the previous day's settlement price in any back month is at the US$0.04 per gallon limit. In the event of a US$0.20 per gallon move in either of the first two contract months, back month limits are expanded to US$0.20 per gallon from the limit in the direction of the move

Quality: generally conforms to industry standards for Simple Model Reformulated Gasoline

Delivery points: FOB seller's facility in New York Harbor ex-shore. All duties, entitlements, taxes, fees, and other charges paid. Requirements for seller's shore facility: capability to deliver into barges. Delivery may also be completed by pipeline, tanker, book transfer, or inter- or intra-facility transfer. Delivery must be made in accordance with applicable federal, state, and local licensing and tax laws

Trading months: trading in New York Harbor unleaded gasoline is specified for 18 consecutive months commencing with the current calendar month

Delivery months: deliveries may only be initiated the day after the fifth business day and must be completed before the last business day of delivery month

Termination of trading: trading terminates at the close of business in the last business day of the month preceding delivery month

New York Harbor unleaded gasoline options

Trading currency and unit (manner of price quotation): dollars and cents per gallon

Trading units (minimum lot size): one NYMEX Division New York Harbor unleaded gasoline futures contract

Trading limits:

Minimum price fluctuation	– US$0.0001 per gallon (US$4.20 per contract)

Strike prices: 1 cent strike prices for the first three months listed at US$0.05 above and below the at-the-money strike price. After that, increments of US$0.02 per gallon, listed only as even numbers. At least 21 strike prices will be listed at all times. 1 cent strike prices will only be listed at levels below US$0.75

Termination of trading: expiration is the Friday immediately preceding the expiration of the underlying futures contract as long as there are three trading days left in the futures contract. In the event there are less than three days to futures expiration, options expiration will be the second Friday prior to futures expiration

Exercise: by a clearing member of the Exchange clearing house not later than 17.30 or 45 minutes after the underlying futures settlement price is posted, whichever is later, on any day up to and including the option's expiration

Gulf Coast unleaded gasoline futures

Trading currency and unit (manner of price quotation): dollars and cents per gallon

Trading units (minimum lot size): 42,000 US gallons (1,000 barrels)

Trading limits:

Minimum price fluctuation	– US$0.0001 per gallon (US$4.20 per contract)
Maximum daily price fluctuation	– US$0.40 per gallon (US$16,800 per contract) for the first two months, to be implemented in two steps. Initial back month limits of US$0.04 per gallon rise to US$0.06 per gallon if the previous settlement price in any back month is at US$0.04. In the event of a US$0.20 per gallon move in either of the first two contract months, back month limits are expanded to US$0.20 per gallon from the limit in the direction of the move

Quality: grade and quality specifications reflect those of Colonial Pipeline Co fungible M Grade gasoline as amended from time to time by Colonial Pipeline, with the following exceptions: Reid Vapor Pressure (RVP) for this contract shall be January and February, 13.5 pounds per square inch (psi); March, April, May, June, July, August, 7.8 psi; September and October, 11.5 psi; November and December, 13.5 psi. In the event that this RVP specification differs from the Colonial Pipeline specification at the time of loading, and RVP adjustment of 0.5 cents per psi per gallon for RVP of 9.0 psi and above, or 0.75 cents per gallon for RVP below 9.0 psi, will apply

Delivery points: FOB the Colonial pipeline at the injection station selected by the seller at Pasadena, Houston, Hebert, or Port Arthur, Texas; Lake Charles, Krotz Springs, or Baton Rouge, Louisiana; Collins, Mississippi; or Moundville, Alabama. Deliveries shall take place during the third Colonial Pipeline cycle of delivery month. Tenders of less than

25 contracts (25,000 barrels) are considered odd lots. Odd lot deliveries require the buyer to inform the seller of the intended take-off point from the Colonial Pipeline

Trading months: 18 consecutive months

Delivery months: delivery shall take place in the third Colonial pipeline cycle of delivery month as follows: where the buyer and seller each are tendering 25 or more contracts, the buyer shall designate whether delivery shall take place in the front half or back half of the delivery cycle. Where the buyer and seller each are tendering less than 25 contracts, delivery shall take place in the back half of the delivery cycle. Where the buyer is tendering 25 or more contracts, but the seller has less than 25 contracts, the buyer shall designate whether delivery shall take place in the front half or back half of the delivery cycle. Where the buyer is tendering less than 25 contracts, but the seller is tendering 25 or more, the seller shall designate whether delivery shall take place in the front half or back half of the delivery cycle. In the event that the third Colonial cycle of delivery month extends beyond the day prior to the last business day of delivery month, delivery may extend through the last day of that cycle

Termination of trading: trading terminates at the close of business in the last business day of the month preceding delivery month

Natural gas futures

Trading currency and unit (manner of price quotation): dollars and cents per MMBtu (million British thermal unit)

Trading units (minimum lot size): 10,000 MMBtu

Trading limits:

Minimum price fluctuation	–	US$0.001 per MMBtu (US$10 per contract)
Maximum daily price fluctuation	–	US$0.750 per MMBtu (US$7,500 per contract) for the first two months. A US$0.750 move in either of the first two months raises the limit an additional US$0.75 in all months. Initial back month limits of US$0.15 per MMBtu, expandable to US$0.30 per MMBtu

Quality: pipeline specifications in effect at time of delivery

Margins: margins are required for open futures and short options positions. The margin requirement for an options purchaser will never exceed the premium paid

Delivery points: Sabine Pipe Line Co's Henry Hub in Louisiana. Seller is responsible for the movement of the gas through the Hub; the buyer, from the Hub. The Hub fee will be paid by seller

Trading months: 30 consecutive months plus a long-dated month, initially listed 36 months out

Delivery months: deliveries shall take place no earlier than the first calendar day of delivery month and shall be completed no later than the last calendar day of delivery month. All deliveries shall be made at as uniform as possible an hourly and daily rate of flow over the course of delivery month

Termination of trading: trading terminates five business days prior to the first calendar day of delivery month

Natural gas options

Trading currency and unit (manner of price quotation): dollars and cents per MMBtu

Trading units (minimum lot size): one NYMEX Division natural gas futures contract

Trading limits:

Minimum price fluctuation	–	US$0.001 per MMBtu (US$10 per contract)

Strike prices: in increments of US$0.05 per MMBtu with at least 15 strike prices above and 15 below the at-the-money strike price. The at-the-money strike price is closest to the previous day's close of the underlying futures contract. Strike price boundaries are adjusted according to the futures price movements

Trading months: 12 consecutive months, plus 18, 24, 30, and 36 months on a June-December cycle

Termination of trading: trading terminates at the close of business on the business day immediately preceding the expiration of the underlying futures contract

Exercise: by a clearing member of the Exchange clearing house not later than 17.30 or 45 minutes after the underlying futures settlement price is posted, whichever is later, on any day up to and including the option's expiration

Propane futures

Trading currency and unit (manner of price quotation): dollars and cents per gallon

Trading units (minimum lot size): 42,000 US gallons (1,000 barrels)

Trading limits:

Minimum price fluctuation	–	US$0.0001 per gallon (US$4.20 per contract)
Maximum daily price fluctuation	–	US$0.40 per gallon (US$16,800 per contract) for the first two contract months. Initial back month limits of US$0.04 per gallon rise to US$0.06 per gallon if the previous settlement price in any back month is at the US$0.04 limit. In the event of a US$0.20 per gallon move in either of the first two contract months, back month limits are expanded to US$0.20 per gallon from the limit in the direction of the move

Quality: conforms to industry standards for fungible liquified propane gas as determined by the Gas Processors Association (GPA-HD-5)

Delivery points: FOB at Texas Eastern Products Pipeline Co (TEPPCO)or, with the agreement of the buyer and seller, at any pipeline, storage facility, or fractionation facility in Mont Belvieu, Texas, with direct pipeline access to TEPPCO. Delivery may be made by in-line or in-well transfer, inter-facility transfer from the seller's facility to TEPPCO, or by book transfer unless either the buyer or seller disagrees with such transfer

Trading months: trading is conducted in 15 consecutive months commencing with the next calendar month

Delivery months: all deliveries must be initiated after the fourth business day and completed by the calendar day prior to the last business day of delivery month

Termination of trading: trading terminates at the close of business on the last business day of the month preceding delivery month

Gold futures

Trading currency and unit (manner of price quotation): dollars and cents per troy ounce

Trading units (minimum lot size): 100 troy ounces

Trading limits:

Minimum price fluctuation	– price changes are registered in multiples of US$0.10 per troy ounce, equivalent to US$10 per contract. A fluctuation of US$1 is equivalent to US$100 per contract
Maximum daily price fluctuation	– initial price limit, based upon the preceding day's settlement price is US$75 per ounce. Two minutes after either of the two most active months trades at the limit, trades in all months of futures and options cease for a 15-minute period. Trading will also cease of either of the two active months is bid at the upper limit or offered at the lower limit for two minutes without trading. Trading will not cease if the limit is reached during the final 20 minutes of a days trading. If the limit is reached during the final half hour of trading, trading will resume no later than 10 minutes before the normal closing time. When trading resumes after a cessation of trading, the price limits will be expanded by increments of 100%

Quality: in fulfilment of each contract, the seller must deliver 100 troy ounces (+/-5%) of refined gold, assaying not less than 0.995 fineness, cast either in one bar or in three one kg bars, and bearing a serial number and identifying stamp of a refiner approved and listed by the Exchange. A list of approved refiners and assayers is available from the Exchange upon request

Delivery points: delivery must be made from a depository located in the borough of Manhattan, New York City, licensed by the Exchange

Trading months: trading is conducted for delivery during the current calendar month, the next two calendar months, and any February, April, August, and October thereafter falling within a 23-month period and any June and December falling within a 60-month period beginning with the current month

Delivery months: the first delivery day is the first business day of delivery month; the last delivery day is the last business day of delivery month

Termination of trading: trading terminates at the close of business on the third last business day of the maturing delivery month

Gold options and 5-day options

Trading currency and unit (manner of price quotation): dollars and cents per troy ounce

Trading units (minimum lot size): one COMEX Division gold futures contract

Trading limits:

Minimum price fluctuation	– price changes are registered in multiples of US$0.10 per troy ounce, equivalent to US$10 per contract. A fluctuation of US$1 is equivalent to US$100 per contract

Strike prices: US$10 per ounce apart from strike prices below US$500, US$20 per ounce apart for strike prices between US$500 and US$1,000, US$50 per ounce apart for strike prices above US$1,000

Trading months: the nearest six of the following contract months: February, April, June, August, October, December. Additional contract months – January, March, May, July, September, November – will be listed for trading for a period of two months. A 24-month option is added on a June-December cycle. Options are American-style and can be exercised at any time up to expiration. On the first day of trading for any options contract month, there will be 13 strike prices each for puts and calls. 5-day gold options are based on the nearest of the following: February, June, August, December – which are delivery months for non-expired conventional gold options. 5-day options are European-style options and may only be exercised upon expiration

Termination of trading: expiry is on the second Friday of the month prior to delivery month of the underlying futures contract. 5-day options are referred to by the day of the week upon which they expire. These options expire on every business day and have a maximum life of five business days

Exercise: until 15.00, New York time, on any business day for which the option is listed for trading. On expiration day, the buyer has until 16.00, New York time, to exercise an option. 5-day options may only be exercised on expiration day

Silver futures

Trading currency and unit (manner of price quotation): cents per troy ounce

Trading units (minimum lot size): 5,000 troy ounces

Trading limits:

Minimum price fluctuation	– price changes for outright transactions,

including EFPs, are in multiples of 1/2 cent per troy ounce, equivalent to US$25 per contract. For straddle or spread transactions, as well as the determination of settlement prices, the price changes are registered in multiples of 1/10 cent per troy ounce, equivalent to US$5 per contract. A fluctuation of 1 cent is equivalent to US$50 per contract

Maximum daily price fluctuation – initial price limit, based upon the preceding day's settlement price is US$1.50 per ounce. Two minutes after either of the two most active months trades at the limit, trades in all months of futures and options cease for a 15-minute period. Trading will also cease if either of the two active months is bid at the upper limit or offered at the lower limit for two minutes without trading. Trading will not cease if the limit is reached during the final 20 minutes of a day's trading. If the limit is reached during the final half hour of trading, trading will resume no later than 10 minutes before the normal closing time. When trading resumes after a cessation of trading, the price limits will be expanded by increments of 100%

Quality: in fulfilment of each contract, the seller must deliver 5,000 troy ounces (+/-6%) of refined silver, assaying not less than 0.999 fineness in cast bars weighing 1,000 or 1,100 troy ounces each and bearing a serial number and identifying stamp of a refiner approved and listed by the Exchange. A list of approved refiners and assayers is available from the Exchange upon request

Delivery points: delivery must be made from an Exchange-licensed warehouse or vault in the City of New York licensed or designated by the Exchange specifically for the storage of silver

Trading months: trading is conducted for delivery during the current calendar month, the next two calendar months, and any January, March, May and September thereafter falling within a 23-month period and any July and December falling within a 60-month period beginning with the current month

Delivery months: the first delivery day is the first business day of delivery month; the last delivery day is the last business day of delivery month

Termination of trading: trading terminates at the close of business on the third last business day of the maturing delivery month

Silver options and 5-day options

Trading currency and unit (manner of price quotation): cents per troy ounce

Trading units (minimum lot size): one COMEX Division silver futures contract

Trading limits:

Minimum price fluctuation – price changes for outright transactions, including EFPs, are in multiples of 1/2 cent per troy ounce, equivalent to US$25 per contract. For straddle or spread transactions, as well as the determination of settlement prices, the price changes are registered in multiples of 1/10 cent per troy ounce, equivalent to US$5 per contract. A fluctuation of 1 cent is equivalent to US$50 per contract

Strike prices: 25 cents per ounce apart for strike prices below US$8, 50 cents per ounce apart for strike prices between US$8 and US$15, and US$1 per ounce apart for strike prices above US$15

Trading months: the nearest five of the following contract months: March, May, July, September, December. Additional contract months – January, February, April, June, August, October, November – will be listed for trading for a period of two months. A 24-month option is added June and December become the 24th month. 5-day silver options are based on the nearest of the following: March, May, July, September, December – which are delivery months for non-expired conventional silver options. 5-day silver options that expire after the expiration of conventional silver options are based on the next cycle futures month. 5-day options are European-style options and may only be exercised upon expiration

Termination of trading: expiry is on the second Friday of the month prior to delivery month of the underlying futures contract. 5-day options are referred to by the day of the week upon which they expire. These options expire on every business day and have a maximum life of five business days

Exercise: until 15.00, New York time, on any business day for which the option is listed for trading. On expiration day, the buyer has until 16.00, New York time, to exercise an option. 5-day options may only be exercised on expiration day

High-grade copper futures

Trading currency and unit (manner of price quotation): cents per pound

Trading units (minimum lot size): 25,000 pounds

Trading limits:

Minimum price fluctuation – price changes are registered in multiples of five 1/100 of 1 cent per pound, equal to US$12.50 per contract. A fluctuation of US$0.01 is equal to US$250 per contract

Maximum daily price fluctuation – initial price limit, based upon the preceding day's settlement price is US$0.20 per pound. Two minutes after either of the two most active months trades at the limit, trading in all months of futures and options cease for a 15-minute period. Trading will also cease if either of the two active months is bid at the upper limit or offered at the lower limit for two minutes without trading. Trading will not cease if the limit is reached during the final 20 minutes of a day's trading. If the limit is reached during the final half hour of trading, trading will resume no later than 10 minutes before the normal closing time. When trading resumes after a cessation of trading, the price limits will be expanded by increments of 100%

Quality: grade 1 electrolytic copper conforming to the specification B115 as to chemical and physical requirements, as adopted by the American Society for the Testing of Materials, and of a brand approved and listed by the Exchange

Delivery: copper may be delivered against the high-grade copper contract only from a warehouse in the United States licensed or designated by the Exchange. Delivery must be made upon a domestic basis; import duties or import taxes, if any, must be paid by the seller, and shall be made without any allowance for freight

Trading months: trading is conducted for delivery during the current calendar month and the next 23 consecutive calendar months

Delivery months: the first delivery day is the first business day of delivery month; the last delivery day is the last business day of delivery month

Termination of trading: trading terminates at the close of business on the third last business day of the maturing delivery month

High-grade copper options and 5-day options

Trading currency and unit (manner of price quotation): cents per pound

Trading units (minimum lot size): one COMEX Division high-grade copper futures contract

Trading limits:

Minimum price fluctuation – price changes are registered in multiples of five 1/100 of 1 cent per pound, equal to US$12.50 per contract. A fluctuation of US$0.01 is equal to US$250 per contract

Strike prices: 1 cent per pound apart for strike prices below 40 cents, 2 cents per pound apart for strike prices between 40 cents and US$1.20, and 5 cents apart for strike prices above US$1.20

Trading months: options are offered for trading in each of the following contract months:

March, May, July, September, December up to one year to expiration. Serial months are also listed so there are always three consecutive nearby months traded. 24-month copper options are listed when July and December become the 24th month. The options are American-style and can be exercised at any time up to expiration. The futures contract underlying 5-day copper options is the nearest of the following cycles – March, May, July, September, December – which are the delivery months for non-expired conventional options contracts. Three calls and three puts are listed daily. 5-day options are European-style options which can only be exercised at expiration

Termination of trading: expiry is on the fourth last business day of the month prior to delivery month of the underlying futures contract. 5-day options are referred to by the day of the week upon which they expire. These options expire on every business day and have a maximum life of five business days

Exercise: until 15.00, New York time, on any business day for which the option is listed for trading. On expiration day, the buyer has until 16.00, New York time, to exercise an option. 5-day options may only be exercised on expiration day

Platinum futures

Trading currency and unit (manner of price quotation): dollars and cents per troy ounce

Trading units (minimum lot size): 50 troy ounces

Trading limits:

Minimum price fluctuation	–	price changes are in multiples of US$0.10 per troy ounce, equal to US$5 per contract.
Maximum daily price fluctuation	–	US$25 per troy ounce (US$1,250 per contract). There is no maximum daily limit during the current delivery month and the three business days preceding it. If the settlement price reaches the maximum daily limit for two consecutive days, the expanded daily limit schedule will go into effect. The maximum expanded daily limit is US$50 per troy ounce (US$2,500 per contract)

Quality: in fulfilment of each contract, the seller must deliver 50 troy ounces (+/-5%) of platinum not less than 0.9995 fineness, with no single piece weighing less than 10 ounces. Each contract unit may consist of ingots or plates, each incised with the lot or bar number, weight, grade, name, or logo of the assayer, and symbol identifying the metal

Inspection: inspection must be made by an Exchange-approved assayer. Assay certificates are valid provided the metal covered is thereby passed directly from the assayer to an Exchange-approved depository by means of an Exchange-approved carrier

Packaging: platinum may be delivered in packaged or unpackaged form. If packaged, the package must be sealed by an Exchange-approved assayer or producer of approved brands so that it cannot be opened without destroying the seal. The package must bear the lot or bar number, weight, grade, name, or logo of the assayer or approved brand mark, and the symbol of the metal

Trading months: trading is conducted over 15 months beginning with the current month and the next two consecutive months before moving into the quarterly cycle of January, April, July, October

Delivery months: delivery notice may be given by the seller to the Exchange on the last business day preceding delivery month or any subsequent business day up to the third business day prior to the end of delivery month. The basis of delivery is the settlement price on the day the delivery notice is issued

Termination of trading: trading terminates at the close of business on the fourth business day prior to the end of the delivery month

Platinum options

Trading currency and unit (manner of price quotation): dollars and cents per troy ounce

Trading units (minimum lot size): one NYMEX Division platinum futures contract

Trading limits:

Minimum price fluctuation	– price changes are in multiples of US$0.10 per troy ounce, equal to US$5 per contract.

Strike prices: strike prices are in increments of US$10. At least seven strike prices will be listed at all times

Trading months: trading is conducted over 15 months beginning with the current month and the next two consecutive months before moving into the quarterly cycle of January, April, July, October

Termination of trading: second Friday of the month prior to delivery month of the options contract traded

Exercise: by a clearing member to the clearing house not later than 17.30, or 45 minutes after the underlying futures settlement price is posted, whichever is later, on any day up to and including the option's expiration

Palladium futures

Trading currency and unit (manner of price quotation): dollars and cents per troy ounce

Trading units (minimum lot size): 100 troy ounces

Trading limits:

Minimum price fluctuation	– price changes are in multiples of US$0.05 per troy ounce, equal to US$5 per contract.
Maximum daily price fluctuation	– US$6 per troy ounce (US$600 per contract). There is no maximum daily limit during the current delivery month and the three business days preceding it. If the settlement price reaches the maximum

daily limit, the expanded daily limit schedule will go into effect the next day. The maximum expanded daily limit is US$12 per troy ounce (US$1,200 per contract)

Quality: in fulfilment of each contract, the seller must deliver 100 troy ounces (+/-5% of palladium not less than 0.9995 fineness, with no single piece weighing less than 10 ounces. Each contract unit may consist of ingots or plates, each incised with the lot or bar number, weight, grade, name, or logo of the assayer, and symbol identifying the metal

Delivery: delivery notice may be given by the seller to the Exchange on the last business day preceding delivery month or any subsequent business day up to the third business day prior to the end of delivery month. The basis of delivery is the settlement price on the day the delivery notice is issued

Inspection: inspection must be made by an Exchange-approved assayer. Assay certificates are valid provided the metal covered is thereby passed directly from the assayer to an Exchange-approved depository by means of an Exchange-approved carrier

Packaging: palladium may be delivered in packaged or unpackaged form. If packaged, the package must be sealed by an Exchange-approved assayer or producer of approved brands so that it cannot be opened without destroying the seal. The package must bear the lot or bar number, weight, grade, name, or logo of the assayer or approved brand mark, and the symbol of the metal. If there is more than one plate or ingot in the package, each plate or ingot must be incised with the lot or bar number and the weight

Trading months: trading is normally conducted over 15 months beginning with the current month and the next two consecutive months before moving into the quarterly cycle of March, June, September, December

Termination of trading: trading terminates at the close of business on the fourth business day prior to the end of delivery month

Eurotop 100 Index futures
Trading units (minimum lot size): US$100 times the value of Eurotop 100 Index
Trading limits:

Minimum price movement – 0.1 index points or US$10 per contract

Trading months: March, June, September, December

Termination of trading: the third Friday of delivery month until 07.00

Settlement date: second business day following last trading day

Settlement: Eurotop 100 futures are cash-settled. The final settlement value is calculated and disseminated by the European Options Exchange on the third Friday of delivery month. The settlement price is based on the average value of the Eurotop 100 index at five-minute intervals during the last 30 minutes trading when all of the primary exchanges are open. This is usually between 06.30 and 07.00 New York time or 12.30 to 13.00 (CET). In the event that a primary exchange is not open for trading on expiration Friday, the final settlement value will be calculated on the first preceding day when all primary exchanges are open

Eurotop 100 Index options
Trading units (minimum lot size): one Eurotop 100 futures contract

Trading limits:

Minimum price fluctuation – 0.5 index points or US$5 per contract

Strike prices: 10 index point intervals. Thirteen strikes are listed for each contract month – six above and six below the settlement price of the underlying futures (rounded up or down to the nearest 10 point interval)

Trading months: March, June, September, December and the next two nearest non-trading months

Termination of trading: March, June, September, December – the third Friday of delivery month until 07.00. Non-regular trading months – the Thursday preceding the third Friday of delivery month

California Oregon Border electricity futures
Trading currency and unit (manner of price quotation): dollars and cents per megawatt hour (Mwh)

Trading units (minimum lot size): 736 Mwh delivered over a monthly period

Trading limits:

Minimum price fluctuation – 1 cent per Mwh (US$7.36 per contract)
Maximum daily price fluctuation – US$3 per Mwh above or below the preceding day's settlement price (the basic maximum fluctuation). Expanded limits apply when the contract settles at the maximum limit

Delivery points: California Oregon Border

Trading months: 18 consecutive months

Delivery months: 16 on-peak hours: hour ending 07.00 prevailing time to hour ending 22.00 prevailing time. (This can also be amended at the time of delivery by mutual consent of the buyer and seller)

Delivery rate: 2 Mw throughout every hour of the delivery period (this can be amended upon mutual agreement of the buyer and seller)

Termination of trading: the fourth business day prior to the first day of delivery month

Scheduling: buyer and seller must follow Western Systems Coordinating Council scheduling practices

Margins: margins are required for open futures and short options positions. The margin requirement for an options purchaser will never exceed the premium paid

California Oregon Border electricity options
Trading currency and unit (manner of price quotation): dollars and cents per megawatt hour (Mwh)

Trading units (minimum lot size): one NYMEX Division electricity futures contract

Trading limits:

Minimum price fluctuation – 1 cent per Mwh (US$7.36 per contract)

Strike prices: at all times at least 11 strike prices are available. Strike prices will be listed in increments of US$1 per Mwh with five strike prices below and five above the at-the-money strike price

Trading months: 12 consecutive months

Termination of trading: expiration occurs on the day preceding the expiration of the underlying futures contract

Exercise: by a clearing member to the Exchange clearing house not later than 17.30 or 45 minutes after the underlying futures settlement price is posted, whichever is later, on any day up to and including the option's expiration

Palo Verde electricity futures

Trading currency and unit (manner of price quotation): dollars and cents per megawatt hour (Mwh)

Trading units (minimum lot size): 736 Mwh delivered over a monthly period

Trading limits:

Minimum price fluctuation	– 1 cent per Mwh (US$7.36 per contract)
Maximum daily price fluctuation	– US$3 per Mwh above or below the preceding day's settlement price (the basic maximum fluctuation). Expanded limits apply when the contract settles at the maximum limit

Delivery points: Palo Verde switchyard in Arizona

Trading months: 18 consecutive months

Delivery months: 16 on-peak hours: hour ending 07.00 prevailing time to hour ending 22.00 prevailing time. (This can also be amended at the time of delivery by mutual consent of the buyer and seller)

Delivery rate: 2 Mw throughout every hour of the delivery period (this can be amended upon mutual agreement of the buyer and seller)

Termination of trading: the fourth business day prior to the first day of the delivery month

Scheduling: buyer and seller must follow Western Systems Coordinating Council scheduling practices

Margins: margins are required for open futures and short options positions. The margin requirement for an options purchaser will never exceed the premium paid

Palo Verde electricity options

Trading currency and unit (manner of price quotation): dollars and cents per megawatt hour (Mwh)

Trading units (minimum lot size): one NYMEX Division electricity futures contract

Trading limits:

Minimum price fluctuation – 1 cent per Mwh (US$7.36 per contract)

Strike prices: at all times at least 11 strike prices are available. Strike prices will be listed in increments of US$1 per Mwh with five strike prices below and five above the at-the-money strike price

Trading months: 12 consecutive months

Termination of trading: expiration occurs on the day preceding the expiration of the underlying futures contract

Exercise: by a clearing member to the Exchange clearing house not later than 17.30 or 45 minutes after the underlying futures settlement price is posted, whichever is later, on any day up to and including the option's expiration

Permian Basin natural gas futures

Trading units (minimum lot size): 10,000 million British thermal units (MMBtu) delivery rateably over the month

Trading limits:

Minimum price fluctuation – US$0.001 per MMBtu (US$10 per contract)

Maximum daily price fluctuation – US$0.100 per MMBtu. No limit for near month contract. Limit can change to 150% or 200% of maximum

Quality: specifications outlined in El Paso Natural Gas Co's FERC approved tariff

Delivery: Permian Pool account transfer or physical transfer in Permian Pool

Product placement: El Paso Pooling Account or El Paso Transportation Service Agreement

Delivery points: low pressure aggregation pool in Keystone, Texas, area

Termination of trading: three business days prior to the first day of delivery month

Permian Basin natural gas options

Trading units (minimum lot size): one NYMEX Division Permian Basin natural gas futures contract

Strike prices: 15 strikes above and below the at-the-money strike price at US$0.05 intervals

Expiration dates: one day prior to futures termination

Volume of trade:

NYMEX Division

	1993	*1994*	*1995*
Palladium	113,681	143,773	166,713
Platinum	651,222	895,805	846,693
No. 2 heating oil, NY	8,625,061	8,986,835	8,266,783

	1993	*1994*	*1995*
Unleaded reg gas, NY	7,407,809	7,470,836	7,071,787
Crude oil	24,868,602	26,812,262	23,613,994
Propane	44,923	45,100	49,532
Natural gas	4,671,533	6,357,560	8,086,718
Gulf Coast unleaded gas	510	300	252
Total futures	46,383,341	50,712,471	48,102,472
Heating oil options	803,216	699,325	703,388
Crude oil options	7,156,518	5,675,072	3,975,611
Unleaded gasoline options	660,886	573,502	766,557
Platinum options	62,661	90,556	43,601
Natural gas options	345,814	493,491	921,520
Gas (crude oil spread options)	0	13,932	64,285
Heating oil (crude oil spread options)	0	13,965	72,969
Total options	9,029,095	7,559,843	6,547,931
Total NYMEX	55,412,436	58,272,314	54,650,403
COMEX Division			
Silver	4,855,924	5,994,345	5,183,236
Gold	8,916,195	8,503,366	7,781,596
High-grade copper	2,064,629	2,737,967	2,519,414
Eurotop 100 index	56,497	62,231	49,328
Gold option	1,717,015	1,589,065	2,006,695
5-day gold option	418	911	688
Silver option	1,094,702	1,316,650	1,146,513
5-day silver option	1,262	368	221
High-grade copper option	146,060	184,125	134,212
5-day copper option	534	41	34
Eurotop 100 index option	533	0	0
Total COMEX	18,853,764	20,389,069	18,821,937
Total exchange	74,266,205	78,661,383	73,472,340

Date of establishment of contracts:

Futures:

Crude oil – 30 March 1983
Heating oil – 14 November 1978
NY Harbor gasoline – 3 December 1984
Natural gas – 3 April 1990
Propane – 21 August 1987
Sour crude oil – 28 February 1992
Gulf Coast gasoline – 18 September 1992
Platinum – December 1956
Palladium – 22 January 1968
Gold – 31 December 1974
Silver – 5 July 1933

High-grade copper – 22 July 1988
Eurotop 100 index – 26 October 1992

Options:

Crude oil – 14 November 1986
Heating oil – 26 June 1987
NY Harbor gasoline – 13 March 1989
Natural gas – 2 October 1992
Platinum – 16 October 1990
Gold – 4 October 1982
5-day gold – 3 September 1991
Silver – 4 October 1984
5-day silver – 10 December 1991
Copper – 29 July 1988
5-day copper – 10 August 1993
Eurotop 100 index – 8 January 1993
Palo Verde electricity – 26 April 1996
California Oregon Border electricity – 26 April 1996

Membership of other organizations: American Gas Association, Fuel Merchants Association of New Jersey, Futures Industry Association, Managed Futures Association, Metropolitan Energy Council, International Precious Metals Institute, National Petroleum Refiners, Swiss Commodities Futures, Texas Independent Producers, Gas Processors Association, New York Women's Agenda, US Chamber of Commerce, Copper Club, Gold Institute, Silver Institute, New York Section of the American Institute of Mining, Metallurgical and Petroleum Engineers, Inc., American Copper Council, North Texas Oil and Gas Association.

Further information: The New York Mercantile Exchange, founded in 1872, is the third largest US futures exchange and the world's largest physical commodity exchange. Since the Exchange merged with Commodity Exchange Inc. on 3 August 1994, trading is conducted through two divisions: the NYMEX Division, and the COMEX Division, which provide risk-management tools and price references for the global energy, precious metals, and copper industries.

PHILADELPHIA

Philadelphia Board of Trade (PBOT)
(a wholly-owned subsidiary of the Philadelphia Stock Exchange)

Established in 1985, the PBOT trades in the foreign currency contracts listed below.

Hours of trading (Eastern time): 02.30 – 14.30
Canadian dollar – 07.00–14.30

Contract details:
Commodities: futures – Australian dollar, British pound, Canadian dollar, Deutschmark, ECU, Swiss franc, French franc, Japanese yen

Trading currency and unit (manner of price quotation):

Australian dollar, British pound, Canadian dollar, Deutschmark, ECU, Swiss franc	– cents per unit
French franc	– 1/10 cent per unit
Japanese yen	– 1/100 cent per unit

Trading unit (minimum lot size):

Australian dollar	– 100,000
British pound	– 62,500
Canadian dollar	– 100,000
Deutschmark	– 125,000
ECU	– 125,000
Swiss franc	– 125,000
French franc	– 500,000
Japanese yen	– 12,500,000

Trading limits:

Minimum price change:

Australian dollar	– US$0.01 per unit (US$10 per contract)
British pound	– US$0.01 per unit (US$6.25 per contract)
Canadian dollar	– US$0.01 per contract (US$10 per contract)
Deutschmark	– US$0.01 per unit (US$12.50 per contract)
ECU	– US$0.01 per unit (US$12.50 per contract)
Swiss franc	– US$0.01 per unit (US$12.50 per contract)
French franc	– US$0.02 per unit (US$10 per contract)
Japanese yen	– US$0.01 per unit (US$12.50 per contract)

Position accountability standards:

Australian dollar, Canadian dollar, Deutschmark, Swiss franc, French franc, Japanese yen	– 6,000 contracts
British pound	– 5,000 contracts
ECU	– 4,000 contracts

Contract months:

Australian dollar, British pound, Canadian dollar, Deutschmark, ECU, Swiss franc, French franc, Japanese yen	– March, June, September, December and two additional near months

Termination of trading:

Australian dollar, British pound, Canadian dollar, Deutschmark, ECU, Swiss franc, French franc, Japanese yen	– Friday before the third Wednesday of the month

Settlement date:

Australian dollar, British pound,
Canadian dollar, Deutschmark, ECU,

Swiss franc, French franc, Japanese yen – third Wednesday of the month

Issuer and guarantor: Intermarket Clearing Corporation (a subsidiary of the Options Clearing Corporation)

Philadelphia Stock Exchange

1900 Market Street, Philadelphia, Pennsylvania 19103–3584
Tel: +1 215 496 5000
Fax: +1 215 496 5653/5567/6729
President & CEO: N A Giordano
Chairman: V J Casella

European office:
39 King Street, London EC2V 8DQ
Tel: +44 171 606 2348
Fax: +44 171 606 3548
Web site: http://www.phlx.com
E-mail: info@phlx.com

Hours of trading (Eastern time):

Sector index options	– 09.30–16.10
Standardized currency options	– 02.30–14.30, Monday to Friday
Canadian dollar	– 07.30–14.30, Monday to Friday

Contract details:
Commodities: currency options – Australian dollar/USD, British pound/USD, Canadian dollar/USD, Deutschmark/USD, ECU/USD, French franc/USD, Japanese yen/USD, Swiss franc/USD, Deutschmark/Japanese yen, British pound/Deutschmark, 3D Deutschmark/USD; sector index options – PHLX/Keefe Bruyette & Woods Inc bank sector, gold/silver sector, national over-the-counter sector, phone sector, semiconductor sector, utility sector, value line composite index, airline sector, US top 100 index, forest and paper products sector, supercap sector

Standardized currency options – trading currency and unit (manner of price quotation):

Australian dollar/USD, British pound/USD, Canadian dollar/USD, Deutschmark/USD, ECU/USD, Swiss franc/USD	– cents per unit
French franc/USD	– tenths of a cent per unit
Japanese yen/USD	– hundredths of a cent per unit
Deutschmark/Japanese yen	– Japanese yen per Deutschmark
British pound/Deutschmark	– Deutschmark per British pound
3D Deutschmark/USD	– US dollar per Deutschmark

Standardized currency options – trading units (minimum lot size):

Australian dollar/USD	– 50,000
British pound/USD	– 31,250
Canadian dollar/USD	– 50,000

Deutschmark/USD	– 62,500
ECU/USD	– 62,500
French franc/USD	– 250,000
Japanese yen/USD	– 6,250,000
Swiss franc/USD	– 62,500
Deutschmark/Japanese yen	– 62,500 DEM
British pound/Deutschmark	– 31,250 GBP
3D Deutschmark/USD	– 62,500 DEM

Standardized currency options – minimum premium change:

Australian dollar/USD	– US$0.01 per unit (US$5 per contract)
British pound/USD	– US$0.01 per unit (US$3.125 per contract)
Canadian dollar/USD	– US$0.01 per unit (US$5 per contract)
Deutschmark/USD	– US$0.01 per unit (US$6.25 per contract)
ECU/USD	– US$0.01 per unit (US$6.25 per contract)
French franc/USD	– US$0.02 per unit (US$5 per contract)
Japanese yen/USD	– US$0.01 per unit (US$6.25 per contract)
Swiss franc/USD	– US$0.01 per unit (US$6.25 per contract)
Deutschmark/Japanese yen	– ¥0.01 per unit (¥625 per contract)
British pound/Deutschmark	– DEM0.002 per unit (DEM6.25 per contract)
3D Deutschmark/USD	– US$0.01 per unit (US$6.25 per contract)

Standardized currency options – margins:

Australian dollar/USD, British pound/USD, Canadian dollar/USD, Deutschmark/USD, ECU/USD, French franc/USD, Japanese yen/USD, Swiss franc/USD, 3D Deutschmark/USD	– US dollars
Deutschmark/Japanese yen	– US dollars or Japanese yen
British pound/Deutschmark	– US dollars or Deutschmark

Standardized currency options – termination of trading:
Providing it is a business day, otherwise the day immediately prior:

Mid-month options	– Friday before the third Wednesday of expiring month
Month-end options	– last Friday of the month
Long-term options	– Friday before the third Wednesday of expiring month
2-week options	– 10.30 ET, every Monday except for holidays

Standardized currency options – settlement date:

Mid-month options	– third Wednesday of expiring month
Month-end options	– Wednesday following the last Friday of the month

Long-term options	– third Wednesday of expiring month
2-week options	– cash settlement in US dollars

Standardized currency options – expiration date:

Mid-month options	– March, June, September, December plus two near-term months
Month-end options	– three nearest months
Long-term options	– 18, 24, 30 and 36 months (June, December)

Standardized currency options – exercise:

Mid-month options, month-end options	– dollar-based: American and European (except ECU, which is American-style only). Cross rates: European
Long-term options, 2-week options	– European-style

Customized currency options – currency pairs:
Any of the currently approved currencies, including the US dollar, may be matched for trading*. Either may represent the base or underlying currency. For example, US dollar/Japanese yen (strike prices expressed in USD per the underlying Japanese yen) or Japanese yen/USD (strike prices expressed in Japanese yen per the underlying USD); DEM/FRF (strike prices expressed in DEM per the underlying FRF) or FRF/DEM (strike prices expressed in FRF per the underlying DEM). A total of 110 possible currency pairs are available for trading.

* Currently, the Australian dollar may be matched only with the US dollar provided that the premium is denominated in US dollars.

Customized currency options – premium:
May be expressed in units of base currency or as a percentage of the underlying currency. For example, the premium of a USD/DEM contract could be expressed in US cents per DEM (a quote of 1.54 = 0.0154 x 62,500 = US$962.50), or a percentage of Deutschmark (a quote of 2.16% = 0.0216 x 62,500 = DEM1,350

Customized currency options – exercise price:
Any price level to four characters. For example, a USD/GBP options could have an exercise price of US$1.543 per GBP

Customized currency options – exercise:
European-style (exercise at expiration only)

Customized currency options – expiration:
A participant may trade a customized currency option with either a standard expiration date (termed a standard-expiry option) or with a customized date (termed a custom-dated option). Standard-expiry options and custom-dated options have distinct exercise and assignment processes

Customized currency options – exercise and assignment:
Standard-expiry options conform to existing exercise and assignment practices for all standardized contracts. Custom-dated options follow a unique exercise and assignment

process on expiration day

Sector index options – exercise:

PHLX/Keefe Bruyette & Woods Inc bank sector, utility sector, value line composite index, airline sector, US top 100 index, forest and paper products sector, supercap sector	– European-style
Gold/silver sector, national over-the-counter sector, phone sector, semiconductor sector	– American-style

Sector index options – position limits:

PHLX/Keefe Bruyette & Woods Inc bank sector	– 12,000 contracts
Gold/silver sector	– 6,000 contracts
National over-the-counter sector	– 25,000 contracts
Phone sector	– 6,000 contracts
Semiconductor sector	– 9,000 contracts
Utility sector	– 12,000 contracts
Value line composite index	– 25,000 contracts
Airline sector	– 12,000 contracts
US top 100 index	– 25,000 contracts
Forest and paper products sector	– 12,000 contracts
Supercap sector	– 5,500 contracts

Sector index options – last trading day for expiring contracts:

PHLX/Keefe Bruyette & Woods Inc bank sector, phone sector, semiconductor sector, airline sector, US top 100 index, forest and paper products sector, supercap sector	– Thursday
Gold/silver sector, national over-the-counter sector, utility sector, value line composite index	– Friday

Clearing house: Options Clearing Corporation (OCC)

Part 4: Commodity Market Trading Members

Commodity Market Trading Members

Australia

Sydney Futures Exchange

Floor Members

All-States Futures Pty Ltd
Level 2, 2 Bridge Street
Sydney NSW 2000
Tel: +61 2 233 1559
Fax: +61 2 221 3644

ANZ McCaughan Futures Ltd
Level 4, 70 Phillip Street
Sydney NSW 2000
Tel: +61 2 257 6170
Fax: +61 2 257 6257

Australian Gilt Futures Ltd
Level 5, Underwood House
37–49 Pitt Street
Sydney NSW 2000
Tel: +61 2 251 8763
Fax: +61 2 251 5961

Bain Refco Commodities Ltd
17th Floor, Grosvenor Place
225 George Street
Sydney NSW 2000
Tel: +61 2 558 1249
Fax: +61 2 258 1133

Bankers Trust Australia Ltd
Level 15, Chifley Tower
2 Chifley Square
Sydney NSW 2000
Tel: +61 2 323 8888
Fax: +61 2 259 9444

Barclays Bank Plc
(Trading as BZW Futures)
Level 21, 255 George Street
Sydney NSW 2000
Tel: +61 2 247 7155
Fax: +61 2 259 5365

C, A & L Bell Commodities Corporation Pty Ltd
Level 33, Grosvenor Place
225 George Street
Sydney NSW 2000
Tel: +61 2 255 7222
Fax: +61 2 251 6992

Citifutures Ltd
Level 12, Citibank Centre
1 Margaret Street
Sydney NSW 2000
Tel: +61 2 239 9100
Fax: +61 2 239 9690

Commonwealth Bank of Australia
Futures Broking & Clearing Institutional Banking
Level 4, 85 Harrington Street
The Rocks
Sydney NSW 2000
Tel: +61 2 251 8733
Fax: +61 2 312 0565

CS First Boston Australia Securities Ltd
Level 31, Gateway
1 Macquarie Place
Sydney NSW 2000
Tel: +61 2 394 4333
Fax: +61 2 394 4390

Fay, Richwhite Futures Australia Ltd
Level 29, 9 Castlereagh Street
Sydney NSW 2000
Tel: +61 2 232 1255
Fax: +61 2 221 1188

FIMAT Australia Pty Ltd
Level 28, Grosvenor Place
225 George Street
Sydney NSW 2000
Tel: +61 2 336 6800
Fax: +61 2 251 1277

HSBC Futures Australia Ltd
Level 10, 1 O'Connell Street
Sydney NSW 2000
Tel: +61 2 225 2211
Fax: +61 2 225 2408

L Quay Futures Brokers Pty Ltd
Level 7, 220 George Street
Sydney NSW 2000
Tel: +61 2 247 6852
Fax: +61 2 247 6876

Macquarie Bank Ltd
Level 22, Exchange Centre
20 Bond Street
Sydney NSW 2000
Tel: +61 2 237 3555
Fax: +61 2 234 4160

McIntosh Futures Ltd
Level 39, 1 Macquarie Place
Sydney NSW 2000
Tel: +61 2 256 8888
Fax: +61 2 256 8889

Merrill Lynch (Australia) Ltd
Level 49, MLC Centre
19–29 Martin Place
Sydney NSW 2000
Tel: +61 2 225 6500
Fax: +61 2 225 6762

J P Morgan Australia Ltd
Level 20, 1 O'Connell Street
Sydney NSW 2000
Tel: +61 2 551 6100
Fax: +61 2 551 6353

National Australia Bank Ltd
29th Floor, National Australia Bank House
255 George Street
Sydney NSW 2000
Tel: +61 2 237 1528
Fax: +61 2 237 1512

ORD Minnet Jardine Fleming Futures Ltd
Level 24, Grosvenor Place
225 George Street
Sydney NSW 2000
Tel: +61 2 220 1555
Fax: +61 2 220 1316

Potter Warburg Securities Pty Ltd
(Trading as Potter Warburg Futures)
Level 25, Grosvenor Phillip Tower
1 Farrer Place
Sydney NSW 2000
Tel: +61 2 375 6700
Fax: +61 2 375 6622

Refco Group Ltd
C/o Bain Refco Commodities Ltd
Level 19, Grosvenor Place
225 George Street
Sydney NSW 2000
Tel: +61 2 258 1222
Fax: +61 2 258 1133

SBC Australia Ltd
Level 6, Grosvenor Place
225 George Street
Sydney NSW 2000
Tel: +61 2 258 2180
Fax: +61 2 258 2202

Schroders Australia Ltd
Level 31, Grosvenor Place
225 George Street
Sydney NSW 2000
Tel: +61 2 258 9500
Fax: +61 2 251 5532

State Bank of New South Wales Ltd
Level 40, Grosvenor Place
225 George Street
Sydney NSW 2000
Tel: +61 2 259 4310
Fax: +61 2 251 8009

Tullett & Tokyo (Australia) Pty Ltd
Level 19, 60 Margaret Street
Sydney NSW 2000
Tel: +61 2 240 5555
Fax: +61 2 240 5030

United Capital Securities Ltd
Level 34, Grosvenor Place
225 George Street
Sydney NSW 2000
Tel: +61 2 247 1666
Fax: +61 2 247 1762

J B Were Futures Pty Ltd
Level 42, Grosvenor Phillip Tower
1 Farrer Place
Sydney NSW 2000
Tel: +61 2 321 8777
Fax: +61 2 321 8621

Brazil

Bolsa Brasileira de Futuros (Brazilian Futures Exchange)

Trading Members

ABC-Roma CVIM SA
Rua Rodrigo Silva, 26/10
Rio de Janeiro RJ 20011–040
Tel: +55 21 296 0022/11 253 3355
Fax: +55 21 307 1803/11 253 5889

Arbi SA SCCTVM
Avenida Almirante Barroso, 52/11
Rio de Janeiro RJ 20051–000
Tel: +55 21 212 8282/8367
Fax: +55 21 220 3457

Ativa SA CTV
Avenida Rio Branco 181/29
Rio de Janeiro RJ 20040–007
Tel: +55 21 210 1201/282 9566
Fax: +55 21 220 5603

Bahia CCVM SA
PC Pio X, 98/5 0 E 7
Rio de Janeiro RJ 20091–040
Tel: +55 21 221 8429/233 0362
Fax: +55 21 233 7069/269 5825

BB DTVM SA
Rua Senador Dantas, 105/26
Rio de Janeiro RJ 20031–201
Tel: +55 21 240 3110/272 7039
Fax: +55 21 213 1450/240 3357

BCO Bamerindus SA
Avenida Cicade de Lima, 147/5
Rio de Janeiro RJ 20220–710
Tel: +55 21 276 5683/41 221 2106
Fax: +55 21 276 5848/276 5406

BCO BVA SA
Avenida Rio Branco, 109/13
Rio de Janeiro RJ 20040–004
Tel: +55 21 224 0025
Fax: +55 21 224 7753

Bittencourt SA CTV
Rua do Mercado, 12/13
Rio de Janeiro RJ 20010–120
Tel: +55 21 221 8127/292 0055
Fax: +55 21 224 3724

Boavista SA CCVM
PC Pio X, 116A/9
Rio de Janeiro RJ 20091–040
Tel: +55 21 211 1443
Fax: +55 21 253 9036

Bozano Simonsen SA CCYM
Avenida Rio Branco, 138/16
Rio de Janeiro RJ 20040–002
Tel: +55 21 271 8020
Fax: +55 21 271 8309

Brascan SA CTV
Avenida Almirante Barroso, 52/31
Rio de Janeiro RJ 20031–000
Tel: +55 21 282 1328
Fax: +55 21 240 3652

Caixa Económica Federal
Avenida Paulista, 1842/3 s39
São Paulo SP 01310–941
Tel: +55 11 253 6601/253 8191
Fax: +55 11 253 1890

Cambial SA CCTVM
Rua Rodrigo Silva, 26/14
Rio de Janeiro 20011–040
Tel: +55 21 296 3100/224 2333
Fax: +55 21 224 3451

CCF Brasil DTVM SA
Rua Rodrigo Silva, 26/16
Rio de Janeiro RJ 2001–040
Tel: +55 21 271 0202
Fax: +55 21 271 0931/11 252 3116

City CCVM Ltda
Avenida Rio Branco, 116/8 Parte
Rio de Janeiro RJ 20040–001
Tel: +55 21 221 2760/224 8558
Fax: +55 21 224 0763

Codepe CV de Pernanbuco SA
Alameda Santos, 223/2
São Paulo SP 01419–002
Tel: +55 11 3061 3966
Fax: +55 11 3064 3340

Cor Nacional FP LTDA
Avenida Rio Branco, 108/6
Rio de Janeiro RJ 20040–001
Tel: +55 21 292 1277
Fax: +55 21 224 2296

Cor Omega VMC SA
PC Pio X, 55/4 E 5
Rio de Janeiro RJ 20040–020
Tel: +55 21 296 4466/11 258 8122
Fax: +55 21 233 4770

Cor Patente SA CVM
Trav do Ouvidor, 5/12
Rio de Janeiro RJ 20040–040
Tel: +55 21 221 1143/11 239 2455
Fax: +55 21 252 1718

DC CCTVM SA
Rua Rodrigo Silva, 26/19
Rio de Janeiro RJ 20010–040
Tel: +55 21 292 7722
Fax: +55 21 221 9809

Dolic CM Ltda
Avenida Rio Branco, 89/601
Rio de Janeiro RJ 20040–004
Tel: +55 21 203 1307/233 7800
Fax: +55 21 269 9980/255 5488

Económico SA CCVM
Rua do Carmo, 71/9
Rio de Janeiro RJ 20011–020
Tel: +55 21 224 7172
Fax: +55 21 221 0911

Elite CCVM Ltda
PC Pio X, 55/11
Rio de Janeiro RJ 20040–020
Tel: +55 21 291 2103/283 7171
Fax: +55 21 253 7044

Equity CP CC Ltda
Avenida Rio Branco, 115/20
Rio de Janeiro RJ 20040–004
Tel: +55 21 221 8808/224 7772
Fax: +55 21 252 9380

Estratégia Invest SA CVC
Praça XV de Novembro, 34/6
Rio de Janeiro RJ 20010–010
Tel: +55 21 210 1381/271 1811
Fax: +55 21 224 0950

Exata SA CTVM
Avenida Rio Branco 123/9
Rio de Janeiro RJ 20040–005
Tel: +55 21 224 8478
Fax: +55 21 252 6759

Factorial CCTVM Ltda
Rua de Quitanda, 50/11
Rio de Janeiro RJ 20011–030
Tel: +55 21 507 1566/507 1233
Fax: +55 21 242 3069

Fator SA CVC
Praça de Botafogo, 228/1001
Rio de Janeiro RJ 22359–900
Tel: +55 21 553 7000/553 9005
Fax: +55 21 553 5835/553 6375

Fonte SA CCV
Rua da Assembléia, 98/16
Rio de Janeiro RJ 20011–000
Tel: +55 21 217 0200
Fax: +55 21 221 3223

Garantia SA CTVM
Avenida Almirante Barroso, 52/3
Rio de Janeiro RJ 20031–000
Tel: +55 21 277 0324/252 4877

Graphus SA CCVM
Avenida Presidente Vargas, 409/17
Rio de Janeiro RJ 20071–003
Tel: +55 21 292 1177
Fax: +55 21 231 2381/507 1914

Intreunion SA CTVC
Avenida Rio Branco, 45/22
Rio de Janeiro RJ 20090–003
Tel: +55 21 212 2300/11 232 5141
Fax: +55 21 263 2899/11 518 1518

Investor SA CCTM
Rua São José, 20/13
Rio de Janeiro RJ 20010–020
Tel: +55 21 239 2277
Fax: +55 21 593 6327

Itaú CV SA
PC Pio X, 99/4
Rio de Janeiro RJ 20040–020
Tel: +55 21 276 2119/11 237 5811
Fax: +55 21 233 6080

Liberal SA CCVM
Rua do Carmo, 7/8
Rio de Janeiro, RJ 20011–020
Tel: +55 21 212 4000/292 5191
Fax: +55 21 212 4167

Marlin SA CCTVM
Rua do Ouvidor, 12/17
Rio de Janeiro RJ 20040–030
Tel: +55 21 252 6020/242 7582
Fax: +55 21 232 3974

Maxima CC Cons Ltda
Rua Rodrigo Silva, 26/21
Rio de Janeiro RJ 20050–005
Tel: +55 21 221 5339/2246191
Fax: +55 21 252 8459

Milbanco CCV SA
Rua Sete de Setembro, 71/5
Rio de Janeiro RJ 20050–005
Tel: +55 21 224 8092/31 271 2255
Fax: +55 21 242 8005

Multiplic CVM SA
Rua da Alfandega, 33/4
Rio de Janeiro RJ 20070–000
Tel: +55 21 291 1212/233 8112
Fax: +55 21 233 4052/11 240 6371

Norsul CCVM Ltda
Rua Primeiro de Marco, 32/7
Rio de Janeiro RJ 20010–000
Tel: +55 21 292 6617
Fax: +55 21 221 2072

Pebb CV Ltda
Rua Gonçalves Dias, 30 A/2
Rio de Janeiro RJ 20031–170
Tel: +55 21 292 1242
Fax: +55 21 507 1758

Premium DTVM Ltda
Rua Sete de Setembro, 99/20
Rio de Janeiro RJ 20050–005
Tel: +55 21 224 5181
Fax: +55 21 232 2973

Prime SA CCV
Rua da Alfandega, 91/9
Rio de Janeiro RJ 20070–001
Tel: +55 21 221 9977/11 232 1333
Fax: +55 21 221 2489

Primus CVC SA
Avenida Republic do Chile, 230/9
Rio de Janeiro RJ 20031–170
Tel: +55 21 210 1229/533 2312
Fax: +55 21 262 6107

Prosper SA CVC
Rua do Passeio, 70/8
Rio de Janeiro RJ 20021–290
Tel: +55 21 297 3141
Fax: +55 21 220 2882

Rural SA CTVM
Avenida Presidente Wilson, 165/6
Rio de Janeiro RJ 20030–020
Tel: +55 21 240 2611/31 271 1622
Fax: +55 21 533 2263

Senior DTVM SA
Avenida Almirante Barroso, 52/30
Rio de Janeiro RJ 20031–000
Tel: +55 21 210 3100/232 4133
Fax: +55 21 240 5398

Senso CCVM SA
Rua Primeiro de Marco, 23/16
Rio de Janeiro RJ 20010–000
Tel: +55 21 292 1222/224 3545
Fax: +55 21 222 1094

Sheck SA DTVM
PC Pio X, 55/7
Rio de Janeiro RJ 20040–020
Tel: +55 21 283 5225/11 288 1114
Fax: +55 21 221 9177

Sinal SA SCV
Avenida Rio Branco, 1/11
Rio de Janeiro RJ 20090–003
Tel: +55 21 216 4272/518 1242
Fax: +55 21 518 1243

Sincerely Cor de Comm Ltda
Rua da Ajuda, 35/908
Rio de Janeiro RJ 20040–000
Tel: +55 21 240 4458
Fax: +55 21 240 4458/220 4833

Sogeral SA CCTVM
Avenida Paulista, 1345/10
São Paulo SP 01311–200
Tel: +55 11 281 5207/5049
Fax: +55 11 251 1763/289 1188

Solidez CCTVM SA
Praça da Liberdade 118/S01
São Paulo SP 01503–101
Tel: +55 11 239 2866
Fax: +55 11 805 1020

Stock SA CCV
Rua Rodrigo Silva, 26/11
Rio de Janeiro RJ 20011–040
Tel: +55 21 507 5445
Fax: +55 21 507 1660/234 0412

Umuarama SA CTVM
Avenida Rio Branco, 16/10
Rio de Janeiro RJ 20040–001
Tel: +55 21 221 0322/2424
Fax: +55 21 252 3736

Unibanco CVM SA
Rua do Ouvidor, 91/4
Rio de Janeiro RJ 20040–030
Tel: +55 21 221 3038/297 2147
Fax: +55 21 216 3524

Vega SA CCVM
Rua Rodrigo Silva, 26/12
Rio de Janeiro RJ 20011–040
Tel: +55 21 216 1133
Fax: +55 21 216 1175/216 1174

Vector CRC SA
Rua do Mercado, 11/7
Rio de Janeiro RJ 20010–120
Tel: +55 21 297 5115/11 232 3913
Fax: +55 21 232 8955

Bolsa de Mercadorias & Futuros, São Paulo

Commodities Brokerage Houses

A Coutinho Comissária Ltda
Rua Marconi, 31/8
São Paulo SP 01047–000
Tel: +55 11 258 3177
Fax: +55 11 258 3054

Adipar DTVM Ltda
Rua Haddock Lobo, 578/1/12
São Paulo SP 01414–000
Tel: +55 11 853 2029
Fax: +55 11 853 9116

Ativa SA CTV
Avenida Paulista, 967/6
São Paulo SP 01311–100
Tel: +55 11 289 8288/8802
Fax: +55 11 283 1809

Atlântica CTVM Ltda
Rua do Ouvidor, 97/6
Rio de Janeiro RJ 20040–030

Baluarte Comm CM Ltda
Rua Boa Vista, 356/14/15
São Paulo SP 01014–000
Tel: +55 11 227 2111
Fax: +55 11 228 6057

Banco Cacique SA
Avenida Cicade Jardim, 803
São Paulo SP 01453–000
Tel: +55 11 3048 5000
Fax: +55 11 3048 5132

Banco Cindam SA
Avenida Presidente Wilson, 231/17
Rio de Janeiro RJ 20030–021
Tel: +55 21 292 3146
Fax: +55 21 220 1854

Banco Divisa SA
Rua de Quitaanda, 52/3
Rio de Janeiro RJ 20011–030
Tel: +55 21 280 6622

Banco de Investimento BMC SA
Avenida Paulista, 302/5
São Paulo SP 01310–000
Tel: +55 11 284 0688
Fax: +55 11 251 5245

Banco Fenícia SA
Avenida das Nações Unidas, 11633/8/9
São Paulo SP 04534–000
Tel: +55 11 505 2644
Fax: +55 11 505 4968

Banco Fiat SA
Avenida Paulista, 967/14
São Paulo SP 01311–100
Tel: +55 11 251 3133
Fax: +55 11 251 3133

Banco Icatu SA
Rua Joaquim Floriano, 71/18, cjs 185/8
São Paulo SP 04534–000
Tel: +55 11 822 0200
Fax: +55 11 827 3938

Banco Itamarati SA
Avenida Juscelino Kubitschek, 1830, Torre 1/12
São Paulo SP 04553–900
Tel: +55 11 827 2000
Fax: +55 11 829 8071/0132

Banco JP Morgan SA
Avenida Paulista, 1294/7/8
São Paulo SP 01310–915
Tel: +55 11 284 4566
Fax: +55 11 285 5811

Banco Marca SA
Avenida Presidente Wilson, 231/20
Rio de Janeiro RJ 20011–040
Tel: +55 21 217 7788
Fax: +55 21 217 7800

Banco Rural SA
Rua Haddock Lobo, 556/2
São Paulo SP 01414–000
Tel: +55 11 851 5511
Fax: +55 11 533 2263

Banco Vega SA
Rua Rodrigo Silva, 26/12
Rio de Janeiro RJ 20011–040
Tel: +55 21 216 1133
Fax: +55 21 216 1175

Bandeirantes CCVM SA
Rua Boa Vista, 162/2
São Paulo SP 01014–000
Tel: +55 11 233 7352/4/5
Fax: +55 11 605 9689

BFB CCVM SA
Avenida Paulista, 1294/2
São Paulo SP 01210–915
Tel: +55 11 238 8259/8369
Fax: +55 11 238 8663

BFC DTVM SA
Avenida Rio Branco, 128/10
Rio de Janeiro RJ 20040–002
Tel: +55 21 221 5177
Fax: +55 21 221 9184/7358

Boasafra DTVM SA
Al Joaquim Eugênio de Lima, 680/11
São Paulo SP 01403–901
Tel: +55 11 284 7822
Fax: +55 11 283 3273

Bonus CCM Ltda
Rua San Bento, 470/4
São Paulo SP 01010–905
Tel: +55 11 239 0133/607 8143
Fax: +55 11 606 9624

Brascan Futuros Ltda
Rua Almirante Barroso, 52/31
Rio de Janeiro RJ 20031–000
Tel: +55 21 282 1328
Fax: +55 21 240 3652

CCF Brasil Comm Part e CM e Fut SA
Rua Jorge Coelho, 16/2
São Paulo SP 01451–020
Tel: +55 11 827 5000
Fax: +55 11 827 5343

Chase Manhattan SA DTVM
Rua Verbo Divino, 1400/1
São Paulo SP 04719–002
Tel: +55 11 546 4275
Fax: +55 11 546 4711/6

Cia Real de Commodities
Avenida Paulista, 1374/16
São Paulo SP 01310–916
Tel: +55 11 251 9030/287 1205/285 3622
Fax: +55 11 283 5849

Coinvalores DTVM Ltda
Rua da Quitanda, 96/1
São Paulo SP 01012–907
Tel: +55 11 606 0151/232 7161
Fax: +55 11 604 8877

Comercial SA CVC
Avenida Paulista, 1439/3 cj 33/4
São Paulo SP 01311–926
Tel: +55 11 283 0599/0953/0348
Fax: +55 11 287 6600

Concórdia SA CVMCC
Rua Líbero Badaró, 425/7
São Paulo SP 01069–900
Tel: +55 11 239 3122
Fax: +55 11 605 6825

DC CM SA
Rua Rodrigo Silva, 16/19
Rio de Janeiro RJ 20011–040
Tel: +55 21 292 7722
Fax: +55 21 221 9809

Dibran DTVM Ltda
Avenida Ipiranga, 318, Block A/14
São Paulo SP 01046–010
Tel: +55 11 256 6188
Fax: +55 11 255 9197

Dimarco Commodities Ltda
Rua Sete de Setembro, 99/11
Rio de Janeiro RJ 20050–002
Tel: +55 21 224 5159
Fax: +55 21 221 0263

Distribuidora Bank of Boston TVM SA
Rua Líbero Badaró, 501
São Paulo SP 01095–900
Tel: +55 11 249 5622
Fax: +55 11 239 3018

Doria & Atherino CM Ltda
Rua Líbero Badaró, 377/24 cj 2402/06
São Paulo SP 01074–900
Tel: +55 11 239 4055
Fax: +55 11 604 0266

Equity CPCC Ltda
Avenida Rio Branco, 115/20
Rio de Janeiro RJ 20040–004
Tel: +55 21 224 7772
Fax: +55 21 507 1526

Esboriol CM Ltda
Praça Pe Manoel da Nóbrega, 16/6
São Paulo SP 01015–900
Tel: +55 11 605 2101/606 9823/232 9531
Fax: +55 11 606 5616

Escritório Lerosa SA CV
Praça Pe Manoel da Nóbrega, 21/7
São Paulo SP 01015–010
Tel: +55 11 239 1733
Fax: +55 11 232 5279

Estructura DTVM Ltda
Rua da Alfândega, 91/15
Rio de Janeiro RJ 20070–001
Tel: +55 21 224 8484
Fax: +55 21 252 3182

Exata CM Ltda
Avenida Rio Branco, 123/9
Rio de Janeiro RJ 20040–005
Tel: +55 21 224 8478
Fax: +55 21 252 6746

Fair CCV Ltda
Almirante Santos, 1800/8/9
São Paulo SP 01418–200
Tel: +55 11 288 0577
Fax: +55 11 289 7412

Factor SA CVC
Avenida Paulista, 1728/5
São Paulo SP 01310–000
Tel: +55 11 253 1577
Fax: +55 11 284 2127

Ficsa SA CCTVM
Rua Álvares Penteado, 65/1
São Paulo SP 01012–001
Tel: +55 11 232 1666
Fax: +55 11 605 6347

Fimat Futures CM SA
Avenida Paulista, 1345/5
São Paulo SP 01311–924
Tel: +55 11 251 5100
Fax: +55 11 288 1893

Finabank CCTVM Ltda
Rua Boa Vista, 63/5
São Paulo SP 01014–001
Tel: +55 11 607 6001/607 4456
Fax: +55 11 606 9588

Futura Commodities CM Ltda
Rua Sao Bento, 470/5
São Paulo SP 01010–001
Tel: +55 11 604 7076/607 6066
Fax: +55 11 604 6876

Intercap Asses e Part SC Ltda
Rua Boa Vista, 280/3
São Paulo 01014–000
Tel: +55 11 605 1041/1131/607 2404
Fax: +55 11 607 7874

Interfloat CM & Futuros Ltda
Praça Pe Manoel de Nóbrega, 21/15
São Paulo SP 01015–010
Tel: +55 11 607 1561
Fax: +55 11 604 6949

Interunion SA CTCV
Avenida Rio Branco, 45/22
Rio de Janeiro RJ 20090–003
Tel: +55 21 223 1300
Fax: +55 21 233 2672/263 2899

Intra CM Ltda
Rua Líbero Badaró, 377/25
São Paulo SP 01074–900
Tel: +55 11 239 2699
Fax: +55 11 606 1091

Ipanema CM Ltda
Rua Boa Vista, 186/10
São Paulo SP 01014–030
Tel: +55 11 239 2899
Fax: +55 11 606 9608

Kronor DTVM SA
Rua do Ouvidor, 97/8
Rio de Janeiro RJ 20040–030
Tel: +55 21 224 0122

Laeco CCM Ltda
Almirante Santos, 1800/7
São Paulo SP 01418–200
Tel: +55 11 284 1400
Fax: +55 11 285 2277

Liberal SA CCVM
Rua Líbero Badaró, 377/7 cj 710
São Paulo SP 01074–900
Tel: +55 11 255 9511
Fax: +55 11 605 1366

Liquidez DTVM Ltda
Rua 7 de Abril, 103/5 cjB
São Paulo SP 01043–000
Tel: +55 11 259 5788
Fax: +55 11 221 4204

Lucro DTVM Ltda
Avenida Rio Branco, 134/19
Rio de Janeiro RJ 20040–002
Tel: +55 21 224 9942/9982
Fax: +55 21 507 1557

Marsham DTVM Ltda
Rua Haddock Lobo, 585/1
São Paulo SP 01414–001
Tel: +55 11 883 6088/6057/6174
Fax: +55 11 881 0036

Master CM Ltda
Avenida Nove de Julho, 5617/7 cjB
São Paulo SP 01407–200
Tel: +55 11 3064 3492/9632/9153/6486
Fax: +55 11 3068 8810

MB DTVM Ltda
Avenida Rio Branco, 89/6, Room 601
Rio de Janeiro RJ 20040–004
Tel: +55 21 233 7800/11 607 2536
Fax: +55 21 253 5488

Mercantil do Brasil Cor SA CTVM
Rua São Bento, 366/1
São Paulo SP 01010–001
Tel: +55 11 607 4333/13
Fax: +55 11 284 6377

Merrill Lynch SA DTVM
Avenida Paulista, 37/3
São Paulo SP 01311–902
Tel: +55 11 245 4001/4094
Fax: +55 11 245 4081

Mesa DTVM Ltda
Rua Dr Miguel Couto, 53/2
São Paulo SP 01008–010
Tel: +55 11 607 6091
Fax: +55 11 607 9077

Next CM Ltda
Rua Líbero Badaró, 377/22 cj2206
São Paulo SP 01074–900
Tel: +55 11 607 7406
Fax: +55 11 604 8664

Performance CM Ltda
Rua São José, 20/4/15
Rio de Janeiro RJ 20010–020
Tel: +55 21 296 2000
Fax: +55 21 296 2000

Planibanc CV SA
Avenida Presidente Juscelino Kubitschek, 1830/5, Torre 2
São Paulo SP 04543–900
Tel: +55 11 866 8788/8996
Fax: +55 11 866 9024

Portus CM Ldta
Rua São Bento, 365/10 cj 100
São Paulo SP 01011–100
Tel: +55 11 607 1131/2536
Fax: +55 11 605 7740

Prime SA CCV
Rua Líbero Baderó, 293/6 cjs A e B
São Paulo SP 01095–900
Tel: +55 11 232 1333
Fax: +55 11 607 2396

Quality CM Ltda
Avenida Presidente Juscelino Kubitschek, 50/9 cj 92
São Paulo SP 04543–000
Tel: +55 11 822 0770
Fax: +55 11 829 1591

Refco Do Brasil CM Ltda
Rua Boa Vista, 254/7
São Paulo SP 01014–907
Tel: +55 11 232 5022
Fax: +55 11 232 9161

Safic CVC Ltda
Rua Vergueiro, 1883/9/10
São Paulo SP 04101–000
Tel: +55 11 549 8266
Fax: +55 11 571 2512

Santander Investment CM Ltda
Avenida Paulista, 37/16
São Paulo SP 01311–000
Tel: +55 11 253 3566
Fax: +55 11 3179 4244/4243/276 5406

SB Commodities CM Ltda
Rua Vergueiro, 2009/1 cj A
São Paulo SP 01014–030
Tel: +55 11 239 0022/2711
Fax: +55 11 606 6492

Senior DTVM SA
Avenida Almirante Barroso, 52/3 cj 3022
Rio de Janeiro RJ 20031–000
Tel: +55 21 210 3100
Fax: +55 21 240 5398

Sítese CMF Ltda
Rua Tenente Negrão, 140/11
São Paulo SP 04530–030
Tel: +55 11 829 9755
Fax: +55 11 829 9755

SLW CVC Ltda
Rua Arnolfo Azevedo, 40
São Paulo SP 01236–030
Tel: +55 11 872 0096
Fax: +55 11 871 5959

Somartec CM E Futuros Ltda
Avenida Paulista, 1765 cj 171
São Paulo SP 01311–000
Tel: +55 11 253 2577/253 6135
Fax: +55 11 288 6677

Stock SA CCv
Rua Líbero Badaró, 377/5 cj 504/5/6
São Paulo SP 01074–900
Tel: +55 11 232 5611/605 7114
Fax: +55 11 239 4667

Talarico CCTM Ltda
Rua Boa Vista, 230/5/6 cj 501/2/601
São Paulo SP 01014–000
Tel: +55 11 604 8126
Fax: +55 11 605 7229

Tática CCM Ltda
Rua Marquês de Itu, 837 cj 43
São Paulo SP 01223–001
Tel: +55 11 255 0599/258 2814
Fax: +55 11 231 5511

Telles CCM Ltda
Rua 15 de Novembro, 269/8 cj 801/6
São Paulo SP 01013–913
Tel: +55 11 605 2450/4862
Fax: +55 11 605 4932

Theca CCM Ltda
Rua Boa Vista, 186/7
São Paulo SP 01014–000
Tel: +55 11 239 4077
Fax: +55 11 239 0772

Trycomm CM Ltda
Avenida 9 de Julho, 4400
São Paulo SP 01406–100
Tel: +55 11 823 2777/2231/2888/2958
Fax: +55 11 280 2749

Umuarama SA CTVM
Avenida Rio Branco, 116/10
Rio de Janeiro RJ 20040–001
Tel: +55 11 221 2424
Fax: +55 11 252 3736

Commodities Brokerage Houses and Clearing Members

Agente CTVM Ltda
Almirante Santos, 1800/7
São Paulo SP 01418–200
Tel: +55 11 285 5511
Fax: +55 11 285 2590

Bahia CCVM SA
Avenida Paulista,
1842/10, Room 108
São Paulo SP 01310–200
Tel: +55 11 169 0500
Fax: +55 11 284 6075

Bamerindus SA CCVM
Avenida Cicade Lima, 147/6
Rio de Janeiro RJ 20220–710
Tel: +55 21 276 5649
Fax: +55 21 276 5406

Bancocidade CVMC Ltda
Praça Dom José Gaspar, 134/7/9
São Paulo SP 01047–010
Tel: +55 11 231 6477
Fax: +55 11 231 6194/6478

Banespa SA CCT
Rua Álvares Penteado, 49 & 53
São Paulo SP 01012–900
Tel: +55 11 231 7544/605 1203/232 7911
Fax: +55 11 232 3964

BMD SA CCVM
Rua 15 de Novembro, 251/6
São Paulo SP 01013–000
Tel: +55 11 232 2600
Fax: +55 11 607 2461

BMG Corretora SA
Almirante Santos, 2335/3
São Paulo SP 01419–002
Tel: +55 11 897 2021/2014
Fax: +55 11 897 2021/2014

Boavista SA CCVM
Rua 15 de Novembro, 331 SSL/3
São Paulo SP 01013–001
Tel: +55 11 3179 8665

Bozano, Simonsen SA CCVM
Avenida Paulista, 1500/2
São Paulo SP 01310–100
Tel: +55 11 252 8072
Fax: +55 11 234 0956

Bradesco SA CTVM
Avenida Ipiranga, 282/11/12
São Paulo SP 01046–010
Tel: +55 11 235 9511/9722
Fax: +55 11 853 9116

Cia América do Sul CCTVM
Rua Senador Paulo Egídio, 72/1, Room 110
São Paulo SP 01006–010
Tel: +55 11 606 9113/607 0101
Fax: +55 11 606 9113

Citibank CCTVM SA
Avenida Paulista, 1111/11
São Paulo SP 01311–920
Tel: +55 11 576 1666/1099/1299
Fax: +55 11 283 1020/289 1035

Convenção SA CVC
Rua Bela Cintra, 986/7
São Paulo SP 01415–000
Tel: +55 11 255 9400
Fax: +55 11 258 4550

Corretora BCN SA VM
Rua Boa Vista, 208/13 cj B
São Paulo SP 01014–000
Tel: +55 11 244 1704
Fax: +55 11 235 1835

Corretora Omega VMC SA
Rua da Consolaçoão, 331/11
São Paulo SP 01301–905
Tel: +55 11 258 8122
Fax: +55 11 258 9982

Corretora Patente SA CVM
Avenida Paulista, 1106/7
São Paulo SP 01310–914
Tel: +55 11 886 9600
Fax: +55 11 886 9700

Corretora Souza Barros CT SA
Rua Líbero Badaró, 293/23
São Paulo SSP 0095–900
Tel: +55 11 232 2233
Fax: +55 11 232 2233

Dias de Souza Valores SC Ltda
Rua Líbero Badaró, 471/16
São Paulo SP 01009–000
Tel: +55 11 607 7506/7507/7508/7509
Fax: +55 11 607 4384

Excel Econômico CCVM Ltda
Rua Agusta, 1638
São Paulo SP 01304–001

Finasa CCVM SA
Rua Líbero Badaró, 377/3
São Paulo 01009–000
Tel: +55 11 607 1171/7065
Fax: +55 11 604 6028

Fonte SA CCV
Rua Líbero Badaró, 425/27 cj 102
São Paulo SP 01069–900
Tel: +55 11 239 5088
Fax: +55 11 607 7875

Garantia SA CTVM
Rua Jorge Coelho, 16/14
São Paulo SP 01451–020
Tel: +55 11 821 6000
Fax: +55 11 821 6900

Geral do Comércio SA CCVM
Rua Funchal, 160/5
São Paulo SP 04551–060
Tel: +55 11 828 7369
Fax: +55 11 820 8403

Graphus SA CCVM
Rua Líbero Badaró, 425/15 cj 154/6
São Paulo SP 01069–900
Tel: +55 11 232 4141
Fax: +55 11 607 7518

Hedging Griffo CV SA
Avenida Presidente Juscelino Kubitschek, 1830
Condomínio Sao Luiz, Torre IV/6 e 7
São Paulo SP 04343–001
Tel: +55 11 866 4953
Fax: +55 11 3040 8666

Indusval SA CTVM
Rua Boa Vista, 356/7–10
São Paulo SP 01014–000
Tel: +55 11 225 6777
Fax: +55 11 225 0130

Ing-Baring CVM SA
Rua Jorge Coelho, 16/11
São Paulo SP 01451–020
Tel: +55 11 827 6000
Fax: +55 11 827 6599

Ing-Guilder CCT SA
Rua Jorge Coelho, 16/8
São Paulo SP 01451–020
Tel: +55 11 827 6000
Fax: +55 11 827 6464

Investor SA CCTM
Rua São José, 20/13–14
Rio de Janeiro RJ 20010–020
Tel: +55 21 533 2899
Fax: +55 21 232 3327

Isoldi SA CVM
Praça Antonio Prado, 33/15
São Paulo SP 01010–900
Tel: +55 11 607 4021
Fax: +55 11 604 2022

Itaú CV SA
Rua Boa Vista, 185/4
São Paulo SP 01014–001
Tel: +55 11 237 5880/5000
Fax: +55 11 232 9840/606 5077

Magliano SA CCVM
Rua Bela Cintra, 986/2
São Paulo SP 01415–000
Tel: +55 11 214 0855
Fax: +55 11 214 4966

Multiplic CVM SA
Avenida Jurubatuba, 83/9
São Paulo SP 04583–100
Tel: +55 11 534 6896/6897/6907
Fax: +55 11 534 6736

Noroeste SA CCTVM
Rua Álvares Penteado, 216/5
São Paulo SP 01012–000
Tel: +55 11 259 2233
Fax: +55 11 606 7573

Novação SA CCM
Avenida Paulista, 1294/4
São Paulo SP 01310–915
Tel: +55 11 251 2877/253 4644
Fax: +55 11 288 9408

Novinvest SA CVM
Rua Boa Vista, 63/10
São Paulo SP 01014–001
Tel: +55 11 607 2161
Fax: +55 11 607 7231

Pebb CV Ltda
Rua São Bento, 470/6 cj ímpar
São Paulo SP 01010–020
Tel: +55 11 605 4145
Fax: +55 11 604 7553

Primus CVC SA
Avenida Paulista, 37/8
São Paulo SP 01311–902
Tel: +55 11 251 4877/251 2300
Fax: +55 11 283 3791

Prosper SA CVC
Rua São Bento, 470/2
São Paulo SP 01010–001
Tel: +55 11 239 1311
Fax: +55 11 829 1591

RMC SA Sociedade Corretora
Avenida Brigadeiro Faria Lima, 1541/20 cj L/M
São Paulo SP 01451–000
Tel: +55 11 816 4141/4155
Fax: +55 11 814 0140

Safra CVC Ltda
Avenida Paulista, 2100/4 & 7, Piso Augusta
São Paulo SP 01310–200
Tel: +55 11 251 7297/7247/7018/8534
Fax: +55 11 251 7105

Santos CCV SA
Avenida Paulista, 1842/5 & 6
Torre Norte
São Paulo SP 01310–200
Tel: +55 11 269 6000
Fax: +55 11 283 2679/2701

São Paulo CV Ltda
Avenida Paulista, 1009/21 & 22
São Paulo SP 01311–919
Tel: +55 11 253 6755
Fax: +55 11 284 6734

Schahin Cury CCVM SA
Rua Vergueiro, 2009/1
São Paulo SP 04101–000
Tel: +55 11 576 8282/8287/8080
Fax: +55 11 576 8333

Sinal SA SCV
Avenida Paulista, 2166/3
São Paulo SP 01310–300
Tel: +55 11 284 4323/3492/251 0255
Fax: +55 11 287 4905

Sistema SA CCVM
Avenida Brigadeiro Faria Lima, 2000/2 & 3
Torre Norte
São Paulo SP 01480–900
Tel: +55 11 816 6422
Fax: +55 11 815 2583

Socopa SC Paulista SA
Rua Boa Vista, 254/2
São Paulo SP 01014–907
Tel: +55 11 239 5800
Fax: +55 11 605 7481

Spinelli SA CVMC
Rua José Bonifácio, 93/6, 10 & 11
São Paulo SP 01003–001
Tel: +55 11 607 4521
Fax: +55 11 606 3539

Sudameris CCVM SA
Avenida Paulista, 1000/7
São Paulo SP 01310–912
Tel: +55 11 289 8066/285 6444
Fax: +55 11 283 9606/9395

Suplicy CCT Ltda
Rua Boa Vista, 254/10
São Paulo SP 01014–907
Tel: +55 11 232 3181/607 9461
Fax: +55 11 232 7343/607 9561

Tendência CCTVM Ltda
Avenida Brigadeiro Faria Lima, 1383/20
São Paulo SP 01451–905
Tel: +55 11 867 0080
Fax: +55 11 210 3197

Unibanco CVM SA
Rua da Quitanda, 157/4
São Paulo SP 01012–010
Tel: +55 11 244 5264/5746
Fax: +55 11 604 2862

Vetor CVC SA
Rua do Mercado, 11/7 & 8
Rio de Janeiro RJ 20010–120
Tel: +55 21 297 5115
Fax: +55 21 232 8955

Votorantim CTVM Ltda
Rua Roque Petroni Junior, 999/16
São Paulo SP 04707–910
Tel: +55 11 536 1700
Fax: +55 11 536 1900

Clearing Members

CCF Brazil CTVM SA
Rua Jorge Coelho, 16/2
São Paulo SP 01451–020
Tel: +55 11 827 5000
Fax: +55 11 827 5343

Cia Real CCVM
Avenida Paulista, 1374/16
São Paulo SP 01310–916
Tel: +55 11 289 8049
Fax: +55 11 283 5849

DC CCTVM SA
Rua do Tesouro, 23/11
São Paulo SP 01013–020
Tel: +55 11 606 0071/604 5713
Fax: +55 11 604 5713

Doria & Atherino SA CCVM
Rua Líbero Badaró
377/24 cj 2402/06
São Paulo SP 01074–900
Tel: +55 11 239 4055
Fax: +55 11 604 0266

Finambrás CCTVM Ltda
Praça Amadeu Amaral, 27/9
São Paulo SP 01327–010
Tel: +55 11 289 8855
Fax: +55 11 604 6028

Icatu Corretora de TVM Ltda
Rua Joaquim Floriano, 72/18
São Paulo SP 04534–000
Tel: +55 11 822 0200
Fax: +55 11 217 1300

Mesa CVM Ltda
Rua Dr Miguel Couto, 53/2
São Paulo SP 01008–010
Tel: +55 11 607 6091
Fax: +55 11 607 9077

Oak CCVM Ltda
Rua Haddock Lobo, 684
São Paulo SP 01414–000
Tel: +55 11 897 3700

Senior CCVF Ltda
Avenida Almirante Barroso, 52/3 cj 3002
Rio de Janeiro RJ 20031–000
Tel: +55 21 210 3100
Fax: +55 21 240 5398

Sheck CTVM Ltda
Almirante Santos, 2224/2 cj 22
São Paulo SP 01418–200
Tel: +55 11 280 6622

Sintese CV Ltda
Rua Tenente Negrão, 140/11
São Paulo SP 04530–030
Tel: +55 11 829 9755
Fax: +55 11 829 9755

SN Crefisul SA SC
Avenida Presidente Juscelino Kubitschek, 1830
Torre II/11
São Paulo SP 04353–900
Tel: +55 11 820 1060/827 2690
Fax: +55 11 827 2693

Theca CCTVM Ltda
Rua Boa Vista, 186/7
São Paulo SP 01014–000
Tel: +55 11 239 4077
Fax: +55 11 239 0772

Agricultural Commodities Brokerage Houses

Aplicação ADM e Serviços Ltda
Largo da Misericórdia, 20/7
São Paulo SP
Tel: +55 11 607 4071
Fax: +55 11 607 3938

Banco Norchem SA
Avenida Paulista, 1842/13
São Paulo SP 01310–200
Tel: +55 11 238 5000
Fax: +55 11 238 5011

Hedging CCM SA
Praça Ramos de Azevedo, 206/13
São Paulo SP 01049–000
Tel: +55 11 223 6822

Intermarket CM Ltda
Rua Dr Sodré, 106
São Paulo SP 04535–110
Tel: +55 11 820 9433
Fax: +55 11 820 3121

Multinvest DTVM Ltda
Avenida Ipiranga, 318/10, Block A
São Paulo SP 01046–010
Tel: +55 11 257 7022/258 2588
Fax: +55 11 255 9059

Termo CM Ltda
Rua Tapinas, 22
São Paulo SP 04531–050
Tel: +55 11 3061 2355
Fax: +55 11 881 9690

Trader CM Ltda
Rua São Bento, 329/2, Room 24
São Paulo SP 01011–000
Tel: +55 11 606 0056
Fax: +55 11 606 0059

Unidade CM SA
Rua Líbero Badaró, 471/23
São Paulo SP 01009–000
Tel: +55 11 607 5131/232 5131
Fax: +55 11 604 0463

Canada

The Montreal Exchange

Active Members

Altamira Securities
250 Bloor Street East
Suite 301
Toronto, Ontario
M4W 1E6
Tel: +1 416 9252512

Beacon Securities Ltd
1707 Grafton Street
Halifax, Nova Scotia
B3J 2C6
Tel: +1 902 4231260

BLC Rousseau Inc
1981, avenue McGill College
Bureau 1985
Montréal, Québec
H8A 3K3
Tel: +1 514 2845333

Brockhouse & Cooper Inc
1250, boul. René-Lévesque Ouest
Bureau 4025
Montréal (Québec)
H3B 4WB
Tel: +1 514 9327171

Bunting Warburg Inc
ECE Place, 161 Bay Street
Suite 4100,
PO Box 617
Toronto, Ontario
M51 2S1
Tel: +1 416 3643293

1010, rue Sherbrooke Ouest
Bureau 2510
Montréal (Québec)
H3A 2R7
Tel: +1 514 8428726

CM Oliver & Co Ltd
750 West Pender Street
2nd Floor
Vancouver, British Columbia
V6C 1B5
Tel: +1 604 6686700

Canaccord Capital Corporation
Pacific Centre
609 Granville Street,
Suite 2200,
PO Box 10337
Vancouver, British Columbia
V7Y 1H2
Tel: +1 604 6437300

Casgrain & Compagnie Limitée
500, boul. René-Lévesque Ouest
Bureau 1625
Montréal (Québec)
H2Z 1W7
Tel: +1 514 8718080

Choulnard, McNamara Inc
1100, boul. René-Lévesque Ouest
Bureau 1300
Montréal (Québec)
H3B 4N4
Tel: +1 514 3933430

CIBC Wood Gundy Securities Inc
BCE Place
161 Bay Street
PO Box 500
Toronto, Ontario
M5J 2S8
Tel: +1 416 5947000

600, boul. de Maisonneuve Ouest
Bureau 3050
Montréal (Québec)
M3A 3J2
Tel: +1 514 8476300

Commission Direct Inc
121 King Street West
PO Box 11, Suite 1010
Toronto, Ontario
M5H 3T9
Tel: +1 416 9415622

Credifinance Securities Ltd
130 Adelaide Street West
Suite 3303
Toronto, Ontario
M5H 3P5
Tel: +1 416 9550159

1501, avenue McGill College
Bureau 1580
Montréal (Québec)
H3Z 1Z4
Tel: +1 514 8434644

CS First Boston (Canada) Inc
121 King Street West
PO Box 111
Suite 2500
Toronto, Ontario
M5H 3T9
Tel: +1 416 9472600

CT Securities International Inc
70 York Street
Suite 950
Toronto, Ontario
M5J 1S9
Tel: +1 416 9477200

1155, boul. René-Lévesque Ouest
Bureau 816
Montréal (Québec)
H3B 2H7
Tel: +1 514 3979073

CT Securities Services Inc
70 York Street
8th Floor
Toronto, Ontario
M5J 1S9
Tel: +1 416 9815000

630, boul. René-Lévesque Ouest
ler étage
Montréal (Québec)
H3V 1S6
514 3979073

CTI Capital Inc
1, Place Ville-Marie
Bureau 1695
Montréal (Québec)
H3B 2B6
Tel: +1 514 8613500

D & B Internat Securities Inc
1115, rue Sherbrooke Ouest
Bureau 1702
Montréal (Québec)
H3A 1H3
Tel: +1 514 8424111

Deacon Capital Corp
320 Bay Street,
PO Box 3
9th Floor
Toronto, Ontario
M5H 4A6
Tel: +1 416 3503250

600, boul. de Maisonneuve Ouest
Bureau 750
Montréal (Québec)
H3A 3J4
Tel: +1 514 4990099

Demers Consell Inc
615, boul. René-Lévesque Ouest
Bureau 1120
Montréal (Québec)
H3B 1P5
Tel: +1 514 8791702

Desjardins Securities Inc
2, Complexe Desjardins
Tour de l'Est, 15e étage
CP 194, Succursale Desjardins
Montréal (Québec)
H5B 1J2
Tel: +1 514 9871749

Deutsche Morgan Grenfell Canada Ltd
Toronto-Dominion Centre
222 Bay Street
PO Box 64
Toronto, Ontario
M5K 1E7
Tel: +1 416 9625151

1501, avenue McGill College
Bureau 1650
Montréal (Québec)
H3A 3M8
Tel: +1 514 2865151

Dlouhy Investments Inc
1350, rue Sherbrooke Ouest
Bureau 1200
Montréal (Québec)
H3G 1J1
Tel: +1 514 6458111

DPM Securities Inc
755, boulevard St-Jean
Bureau 602
Pointe-Claire (Québec)
H9R 5M9
Tel: +1 514 6307500

Dubeau Capital & Compagnie ltée
5600, boulevard des Galeries
Bureau 530
Québec (Québec)
G2K 2H6
Tel: +1 418 6285593

Edward D Jones & Co
90 Burnhamthorpe Road West
Suite 902
Mississauge, Ontario
L5B 3C3
Tel: +1 905 2738400

RCG Securities Corp
145 King Street West
Suite 2750
Toronto, Ontario
M5H 1J8
Tel: +1 416 3648600

Fairvest Securities Corp
8 King Street East
Suite 700
Toronto, Ontario
M5C 1B5
Tel: +1 416 3649000

Fimat Derivatives Canada Inc
1501, avenue McGill College
Bureau 1800
Montréal (Québec)
H3A SM8
Tel: +1 514 8416200

First Marathon Securities Ltd
The Stock Exchange Tower
PO Box 21, Suite 3200
2 First Canadian Place
Toronto, Ontario
M5X 1J9
Tel: +1 416 8693707

1155, rue Metcalfe
Bureau 2160
Montréal (Québec)
H9B 2X8
Tel: +1 514 8754859

Fortune Financial Corp
One Corporate Plaza
2075 Kennedy Road
Suite 608
Scarborough, Ontario
M1T 3V3
Tel: +1 416 2914400

1165, boulevard Lebourgneuf
Bureau 320
Québec (Québec)
G2K 2C9
Tel: +1 418 6294707

Friedberg Mercantile Group
BCE Place
181 Bay Street
PO Box 866
Suite 250
Toronto, Ontario
M5J 2T3
Tel: +1 416 3642700

Georgia Pacific Securities Corp
Two Bentall Centre
535 Burrard Street
16th Floor
Vancouver, British Columbia
V7X 1S6
Tel: +1 604 6681800

Goepel Shields & Partners Inc
Pacific Centre
701 West Georgia Street
Suite 1400,
PO Box 10111
Vancouver, British Columbia
V7Y 1C6
Tel: +1 604 6611777

Golden Capital Securities Ltd
1177 West Hastings Street
Suite 168
Vancouver, British Columbia
V6E 2K3
Tel: +1 604 6881898

Goldman Sachs Canada
150 King Street West
Suite 1201
Toronto, Ontario
M5H 1J9
Tel: +1 416 3438900

600, boul. de Maisonneuve Ouest
Bureau 2350
Montréal (Québec)
H3A 3J2
Tel: +1 514 4991510

Gordon Capital Corp
Toronto-Dominion Centre
PO Box 67
Suite 5300
Toronto, Ontario
M5K 1E7
Tel: +1 416 3649393

1, Place Ville-Marie
Bureau 4130
Montréal (Québec)
H3B 3P9
Tel: +1 514 8619751

Great Pacific Management Co Ltd
1125 Howe Street
4th Floor
Vancouver, British Columbia
V6Z 2K8
Tel: +1 604 6691143

Groupe Option Retraite Inc (Le)
455, rue Sainte-Antoine Ouest
Suite 201
Montréal (Québec)
H2Z 1J1
Tel: +1 514 8610777

James Capel Canada Inc
One Financial Place
1 Adelaide Street East
Suite 2400
Toronto, Ontario
M5C 2V9
Tel: +1 416 9472700

1501, avenue McGill College
Bureau 1530
Montréal (Québec)
H3A 3M8
Tel: +1 514 8448799

John Pasztor & Associates Inc
19 Shorncliffe Avenue
Toronto, Ontario
M4V 1S9
Tel: +1 416 9221326

Lafferty, Harwood & Partners Ltd
2020, rue University
Bureau 1920
Montréal (Québec)
H3A 2A5
Tel: +1 514 2877306

Leduc & Associés, valeurs mobilières Inc
2020, rue University
Bureau 2300
Montréal (Québec)
H3A 2A5
Tel: +1 514 4991066

Lévesque Beaubien Geoffrion Inc
Edifice Sun Life
1155, rue Metcalfe,
5e étage
Montréal (Québec)
H3B 4S9
Tel: +1 514 8792222

Loewen, Ondaatje, McCutcheon Ltd
Hazelton Lanes, East Tower
55 Avenue Road
Suite 2250
Toronto, Ontario
M5R 3L2
Tel: +1 416 9644455

1200, avenue McGill College
Bureau 2010
Montréal (Québec)
H3B 4G7
Tel: +1 514 3934600

MacDougall, MacDougall & MacTier Inc
Place du Canada
Bureau 2000
Montréal (Québec)
H3B 4J1
Tel: +1 514 3943000

MacDougall, Meyer Inc
2050, rue Mansfield
Bureau 1500
Montréal (Québec)
H3A 1Y9
Tel: +1 514 2888823

Maison Placements Canada Inc
Place du Canade
Bureau 2230
Montréal (Québec)
H3B 2N2
Tel: +1 514 8791662

Marieau, Lemire Securities Inc
1, Place Ville-Marie
Bureau 3601
Montréal (Québec)
H3B 3P2
Tel: +1 514 8773800

Maxima Capital Inc
266, rue St-Paul Est
Montréal (Québec)
H2V 1G9
Tel: +1 514 8782525

Merit Investment Corp
55 University Avenue
Suite 1000
Toronto, Ontario
M5J 2P8
Tel: +1 416 8676000

Merrill Lynch Canada Inc
Merrill Lynch Canada Tower
200 King Street West
Toronto, Ontario
M5H 3W3
Tel: +1 416 5866000

Place Montréal Trust
1600, avenue McGill College
Bureau 2500
Montréal (Québec)
H3A 3J6
Tel: +1 514 9822700

Midland Welwyn Capital Inc
BCE Place, Bay Wellington Tower
181 Bay Street
Suite 400
Toronto, Ontario
M5J 2V8
Tel: +1 416 3697400

1250, boul. René-Lévesque Ouest
Bureau 3100
Montréal (Québec)
H3B 4W8
Tel: +1 514 8461050

Morgan Stanley Canada Ltd
181 Bay Street,
Suite 3700,
PO Box 776
Toronto, Ontario
M5J 2T3
Tel: +1 416 9438400

1501, avenue McGill College
Bureau 2310
Montréal (Québec)
H3A 3M8
Tel: +1 514 8477400

National Bank Securities Inc
1100, rue University
7e étage
Montréal (Québec)
H3B 2G7
Tel: +1 514 3945000

Nesbitt Burns Ltd
1501, avenue McGill College
Bureau 3200
Montréal (Québec)
H3A 3M8
Tel: +1 514 2867200

Newcrest Capital Inc
55 Yonge Street
Suite 1200
Toronto, Ontario
M5E 1J4
Tel: +1 416 8629160

1501, avenue McGill College
Bureau 2250
Montréal (Québec)
H3A 3M8
Tel: +1 514 8454262

Odium Brown Ltd
Pacific Centre
1800 – 609 Granville Street
PO Box 10012
Vancouver, British Columbia
V7T 1A3
Tel: +1 604 6691600

Pensec Inc
55 Metcalfe Street
Suite 860
Ottawa, Ontario
K1P 6L5
Tel: +1 613 7245434

Pictet (Canada) and Co, Ltd
1800, avenue McGill College
Bureau 2900
Montréal (Québec)
H3A 3J6
Tel: +1 514 2888161

Pollitt & Co, Inc
Commerce Court North
25 King Street West
Suite 1101,
PO Box 94
Toronto, Ontario
M5L 1B9
Tel: +1 416 3653313

625, boul. René-Lévesque Ouest
Bureau 1110
Montréal (Québec)
H3B 1R2
Tel: +1 514 3958910

RBC Dominion Securities Inc
PO Box 21
Commerce Court South
Toronto, Ontario
M5L 1A7
416 8644000

1, Place Ville-Marie
3e étage
Montréal (Québec)
H9B 4R8
Tel: +1 514 8787000

Refco Futures (Canada) Ltd
800, Square Victoria
Bureau 4110, BP 913
Montréal (Québec)
H4Z 1G8
Tel: +1 514 8661000

Research Capital Corp
Ernst & Young Tower
Suite 1500
Toronto Dominion Centre
PO Box 265
Toronto, Ontario
M5K 1J5
Tel: +1 416 8607600

1555, rue Peel
Bureau 900
Montréal (Québec)
H3A 1X6
Tel: +1 514 2811800

Richardson Greenshields of Canada Ltd
One Lombard Place
Winnipeg, Manitoba
R3B 0Y2
Tel: +1 204 9345858

4, Place Ville-Marie
ler étage
Montréal (Québec)
H3B 2E8
Tel: +1 1514 3972000

ScotiaMcLeod Inc
Scotia Plaza
40 King Street West
PO Box 4085
Station A
Toronto, Ontario
M5W 2X6
Tel: +1 416 8697411

Tour Scotia
1002, rue Sherbrooke Ouest
6e étage
Montréal (Québec)
H3A 3L6
Tel: +1 514 2873600

Sociéte Générale Securities Inc
1501, avenue McGill College
Bureau 1800
Montréal (Québec)
H3A 3M8
Tel: +1 514 8416150

Sprott Securities Ltd
Royal Bank Plaza, South Tower
PO Box 63, Suite 2300
Toronto, Ontario
M5J 2J2
Tel: +1 416 3627485

500, boul. René-Lévesque Ouest
Bureau 1605
Montréal (Québec)
H2Z 1W7
Tel: +1 514 8780009

Tassé & Associates Ltd
630, boul. René-Lévesque Ouest
Bureau 1200
Montréal (Québec)
H3B 1S6
Tel: +1 514 8792100

TD Securities Inc
Toronto Dominion Bank Tower
Toronto Dominion Centre
18th Floor
PO Box 100
Toronto, Ontario
M5K 1A2
Tel: +1 416 9827800

500, rue St-Jacques
7e étage
Montréal (Québec)
H2Y 1S1
Tel: +1 514 2890407

Thomson Kernaghan & Co Ltd
365 Bay Street
2nd Floor
Toronto, Ontario
M5H 2V2
Tel: +1 416 8608800

500, boul. René-Lévesque Ouest
Bureau 1501
Montréal (Québec)
H2Z 1W7
Tel: +1 514 3931144

Versus Brokerage Services Inc
BCE Place
181 Bay Street
Suite 3810
PO Box 751
Toronto, Ontario
M5J 2T9
Tel: +1 416 2141960

WD Latimer Co Ltd
Toronto Dominion Centre
PO Box 96
Toronto, Ontario
M5K 1G8
Tel: +1 416 3635631

Tour de la Bourse
800, Square Victoria,
Niveau Mezzanine, CP 174
Montréal (Québec)
H4Z 1C8
Tel: +1 514 8734359

Whalen, Béllveau & Associates Inc
1010, rue Sherbrooke Ouest
Bureau 600
Montréal (Québec)
H3A 2R7
Tel: +1 514 8445443

Yamaichi International (Canada) Ltd
600, boul. de Maisonneuve Ouest
Bureau 2900
Montréal (Québec)
H3A 3J2
Tel: +1 514 4991110

Yorkton Securities Inc
Stock Exchange Tower
2 First Canadian Place
Suite 3640
PO Box 379
Toronto, Ontario
M5X 1J8
Tel: +1 416 8643500

Electronic Access Members

Dariar, Hentsch (Canada) Inc
Desauiniers, André
Transatlantic Securities Co

Individual Members

Brunet, Jacques
Costa, Remo
Scott, John

Jitney Members

Casey, Gerald P.
Cavanagh, Frank

Montréal Exchange

Members

AIS Securities
250 Bloor Street East
Suite 301
Toronto, Ontario
M4W 1E6
Tel: +1 416 9252512
Fax: +1 416 9255352

Beacon Securities Ltd
1707 Grafton Street
Halifax, Nova Scotia
B3J 2C6
Tel: +1 902 4231260
Fax: +1 902 4255237

BLC Rousseau Inc
Tour de la Banque Laurentienne
1981, avenue McGill College
Bureau 1985
Montréal, Québec
H3A 3K3
Tel: +1 514 2845333
Fax: +1 514 2846224

Brockhouse & Cooper Inc
1250 boulevard René-Lévesque Ouest
Bureau 4015
Montréal, Québec
H3B 4W8
Tel: +1 514 9327171
Fax: +1 514 9328288

Bunting Warburg Inc
BCE Place
161 Bay Street
Suite 4100, PO Box 617
Toronto, Ontario
M5J 2S1
Tel: +1 416 3643293
Fax: +1 416 3641221

BZW Canada Ltd
Royal Bank Plaza
304 Bay Street
Toronto, Ontario
M5H 2P2
Tel: +1 416 3503200
Fax: +1 416 3503201

CM Oliver & Co Ltd
750 West Pender Street
2nd Floor
Vancouver, British Columbia
V6C 1B5
Tel: +1 604 6686700
Fax: +1 604 6818964

Canaccord Caoital Corporation
PO Box 10337, Pacific Centre
2200–609 Granville Street
Vancouver, British Columbia
V7Y 1H2
Tel: +1 604 6437300
Fax: +1 604 6437606

Casgrain & Co Ltd
500 boulevard René-Lévesque Ouest
Bureau 1625
Montréal, Québec
H2Z 1W7
Tel: +1 514 8718080
Fax: +1 514 8711943

Chouinard, McNamara Inc
1100 boulevard René-Lévesque Ouest
Bureau 1300
Montréal, Québec
H3B 4N4
Tel: +1 514 3933430
Fax: +1 514 3931110

Commission Direct Inc
121 King Street West
PO Box 11, Suite 1010
Toronto, Ontario
M5H 3T9
Tel: +1 416 9415622
Fax: +1 416 9415626

Credifinance Securities Ltd
130 Adelaide Street West
Suite 3303
Toronto, Ontario
M5H 3P5
Tel: +1 416 5040159
Fax: +1 416 3641522

CS First Boston (Canada) Inc
121 King Street West
Suite 2500, PO Box 11
Toronto, Ontario
M5H 3T9
Tel: +1 416 9472600
Fax: +1 416 9472695

CT Securities International Inc
70 York Street
Suite 950
Toronto, Ontario
M5G 1S9
Tel: +1 416 9477200
Fax: +1 416 9477213

CT Securities Services Inc
70 York Street
8th Floor
Toronto, Ontario
M5J 1S9
Tel: +1 416 9815000
Fax: +1 416 9477190

CTI Capital Inc
1 Place Ville-Marie
Bureau 1635
Montréal, Québec
H3B 2B6
Tel: +1 514 8613500
Fax: +1 514 8613230

D&B International Securities Inc
1115 rue Sherbrooke Ouest
Bureau 1702
Montréal, Québec
H3A 1H3
Tel: +1 514 8424111
Fax: +1 514 8423600

Demers Conseil Inc
615 boulevard René-Lévesque Ouest
Bureau 1120
Montréal, Québec
H3B 1P5
Tel: +1 514 8791702
Fax: +1 514 8795977

Desjardins Securities Inc
2 Complexe Desjardins
Tour de lEst, 15e étage
Casier Postal, 394, Succursale Desjardins
Montréal, Québec
H5B 1J2
Tel: +1 514 9871749
Fax: +1 514 8423137

DFI Securities Inc
150 York Street
Suite 1814
Toronto, Ontario
M5H 3S5
Tel: +1 416 3627747
Fax: +1 416 3624924

Dlouhy Investments Inc
1350 rue Sherbrooke Ouest
Bureau 1200
Montréal, Québec
H3G 1J1
Tel: +1 514 8458111
Fax: +1 514 8450200

DPM Securities Inc
755 boulevard St Jean
Bureau 602
Pointe Claire, Québec
H9R 5M9
Tel: +1 514 6307500
Fax: +1 514 6307347

Dubeau Capital & Co Ltd
5600 boulevard des Galeries
Bureau 530
Québec, Québec
G2K 2H6
Tel: +1 418 6285533
Fax: +1 418 6287844

Edward D Jones & Co
90 Burnhamthorpe Road West
Suite 902
Mississauga, Ontario
L5B 3C3
Tel: +1 905 2738400
Fax: +1 905 2738424

FCG Securities Corporation
145 King Street West
Suite 2750
Toronto, Ontario
M5H 1J8
Tel: +1 416 3648600
Fax: +1 416 3644812

Fairvest Securities Corporation
8 King Street East
Suite 700
Toronto, Ontario
M5C 1B5
Tel: +1 416 3649000
Fax: +1 416 3646710

Fimat Derivatives Canada Inc
1501 avenue McGill College
Bureau 1800
Montréal, Québec
H3A 3M8
Tel: +1 514 8416200
Fax: +1 514 8416254

First Marathon Securities Ltd
The Stock Exchange Tower
2 First Canadian Place
PO Box 21, Suite 3200
Toronto, Ontario
M5X 1J9
Tel: +1 416 8693707
Fax: +1 416 8690089

Fortune Financial Corporation
One Corporation Plaza
2075 Kennedy Road
Suite 608
Scarborough, Ontario
M1T 3V3
Tel: +1 416 2914400
Fax: +1 416 2914457

Friedberg Mercantile Group
BCE Place
181 Bay Street
Suite 250, PO Box 866
Toronto, Ontario
M5J 2T3
Tel: +1 416 3642700
Fax: +1 416 3645385

Georgia Pacific Securities Corporation
Two Bentall Centre
555 Burrard Street
16th Floor
Vancouver, British Columbia
V7X 1S6
Tel: +1 604 6681800
Fax: +1 604 6681816

Goepel Shields & Partners Inc
701 West Georgia Street
Suite 1400
Pacific Centre, PO Box 10111
Vancouver, British Columbia
V7Y 1C6
Tel: +1 604 6611777
Fax: +1 604 6840485

Golden Capital Securities Ltd
1177 West Hastings Street
Suite 168
Vancouver, British Columbia
V6E 2K3
Tel: +1 604 6881898
Fax: +1 604 6828874

Goldman Sachs Canada
150 West King Street
Suite 1201
Toronto, Ontario
M5H 1J9
Tel: +1 416 3438900
Fax: +1 416 5938506

Gordon Capital Corporation
Toronto-Dominion Centre
Suite 5300, PO Box 67
Toronto, Ontario
M5K 1E7
Tel: +1 416 3649393
Fax: +1 416 8686730

Great Pacific Management Co Ltd
1125 Howe Street
4th Floor
Vancouver, British Columbia
V6Z 2K8
Tel: +1 604 6691143
Fax: +1 604 6690210

Green Line Investor Services Inc
17th Floor, Royal Trust Tower
PO Box 1, Toronto-Dominion Centre
Toronto, Ontario
M5K 1A2
Tel: +1 416 9827800
Fax: +1 416 9824180

Groupe Option Retraite Inc
455 rue Saint-Antoine Ouest
Bureau 201
Montréal, Québec
H2Z 1J1
Tel: +1 514 8610777
Fax: +1 514 8611976

James Capel Canada Inc
One Financial Place
1 Adelaide Street East
Suite 2400
Toronto, Ontario
M5C 2V9
Tel: +1 416 9472700
Fax: +1 416 9472730

John Pasztor & Associates Inc
19 Shorncliffe Avenue
Toronto, Ontario
M4V 1S9
Tel: +1 416 9221326
Fax: +1 416 9221110

Lafferty, Harwood & Partners Ltd
2020, rue University
Bureau 1920
Montréal, Québec
H3A 2A5
Tel: +1 514 2877306
Fax: +1 514 2877123

Leduc & Associés Valeurs Mobilières Inc
2020 rue University
Bureau 2300
Montréal, Québec
H3A 2A5
Tel: +1 514 4991066
Fax: +1 514 4991071

Levesque Beaubien Geoffrion Inc
Édifice Sun Life
1155 rue Metcalf, 5e étage
Montréal, Québec
H3B 4S9
Tel: +1 514 8792222
Fax: +1 514 8795142

Loewen, Ondaatje, McCutcheon Ltd
Hazelton Lanes, East Tower
55 Avenue Road
Suite 2250
Toronto, Ontario
M5R 3L2
Tel: +1 416 9644455
Fax: +1 416 9644490

MacDougall, MacDougall & MacTier Inc
Place du Canada
Bureau 2000
Montréal, Québec
H3B 4J1
Tel: +1 514 3943000
Fax: +1 514 8711481

MacDougall, Meyer Inc
2050 rue Mansfield
Bureau 1500
Montréal, Québec
H3A 1Y9
Tel: +1 514 2888823
Fax: +1 514 2883272

Maison Placements Canada Inc
Place du Canada
Bureau 2300
Montréal, Québec
H3B 2N2
Tel: +1 514 8791662
Fax: +1 514 8791673

Marleau, Lemire Securities Inc
1 Place Ville-Marie
Bureau 3601
Montréal, Québec
H3B 3P2
Tel: +1 514 8773800
Fax: +1 514 8750398

Maxima Capital Inc
266 rue St-Paul Est
Montréal, Québec
H2Y 1G9
Tel: +1 514 8782525
Fax: +1 514 8782393

McLean McCarthy Inc
Toronto-Dominion Centre
222 Bay Centre
PO Box 64
Toronto, Ontario
M5K 1E7
Tel: +1 416 3625151
Fax: +1 416 3680085

Merit Investment Corporation
55 University Avenue
Suite 1000
Toronto, Ontario
M5J 2P8
Tel: +1 416 8676000
Fax: +1 416 8676137

Merrill Lynch Canada Inc
Merrill Lynch Canada Tower
200 King Street West
Toronto, Ontario
M5H 3W3
Tel: +1 416 5866000
Fax: +1 416 5866076

Midland Walwyn Capital Inc
BCE Place
Bay Wellington Tower
181 Bay Street, Suite 400
Toronto, Ontario
M5J 2V8
Tel: +1 416 3697400
Fax: +1 416 3698172

Morgan Stanley Canada Ltd
181 Bay Street
Suite 3700, PO Box 776
Toronto, Ontario
M5J 2T3
Tel: +1 416 9438400
Fax: +1 416 3680796

National Bank Securities Inc
1100 rue University
7e étage
Montréal, Québec
H3B 2G7
Tel: +1 514 3945000
Fax: +1 514 3945510

Nesbitt Burns Ltd
355 rue St-Jacques Ouest
Montréal, Québec
H2Y 1P1
Tel: +1 514 2825800
Fax: +1 514 2825883

Odlum Brown Ltd
1800–609 Granville Street
PO Box 10012, Pacific Centre
Vancouver, British Columbia
V7Y 1A3
Tel: +1 604 6691600
Fax: +1 604 6818310

Pensec Inc
55 Metcalfe Street
Suite 860
Ottowa, Ontario
K1P 6L5
Tel: +1 613 7245434
Fax: +1 613 2323113

Pictet (Canada) & Co Ltd
1800 avenue McGill College
Bureau 2900
Montréal, Québec
H3A 3J6
Tel: +1 514 2888161
Fax: +1 514 2885473

Pollitt & Co Inc
Commerce Court North
25 King Street West
Suite 1101, PO Box 94
Toronto, Ontario
M5L 1B9
Tel: +1 416 3653313
Fax: +1 416 3680141

RBC Dominion Securities Inc
Commerce Court South
PO Box 21
Toronto, Ontario
M5L 1A7
Tel: +1 416 8644000
Fax: +1 416 8648816

Refco Futures (Canada) Ltd
Canada Trust Tower
BCE Place
161 Bay Street
Suite 3630
Toronto, Ontario
M5J 2S1
Tel: +1 416 8627000
Fax: +1 416 8620576

Research Capital Corporation
Ernst & Young Tower
Suite 1500, Toronto-Dominion Centre
PO Box 265
Toronto, Ontario
M5K 1J5
Tel: +1 416 8607600
Fax: +1 416 8607674

Richardson Greenshields of Canada Ltd
One Lombard Place
Winnipeg, Manitoba
R3B 0Y2
Tel: +1 204 9345858
Fax: +1 204 9345875

Sanwa McCarthy Securities Ltd
55 Yonge Street
Suite 1200
Toronto, Ontario
M5E 1J4
Tel: +1 416 8629160
Fax: +1 416 8628053

ScotiaMcLeod Inc
Scotia Plaza
40 King Street West
PO Box 4085, Station A
Toronto, Ontario
M5W 2X6
Tel: +1 416 8637411
Fax: +1 416 8637751

Société Générale Securities Inc
1155 rue University
Bureau 709
Montréal, Québec
H3B 3A7
Tel: +1 514 9542300
Fax: +1 514 8758136

Sprott Securities Ltd
Royal Bank Plaza, South Tower
PO Box 63, Suite 2300
Toronto, Ontario
M5J 2J2
Tel: +1 416 3627485
Fax: +1 416 3620459

Tasse & Associates Ltd
630 boulevard René-Lévesque Ouest
Bureau 1200
Montréal, Québec
H3B 1S6
Tel: +1 514 8792100
Fax: +1 514 8793903

Thompson Kernaghan & Co Ltd
365 Bay Street, 2nd Floor
Toronto, Ontario
M5H 2V2
Tel: +1 416 8608800
Fax: +1 416 3678055

Toronto Dominion Securities inc
Toronto-Dominion Bank Tower, 18th Floor
Toronto-Dominion Centre, PO Box 100
Toronto, Ontario
M5K 1G8
Tel: +1 416 9826160
Fax: +1 416 9826625

Versus Brokerage Services Inc
BCE Place
181 Bay Street
Suite 3810, PO Box 751
Toronto, Ontario
M5J 2T3
Tel: +1 416 2141960
Fax: +1 416 8643918

WD Latimer Co Ltd
PO Box 96
Toronto-Dominion Centre
Toronto, Ontario
M5K 1G8
Tel: +1 416 3635631
Fax: +1 416 3638022

Whalen, Béliveau & Associates Inc
1010 Sherbrooke Ouest
Bureau 600
Montréal, Québec
H3A 2R7
Tel: +1 514 8445443
Fax: +1 514 8445216

Wood Gundy Inc
BCE Place
161 Bay Street, PO Box 500
Toronto, Ontario
M5J 2S8
Tel: +1 416 5947000
Fax: +1 416 5947618

Yamaichi International (Canada) Ltd
600 boulevard de Maisonneuve Ouest
Bureau 2300
Montréal, Québec
H3A 3J2
Tel: +1 514 4991110
Fax: +1 514 4991113

Yorkton Securities Inc
Stock Exchange Tower
Suite 3640, PO Box 379
2 First Canadian Place
Toronto, Ontario
M5X 1J8
Tel: +1 416 8643500
Fax: +1 416 8649134

Toronto Futures Exchange

Futures Commission Merchants

Bunting Warburg Inc
BCE Place, Suite 4100
161 Bay Street
Toronto, Ontario
M5J 2SI
Tel: +1 416 3643293
Fax: +1 416 3541976

Canaccord Capital Corporation
609 Granville Street
Suite 2200
Vancouver, British Columbia
V7Y 1H2
Tel: +1 604 6437300
Fax: +1 604 6437606

CIBC Wood Gundy Securities Inc
BCE Place, PO Box 500
161 Bay Street
Toronto, Ontario
M5J 2S8
Tel: +1 416 5948559
Fax: +1 416 5948796

Derivative Services Inc
372 Bay Street
Suite 1602
Toronto, Ontario
M5H 2WP
Tel: +1 416 9551856
Fax: +1 416 9551854

First Marathon Securities Ltd
2 First Canadian Place
The Exchange Tower, Suite 3100
Toronto, Ontario
M5X 1J9
Tel: +1 416 86 3707
Fax: +1 416 8690089

Friedberg Mercantile Group
BCE Place, 181 Bay Street
Suite 250
Toronto, Ontario
M5J 2T3
Tel: +1 416 3502907
Fax: +1 416 3645385

Goldman Sachs Canada Inc
150 King Street
Suite 1201
Toronto, Ontario
M5H 1S9
Tel: +1 416 3438900
Fax: +1 416 5938506

Gordon Capital Corporation
Suite 5300, PO Box 67
Toronto-Dominion Centre
Toronto, Ontario
M5K 1E7
Tel: +1 416 8685417
Fax: +1 416 8683077

G W Welkin Capital Corporation of Canada
15 Wertheim Court, Suite 312
Richmond Hill, Ontario
L4B 3H7
Tel: +1 905 8860212
Fax: +1 905 8860200

Lévesque Beaubien Geoffrion Inc
1155 Metcalfe Street
Montréal, Québec
H3B 4S9
Tel: +1 514 8792222
Fax: +1 514 8795142

Lévesque Securities Inc
121 King Street West
Suite 600
Toronto, Ontario
M5H 3T9
Tel: +1 416 8657400
Fax: +1 416 8657605

Marleau, Lemire Securities Ltd
1 Place Ville Marie
Suite 3601
Montréal, Québec
H3B 3P2
Tel: +1 514 8773800
Fax: +1 514 8758593

Merrill Lynch Canada Inc
Merrill Lynch Canada Tower
200 King Street West
Toronto, Ontario
M5H 3W3
Tel: +1 416 5866000
Fax: +1 416 5866601

Midland Walwyn Capital Inc
BCE Place, Suite 400
181 Bay Street
Toronto, Ontario
M5J 2V8
Tel: +1 416 3697524
Fax: +1 416 36998778

Morgan Stanley Canada Ltd
181 Bay Street
37th Floor
Toronto, Ontario
M5J 2T3
Tel: +1 416 9438300
Fax: +1 416 9438383

Nesbitt Burns Inc
1 First Canadian Place
3rd Floor Podium
Toronto, Ontario
M5X 1H3
Tel: +1 416 3594717
Fax: +1 416 3594841

Polar Securities Inc
350 Bay Street
13th Floor
Toronto, Ontario
M5H 2S6
Tel: +1 416 3674364
Fax: +1 416 3670564

RBC Dominion Securities Inc
PO Box 21
Commerce Court South
Toronto, Ontario
M5L 1A7
Tel: +1 416 8644000

Refco Futures Canada Ltd
1 First Canadian Place
Suite 4640
Toronto, Ontario
M5X 1H3
Tel: +1 416 8627000
Fax: +1 416 8620576

Richardson Greenshields of Canada Ltd
140 Adelaide Street West
Toronto, Ontario
M5H 1T8
Tel: +1 416 8607529
Fax: +1 416 8603460

ScotiaMcleod Inc
PO Box 433, Commercial Union Tower
Toronto-Dominion Centre
Toronto, Ontario
M5K 1M2
Tel: +1 416 8637511
Fax: +1 416 8623005

Yorkton Securities Inc
Stock Exchange Tower
2 First Canadian Place
Suite 3640, PO Box 379
Toronto, Ontario
M5X 1J8
Tel: +1 416 8643500
Fax: +1 416 8649134

Winnipeg Commodity Exchange

Registered Members

Access Traders Inc
Winnipeg, MB
Tel: +1 204 9430661
Contact: A D Cattani

ADM Agri-Industries Ltd
Windsor, ON
Tel: +1 519 9728100
Fax: +1 519 9690414
Contact: J D McNamara

AgPro Grain Inc
Winnipeg, MB
Tel: +1 204 9422470
Fax: +1 204 9490936
Contact: L Rankin

AgPro Grain Inc
Winnipeg, MB
Tel: +1 204 9422470
Fax: +1 204 9490936
Contact: J Brasier

Alberta Wheat Pool
Winnipeg, MB
Tel: +1 204 9498608
Fax: +1 204 9431709
Contact: J E Mendella

Alberta Wheat Pool
Calgary, AB
Tel: +1 403 2904716
Fax: +1 403 2905555
Contact: B G George

Alberta Wheat Pool
Winnipeg, MB
Tel: +1 204 9498608
Fax: +1 204 9431709
Contact: C M Gosse

Appointed Governor
Winnipeg, MB
Tel: +1 403 7642629
Fax: +1 403 7642629
Contact: K M Motiuk

Appointed Governor
Winnipeg, MB
Tel: +1 204 9343244
Fax: +1 204 9250765
Contact: O Lang

Appointed Governor
Winnipeg, MB
Tel: +1 204 4895551
Fax: +1 204 4895551
Contact: A S Leach

Appointed Governor
Winnipeg, MB
Tel: +1 204 2223758
Fax: +1 204 2220076
Contact: D James

Appointed Governor
Wawota, SK
Tel: +1 306 7392600
Fax: +1 306 7392841
Contact: K Lewis

T C Arhontas
Desplaines, IL
Tel: +1 708 7501589

Benson-Quinn Commodities Inc
Winnipeg, MB
Tel: +1 204 9827949
Fax: +1 204 9428077
Contact: L P S Hooge

Benson-Quinn Commodities Inc
Winnipeg, MB
Tel: +1 204 9827949
Fax: +1 204 9428077
Contact: K Chester

Benson-Quinn Commodities Inc
Minneapolis, MN
Tel: +1 612 3405923
Fax: +1 612 3352960
Contact: L Neumann

Benson-Quinn Commodities Inc
Winnipeg, MB
Tel: +1 204 9827949
Fax: +1 204 9428077
Contact: D B McGregor

Benson-Quinn Commodities Inc
Saskatoon, SK
Tel: +1 306 2423522
Fax: +1 306 2404969
Contact: K Blair

A P Beutel
Winnipeg, MB
Tel: +1 204 9882900
Fax: +1 204 9437957

S E Brand
Nisku, AB
Tel: +1 403 9558850
Fax: +1 403 9552663

H Brownlee
Crystal City, MB
Tel: +1 204 8732288

Bunge of Canada Ltd
Winnipeg, MB
Tel: +1 204 9490066
Fax: +1 204 9490068
Contact: E C Chunick

D A Burneski
Surrey, BC
Tel: +1 604 5975060
Fax: +1 604 5974933

Canada Malting Co Ltd
Winnipeg, MB
Tel: +1 204 9427268
Fax: +1 204 9565320
Contact: J R Tye

Canadian National Railways
Winnipeg, MB
Tel: +1 204 9888251
Fax: +1 204 9888517
Contact: S Mielitz

Canadian Oilseed Processors Assoc
Winnipeg, MB
Tel: +1 204 9569500
Fax: +1 204 9569506
Contact: R J Broeska

CanAmera Foods Ltd
Winnipeg, MB
Tel: +1 204 9251854
Fax: +1 204 7743314
Contact: K Galloway

Canbra Foods Ltd
Lethbridge, AB
Tel: +1 403 3295556
Fax: +1 403 3287933
Contact: L McNamara

Cargill Incorporated
Wayzata, MN
Tel: +1 612 7426081
Fax: +1 612 7426301
Contact: F L Sims

Cargill Investor Services Inc
Chicago, IL
Tel: +1 312 4604000
Fax: +1 312 4604015
Contact: H T Hansen

Cargill Ltd
Winnipeg, MB
Tel: +1 204 9476219
Fax: +1 204 9560995
Contact: S B Benning

Cargill Ltd
Winnipeg, MB
Tel: +1 204 9476212
Fax: +1 204 9476444
Contact: A Bonneteau

Cargill Ltd
Winnipeg, MB
Tel: +1 204 9476209
Fax: +1 204 9476444
Contact: P N Butters

Cargill Ltd
Winnipeg, MB
Tel: +1 204 9476212
Fax: +1 204 9476444
Contact: R J Eyemoto

Cargill Ltd
Winnipeg, MB
Tel: +1 204 9476335
Fax: +1 204 9476444
Contact: M Fouillard

Cargill Ltd
Winnipeg, MB
Tel: +1 204 9476206
Fax: +1 204 9476444
Contact: G Manaigre

Cargill Ltd
Winnipeg, MB
Tel: +1 204 9476207
Fax: +1 204 9476235
Contact: A Marceau

Cargill Ltd
Winnipeg, MB
Tel: +1 204 9476215
Fax: +1 204 9476444
Contact: R E McRae

Cargill Ltd
Winnipeg, MB
Tel: +1 204 9476131
Fax: +1 204 9476444
Contact: P Oswald

Cargill Ltd
Winnipeg, MB
Tel: +1 204 9476254
Fax: +1 204 9476444
Contact: D C Paterson

Cargill Ltd
Winnipeg, MB
Tel: +1 204 9476450
Fax: +1 204 9476235
Contact: P J Rowe

Cargill Ltd
Winnipeg, MB
Tel: +1 204 9470141
Fax: +1 204 9476235
Contact: C Slade

Cargill Ltd
Winnipeg, MB
Tel: +1 204 9476206
Fax: +1 204 9476444
Contact: P Weisshaar

Cargill Ltd
Winnipeg, MB
Tel: +1 204 9476205
Fax: +1 204 9476444
Contact: R Whyte

A Cheveldayoff
Blaine Lake, SK
Tel: +1 306 4972528

R K Cheveldayoff
Blaine Lake, SK
Fax: +1 306 4973314

Chinook Agri Marketing Inc
Didsbury, AB
Tel: +1 403 3353056
Fax: +1 403 3353088
C W Ausenhus

Chinook Agri Marketing Inc
Didsbury, AB
Tel: +1 403 3353056
Fax: +1 403 3353088
Contact: K Blakely

CIBC Wood Gundy Securities Inc
Winnipeg, MB
Tel: +1 416 5947000
Fax: +1 416 5948237
Contact: P McLernon

Co-op Atlantic
Winnipeg, MB
Tel: +1 204 9438565
Fax: +1 204 9422603
Contact: L Miller

ConAgra Grain, Canada (A division of ConAgra Ltd)
Winnipeg, MB
Tel: +1 204 9425550
Fax: +1 204 9434012
Contact: M M Schmidt

Continental Grain Co (Canada) Ltd
Vancouver, BC
Tel: +1 604 6847292
Fax: +1 604 6848031
Contact: G W McClintock

Continental Grain Co (Canada) Ltd
Winnipeg, MB
Tel: +1 204 9425181
Fax: +1 204 9434492
Contact: R J McNab

Continental Grain Co (Canada) Ltd
Winnipeg, MB
Tel: +1 204 9425181
Fax: +1 204 9434492
Contact: G S Kostal

Continental Grain Co (Canada) Ltd
Winnipeg, MB
Tel: +1 204 9425181
Fax: +1 204 9434492
Contact: D G Drolet

Coopérative Fédérée De Québec
Montreal, QB
Tel: +1 514 8582667
Fax: +1 514 3840511
Contact: P L S Lauzier

W J Craddock
Winnipeg, MB
Tel: +1 204 9430661

daex Commodities Inc
Winnipeg, MB
Tel: +1 204 9491777
Fax: +1 204 4880120
Contact: D Eschmann

daex Commodities Inc
Winnipeg, MB
Tel: +1 204 9491777
Fax: +1 204 4880120
Contact: V I Eschmann

P Dagenals
Ste-Rosalie, QB
Tel: +1 514 7995550
Fax: +1 514 7991106

J B Degeus
Winnipeg, MB
Tel: +1 204 2539071

Delta Asia Credit Ltd
Hong Kong
Tel: +1 852 25330800
Fax: +1 852 28104495
S C K Au

J C DePape
Winnipeg, MB
Tel: +1 204 4893244

Dominion Malting Ltd
Winnipeg, MB
Tel: +1 204 9430741
Fax: +1 204 9476791
Contact: J Venn

Don Stewart Grain Ltd
Winnipeg, MB
Tel: +1 204 9430661
Contact: D C Stewart

M Dorchak
Winnipeg, MB
Tel: +1 204 9430661

Dreman & Co Ltd
Winnipeg, MB
Tel: +1 204 9430691
Contact: I J Dreman

J C Dunn
Winnipeg, MB
Tel: +1 204 8325643

J L Duvenaud
Winnipeg, MB
Tel: +1 204 9421459
Fax: +1 204 9427652

K D Eidse
Morris, MB
Tel: +1 204 7468182

R Eikanger
Pierson, MB
Tel: +1 204 6342319

S Farkas
Winnipeg, MB
Tel: +1 204 3390690

FIMAT Derivatives Canada, Inc
Montreal, QB
Tel: +1 514 8416200
Fax: +1 514 8416254
Contact: J P Gallardo

T A Fjeldsted
Winnipeg, MB
Tel: +1 204 9445164
Fax: +1 204 9438347

Flaherty Grain Co Ltd
Winnipeg, MB
Tel: +1 204 9491343
Fax: +1 204 9470076
Contact: B Flaherty

G F Florentine
Winnipeg, MB
Tel: +1 204 9430661

R C Fugle
Winnipeg, MB
Tel: +1 204 9430661

B E Futz
Winnipeg, MB
Tel: +1 204 9430661

Gallie Grain Ltd
Winnipeg, MB
Tel: +1 204 9432516
Contact: A D Gallie

Gallie Grain Ltd
Winnipeg, MB
Tel: +1 204 9432516
Contact: D J Gallie

Geldermann Inc
Chicago, IL
Tel: +1 312 6637500
Fax: +1 312 6637710
Contact: J R Curley

M A Girardin
Winnipeg, MB
Tel: +1 204 9425528
Fax: +1 204 9475160

A Grande
Winnipeg, MB
Tel: +1 204 9430661

C L Grapentine
Winnipeg, MB
Tel: +1 204 9471285

H Green
Anchorage, AL
Tel: +1 907 2762054
Fax: +1 907 5629433

S Griffith
Winnipeg, MB
Tel: +1 204 9430661

Hantec Futures Ltd
Hong Kong
Tel: +1 852 28159060
Fax: +1 852 28518601
Contact: K M Wong

R W Harden
Winnipeg, MB
Tel: +1 204 9853030
Fax: +1 204 9853106

B Hayles
Winnipeg, MB
Tel: +1 204 9425153
Fax: +1 204 9472816

B K Heiman
Winnipeg, MB
Tel: +1 204 9430661

HSBC James Capel Asia Derivatives Ltd
Hong Kong
Tel: +1 852 28439111
Fax: +1 852 28107673
Contact: I R Martin

Itochu Int Inc
New York, NY
Tel: +1 212 8188310
Fax: +1 212 8188328
Contact: T Konishi

H Kuhl
Bagot, MB
Tel: +1 204 2742467
Fax: +1 204 2742204

Lake Shippers' Clearance Assoc
Winnipeg, MB
Tel: +1 204 9422424
Fax: +1 204 9473740
Contact: R W MacDonald

T K C Lau
North York, ON
Tel: +1 416 3913329
Fax: +1 416 3914930

Lévesque Securities Inc
Montreal, QB
Tel: +1 514 8795346
Fax: +1 514 8795321
Contact: G Normandin

LFG, LLC
Winnipeg, MB
Tel: +1 204 9889712
Fax: +1 204 9567670
Contact: R Dzisiak

LFG, LLC
Winnipeg, MB
Tel: +1 204 9889710
Fax: +1 204 9889718
Contact: P E Erickson

LFG, LLC
Winnipeg, MB
Tel: +1 204 9889710
Fax: +1 204 9567670
Contact: L Gwyllt

Linear Grain Inc
Carman, MB
Tel: +1 204 7456747
Fax: +1 204 7456573
Contact: R McKnight

Louis Dreyfus Canada Ltd
Winnipeg, MB
Tel: +1 204 9433546
Fax: +1 204 9441307
Contact: J M Anderson

Louis Dreyfus Canada Ltd
Winnipeg, MB
Tel: +1 204 9433546
Fax: +1 204 9441307
Contact: D Shannon

Louis Dreyfus Canada Ltd
Winnipeg, MB
Tel: +1 204 9433546
Fax: +1 204 9441307
Contact: A P Temple

A Lum
Winnipeg, MB
Tel: +1 204 9476627

Malchy Grain Co Ltd
Winnipeg, MB
Tel: +1 204 9449328
Fax: +1 204 9472271
Contact: B Grushko

Manitoba Pool Elevators
Winnipeg, MB
Tel: +1 204 9340522
Fax: +1 204 9340451
Contact: R C Bradbury

Manitoba Pool Elevators
Winnipeg, MB
Tel: +1 204 9471171
Fax: +1 204 9420570
Contact: M Davey

Manitoba Pool Elevators
Winnipeg, MB
Tel: +1 204 9471171
Fax: +1 204 9420570
Contact: R F V Green

Manitoba Pool Elevators
Winnipeg, MB
Tel: +1 204 9471171
Fax: +1 204 9420570
Contact: D W Hunter

Manitoba Pool Elevators
Winnipeg, MB
Tel: +1 204 9471171
Fax: +1 204 9420570
Contact: L R Karnafel

Marubeni America Corporation
New York, NY
Tel: +1 212 4500585
Fax: +1 212 4500773
Contact: H Tamai

L Megaw
Winnipeg, MB
Tel: +1 204 9852427

Merrill Lynch Canada Inc
Toronto, ON
Tel: +1 416 5866417
Fax: +1 416 5866616
Contact: G B Dunn

MHS Futures Ltd
Hong Kong
Tel: +1 852 28431431
Fax: +1 852 28451841
Contact: C Broadhurst

Midland Walwyn Capital Inc
Toronto, ON
Tel: +1 416 3697400
Fax: +1 416 3697438
Contact: B J Geisler

Midland Walwyn Capital Inc
Winnipeg, MB
Tel: +1 204 9420311
Fax: +1 204 9432350
Contact: J Oneschuk

Midland Walwyn Capital Inc
Winnipeg, MB
Tel: +1 204 9420311
Fax: +1 204 9432350
Contact: W L Stebbe

Midland Walwyn Capital Inc
Winnipeg, MB
Tel: +1 204 9433729
Fax: +1 204 9432350
Contact: D J Tougher

Milsul & Co (Canada) Ltd
Vancouver, BC
Tel: +1 604 3313162
Fax: +1 604 3313129
Contact: Y Muramatsu

L M Mistelbacher
Winnipeg, MB
Tel: +1 204 9881700
Fax: +1 204 2350954

Mitsubishi Canada Ltd
Vancouver, BC
Tel: +1 604 6548000
Fax: +1 604 6548228
Contact: K Nakaso

Morgan Stanley Futures (Hong Kong) Ltd
Hong Kong
Tel: +1 852 28485200
Fax: +1 852 28451012
Contact: N A Shear

Morrow Inc, AR
Winnipeg, MB
Tel: +1 204 9438579
Fax: +1 204 9430575
Contact: A R Morrow

A D Muggaberg
Winnipeg, MB
Tel: +1 204 9430661

J Murphy
Winnipeg, MB
Tel: +1 204 9884071
Fax: +1 204 9422822

T Naber
Melfort, SK
Tel: +1 306 7524115
Fax: +1 306 7522909

Nesbitt Burns Inc
Winnipeg, MB
Tel: +1 204 9471501
Fax: +1 204 9449562
Contact: T D A Waitt

Northern Sales Co Ltd
Winnipeg, MB
Tel: +1 204 9491456
Fax: +1 204 9570350
Contact: J P Middagh

Northern Sales Co, Ltd
Winnipeg, MB
Tel: +1 204 9491456
Fax: +1 204 9570350
Contact: J M Schindle

Northern Sales Co, Ltd
Winnipeg, MB
Tel: +1 204 9491456
Fax: +1 204 9570350
Contact: C E Swartz

Northern Sales Co, Ltd
Winnipeg, MB
Tel: +1 204 9496270
Fax: +1 204 9570350
Contact: K E Swartz

PaineWebber Inc
Chicago, IL
Tel: +1 312 6836153
Fax: +1 312 6836177
Contact: W A Kizka

Palliser Commodities Corp
Winnipeg, MB
Tel: +1 403 2505020
Fax: +1 403 2505041
Contact: J R Harriman

Palliser Grain Co Ltd
Winnipeg, MB
Tel: +1 403 2914450
Fax: +1 403 2501739
Contact: J R Harriman

Palmer Grain Ltd
Winnipeg, MB
Tel: +1 204 9421999
Contact: W Palmer

Parrish & Heimbecker Ltd
Winnipeg, MB
Tel: +1 204 9562030
Fax: +1 204 9438233
Contact: J W Astwood

Parrish & Heimbecker Ltd
Winnipeg, MB
Tel: +1 204 9562030
Fax: +1 204 9438233
Contact: R Baldwin

Parrish & Heimbecker, Ltd
Toronto, ON
Tel: +1 416 3630431
Fax: +1 416 3637957
Contact: H C Heimbecker

Parrish & Heimbecker Ltd
Winnipeg, MB
Tel: +1 204 9562030
Fax: +1 204 9438233
Contact: J Heimbecker

Parrish & Heimbecker Ltd
Winnipeg, MB
Tel: +1 204 9542030
Fax: +1 204 9438233
Contact: W B Parrish

Parrish & Heimbecker Ltd
Winnipeg, MB
Tel: +1 204 9562030
Fax: +1 204 9438233
Contact: W S Parrish

Paterson & Sons Ltd, NM
Winnipeg, MB
Tel: +1 204 9562090
Fax: +1 204 9472386
Contact: K Bruch

Paterson & Sons Ltd, NM
Winnipeg, MB
Tel: +1 204 9562090
Fax: +1 204 9475158
Contact: D Couldwell

Paterson & Sons Ltd, NM
Winnipeg, MB
Tel: +1 204 9562090
Fax: +1 204 9472386
Contact: D Koskie

Paterson & Sons Ltd, NM
Winnipeg, MB
Tel: +1 204 9562090
Fax: +1 204 9472386
Contact: A B Paterson

Paterson & Sons Ltd, NM
Winnipeg, MB
Tel: +1 204 9562090
Fax: +1 204 9472386
Contact: D S Paterson

Peace Town Futures Ltd
Hong Kong
Tel: +1 852 28228338
Fax: +1 852 28770133
Contact: S Chan

Pioneer Grain Co Ltd
Winnipeg, MB
Tel: +1 204 9345660
Fax: +1 204 9575614
Contact: A Anderson

Pioneer Grain Co Ltd
Winnipeg, MB
Tel: +1 204 9345223
Fax: +1 204 9575614
Contact: C Bredin

Pioneer Grain Co Ltd
Winnipeg, MB
Tel: +1 204 9345961
Fax: +1 204 9575614
Contact: J R Hamilton

Pioneer Grain Co Ltd
Winnipeg, MB
Tel: +1 204 9345961
Fax: +1 204 9575614
Contact: P Koltek

Pioneer Grain Co Ltd
Winnipeg, MB
Tel: +1 204 9345963
Fax: +1 204 9575614
Contact: J W Rea

Pioneer Grain Co Ltd
Winnipeg, MB
Tel: +1 204 9345961
Fax: +1 204 9430942
Contact: C R Vossen

Pioneer Grain Terminal Ltd
Winnipeg, MB
Tel: +1 204 9345657
Fax: +1 204 9575614
Contact: R J Miles

Pool Commodity Trading Service
Winnipeg, MB
Tel: +1 204 9494643
Fax: +1 204 9424167
Contact: S P Bloss

Pool Commodity Trading Service
Winnipeg, MB
Tel: +1 204 9494515
Fax: +1 204 9424167
Contact: K Ferley

Pool Commodity Trading Service
Winnipeg, MB
Tel: +1 204 9494644
Fax: +1 204 9491057
Contact: T Tryhuk

D A Purves
Vancouver, BC
Tel: +1 604 2616369

R P Purves
Winnipeg, MB
Tel: +1 204 9427457
Fax: +1 204 9427458

Quantum Financial Services (Canada) Ltd
Vancouver, BC
Tel: +1 604 8211933
Fax: +1 604 8211911
Contact: J M S Ho

Range Grain Co Ltd
Winnipeg, MB
Tel: +1 204 9436407
Fax: +1 204 9470677
Contact: D Metraux

RBC Dominion Securities Inc
Winnipeg, MB
Tel: +1 204 9822632
Fax: +1 204 9475213
Contact: E A McLaughlin

Refco Futures (Canada) Ltd
Toronto, ON
Tel: +1 416 8627000
Fax: +1 416 8620576
Contact: P Gloutney

D W Reimann
Winnipeg, MB
Tel: +1 204 9430661

Richardson & Sons Ltd, James
Winnipeg, MB
Tel: +1 204 9345811
Fax: +1 204 9426339
Contact: D W Champion

Richardson & Sons Ltd, James
Winnipeg, MB
Tel: +1 204 9345690
Fax: +1 204 9560287
Contact: D Fisher

Richardson & Sons Ltd, James
Winnipeg, MB
Tel: +1 204 9345623
Fax: +1 204 9436065
Contact: T James

Richardson & Sons Ltd, James
Winnipeg, MB
Tel: +1 204 9345627
Fax: +1 204 9560287
Contact: D G Kerr

Richardson & Sons Ltd, James
Winnipeg, MB
Tel: +1 204 9345933
Fax: +1 204 9560287
Contact: G T Richardson

Richardson & Sons Ltd, James
Winnipeg, MB
Tel: +1 204 9345933
Fax: +1 204 9560287
Contact: R Tkatchuk

Richardson Greenshields of Canada Ltd
Winnipeg, MB
Tel: +1 204 9345941
Fax: +1 204 9570141
Contact: H A Benham

Richardson Greenshields of Canada Ltd
Winnipeg, MB
Tel: +1 204 9345933
Fax: +1 204 9570139
Contact: R J W Bradley

Richardson Greenshields of Canada Ltd
Winnipeg, MB
Tel: +1 204 9345531
Fax: +1 204 9345875
Contact: K A Debus

Richardson Greenshields of Canada Ltd
Winnipeg, MB
Tel: +1 204 9345722
Fax: +1 204 9345875
Contact: K Dyer

Richardson Greenshields of Canada Ltd
Winnipeg, MB
Tel: +1 204 9345835
Fax: +1 204 9570141
Contact: P S Gerstein

Richardson Greenshields of Canada Ltd
Winnipeg, MB
Tel: +1 204 9345835
Fax: +1 204 9345875
Contact: A R Hargest

Richardson Greenshields of Canada Ltd
Winnipeg, MB
Tel: +1 204 9345698
Fax: +1 204 9345875
Contact: M D Mestdagh

Richardson Greenshields of Canada Ltd
Winnipeg, MB
Tel: +1 204 9345149
Fax: +1 204 9570139
Contact: R D Pujo

Richardson Greenshields of Canada Ltd
Winnipeg, MB
Tel: +1 204 9345835
Fax: +1 204 9345875
Contact: D C Turk

Richardson Greenshields of Canada Ltd
Winnipeg, MB
Tel: +1 204 9345698
Fax: +1 204 9570139
Contact: R A Wiebe

Richardson Terminals Ltd
Winnipeg, MB
Tel: +1 204 9345712
Fax: +1 204 9436065
Contact: W Fox

Richardson Terminals Ltd
Winnipeg, MB
Tel: +1 204 9345107
Fax: +1 204 9436065
Contact: A J Weir

P V Riese
Lockport, MB
Tel: +1 204 4824941

R Ripstein
Winnipeg, MB
Tel: +1 204 9433946

Roberts Grain Inc
Winnipeg, MB
Tel: +1 204 9430654
Fax: +1 204 9560282
Contact: D K Roberts

R G Rogers
Winnipeg, MB
Tel: +1 204 2695546

R L Russell
Winnipeg, MB
Tel: +1 204 9438714

Saskatchewan Wheat Pool
Winnipeg, MB
Tel: +1 204 9881308
Fax: +1 204 9472777
Contact: W Taylor

Saskatchewan Wheat Pool
Winnipeg, MB
Tel: +1 204 9881306
Fax: +1 204 9472777
Contact: R Teffaine

Saskatchewan Wheat Pool
Winnipeg, MB
Tel: +1 204 9881307
Fax: +1 204 9472777
Contact: G J Walters

Saskatchewan Wheat Pool
Winnipeg, MB
Tel: +1 294 9881300
Fax: +1 204 9881318
Contact: R Wansbutter

ScotiaMcLeod Inc
Winnipeg, MB
Tel: +1 204 9469222
Fax: +1 204 9469236
Contact: R Gigiel

ScotiaMcLeod Inc
Winnipeg, MB
Tel: +1 204 9440025
Fax: +1 204 9469236
Contact: H W Hanec

ScotiaMcLeod Inc
Toronto, ON
Tel: +1 416 8637411
Fax: +1 416 8623132
Contact: W C Kennedy

Seapower Forex Ltd
Hong Kong
Tel: +1 852 28474888
Fax: +1 852 28681911
Contact: K L Siu

N R Shodine
Winnipeg, MB
Tel: +1 204 9430661

F V Siemens
Winnipeg, MB
Tel: +1 204 9255001;
204 9255002
Fax: +1 204 9435448

Smith Barney Inc
New York, NY
Tel: +1 212 7235600
Fax: +1 212 7238991
Contact: B P Pinchichero

E Sochaski
Winnipeg, MB
Tel: +1 204 9889726

G E Sproule
Winnipeg, MB
Tel: +1 204 9430661

K Stiwich
Manitou, MB
Tel: +1 204 2422658

M E Thompson
Chicago, IL
Tel: +1 312 8555272
Fax: +1 312 4274489

Toefer (Canada) Ltd, Alfred C
Winnipeg, MB
Tel: +1 204 9250468
Fax: +1 204 9560282
Contact: C E Pauls

Toepfer (Canada) Ltd, Alfred C
Winnipeg, MB
Tel: +1 204 9250471
Fax: +1 204 9560282
Contact: L R Yaklelashek

United Grain Growers Ltd
Winnipeg, MB
Tel: +1 204 9445632
Fax: +1 204 9471779
Contact: B Anderson

United Grain Growers Ltd
Winnipeg, MB
Tel: +1 204 9445690
Fax: +1 204 9471779
Contact: D Bellisario

United Grain Growers Ltd
Winnipeg, MB
Tel: +1 204 9445421
Fax: +1 204 9471779
Contact: B E Fowler

United Grain Growers Ltd
Winnipeg, MB
Tel: +1 204 9445406;
204 9445411
Fax: +1 204 9445415
Contact: B Hayward

United Grain Growers Ltd
Winnipeg, MB
Tel: +1 204 9445725
Fax: +1 204 9471779
Contact: D R Hilderman

United Grain Growers Ltd
Winnipeg, MB
Tel: +1 204 9445522
Fax: +1 204 9471779
Contact: W E Hill

United Grain Growers Ltd
Winnipeg, MB
Tel: +1 204 9445411
Fax: +1 204 9471779
Contact: C W Hunnie

United Grain Growers Ltd
Winnipeg, MB
Tel: +1 204 9445411
Fax: +1 204 9471779
Contact: T Letkeman

United Grain Growers Ltd
Winnipeg, MB
Tel: +1 204 9445411
Fax: +1 204 9445454
Contact: I R Luff

United Grain Growers Ltd
Winnipeg, MB
Tel: +1 204 9445411
Fax: +1 204 9471779
Contact: S M MacKay

United Grain Growers Ltd
Winnipeg, MB
Tel: +1 204 9449393;
204 9255050
Fax: +1 204 9441124
Contact: D R McLaughlin

United Grain Growers Ltd
Winnipeg, MB
Tel: +1 204 9445405
Fax: +1 204 9471779
Contact: D R Parsons

United Grain Growers Ltd
Winnipeg, MB
Tel: +1 204 9445411
Fax: +1 204 9471779
Contact: J P Rowan

United Grain Growers Ltd
Winnipeg, MB
Tel: +1 204 9445411
Fax: +1 204 9471779
Contact: G Tougher

United Grain Growers Ltd
Winnipeg, MB
Tel: +1 204 9445404
Fax: +1 204 9471779
Contact: B G Troup

United Grain Growers Ltd
Calgary, AB
Tel: +1 403 9743680
Fax: +1 403 9743655
Contact: B E Vannan

Wardley Futures Ltd
Winnipeg, MB
Tel: +1 852 25211661
Fax: +1 852 28100145
Contact: D T Y Shang

Weyburn Inland Terminal Ltd
Weyburn, SK
Tel: +1 306 8427436
Fax: +1 306 8420303
Contact: S B McCormick

Winnipeg Commodity Clearing Ltd
Winnipeg, MB
Tel: +1 204 9426936
Fax: +1 204 9440319
Contact: R D Willerton

R A Wright
Winnipeg, MB
Tel: +1 204 9430661
Fax: +1 204 6544251

XCAN Grain Pool Ltd
Winnipeg, MB
Tel: +1 204 9494500
Fax: +1 204 9491057
Contact: B G Clunie

XCAN Grain Pool Ltd
Winnipeg, MB
Tel: +1 204 9494500
Fax: +1 204 9491057
Contact: K DeGroot

XCAN Grain Pool Ltd
Winnipeg, MB
Tel: +1 204 9494500
Fax: +1 204 9491057
Contact: V Janzen

XCAN Grain Pool Ltd
Winnipeg, MB
Tel: +1 204 9494681
Fax: +1 204 9491057
Contact: B Litke

XCAN Grain Pool Ltd
Winnipeg, MB
Tel: +1 204 9491388
Fax: +1 204 9491057
Contact: P G Lloyd

XCAN Grain Pool Ltd
Winnipeg, MB
Tel: +1 204 9494500
Fax: +1 204 9491057
Contact: K L Matchett

XCAN Grain Pool Ltd
Winnipeg, MB
Tel: +1 204 9494500
Fax: +1 204 9491057
Contact: M W Miller

XCAN Grain Pool Ltd
Winnipeg, MB
Tel: +1 204 9494500
Fax: +1 204 9491057
Contact: C J Paul

XCAN Grain Pool Ltd
Winnipeg, MB
Tel: +1 204 9494522
Fax: +1 204 9491057
Contact: M L Wilson

R Zimmerman
Winnipeg, MB
Tel: +1 204 2539945

Registered Companies

ADM Agri-Industries Ltd
5550 Maplewood Drive
PO Box 7128
Windsor, Ontario
N9C 4G9
Tel: +1 519 9728100
Fax: +1 519 9690414
Contact: J D McNamara

Access Traders Inc
Suite 470 – 360 Main Street
Winnipeg, Manitoba
R3C 3Z4
Tel: +1 204 9430661
Contact: A D Cattani

AgPro Grain Inc
Suite 1504 – 201 Portage Ave
Winnipeg, Manitoba
R3B 3K6
Tel: +1 204 9422470
Fax: +1 204 9490936
Contact: L Rankin

Alberta Wheat Pool
Suite 1010 – 220 Portage Ave
Winnipeg, Manitoba
R3C 0A5
Tel: +1 204 9498605
Fax: +1 204 9431709
Contact: B G George

Benson-Quinn Commodities Inc
Suite 970 – 360 Main Street
Winnipeg, Manitoba
R3C 3Z4
Tel: +1 204 9829749
Fax: +1 204 9428077
Contact: L Neumann

Bunge of Canada Ltd/Bunge du Canada Ltée
Suite 812 – 167 Lombard Ave
Winnipeg, Manitoba
R3B 0V3
Tel: +1 204 9490066
Fax: +1 204 9490068
Contact: E C Chunick

CIBC Wood Gundy Securities Inc
161 Bay Street
PO Box 500
BCE Place
Toronto, Ontario
M5J 2S8
Tel: +1 416 5947000
Fax: +1 416 5947067
Contact: P McLernon

Canada Malting Co Ltd
Suite 2080 – 360 Main Street
Winnipeg, Manitoba
R3C 3Z3
Tel: +1 204 9427268
Fax: +1 204 9565320
Contact: J R Tye

Canadian National Railways
Suite 890 – 360 Main Street
Winnipeg, Manitoba
R3C 3Z4
Tel: +1 204 9888251
Fax: +1 204 9888517
Contact: S Mielitz

Canadian Oilseed Processors Assoc
Suite 2150 – 360 Main Street
Winnipeg, Manitoba
R3C 3Z3
Tel: +1 204 9569500
Fax: +1 204 9569506
Contact: R J Broeska

CanAmera Foods Inc
Suite 408 – 1780 Wellington Ave
Winnipeg, Manitoba
R3H 1B3
Tel: +1 204 9251754
Fax: +1 204 7743314
Contact: K Galloway

Canbra Foods Ltd
PO Box 99
Lethbridge, Alberta
T1J 3Y4
Tel: +1 403 3295556
Fax: +1 403 3287933
Contact: L McNamara

Cargill Inc
15407 McGinty Road West
PO Box 930
Wayzata, Minnesota
Tel: +1 612 4757575
Fax: +1 612 7426079
Contact: F L Sims

Cargill Investor Services Inc
Suite 2300, Sears Tower
233 South Wacker Drive
Chicago, Illinois
60606
Tel: +1 312 4604000
Fax: +1 312 4604017
Contact: H T Hansen

Cargill Ltd
Suite 300 – 240 Graham Ave
Winnipeg, Manitoba
R3C 0J7
Tel: +1 204 9470141
Fax: +1 204 9560995
Contact: K L Hawkins

Chinook Agri Marketing Inc
Box 910
Didsbury, Alberta
T0M 0W0
Tel: +1 403 3353056
Fax: +1 403 3353088
Contact: C W Ausenhus

Co-op Atlantic
Suite 540 – 167 Lombard Ave
Winnipeg, Manitoba
R3B 0V3
Tel: +1 204 9585970
Fax: +1 204 9422603
Contact: L Miller

ConAgra Grain, Canada (A Division of ConAgra Ltd)
Suite 2100 – 360 Main Street
Winnipeg, Manitoba
R3C 3Z3
Tel: +1 204 9425550
Fax: +1 204 9434012
Contact: M M Schmidt

Continental Grain Co (Canada) Ltd
Suite 2500 – 200 Granville Street
Vancouver, British Columbia
V6C 1S4
Tel: +1 604 6847292
Fax: +1 604 6848031
Contact: G W McClintock

Coopérative Fédérée de Québec
Boul De L'Acadie, Chambre 200
Montreal, Quebec
H4N 3H7
Tel: +1 514 8582667
Fax: +1 514 3840551
Contact: P L S Lauzier

daex Commodities Inc
3 Lindenwood Place
Winnipeg, Manitoba
R3P 1M3
Tel: +1 204 9491777
Fax: +1 204 4880120
Contact: D Eschmann

Delta Asia Credit Ltd
1 Connaught Place
31st Floor, Jardine House
Hong Kong
Tel: +1 852 25247106
Fax: +1 852 28104495
Contact: S C K Au

Dominion Malting Ltd
Suite 953 – 167 Lombard Avenue
Winnipeg, Manitoba
R3B 0V3
Tel: +1 204 9430741
Fax: +1 204 9476791
Contact: J Venn

Dreman & Co Ltd
6th Floor – 238 Portage Ave
Winnipeg, Manitoba
R3C 0B1
Tel: +1 204 9430691
Contact: I J Dreman

Dreyfus Canada Ltd, Louis
Suite 1690 – 360 Main Street
Winnipeg, Manitoba
R3C 3Z3
Tel: +1 204 9433546
Fax: +1 204 9441307
Contact: A P Temple

FIMAT Derivatives Canada Inc
Suite 1800 – 1501 McGill College Ave
Montréal, Quebec
H3A 3M8
Tel: +1 514 8416200
Fax: +1 514 8416254
Contact: J P Gallardo

Flaherty Grain Co Ltd
Suite 426 – 360 Main Street
Winnipeg, Manitoba
R3C 3Z3
Tel: +1 204 9491343
Fax: +1 204 9470076
Contact: B Flaherty

Gallie Grain Ltd
Suite 408 – 360 Main Street
Winnipeg, Manitoba
R3C 2Z4
Tel: +1 204 9432516
Contact: D J Gallie

Geldermann Inc
440 South La Salle Street
One Financial Place – 20th Floor
Chicago, Illinois
60605
Tel: +1 312 6637500
Fax: +1 312 6637710
Contact: J R Curley

HSBC James Capel Asia Derivatives Ltd
1 Queen's Road Central
Level 17
Hong Kong
Tel: +1 852 28439111
Fax: +1 852 28107673
Contact: I R Martin

Hantec Futures Ltd
168 Des Voeux Road Central
5/F Lee Kam Kee Building
Hong Kong
Tel: +1 852 28159060
Fax: +1 852 28518601
Contact: K M Wong

Itochu International Inc
335 Madison Avenue
New York, New York
10017
Tel: +1 212 8188000
Fax: +1 212 8188328
Contact: T Konishi

LFG, LLC
Suite 310 – 360 Main Street
Winnipeg, Manitoba
R3C 3Z3
Tel: +1 204 9889710
Fax: +1 204 9567670
Contact: R Dzisiak

Lake Shippers' Clearance Assoc
Suite 510 – 360 Main Street
Winnipeg, Manitoba
R3C 3Z3
Tel: +1 204 9422424
Fax: +1 204 9473740
Contact: R W MacDonald

Levesque Securities Inc
Suite 600 – 1155 Rue Metcalfe
Montréal, Quebec
H3B 4S9
Tel: +1 514 8795346
Fax: +1 514 8792204
Contact: G Normandin

Linear Grain Inc
67 Centre Ave, West
Carman, Manitoba
R0G 0J0
Tel: +1 204 7456747
Fax: +1 204 7456573
Contact: R McKnight

MHS Futures Ltd
1 Garden Road Central
37A, Bank of China Tower
Hong Kong
Tel: +1 852 28431841
Fax: +1 852 28459036
Contact: C Broadhurst

Malchy Grain Co Ltd
Suite 975 – 167 Lombard Ave
Winnipeg, Manitoba
R3B 0V3
Tel: +1 204 9449328
Fax: +1 204 9472271
Contact: B Grushko

Manitoba Pool Elevators
220 Portage Ave
Box 9800
Winnipeg, Manitoba
R3C 3K7
Tel: +1 204 9471171
Fax: +1 204 9420570
Contact: D W Hunter

Marubeni America Corp
405 Lexington Avenue
New York, New York
10017
Tel: +1 212 4500585
Fax: +1 212 4500773
Contact: H Tamai

Merrill Lynch Canada Inc
200 King Street West
Toronto, Ontario
M5H 3W3
Tel: +1 416 5866417
Fax: +1 416 5866616
Contact: G B Dunn

Midland Walwyn Capital Inc
Ste 400 – BCE Place
181 Bay Street
Toronto, Ontario
M5J 2V8
Tel: +1 416 3697400
Fax: +1 416 3697438
Contact: B J Geisler

Mitsubishi Canada Ltd
Suite 2800 – 200 Granville Street
Vancouver, British Columbia
V6C 1G6
Tel: +1 604 6548000
Fax: +1 604 6548222
Contact: K Nakaso

Mitsui & Co (Canada) Ltd
1055 Dunsmuir Street, 32nd Floor
Vancouver, British Columbia
V7X 1E6
Tel: +1 604 3313100
Fax: +1 604 3313129
Contact: Y Muramatsu

Morgan Stanley Futures (Hong Kong) Ltd
8 Connaught Place
31st Floor, Central
Hong Kong
Tel: +1 852 28485200
Fax: +1 852 28451012
Contact: N A Shear

Morrow Inc, AR
Suite 602 – 191 Lombard Ave
Winnipeg, Manitoba
R3B 0X1
Tel: +1 204 9438579
Fax: +1 204 9430575
Contact: A R Morrow

Nesbitt Burns Inc
Suite 1300 – 360 Main Street
Winnipeg, Manitoba
R3C 3Z3
Tel: +1 204 9471501
Fax: +1 204 9449562
Contact: T D A Waitt

Northern Sales Co Ltd
135 Lombard Ave
Winnipeg, Manitoba
R3B 0T4
Tel: +1 204 9491456
Fax: +1 204 9570350
Contact: J P Middagh

PaineWebber Inc
181 West Madison Street
Chicago, Illinois
60602
Tel: +1 312 6836153
Fax: +1 312 6836177
Contact: W A Kiszka

Palliser Commodities Corp
Suite 102 Stockman's Center
2116 – 27 Avenue NE
Calgary, Alberta
T2E 7A6
Tel: +1 403 2505020
Fax: +1 403 2505041
Contact: J R Harriman

Palliser Grain Co Ltd
Suite 102 Stockman's Center
2116 – 27 Avenue NE
Calgary, Alberta
T2E 7A6
Tel: +1 403 2914450
Fax: +1 403 2501739
Contact: J R Harriman

Palmer Grain Ltd
Suite 430 – 360 Main Street
Winnipeg, Manitoba
R3C 3Z3
Tel: +1 204 9421999
Contact: W Palmer

Parrish & Helmbecker, Ltd
Suite 700 – 360 Main Street
Winnipeg, Manitoba
R3C 3Z3
Tel: +1 204 9562030
Fax: +1 204 9438233
Contact: W B Parrish

Paterson & Sons Ltd, NM
Suite 609 – 167 Lombard Ave
Winnipeg, Manitoba
R3B 0V5
Tel: +1 204 9562090
Fax: +1 204 9472386
Contact: A B Paterson

Peace Town Futures Ltd
89 Queensway
40/F Liffo Tower
Hong Kong
Tel: +1 852 28228338
Fax: +1 852 28770133
Contact: S Chan

Pioneer Grain Co Ltd
Suite 2500 – One Lombard Place
Winnipeg, Manitoba
R3B 0X8
Tel: +1 204 9345961
Fax: +1 204 9345275
Contact: C R Vossen

Pioneer Grain Terminal Ltd
26th Floor – One Lombard Place
Winnipeg, Manitoba
R3B 0X8
Tel: +1 204 9345657
Fax: +1 204 9570677
Contact: R J Miles

Pool Commodity Trading Service
Suite 1200 – 201 Portage Avenue
Winnipeg, Manitoba
R3B 3K6
Tel: +1 204 9494643
Fax: +1 204 9424167
Contact: S P Bloss

Quantum Financial Services (Canada) Ltd
800 – 5951, No 3 Road
Richmond, British Columbia
V6X 2E3
Tel: +1 604 8211933
Fax: +1 604 7238991
Contact: J M S Ho

RBC Dominion Securities Inc
Suite 900 – 360 Main Street
Winnipeg, Manitoba
R3C 2G9
Tel: +1 204 9822600
Fax: +1 204 9479540
Contact: E A McLaughlin

Range Grain Co Ltd
Suite 960 – 360 Main Street
Winnipeg, Manitoba
R3C 3Z3
Tel: +1 204 9436407
Fax: +1 204 9470677
Contact: D Metraux

Refco Futures (Canada) Ltd
Suite 3630 – 161 Bay Street
Toronto, Ontario
M5J 2S1
Tel: +1 416 8627000
Fax: +1 416 8620576
Contact: P Gloutney

Richardson & Sons Ltd, James
30th Floor – One Lombard Place
Winnipeg, Manitoba
R3B 0Y1
Tel: +1 204 9345933
Fax: +1 204 9560287
Contact: G T Richardson

Richardson Greenshields of Canada Ltd
Suite 2800 – One Lombard Place
Winnipeg, Manitoba
R3B 0Y2
Tel: +1 204 9345698
Fax: +1 204 9570141
Contact: R A Wiebe

Richardson Terminals Ltd
Suite 2500 – One Lombard Place
Winnipeg, Manitoba
R3B 0X8
Tel: +1 204 9345712
Fax: +1 204 9436065
Contact: W Fox

Roberts Grain Inc
Suite 448 – 360 Main Street
Winnipeg, Manitoba
R3C 3Z3
Tel: +1 204 9436054
Contact: D K Roberts

Saskatchewan Wheat Pool
11th Floor – 201 Portage Ave
Winnipeg, Manitoba
R3B 3R6
Tel: +1 204 9881300
Fax: +1 204 9881318
Contact: R Wansbutter

ScotiaMcLeod Inc
40 King Street West
PO Box 4085, Station A
Toronto, Ontario
M5W 2X6
Tel: +1 416 8637411
Fax: +1 416 8623132
Contact: W C Kennedy

Seapower Forex Ltd
Suite 32–35F, Alexandra House
16–20 Chater Road
Central, Hong Kong
Tel: +1 852 28474888
Fax: +1 852 28681911
Contact: K L Slu

Smith Barney Inc
1st Floor – 390 Greenwich Street
New York, New York
10013
Tel: +1 212 7235600
Fax: +1 212 7238991
Contact: B P Pichichero

Stewart Grain Ltd, Don
Suite 470 – 360 Main Street
Winnipeg, Manitoba
R3C 3Z4
Tel: +1 204 9430661
Contact: D C Stewart

Toepfer (Canada) Ltd, Alfred C
Suite 709 – 167 Lombard Ave
Winnipeg, Manitoba
R3B 0V3
Tel: +1 204 9250468
Fax: +1 204 9560282
Contact: C E Pauls

United Grain Growers Ltd
26th Floor – 201 Portage Ave
Winnipeg, Manitoba
R3C 3A7
Tel: +1 204 9445517
Fax: +1 204 9471779
Contact: W E Hill

Wardley Futures Ltd
10 Harcourt Road
Suite 3/F Hutchison House
Central, Hong Kong
Tel: +1 852 25211661
Fax: +1 852 28100145
Contact: D T Y Shang

Weyburn Inland Terminal Ltd
PO Box 698
Weyburn, Saskatchewan
S4H 2K8
Tel: +1 306 8427436
Fax: +1 306 8420303
Contact: S B McCormick

Winnipeg Commodity Clearing Ltd
Suite 480 – 360 Main Street
Winnipeg, Manitoba
R3C 3Z3
Tel: +1 204 9426936
Fax: +1 204 9440319
Contact: R Willerton

XCAN Grain Pool Ltd
Suite 1200 – 201 Portage Ave
Winnipeg, Manitoba
R3B 3K6
Tel: +1 204 9494500
Fax: +1 204 9491057
Contact: K L Matchett

Registered Futures Commission Merchants

Benson-Quinn Commodities Inc
Winnipeg, Manitoba

CIBC Wood Gundy Securities Inc
Toronto, Ontario

Cargill Investor Services Inc
Chicago, Illinois

Cargill Ltd
Winnipeg, Manitoba

Chinook Agri-Marketing Inc
Didsbury, Alberta

daex Commodities Inc
Winnipeg, Manitoba

FIMAT Derivatives Canada, Inc
Montreal, Quebec

Geldermann Inc
Chicago, Illinois

HSBC James Capel Asia Derivatives Ltd
Hong Kong

Hanec Futures Ltd
Hong Kong

LFG, LLC
Winnipeg, Manitoba

Levesque Securities Inc
Montreal, Quebec

Linear Agra (Man) Ltd
Carman, Manitoba

MHS Futures Ltd
Hong Kong

Merrill Lynch Canada Inc
Toronto, Ontario

Midland Walwyn Capital Inc
Toronto, Ontario

Morgan Stanley Futures (Hong Kong) Commodities Inc
Hong Kong

Nesbitt Burns Inc
New York, New York

Northern Sales Co Ltd
Winnipeg, Manitoba

PaineWebber Inc
Chicago, Illinois

Palliser Commodities Corp
Calgary, Alberta

Parrish & Heimbecker Ltd
Winnipeg, Manitoba

Peace Town Futures Ltd
Hong Kong

Pool Commodity Trading Service
Winnipeg, Manitoba

Quantum Financial Services (Canada) Ltd
Vancouver, British Columbia

RBC Dominion Securities Inc
Winnipeg, Manitoba

Refco Futures (Canada) Ltd
Toronto, Ontario

Richardson Greenshields of Canada Ltd
Winnipeg, Manitoba

ScotiaMcLeod Inc
Winnipeg, Manitoba

Smith Barney Inc
New York, New York

Toepfer (Canada) Ltd, Alfred C
Winnipeg, Manitoba

United Grain Growers Ltd
Winnipeg, Manitoba

Wardley Futures Ltd
Hong Kong

Registered Clearing Members

ADM Agri-Industries Ltd
Windsor, Ontario

Access Traders Inc
Winnipeg, Manitoba

AgPro Grain Inc
Winnipeg, Manitoba

Alberta Wheat Pool
Winnipeg, Manitoba

Benson-Quinn Commodities Ltd
Winnipeg, Manitoba

H Brownlee
Crystal City, Manitoba

Bunge of Canada Ltd
Winnipeg, Manitoba

Canada Malting Co Ltd
Winnipeg, Manitoba

Cargill Ltd
Winnipeg, Manitoba

ConAgra Grain, Canada (A Division of ConAgra Ltd)
Winnipeg, Manitoba

Continental Grain Co (Canada) Ltd
Vancouver, British Columbia

W J Craddock
Winnipeg, Manitoba

daex Commodities Inc
Winnipeg, Manitoba

J C DePape*
Winnipeg, Manitoba

Dominion Malting Ltd
Winnipeg, Manitoba

Don Stewart Grain Ltd
St Adolphe, Manitoba

Dreman & Co Ltd
Winnipeg, Manitoba

Dreyfus Canada Ltd, Louis
Winnipeg, Manitoba

Flaherty Grain Co Ltd
Winnipeg, Manitoba

B E Futz
Winnipeg, Manitoba

Gallie Grain Ltd
Winnipeg, Manitoba

A Grande
Winnipeg, Manitoba

LFG, LLC
Winnipeg, Manitoba

Malchy Grain Co Ltd
Winnipeg, Manitoba

Manitoba Pool Elevators Ltd
Winnipeg, Manitoba

Merrill Lynch Canada Inc
Toronto, Ontario

Midland Walwyn Capital Inc
Toronto, Ontario

Morrow Inc, A R
Winnipeg, Manitoba

A D Muggaberg
Winnipeg, Manitoba

Northern Sales Co Ltd
Winnipeg, Manitoba

Palmer Grain Ltd
Winnipeg, Manitoba

Parrish & Heimbecker, Ltd
Winnipeg, Manitoba

Paterson & Sons Ltd, N M
Winnipeg, Manitoba

Pioneer Grain Co, Ltd
Winnipeg, Manitoba

Pool Commodity Trading Service
Winnipeg, Manitoba

Quantum Financial Services (Canada) Ltd
Richmond, British Columbia

RBC Dominion Securities Inc
Winnipeg, Manitoba

Range Grain Co Ltd
Winnipeg, Manitoba

D W Reimann
Winnipeg, Manitoba

Richardson & Sons Ltd, James
Winnipeg, Manitoba

Richardson Greenshields of Canada Ltd
Winnipeg, Manitoba

Richardson Terminals Ltd
Winnipeg, Manitoba

Roberts Grain Inc
Winnipeg, Manitoba

Saskatchewan Wheat Pool
Winnipeg, Manitoba

ScotiaMcLeod Inc
Winnipeg, Manitoba

N R Shodine
Winnipeg, Manitoba

E Sochaski
Winnipeg, Manitoba

G E Sproule
Winnipeg, Manitoba

Toepfer (Canada) Ltd, Alfred C
Winnipeg, Manitoba

United Grain Growers Ltd
Winnipeg, Manitoba

R A Wright
Winnipeg, Manitoba

XCAN Grain Pool Ltd
Winnipeg, Manitoba

*Non-active clearing member

France

MATIF

* General clearing member
† Individual clearing member
‡ Negotiating broker

BA Futures SA†
43-47 avenue de la Grand Armée
75782 Paris
Tel: +33 1 45 02 68 70

Bankers Trust Futures (Europe) GIE*
12-14 Rond-point des Champs Elysées
75386 Paris
Tel: +33 1 42 99 30 00

Banque d'Escompte†
13 boulevard Haussman
75009 Paris
Tel: +33 1 48 24 85 44

Banque Fédérative du Crédit Mutuel†
34 rue du Wacken
67000 Strasbourg
Tel: +33 16 88 14 88 14

Banque Bruxelles Lambert France†
Immeuble Kupka – B
16 rue Hoche
92906 Paris
Tel: +33 1 41 26 70 00

Banque Française du Commerce Extérieur (BFCE)†
21 boulevard Haussmann
75009 Paris
Tel: +33 1 48 00 48 00

Banque Générale du Phénix et du Crédit Chimique†
6 avenue Kléber
75116 Paris
Tel: +33 1 44 17 21 00

Banque Internationale de Placement (BIP)†
108 boulevard Haussmann
75008 Paris
Tel: +33 1 44 70 80 80

Banque Lehman Brothers†
56 rue du Fg St Honoré
75008 Paris
Tel: +33 1 44 56 41 00

Banque Nationale de Paris (BNP)†
20 boulevard des Italiens
75009 Paris
Tel: +33 1 40 14 45 46

Banque Nomura France†
164 rue Rivoli
75001 Paris
Tel: +33 1 42 97 19 00

Banque Paribas
3 rue d'Antin
75002 Paris
Tel: +33 1 42 98 12 34

Banque Régionale d'Escompte et de Dépôts (BRED)†
18 Quai de la Rapée
75012 Paris
Tel: +33 1 48 98 60 00

Banque San Paolo*
52 avenue Hoche
75008 Paris
Tel: +33 1 47 54 40 40

Barclays Bank Plc†
21 rue Lafitte
75009 Paris
Tel: +33 1 44 79 79 79

BNP Finance†
9 boulevard des Italiens
75002 Paris
Tel: +33 1 40 14 16 01

BZW Société de Bourse†
21 boulevard de la Madeleine
75038 Paris Cedex 01
Tel: +33 1 44 58 32 32

Caisse Centrale de Crédit Coopératif (CCCC)†
Parc de la Défense/BP 211
33 rue des 3 Fontanot
92002 Nanterre Cedex
Tel: +33 1 47 24 85 00

Caisses Centrale des Banques Populaires (CCBP)†
115 rue Montmartre
75002 Paris
Tel: +33 1 40 39 30 00

Caisses des Dépôts et Consignations (CDC)*
56 rue de Lille
75007 Paris
Tel: +33 1 45 96 16 16

Cardif Bancaire Transaction (CBT)†
4 rue des Fréres Caudron
92858 Rueol Malmaison Cedex
Tel: +33 1 41 42 83 00

Cargill Investor Services SNC†
46 rue Notre-Dame des Victoires
75002 Paris
Tel: +33 1 44 82 31 60

CCF Elysées Bourse†
103 avenue des Champs Elysées
75008 Paris
Tel: +33 1 40 70 33 49

Cheuvreux de Virieu SA†
44-46 rue de Courselles
75008 Paris
Tel: +33 1 44 95 24 24

Cholet Dupont SA†
3 rue de Gramont
75002 Paris
Tel: +33 1 44 77 15 15

Citibank SA†
19 Parvis de la Défense
La Défense 7
92073 Paris La Défense
Tel: +33 1 49 06 10 10

Compagnie Parisienne de Reescompte (CPR)†
30 rue Saint Georges
75312 Paris Cedex 09
Tel: +33 1 45 96 16 16

Concord Matif†
24 rue des Jeûners
75002 Paris
Tel: +33 1 44 82 14 14

Courcoux Bouvet SNC†
32 avenue de l'Opéra
75002 Paris
Tel: +33 1 40 17 50 00

Crédit Agricole Futures SNC†
Immeuble Cotentin
90 boulevard Pasteur
75015 Paris
Tel: +33 1 43 23 52 02

Crédit Commercial de France (CCF)†
103 avenue des Champs Elysées
75008 Paris
Tel: +33 1 40 70 70 40

Crédit Lyonnais Rouse (France) SNC*
6-8 rue Ménars
Boîte Courrier No 22,31
75002 Paris
Tel: +33 1 42 21 25 25

Daiwa Europe (France) SA†
26 avenue des Champs Elysées
75008 Paris
Tel: +33 1 44 35 56 00

Deutsche Bank AG†
3 avenue de Friedland
75008 Paris
Tel: +33 1 44 95 64 00

Dupont Denant SA†
100 rue Réaumur
75008 Paris
Tel: +33 1 40 75 41 75

ED & F Man International SA†
13 boulevard Haussmann
75009 Paris
Tel: +33 1 53 34 50 00

Ferri SA†
11 avenue Delcassé
75008 Paris
Tel: +33 1 40 75 41 75

Finacor Vendôme†
52 avenue des Champs Elysées
75008 Paris
Tel: +33 1 40 74 15 15

Financière des Marchés à Terme SNC (FIMAT)*
32 rue de Trévise
75009 Paris
Tel: 33 1 44 79 20 20

France Compensation Futures GIE*
34-36 avenue de Friedland
75008 Paris
Tel: +33 1 47 54 80 00

Galfi Futures†
103 avenue de Champs Elysées
75008 Paris
Tel: +33 1 40 70 70 40

Goldman Sachs Paris Inc et Cie†
2 rue de Thann
75017 Paris
Tel: +33 1 42 12 10 00

IBJ (France) SA†
Washington Plaza
42 rue Washington
75408 Paris
Tel: +33 1 53 83 41 00

IFF SNC*
9-11 rue de Vienne
75008 Paris
Tel: +33 1 44 69 69 60

Ifitec†
49 avenue de l'Opéra
75002 Paris
Tel: +33 1 47 42 31 22

Indosuez Carr Futures GIE*
199 rue Réaumur
75002 Paris
Tel: +33 1 44 82 86 86

ING Bourse SA†
21 boulevard de la Madeleine
75001 Paris
Tel: +33 1 44 55 86 00

JP Morgan SA‡
21 Place du Marché St Honoré
75001 Paris
Tel: +33 1 40 15 48 00

JP Morgan & Cie SA*
21 Place du Marché St Honoré
75001 Paris
Tel: +33 1 40 15 45 00

Jean-Pierre Pinatton SA‡
69 boulevard Haussmann
75009 Paris
Tel: +33 1 40 17 52 00

Louis Dreyfus Finance (Banque) SA†
87 avenue de la Grande Armée
75782 Paris Cedex 16
Tel: +33 1 40 66 11 11

Lyonnaise de Banque†
24 rue de la Banque
75002 Paris
Tel: +33 1 49 27 68 68

Merrill Lynch Capital Markets (France) SA†
96 avenue d'Iéna
75116 Paris
Tel: +33 1 40 69 15 00

MFK Futures SNC†
3 avenue Hoche
75388 Paris Cedex 8
Tel: +33 1 44 29 46 60

Midland Bank Plc†
20 bis, Avenue Rapp
75332 Paris
Tel: +33 1 44 42 73 61

Morgan Stanley SA†
25 rue Balzac
75008 Paris
Tel: +33 1 53 77 70 00

MR Futures SNC †
16 boulevard Montmartre
75009 Paris
Tel: +33 1 42 46 72 64

Natwest Sellier†
12 rue d'Uzès
75002 Paris
Tel: +33 1 44 76 50 00

Nikko France SA‡
10 rue de la Paix
75002 Paris
Tel: +33 1 44 58 39 00

Nord Futures GIE*
6-8 boulevard Haussmann
75009 Paris
Tel: +33 1 40 22 43 10

Oddo Futures†
12 boulevard de la Madeleine
75009 Paris
Tel: +33 1 44 51 85 00

Painewebber France SA†
56 rue du Fg St Honoré
75008 Paris
Tel: +33 1 44 71 13 00

Patrick du Bouzet SA†
10 Cité Rougemont
75009 Paris
Tel: +33 1 40 22 19 92

Refco SA†
29 rue du Louvre
75002 Paris
Tel: +33 1 44 88 10 00

Salomon Brothers SA†
4 avenue Hoch
75008 Paris
Tel: +33 1 47 63 79 07

Scandinaviska Enskilda Banken (SKA)†
25 rue Balzac
75008 Paris
Tel: +33 1 42 97 19 00

Securité Futures GIE*
12 rue Gaillon
75002 Paris
Tel: +33 1 44 94 24 50

Smith Barney SA†
112 avenue Kléber
75116 Paris
Tel: +33 1 53 70 28 00

Société Générale†
Tour Société Générale
92987 Paris La Défense Cedex
Tel: +33 1 42 14 20 00

Société de Transactions et d'Arbitrage sur Futurs Financiers (STAFF)‡
42 rue d'Anjou
75008 Paris
Tel: +33 1 47 42 70 20

Transoptions Compensation†
20 rue de la Baume
75008 Paris
Tel: +33 1 40 75 62 62

Trifutures‡
119 rue Réaumur
75002 Paris
Tel: +33 1 44 82 12 34

Tullett & Tokyo (Futures & Traded Options) Paris SA‡
27 rue du Quatre Septembre
75002 Paris
Tel: +33 1 44 51 63 63

UBS France SA†
69 boulevard Haussmann
75008 Paris
Tel: +33 1 44 56 45 45

Viel Monetaire Futurs†
42 rue d'Anjou
75008 Paris
Tel: +33 1 47 42 70 20

Germany

Frankfurt Corn and Produce Exchange

Members

Agrarhandel Hessen GmbH
Bahnhofstraße 18 b
61250 Usingen

Ludwig Amend
Roggen- und Weizenmühle
Mühlweg 23
35633 Lahnau-Dorlar
Tel: +49 64 41 61929

ABN AMRO Bank (Deutschland) AG
Niederlassung Frankfurt
Grüneburgweg 18
60322 Frankfurt

ARAL Rhein-Main GmbH
Stiftstraße 30, 60313 Frankfurt
per Adr Theodor-Heuss-Straße 57
61118 Bad Vilbel
Tel: +49 61 01 52660
Fax: +49 61 01 526666

Beckmann Mineralölhandel GmbH
Niederlassung
Karl-Benz-Straße 35
60386 Frankfurt
Tel: +49 69 424044

BP Handel GmbH
Ehrichstraße 10
63450 Hanau
Tel: +49 69 15480
Fax: +49 69 289900

BP Handel GmbH
Uferstraße 37
55116 Mainz
Tel: +49 61 21 371031

DEA Mineralölverkauf Hessen GmbH
Zweigniederl Müller & Sinnig
Karl-Benz-Straße 4–6
60314 Frankfurt
Tel: +49 69 40930

DEA Mineralölhandel Rhein-Hessen GmbH
Rheinhessenstraße 3
55129 Mainz
Tel: +49 61 31 59001
Fax: +49 61 31 508188

Emil Doelzer KG
Getreide- Futtermittelgroßhandel
Waldstraße 64
63477 Maintal
Tel: +49 61 09 63777 und 62157

ESSO Südwest Mineralölvertrieb GmbH
Hanauer Landstraße 208–216
60314 Frankfurt
Tel: +49 69 430246
Fax: +49 69 490676

Farm-ei GmbH & Co KG
Assar Gabrielsson-Straße 19
63128 Dietzenbach-Steinberg
Tel: +49 60 74 85060
Fax: +49 60 74 41289

Reinhard Frischmann GmbH
Vermittlung, Großhandel, Import, Export, Speise-, Pflanz-, Futter-, Industrie-Kartoffeln, Zwiebeln, in- u ausl Herkünfte
In den Grummetwiesen 15
60488 Frankfurt
Tel: +49 69 769035 und 36
Fax: +49 69 769075

Toni Geisler
Roederweg 9
65232 Taunusstein
Tel: +49 61 28 44233

Carl Georg
Inh Dieter Benner
Donsbacher Straße 4
35708 Haiger
Tel: +49 27 73 4613

HANIEL Umschlag und Lager GmbH
Hafenstraße 10
63450 Hanau
Tel: +49 61 81 3030
Fax: +49 61 81 303122

Hengstenberg & Co KG
Berliner Straße 262
65205 Wiesbaden
Tel: +49 06 11 701025

Friedrich Jung KG
Mineralöl-Großhandel
Gwinnerstraße 30–32
60388 Frankfurt 60
Tel: +49 69 411805
Fax: +49 69 425282

Kampfmeyer Mühlen GmbH
Werk Hildebrandmühlen Frankfurt
Franziusstraße 15
60314 Frankfurt
Tel: +49 69 407200
Fax: +49 69 4072210

Friedrich Kilian oHG
Inh Helmut Kilian
Säcke- und Planen-Fabrik
Edisonstraße 9
60388 Frankfurt
Tel: +49 61 09 33857

Klöckner & Co
Aktiengesellschaft
Zweigniederl Frankfurt
Gotenstraße 53
65929 Frankfurt
Tel: +49 69 3300840
Fax: +49 69 330084–49

Hrch Frz Knecht Söhne
Getreidemühle
Mühlstraße 7
63785 Obernburg am Main
Tel: +49 60 22 31200

Klaus Kropp
Eiergroßhandel-Frischeidienst GmbH
Bornwiesenweg 6
61130 Nidderau
Tel: +49 61 87 25473

Karl Hans Mehl
Hofgut
Auf der Steinritz 12
60437 Frankfurt Nieder-Erlenbach
Tel: +49 61 01 42392

Walter Mumm
Getreide- und Futtermittelmakler
c/o Rhenania Umschlag und Lagerei GmbH
Schmickstraße 13
60314 Frankfurt-Osthafen
Tel: +49 69 94 332018

Neumühle
Otto Gräf
35633 Lahnau
Tel: +49 64 41 62031
Fax: +49 64 41 62715

Franz Pfeiffer
Landesprodukte KG
Taunusstraße 40
65835 Liederbach
Tel: +49 69 313301

Raiffeisen
Hauptgenossenschaft Frankfurt eG
Ben-Gurion-Ring 174
60437 Frankfurt
Tel: +49 69 50031
Fax: +49 69 5003211 und 5003230

Raiffeisen-Warenzentrale Hessenland GmbH
Staendeplatz 1–3
34117 Kassel
Tel: +49 5 61 71220
Fax: +49 5 61 7122–444/445

Rein Energie Logistik Wärme GmbH
Platanenstraße 25
65187 Wiesbaden
Tel: +49 6 11 8020

Phillipp Remsberger jr
Wiesenstraße 7
65439 Flörsheim
Tel: +49 61 45 32514

Rhenania Umschlag und Lagerei GmbH
Zweigniederl Frankfurt am Main
Schmickstraße 13
60314 Frankfurt
Tel: +49 69 94 33200

Rhenus Aktiengesellschaft
Hafenstraße 16–20
63450 Hanau
Tel: +49 61 81 36010

Otto Simon
Landesprodukte
Rodheimer Straße 6
61191 Rosbach
Tel: +49 60 03 7118

Winand Simons
Gut Weilerhof
64560 Riedstadt
Tel: +49 61 55 2046
A Schaefer
Hehrmühle
36110 Schlitz 1
Tel: +49 66 42 5078
Fax: +49 66 42 5070

Schauenburg & Garthe
Orber Straße 10
60386 Frankfurt
Tel: +49 69 41 5005–07
Fax: +49 69 51 5057

Adolf W Scheibel
Inh Alfred Scheibel
Usinger Straße 81
61239 Ober Mörlen
Tel: +49 60 02 328 oder 5310

Bernd Schilly
Brennstoff-Dienste
Herrngartenstraße 18
65185 Wiesbaden
Tel: +49 6 11 376303

Heinrich Schulmeyer 23
Inh Scholl, Landesprodukte
Langener Straße 38
64546 Mörfelden-Walldorf
Tel: +49 61 05 22213

Shell Mineralölhandel und Heizungs-Dienst GmbH
Niederlassung Wiesbaden
Daimlerstraße 41 a
65197 Wiesbaden
Tel: +49 6 11 422025

Friedrich Strauß
Tierwirtschaftsmeister
Dörnbachstraße 10
64351 Reinheim-Georgenhausen

Friedrich Thelen
Mineralölvertrieb, Wärmetechnik, Heizungbau
Gassnerallee 14
55120 Mainz
Tel: +49 61 31 677018

Heinrich Thylmann
Kilianstädtermühle
Frankfurter Straße 58
61137 Schöneck
Tel: +49 61 87 95080

Geflügelhof Nagel
Hanauer Straße 58
61197 Florstadt-Stammheim
Tel: +49 60 35 6675

Total Deutschland GmbH
Verkaufsbüro Frankfurt
Daimlerstraße 38
60314 Frankfurt
Tel: +49 69 418014

Valentin Gas & Oel GmbH & Co
Rheinallee 187
55120 Mainz
Tel: +49 61 31 6950
Fax: +49 61 31 695262
Telex: 4787364

Veba Oel Vertrieb GmbH
Hanauer Landstraße 187–189
60314 Frankfurt
Tel: +49 69 40504
Fax: +49 69 40505499

Veba Oel Vertrieb GmbH
Obere Austraße 9
55120 Mainz
Tel: +49 61 31 677005

DTB Member List

NCM Non Clearing Member
DCM Direct Clearing Member
GCM General Clearing Member
MM Market Maker

ABN AMRO Bank (Deutschland) AG
Mainzer Landstraße 65
60329 Frankfurt am Main
Germany
DCM
Tel: +49 69 26900660
Contact: Olaf Gerbig

Alumo BV
Dam 27
1012 JS Amsterdam
Netherlands
NCM, MM
Tel: +31 20 5551297
Contact: Duco A Lambers

Amsterdam Options Traders (AOT) GmbH
Komödienstraße 44–46
50667 Köln
Germany
NCM, MM
Tel: +49 221 133003
Contact: Adrianus van den Brink

Amsterdam Options Traders NV
Oudezijds Voorburgwal 282
1012 GL Amsterdam
Netherlands
NCM, MM
Tel: +31 20 6267050
Contact: Koenrad J Dreesens

Apollo Derivatives Group Frankfurt GmbH
c/o MeesPierson
Goethestraße 32
60313 Frankfurt
Germany
NCM, MM
Tel: +49 69 28602
Contact: Arthur Duquette

Archelon Deutschland GmbH
Oberlindau 7
60323 Frankfurt am Main
Germany
NCM, MM
Tel: +49 69 175289
Contact: Charles Tall

B Metzler seel Sohn & Co KGaA
Große Gallusstraße 18
60311 Frankfurt am Main
Germany
DCM, MM
Tel: +49 69 2104591
Contact: Michael Klaus

Baden-Württembergische Bank AG
Kleiner Schloßplatz 11
70173 Stuttgart
Germany
GCM, MM
Tel: +49 711 2094427
Contact: Wolf-Dieter Ihle

Ballmaier & Schultz Wertpapier AG
Bleidenstraße 6
60311 Frankfurt am Main
Germany
NCM, MM
Tel: +49 69 1388111
Contact: Volker Handon

Bank J Vontobel & Co KG
Bahnhofstraße 3
8022 Zürich
Switzerland
NCM
Tel: +41 1 2837111
Contact: R Angst

Bank of Tokyo-Mitsubishi (Deutschland) AG
Mainzer Landstraße 16
60325 Frankfurt am Main
Germany
DCM
Tel: +49 69 7176240
Contact: Yasushi Watanabe

Bankers Trust International Plc
Frankfurt Branch
Grüneburgweg 16
60322 Frankfurt am Main
Germany
DCM
Tel: +49 69 15301284
Contact: Thomas Eckert

Bankgesellschaft Berlin AG
Hardenbergstraße 32
10623 Berlin
Germany
GCM
Tel: +49 30 31093836
Contact: Serge Demoliére

Bankhaus Gebrüder Bethmann
Bethmannstraße 7–9
60311 Frankfurt am Main
Germany
NCM
Tel: +49 69 2177349
Contact: Herbert Fleckenstein

Bankhaus H Aufhäuser
Kaiserhofstraße 16
60313 Frankfurt am Main
Germany
NCM
Tel: +49 69 285340
Contact: Michael Lex

Bankhaus Hermann Lampe KG
Jägerhofstraße 10
40479 Düsseldorf
Germany
DCM
Tel: +49 211 4952334
Contact: Heidi Diekmann

Bankhaus Reuschel & Co
Maximilianplatz 13
80333 München
Germany
DCM
Tel: +49 89 2395350
Contact: Lothar Krüger

Banque Nationale de Paris SA
Niederlassung Frankfurt
Bockenheimer Landstraße 22
60323 Frankfurt
Germany
GCM, MM
Tel: +49 69 7193149
Contact: Stephen Soulas

Bayerische Hypotheken- und
Wechsel-Bank AG
Arabellastraße 12
81925 München
Germany
GCM, MM
Tel: +49 89 92443047
Contact: Günther Werner (Abteilung O-EDV-AE3)

Bayerische Landesbank
- Girozentrale -
Brienner Straße 20
80333 München
Germany
DCM
Tel: +49 89 21713389
Contact: Alfred Mundner

Bayerische Vereinsbank AG
Am Tucherpark 1
80538 München
Germany
GCM, MM
Tel: +49 69 27173860
Contact: Stefan Schliemann (Leiter Aktienhandel)

Beekman Trading BV
Dam 27
1012 JS Amsterdam
Netherlands
NCM, MM
Tel: +31 20 5551278
Contact: Johannes S A Overbeek

BfG Bank AG
Gruppe Credit Lyonnais
Mainzer Landstraße 16
60325 Frankfurt am Main
Germany
GCM, MM
Tel: +49 69 97271174
Contact: François Menard

BHF-BANK
Aktiengesellschaft
Bockenheimer Landstraße 10
60323 Frankfurt am Main
Germany
GCM, MM
Tel: +49 69 7183262
Contact: Rüdiger Wolf

Birkert & Partner GmbH
Börsenstraße 7–11
60313 Frankfurt am Main
Germany
NCM
Tel: + 49 69 94507265
Contact: Rolf Birkert

BMP Wertpapiere und Optionen GmbH
Niedenau 36
60325 Frankfurt am Main
Germany
NCM, MM
Tel: +49 69 9714460
Contact: Brian D Sparks

BPT Trading SA
Rue Langallerie 9
PO Box 2552
1002 Lausanne
Switzerland
NCM, MM
Tel: +41 21 3201991
Contact: Patrick Girondi

Bremer Landesbank
Kreditanstalt Oldenburg
– Girozentrale –
Domshof 26
28195 Bremen
Germany
DCM
Tel: +49 421 3322618
Contact: Pierre Schwital (Aktien-Derivate)
Tel: +49 421 3322617
Contact: B Mosegart-Hansen (Sales)
Tel: +49 421 3322622
Contact: Uwe Harms (Renten-Derivate)

BZW Deutschland Branch of Barclays Bank Plc
Bockenheimer Landstraße 38–40
60323 Frankfurt am Main
Germany
NCM
Tel: +49 69 71611414
Contact: George Austin

BZW Société de Bourse SA
21, boulevard de la Madeleine
75038 Paris
France
NCM
Tel: +33 1 44583232
Contact: Thierry Altmann

Caisse des Dépôts et Consignations GmbH
Bockenheimer Landstraße 51–53
60325 Frankfurt
Germany
GCM, MM
Tel: +49 69 97133354
Contact: Wilhelm Teitscheid

Cargill Investor Services SNC
46, rue Notre Dame des Victoires
75002 Paris
France
NCM
Tel: +33 1 44823181
Contact: Alicia Maurin
Tel: +33 1 44823179
Contact: Grainne Dosley

Carl Kliem Börsen-Service GmbH
An der Hauptwache 7
60313 Frankfurt
Germany
NCM
Tel: +49 69 9201629
Contact: Peter-Joachim Noack

Chicago International Arbitrage GmbH
Börsenstraße 7–11
60313 Frankfurt
Germany
NCM, MM
Tel: +49 69 94507226
Contact: Jim Phelen

Citibank AG
Neue Mainzer Straße 75
60311 Frankfurt am Main
Germany
GCM, MM
Tel: +49 69 13663930
Contact: William Luterman

Commerz Financial Products GmbH
Neue Mainzer Straße 32–36
60261 Frankfurt am Main
Germany
NCM, MM
Tel: +49 69 929037789
Contact: Laurent Giannesini

Commerzbank AG
Neue Mainzer Straße 32–36
60311 Frankfurt am Main
Germany
GCM
Tel: +49 69 13629126
Contact: Thomas Knipping

CPR-Compagnie
Parisienne de Réescompte
30, rue Saint Georges
75009 Paris
France
NCM
Tel: +33 1 45962424
Contact: Eric Marcombes

Crédit Commercial de France
103, avenue des Champs-Elysées
75419 Paris Cédex 08
France
NCM
Tel: +33 1 40707068
Contact: Marc Legendre

Credit Lyonnais Rouse Ltd
Broadwalk House
5 Appold Street
London EC2A 2DA
Great Britain
NCM
Tel: +44 171 6380293
Contact: Alex Cooper

Credit Suisse (Deutschland) AG
Messeturm
60308 Frankfurt am Main
Germany
DCM
Tel: +49 69 75382334
Contact: Norbert Geus

CS First Boston Effectenbank AG
Messeturm
60308 Frankfurt am Main
Germany
DCM
Tel: +49 69 75343775
Contact: Michael Lamp

DAIWA Europe (Deutschland) GmbH
Mainzer Landstraße 46
60325 Frankfurt am Main
Germany
DCM
Tel: +49 69 71708141
Contact: Paul Rotter

Dean Witter International Ltd
1 Appold Street
London EC2A
Great Britain
NCM
Tel: +44 171 2948596
Contact: Richard Seaman

Delbrück & Co Privatbankiers
Neue Mainzer Str 75
60311 Frankfurt am Main
Germany
DCM
Tel: +49 69 1331229
Contact: Karl-Heinz Nowak

Derivative Trading System AG
Bundesplatz 2
6500 Zug
Switzerland
NCM, MM
Tel: +41 42 225707
Contact: Jorgen Molen

Deutsche Bank AG
Taunusanlage 12
60325 Frankfurt am Main
Germany
GCM, MM
Tel: +49 69 91038439
Contact: Stefan Raida

Deutsche Girozentrale Deutsche Kommunalbank
Taunusanlage 10
60329 Frankfurt am Main
Germany
DCM
Tel: +49 69 2693620
Contact: Roland Schulz

DG Bank Deutsche Genossenschaftsbank
Am Platz der Republik
60325 Frankfurt am Main
Germany
GCM
Tel: +49 69 74476373
Contact: Stephan Hink

Dresdner Bank AG
Jürgen-Ponto-Platz 1
60329 Frankfurt am Main
Germany
GCM, MM
Tel: +49 69 2638332
Contact: Jens Hansen

DTS Derivative Trading System GmbH
Börsenstraße 7–11
60313 Frankfurt am Main
Germany
NCM, MM
Tel: +49 69 94507285
Contact: Patrick S McEvoy

Dyna Option GmbH
Mainzer Landstraße 46
60325 Frankfurt am Main
Germany
NCM, MM
Tel: +49 69 97201930
Contact: Alain Perrollaz (President)

Dynamic Hedge Wertpapierhandelsgesellschaft mbH
Börsenstraße 7–11
60313 Frankfurt am Main
Germany
NCM
Tel: +49 69 94507261
Contact: Tony Saliba

ED&F Man International Ltd
Sugar Quay
Lower Thames Street
London EC3R 6DU
NCM
Tel: +44 171 2853000
Contact: Marc Satterthwaite

Estlander & Rönnlund GmbH*
An der Staufenmauer 6
60311 Frankfurt am Main
Germany
NCM, MM
Tel: +49 69 91399507
Contact: Kaj M Rönnlund

Extra Clearing BV
Zweigniederlassung Frankfurt
Blanchardstraße 17
60487 Frankfurt
Germany
NCM, MM
Tel: +31 20 5301301
Contact: Roelof Veenstra (Managing Director)

Extra Clearing GmbH & Co Service KG
Blanchardstraße 17
60487 Frankfurt
Germany
NCM, MM
Tel: +49 69 9706220
Contact: Hans de Theye

F & O Capital Management AG
Bellerivestraße 49
8008 Zürich
Switzerland
NCM, MM
Tel: +41 1 4223102
Contact: Filippo Arnieri

FCT Europe Ltd
Buckingham House, 1st Floor
62–63 Queen Street
London EC4R 1AD
NCM
Tel: +44 171 3344825
+44 171 3344800
Contact: Julian A Foster

Ferri SA
11, avenue Delcasse
75008 Paris
France
NCM
Tel: +33 1 40754197
Contact: Roch Maes

Fimat International Banque SA
Niederlassung Frankfurt
Mainzer Landstraße 46
60325 Frankfurt am Main
Germany
GCM
Tel: +49 69 7107760
Contact: François Bloch (General Manager)

First Marathon Bank GbmH
Feuerbachstraße 26–32
60325 Frankfurt am Main
Germany
DCM
Tel: +49 69 97166151
Contact: Peter Ertel

Frankfurter Sparkasse
Neue Mainzer Straße 47–53
60311 Frankfurt am Main
Germany
GCM, MM
Tel: +49 69 26412410
Contact: Peter Ensel

Fritz Nols KG
Hochstraße 31
60313 Frankfurt am Main
Germany
NCM
Tel: +49 69 920240
Contact: Fritz Nols
Tel: +49 69 92924184
Contact: René Kreiss

Georg Hauck & Sohn Bankiers KGaA
Kaiserstraße 24
60311 Frankfurt am Main
Germany
DCM
Tel: +49 69 2161219
Contact: Andreas Jilg

GIE Oddo Futures
12, boulevard de la Madeleine
75009 Paris
France
NCM, MM
Tel: +33 1 44518547
Contact: Sébastian Moriseau

GIE Sécurité Futures
12, rue Gaillon
75002 Paris
France
NCM
Tel: +33 1 44942450
Contact: Pauline Denis-Charneau

Goldman, Sachs & Co oHG
Friedrich-Ebert-Anlage 49 (Messeturm)
60308 Frankfurt am Main
Germany
NCM
Tel: +49 69 75322058
Contact: Michael Roczinski

Grindstone Investments BV
Paleisstraat 1
1012 RB Amsterdam
Netherlands
NCM, MM
Tel: +31 20 6387918
+31 20 5212124
Contact: Pascal de Wit

Hamburgische Landesbank
– Girozentrale –
Gerhart-Hauptmann-Platz 50
20095 Hamburg
Germany
GCM, MM
Tel: +49 40 33333566
Contact: Dieter Bohlens

Hamburger Sparkasse
Individualkunden Abteilung
Brandstwiete 1`
20457 Hamburg
Germany
DCM
Tel: +49 40 35793360
Contact: Knut Hochwald

HJM Trading Advisors
In der Au 27
61440 Oberursel
Germany
NCM
Tel: +49 6171 58800
Contact: Hans Meßner

Hull Trading GmbH
Friedrichstraße 2–6
60323 Frankfurt am Main
Germany
NCM, MM
Tel: +49 69 97200520
Contact: Mark Carroll

Indosuez Carr Futures SNC
119, rue Réaumur
75002 Paris
France
NCM
Tel: +33 1 44828675
Contact: Phillippe Weber

Industriebank von Japan (Deutschland) AG
Niedenau 13–19
60325 Frankfurt
Germany
DCM
Tel: +49 69 71405101
Contact: Jürgen Ganßleben

ING-Bank Internationale Nederlanden Bank NV
Strawinskylaan 2631
1077 ZZ Amsterdam
Netherlands
NCM, MM
Tel: +31 20 5415500
Contact: GJA van der Lugt

IS-Futures Trading GmbH
Bismarkstraße 191
63067 Offenbach
Germany
NCM, MM
Tel: +49 69 92076418
Contact: Stefan Lang

JP Morgan GmbH
Börsenstraße 2–4
60313 Frankfurt am Main
Germany
GCM
Tel: +49 69 71241287
Contact: Susanne Kaap

JP Morgan SA
Société de Bourse
27, boulevard des Capucines
75002 Paris
France
NCM
Tel: +33 1 40154500
Contact: Jérôme Kemp

Juno Limited
1st Floor Prince Rupert House
64 Queen Street
London EC4R 1AD
Great Britain
NCM
Tel: +44 171 7767600
Contact: Richard R Hogan

KBW Effectenbank NV
De Ryterkade 113
1011 AB Amsterdam
Netherlands
NCM
Tel: +31 20 6261811
Contact: Mark Kellerman

Kessler Asher Derivatives GmbH iG
Große Eschenheimer Straße 1
60313 Frankfurt am Main
Germany
NCM, MM
Tel: +49 69 92076423
Contact: Mark Lyons

Kingstone Derivatives Trading GmbH
Altkönigstraße 7
61462 Königstein
Germany
NCM
Tel: +49 6174 936630
Contact: Wilhelm Delp

Kredietbank-Bankverein Ag
Niederlassung Frankfurt
Mendelssohnstraße 75–77
60325 Frankfurt
Germany
NCM
Tel: +69 75 619338
Contact: Dirk Vereeken

Landesbank Berlin
– Girozentrale –
Bundesallee 171
10715 Berlin
Germany
DCM
Tel: +49 30 8694924
Contact: Richard Tangermann

Landesbank Hessen-Thüringen*
– Girozentrale –
Neue Mainzer Straße 46–50
60311 Frankfurt am Main
Germany
DCM
Tel: +49 69 1323163
Contact: Jürgen Lösche

Landesbank Rheinland-Pfalz
– Girozentrale –
Große Bleiche 54–56
55116 Mainz
Germany
DCM
Tel: +49 6131 133155
Contact: Elke Marten

Landesbank Saar
– Girozentrale –
Ursulinenstraße 2
66111 Saarbrücken
Germany
NCM
Tel: +49 681 3006653
Contact: Gerd Kothe

Landesbank Schleswig-Holstein
– Girozentrale –
Martensdamm 6
24103 Kiel
Germany
DCM
Tel: +49 431 9001990
Contact: Jörg Kaminski

Landesgirokasse öffentliche Bank und
Landessparkasse
Königstraße 3–5
70173 Stuttgart
Germany
DCM
Tel: +49 711 1243070
Contact: Nikolaus Stetter

Lehman Brothers Bankhaus AG
Grüneburgweg 18
60322 Frankfurt am Main
Germany
DCM
Tel: +49 69 15307320
Contact: Uwe Eilers

Local Traders Ltd
Camomile Court
23 Camomile Street
London EC3A 7PP
Great Britain
NCM
Tel: +44 171 2821000
Contact: Donald Wilson

Marquette Trading GmbH
Börsenstraße 7–11
60313 Frankfurt am Main
Germany
NCM, MM
Tel: +49 69 94507274
Contact: John Witt

MeesPierson NV
Niederlassung Frankfurt
Börsenstraße 7–11
60313 Frankfurt am Main
Germany
GCM
Tel: +49 69 94507152
Contact: Evert van den Brink

Merck Finck & Co Privatbankiers
Neue Mainzer Straße 55
60311 Frankfurt am Main
Germany
DCM
Tel: +49 69 2564201
Contact: Ariane Markert

Merrill Lynch Bank AG
Neue Mainzer Straße 75
60311 Frankfurt am Main
Germany
DCM
Tel: +49 69 2994257
Contact: Bernd Limberg

Metallbank GmbH
Reuterweg 14
60323 Frankfurt am Main
Germany
DCM
Tel: +49 69 1593460
Contact: Jürgen Raabe

MFK Futures
3, avenue Hoche
75008 Paris
France
NCM
Tel: +33 1 44294664
Contact: Laurent Fille

MM Warburg & Co KGaA
Ferdinandstraße 75
20095 Hamburg
Germany
DCM, MM
Tel: +49 40 32822692
Contact: Rainer Oehr(Eigenhandel + MM)
Tel: +49 40 32822638
Contact: Bettina Hüls (Kommissionshandel DTB)

Morgan Stanley Bank AG
Rahmhofstraße 2–4
60313 Frankfurt am Main
Germany
DCM, MM
Tel: +49 69 21661011
Contact: Dietrich Heitmann

MTH-Midas Trading House (Ireland) Ltd
Dublin Exchange Facility, IFSC
Dublin 1
Ireland

National Westminster Bank Plc
Niederlassung Frankfurt
Feldbergstraße 35
60323 Frankfurt am Main
Germany
NCM
Tel: +49 69 97260373
Contact: Heinz Matthies

Nations-CRT Overseas Inc & Co (Germany)
Eschersheimer Landstraße 55
60322 Frankfurt am Main
Germany
NCM, MM
Tel: +49 69 95512214
Contact: Kurt Korte

Nikko Bank (Deutschland) GmbH
Kaiserstraße 29
60311 Frankfurt am Main
Germany
DCM
Tel: +49 69 23851816
Contact: Manfred Bohn

Nomura Bank (Deutschland) GmbH
Hamburger Allee 2–10
60486 Frankfurt am Main
Germany
DCM
Tel: +49 69 97552163
Contact: Murat Baygeldi
Tel: +49 69 97552167
Contact: Kerstin Kalz

Norddeutsche Landesbank
– Girozentrale –
Georgsplatz 1
30159 Hannover
Germany
GCM
Tel: +49 51 13615321
Contact: Dirk Niemeyer

OFT Options & Futures Trading GmbH
Börsenstraße 7–11
60313 Frankfurt am Main
Germany
NCM
Tel: +49 69 94507231
Contact: Tomo Matasic (Geschäftsführer)

Optrix BV
Papenbroekssteeg 2
1012 NW Amsterdam
Netherlands
NCM, MM
Tel: +31 20 6386991
Contact: Johann G Kaemingk

Öro Futures GmbH
Königsalle 88
40212 Düsseldorf
Germany
NCM
Tel: +31 20 5551200
Contact: Albertus ter Horst

PaineWebber France SA
56, rue du Faubourg Saint Honoré
75008 Paris
France
NCM
Tel: +33 1 44711300
Contact: Michael Lück

Rabobank Deutschland AG
Solmsstraße 2–26
60486 Frankfurt am Main
Germany
DCM, MM
Tel: +49 69 79206223
Contact: Valerie Schlegel (Leiterin Handel)

Rational Trading BV
Valeriusstraat 183
1075 EW Amsterdam
Netherlands
NCM, MM
Tel: +31 20 5551281
Contact: Randall Max Liss

Refco SA
29, rue du Louvre
75002 Paris
France
NCM
Tel: +33 1 44881004
Contact: Francis Desrousseaux

Ressang Options & Securities Trading BV
Dam 27
1012 JS Amsterdam
Netherlands
NCM, MM
Tel: +31 20 5551296
Contact: Abdul A Ressang

RMT Rhein-Main Trading Börsenmakler GmbH
Große Bockenheimer Straße 30
60313 Frankfurt am Main
Germany
NCM
Tel: +49 69 29705413
Contact: Axel Pufal

S & J Derivatives Trading GmbH
Oberlindau 7
60323 Frankfurt
Germany
NCM
Tel: +49 69 97202392
Contact: Dale S Scales

Sal Oppenheim jr & Cie KGaA
Privatbankiers seit 1789
Bockenheimer Landstraße 20
60323 Frankfurt am Main
Germany
GCM, MM
Tel: +40 69 71345427
Contact: Heike Dürrenberger

Salomon Brothers AG
Eurotower
Kaiserstraße 29
60311 Frankfurt am Main
Germany
DCM, MM
Tel: +49 69 2607290
Contact: Alfred Kirchmann

Saratoga Ltd
65–66 Queen Street
London EC4R 1EB
Great Britain
NCM, MM
Tel: +44 171 3290339
Contact: Paul Leifer

Schmidt Bank
Zentraler Wertpapierbereich
Johannesgasse 20
90402 Nürnberg
Germany
DCM
Tel: +49 911 2470210
Contact: Josef Dill

Schröder Münchmeyer Hengst & Co
Friedensstraße 6–10
60311 Frankfurt am Main
Germany
DCM, MM
Tel: +49 69 2179718
Contact: Thomas Plüer

Schweizerische Bankgesellschaft
(Deutschland) AG
Bleichstraße 52
60313 Frankfurt am Main
Germany
DCM, MM
Tel: +49 69 13691890
Contact: Reto Meroni

Schweizerischer Bankverein
(Deutschland) AG
Ulmenstraße 30
60325 Frankfurt am Main
Germany
DCM, MM
Tel: +49 69 71401361
Contact: André Brisacher

SGZ-Bank AG
Südwestdeutsche Genossenschafts-
Zentralbank AG
Bockenheimer Anlage 46
60322 Frankfurt
Germany
DCM
Tel: +49 69 71391268
Contact: Marisa Duill

Société de Banque Suisse (France) SA
65, rue de Courcelles
75008 Paris
France
NCM
Tel: +33 1 48883030
Contact: Alan Genn

Société Générale SA
Zweigniederlassung
Frankfurt
Mainzer Landstraße 36
60325 Frankfurt am Main
Germany
GCM, MM
Tel: +49 69 7174370
Contact: Berthold Naumann

Stadtsparkasse München
Sparkassenstraße 2
80331 München
Germany
DCM
Tel: +49 89 21675414
Contact: Manfred Schmitt

STAFF
42, rue d'Anjou
75008 Paris
France
NCM
Tel: +33 1 47427020
Contact: Dominique Chesneau

Südwestdeutsche Landesbank
– Girozentrale –
Am Hauptbahnhof 2
70173 Stuttgart
Germany
GCM
Tel: +49 711 1275051
Contact: Hans-Ulrich Haller

Susquehanna Securities Trading GmbH
Oberlindau 7
60323 Frankfurt am Main
Germany
NCM
Tel: +49 69 174406
Contact: Johann Koehne

Taurus Finanz GmbH
Niederlassung
Frankfurt
Börsenstraße 7–11
60313 Frankfurt
Germany
NCM
Tel: +49 69 94507215
Contact: Michael Kuhn

TGS Vermögensverwaltungs-gesellschaft mbH
Zweigniederlassung Frankfurt
Guilettstraße 24
60325 Frankfurt am Main
Germany
NCM
Tel: +49 211 9102295
Contact: Paul Hagen

The Hague Options International BV
Dam 27
1012 JS Amsterdam
Netherlands
NCM, MM
Tel: +31 20 5551257
Contact: Eugene ten Brink

Timber Hill Deutschland GmbH
Steinweg 7
60313 Frankfurt am Main
Germany
NCM, MM
Tel: +49 69 92072712
Contact: Robert E Prior

Timber Hill Europe AG
Gotthardstraße 3 Ost
6300 Zug
Switzerland
NCM, MM
Tel: +41 41 7265060
Contact: Jonathan Chait (Geschäftsführer)

Transoptions Compensation GIE
26, rue de la Baume
75008 Paris
France
NCM, MM
Tel: +33 1 40756396
Contact: Mourad Amellal

Transoptions SA
4, avenue Sainte-Luce
1003 Lausanne
Switzerland
NCM, MM
Tel: +41 21 3115205
Contact: Karl Stöcklin

Trifutures
119, rue Réaumur
75002 Paris
France
NCM
Tel: +33 1 44821234
Contact: Bertrand Dautresme

Trinkaus & Burkhardt KGaA
Königsallee 21–23
40212 Düsseldorf
Germany
GCM, MM
Tel: +49 211 91063
Contact: Marc Cringle

Trinkaus Consult GmbH
Königsallee 21–23
40212 Düsseldorf
Germany
NCM, MM
Tel: +49 211 9102464
Contact: Victor Maessen

Van der Moolen (Deutschland) GmbH
Graf Adolf Straße 86–88
40210 Düsseldorf
Germany
NCM, MM
Tel: +49 211 1730621
Contact: Ralf Seithümmer

Vereins- und Westbank AG
Alter Wall 22
20457 Hamburg
Germany
DCM, MM
Tel: +49 40 36922476
Contact: Timothy P Lew

Westdeutsche Genossenschafts-Zentralbank eG
Ludwig-Erhard-Allee 20
40227 Düsseldorf
Germany
DCM
Tel: +49 211 7782600
Contact: Karl-Heinz Moll

Westdeutsche Landesbank
– Girozentrale –
Herzogstraße 15
40217 Düsseldorf
Germany
GCM, MM
Tel: +49 211 8266751
Contact: Rainer Schmitz (Bereichsleiter)
Tel: +49 211 8264555
Contact: Friedhelm Breuers

Westfalenbank AG
Huestraße 21–25
44787 Bochum
Germany
DCM
Tel: +49 234 6164693
Contact: Holger Schmidt

Yamaichi Bank (Deutschland) GmbH
Feuerbachstraße 26
60325 Frankfurt am Main
Germany
NCM
Tel: +49 69 7102126
Contact: Sabine Hüttermann

Euro-Terminals located at a branch of a member company

Apollo Derivatives Group - Frankfurt
GmbH Germany
London Branch
Walbrook House
23–29 Walbrook
London EC4N 8BT
Great Britain

BZW Futures/Barclays Bank Plc
Ebbgate House
2 Swan Lane
London EC4R 3TS
Great Britain

Commerzbank AG
London Branch
PO Box 286
London EC2P 2JD
Great Britain

Deutsche Bank AG
Succursale de Paris
3, avenue de Friedland
75008 Paris
France

Estlander & Rönnlund GmbH
Vsaesplanaden 14 D
65100 Vaasa
Finland

Estlander & Rönnlund GmbH
Zweigniederlassung Zug
Baarerstraße 112
6300 Zug
Switzerland

Extra Clearing Services GmbH & Co KG
Niederlassung Amsterdam
Rokin Plaza
Papenbroeksteeg 2
1012 NW Amsterdam
Netherlands

Landesbank Hessen-Thüringen
London Branch
8 Moorgate
London EC2R 6DD
Great Britain
DCM, MM

National Westminster Bank Plc
135 Bishopsgate
London EC3M 3UR
Great Britain

Öro Futures GmbH
Zweigniederlassung Amsterdam
Rokin 68
1012 KW Amsterdam
Netherlands

IBIS Members

ABN Amro Bank (Deutschland) AG
Kreditinstitut (7034)
Grüneburgweg 18
60322 Frankfurt
Tel: +49 69 29600650
Contact: Winfried Hauske

Gerhard Anhoff
Kursmakler (1188)
Fasanenstr 3
10623 Berlin
Tel: +49 30 3122359

AOT Amsterdam Options Traders GmbH
Wertpapierhandelshaus (9241)
Komödienstraße 44–46
50667 Köln
Tel: +49 221 133003
Contact: Adrianus van den Brink

Archelon (Deutschland) GmbH
Wertpapierhandelshaus (9173)
Oberlindau 7
60323 Frankfurt
Tel: +49 69 175289
Contact: Charles Tall

Arne Albrecht AG
Freimakler (3898)
Obernstr 2-12
28195 Bremen
Tel: +49 421 3365656
Contact: Arne Albrecht

Frank Arnold
Kursmakler (4189)
Ernst-Schneider-Platz 1
40489 Düsseldorf
Tel: +49 211 8902131

Gisela Baasner
Kursmakler (7839)
Kaiserstr 1
60311 Frankfurt
Tel: +49 69 21731839

Baden-Württembergische Bank AG
Kreditinstitut (6005)
Kleiner Schloßplatz 11
70173 Stuttgart
Tel: +49 711 1801491
Contact: Rainer Helbig

Ballmaier & Schultz
Wertpapier Aktiengesellschaft
Freimakler (3881)
Bleidenstr 6
60311 Frankfurt
Tel: +49 69 13881312
Contact: Stefan Richter

Ballmaier & Schultz
Wertpapier Aktiengesellschaft
Freimakler (7881)
Bleidenstr 6
60311 Frankfurt
Tel: +49 69 13881312
Contact: Stefan Richter

Bank Julius Bär (Deutschland) AG
Kreditinstitut (7226)
Friedrich-Ebert-Anlage 49/Messeturm
60327 Frankfurt
Tel: +49 69 75696162
Contact: Lutz Michel

Bank of Tokyo (Deutschland) AG
Kreditinstitut (7047)
Mainzer Landstr 16, Trianon-Haus
60325 Frankfurt
Tel: +49 69 7176224
Contact: Issei Inoue

Bankers Trust International PLC
Zweigniederlassung Frankfurt am Main
Kreditinstitut (7103)
Bockenheimer Landstraße 39
60325 Frankfurt
Tel: +49 69 15301363
Contact: Thomas Eckert
Bankgesellschaft Berlin AG
w/Landesbank Berlin
Kreditinstitut (1051)
Alexanderplatz 2
10178 Berlin
Tel: +49 30 24562461
Contact: Wolfgang Lierck

Bankgesellschaft Berlin AG
Kreditinstitut (1011)
Hardenbergstraße 32
10623 Berlin
Tel: +49 30 31093927
Contact: Bartho Schröder

Bankhaus Carl F Plump & Co
Kreditinstitut (3311)
Am Markt 19
28195 Bremen
Tel: +49 421 3685262 oder 259
Contact: Frank Fischer

Bankhaus Gebrüder Bethmann
Kreditinstitut (7038)
Bethmannstraße 7–9
60311 Frankfurt
Tel: +49 69 2177362
Contact: Kurt Goettgens

Bankhaus Hermann Lampe KG
Kreditinstitut (4058)
Jägerhofstraße 10
40479 Düsseldorf
Tel: +49 211 4952436
Contact: Caroline Ringel

Bankhaus H Aufhäuser
Kreditinstitut (7118)
Kaiserhofstraße 16
60313 Frankfurt
Tel: +49 69 281629
Contact: Fidel Helmer

Bankhaus H Aufhäuser
Kreditinstitut (2025)
Löwengrube 18–20
80333 München
Tel: +49 89 23932400
Contact: Peter Höß

Bankhaus Löbbecke & Co
Kreditinstitut (7031)
Lidenstraße 27
60325 Frankfurt
Tel: +49 69 75305352
Contact: Heinz Dieruff

Bankhaus Max Flessa & Co
Kreditinstitut (2015)
Schwanthalerstraße 16
80336 München
Tel: +49 89 55870257
Contact: Manfred Tröppner

Bankhaus Metzler Seel Sohn & Co KGaA
Kreditinstitut (7052)
Rembrandtstraße 13
60596 Frankfurt
Tel: +49 69 2104368
Contact: Detlev Klug

Bankhaus Neelmeyer AG
Kreditinstitut (3309)
AM Markt 14–16
28195 Bremen
Tel: +49 421 3603286
Contact: Karl-Adolf Stock

Bankhaus Reuschel & Co
Kreditinstitut (2021)
Maximiliansplatz 13
80333 München
Tel: +49 89 2395350
Contact: Lothar Krüger

Banque Nationale de Paris SA
Niederlassung Frankfurt
Kreditinstitut (7076)
Bockenheimer Landstraße 22
60323 Frankfurt
Tel: +49 69 728139
Contact: Matthias-Klaus Fried

Banque Paribas (Deutschland) OHG
Kreditinstitut (7108)
Grüneburgwerg 14
60322 Frankfurt
Tel: +49 69 5970111
Contact: Michael Hoffmann

Barclays Bank PLC
Zweigniederlassung Frankfurt
Kreditinstitut (7244)
Bockenheimer Landstraße 38–40
60323 Frankfurt
Tel: +49 69 71611010
Contact: Andrea Repp

Bayerische Hypotheken- und
Wechselbank AG
Kreditinstitut (7032)
Kleiner Hirschgraben 16
60311 Frankfurt
Tel: +49 69 29808260
Contact: Martin Haider

Bayerische Hypotheken- und
Wechselbank AG
Kreditinstitut (6030)
Hospitalplatz 17–19
70174 Stuttgart
Tel: +49 711 299451
Contact: Raimund Krauss

Bayerische Hypotheken- und
Wechselbank AG
Kreditinstitut (3009)
Graskeller 2
20475 Hamburg
Tel: +49 40 36953315
Contact: Holger Krohn

Bayerische Hypotheken- und
Wechselbank AG
Kreditinstitut (4006)
Königsallee 17
40212 Düsseldorf
Tel: +49 211 1372355
Contact: Lothar Neumann

Bayerische Hypotheken- und
Wechselbank AG
Kreditinstitut (2009)
Arabellastraße 12
81925 München
Tel: +49 89 92446363
Contact: Claudia Radmiller

Bayerische Hypotheken- und
Wechselbank AG w/London
Kreditinstitut (2069)
Arabellastraße 12
81925 München
Tel: +49 89 92446363
Contact: Claudia Radmiller

Bayerische Landesbank
– Girozentrale –
Kreditinstitut (2007)
Brienner Straße 18
80333 München
Tel: +49 89 21713353
Contact: Hans-Peter Goth

Bayerische Landesbank
—Girozentrale –
Kreditinstitut (7106)
Bockenheimer Landstraße 19
60325 Frankfurt
Tel: +49 69 173101
Contact: Otto Kohl

Bayerische Vereinsbank AG
Kreditinstitut (2013)
Am Tucherpark 1
80311 München
Tel: +49 89 37818123
Contact: Regina Nowakowski

Bayerische Vereinsbank AG
Kreditinstitut (7084)
Mainzer Landstr 23
60329 Frankfurt
Tel: +49 69 27172156
Contact: Norbert Wentzien

Bear Stearns Bank GmbH
Kreditinstitut (7323)
Grüneburgweg 16
60322 Frankfurt
Tel: +49 69 15304180
Contact: Volker Kobel

Wolfgang Becker
Kursmakler (4186)
Im Grund 83
40489 Düsseldorf
Tel: +49 211 8902103

Berenberg, Gossler & Co, Joh
Kreditinstitut (7036)
Niedenau 61–63
60325 Frankfurt
Tel: +49 69 9715833
Contact: Peter Estelmann

Berliner Volksbank eG
Kreditinstitut (1623)
Kaiserdamm 86
14057 Berlin
Tel: +49 30 30631251
Contact: Dieter Smolibocki

BfG Bank AG
Kreditinstitut (7104)
Ben-Gurion-Ring 62
60437 Frankfurt
Tel: +49 69 2585250
Contact: Matthias Gramb

BHF Bank AG
Kreditinstitut (7001)
Bockenheimer Landstraße 10
60323 Frankfurt
Tel: +49 69 7182739
Contact: Matthias Rind

BHF Bank AG
Kreditinstitut (1026)
Uhlandstraße 165–166
10719 Berlin
Tel: +49 30 88417234
Contact: Robert Schulz

BHF Bank AG
Niederlassung Düsseldorf
Kreditinstitut (4060)
Pempelforter Straße 11
40211 Düsseldorf
Tel: +49 211 3663213
Contact: Helmut Zils

BHF Bank AG Filiale Hamburg
Kreditinstitut (3045)
Paulstraße 5
20095 Hamburg
Tel: +49 40 3009223
Contact: Edgar Schröder

BHF Bank AG Fil München
Kreditinstitut (2076)
Max-Joseph-Straße 6
80333 München
Tel: +49 89 55173217
Contact: Dieter Silmen

Bierbaum & Co Effekten GmbH
Freimakler (7856)
Stephanstraße 3
60313 Frankfurt
Tel: +49 69 290357
Contact: Heinfried Reiche

BMP Wertpapiere und Optionen GmbH
Wertpapierhandelshaus (9174)
Niedenau 36
60325 Frankfurt
Tel: +49 69 9714460
Contact: Brian D Sparks

Adolf Bonfig
Kursmakler (7803)
Hochstraße 39
60313 Frankfurt
Tel: +49 69 285154–6

Brauburger Rolf
Kursmakler (7821)
Kaiserstr 1
60311 Frankfurt
Tel: +49 69 21731821

Bremer Bank
Kreditinstitut (3413)
Domshof 8–9
28195 Bremen
Tel: +49 421 3662286
Contact: Ralf Wottge

Bremer Landesbank
Kreditinstitut (3305)
Domshof 26
28195 Bremen
Tel: +49 421 3322888
Contact: Helmut Hoppe

Bruker Wertpapierhandelsges mbH
Kursmakler (6182)
Königstraße 28
70173 Stuttgart
Tel: +49 711 221472
Contact: Hans-Peter Bruker

Peter Buch
Kursmakler (7887)
Kaiserstr 1
60311 Frankfurt
Tel: +49 69 21731887

Albert Bürger
Kursmakler (4194)
Ernst-Schneider-Platz 1
40489 Düsseldorf
Tel: +49 211 8902101

Caisse des Dépôts et Consignations GmbH
Kreditinstitut (7092)
Bockenheimer Landstraße 51–53
60325 Frankfurt
Tel: +49 69 97133363
Contact: Thomas Lay

Carl Kliem & Co
Freimakler (7834)
An der Hauptwache 7
60313 Frankfurt
Tel: +49 69 20204
Contact: Rainer Thormann

CFP Commerz Financial Products GmbH
Freimakler (9172)
Neue Mainzer Str 32–36
60313 Frankfurt
Tel: +49 69 13624868
Contact: Günther Wudy

Commerzbank AG
Filiale Stuttgart
Kreditinstitut (6002)
Königstraße 11–15
70173 Stuttgart
Tel: +49 711 2002451
Contact: Werner Fronk

Commerzbank AG
Kreditinstitut (4013)
Breite Straße 25
40213 Düsseldorf
Tel: +49 211 8272456
Contact: Klaus Meuskens

Commerzbank AG
Kreditinstitut (7004)
Neue Mainzer Str 32–36
60311 Frankfurt
Tel: +49 69 13622259
Contact: Stefan Spies

Commerzbank AG
Kreditinstitut (3004)
Neß 7–9
20457 Hamburg
Tel: +49 40 36834600
Contact: Michael von Unruh

Concord Effecten GmbH & Co KG
Freimakler (7841)
Roßmarkt 23
60311 Frankfurt
Tel: +49 69 29704413
Contact: Dag Liedtke

Conrad Hinrich Donner Bank
Kreditinstitut (3043)
Ballindamm 27
20095 Hamburg
Tel: +49 40 30217280
Contact: Klaus Wenzel

Credit Suisse (Deutschland) Aktiengesellschaft
Kreditinstitut (7005)
Messeturm
60308 Frankfurt
Tel: +49 69 75382959
Contact: Thomas Schlawinsky

CS First Boston Effectenbank AG
Kreditinstitut (7191)
Messeturm
60308 Frankfurt am Main
Tel: +49 69 75343780
Contact: Dennis Patrikios

Klaus-Dieter Dahm
Kursmakler (3828)
Glashütter Landstr 209
22417 Hamburg
Tel: +49 40 5373996`

Daiwa Bank (Deutschland) AG
Kreditinstitut (7197)
Im Trutz Frankfurt 55
60322 Frankfurt
Tel: +49 69 15407107
Contact: Boris Pasternak

Delbrück & Co Provatbankiers
Kreditinstitut (7100)
Neue Mainzer Str 75
60311 Frankfurt
Tel: +49 69 1331220
Contact: Andreas Busse

Deutsche Apotheker und Ärztebank eG
Kreditinstitut (4011)
Emanuel-Leutze-Straße 8
40547 Düsseldorf
Tel: +49 21 15998303
Contact: Jürgen Wamers

Deutsche Bank AG
Kreditinstitut (2005)
Promenadeplatz 15
80333 München
Tel: +49 89 23902542
Contact: Helmut Breu

Deutsche Bank AG
Niederlassung Bremen
Kreditinstitut (3407)
Domshof 22–25
28195 Bremen
Tel: +49 42 13674361
Contact: Klaus Holst

Deutsche Bank AG
Kreditinstitut (6004)
Theodor-Heuss-Straße 3
70174 Stuttgart
Tel: +49 711 1252610
Contact: Gert-Michael Hommel

Deutsche Bank AG
Kreditinstitut (8020)
Georgsplatz 20
30159 Hannover
Tel: +49 511 365265
Contact: Georg Hudalle

Deutsche Bank AG
Kreditinstut (3007)
Alter Wall 37/53
20457 Hamburg
Tel: +49 40 37013162
Contact: Lars Hufediener

Deutsche Bank AG
Kreditinstitut (4001)
Königsallee 45–47
40189 Düsseldorf
Tel: +49 211 8832000
Contact: Gerhard Jäckel

Deutsche Bank AG
Kreditinstitut (4098)
Unter Sachsenhausen 11–27
50587 Köln
Tel: +49 221 1422280
Contact: Hans Müller

Deutsche Bank AG
Kreditinstitut (7003)
Taunusanlage 12
60325 Frankfurt
Tel: +49 69 91038401
Contact: Edeltraud Plünnecke

Deutsche Bank AG, Filiale Berlin
Kreditinstitut (1007)
Otto-Suhr-Allee 6–16
10585 Berlin
Tel: +49 30 34072966
Contact: Jörg Wiese

Deutsche Bank AG
Kreditinstitut (7078)
P7, 10–15
68161 Mannheim
Tel: +49 62 11693131
Contact: Peter Wilhelm

Deutsche Bundesbank
Kreditinstitut (7073)
Wilhelm-Epstein-Straße 14
60431 Frankfurt
Tel: +49 69 95663027
Contact: Bernhard Oppenheim

Deutsche Verkehrs-Bank AG
Kreditinstitut (7096)
Untermainkai 23–25
60329 Frankfurt
Tel: +49 69 2648426
Contact: Ulrich Berner

DGZ Deutsche Girozentrale
– Deutsche Kommunalbank –
Kreditinstitut (7079)
Taunusanlage 10
60329 Frankfurt
Tel: +49 69 2693602
Contact: Helmut Vogel

DG-Bank
Kreditinstitut (7030)
Am Platz der Republik
60325 Frankfurt
Tel: +49 69 74476584
Contact: Theo Stenner

Die Sparkasse in Bremen
Kreditinstut (3306)
Am Brill 1–3
28195 Bremen
Tel: +49 421 1793505
Contact: Ulrich Dopmeyer

Diederich Kursmaklerges mbH
Kursmakler (1181)
WInkler Straße 18 D
14193 Berlin
Tel: +49 30 3127891
Contact: Claus-Jürgen Diederich

Hans Dittmar
Kursmakler (7818)
Schillerstraße 10
60313 Frankfurt
Tel: +49 69 20426

Dresdner Bank AG
Kreditinstitut (6001)
Königstraße 9
70173 Stuttgart
Tel: +49 711 1852422
Contact: Rudolf Gläsche

Dresdner Bank AG
Kreditinstitut (7002)
Jürgen-Ponto-Platz 1
60301 Frankfurt
Tel: +49 69 2632671
Contact: Frank Henning

Dresdner Bank AG Ndl Hbg
Kreditinstitut (3008)
St Valentinskamp 91
20349 Hamburg
Tel: +49 40 35012303
Contact: Peter Rathje

Dresdner Bank AG in Berlin
Kreditinstitut (1008)
Uhlandstr 9–11
10623 Berlin
Tel: +49 30 315332358
Contact: Erhardt Rothe

Dresdner Bank AG in Düsseldorf
Kreditinstitut (4037)
Königsallee 37
40212 Düsseldorf
Tel: +49 211 32173
Contact: Horst Steiner

Dresdner Bank AG
Kreditinstitut (8018)
Rathenaustraße 4
30159 Hannover
Tel: +49 511 3662381
Contact: Lisa Wiese-Rosenbrock

Dresdner Bank AG
Kreditinstitut (2004)
Promenadeplatz 7
80333 München
Tel: +49 89 21392705
Contact: Michael Wimmer

Dyna Option GmbH
Wertpapierhandelshaus (9272)
Mainzer Landstr 46
60325 Frankfurt
Tel: +49 69 97201930
Contact: Bruno Hery

Eckes Effekten-Handelsges mbH
Freimakler (7845)
Kaiserstraße 8
60311 Frankfurt
Tel: +49 69 9130150
Contact: Ulrich Thaler

Estlander & Rönnlund GmbH
Wertpapierhandelshaus (9175)
An der Staufenmauer 6
60311 Frankfurt
Tel: +49 04 684631018
Contact: Martin Estlander

Extra Clearing GmbH & Co Service KG
Wertpapierhandelshaus (9240)
Blanchardstr 17
60487 Frankfurt
Tel: +49 03 1205301301
Contact: Hans de Theye

F & O Capital Management Ag
Wertpapierhandelshaus (9770)
Bellerivestr 49
8008 Zürich
Tel: +49 04 113882323
Contact: George W Fleming

Wilhelm Faust
Kursmakler (7820)
Goethestraße 21
60313 Frankfurt
Tel: +49 69 20469

Norbert Fey
Kursmakler (7819)
Kaiserhofstraße 10
60313 Frankfurt
Tel: +49 69 284645

FIMAT Internat Banque SA
Zweigniederlassung Frankfurt
Kreditinstitut (7328)
Mainzer Landstr 46
60325 Frankfurt
Tel: +49 69 71070
Contact: François Bloch

Finacor Deutschland GmbH
Freimakler (2175)
Residenzstraße 22
80333 München
Tel: +49 89 293526
Contact: Gert Pfannenstiel

First Marathon Bank GmbH
Kreditinstitut (7165)
Feuerbachstraße 26–32
60325 Frankfurt am Main
Tel: +49 69 97166
Contact: Christoph Busch

Frankfurter Sparkasse
Kreditinstitut (7029)
Neue Mainzer Str 47–53
60255 Frankfurt
Tel: +49 69 26412410
Contact: Peter Ensel

Frankfurter Volksbank eG
Kreditinstitut (7009)
Börsenstraße 1
60313 Frankfurt
Tel: +49 69 21721222
Contact: Thomas Fleischmann

Helmut Fuhr
Kursmakler (4180)
Ernst-Schneider-Platz 1
40212 Düsseldorf
Tel: +49 211 8902128

Fürst Fugger Privatbank
Kreditinstitut (2042)
Maximilianstraße 38
86150 Augsburg
Tel: +49 82 13201211
Contact: Wolfgang Grau

Lothar Gautsch
Freimakler (7878)
Große Bockenheimer Straße 35
60313 Frankfurt
Tel: +49 69 920320
Contact: Lothar Gautsch

Michael Gebhard
Kursmakler (2196)
Lenbachplatz 2 A
80333 München
Tel: +49 89 55190820

Geestemünder Bank AG
Kreditinstitut (3312)
Am Alten Hafen 118
27568 Bremerhaven
Tel: +49 471 4822215
Contact: Lars P Wollesen

Genossenschaftliche Zentralbank AG
Kreditinstitut (6018)
Heilbronner Str 41
70191 Stuttgart
Tel: +49 711 9402324
Contact: Manfred Häfner

Georg Hauck & Sohn Bankiers
Kreditinstitut (7057)
Kaiserstraße 24
60311 Frankfurt
Tel: +49 69 2161222
Contact: Dieter Arlt

Goldman, Sachs & Co OHG
Kreditinstitut (7246)
Friedr-Ebert-Anl 49/Messeturm
60327 Frankfurt
Tel: +49 69 75321950
Contact: Thomas Behrens

Grundkreditbank eG
Kreditinstitut (1625)
Budapester Straße 35
10787 Berlin
Tel: +49 30 26981472
Contact: Chana Krzeszower

Roland Grundstein
Kursmakler (7806)
Kaiserstrasse 1
60311 Frankfurt
Tel: +49 69 21731806

Norbert Gruner
Kursmakler (7826)
Kaiserstr 1
60311 Frankfurt
Tel: +49 69 21731826

Hamburger Sparkasse
Kreditinstitut (3057)
Großer Burstah 6
20454 Hamburg
Tel: +49 40 35793724
Contact: Martin Kruse

Hamburgische Landesbank -GZ-
Kreditinstitut (3005)
Gerhart-Hauptmann-Platz 50
20095 Hamburg
Tel: +49 40 33333561
Contact: Rüdiger Munzke

Hans Bauer Börsenmakler GmbH
Freimakler (2179)
Sonnenstr 13
86923 Finning
Tel: +49 88 0692140
Contact: Hans Bauer

Wolfgang Hein
Freimakler (3804)
Adolf-Platz 1
20457 Hamburg
Tel: +49 40 3698930

Dieter Heinemann
Kursmakler (7822)
Kaiserstr 1
60311 Frankfurt
Tel: +49 69 21731822

Herbert Bendel GmbH
Börsenmakler
Freimakler (7889)
Große Eschenheimer Straße 13 A
60313 Frankfurt
Tel: +49 69 280098
Contact: Herbert Bendel

Alf-Dietrich Herforth
Kursmakler (7866)
Kaiserstr 1
60311 Frankfurt
Tel: +49 69 21731866

Rüdiger Hinkel
Kursmakler (7828)
Kaiserstr 1
60311 Frankfurt
Tel: +49 69 21731828

Peter Hirthammer
Kursmakler (1189)
Fasanenstr 3
10623 Berlin
Tel: +49 30 3137802

Thomas Hofacker
Freimakler (4279)
Ernst-Schneider-Platz 1
40212 Düsseldorf
Tel: +49 211 1389111

HSBC James Capel
Kreditinstitut (9772)
10 Queen Street Place
London EC4R 1BL
Tel: +44 171 3362430
Contact: David Price

Josef Huf
Kursmakler (7813)
Kaiserstrasse 1
60311 Frankfurt
Tel: +49 69 21731813

Hull Trading GmbH
Wertpapierhandelshaus (9274)
Friedrichstr 2–6
60323 Frankfurt
Tel: +49 69 97200520
Contact: Mark Carroll

Horst Hüfner
Kursmakler (7882)
An der Hauptwache 11
60313 Frankfurt
Tel: +49 69 20662

IKB Deutsche Industriebank AG
Kreditinstitut (4061)
Karl-Theodor-Straße 6
40213 Düsseldorf
Tel: +49 211 8221270
Contact: Gert Neubeck

ING Bank NV
Kreditinstitut (9771)
PO Box 1800
1000 BV Amsterdam
Tel: +49 03 1205638639
Contact: Theo M Bakkum

Instinet GmbH
Freimakler (7844)
Kaiserstraße 5
60311 Frankfurt
Tel: +49 69 92007916
Contact: Harald Breitenbach

1st Bancario S Paolo Di Torino
Kreditinstitut (7175)
Eschersheimer Landstr 55
60322 Frankfurt
Tel: +49 69 15681180
Contact: Rudolf Weber

Lothar Jäger
Kursmakler (7824)
Kaiserstr 1
60311 Frankfurt
Tel: +49 69 21731824

Joh Berenberg, Gossler & Co -
Berenbergbank, Hamburg
Kreditinstitut (3048)
Neuer Jungfernstieg 20
20354 Hamburg
Tel: +49 40 349677
Contact: Dieter Lügering

JP Morgan GmbH
Kreditinstitut (7080)
Börsenstr 2–4
60313 Frankfurt
Tel: +49 69 71241160
Contact: Frank Röser

Paul Kappes
Freimakler (4170)
Ernst-Schneider-Platz 1
40212 Düsseldorf
Tel: +49 211 1389304

Georg Kaul
Kursmakler (7809)
Große Eschenheimerstr 39
60313 Frankfurt
Tel: +49 69 287492

Keller & Treichel GmbH
Harald Treichel
Freimakler (6172)
Königstraße 28
70173 Stuttgart
Tel: +49 711 2261083
Contact: Gerrit Keller

Helmuth Klein
Kursmakler (3807)
Am Kiekeberg 20
22587 Hamburg
Tel: +49 40 867787

Kling & Jelko
Börsenmakler AG
Freimakler (7862)
Goethestr 7
60313 Frankfurt
Tel: +49 69 294057
Contact: Rona Jungeblut

Klaus König
Kursmakler (4193)
Ernst-Schneider-Platz 1
40212 Düsseldorf
Tel: +49 211 8902130

Frank Kraul
Kursmakler (8882)
In der Feddel 8
30952 Ronnenberg
Tel: +49 511 363434

Krähling GmbH
Freimakler (7871)
Schillerstr 20
60313 Frankfurt
Tel: +49 69 5970705
Contact: Hans Krähling

Kredietbank – Bankverein AG
Kreditinstitut (7195)
Mendelssohnstraße 75–77
60325 Frankfurt
Tel: +49 69 740729
Contact: Michael Laufenberg

Kreissparkasse in Siegburg
Kreditinstitut (4126)
An der Stadtmauer 1–5
53721 Siegburg
Tel: +49 22 41100617
Contact: Fritz Broszehl

Kreissparkasse Köln
Kreditinstitut (4128)
Neumarkt 18–24
50667 Köln
Tel: +49 221 2272204
Contact: Manfred Nickel

K-H Möser Börsenmakler GmbH
Freimakler (7886)
Schillerstraße 18
60313 Frankfurt
Tel: +49 69 1310741
Contact: Karl-Heinz Möser

Landesbank Hessen-Thüringen GZ
Kreditinstitut (7010)
Neue Mainzer Straße 46–50
60311 Frankfurt
Tel: +49 69 1323040
Contact: Klaus Hartmann

Landesbank Rheinland-Pfalz -GZ-
Kreditinstitut (7018)
Große Bleiche 54–56
55098 Mainz
Tel: +49 61 3127510
Contact: Hans-Josef Wucher

Landesbank Saar -GZ-
Kreditinstitut (7048)
Ursulinenstraße 2
66111 Saarbrüken
Tel: +49 681 3006681
Contact: Ralph Amorosi

Landesbank Schleswsig-Holstein
Kreditinstitut (3212)
Martensdamm 6
24103 Kiel
Tel: +49 431 9001128
Contact: Gert-Horst Harpeng

Landesgirokasse Stuttgart
Kreditinstitut (6061)
Königstraße 3–5
70173 Stuttgart
Tel: +49 711 1242121
Contact: Helmut Oßwald

Landesgirokasse Stuttgart
Niederlassung Frankfurt
Kreditinstitut (7179)
Zeil 65–69
60313 Frankfurt
Tel: +49 69 20534
Contact: Klaus Pätz

Lang & Schwartz Börsenmakler GmbH
Freimakler (4273)
Ernst-Schneider-Platz 1
40212 Düsseldorf
Tel: +49 211 138400
Contact: Jörg Schwarz

Lehman Brothers Bankhaus AG
Kreditinstitut (7059)
Grüneburgweg 18
60322 Frankfurt
Tel: +49 69 15307255
Contact: Claudia Hauser

LGT Bank in Liechtenstein
(Deutschland) GmbH
Kreditinstitut (7154)
Bleichstraße 60–62
60313 Frankfurt
Tel: +49 69 29807170
Contact: Detlev Claas

Hainz Maier
Kursmakler (2191)
Lenbachplatz 2 A
80333 München
Tel: +49 89 555927

Klaus Massing
Kursmakler (4184)
Ernst-Schneider-Platz 1
40489 Düsseldorf
Tel: +49 211 8902113

Klaus Mathis
Kursmakler (4288)
Ernst-Schneider-Platz 1
40212 Düsseldorf
Tel: +49 211 8902153

MeesPierson NV
Niederlassung Frankfurt
Kreditinstitut (7326)
Börsenstraße 7–11
60313 Frankfurt am Main
Tel: +49 69 94507201
Contact: Heiko Friedrich

Dieter Menzel
Kursmakler (7876)
Kaiserstr 1
60311 Frankfurt
Tel: +49 69 21731876

Merck Finck & Co
Kreditinstitut (7061)
Neue Mainzer Str 55
60311 Frankfurt
Tel: +49 69 2564233
Contact: Christian Recker

Merck, Finck & Co
Kreditinstitut (4104)
Steinstraße 4
40212 Düsseldorf
Tel: +49 211 8229251
Contact: Harald Klöckner

Merrill Lynch Bank AG
Kreditinstitut (7042)
Neue Mainzer Straße 75
60311 Frankfurt
Tel: +49 69 2994340
Contact: Michael Failing

Metallbank GmbH
Kreditinstitut (7056)
Reuterweg 14
60323 Frankfurt
Tel: +49 69 1593460
Contact: Jürgen Raabe

Werner Meyer
Kursmakler (3893)
Obernstraße 2–12
28195 Bremen
Tel: +49 421 321492

Montag, Pöpper und Partner GmbH
Freimakler (7850)
Große Bockenheimer Straße 45
60313 Frankfurt
Tel: +49 69 920231
Contact: Volker Gilbert

Karl-Heinz Moog
Kursmakler (4183)
Fritz-Reuter-Str 36
40699 Erkrath
Tel: +49 211 1389161

Morgan Stanley Bank AG
Kreditinstitut (7171)
Rahmhofstraße 2–4
60313 Frankfurt
Tel: +49 69 21661110
Contact: Dietmar Schmidt

Thomas Munz
Kursmakler (6183)
Königstraße 28
70173 Stuttgart
Tel: +49 711 221472

MWB Wertpapierhandels- und
Börsenmaklergesellschaft mbH
Freimakler (2190)
Lenbachplatz 2 A
80333 München
Tel: +49 89 8543073
Contact: Thomas Posovatz

M M Warburg & Co
Kommanditges, auf Aktien
Kreditinstitut (3049)
Ferdinandstraße 75
20095 Hamburg
Tel: +49 40 3282676
Contact: Peter Ripke

M M Warburg & Co Kommanditges auf Aktien
Kreditinstitut (7150)
Liebigstraße 6
60323 Frankfurt
Tel: +49 69 7100640
Contact: Christine Schmidt

Nassauische Sparkasse
Kreditinstitut (7006)
Abraham-Lincoln-Str 34
65189 Wiesbaden
Tel: +49 61 1364339
Contact: Peter Seifert
National Bank AG
Kreditinstitut (4029)
Theaterlatz 8
45219 Essen
Tel: +49 201 8115276
Contact: Bernd Andersen

National Westminster Bank Plc
Niederlassung Frankfurt
Kreditinstitut (7126)
Feldbergstr 35
60323 Frankfurt
Tel: +49 69 9726210
Contact: Thomas Böckenfeld

Nations-CRT Overseas Inc & Co (Germany)
Wertpapierhandelshaus (9177)
Eschersheimer Landstr 55
60322 Frankfurt am Main
Tel: +49 69 95512223
Contact: Stefan Durdic

Nikko Bank (Deutschland) AG
Kreditinstitut (7135)
Willy-Brandt-Platz 2
60311 Frankfurt
Tel: +49 69 23851832
Contact: Claudia Wiemann

Dr Karl Emil Nohe
Freimakler (2177)
Lenbachplatz 2A
80333 München
Tel: +49 17 26676543

Nols Fritz KG
Freimakler (7854)
Hochstr 31
60313 Frankfurt
Tel: +49 69 920240
Contact: Eric Nols

Nomura Bank (Deutschland) GmbH
Kreditinstitut (7136)
Hamburger Allee 2–10
60486 Frankfurt
Tel: +49 69 97552272
Contact: Hermann H Tilk

Nord LB -GZ-
Kreditinstitut (8019)
Georgsplatz 1
30159 Hannover
Tel: +49 511 3614718
Contact: Herr Ahrent
Nord LB -GZ-
Kreditinstitut (7168)
Rahmhofstraße 2–4
60313 Frankfurt
Tel: +49 69 92044124
Contact: Udo Glafenhein

Noris Verbraucherbank GmbH
Kreditinstitut (3044)
Große Bäckerstraße 11
20095 Hamburg
Tel: +49 40 3699332
Contact: Inga Lupinski

Oldenburgische Landesbank AG
Kreditinstitut (7347)
Stau 15/17
26122 Oldenburg
Tel: +49 441 2211228
Contact: Bernd Claaßen

Optiver GmbH
Wertpapierhandelshaus (9176)
Börsenstr 7–11
60313 Frankfurt am Main
Tel: +49 03 1206386991
Contact: Jan Dobber

Heinz Osterkamp
Kursmakler (7830)
Kaiserstrasse 1
60311 Frankfurt
Tel: +49 69 21731830

Otto M Schröder Bank AG
Kreditinstitut (3112)
Alsterarkaden 27
20354 Hamburg
Tel: +49 40 335928223
Contact: Malte Struefing

PantaCon GmbH Wertpapierhandels- und Kapitalbetreuungsgesellschaft
Freimakler (2188)
Bavariastraße 7
80336 München
Tel: +49 89 74616850
Contact: Isabella Medri

Karl-Heinz Pfeiffer
Kursmakler (6186)
Königstraße 28
70173 Stuttgart
Tel: +49 711 221472

Rabe & Partner Börsenmakler GmbH
Freimakler (7852)
Hochstraße 43
60313 Frankfurt
Tel: +49 69 282448
Contact: Harald Göbel

Rabobank Deutschland AG
Kreditinstut (7007)
Solmsstr 2–26
60486 Frankfurt
Tel: +49 69 79206356
Contact: Jürgen Scharnowske

Uwe Radeke
Kursmakler (3829)
Trostbrücke
1 20457 Hamburg
Tel: +49 40 367892

RBS Effectenhandelsges mbH
Freimakler (7896)
Jahnstr 45
60318 Frankfurt
Tel: +49 69 558776
Contact: Christian Schlegel

Hans-Jörg Reder
Kursmakler (6185)
Königstraße 28
70173 Stuttgart
Tel: +49 711 221472

Reich & Partner GmbH
Freimakler (7869)
Schillerstraße 14
60313 Frankfurt
Tel: +49 69 2998010
Contact: Udo Wedeward

Peter Renell
Kursmakler (7810)
Kaiserhofstraße 13
60313 Frankfurt
Tel: +49 69 295181

RMT Rhein Main Trading Börsenmakler GmbH
Freimakler (7842)
Große Bockenheimer Str 30
60313 Frankfurt
Tel: +49 69 2970540
Contact: Frank Linden

Robert Fleming (Deutschland) GmbH
Kreditinstitut (7228)
Im Trutz Frankfurt 55
60322 Frankfurt
Tel: +49 69 15209125
Contact: Jörg Blättermann

Rolf-R Warnholtz, Detlef Lübbe, Christian Kalischer GmbH
Kursmakler (3846)
Adolfsplatz 1
20457 Hamburg
Tel: +49 40 372351 und 52
Contact: Christian Kalischer

Rainer Roubal
Kursmakler (7827)
Kaiserstr 1
60311 Frankfurt
Tel: +49 69 21731827

Franz Röhrig
Kursmakler (4198)
Clemens-Brentano-Straße 25
40489 Düsseldorf
Tel: +49 211 8902163

RST Börsenmakler GmbH
Freimakler (2165)
Gernerstr 7
80683 München
Tel: +49 89 1595040
Contact: Michael Teppert

Sachsen LB
Landesbank Sachsen Girozentrale
Kreditinstitut (9279)
Hauptstr 105
04416 Markkleeberg
Tel: +49 34 19794200
Contact: William Klein

Salomon Brothers AG
Kreditinstitut (7166)
Wiesenhüttenstraße 10
60329 Frankfurt
Tel: +49 69 2607262
Contact: Rainer Karsten

Sal Oppenheim Jr & Cie KGaA
Kreditinstitut (4135)
Bockenheimer Landstraße 20
60323 Frankfurt
Tel: +49 69 71345330
Contact: Arno Radermacher

Sanwa Bank (Deutschland) AG
Kreditinstitut (7193)
Bockenheimer Landstraße 42
60323 Frankfurt
Tel: +49 69 170094123
Contact: Erich Gonder

Saunders & Zellweger GmbH
Freimakler (3843)
Bleichenbrücke 11
20354 Hamburg
Tel: +49 40 3554444
Contact: Christopher Saunders

Scheich & Partner GmbH
Freimakler (7863)
Große Eschenheimer Straße 13A
60313 Frankfurt
Tel: +49 69 280786
Contact: Wolfgang Brandt

Schierburg & Partner GmbH
Freimakler (4258)
Wagnerstraße 4
40212 Düsseldorf
Tel: +49 211 1649086
Contact: Hans-Joachim Geilenkirchen

SchmidtBank Zentral Wertpapier
Kreditinstitut (2060)
Johannesgasse 20
90402 Nürnberg
Tel: +49 911 24702210
Contact: Josef Dill

Clemens Schmittner
c/o Kursmakler Service Gesellschaft
Kursmakler (7837)
Kaiserstr 1
60311 Frankfurt
Tel: +49 69 21731837

Schnigge & Partner Börsenmakler GmbH
Freimakler (7816)
Oederweg 15
60318 Frankfurt
Tel: +49 69 156840
Contact: Karl A Schnigge

Schröder Münchmeyer Hengst & Co
Kreditinstitut (7008)
Friedensstraße 6–10
60311 Frankfurt
Tel: +49 69 2179223
Contact: H-G Raven

Schröder Münchmeyer Hengst & Co
Kreditinstitut (3041)
Ballindamm 33
20095 Hamburg
Tel: +49 40 3295232
Contact: Klaus Reichenbach

Wolfgang Schulz
Kursmakler (3827)
Lilienstraße 32
20095 Hamburg
Tel: +49 40 335751

Herbert Schuster
Kursmakler (2182)
Kreuzlingerstraße 36
82110 Germering
Tel: +49 89 55190821

Schweizerische Bankgesellschaft
(Deutschland) AG
Kreditinstitut (7163)
Bleichstraße 52
60313 Frankfurt
Tel: +49 69 13691866
Contact: Markus Laifle

Schweizerischer Bankverein
(Deutschland) AG
Kreditinstitut (7158)
Ulmenstr 30
60325 Frankfurt
Tel: +49 69 71401870
Contact: Günther Kapitza

Seydler Dieter Börsenmakler GmbH
Freimakler (7890)
Hochstraße 43
60313 Frankfurt
Tel: +49 69 92054201
Contact: Klaus Ding

SGZ - Bank AG
Kreditinstitut (7051)
Bockenheimer Anlage 46
60322 Frankfurt
Tel: +49 69 71391215
Contact: Erwin Muthspiel

Skandinaviska Enskilda Banken AG
Kreditinstitut (7066)
Rahmhofstraße 2–4
60313 Frankfurt
Tel: +49 69 92021540
Contact: Ursula Wolter

Société Générale Strauss Turnbull Sec Ltd
Wertpapierhandelshaus (9773)
Exchange House, Primrose Street
London EC2A 2DD
Tel: +44 1717625053
Contact: David Wilson

Société Générale SA
Kreditinstitut (7082)
Mainzer Landstraße 36
60325 Frankfurt
Tel: +49 69 7174370
Contact: Berthold Naumann

Spütz Aktiengesellschaft
Freimakler (4277)
Bleidenstr 6
60311 Frankfurt
Tel: +49 69 13300
Contact: Helmuth Fröhlich

Spütz Aktiengesellschaft
Freimakler (7848)
Bleidenstr 6
60311 Frankfurt
Tel: +49 69 13300
Contact: Helmuth Fröhlich

Stadtsparkasse München
Kreditinstitut (2027)
Sparkassenstraße 2
80331 München
Tel: +49 89 21675447/Bö-5463
Contact: Alfred Fischer

Stadtsparkasse Köln
Kreditinstitut (4148)
Hahnenstr 57
50667 Köln
Tel: +49 221 2262375
Contact: Dieter Loreng

Stadsparkasse Düsseldorf
Kreditinstitut (4079)
Berliner Allee 33
40489 Düsseldorf
Tel: +49 211 8781
Contact: Reinke-Welger

Steubing GmbH
Freimakler (7873)
Schillerstraße 20–40
60313 Frankfurt
Tel: +49 69 295455
Contact: Wolfgang Steubing

Albert Strauß
Kursmakler (2189)
Staltacher Straße 18
82393 Iffeldorf
Tel: +49 89 55190860

Stuttgarter Bank AG
Kreditinstitut (6013)
Schloßstraße 56
70176 Stuttgart
Tel: +49 711 1812409
Contact: Detlef Dauses

Susquehanna Securities Trading GmbH
Wertpapierhandelshaus (9178)
Oberlindau 7
60323 Frankfurt
Tel: +49 69 174406
Contact: Marc Dooley

Südwestdeutsche Landesbank
– Girozentrale –
Kreditinstitut (6062)
Am Hauptbahnhof 2
70173 Stuttgart
Tel: +49 711 1275846
Contact: Walter Schaal

Tacken Börsenmakler GmbH
Freimakler (4166)
Ernst-Schneider-Platz 1
40212 Düsseldorf
Tel: +49 211 3239095

Jürgen Thurner
Kursmakler (6180)
Königstraße 28
70173 Stuttgart
Tel: +49 711 221472

Timber Hill Deutschland GmbH
Freimakler (7892)
Steinweg 7
60313 Frankfurt
Tel: +49 69 92072720
Contact: J Lutz Landsrath

Andreas Tremmel
Freimakler (7861)
Große Eschenheimer Straße 13 A
60313 Frankfurt
Tel: +49 69 284093

Trinkaus & Burkhardt KGaA
Kreditinstitut (4043)
Königsallee 21/23
40212 Düsseldorf
Tel: +49 211 326119
Contact: Gerd Goetz

Klaus Tuxhorn
Kursmakler (4297)
Ernst-Schneider-Platz 1
40212 Düsseldorf
Tel: +49 211 8902126

Jörg Urban
Kursmakler (3820)
Doktorberg 25
21029 Hamburg
Tel: +49 40 7211597

Van der Moolen (Deutschland) GmbH
Wertpapierhandelshaus (9242)
Graf-Adolf-Str 86–88
40210 Düsseldorf
Tel: +49 211 173060
Contact: Ralf Seithümmer

Vereins- und Westbank AG
Kreditinstitut (7159)
Mainzer Landstraße 23
60329 Frankfurt
Tel: +49 69 232462
Contact: Günther Debus

Vereins- und Westbank AG Hauptfiliale Hannover
Kreditinstitut (8087)
Rathenaustraße 5–6
30159 Hannover
Tel: +49 511 3664235
Contact: Klaus-Dieter Hölscher

Vereins- und Westbank AG
Kreditinstitut (3029)
Alter Wall 22
20457 Hamburg
Tel: +49 40 36922142
Contact: Rainer J Martensen

Westdeutsche Landesbank -GZ-
Kreditinstitut (4059)
Friedrichstr 56
40489 Düsseldorf
Tel: +49 211 8263389
Contact: Jörg Althoff

Westfalenbank AG
Kreditinstitut (4086)
Huestraße 21–25
44787 Bochum
Tel: +49 211 8227260
Contact: Klaus Rose

WGZ-Bank, Westdeutsche Genossenschafts-Zentralbank eG
Kreditinstitut (4033)
Ludwig-Erhard-Allee 20
40227 Düsseldorf
Tel: +49 211 7782600
Contact: Karl-Heinz Moll

Köthe Wolfgang
Kursmakler (1183)
Sulzaer Straße 8
14199 Berlin
Tel: +49 30 3121939

Wüstenrot Bank AG
Kreditinstitut (6065)
Im Tambour 1
71638 Ludwigsburg
Tel: +49 71 41164132
Contact: Ulrich Ibach

Yamaichi Bank (Deutschland) GmbH
Kreditinstitut (7139)
Feuerbachstraße 26
60325 Frankfurt
Tel: +49 69 7102117
Contact: Manuel Auth

Franz Zech
Kursmakler (7812)
Kaiserstr 1
60311 Frankfurt
Tel: +49 69 21731812

Zöll Börsenmakler GmbH
Freimakler (4172)
Ernst-Schneider-Platz 1
40212 Düsseldorf
Tel: +49 211 131001
Contact: Jörg Gillrath

Hong Kong

The Chinese Gold and Silver Exchange

Active Dragon
Rm 712 Fu Hang
Industrial Bldg, 1 Hok
Yuen St East, KLN, Hong Kong
Tel: +852 26270833
Contact: Chau Chi Yiu

Asian Pacific Capital Co Ltd
Rm 506–8 One Exchange
Square, Hong Kong
Tel: +852 25256122
Contact: Lau Ka Ping

B M Co
Rm 517 East Ocean
Centre, 98 Granville Rd, KLN
Tel: +852 27214361
Contact: Choy Yiu Kwong

Berich Bullion Co
Rm 2303 Wing Shan
Tower, 173 Des Voeux Rd, C,
Hong Kong
Tel: +852 28155662
Contact: Lam Kwok Fai

Best Profit Gold Dealer
Rm 603 Gold & Silver
Comm Bldg, 12 Mercer St,
Hong Kong
Tel: +852 28542074
Contact: Leung Kin Man

Bond Tak Bullion Co
Rm 3201–5, Shui On
Centre, 6 Harbour Rd
Hong Kong
Tel: +852 28022380
Contact: Chang Shu Tong

Brilliant Prospect Bullion
Flat B–C, 18/F, Success Industrial Bldg,
17 Sheung Hei St, KLN
Tel: +852 23207275
Contact: Cheng Koon Chung

C & C Co
18/F, Chuang's Tower,
3D Connaught Rd C,
Hong Kong
Tel: +852 25373033
Contact: Chim Pui Chung

Campbell Bullion Co
Flat B1, 13/F, United Centre
95 Queensway
Hong Kong
Tel: +852 27991111
Contact: Wong Kwok On

Charleswin Co
Rm 1501 Tung Ning Bldg
125 Connaught Rd, C
Hong Kong
Tel: +852 25441055
Contact: Chong Chin

Cheerful (International) Securities & Investment Ltd
Rm 2104–5 World Wide
Hse, 19 Des Voeux Rd, C
Hong Kong
Tel: +852 25236131
Contact: Lee Yiu Sun

Cheong Fat Bullion Co
Rm 902 Silver Cord
Tower 1, 30 Canton Rd
KLN
Tel: +852 23752262
Contact: Chan Wai Hei

Cheow Seng Bullion Co Ltd
Rm 1312 Shun Tak Centre
200 Connaught Rd, C
Hong Kong
Tel: +852 25494196
Contact: Cheung Tsang Wing

Cheung On Fat
11/F, H K & Macau Bldg
156 Connaught Rd, C
Hong Kong
Tel: +852 25448286
Contact: Tam Cham Yuk

Cheung's Gold Dealers
Rm 1901–6 Bank Centre,
636 Nathan Rd, KLN
Tel: +852 23323711
Contact: Cheong Yan Lung

Chief Co
20/F, Regent Centre
86 Queen's Rd, C
Hong Kong
Tel: +852 25223686
Contact: Chau Chung Kai

Chin Luck Gold Dealer
34/F, World Trade Centre
280 Gloucester Rd
Hong Kong
Tel: +852 28811612
Contact: Zhen Shu Cheng

Chow Sang Sang Bullion Dealers Ltd
4/F, 299 Nathan Rd, KLN
Tel: +852 27300111
Contact: Chow Wing Shing

Chow Tai Fook Jewellery Co Ltd
31/F, New World Tower
16 Queen's Rd, C
Hong Kong
Tel: +852 25243166
Contact: Cheng Poon

Chuen Kee
C/O 36/F, Jardine Hse
Connaught Rd, C
Hong Kong
Tel: +852 25262211
Contact: Wu Yue Hing

Chung Hing Gold Dealer
Flat H, 22/F, Everwin Bldg
406 King's Rd
Hong Kong
Tel: +852 25663564
Contact: So Sun Yuen

Chunlong Gold Trader
Rm 1705–6 Hong Kong Plaza
186 Connaught Rd, W
Hong Kong
Tel: +852 28584880
Contact: Ng Cheuk Chun

Corporate Gold Bullion Ltd
4/F, Allied Capital Resources Bldg
32 Ice Hse, St
Hong Kong
Tel: +852 25218456
Contact: Chan Chiu Hung

Cosmos Rich Co
11/F, Gold & Silver Comm Bldg
12 Mercer St
Hong Kong
Tel: +852 25448330
Contact: Yan Man Sing

Dao Heng Bank Ltd
32–35/F, Wu Chung Hse
213 Queen's Rd, E
Hong Kong
Tel: +852 28315000
Contact: Tung Hsi Hui

Dao Heng Finance Ltd
9–10F, Sincere Insurance Bldg
4 Hennessy Rd
Hong Kong
Tel: +852 28610883
Contact: Tam Ping Shing

Deborah Gold Trader
Flat B, 6/F, Yuen Ming Bldg
13 Caine Rd
Hong Kong
Tel: +852 27423428
Contact: So Chian Su

Deluxe Gold Dealer Ltd
Rm 1004, Hang Sang Bldg
77 Des Voeux Rd, C
Hong Kong
Tel: +852 25269889
Contact: Cheung Wai Sang

Diamount Bullion Co
Rm 503 Far East Consortium Bldg
121 Des Voeux Rd, C
Hong Kong
Tel: +852 25414771
Contact: Zai Chung Ling

Emperor Gold & Silver Co, Ltd
28/F, Emperor Group Centre
288 Hennessy Rd
Hong Kong
Tel: +852 28356688
Contact: Wong Chi Fai

Fair Eagle Gold Dealing Co, Ltd
Unit A, 12/F Entertainment Bldg
30 Queen's Rd, C
Hong Kong
Tel: +852 25263471
Contact: Wong Kwong Ho

Far East (HK) Co
15/F, BUPA Centre
141 Connaught Rd, W
Hong Kong
Tel: +852 25480179
Contact: Lee Sik Ming

Faµ Tak
Flat F, 7/F, 30 Johnston Rd
Hong Kong
Contact: Yuen Chung Kwong

Financial Strategic Resources Ltd
Rm 1601–4, Ligna Tower
482 Jaffe Rd
Hong Kong
Tel: +852 28151335
Contact: Cheung Chi Kuen

Foo Kee & Co
Rm 707A Wing On Hse
71 Des Voeux Rd, C
Hong Kong
Tel: +852 25218068
Contact: Chan Ying Lun

Fook Luen Gold Dealer
11/F, Richmake Comm Bldg
198 Queen's Rd, C
Hong Kong
Tel: +852 25458639
Contact: Tong Chun Man

Fook Tai Co
Rm 905–8 New World Tower
18 Queen's Rd, C
Hong Kong
Tel: +852 25251001
Contact: Fu Sau Chun

Forex Fix Gold Dealers
Unit A, 10/F, Entertainment Bldg
30 Queen's Rd, C
Hong Kong
Tel: +852 25010355
Contact: Yu Wing Cheuk

Fu Hang
Rm 501 On Lok Yuen Bldg, 25 Des Voeux Rd, C
Hong Kong
Tel: +852 25231525
Contact: Ng Wa Yee

Get Nice Gold Co
23/F, Euro Trade Centre
13 Connaught Rd, C
Hong Kong
Tel: +852 25267738
Contact: Hung Hon Man

Global Gold Co
7/F, Kam Shek Comm Bldg
17 Waterloo Rd, KLN
Tel: +852 23321521
Contact: Lam Shun Kam

Gold City Bullion Co
7/F, Kam Sang Bldg
255 Des Voeux Rd, C
Hong Kong
Tel: +852 28152523
Contact: Wong Tung Chi

Golden Eagle Bullion Co
Flat A, 2/F, Haywood Mansion
57 Paterson St
Hong Kong
Tel: +852 28949808
Contact: Tsang Shiu Hong

Goldion Gold Traders
Rm 1405 Cheong Kee Bldg
84 Des Voeux Rd, C
Hong Kong
Tel: +852 28158777
Contact: Chan Wing Kwei

Goldlion Co
15 Sze Shan St, Yau Tong Bay, KLN
Tel: +852 23400111
Contact: Cheng Sau Kam

Grand Gold Dealers Ltd
8/F, OTB Bldg
259 Des Voeux Rd, C
Hong Kong
Tel: +852 28158862
Contact: Lee Tak Lun

Hai Lung Co
Rm 607 Melbourne Plaza
33 Queens Rd, C
Hong Kong
Tel: +852 25232709
Contact: Cheung Kwok Leung

Hang Fong
16/F, Wong Hse
26 Des Voeux Rd, W
Hong Kong
Tel: +852 25497576
Contact: Wong Yee On

Hang Seng Bullion Co Ltd
83 Des Voeux Rd, C
Hong Kong
Tel: +852 28255111
Contact: Tong Kwok Hung

Hang Yick
6/F, World Wide Hse
19 Des Voeux Rd, C
Hong Kong
Tel: +852 25255977
Contact: Lee Shau Kee

Hantec Bullion Co
5/F, Lee Kum Kee Bldg
168 Des Voeux Rd, C
Hong Kong
Tel: +852 28159060
Contact: Tsai Hsui Ping

Hing Fung Goldsmith & Refinery Ltd
16/F, Cheung Fat Bldg
7 Hill Rd
Hong Kong
Tel: +852 28032888
Contact: Chan Fat Chu

Hing Yep Gold Dealers
10/F, 9 Queen's Rd, C
Hong Kong
Tel: +852 25254422
Contact: Ng Chun Ping

Hon Hing Hong
27/F, Asia Pacific Finance Tower, Citibank Plaza
3 Garden Rd
Hong Kong
Tel: +852 28773877
Contact: Tao Hak Ping

Hsing Lung Co
Rm 2502 Admiralty Centre
Tower 1, 18 Harcourt Rd
Hong Kong
Tel: +852 25273715
Contact: Lee Woo Sing

Hung Tak
Rm 702 Gold & Silver Comm Bldg
12 Mercer St
Hong Kong
Tel: +852 25438079
Contact: Li Kam Chuan

J A Livermore Bullion Co
20/F, Admiralty Centre
Tower 2, 18 Harcourt Rd
Hong Kong
Contact: Ho Kai Cheung

John Lok Investments Ltd
19/F, Sun Hse
181 Des Voeux Rd, C
Hong Kong
Tel: +852 25458618
Contact: Lok Hsiao Pei

Ka Wah
12/F, Hang Seng Bldg
77 Des Voeux Rd, C
Hong Kong
Tel: +852 28468111
Contact: Leung Kwong Sang

Kam Kee Gold Co
Flat A, 1/F, 201 Prince Edward Rd, KLN
Tel: +852 27135377
Contact: Li Yu Chun

Kam Tat Gold Co
Flat 213, Blk, U, Telford Garden
33 Wai Yip St, KLN
Tel: +852 27960219
Contact: Tam Yuk Ling

Karl-Thomson Bullion Co
Shop 9A, Lucky Plaza, G/F, Shatin, NT
Tel: +852 26922244
Contact: Lam Kwok Yin

Kee Shing Bullion Co
3/F, QPL-Ksip Holdings Centre
74 Kimberley Rd, KLN
Tel: +852 23661211
Contact: Leung Shu Wing

Kin Shing
Rm 702 Gold & Silver Comm Bldg
12 Mercer St
Hong Kong
Tel: +852 25438060
Contact: Li Kam Chuan

King Fook Gold & Jewellery Co Ltd
30 Des Voeux Rd, C, G/F
Hong Kong
Tel: +852 25235111
Contact: Yeung Ping Leung

King Hing Co
Rm 1001 Admiralty Centre
Tower 2, 18 Harcourt Rd
Hong Kong
Tel: +852 25291020
Contact: Ho Hau Hay

King Sang Gold Dealer
Rm 1303 Gold & Silver Comm Bldg
12 Mercer St
Hong Kong
Tel: +852 25414848
Contact: Lui Wing Kai

King Shing Bullion Traders & Finance Co Ltd
G/F, 30–32 Des Voeux Rd, C
Hong Kong
Tel: +852 28228565
Contact: Yeung Bing Yin

Kingly Gold Co
9/F, Wing's Bldg
110 Queen's Rd, C
Hong Kong
Tel: +852 28152223
Contact: Choi Yau Man

Kingston Bullion Co
10/F, Wings Bldg
110 Queen's Rd, C
Hong Kong
Tel: +852 28508333
Contact: Chu Yuet Wah

KMC Bullion Trading Co
26/F, 88 Lockhart Rd
Hong Kong
Tel: +852 25281393
Contact: Chi Chun Nam

Kui Shing Gold Trader
RM 1501 Wing Hang Bank Bldg
161 Queen's Rd, C
Hong Kong
Tel: +852 25421128
Contact: Yim Kam Hung

Kung Lee
5 Li Yuen St, W, 5/F
Hong Kong
Tel: +852 25414898
Contact: David Kung

Kung Yue
Rm 600
12 Queen's Rd, C
Hong Kong
Contact: Cheng Wai Chai

Kwong Cheung Co
M/F 54A Tonkin St, KLN
Tel: +852 27205241–4
Contact: Chan Yan

Kwong Fat
6/F, Kwong Fat Hong Bldg
1 Rumsey St
Hong Kong
Tel: +852 25433327
Contact: Cham Siu Leun

Lai Kee Gold Co Ltd
Rm, 401–2 V-Heun Bldg
138 Queen's Rd, C
Hong Kong
Tel: +852 25443102–3
Contact: Lai Po Hung

Lam Tai Shing Gold Dealer
2/F, Long To Bldg
654 Castle Peak Rd, KLN
Tel: +852 23101111
Contact: Lam Man Yan

Lee Cheong Gold Dealers Ltd
Rm, 705 Wing On Hse
71 Des Voeux Rd, C
Hong Kong,
Tel: +852 25213106
Contact: Wu King Cheong

Lee On Hong
Flat C, 8/F, Wing Cheong Comm Bldg
19 Jervois St
Hong Kong
Tel: +852 25437743
Contact: Chan Cheong Yip

Lee Sang Co
Rm 501 Tien Cheung Hong Bldg
77 Jervois St
Hong Kong
Tel: +852 25444138
Contact: Chan Yun Hoi

Lee Shing
Rm 1302 Gold & Silver Comm Bldg
12 Mercer St
Hong Kong
Tel: +852 25439093
Contact: Ip Ngai Wo

Legarleon Gold Traders
Rm 308 Yu Yuet Lai Bldg
43 Wyndham St
Hong Kong
Tel: +852 25262061
Contact: Lo Kwong Hung

Li Kee Hong
Rm 3501–1 Central Plaza
18 Harbour Rd
Hong Kong
Tel: +852 28458188
Contact: Fung Ho Sum

Loong Shing Ho
Flat B, 21/F, Wing Hing Court
110 Tung Lo Wan Rd
Hong Kong
Contact: Kan Yau Chung

Lotus Gold & Silver Co
13/F, Kaiseng Comm Centre
4 Hankow Rd, KLN
Tel: +852 23691460
Contact: Kong Ho Pak

Luen Fat
Flat B, 16/F, Blk 17, Chi Fu Fa Yuen
Hong Kong
Tel: +852 25508363
Contact: Mui Kin

Luen Hing (HK) Co
40 Connaught Rd, W, 1/F
Hong Kong
Tel: +852 25496681
Contact: Chan Wai Dan

Luen On Kam Ho
Flat A, 8/F, Hip Kee Comm Bldg
205 Wing Lok St, W
Hong Kong
Tel: +852 25434254
Contact: Yeung Sui Mau

Luen Thai Co
Rm 701 Finance Bldg
254 Des Voeux Rd, C
Hong Kong
Tel: +852 25458668
Contact: Wu Ting Fai

Lui Hing Hop Cheung Kee Finance Ltd
G/F, 18 Des Voeux Rd, W
Hong Kong
Tel: +852 25408998
Contact: Lui Kao Boon

Malahon Bullion Co
5 & 6/F, Malahon Centre
10 Stanley St
Hong Kong
Tel: +852 28680628
Contact: Hung Sheung Hang

Man Fat & Co
33/F, Jardine Hse
Connaught Rd, C
Hong Kong
Contact: Ng Kai Kwong

Man Loong Co
Rm 1504 Crocodile Hse 2
55 Connaught Rd, C
Hong Kong
Tel: +25811827
Contact: Yue Tsong Nyeu

Man Shing Co
Front Door, 2/F
315 Nathan Rd, KLN
Contact: Lau Yau Kwun

Man Sun
Rm 905–8 New World Tower
18 Queen's Rd, C
Hong Kong
Tel: +852 25251001
Contact: Foo Wai Yu

Manin Hing Co
Rm 2202 Bank of America Tower
12 Harcourt Rd
Hong Kong
Tel: +852 25255407
Contact: Ho Hau Wing

Mansion House Bullion Co
Flat A, 37/F, Bank of China Tower
1 Garden Rd
Hong Kong
Tel: +852 28431431
Contact: Evans Carrera

Maryloone Gold Dealers
Rm 2210 Peregrine Tower
Lippo Centre
89 Queensway
Hong Kong
Tel: +852 28698683
Contact: Chu Nam Yeung

Mass Fine Co
Unit A&B, 19/F, Sang Woo Bldg
227 Gloucester Rd
Hong Kong
Tel: +852 28384223
Contact: Lau Siu Wai

Mayfair Bullion Ltd
10/F, Hong Kong & Macau Bldg
156 Connaught Rd, C
Hong Kong
Tel: +852 25411848
Contact: Fan Kwok Ching

Ming Fung Gold Trader
6/F, Golden Centre
188 Des Voeux Rd, C
Hong Kong
Tel: +852 25455300
Contact: Chan Kwong Hung

Ming Hing
Flat D, 1/F, Skyscraper
138 Tin Hau Temple Rd
Hong Kong
Tel: +852 28072112
Contact: Chan Wing Tung

Ming Tai Co
5/F, Harbour Comm Bldg
122 Connaught Rd, C
Hong Kong
Tel: +852 28540950
Contact: Chan Wai Sang

National
58/F, Bank of China Tower
1 Garden Rd
Hong Kong
Tel: +852 25227131
Contact: Fok Ying Tung

National Harvest Bullion Co
Unit B-C, 24/F, United Centre
95 Queensway
Hong Kong
Tel: +852 25271223
Contact: Lee Shing Kwong

O & S Bullion Co
1/F, Dragon Hse
7 Cameron Rd, KLN
Tel: +852 23135110
Contact: Chua Nai Tuen

On Lung Gold & Silver Co Ltd
G/F, 276 Queen's Rd, C
Hong Kong
Tel: +852 25439512
Contact: Chan Yu Yuk

Onmate Ltd
S1, 2/F, Wong Tai Sin Shopping Centre
KLN
Tel: +852 27511488
Contact: Cheung Chi Wai

Oriental Crystal Bullion Co
22/F, Oriental Crystal Comm Bldg
46 Lyndhurst Terrace
Hong Kong
Tel: +852 25448899
Contact: Li Chak Man

Pak Kai Gold Co
G/F, 595 Shanghai St, KLN
Tel: +852 23917151
Contact: Yu Kwei Yuk

Pak Lok Co
2/F, Oriental Daily News Bldg
6 Kwei Chow St, KLN
Tel: +852 27746362
Contact: Pui Jun Kuen

Patco Bullion Co
Rm 701 Gold & Silver Comm Bldg
12 Mercer St
Hong Kong
Tel: +852 28519534
Contact: Kuan Ian Leong

Peace Town Gold & Silver Co Ltd
Rm 4001 Lippo Tower, Lippo Centre
89 Queensway
Hong Kong
Tel: +852 28228338
Contact: Chan Sheung Chi

Peregrine Bullion Ltd
23/F, New World Tower
16 Queen's Rd, C
Hong Kong
Tel: +852 28251888
Contact: Wong Wing Cheong

Po Fung Bullion Co
Rm 1801–3 Two Exchange Square
8 Connaught Place
Hong Kong
Tel: +852 25215451
Contact: Cheung Wah Fung

Po Sang Bank Ltd
1/F, Wing On Hse
71 Des Voeux Rd, C
Hong Kong
Tel: +852 28436111
Contact: Chao Shing On

Po Tai Bullion Co
Flat D, 22/F, Wing Cheong Comm Bldg
19 Jervois St
Hong Kong
Tel: +852 25433080
Contact: Kwok Ping Kap

Poly Enterprises
Rm, 808 Yu Sung Boon Bldg
111 Des Voeux Rd, C
Hong Kong
Tel: +852 25412389
Contact: Cheng To

Safe Margin Gold Dealer
Shop B, G/F & 1/F
Fai Hon Bldg
15 Ngan Mok St
Hong Kong
Tel: +852 25446880
Contact: Wong On Chak

Sai Shing
Rm 2206 Wing On Hse
71 Des Voeux Rd, C
Hong Kong
Tel: +852 25255777
Contact: Pau Lap Kwan

San Fu & Co
Rm 2001–3 Far East Consortium Bldg
121 Des Voeux Rd, C
Hong Kong
Tel: +852 28532107
Contact: Chan Chieh Chung

Seapower Bullion Co Ltd
32–34/F, Alexandra Hse
16 Chater Rd
Hong Kong
Tel: +852 28474888
Contact: So Kam Wing

Shing Tak Gold Trader
Flat A, 17/F, World Trust Tower
50 Stanley St
Hong Kong
Tel: +852 25861318
Contact: Yeung Shing Fung

Shui Cheong
Flat 19/F, Wing Cheong Comm Bldg
19 Jervois St
Hong Kong
Tel: +852 25446436
Contact: Chan Cheong Wai

Shun Kai Bullion Co
Rm 703 Chuk On Bldg
23 Mercer St
Hong Kong
Tel: +852 25451708
Contact: Yeung Pui Ying

Shun Lee Gold Traders Co
Rm 1703–6 World International Hse
20 Pedder St
Hong Kong
Tel: +852 25265600
Contact: Lau Wai Shing

Shun Loong Bullion Ltd
Rm 2502 Admiralty Centre
Tower 1, 18 Harcourt Rd
Hong Kong
Tel: +852 25200111
Contact: Zee Kwoh Kung

Sing Lung Gold Trader Co
Rm 710 Wing On Hse
71 Des Voeux Rd, C
Hong Kong
Contact: Lee Chun Kwok

Solid Commodities Co
Rm 1905–6, 19/F, Vicwood Plaza
199 Des Voeux Rd, C
Hong Kong
Tel: +852 25456563
Contact: Wang Chun King

South China Bullion Co
28/F, Bank of China Tower
1 Garden Rd
Hong Kong
Tel: +852 28206333
Contact: Ng Hung Sang

Standard Bullion
Rm 2706–11 Asia Pacific Finance Tower
Citibank Plaza
3 Garden Rd
Hong Kong
Tel: +852 28773877
Contact: Yau Pui Kee

Sun Hing Bullion Co Ltd
3/F, Admiralty Centre
Tower 2, 18 Harcourt Rd
Hong Kong
Tel: +852 28225684
Contact: Chan Chiu Chung

Sun Hung Kai Bullion Co Ltd
3/F, Admiralty Centre, Tower 2
18 Harcourt Rd
Hong Kong
Tel: +852 28225679
Contact: Law Ding Ming

Sun Kwong Co
Rm 703 Gold & Silver Comm Bldg
12 Mercer St
Hong Kong
Tel: +852 25441468
Contact: Chan Sek Kam

Sun Wing Yuen Bullion Co
22/F, Onfem Centre
135 Des Voeux Rd, C
Hong Kong
Tel: +852 25413821
Contact: Ng Kun Man

Sunnymen & Co
Flat C4, 21/F, Parker Lodge
10 Hong Pak Path
Quarry Bay
Hong Kong
Tel: +852 25643635
Contact: Ng Hon Yeung

Sze Lee Gold Dealers Ltd
G/F, 5 Hillier St
Hong Kong
Tel: +852 25440201–2
Contact: Leung Che Keung

T & L Gold Dealer
Rm 2905–6 Central Plaza
18 Harbour Rd
Hong Kong
Tel: +852 28779188
Contact: Pu Mei Lee

Tah Hsin Gold Dealer
Flat A, 20/F, Kam Tao Bldg
4 Whitfield Rd
Hong Kong
Tel: +852 25787089
Contact: Yip Nuen Ting

Tai Heng & Co
28/F, Tai Sang Comm Bldg
24 Hennessy Rd
Hong Kong
Contact: Ma Ching Chung

Tai Lee Gold Traders
Rm 601, Hua Chiao Comm Bldg
88 Des Voeux Rd, C
Hong Kong
Contact: Lung Hon Wing

Tai Sang Bank Ltd
Tai Sang Bank Bldg
130 Des Voeux Rd, C
Hong Kong
Tel: +852 25445011
Contact: Ma Kam Ming

Tai Yau
16/F, Tak Shing Hse
20 Des Voeux Rd, C
Hong Kong
Tel: +852 25229002
Contact: Ko Fook Kau

Tak Shun
Rm 802 Cosmopolitan Bldg
10 Stanley St
Hong Kong
Contact: Ho Hung Cheung

Tak Sum Gold Co
Flat B1, 8/F, Kiu Hing Mansion
14 King's Rd
Hong Kong
Tel: +852 25470108
Contact: Lee Hou Cheong

Tak Wo & Co
Flat 5/F, 58 Bonham Strand E
Hong Kong
Tel: +852 25442993
Contact: Chung Kwong

Tak Yue
NA
Contact: Lai Man Sun

Tang Kee
Rm 203–B Pedder Bldg
12 Pedder St
Hong Kong
Tel: +852 25221792
Contact: Fung Pak Fai

Tanrich & Co
Rm 1601–2 Central Plaza
18 Harbour Rd
Hong Kong
Tel: +852 28028838
Contact: Yip Man Fan

Target Champion Investment Ltd
Rm 802 Chinachem Tower
34 Connaught Rd, C
Hong Kong
Tel: +852 28508333
Contact: Ng Kei Choy

Tin Fook
12/F, Gold & Silver Comm Bldg
12 Mercer St
Hong Kong
Tel: +852 25422109
Contact: Chan Kwok Tuen

Tse Sui Luen Jewellery Co Ltd
Blk B, G/F, Summit Bldg
30 Man Yue St, KLN
Tel: +852 23334221
Contact: Tse Sui Luen

U B Bullion Co Ltd
3/F, Union Bank Tower
122 Queen's Rd, C
Hong Kong
Tel: +852 25411190
Contact: Liao Chin Shen

Unicomex Gold Trader
Rm 3607 Shun Tak Centre
200 Connaught Rd, C
Hong Kong
Tel: +852 25497132
Contact: Chung Kai Sing

Universal (Investment) Co
Rm 504 Mong Kok Comm Centre
16 Argyle St, KLN
Tel: +852 23944693
Contact: Kong Chuk Lun

Upbest Bullion Co Ltd
2/F, Wah Kit Comm Bldg
302 Des Voeux Rd, C
Hong Kong
Tel: +852 25453298
Contact: Cheng Kai Ming

Uptrend Bullion Co
Rm 705 West Coast International Bldg
290 Un Chau St, KLN
Tel: +852 23862214
Contact: Lam Foon

Vanrich Gold Traders
Flat H3, 13/F, Hunghom Bay Centre
KLN
Tel: +852 23342292
Contact: Jose Chong

Vanroy Gold Traders
Rm 1003–6, Wai Fung Plaza
664 Nathan Rd, KLN
Tel: +852 23980838
Contact: Ho Sing

Wah Tai Co
Rm 1703 Tai Sang Comm Bldg
24 Hennessy Rd
Hong Kong
Tel: +852 25276121–3
Contact: Ma Ching Leong

Wai Chong Co
Rm B4, 9/F, Kingston Bldg
2 Kingston St
Hong Kong
Tel: +852 25772484
Contact: Siu Chak Lam

Wang Tai Gold Dealers
Rm 2902 Yat Chau Intl Plaza
118 Connaught Rd, W
Hong Kong
Tel: +852 25595228
Contact: Cheung Man Tat

Wayfoong Bullion Co
3/F, Hutchison Hse
10 Harcourt Rd
Hong Kong
Tel: +852 25211661
Contact: To Man Hung

Weal & Well Bullion Co
29/F, Bank of America Tower
12 Harcourt Rd
Hong Kong
Tel: +852 28686100
Contact: Kook Ying Tai

Wellsun Gold Dealer
12/F, Gold & Silver Comm Bldg
12 Mercer St
Hong Kong
Tel: +852 25415626
Contact: Ho Ying

Whitehall Bullion Co
2D Conway Mansion
29 Conduit Rd
Hong Kong
Tel: +852 28585188
Contact: Lam Ma Ching Miu

Winfaith Bullion Co
Flat 5A, Tern Center
Tower 2, 251 Queen's Rd, C
Hong Kong
Tel: +852 28540171
Contact: Wong Kwan Ming

Wing Hang Commodities Co Ltd
1/F, 161 Queen's Rd, C
Hong Kong
Tel: +852 28525111
Contact: Fung Yuk Sing

Wing Lung Credit Ltd
45 Des Voeux Rd, C,
Hong Kong
Tel: +852 28268333
Contact: Wu Po Him

Wing On Gold Dealer
Rm 2701 Wing On Centre
111 Connaught Rd, C
Hong Kong
Tel: +852 28530111
Contact: Kwok Man Cho

Wing Shing Loong Goldsmith &
Refinery Co Ltd
16/F, Cheung Fat Bldg
7 Hill Rd
Hong Kong
Tel: +852 28032888
Contact: Tsui Muk Ming

Wing Wah
12/F, Hang Seng Bldg
77 Des Voeux Rd, C
Hong Kong
Tel: +852 28468111
Context: Lee Kam Woon

Wings Investment Co Ltd
45 Des Voeux Rd, C
Hong Kong
Tel: +852 28268333
Contact: Wu Po Cheung

Wo Cheong Hong
G/F, 21 Bonham Strand W
Hong Kong
Tel: +852 25437722
Contact: Lam Hoi Loy

Wong Sha Co Ltd
Rm 1203–5 East Asia Aetna Tower
308 Des Voeux Rd, C
Hong Kong
Tel: +852 28542818
Contact: Chung Foo Chor

Wu Leung Lee Gold Dealer
18/F, Wing Tuck Comm Centre
177 Wing Lok St, W
Hong Kong
Tel: +852 25418111
Contact: Wu Ming Hung

Yan Tai
Flat F, 7/F, Hoi Sing Mansion
Sing Fai Terrace
Taikoo Shing
Hong Kong
Tel: +852 25686506
Contact: Cheuk Wing Cheong

Yat Lung
16/F, Cheung Fat Bldg
7 Hill Rd
Hong Kong
Tel: +852 28032888
Contact: Chan Fat Leung

Yau Hang Ho
Rm 820 Lai Fu Hse
Lai-Kok Estate
Cheung Sha Wan, KLN
Contact: Chan Yee Yin

Yau Hing
RM 503 Gold & Silver Comm Bldg
12 Mercer St
Hong Kong
Tel: +852 25459856
Contact: Chan Po Chuen

Yau Seng Bullion Co
Rm 507 Gold & Silver Comm Bldg
12 Mercer St
Hong Kong
Tel: +852 25411035
Contact: Lee Chi Kin

Yau Wing Gold Dealer
Top Floor, Wing Shun Bldg
64 Bonham Strand W
Hong Kong
Tel: +852 25497576
Contact: Wong Chung Sze

Yee Fi Co
Flat B, 18/F, Lucky Plaza
315 Lockhart Rd
Hong Kong
Tel: +852 28363966
Contact: Ching Man Kit

Yick Hing Bullion Co
Rm 901–3 Regent Centre
88 Queen's Rd, C
Hong Kong
Tel: +852 28682287
Contact: Wong Yik Nin

Yiu Wing Gold Traders
G/F, 32 Apliu St
Shamshuipo, KLN
Tel: +852 23812332
Contact: Cheung Yiu Wing

Yong Tong Gold Dealer
Rm, 2809 Wu Chung Hse
197 Queen's Rd, E
Hong Kong
Tel: +852 28329991
Contact: Yeung Ki Yuen

Yorkwell Investment Co
20/F, Wyndham Place
40 Wyndham St
Hong Kong
Tel: +852 28105023
Contact: Chua Nai King

Yue Fu Gold Dealer
Shop C, G/F, Fund Yip Bldg
347 Des Voeux Rd, W
Hong Kong
Tel: +852 28574120
Contact: Wong Lee Ching

Yue Sang Ho
71 Des Voeux Rd, C, 1/F
Hong Kong
Tel: +852 28436111
Contact: Fung Kin

Yuen Yee Co
Rm 901 Gold & Silver Comm Bldg
12 Mercer St
Hong Kong
Tel: +852 25440362
Contact: Cheung Hon Cheung

Hong Kong Futures Exchange Ltd

Member List

Trader	(T)
Broker	(B)
Futures Commission Merchant	(FCM)
Merchant Trader	(MT)

ASG Futures Ltd (FCM)
24/F, Nine Queen's Road
Central, Hong Kong
Tel: +852 25265338
Fax: +852 25375818

Alpha Futures Co Ltd (FCM)
Rms 3401–2, Two Exchange Square,
Connaught Place,
Central, Hong Kong
Tel: +852 25252373
Fax: +852 28450236

Amsteel Futures (HK) Ltd (FCM)
12/F, Bank of East Asia Bldg
10 Des Voeux Road
Central, Hong Kong
Tel: +852 28483688
Fax: +852 28483628

Asia Financial Futures Ltd (FCM)
12/F, Asia Financial Centre
120 Des Voeux Road
Central, Hong Kong
Tel: +852 28534675
Fax: +852 25451253

BNP Futures (Hong Kong) Ltd (FCM)
1/F, Central Building
23 Queen's Road
Central, Hong Kong
Tel: +852 25329288
Fax: +852 28652523

BZW Futures Asia Ltd (FCM)
42/F, Citibank Tower
Citibank Plaza
3 Garden Road, Hong Kong
Tel: +852 29032000
Fax: +852 29032296

C A Pacific Futures Ltd (FCM)
Room 603–606, 6/F, No 9 Queen's
Road,
Central, Hong Kong
Tel: +852 28448188
Fax: +852 25249742

CS First Boston (Hong Kong) Futures
Ltd (FCM)
9/F, One Exchange Square
8 Connaught Place
Central, Hong Kong
Tel: +852 28470388
Tel: +852 28452456

Central Options and Securities Ltd (B)
8/F, Prince's Bldg
10 Chater Road
Central, Hong Kong
Tel: +852 25240595

Cheerful Commodities Co Ltd (FCM)
Room 2105, Worldwide House
19 Des Voeux Road
Central, Hong Kong
Tel: +852 25236131
Fax: +852 28680146

Chief Commodities Ltd (FCM)
20/F, Regent Centre
88 Queen's Road
Central, Hong Kong
Tel: +852 25223686
Tel: +852 25216893

China Nonferrous Metals Futures Co Ltd
(FCM)
Room 2005, New World Tower
16–18 Queen's Road
Central, Hong Kong
Tel: +852 28456161
Fax: +852 25960505

China Top Commodities & Futures Ltd (FCM)
6/F, Liu Chong Hing Bank Bldg
24 Des Voeux Road
Central, Hong Kong
Tel: +852 28682222
Fax: +852 28684103

Chow Sang Sang Futures Ltd (FCM)
G/F–4/F, Chow Sang Sang Bldg
229 Nathan Road, Kowloon
Tel: +852 27300111
Tel: +852 27309683

Chung Mao Commodities & Futures Ltd (FCM)
1/F, Bank of China Bldg
2A Des Voeux Road
Central, Hong Kong
Tel: +852 28676336
Fax: +852 25303345

Chung Nam Commodities Ltd (FCM)
23/F, Asia Orient Tower
Town Place
33 Lockhart Road, Hong Kong
Tel: +852 28666389
Fax: +852 28042238

Clover Futures Co Ltd (FCM)
19/F, CMA Building
64–66 Connaught Road
Central, Hong Kong
Tel: +852 28519019
Fax: +852 28517048

Compu-Chart Investment Adviser Ltd (FCM)
Room 405, Alliance Bldg
130–136 Connaught Road
Central, Hong Kong
Tel: +852 25434399
Fax: +852 25439878

Corporate Commodities Ltd (FCM)
8–9/Floor, Radio City 505, Hennessy Road
Causeway Bay, Hong Kong
Tel: +852 28320139
Fax: +852 28921090

Credit Lyonnais Securities Futures Ltd (FCM)
33/F, Peregrine Tower, Lippo Centre
89 Queensway, Hong Kong
Tel: +852 28109338
Fax: +852 28680189

DBS Futures Hong Kong Ltd (FCM)
33 & 34/F, Two Pacific Place
88 Queensway, Hong Kong
Tel: +852 25262002
Fax: +852 28771936

Daiwa Futures (Asia) Ltd (FCM)
Level 26, One Pacific Place
88 Queensway, Hong Kong
Tel: +852 25250121
Fax: +852 28484099

Dao Heng Commodities Ltd (FCM)
21/F, Entertainment Building
30 Queen's Road
Central, Hong Kong
Tel: +852 25255091
Fax: +852 28459237

Delta Asia Financial Futures Ltd (FCM)
31/F, Jardine House
1 Connaught Place
Central, Hong Kong
Tel: +852 25330800
Fax: +852 28104495

Deutsche Morgan Grenfell Futures Hong Kong Ltd (FCM)
28/F, One Pacific Place
88 Queensway, Hong Kong
Tel: +852 28680388
Fax: +852 28450228

Dharmala Futures Ltd (FCM)
29/F, Jardine House
1 Connaught Place
Central, Hong Kong
Tel: +852 28472222
Fax: +852 25301822

Diamond Futures Ltd (FCM)
Rm 503A, Golden Centre
188 Des Voeux Road
Central, Hong Kong
Tel: +852 25230282
Fax: +852 25419796

Emperor Futures Ltd (FCM)
23–24/F, Emperor Group Centre
288 Hennessy Road
Wanchai, Hong Kong
Tel: +852 28362600
Tel: +852 25742622

Euro Manor Investment Ltd (B)
Flat A, 11/F, Harbour Comm Bldg
122–124 Connaught Road
Central, Hong Kong
Tel: +852 28680611
Fax: +852 28400825

Excalibur Futures Ltd (FCM)
3505–6 Edinburgh Tower
15 Queen's Road
Central, Hong Kong
Tel: +852 25260388
Fax: +852 25260618

Fair Eagle Futures Co Ltd (FCM)
Unit A, 12/F, Entertainment Bldg
30 Queen's Road
Central, Hong Kong
Tel: +852 25263471
Fax: +852 28455731

Fimat Futures (Hong Kong) Ltd (FCM)
1907–08, One Exchange Square
8 Connaught Place
Central, Hong Kong
Tel: +852 28483300
Fax: +852 28694615

First Shanghai Futures Ltd (FCM)
Rm 1905, Wing On House
71 Des Voeux Road
Central, Hong Kong
Tel: +852 25222101
Fax: +852 28106789

Frankwell Commodities Ltd (FCM)
Room 810, Tower A
New Mandarin Plaza
14 Science Museum Road,
Tsimshatsui East, Kowloon
Tel: +852 28023488
Fax: +852 25114930

Fuji Hong Kong Commodities Co Ltd (FCM)
Rm 1203–1204, Singga Commercial Centre
144 Connaught Road West
Hong Kong
Tel: +852 25591041
Fax: +852 25594526

Get Nice Futures Co Ltd (FCM)
23/F, Euro Trade Centre
13–14 Connaught Road
Central, Hong Kong
Tel: +852 25267738
Fax: +852 25225437

Goodwill Commodities Ltd (FCM)
20/F, Nine Queen's Road
Central, Hong Kong
Tel: +852 25339898
Fax: +852 25339888

Grand Futures Ltd (FCM)
8/F, OTB Building
259–265 Des Voeux Road
Central, Hong Kong
Tel: +852 28158862
Fax: +852 25419131

Grand Generale Commodities & Futures Ltd (FCM)
Room 501, Admiralty Centre
Tower I, 18 Harcourt Road, Hong Kong
Tel: +852 28655099
Fax: +852 28660186

HG Asia Futures Ltd (FCM)
30/F, Edinburgh Tower
The Landmark
Central, Hong Kong
Tel: +852 28680368
Tel: +852 28104932

HSBC James Capel Asia Futures Hong Kong Ltd (FCM)
Level 17
Hongkong Bank Building
1 Queen's Road
Central, Hong Kong
Tel: +852 28439111
Fax: +852 28107673

Harvester (Futures) Co Ltd (FCM)
Suite 2408–9
Peregrine Tower Lippo Centre
89 Queensway, Hong Kong
Tel: +852 25010882
Fax: +852 25010208

Hase Futures Ltd (FCM)
16/F, Hang Seng Building
77 Des Voeux Road
Central, Hong Kong
Tel: +852 28255653
Fax: +852 28684544

Henchman Futures Ltd (FCM)
10/F, Nine Queen's Road
Central, Hong Kong
Tel: +852 2524422
Fax: +852 28452145

Hing Fung Futures Ltd (FCM)
16/F, Cheung Fat Building
7–9 Hill Road
Western District, Hong Kong
Tel: +852 28032888
Fax: +852 28575294

Hon Hing Futures Ltd (FCM)
Room 2606, Convention Plaza
No 1 Harbour Road
Wanchai, Hong Kong
Tel: +852 25237936
Fax: +852 28683748

Honfirst Investment Ltd (FCM)
2/F, Chekiang First Bank Centre
1 Duddell Street
Central, Hong Kong
Tel: +852 25259755
Fax: +852 28772573

Honour Futures Ltd (FCM)
45/F, Sun Hung Kai Centre
30 Harbour Road
Wanchai, Hong Kong
Tel: +852 28278111
Fax: +852 28272862

Hull Trading Asia Ltd (FCM)
18/F, Peregrine Tower
Lippo Centre
89 Queensway, Hong Kong
Tel: +852 28489154
Fax: +852 28691126

I & P Commodities Ltd (FCM)
7/F, Wings Building, 110–116 Queen's Road
Central, Hong Kong
Tel: +852 28150188
Fax: +852 28155370

ICA Enterprise Co Ltd (FCM)
UG/F, Flat C, Hop Hing Ind Bldg
704 Castle Peak Road, Kowloon
Tel: +852 27852681
Fax: +852 27862155

ING Futures & Options (Hong Kong) Ltd (FCM)
8/F, Three Exchange Square
8 Connaught Place
Central, Hong Kong
Tel: +852 28488488
Fax: +852 28014502

JP Morgan Futures Hong Kong Ltd (FCM)
22/F, Edinburgh Tower
15 Queen's Road
Central, Hong Kong
Tel: +852 28411311
Fax: +852 28411139

Jardine Fleming Futures Ltd (FCM)
46/F, Jardine House
1 Connaught Place
Central, Hong Kong
Tel: +852 28438888
Fax: +852 25215818

Jin Loong Futures Ltd (FCM)
2305 Shun Tak Centre
200 Connaught Road
Central, Hong Kong
Tel: +852 28598168
Fax: +852 25497572

Karl-Thomson Commodities Co Ltd (FCM)
Room 1201, Lippo Tower
Lippo Centre
89 Queensway, Hong Kong
Tel: +852 28779266
Fax: +852 25220170

Kim Eng Futures (HK) Ltd (FCM)
8/F, Alexandra House
16–20 Chater Road
Central, Hong Kong
Tel: +852 28107755
Fax: +852 25305078

King Fook Commodities Co Ltd (FCM)
8/F, King Fook Building
30–32 Des Voeux Road
Central, Hong Kong
Tel: +852 28228633
Fax: +852 28046481

Kingston Futures Ltd (FCM)
10/F, Wings Building
110–116 Queen's Road
Central, Hong Kong
Tel: +852 28508333
Fax: +852 25526666

Kongson Commodities Ltd (FCM)
2805–2806, Bank of America Tower
12 Harcourt Road, Hong Kong
Tel: +852 28108382
Fax: +852 28451635

Lee Fung Hong (International) Futures Ltd (FCM)
19/F, Bank Centre
636 Nathan Road, Kowloon
Tel: +852 23593300
Fax: +852 23847821

Lee On Tat Commodity Ltd (FCM)
2/F, Unicorn Trade Centre
127–131 Des Voeux Road
Central, Hong Kong
Tel: +852 25450653
Fax: +852 25417920

Lehman Brothers Futures Asia Ltd (FCM)
Level 38, One Pacific Place
88 Queensway
Central, Hong Kong
Tel: +852 28693000
Fax: +852 28693690

Lippo Futures Ltd (FCM)
Rm 2302, Lippo Tower
Lippo Centre
89 Queensway, Hong Kong
Tel: +852 28457711
Fax: +852 28452250

MHS Futures Ltd (FCM)
37A Bank of China Tower
1 Garden Road
Central, Hong Kong
Tel: +852 28431431
Fax: +852 28459036

Magusta Futures Ltd (FCM)
Suite 706, 7/F, Nine Queen's Road
Central, Hong Kong
Tel: +852 28454113
Fax: +852 25879878

Makindo Futures (Hong Kong) Ltd (FCM)
Unit 9A/9D, World Trust Tower
50 Stanley Street
Central, Hong Kong
Tel: +852 25373833
Fax: +852 28016790

Mayfair Commodities Ltd (FCM)
10/F, Hong Kong & Macau Building
156–157 Connaught Road
Central, Hong Kong
Tel: +852 25411848
Fax: +852 28155652

Merrill Lynch Futures (HK) Ltd (FCM)
18/F, Asia Pacific Finance Tower
Citibank Plaza
3 Garden Road, Hong Kong
Tel: +852 25363888
Fax: +852 25363199

Morgan Stanley Futures (Hong Kong) Ltd (FCM)
31/F, Three Exchange Square
8 Connaught Place
Central, Hong Kong
Tel: +852 28485200
Fax: +852 28451012

NSC Futures Ltd (FCM)
Suite 1218 Central Building
1 Pedder Street
Central, Hong Kong
Tel: +852 25868288
Fax: +852 25868300

Nations-CRT Hong Kong Ltd (FCM)
2705 Lippo Tower
Lippo Centre
89 Queensway, Hong Kong
Tel: +852 28692295
Fax: +852 25010699

New Trend Futures Ltd (FCM)
4/F, 139 Bonham Stand E, Hong Kong
Tel: +852 25417196
Fax: +852 25413996

Nomura Futures (Hong Kong) Ltd (FCM)
20/F–21/F, Citibank Plaza
3 Garden Road, Hong Kong
Tel: +852 25361111
Fax: +852 25361758

Norman Kong Commodities Co Ltd (B)
504 Mongkok Commercial Centre
16 Argyle Street
Mongkok, Kowloon
Tel: +852 23944693
Fax: +852 23942753

OSK Asia Futures Ltd (FCM)
Rm 2001–5, Wheelock House
20 Pedder Street
Central, Hong Kong
Tel: +852 28100133
Fax: +852 25232932

Okachi (Hong Kong) Co Ltd (FCM)
6/F, Euro Trade Centre
13–14 Connaught Road
Central, Hong Kong
Tel: +852 28680968
Fax: +852 28101702

Oriental Crystal Futures Ltd (FCM)
23/F, Oriental Crystal Comm Bldg
46 Lyndhurst Terrace
Central, Hong Kong
Tel: +852 25448899
Fax: +852 28342218

PaineWebber International Futures (Asia) Ltd (FCM)
Suite 3206–11, Asia Pacific Finance Tower
Citibank Plaza
3 Garden Road, Hong Kong
Tel: +852 2842060
Fax: +852 25093939

Peace Town Futures Ltd (FCM)
40/F, Lippo Tower
Lippo Centre
89 Queensway, Hong Kong
Tel: +852 28228338
Fax: +852 28770133

Peregrine Futures Hong Kong Ltd (FCM)
22/F, New World Tower
16–18 Queen's Road
Central, Hong Kong
Tel: +852 28251888
Fax: +852 28450565

Phillip Commodities (HK) Ltd (FCM)
14/F, Regent Centre, 88 Queen's Road
Central, Hong Kong
Tel: +852 25221138
Fax: +852 28685307

Po Sang Futures Ltd (FCM)
2/F, Cheong Kee Building
84–86 Des Voeux Road
Central, Hong Kong
Tel: +852 28051077
Fax: +852 28541955

Power Range Futures Co Ltd (FCM)
Room 3004, 30/F, No 9 Queen's Road
Central, Hong Kong
Tel: +852 28667679
Fax: +852 25206333

Prudential Index Trading Co Ltd
9/F, Grand Building
15–18 Connaught Road
Central, Hong Kong
Tel: +852 25213251
Fax: +852 28457823

Prudential-Bache Futures (Hong Kong) Ltd (FCM)
40/F, Asia Pacific Finance Tower
3 Garden Road
Central, Hong Kong
Tel: +852 28682002
Fax: +852 28412841

Refco Futures (Hong Kong) Ltd (FCM)
10/F, Hutchison House
10 Harcourt Road, Hong Kong
Tel: +852 28105556
Fax: +852 25099222

Roctec Futures Trading Co Ltd (FCM)
11/F, Dina House
11 Duddell Street
Central, Hong Kong
Tel: +852 28413300
Fax: +852 28452168

SBC Warburg Derivatives Ltd (FCM)
20/F, One Exchange Square
8 Connaught Place
Central, Hong Kong
Tel: +852 28446388
Fax: +852 25371862

SPS Commodities Ltd (FCM)
10/F, Century Square, 1–13 D'Aguilar Street
Central, Hong Kong
Tel: +852 28690638
Tel: +852 25222320

Salomon Brothers Hong Kong Futures Ltd
20/F, Three Exchange Square
8 Connaught Place
Central, Hong Kong
Tel: +852 25012000
Fax: +852 25018105

Sassoon Futures Ltd (FCM)
36/F, One Exchange Square
8 Connaught Place
Central, Hong Kong
Tel: +852 28432100
Fax: +852 28100300

Schroders Asia Futures Ltd (FCM)
25/F, Two Exchange Square
8 Connaught Place
Central, Hong Kong
Tel: +852 25211633
Fax: +852 28681023

Seapower Futures Ltd (FCM)
32–34/F, Alexandra House
16–20 Chater Road
Central, Hong Kong
Tel: +852 28474888
Fax: +852 28681911

Shacom Futures Ltd (FCM)
12 Queen's Road, Central, Hong Kong
Tel: +852 28415283
Fax: +852 28771457

Shanghai International Futures (HK) Ltd (FCM)
28/F, Citibank Tower
Citibank Plaza
3 Garden Road, Hong Kong
Tel: +852 25098333
Fax: +852 25090319

Shun Loong Futures Ltd (FCM)
Rm 2502, Admiralty Centre
Tower I, 18 Harcourt Road, Hong Kong
Tel: +852 25200111
Fax: +852 28657017

Siu Yip Commodity Ltd (FCM)
6/F, Kwong Fat Hong Bldg
1 Rumsey Street
Central, Hong Kong
Tel: +852 25433327
Fax: +852 25417144

South China Commodities Ltd (FCM)
28/F, Bank of China Tower
1 Garden Road
Central, Hong Kong
Tel: +852 28206333
Fax: +852 28455765

Standard Capital Commodities Ltd (FCM)
12/F, St George's Building
2 Ice House Street
Central, Hong Kong
Tel: +852 29783838
Fax: +852 29783839

Standard Chartered Futures (HK) Ltd (FCM)
23/F, Bank of China Tower
1 Garden Road, Hong Kong
Tel: +852 28226752
Fax: +852 25215201

Stockwell Commodities Ltd (B)
1/F, Dragon House
7–7B Cameron Road, TST, Kowloon
Tel: +852 23135110
Tel: +852 27215990

Sun Hung Kai Commodities Ltd (FCM)
3/F, Tower I
Admiralty Centre
18 Harcourt Road, Hong Kong
Tel: +852 28225678
Fax: +852 28225486

Sun Hung Kai International Commodities Ltd (FCM)
3/F, Tower I
Admiralty Centre
18 Harcourt Road, Hong Kong
Tel: +852 28225678
Fax: +852 28225664

Sun's Future Ltd (FCM)
Rm 1104, Hang Seng Bldg
77 Des Voeux Road
Central, Hong Kong
Tel: +852 25222072
Fax: +852 28105885

Tai Fook Futures Ltd (FCM)
25/F, New World Tower
16–18 Queen's Road
Central, Hong Kong
Tel: +852 28016168
Fax: +852 25377647

Tai Yip Commodities & Futures Ltd (FCM)
304–307 China Insurance Group Building
141 Des Voeux Road
Central, Hong Kong
Tel: +852 25421322
Fax: +852 25410428

Taiyo General International Ltd (FCM)
2508 Asia Pacific Finance Tower
Citibank Plaza
3 Garden Road
Central, Hong Kong
Tel: +852 25262141
Fax: +852 28459148

Tak Fung Commodities Ltd (FCM)
8/F, Wah Yuen Building
145–149 Queen's Road
Central, Hong Kong
Tel: +852 25439382
Fax: +852 25451209

Tanrich Futures Ltd (FCM)
1601–2, Central Plaza
18 Harbour Road
Wanchai, Hong Kong
Tel: +852 28028838
Fax: +852 28028710

The New China Hong Kong Futures Ltd (FCM)
11/F, Nine Queen's Road
Central, Hong Kong
Tel: +852 28464200
Fax: +852 25302245

The Nikko Futures (Hong Kong) Ltd (FCM)
19/F, One Pacific Place
88 Queensway, Hong Kong
Tel: +852 28421111
Fax: +852 25309984

Timber Hill Hong Kong Ltd (B)
33/F, Asia Pacific Finance Tower
Citibank Plaza
3 Garden Road
Central, Hong Kong
Tel: +852 29212906
Fax: +852 25094102

Top Equity Derivatives Ltd (FCM)
Room 1002, 10th Floor
9 Queen's Road
Central, Hong Kong
Tel: +852 25262833
Fax: +852 25218722

Tung Shing Futures Ltd (FCM)
6/F, Bank of East Asia Bldg
10 Des Voeux Road
Central, Hong Kong
Tel: +852 28423448
Fax: +852 25267992

UB Futures Ltd (FCM)
3/F, Union Bank Tower
122–126 Queen's Road
Central, Hong Kong
Tel: +852 25411190
Fax: +852 28541326

Upworth Futures Ltd (FCM)
Suite 2108, Two Pacific Place
88 Queensway, Hong Kong
Tel: +852 25337888
Fax: +852 28015733

Vickers Ballas Hong Kong Futures Ltd (FCM)
39/F, Citibank Tower, Citibank Plaza
3 Garden Road
Central, Hong Kong
Tel: +852 28204888
Fax: +852 25236055

W I Carr (Futures) Ltd (FCM)
43/F, One Exchange Square
8 Connaught Place
Central, Hong Kong
Tel: +852 28207373
Fax: +852 28681524

Wardley Futures (HK) Ltd (FCM)
3/F, Hutchison House
10 Harcourt Road, Hong Kong
Tel: +852 25211661
Fax: +852 28100145

Well & Well Commodities Ltd (FCM)
29/F, Bank of America Tower
12 Harcourt Road, Hong Kong
Tel: +852 28686100
Fax: +852 25239598

Wheelock NatWest Futures Ltd (FCM)
43/F, NatWest Tower
Times Square
Causeway Bay, Hong Kong
Tel: +852 21158888
Fax: +852 21158604

Winfull Commodities Ltd (FCM)
Room 1902, New World Tower
16–18 Queen's Road
Central, Hong Kong
Tel: +852 25257361
Fax: +852 28685444

Wing Lung Futures Ltd (FCM)
45 Des Voeux Road
Central, Hong Kong
Tel: +852 25433599
Fax: +852 25442289

Wing On Cheong China Development Co Ltd (FCM)
24/F, Wing On Cheong Bldg
5 Wing Lok Street
Central, Hong Kong
Tel: +852 25430303
Fax: +852 28052528

Winton Commence Ltd (FCM)
6/F, Golden Centre
188 Des Voeux Road
Central, Hong Kong
Tel: +852 25455300
Tel: +852 25459326

Wocom Ltd (FCM)
Rm 2701, Wing On Centre
111 Connaught Road
Central, Hong Kong
Tel: +852 28530111
Fax: +852 28543822

Worldsec Futures Ltd (FCM)
11/F, Bank of America Tower
Harcourt Road
Central, Hong Kong
Tel: +852 28677288
Fax: +852 25265311

YF Futures Co Ltd (FCM)
17/F, SUP Tower, 75–83 King's Road
North Point, Hong Kong
Tel: +852 25713923
Fax: +852 25718446

Yamaichi Futures (Hong Kong) Ltd (FCM)
30/F, Two Pacific Place
88 Queensway, Hong Kong
Tel: +852 28260700
Fax: +852 25232268

Yardley Futures Ltd (FCM)
14/F, Wyndham Place
40–44 Wyndham Street
Central, Hong Kong
Tel: +852 28108068
Fax: +852 28685070

Yu On Commodities Co Ltd (FCM)
11/F, V Heun Building
138 Queen's Road
Central, Hong Kong
Tel: +852 25433255
Fax: +852 2541418

Hungary

Budapest Stock Exchange

Members of the Futures Market

ABN Amro Hoare Govett (Hungary) Co
Bajcsi-Zsilinszky u 12
1054 Budapest
Tel: +36 1 266 6113
Fax: +36 1 267 4205

Budapest Investment Co
Deák F u 5
1052 Budapest
Tel: +36 1 266 2251
Fax: +36 1 266 2250

Concorde Securities Ltd
Váci u 15, II, 1
1052 Budapest
Tel: +36 1 266 8035
Fax: +36 1 266 8036

Co-Nexus Securities Co
Roham u 1
1013 Budapest
Tel: +36 1 212 2490
Fax: +36 1 156 9493

Corvinbroker Ltd
Hold u 25
1054 Budapest
Tel: +36 1 132 0320
Fax: +36 1 111 6327

Creditanstalt Securities Ltd
Nagysándor J u 10
1054 Budapest
Tel: +36 1 269 0711
Fax: +36 1 269 0699

Csiky Securities Ltd
Révay u 10
1065 Budapest
Tel: +36 1 269 1200
Fax: +36 1 269 1030

Daiwa-MKB Co
Rákóczi u 1–3, III/38
1088 Budapest
Tel: +36 1 266 0364
Fax: +36 1 266 4762

Égszi Börze Ltd
Bartók Béla u 152
1054 Budapest
Tel: +36 1 161 3210
Fax: +36 1 186 9870

Equitas Broker Co
Régiposta u 4 II/20
1052 Budapest
Tel: +36 1 138 4327
Fax: +36 1 266 0757

First German Securities Ltd
Fehérhajó u 8–10
1052 Budapest
Tel: +36 1 117 3911
Fax: +36 1 117 3339

Girocredit Investment Co
Madách u 13–15
1075 Budapest
Tel: +36 1 266 2733
Fax: +36 1 268 1577

Góg Securities Ltd
Váci u 9
1052 Budapest
Tel: +36 1 266 5354
Fax: +36 1 266 5356

Inter-Europa Ltd
Szabadság tér 15
1054 Budapest
Tel: +36 1 269 3730
Fax: +36 1 111 9233

Investbank Investment Co
Képíró u 9
1053 Budapest
Tel: +36 1 117 5333/4149
Fax: +36 1 266 5033

K & H Broker Ltd
Váci u 40, IV em
1056 Budapest
Tel: +36 1 117 7666
Fax: +36 1 117 7377

Maygar-Daewoo Securities Ltd
Apáczai Csere János u 11
1052 Budapest
Tel: +36 1 266 4920
Fax: +36 1 266 4922

MKB Securities & Investment Co
Szent István tér 11
1051 Budapest
Tel: +36 1 268 7138
Fax: +36 1 268 7169

New York Broker Budapest Ltd
Váci u 19–21
1052 Budapest
Tel: +36 1 269 6645
Fax: +36 1 269 6649

Pakett Broker Securities Co
Semelweis u 2 I/5
1052 Budapest
Tel: +36 1 118 5022
Fax: +36 1 137 7663

Postabank Securities Selling & Investment Co
Pauler u 11 I em
1013 Budapest
Tel: +36 1 202 6991
Fax: +36 1 202 6643

Procent Hungaria Securities &
Investment Co
Régipost u 5 IV/6
1052 Budapest
Tel: +36 1 118 5766
Fax: +36 1 118 0517

Ireland

Irish Futures & Options Exchange

Members

ABN Amro Bank (Ireland) Ltd
121–122 Stephen's Green
Dublin 2

ACC Bank
ACC House
Upper Hatch Street
Dublin 2

AIB Investment Managers
AIB House
Percy Place
Dublin 4

Allied Irish Banks Plc
AIB International Centre
IFSC
Dublin 1

Anglo Irish Bank Corporation Plc
18–21 St Stephen's Court
Dublin 2

Bank of Ireland Asset Management
26 Fitzwilliam Place
Dublin 2

Banque Nationale de Paris
Dublin Branch
111 St Stephen's Green
Dublin 2

Bloxham Maguire Futures Ltd
10 Fleet Street
Dublin 2

Citifutures Ltd
71 St Stephen's Green
Dublin 2

Davy Futures Ltd
Hibernian Way
Dawson Street
Dublin 2

Eagle Star Insurance Co (Ireland) Ltd
Frascati Road
Blackrock
Co Dublin

Gandon Securities Ltd
Andersen House
1 Harbour Master Place
Dublin 1

Goodbody (Financial Futures) Ltd
122 Pembroke Road
Ballsbridge
Dublin 4

The Governor and Company of the Bank of Ireland
Lower Baggot Street
Dublin 2

Hibernian Insurance Co Ltd
Hibernian House
Haddington Road
Dublin 4

ICC Bank Plc
31 Harcourt Street
Dublin 2

Irish Life Assurance Plc
Irish Life Centre
Lower Abbey Street
Dublin 1

Irish Permanent Plc
56 St Stephen's Green
Dublin 2

ITI Plc
North Block
IFSC
Dublin 1

National Irish Bank
7–8 Wilton Terrace
Blackrock Hall
Dublin 2

NCB Stockbrokers Ltd
48–53 Lower Mount Street
Dublin 2

Riada Stockbrokers Ltd
1 College Green
Dublin 2

Ulster Bank Ltd
33 College Green
Dublin 2

Woodchester Investment Bank Ltd
Golden Lane
Dublin 8

Japan

Tokyo Commodity Exchange

General Members

All Enterprise Co Ltd

Asahi Chemical Laboratory Co Ltd

Asahi Trust Co Ltd

Astmax Co Ltd

Bear Co Ltd

Bridgestone Corp

Cargill Japan Ltd

Central Shinyo Co Ltd

Chubu Daiichi Shohin Co Ltd

Chugai Mining Co Ltd

Chuo Co Ltd

Chuo Trading Co Ltd

Credit Suisse Bullion Japan Ltd

Dah Chong Hong (Japan) Ltd

Daiko Investment Management Co Ltd

Daiwa Investment Management Co Ltd

Daiwa Precious Metals Co Ltd

Dowa Mining Co Ltd

Eguchi Futures Co Ltd

Eiko Kigyo Co Ltd

Engelhard Metals Japan Ltd

Fukutani Co Ltd

Fukuwa Gomu Co Ltd

Furukawa Co Ltd

Gold Tokai Co Ltd

Gomi Sangyo Co Ltd

Ichida Co Ltd
Ido Shoten Co Ltd

Itochu Co Ltd

Ito Shoji Co Ltd

Iwasaki Shoji Co Ltd

Japan of Commodities Exchange

Kagawa Tokei Shokai Co Ltd

Kanematsu Co Ltd

Kasho Co Ltd

Kato Sansho Co Ltd

Kawachi Co Ltd

Kawano Shoji Co Ltd

Kawashima Co Ltd

Kinsho-Mataich Corp

Kohoku Bussan Co Ltd

Kushida Co Ltd

Kuwayama Corp

Kyuko Shoji Co Ltd

Marubeni Corp

Marugo Shoji Co Ltd

Maruichi & Co Ltd

Marumoto Co Ltd

Maruume Co Ltd

Million Trading Co Ltd

Mitsubishi Corp

Mitsubishi Materials Corp

Mitsui & Co Ltd

Mitsui Mining & Smelting Co Ltd

Mitsukoshi Ltd

Murakami Kinzoku Sangyo Co Ltd

Nagahori Corp

Naruoka Co Ltd

Nichimen Corp

Nihon Agricultural Products Co Ltd

Nikko Commodities Co Ltd

Nippon Mining & Metals Co Ltd
Nishida Co Ltd
Nishimura Co Ltd
Nissin Trading Co Ltd
Nittetsu Mining Co Ltd
Olympic Gold Co Ltd
Okato Investment Management Co Ltd
Okura & Co Ltd
Orient Trading Inc
Orion Koeki Co Ltd
Orix Commodities Corp
Osaka Oishi Shoji Co Ltd
Osaka Oroshi Iryo Co Ltd
Otobe Beikoku Co Ltd
Otsuya Co Ltd
Ozawa Tokeiten Co Ltd
Pacific Futures Co Ltd
Sanchu & Co Ltd
Sanki Shoji Co Ltd
Sanki Shoji Co Ltd
Sanmenard Co Ltd
Sanyo Commodities Co Ltd
Senda Munetaka Shoten
Shinko Shoji Co Ltd
Shinnihon Kishi Co Ltd
Shinnihon Shohin Co Ltd
Shinyei Trading Co Ltd
Sumitomo Metal Mining Co Ltd
Taiheiyo Bussan Co Ltd
Taisei Koeki Kaisha Ltd
Taiyo Bussan Kaisha Ltd
Taiyo General Corp
Tamurakoma & Co Ltd
The Yokohama Rubber Co Ltd
Toko Shotori Shinko Co Ltd
Tomen Corp
Toyo Lex Co Ltd
Toyoshima & Co Ltd
Toyota Tsusho Corp
Tsutsui Shoten Co Ltd
Ueno Sugar Co Ltd
Ueno & Co Ltd
Yagi & Co Ltd
Yamabun Sangyo Co Ltd
Yamacho Co Ltd
Yamadai Shoji Co Ltd
Yamago Shoji Co Ltd

Futures Commissions Merchants

Ace Koeki Co Ltd
Alphix Co Ltd
Asahi Trust Co Ltd
Central Shoji Co Ltd
Chubu Daiichi Shohin Co Ltd
Chuo Co Ltd
Comtex Co Ltd
Dai-Ichi Commodities Co Ltd
Daiki Sangyo Co Ltd
Daiwa Futures Co Ltd
Daiyusha Sakimono Co Ltd
Doi Shoji Co Ltd
Fuji Futures Corp
Fujichu Shoji Co Ltd
Fujitomi Co Ltd
Globaly Co Ltd
Harbest Futures Inc
Hiro Shoji Co Ltd
Hokushin Bussan Co Ltd
Hokushin Shohin Co Ltd
Imex Co Ltd
International Trading Corp

Itochu Co Ltd

Japan of Commodities Exchange

Kanematsu Co Ltd

Kanetsu Shoji Co Ltd

Kobayashi Yoko Co Ltd

Kometsune Co Ltd

Kowa Futures Co Ltd

Koyo Futures Co Ltd

Kydei Bussan Co Ltd

Marubeni Corp

Marumura Shoji Co Ltd

Meiji Bussan Co Ltd

Million Trading Co Ltd

Mitsubishi Corporation Futures Ltd

Mitsui & Co Ltd

Mitshi Bussan Futures Ltd

Naruoka Co Ltd

Nichimen Corp

Nihon Unicom Corp

Nikko Commodities Co Ltd

Nissho-Iwai Corp

Nissin Trading Co Ltd

Nomura Trading Co Ltd

Oishi Shoji Co Ltd

Okachi & Co Ltd

Okato Shoji Co Ltd

Okayasu Shoji Co Ltd

Omnico Co Ltd

Orient Trading Inc

Orion Koeki Co Ltd

Sanki Shoji Co Ltd

Sanko Shoji Co Ltd

Sanko Shokuhin Co Ltd

Sanward Trading Inc

Seiyu Shoji Co Ltd

Senda Munetaka Shoten

Shinnihon Kishi Co Ltd

Shinnihon Shohin Co Ltd

S Nishida Co Ltd

Sumitomo Corp

Sunrise Trading Corp

Taichi Shoji Co Ltd

Taiheiyo Bussan Co Ltd

Taisei Commodity Co Ltd

Taiyo General Corp

Tokyo General Corp

Tomen Corp

Toyo Lex Co Ltd

Yamabun Sangyo Co Ltd

Yamanashi Shoji Co Ltd

Yamatane Bussan Co Ltd

Yamazen Shoji Co Ltd

Yutaka Shoji Co Ltd

Tokyo Grain Exchange

Futures Commissions Merchants

Ace Koeki Co Ltd
1–9–9 Roppongi Minato-ku
Tokyo 106

Alphix Co Ltd
1–15–2 Nishi-Nakajima Yodogawa-ku
Osaka 532

Asahi Trust Co Ltd
1–1–8 Nihonbashi Honcho Chuo-ko
Tokyo 103

Asahi Universal Trading Inc
1–8–13 Hiranocho Chuo-ku
Osaka 541

Central Shoji Co Ltd
1–7–9 Nihonbashi Kakigara-cho Chuo-ku
Tokyo 103

Chubu Daiichi Shohin Co Ltd
1–9–26 Higashi-Sakura Higaashi-ku
Nagoya 461

Chuo Co Ltd
3–21–23 Sakae Naka-ku
Nagoya 460
Comtex Ltd
1–10–14 Awaza Nishi-ku
Osaka 550

Cosmo Futures Co Ltd
2–9–1 Higashi Hakataeki Hataka-ku
Fukuoka 812

Daiichi Commodities Co Ltd
10–10 Shinsencho Shibuya-ku
Tokyo 150

Dalki Sangyo Co Ltd
2–2–13 Nishiki Naka-ku
Nagoya 460

Daiwa Futures Co Ltd
1–11–1 Kaigan Minato-ku
Tokyo 105

Daiyusha Futures Co Ltd
49 Kayamachi Toyohashi-shi 440

Doi Shoji Co Ltd
2–8–5 Sakae Naka-ku
Nagoya 460

Fujichu Co Ltd
2–3–7 Funakoshicho Chuo-ku
Osaka 540

Fuji Futures Corporation
1–8–6 Nihonbashi Muromachi Chuo-ku
Tokyo 103

Fujitomi Co Ltd
1–3–17 Okubu Shinjuku-ku
Tokyo 169

Fukutani Corporation
1–9–16 Sakae Naka-ku
Nagoya 460

Globaly Corporation
3–14–17 Aoi Higashi-ku
Nagoya 461

Harbest Futures Co Ltd
1–1–4 Shibuya Shibuya-ku
Tokyo 150

Hokushin Shoshin Co Ltd
3–2–1 Nichi-Azabu Minato-ku
Tokyo 106

Hoxsin Bussan Co Ltd
1–9–2 Nihonbashi Kayabacho Chuo-ku
Tokyo 103

Imex Co Ltd
2–11–7 Sakac Naka-ku
Nagoya 460

International Trading Corporation
1–2–5 Hakataekimae Hakata-ku
Fukuoka 812

Itochu Corporation
2–5–1 Kita-Aoyama Minato-ku
Tokyo 107

Kanetsu Shoji Co Ltd
1–11–5 Nihonbashi Kakigaracho Chuo-ku
Tokyo 103

Kanto Sugar Co Ltd
1–2–7 Nihonbashi Kakigaracho Chuo-ku
Tokyo 103

Kita Nihon Shoshinn Co Ltd
1–8–16 Yaesu Chuo-ku
Tokyo 103

Kobayashi Yoko Co Ltd
1–15–5 Nihonbashi Kakigaracho Chuo-ku
Tokyo 103

Kohwa Futures Co Ltd
1–13–15 Nihonbashi Kakigaracho Chuo-ku
Tokyo 103

Kometsune Corporation
1–45 Shiga Hondori Kita-ku
Nagoya 462

Koyo Futures Corporation
1–3–5 Tanimachi Chuo-ku
Osaka 540

Kyoei Bussan Co Ltd
1–6–1 Hatchbori Chuo-ku
Tokyo 104

Marubeni Corporation
1–4–2 Otemachi Chiyoda-ku
Tokyo 100

Maruha Corporation
1–1–2 Otemachi Chiyoda-ku
Tokyo 100

Maruichi & Co Ltd
1–7–1 Saga Koto-ku
Tokyo 135

Marumoto & Co Ltd
1–13–16 Awaza Nishi-ku
Osaka 550

Maruume Co Ltd
2–17–9 Nihonbashi Kayabacho Chuo-ku
Tokyo 103

Meiji Bussan Co Ltd
1–1–23 Nihonbashi Ningyocho Chuo-ku
Tokyo 103

Meiji Trading Corporation
2–4–17 Kyobashi Chuo-ku
Toyko 104

Million Trading Co Ltd
1--8–20 Marunouchi Naka-ku
Nagoya 460

Mitsubishi Corporation Futures Ltd
1–14–8 Nihonbashi Ningyocho Chuo-ku
Tokyo 103

Mitsui Bussan Futures Ltd
6–6 Nihonbashi Kobunacho Chuo-ku
Tokyo 103

Nihon Agricultural Products Co Ltd
1–10 Kitasanjo-Nishi Chuo-ko
Sapporo 060

Nihon Koeki Co Ltd
7–4–4 Nishi-Shinjuku Shinjuku-ku
Tokyo 160

Nihon Unicom Corporation
1–6–10 Nihonbashi Ningyocho Chuo-ku
Tokyo 103

Nikko Shohin Co Ltd
2–13–2 Higashi-Nihonbashi Chuo-ku
Tokyo 103

Nissho Iwai Corporation
2–4–5 Akasaka Minato-ku
Tokyo 107

Nissin Cup Co Ltd
14–1 Nihonbashi Koamicho Chuo-ku
Tokyo 103

Nissin Trading Co Ltd
3–24 Sakaecho
Otaru 047

Nozaki & Co Ltd
2–2–6 Nihonbashi Bakurocho Chuo-ku
Tokyo 103

Okachi & Co Ltd
3–7–29 Sakae Nakaku
Nagoya 460

Okatu Shoji Co Ltd
3–12–11 Honmachi
Osaka 451

Okayasu Shoji Co Ltd
2–3–8 Kitahama Chuo-ku
Osaka 541

Onishi Shoji Co Ltd
22–14 Nabecho
Shimonoseki 750

Orient Boeki Co Ltd
5–24–30 Wantanabe-dori Chuo-ku
Fukuoka 810

Orion Trading Inc
113–1 Higashicho Chuo-ku
Kobe 650

Oshima Shoten Co Ltd
1–3 Nihonbashi Koami-cho Chuo-ku
Tokyo 103

Pacific Futures Co Ltd
1–17–12 Awaza Nishi-ku
Osaka 550

Sanchu Shoji Corporation
1–19–9 Nihonbashi Kakigaracho Chuo-ku
Tokyo 103

Seiyu Shoiji Co Ltd
1–10–11 Nihonbashi Horidomecho Chou-ku
Tokyo 103

Sinnihon Shohin Co Ltd
3–14–13 Ginza Chuo-ku
Tokyo 104

S Nishida & Co Ltd
1–1–27 Kitahama Chuo-ku
Osaka 541

Sugiyama Shoji Co Ltd
13–3 Nihonbashi Koami-cho Chuo-ku
Tokyo 103

Sumitomo Corporation
3–24–1 Kanda Nishikicho Chiyoda-ku
Tokyo 101

Sunrise Trading Corporation
1–19–4 Higashi-Ikebukuro Toshima-ku
Tokyo 170

Sunward Trading Inc
4–6–1 Odori-Nishi Chuo-ku
Sapporo 060

The Sansiao Trading Co Ltd
3–2–9 Nihonbashi Chuo-ku
Tokyo 103

Taichi Shoji Co Ltd
1–13–13 Nihonbashi Kayabacho Chuo-ku
Toyko 103

Taihelyo Bussan Co Ltd
1–11–2 Nihonbashi Kakigaracho Chuo-ku
Tokyo 103

Taisel Commodity Co Ltd
2–2–7 Honmachi Chuo-ku
Osaka 541
Taiyo General Corporation
8–12–7 Ginza Chuo-ku
Tokyo 104

Takara Futures Co Ltd
1–2–14 Ginza Chuo-ku
Tokyo 104

Tokyo General Corporation
4–3–1 Toranomon Minato-ku
Tokyo 105

Tokyo-to Chuo Shokuro Cooperative Association
16–16 Nihonbashi Koamicho Chuo-ku
Tokyo 103

Toshoku Ltd
2–4–3 Nihonbashi Muromachi Chuo-ku
Tokyo 103

Toyo Lex Co Ltd
1–1–16 Saga Koto-ku
Tokyo 135

Yamabun Sangyo Co Ltd
2–5–12 Iwamotocho Chiyoda-ku
Tokyo 101

Yamadi Shoji Co Ltd
3–12–9 Nihonbashi Kayabacho Chuo-ku
Tokyo 103

Yamanashi Shoji Co Ltd
2–60–6 Nihonbashi Hamacho Chuo-ku
Tokyo 103

Yamatane Bussan Co Ltd
1–1–1 Nihonbashi Ningyocho Chuo-ku
Tokyo 103

Yamato Sangyo Co Ltd
1–14–4 Shinmachi Nichi-ku
Nagoya 451

Yamazen Shoji Co Ltd
1–9–9 Nihonbashi Kakigaracho Chuo-ku
Tokyo 103

Yutaka Shoji Co Ltd
1–16–12 Nihonbashi Kakigaracho Chuo-ku
Tokyo 103

Kobe Rubber Exchange

Members

Trade member *
Commission merchant †

Ace Koeki Co Ltd
9–9 Roppongi 1-chome, Minato-ku
Tokyo 106
Tel: +81 3 3587 4649
Fax: +81 3 3589 4699
RSS3: †
Index: †

Alphix Co Ltd
15–2 Nishi-Nakajima 1-chome
Yodogawa-ku
Osaka 552
Tel: +81 6 3045071
Fax: +81 6 304 6196
RSS3: †
Index: *

Asahi Universal Trading Inc
8–13 Hiranocho 1-chome, Chuo-ku
Osaka 541
Tel: +81 6 201 2711
Fax: +81 6 201 2660
RSS3: †
Index: †

Comtex Ltd
10–14 Awaza 1-chome, Nishi-ku
Osaka 550
Tel: +81 6 543 2118
Fax: +81 6 543 2394
RSS3: †
Index: †

Cosmo Futures Co Ltd
9–1 Hakataeki-Higashi 2-chome
Kakata-ku
Fukuoka 812
Tel: +81 92 4722 2191
Fax: +81 92 472 2187
RSS3: †
Index: †

Daiichi Commodities Co Ltd
10–10 Shinsen-cho, Shibuya-ku
Tokyo 150
Tel: +81 3 3462 8011
Fax: +81 3 3476 0819
Index: †

Daiki Sangyo Co Ltd
2–13 Nichiki 2-chome, Naka-ku
Nagoya 460
Tel: +81 52 201 6311
Fax: +81 52 220 1593
RSS3: *

Daiusha Futures Co Ltd
49 Kaya-machi, Toyohashi
Aichi 440
Tel: +81 532 55 1177
Fax: +81 532 53 7006
RSS3: †
Index: †

Daiwa Futures Co Ltd
11–1 Kaigan 1-chome, Minato-ku
Tokyo 105
Tel: +81 3 5400 3400
Fax: +81 3 5472 7510
RSS3: †
Index: †

Eguchi Futures Co Ltd
17–9 Izumi 3-chome, Higashi-ku
Nagoya 461
Tel: +81 52 931 0111
Fax: +81 52 932 0800
RSS3: †
Index: †

Fujichu Co Ltd
3–7 Funakoshicho 2-chome, Chuo-ku
Osaka 540
Tel: +81 6 942 2131
Fax: +81 6 947 0676
RSS3: †
Index: †

Globaly Co Ltd
14–17 Aoi 3-chome, Higasi-ku
Nagoya 461
Tel: +81 52 932 7000
Fax: +81 52 932 7055
RSS3: †
Index: †

Goryo Shoji Co Ltd
13–6 Nihonbashi-Kakigaracho 2-chome
Chuo-ku
Tokyo 103
Tel: +81 3 5640 5600
Fax: +81 3 5645 8961
RSS3: †
Index: *

Hiro Shoji Co Ltd
4–16 Kyomachiboro 1-chome, Nishi-ku
Osaka 550
Tel: +81 6 441 3521
Fax: +81 6 459 4707
RSS3: †
Index: †

Hokushin Shohin Co Ltd
2–1 Nishi-Azabu 3-chome, Minato-ku
Tokyo 106
Tel: +81 3 3403 3111
Fax: +81 3 3479 2704
RSS3: †
Index: †

Hoxsin Bussan Co Ltd
9–2 Nihonbashi-Ningyocho 1-chome
Chuo-ku
Tokyo 103
Tel: +81 3 3688 8111
Fax: +81 3 3668 4417
Index: †

Imex Co Ltd
11–7 Sakae 2-chome, Naka-ku
Nagoya 460
Tel: +81 52 201 2011
Fax: +81 52 201 2041
RSS3: †
Index: *

International Trading Corporation
2–5 Hakataekimae 1-chome, Hakata-ku
Fukuoka 812
Tel: +81 92 475 8800
Fax: +81 92 475 8444
Index: †

Itochu Corporation
1–3 Kyutaro-machi 4-chome, Chuo-ku
Osaka 541–77
Tel: +81 6 241 3957
Fax: +81 6 241 4593
RSS3: *
Index: *

Kanetsu Shoji Co Ltd
11–5 Nihonbashi-Kakigaracho 1-chome
Chou-ku
Tokyo 103
Tel: +81 3 3662 0111
Fax: +81 6 3664 1010
RSS3: †
Index: †

Kansai Futures Co Ltd
2–9–12 Higashi-Noda, Miyakojima-ku
Osaka 534
Tel: +81 6 352 2241
Fax: +81 6 352 2240
RSS3: *
Index: *

Kasho Co Ltd
14–9 Nihonbashi 2-chome, Chuo-ku
Tokyo 103
Tel: +81 3 3276 7641
Fax: +81 3 3281 0408
RSS3: *
Index: *

Kobayashi Yoko Co Ltd
15–5 Nihonbashi-Kakigaracho 1-chome
Chuo-ku
Tokyo 103
Tel: +81 3 3669 4111
Fax: +81 3 3669 6249
RSS3: †
Index: †

Kobe Gomutori Daiko Kaisha Ltd
5–28 Kyutaro-machi 2 chome, Chuo-ku
Osaka 541
Tel: +81 6 244 2191
Fax: +81 6 243 4427
RSS3: *

Kometsune Co Ltd
45 Shiga-Hondori 1-chome, Kita-ku
Nagoya 462
Tel: +81 52 981 3571
Fax: +81 52 911 1321
RSS3: †
Index: †

Kyoei Bussan Co Ltd
6–1 Hacchobori 1-chome, Chuo-ku
Tokyo 104
Tel: +81 3 3553 4151
Fax: +81 3 3553 4827
RSS3: †
Index: †

Kyuko Shoji Co Ltd
5–28 Hakataeki-Higashi 2-chome
Hakata-ku
Fukuoka 812
Tel: +81 92 471 1701
Fax: +81 92 473 7023
RSS3: †
Index: †

Marubeni Corporation
5–7 Honmachi 2-chome, Chuo-ku
Osaka 541–88
Tel: +81 6 266 4351
Fax: +81 6 266 4286
RSS3: *
Index: *

Marugo Shoji Co Ltd
7–20 Nishi-Tenma 1-chome, Kita-ku
Osaka 530
Tel: +81 6 366 0051
Fax: +81 6 366 0058
RSS3: †
Index: *

Marumura Co Ltd
11–26 Nishiki 3-chome, Naka-ku
Nagoya 460
Tel: +81 52 231 7341
Fax: +81 52 212 2938
RSS3: †
Index: †

Meiji Bussan Co Ltd
1–23 Nihonbashi-Ningyocho 1-chome
Chuo-ku
Tokyo 103
Fax: +81 3 3666 2511
Fax: +81 3 3666 9280
RSS3: *
Index: *

Mitsubishi Corporation Futures Ltd
14–8 Nihonbashi-Ningyocho 1-chome
Chuo-ku
Tokyo 103
Tel: +81 3 3668 0651
Fax: +81 3 3668 0667
Index: †

Mitsui Bussan Futures Ltd
6–6 Nihonbashi-Nongyocho 1-chome
Chuo-ku
Tokyo 103
Tel: +81 3 3660 6800
Fax: +81 3 3660 6899
Index: †

Nihon Unicom Corporation
6–10 Nihonbashi-Nongyocho 1-chome
Chuo-ku
Tokyo 103
Tel: +81 3 3868 2331
Fax: +81 3 3639 3690
Index: †

Nomura Trading Co Ltd
4–5 Bingo-cho 1-chome, Chuo-ku
Osaka 541
Tel: +81 6 268 8353
Fax: +81 6 268 8270
RSS3: *
Index: *

Ohtsuya Co Ltd
15–2 Nishi-Nakajima 1-chome
Yodogawa-ku
Osaka 532
Tel: +81 6 304 2911
Fax: +81 6 304 5376
RSS3: *
Index: *

Okachi & Co Ltd
7–29 Sakae 3-chome, Naka-ku
Nagoya 460
Tel: +81 52 261 3311
Fax: +81 52 262 6717
RSS3: †
Index: *

Okato Shoji Co Ltd
2–11 Honmachi 3-chome, Chuo-ku
Osaka 541
Tel: +81 6 261 7671
Fax: +81 6 258 2125
RSS3: †
Index: †

Orient Trading Inc
24–30 Watanabe-dori 5-chome, Chuo-ku
Fukuoka 810
Tel: +81 92 712 3111
Fax: +81 92 712 3117
RSS3: †
Index: †

Orion Koeki Co Ltd
113–1 Higashi-cho, Chuo-ku
Kobe 650
Tel: +81 78 391 7391
Fax: +81 78 391 4766
RSS3: †
Index: †

Osaka Oishi Shoki Co Ltd
5–24 Minami-Senba 2-chome, Chuo-ku
Osaka 542
Tel: +81 6 261 4231
Fax: +81 6 261 0461
RSS3: †
Index: †

Osaka Oroshi-Iryo Co Ltd
1–10 Koraibashi 2-chome, Chuo-ku
Osaka 541
Tel: +81 6 203 5341
Fax: +81 6 203 6344
RSS3: †
Index: †

Pacific Futures Co Ltd
7–12 Awaza 1-chome, Nishi-ku
Osaka 550
Tel: +81 6 537 2211
Fax: +81 6 531 8652
RSS3: †

S Nishida & Co Ltd
1–27 Kitahama 1-chome, Chuo-ku
Osaka 541
Tel: +81 6 233 6310
Fax: +81 6 233 6351
RSS3: †
Index: *

Sanko Shoji Co Ltd
19–9 Nihonbashi-Hamacho 2-chome, Chuo-ku
Tokyo 103
Tel: +81 3 3249 3500
Fax: +81 3 3249 3716
RSS3: †
Index: †

Santomi & Co Ltd
1–1–1 4th Floor Shinkobe Building
Sannomiya-cho, Chuo-ku
Kobe 650
Tel: +81 78 331 2525
Fax: +81 78 321 5072
RSS3: †
Index: †

Sanyo Trading Co Ltd
11 Kanda-Nishikicho 2-chome, Chuo-ku
Tokyo 101
Tel: +81 3 3233 5701
Fax: +81 3 3233 5777
RSS3: *
Index: *

Seiyu Shoji Co Ltd
10–11 Nihonbashi-Horidomecho
1-chome, Chuo-ku
Tokyo 103
Tel: +81 3 3663 5711
Fax: +81 3 3669 0410
RSS3: †
Index: †

Sunrise Trading Corporation
19–4 Higashi-Ikebukuro 1-chome, Toshima-ku
Tokyo 170
Tel: +81 3 3988 7351
Fax: +81 3 3985 9007
Index: †

Sunward Trading Inc
6–1 Ohdori-Nishi 4-chome, Chuo-ku
Sapporo 060
Tel: +81 11 221 5311
Fax: +81 11 222 6406
Index: *

Taisei Commodity Co Ltd
2–7 Honmachi 2-chome, Chuo-ku
Osaka 541
Tel: +81 6 264 2181
Fax: +81 6 264 2191
RSS3: †
Index: †

Taisei Koeki Kaisha Co Ltd
7–4 Nihonbashi 1-chome, Chuo-ku
Tokyo 103
Tel: +81 3 3271 1005
Fax: +81 3 3275 0885
RSS3: *

Taiyo General Inc
12–7 Ginza 8-chome, Chuo-ku
Tokyo 104
Tel: +81 3 3545 6111
Fax: +81 3 3546 0236
RSS3: †
Index: †

Tokyo General Corporation
3–1 Toranomon 4-chome, Minato-ku
Tokyo 105
Tel: +81 3 5401 6111
Fax: +81 3 5404 3333
RSS3: †
Index: †

Yutaka Shoji Co Ltd
16–12 Nihonbashi-Kakigaracho 1-chome
Chuo-ku
Tokyo 103
Tel: +81 3 3667 5211
Fax: +81 3 5695 1923
RSS3: †
Index: †

Associate Members

Cargill International Trading Pte Ltd
300 Beach Road
23–01 The Concourse
Singapore
Tel: +65 295 1115
Fax: +65 390 9898

Centrotrade Singapore Pte Ltd
10 Collyer Quay
07–07 Ocean Building
Singapore 0140
Tel: +65 535 9133
Fax: +65 534 1345

Guthrie Symington Ltd
Devon House, 58–60 St Katharine's Way
London E1 9LB
United Kingdom
Tel: +44 171 248 0821
Fax: +44 171 248 7246

Joo Cheong Co Pte Ltd
470 North Bridge Road
04–20 Singapore Finance House
Singapore
Tel: +65 338 0101
Fax: +65 339 3215

Kanetsu Singapore Pte Ltd
11 Collyer Quay
The Arcade
Singapore 0104
Tel: +65 220 0268
Fax: +65 224 0214

Kautschuk-Gesellschaft GmbH
Reuterweg, 14
60323 Frankfurt am Main
Germany
Tel: +49 69 159 2117
Fax: +49 69 159 3481

L Wurfbain & Co BV
Mahoniehout, 24
1507 Zaandam
Netherlands
Tel: +31 75 810810
Fax: +31 75 705296

Marubeni International Commodities (Singapore) Pte Ltd
16 Raffles Quay
18–02 Hong Leong Building
Singapore 0104
Tel: +65 227 7622
Fax: +65 227 9293

New Continent Enterprises Pte Ltd
3 Shenton Way
15–04 Shenton House
Singapore 0106
Tel: +65 227 1539

Nordmann, Rassmann GmbH & Co
Kajen, 2
2000 Hamburg 11
Germany
Tel: +49 40 368870
Fax: +49 40 368 7415

Okato Shoji Singapore Pte Ltd
138 Robinson Road
17–08 Hong Leong Centre
Singapore 0106
Tel: +65 224 9301
Fax: +65 224 0214

Sang Tong Rubber Co Ltd
29 Si Phuwanat Nye Road
Haadyai, Songkhla
South Thailand
Tel: +66 74 253051
Fax: +66 74 253050

Singapore Tong Teik Pte Ltd
3 Shenton Way
15–01 Shenton House
Singapore 0106
Tel: +65 744 3648
Fax: +65 225 4716

Yakuta Shoji Singapore Pte Ltd
10 Anson Road
27–06 International Plaza
Singapore 0207
Tel: +65 226 2829
Fax: +65 220 8179

Kenya

East African Tea Trade Association

Producer Members

Africa Highlands Produce Co Ltd
PO Box 72244
Nairobi
& PO Box 71
Kericho

Brooke Bond Kenya Ltd
PO Box 42011
Nairobi
& PO Box 20
Kericho

EA Tea Plantations
PO Box 94
Nandi Hills

Eastern Produce Kenya Ltd
PO Box 45560
Nairobi

George Williamson Kenya Ltd
PO Box 42281
Nairobi

Kapchorua Tea Co
PO Box 42281
Nairobi

Kaimosi Tea Estates Ltd
PO Box 42281
Nairobi

Kaisugu Ltd
PO Box 37
Kericho

Kakuzi Ltd
PO Box 30572
Nairobi

Karirana Estates Ltd
PO Box 39
Limuru
Kenya Tea Development Authority
PO Box 30213
Nairobi

Kibwari Tea Estates Ltd
PO Box 45560
Nairobi

Kipkebe Ltd
Private Bag
Sotik

Kiptagich Tea estate
PO Box 1
Olenguruone

Kip Koimet Tea Co
PO Box 45560
Nairobi

Koisagat Tea Estates Ltd
PO Box 53104
Nairobi

Mau Forest Ltd
PO Box 377
Kericho

Nandi Tea Estates Ltd
PO Box 26
Nandi Hills

Ngorongo Tea Co Ltd
PO Box 364
Kiambu

Nyayo Tea Zones Development
Corporation
PO Box 48552
Nairobi

Sotik Highland Tea Estate
Private Bag
Sotik

Sotik Tea Co
Private Bag
Sotik

Subukia Tea Co Ltd
PO Box 568
Nakuru

Tinderet Tea Estates Ltd
PO Box 144
Songhor

Uganda

Dayalbhai Madanji & Co
PO Box 2093
Kampala

Mwera Tea Estates Ltd
PO Box 54
Jinja

Toro & Mityana Tea Co Ltd
PO Box 6641
Kampala

Uganda Tea Corporation
PO Box 8955
Kampala

Uganda Tea Growers' Corporation
PO Box 7157
Kampala

Rwenzori Commodities Ltd
PO Box 20072
Kampala

Rwenzori Highlands Tea Co Ltd
PO Box 7790
Kampala

Tanzania

Tanzania Tea Authority
PO Box 2663
Dar es Salaam

Tea Association of Tanzania
PO Box 2177
Dar es Salaam

Rwanda

Office des Cultures Industrielle du Rwanda (OCIR)
PO Box 1344
Kigali

Malawi

Malawi Tea Factory Co Ltd
PO Box 135
Mulanje

Zaire

Sipef SA Kasteel Colesberg
B-2900 Schoten Belgium

Burundi

Office du Thé
PO Box 2680
Bujumbura

Broker Members

African Tea Brokers Ltd
PO Box 81883
Mombasa

Anjeli Ltd
PO Box 90020
Mombasa

Bicorn Exim Ltd
PO Box 99530
Mombasa

Combrok Ltd
PO Box 87411
Mombasa

Choice Tea Brokers Ltd
PO Box 62297
Nairobi

Prudential Tea Brokers (EA) Ltd
PO Box 87193
Mombasa

Tea Brokers East Africa Ltd
PO Box 87296
Mombasa

Union Tea Brokers Ltd
PO Box 81120
Mombasa

Venus Tea Brokers Ltd
PO Box 57671
Nairobi

Victory Tea Brokers Ltd
PO Box 84716
Mombasa

Warehouse Members

Bahari Transport Co Ltd
PO Box 81829
Mombasa

Consolidated (Msa) Ltd
PO Box 90400
Mombasa

Express Kenya Ltd
PO Box 90631
Mombasa

Kenya Transit & Trading Co Ltd
PO Box 90403
Mombasa

Mbaraki Port Warehouses (K) Ltd
PO Box 80066
Mombasa

Mitchell Cotts Kenya Ltd
PO Box 90141
Mombasa

Multimodal Forwarders Ltd
PO Box 89003
Mombasa

SGS Kenya Ltd
PO Box 90264
Mombasa

Siginon Freight Ltd
PO Box 99646
Mombasa

Swife Ltd
PO Box 99434
Mombasa

Topaz Transport Co Ltd
PO Box 89051
Mombasa

Transami (Kenya) Ltd
PO Box 90263
Mombasa

Ufanisi Freighters (Kenya) Ltd
PO Box 980
Mombasa

Buyer Members

Abbas Traders Ltd
PO Box 80240
Mombasa

Adex Kenya Ltd
PO Box 84569
Mombasa

African Highlands Produce Co Ltd
PO Box 84619
Mombasa

Albarakah Trading Co Ltd
PO Box 529
Mombasa

Alibhai Ramji (Msa) Ltd
PO Box 80398
Mombasa

Alyameen Trading Co
PO Box 99178
Mombasa

Al-Emir Ltd
PO Box 81254
Mombasa

Al-Hamudi Investments Co Ltd
PO Box 88165
Mombasa

Al Nakhil Enterprises
PO Box 88072
Mombasa

Al Noor Feisal & Co
PO Box 14766
Nairobi

Al Yasin Trading & Contracting Co Ltd
PO Box 40
Mombasa

Anchor Africa Ltd
PO Box 11274 and 63039
Nairobi

Bico Ltd
PO Box 84745
Mombasa

Brooke Bond Mombasa
PO Box 95105
Mombasa

Chai Exports (Kenya) Ltd
PO Box 84078
Mombasa

Cofftea Agencies Ltd
PO Box 217
Mombasa

Commodity House Ltd
PO Box 34625
Nairobi

Cornfields Investments Ltd
PO Box 42863
Nairobi

Devchand Keshavji (K) Ltd
PO Box 80478
Mombasa

DJ Lowe & Co Ltd
PO Box 86232
Mombasa

East African Tea Exporters Ltd
PO Box 82339
Mombasa

Economic Carriers
PO Box 86489
Mombasa

Elamin Trading Co Ltd
PO Box 81112
Mombasa

El Reza Tea Exports Ltd
PO Box 87563
Mombasa

Femo Works Ltd
PO Box 11798
Nairobi

Fin Tea Ltd
PO Box 2101
Mombasa

Gishungo Ltd
PO Box 84251
Mombasa

Global Tea & Commodities (K)
PO Box 98459
Mombasa

I Lutax Ltd
PO Box 27775
Nairobi
& PO Box 498
Kericho

Jakal Services Ltd
PO Box 86874
Mombasa

James Finlay Kenya Ltd
PO Box 84619
Mombasa

Juja Coffee Exporters Ltd
PO Box 85039
Mombasa

Kambugi Supplies Ltd
PO Box 99136
Mombasa

Kenya Bestea Packers Ltd
PO Box 81112
Mombasa

Khaku Exporters
PO Box 88265
Mombasa

Kigless Ltd
PO Box 82037
Mombasa

Kilindini Warehouses (K) Ltd
PO Box 82693
Mombasa

LAB International Kenya Ltd
PO Box 99883
Mombasa

Lipton Ltd
PO Box 83067
Mombasa

Maccani Investments Ltd
PO Box 2438
Mombasa

Malanga Tea Trading Co Ltd
PO Box 47147
Mombasa

Meadow Trading Co Ltd
PO Box 8940
Nairobi

Meleen Enterprises
PO Box 75844
Nairobi

Mella Corporation
PO Box 84904
Mombasa

Mirage Trading Co Ltd
PO Box 40876
Mombasa

MJ Clarke
PO Box 84321
Mombasa

Mombasa Coffee
PO Box 88623
Mombasa

Mombasa Packers Ltd
PO Box 87148
Mombasa

Mountain Produce Ltd
PO Box 56954
Nairobi

MS Bawazir & Co
PO Box 80326
Mombasa

Nchoke Ltd
PO Box 58119
Nairobi

Nairobi Tea Packers Ltd
PO Box 72889
Nairobi

Nyaga Art & Handicraft Co-Op Society
PO Box 95
Ruiru

Oriental Tea Expo Ltd
PO Box 50042
Nairobi

Pegasus Tea Ltd
PO Box 41696
Mombasa

Pekiwa Investments Co Ltd
PO Box 60431
Nairobi

Phillips Kenya Tea Ltd
PO Box 90244
Mombasa

Prodex International Ltd
PO Box 56789
Nairobi

Rooh Ltd
PO Box 84464
Mombasa

Seyffert & Co Ltd
PO Box 87259
Mombasa

Shakab Imports Exports Ltd
PO Box 2078
Mombasa

Shigog Investment Ltd
PO Box 99296
Mombasa

Stansand (Africa) Ltd
PO Box 90683
Mombasa

Tanjal Investments Ltd
PO Box 88999
Mombasa

Teawise (EA) Agencies Ltd
PO Box 42524
Mombasa

Ufanisi Freighters (K) Ltd
PO Box 980
Mombasa

Uneximp Ltd
PO Box 30657
Nairobi

Unitea Ltd
PO Box 56789
Nairobi

Unitrad Ltd
PO Box 89997
Mombasa

Valley Tea Ltd
PO Box 84285
Mombasa

Van Rees Ltd
PO Box 83835
Mombasa

Associate Members

Abosi Traders Ltd
PO Box 119
Kericho

Afrimex Global Ltd
PO Box 71058
Nairobi

Aristocrats Coffee & Tea Ltd
PO Box 49729
Nairobi

Arkay Industries Ltd
PO Box 679
Eldoret

Asad Ltd
PO Box 49726
Nairobi

Chai Ltd
PO Box 72889
Nairobi

Diamond Tea Exporters Kenya Ltd
PO Box 81306
Mombasa

Diara Ltd
PO Box 52447
Nairobi

Esco Kenya Ltd
PO Box 43387
Nairobi

Green Gulf Enterprises
PO Box 67303
Nairobi

Hydery Printers Ltd
PO Box 82576
Mombasa

International Shipping Co Agencies
PO Box 85634
Mombasa

Kenya Bonded Warehouses
PO Box 80522
Mombasa

Lyalroc Enterprises Ltd
PO Box 11444
Nairobi

MA Panju Bros Ltd
PO Box 82985
Mombasa

MG Habib & Co
PO Box 87491
Mombasa

Merali Devji & Sons Ltd
PO Box 80214
Mombasa

Moledina Enterprises
PO Box 83152
Mombasa

Nexus Ltd
PO Box 58198
Nairobi

Packaging Manufacturers Ltd
PO Box 82571
Mombasa

Pakken Exports Ltd
PO Box 536
Mombasa

Purshottam Bhimji & Sons
PO Box 80545
Mombasa

Rashid Moledina & Co
PO Box 80324
Mombasa

Rielco Ltd
PO Box 25932
Nairobi

Sea Air Forwarders International Ltd
PO Box 83354
Mombasa

Seeta Ltd
PO Box 57457
Nairobi

Shah Meghji & Hirji Ltd
PO Box 48162
Nairobi

SM Maina Coffee Ltd
PO Box 47687
Nairobi

Splendid View Cafe
PO Box 80901
Mombasa

Tasty Tea Ltd
PO Box 43762
Nairobi

Telo Food Products Ltd
PO Box 88993
Mombasa

Toumalin Tea Co Ltd
PO Box 75591
Nairobi

Wayne Ltd
PO Box 42844
Nairobi

Wanjoo Trading Co Ltd
PO Box 57610
Nairobi

Zubedi Tea & Produce Centre
PO Box 81264
Mombasa

Packer Members

Africom Agencies
PO Box 16699
Mombasa

Annfred Investments Ltd
PO Box 40459
Nairobi

Belken Enterprises Ltd
PO Box 7376
Nairobi

Carina Drinks
PO Box 52026
Nairobi

Caspian Packers Ltd
PO Box 52361
Nairobi

Chai Halisi Packers
PO Box 39
Samburu

David Sunshine Agencies
PO Box 51393
Nairobi

Global Tea Packers
PO Box 33397
Nairobi

Gitogothi Enterprises
PO Box 425
Limuru

Grawan Enterprises
PO Box 61773
Nairobi

Hygrown Packers Ltd
PO Box 757
Limuru

Jatepa Enterprises
PO Box 77473
Nairobi

Jenga Tea Packers Co Ltd
PO Box 68067
Nairobi

Jimden Enterprises
PO Box 21194
Nairobi

Josdama Enterprises
PO Box 12822
Nakuru

Kanjo General Traders
PO Box 1064
Limuru

Kimac Ltd
PO Box 75015
Nairobi

Kisumu Tea Packers
PO Box 2916
Kisumu

Korokoro Investments
PO Box 198
Taveta

Limarge Co Ltd
PO Box 997
Embu

Limland Tea Packers
PO Box 984
Limuru

Magharibi Chai
PO Box 964
Limuru

Majani Tea Packers
PO Box 50309
Nairobi

Malakisi Agencies Ltd
PO Box 17645
Nairobi

Marga Enterprise
PO Box 56654
Nairobi

Melvin Marsh International Ltd
PO Box 40270
Nairobi

Milford Ltd
PO Box 65706
Nairobi

Mt Kenya Food Products Ltd
PO Box 42
Nkubu-Meru

Okay Tea Packers
PO Box 82403
Mombasa

Pembu Tea Packers
PO Box 45019
Nairobi

Penkar Tea Packers
PO Box 8853
Nairobi

Royal Tea Ltd
PO Box 42017
Mombasa

Rurigi Enterprises Ltd
PO Box 72417
Nairobi

Spiced Tea Co
PO Box 84580
Mombasa

Sunrise Tea Packers, Retailers Imports & Exports Ltd
PO Box 55292
Nairobi

Thiririka Tea Farm Ltd
PO Box 44911
Nairobi

Thumwi Ltd
PO Box 90797
Mombasa

Wamaria Tea Packers
PO Box 191
Chuka

Worldwide Tea Packers
PO Box 451
Ruiru

Zonic Ltd
PO Box 70624
Nairobi

Malaysia

Kuala Lumpur Commodity Exchange (KLCE)

Clearing Members

EPA Futures Sdn Bhd
Suite 2.02, 2nd Floor
Wisma Song Pang Seng
32 Jalan Imbi
55100 Kuala Lumpur
Malaysia
Tel: +60 3 2482355/2428706
Fax: +60 3 2487360/2482563
Contact: Peter Wong

Guan Soon Heng Futures Trading Sdn Bhd
290, Jalan Raja Laut
50350 Kuala Lumpur
Malaysia
Tel: +60 3 2915233
Fax: +60 3 2915970
Contact: S T Kheoh

Maika Futures Sdn Bhd (formerly known as Maika Commodities Sdn Bhd)
7th Floor, Menara Manickavasagam
No 1 Jalan Rahmat
Off Jalan Tun Ismail
50350 Kuala Lumpur
Malaysia
Tel: +60 3 4427286/4427290
Fax: +60 3 4415805
Contact: R Palanisamy

Branch Office:
*No 2, 2nd Floor, Block G
Ruang Singgah Asia City
88000 Kota Kinabalu, Sabah
Tel: +60 88 715346
Fax: +60 88 268606
Contact: Geevanathan

Multi-Purpose Commodity Trading Sdn Bhd
No 42–2A Jalan Sultan Ismail
50250 Kuala Lumpur
Malaysia
Tel: +60 3 2446690
Fax: +60 3 2447903
Contact: Sia Kee Siong

Branch Offices:
*1st Floor, Wisma K S Equity
No 1 Jalan Lintang Pekan Baru
Off Jalan Meru
41050 Klang
Selangor
Tel: +60 3 3437359/69
Fax: +60 3 3437354
Contact: Toh Chee Leong

*Block C, 1st Floor, Singgah Mata Urban Development (Asia City)
88000 Kota Kinabalu
Sabah
Tel: +60 88 250050
Fax: +60 88 250070
Contact: Jack Stephen Juman

Okachi (M) Sdn Bhd
Suite 51A & 51B
51st Floor, Empire Tower
Jalan Tun Razak
50400 Kuala Lumpur
Malaysia
Tel: +60 3 2644633
Fax: +60 3 2644601/2
Contact: H Hishinuma

Phillip Commodities Sdn Bhd
30th Floor, Menara Tun Razak
Jalan Raja Laut
50350 Kuala Lumpur
Malaysia
Tel: +60 3 2939836
Fax: +60 3 2936417
Contact: Dennis Lai

Branch Offices:
*1G, 1st Floor
Penang Street
10200 Penang
Tel: +60 4 2634788
Fax: +60 4 2634787
Contact: Chong Peng Lum

*Room 3–7, 3rd Floor
Wisma Kota Emas
Jalan Osborne
30300 Ipoh
Perak
Tel: +60 5 2412561
Fax: +60 5 2412353
Contact: Loh Kim Swee

*67A, Jalan Meranti Merah
Melodies Garden
80250 Johor Bahru
Tel: +60 7 3340771/6/80
Fax: +60 7 3340771
Contact: Foo Chee Suan

Pro Futures Sdn Bhd
17–1, Jalan Telawi Dua
Bangsar Baru
59100
Kuala Lumpur
Malaysia
Tel: +60 3 2824706
Fax: +60 3 2824715
Contact: J B Lim

Sunny Futures Sdn Bhd
Suite 19–11–3
Level 11, UOA Centre
No 19, Jalan Pinang
50450 Kuala Lumpur
Malaysia
Tel: +60 3 2644468/69/70/72
Fax: +60 3 2644590
Contact: K C Low

Non-Clearing Members

Comtra Sdn Bhd
Room 6.02, 6th Floor
Lee Yan Lian Building
Jalan Tun Perak
50050 Kuala Lumpur
Malaysia
Tel: +60 3 2304777
Fax: +60 3 2304780
Contact: Chong Wee Chee

Convest Sdn Bhd
Lot 202, 2nd Floor, Wisma HLA
Jalan Raja Chulan
50200 Kuala Lumpur
Malaysia
Tel: +60 3 2023233/2484888
Fax: +60 3 2489525
Contact: Quah Boo Huat

Fontannaz Futures Sdn Bhd
Suite 1208, 12th Floor
Pernas International Building
Jalan Sultan Ismail
50250 Kuala Lumpur
Malaysia
Tel: +60 3 2633722/2634857
Fax: +60 3 2634873
Contact: Pang Shio Hin

Kelly Futures Sdn Bhd
17th Floor, Wisma Denmark
86 Jalan Ampang
50450 Kuala Lumpur
Malaysia
Tel: +60 3 2018833
Fax: +60 3 2022733
Contact: Chee Kok How

LPC Futures (M) Sdn Bhd
Lot 3.13, 3rd Floor
Wisma Stephens
Jalan Raja Chulan
50200 Kuala Lumpur
Malaysia
Tel: +60 3 2419555
Fax: +60 3 2416378
Contact: Yeoh Oon Chye

Marpro Oils & Grains Sdn Bhd
Room 905, 9th Floor, Wisma HLA
Jalan Raja Chulan
50200 Kuala Lumpur
Malaysia
Tel: +60 3 2425311
Fax: +60 3 2423034
Contact: Chua Seow Yang

Sri Comm Options & Futures Sdn Bhd
44 Jalan Tun Sambanthan 3
Brickfields
50470 Kuala Lumpur
Malaysia
Tel: +60 3 2731813
Fax: +60 3 2735945/2732117
Contact: Zaha Rina Hj Zahari

Transcommodities Futures (M) Sdn Bhd
301 303 1st Floor
1 1/4 Miles, Jalan Ipoh
51200 Kuala Lumpur
Malaysia
Tel: +60 3 4447777
Fax: +60 3 4443807
Contact: Lim Soo Kok

Kuala Lumpur Tin Market

Members

Escoy Smelting Sdn Bhd
73 Jalan Datuk Keramat
PO Box 280
10150 Penang
Tel: +60 4 374966/344
Fax: +60 4 2272273
Contact: Nazir Ariff b Hj Mushir Ariff

H H Bhatt Trading Sdn Bhd
90 Penang Street
10200 Penang
Tel: +60 4 2610326
Fax: +60 4 2620125
Contact: Arunkumar s/o Himatlal Bhatt

Kay Minerals Sdn Bhd
Letter Box No 72
4th Flr, Ubn Tower
10 Jalan P Ramlee
50250 Kuala Lumpur
Tel: +60 3 2021610
Fax: +60 3 2021894
Contact: Encik Abdul Hamid Hussain

Malaysia Smelting Corp Bhd
27 Jalan Pantal
PO Box 2
12000 Penang
Tel: +60 4 3333600
Fax: +60 4 3317405
Contact: Dato' Mohd Ajib b Hj Anuar

KL Office
Tkt 37, Menara PNB
Jalan Tun Razak
50400 Kuala Lumpur
Tel: +60 3 2616000/2742204
Fax: +60 3 2614370
Contact: Ong Kee Beng

MMC Marketing Sdn Bhd
Tkt 31, Menara PNB
Jalan Tun Razak
50400 Kuala Lumpur
Tel: +60 3 2633888
Fax: +60 3 2610385
Contact: Encik Wan Ahamad Sabri

Mitsui & Co Ltd
5th Flr, Regent Office Block
160 Jalan Bukit Bintang
55100 Kuala Lumpur
Tel: +60 3 2418099
Fax: +60 3 2423644
Contact: A Enoki

Shell Malaysia
11th Flr, Bangunan Shell Malaysia
Off Jalan Semantan
PO Box 11027
50732 Kuala Lumpur
Tel: +60 3 2559144
Fax: +60 3 2512957
Contact: Encik Zain Yusoff

Sinar Berlian Sdn Bhd
15th Flr, Pernas International
Jalan Sultan Ismail
50200 Kuala Lumpur
Tel: +60 3 2611255/58
Fax: +60 3 2631876
Contact: Ryoichi Fukuda

Thailand Smelting & Refining Co Ltd
7th Flr, Shell Building
No 10 Soonthornkosa Road
Klongtoey, Bangkok 10110
Thailand
Tel: +60 7 62 2490491
Fax: +60 7 662 2498335
Contact: David S Ratcliffe

Toyota Tsusho (M) Sdn Bhd
Room 1404, Wisma Lim Foo Yong
No 86 Jalan Raja Chulan
50200 Kuala Lumpur
Tel: +60 3 2423366/5622
Fax: +60 3 2425809
Contact: Sadao Miyamoto

Netherlands

ATA Agrarische Termijnmarkt Amsterdam BV (Agricultural Futures Exchange Amsterdam)

Brokers

AOT Kreeuwen BV
PO Box 3733
1001 AM Amsterdam
Tel: +31 20 624 8897/4311
Fax: +31 20 623 8014

G de Vries Termijnmarkt BV
Damrak 379
1012 ZJ Amsterdam
Tel: +31 20 620 5001
Fax: +31 20 620 6326

Klaas Brouwer Termijnmarkt BV
PO Box 18
7707 ZG Balkbrug
Tel: +31 20 623 6099
Fax: +31 523 657447

Maas & Daemen BV
Damrak 385
1012 ZJ Amsterdam
Tel: +31 20 421 2124
Fax: +31 20 421 1777

Manger Intermedia BV
PO Box 120
1720 AC Broek op Langedijk
Tel: +31 226 313122
Fax: +31 226 316644

Proterma BV
PO Box 10215
1001 EE Amsterdam
Tel: +31 20 626 7635
Fax: +31 20 624 7620

SA Bryonterme
Damrak 257
1012 ZJ Amsterdam
Tel: +31 20 620 4241
Fax: +31 20 638 3559

Van Zanten & Van Westen BV
Pr Hendrikkade 48
1012 AC Amsterdam
Tel: +31 20 626 2206
Fax: +31 20 420 3346

WF Westermann & Co BV
PO Box 3445
1001 AE Amsterdam
Tel: +31 20 626 2784
Fax: +31 20 622 3046

New Zealand

New Zealand Futures & Options Exchange Ltd (NZFOE)

(PB) Public brokers
(IB) Introducing brokers
(PT) Principal traders
(TPH) Trading permit holders

New Zealand Dealers

AMP Investments (NZ) Ltd (PT)
PO Box 3764, Wellington
Level 4, City Tower
95 Customhouse Quay
Wellington
Tel: +64 4 489 8000
Fax: +64 4 498 8221

ANZ Banking Group (NZ) Ltd (PB, TPH)
PO Box 1492, Wellington
New Zealand Treasury
215–229 Lambton Quay
Wellington
Tel: +64 4 473 1960
Fax: +64 4 496 8639

ASB Bank Ltd (PT, TPH)
PO Box 35, Auckland 1050
Level 9, ASB Bank Centre
Corner of Albert & Wellesley Streets
Auckland
Tel: +64 9 377 8930
Fax: +64 9 307 8010

Bank of New Zealand (PT, TPH)
PO Box 2392, Wellington
Head Office, Group Treasury
Level 21, BNZ Centre
1 Willis Street
Wellington
Tel: +64 4 474 6999
Fax: +64 4 474 6446

BT Futures New Zealand Ltd (PB, THP)
(authorized as Clearing Member of the Sydney Futures Exchange Clearing House Ltd)
PO Box 6900
Wellesley Street
Auckland
Level 8, Stock Exchange Centre
191 Queen Street
Auckland
Tel: +64 9 309 3226
Fax: +64 9 303 1851

Citibank NA (New Zealand Branch) (PT, TPH)
PO Box 3429, Auckland
Citibank Centre
23 Custom Street East
Auckland
Tel: +64 9 302 3128
Fax: +64 9 308 9928

Clarke Wycherley Investments Ltd (IB)
PO Box 5595, Wellesley Street
Auckland
Level 7, Tower 2
The Shortland Centre
55–56 Shortland Street
Auckland
Tel: +64 9 366 4689
Fax: +64 9 366 4692

First NZ Capital Futures Ltd (IB)
PO Box 3394, Wellington
10th Floor, Caltex Tower
282–292 Lambton Quay
Wellington
Tel: +64 4 474 4400
Fax: +64 4 474 4060

CS First Boston NZ Futures Ltd (PB, TPH)
PO Box 3394, Wellington
10th Floor, Caltex Tower
282–292 Lambton Quay
Wellington
Tel: +64 4 474 4400
Fax: +64 4 474 4432

Egden Wignall & Co Futures Ltd (PB, TPH)
PO Box 2335, Christchurch
Exchange House
112 Hereford Street
Christchurch
Tel: +64 3 379 2600
Fax: +64 3 379 1196

Electricity Corporation of New Zealand Ltd (PT)
PO Box 930, Wellington
Treasury Division
Level 10, Rutherford House
23 Lambton Quay
Wellington
Tel: +64 4 474 2314
Fax: +64 4 473 3189

Fixed Interest Brokers (NZ) Ltd (PB, TPH)
PO Box 11–274, Wellington
6th Floor, 107 Customhouse Quay
Wellington
Tel: +64 4 499 0009
Fax: +64 4 499 0074

Holroyd Capital Management Ltd (IB)
PO Box 3256, Auckland
6/90 Remuera Road
Remuera
Auckland
Tel: +64 9 524 4461
Fax: +64 9 523 3361

JB Were Futures Pty Ltd (PB, TPH, CM)
New Zealand Branch
PO Box 887, Auckland
Level 21, Coopers & Lybrand Tower
23–29 Albert Street
Auckland
Tel: +64 9 309 9800
Fax: +64 9 309 9861

McIntosh Futures Ltd (PB, TPH, CM)
New Zealand Branch
PO Box 817, Auckland
Westpac Tower
120 Albert Street
Auckland
Tel: +64 9 356 2929
Fax: +64 9 356 2933

MS Capital Management Ltd (IB)
3 Dryden Street
Grey Lynn
Auckland
Tel: +64 9 378 7183
Fax: +64 9 378 7184

Ord Minnett Jardine Fleming Futures (NZ) Ltd (PB, TPH)
PO Box 5830, Auckland
Head Office, Level 8
Arthur Andersen Tower
205 Queen Street
Auckland
Tel: +64 9 356 1300
Fax: +64 9 356 1323

Ord Minnett Jadine Fleming Futures (NZ) Ltd (Christchurch)
PO Box 13–186, Armagh
Christchurch
Level 17, 764 Colombo Street
Christchurch
Tel: +64 3 366 8851
Fax: +64 3 366 8852

SBC Warburg New Zealand Futures Ltd
PO Box 45, Auckland
Level 23, Stock Exchange Centre
191 Queen Street
Auckland
Tel: +64 9 307 4800
Fax: +64 9 307 4888

Strategic Futures & Options Ltd (IB)
35 Lynfield Avenue
Christchurch 4
Tel: +64 3 358 2491

The Hongkong & Shanghai Banking Corporation Ltd (PT, TPH)
PO Box 5947, Wellesley Street
Auckland
8th Floor, Hongkong Bank House
290 Queen Street, Auckland
Tel: +64 9 309 3800
Fax: +64 9 302 0116

The National Bank of New Zealand Ltd (PB, TPH)
Wholesale Audit Services
PO Box 1791
Wellington
Level 9, National Bank House
170–186 Fetherston Street
Wellington
Tel: +64 4 494 4058
Fax: +64 4 802 2021

Trust Bank New Zealand Ltd (PB, TPH)
PO Box 2260, Wellington
Levels 14 & 15, Trust Bank Centre
125 The Terrace
Wellington
Tel: +64 4 473 2807
Fax: +64 4 471 1981

Westpac Banking Corporation (PT, TPH)
PO Box 691, Wellington
Level 4, Westpac House
318–324 Lambton Quay
Wellington
Tel: +64 4 498 1275
Fax: +64 4 473 7879

Australian Dealers

ANZ Capel Court Ltd (PB, CM)
Level 35–36, Chifley Tower
2 Chifley Square
Sydney NSW 2000
Tel: +61 2 322 6520
Fax: +61 2 233 4794

ANZ McCaughan Futures Ltd (PB, TPH)
Levels 35–36, Chifley Tower
2 Chifley Square
Sydney NSW 2000
Tel: +61 2 322 6170
Fax: +61 2 232 8590

Australian Gilt Securities Ltd (PB, TPH, CM)
Level 5, Underwood House
37–49 Pitt Street
Sydney NSW 2000
Tel: +61 2 251 4177
Fax: +61 2 251 5961

Bain Refco Commodities Ltd (PB, TPH)
17th Level, Grosvenor Place
225 George Street
Sydney NSW 2000
Tel: +61 2 258 1222
Fax: +61 2 258 1133

Barclays Bank Plc (PB, TPH, CM)
(Trading as BZW Futures)
Level 23, NAB Building
255 George Street
Sydney NSW 2000
Tel: +61 2 259 5711
Fax: +61 2 259 5265

Bankers Trust Australia Ltd (PB, TPH, CM)
Level 2, Chifley Tower
2 Chifley Square
Sydney NSW 2000
Tel: +61 2 259 3555
Fax: +61 2 259 9800

C, A & L Bell Commodities Corporation Pty Ltd (PB, TPH)
Level 33, 101 Collins Street
Melbourne VIC 3000
Tel: +61 3 656 7333
Fax: +61 3 654 3391

Citifutures Ltd (PB, CM)
Level 12, Citibank Centre
1 Margaret Street
Sydney NSW 2000
Tel: +61 2 239 9174
Fax: +61 2 251 1894

Commonwealth Bank of Australia (PB, TPH, CM)
Futures Broking and Clearing
Institutional Banking, Level 4
85 Harrington Street
Sydney NSW 2000
Tel: +61 2 312 0555
Fax: +61 2 312 0565

CS First Boston Australia Securities Ltd (PB, TPH, CM)
Level 31, 1 Macquarie Place
Sydney NSW2000
Tel: +61 2 394 4333
Fax: +61 2 394 4390

Deutsche Bank AG (PB, CM)
Level 20, Grosvenor Place
225 George Street
Sydney NSW 2000
Tel: +61 2 258 3722
Fax: +61 2 258 1000

FIMAT Australia Pty Ltd (PB, TPH, CM)
Level 28, Grosvenor Place
225 George Street
Sydney NSW 2000
Tel: +61 2 336 6800
Fax: +61 2 251 1277

HSBC Futures Australia Ltd (PB, TPH)
Level 6, 1 O'Connell Street
Sydney NSW 2000
Tel: +61 2 252 1166
Fax: +61 2 255 2409

JB Were Futures Pty Ltd (PB, TPH, CM)
Level 42, Governor Phillips Tower
1 Farrer Place
Sydney NSW 2000
Tel: +61 2 321 8777
Fax: +61 2 321 8500

JB Were Futures Pty Ltd (Melbourne)
101 Collins Street
Melbourne VIC 3000
Tel: +61 3 9679 1356
Fax: +61 3 9679 1330

JB Were Futures Pty Ltd
New Zealand Branch
PO Box 887, Auckland
Level 21, Coopers & Lybrand Tower
23–29 Albert Street
Auckland
Tel: +64 9 309 9800
Fax: +64 9 309 9861

JP Morgan Australia Ltd (PB, TPH, CM)
Level 20, 1 O'Connell Street
Sydney NSW 2000
Tel: +61 2 551 6100
Fax: +61 2 551 6353

L Quay Futures Brokers Pty Ltd (PB, TPH)
Suite 701, 220 George Street
Sydney NSW 2000
Tel: +61 2 247 6852
Fax: +61 2 247 6876

Macquarie Bank Ltd (PB, TPH, CM)
Level 22, Exchange Centre
20 Bond Street
Sydney NSW 2000
Tel: +61 2 237 3350
Fax: +61 2 237 3333

McIntosh Futures Ltd
Level 39, Gateway
1 Macquarie Place
Sydney NSW 2000
Tel: +61 2 256 8882
Fax: +61 2 256 8889

McIntosh Futures Ltd
New Zealand Branch
PO Box 817, Auckland
Level 17, Westpac Tower
120 Albert Street
Auckland
Tel: +64 9 356 2929
Fax: +64 9 356 2933

Merrill Lynch (Australia) Futures Ltd (PH, TPH)
Level 49, MLC Centre
19–29 Martin Place
Sydney NSW 2000
Tel: +61 2 225 6500
Fax: +61 2 232 3519

Midland Bank Plc (PB, CM)
Level 8, 1 O'Connell Street
Sydney NSW 2000
Tel: +61 2 255 2888
Fax: +61 2 255 2408

National Australia BAnk Ltd (PB, CM)
29th Floor, NAB House
255 George Street
Sydney NSW 2000
Tel: +61 2 237 1529
Fax: +61 2 237 1512

NatWest Capital Markets Australia Ltd (PB, TPH)
Level 16, Grosvenor Place
225 George Street
Sydney NSW 2000
Tel: +61 2 321 4567
Fax: +61 2 251 2198

Ord Minnett Jardine Fleming Futures Ltd (PB, TPH, CM)
Level 25, Grosvenor Place
225 George Street
Sydney NSW 2000
Tel: +61 2 220 1666
Fax: +61 2 220 1316

SBC Warburg Australia Ltd (PB, TPH, CM)
Level 25, Governor Phillips Tower
1 Farrer Place
Sydney NSW 2000
Tel: +61 2 375 6700
Fax: +61 2 375 6581

Singapore

Singapore International Monetary Exchange

Clearing Members

BA Futures Inc
78 Shenton Way, #19–00
Singapore 079120
Tel: +65 3203389
Fax: +65 3203390

BOT Futures (Singapore) Pte Ltd
16 Raffles Quay
#01–06 Hong Leong Building
Singapore 048581
Tel: +65 2208111
Fax: +65 2244965

BT Futures (Singapore) Ltd
5 Temasek Boulevard
#08–00 Suntec City Tower
Singapore 038985
Tel: +65 3383138
Fax: +65 3366056

BZW Futures (Singapore) Pte Ltd
50 Raffles Place
#21–01 Shell Tower
Singapore 048623
Tel: +65 3223902
Fax: +65 3223911

Cargill Investor Services (Singapore) Pte Ltd
4 Robinson Road
#03–00 Commercial Union House
Singapore 048543
Tel: +65 4351100
Fax: +65 4351101

Citicorp Futures Ltd
5 Shenton Way
#30–01 UIC Building
Singapore 068808
Tel: +65 2259422
Fax: +65 2258924

Credit Lyonnais Rouse (Pte) Ltd
50 Raffles Place
#11–02/04 Shell Tower
Singapore 048623
Tel: +65 2213380
Fax: +65 2261538

DBS Trading (Private) Ltd
6 Shenton Way
2nd Floor DBS Building
Singapore 068809
Tel: +65 2233064/2233067
Fax: +65 2252963

Daiwa Futures Pte Ltd
6 Shenton Way
#26–08 DBS Building
Tower Two
Singapore 068809
Tel: +65 2203666
Fax: +65 2260758

Fimat Futures Asia Pte Ltd
80 Robinson Road, #27–00
Singapore 068898
Tel: +65 3235711
Fax: +65 3235722

The Fuji Futures (Singapore) Pte Ltd
1 Raffles Place
#20–00 OUB Centre
Singapore 048616
Tel: +65 5343500
Fax: +65 5323690

Goldman Sachs Futures Pte Ltd
50 Raffles Place
#29–01 Shell Tower
Singapore 048623
Tel: +65 2288146/8147
Fax: +65 2288148

HSBC Futures (Singapore) Pte Ltd
21 Collyer Quay
#03–01 HongKong Bank Building
Singapore 049320
Tel: +65 5366255
Fax: +65 5360928

ING Futures & Options (Singapore) Pte Ltd
20 Raffles Place
14th Floor Ocean Towers
Singapore 048620
Tel: +65 5396633
Fax: +65 5361998

Indosuez Carr Futures Pte Ltd
6 Raffles Quay
#18–07 John Hancock Tower
Singapore 048580
Tel: +65 5385232/6911
Fax: +65 5385212

Keppel Bullion & Futures Pte Ltd
20 Raffles Place
#13–06 Ocean Towers
Singapore 048620
Tel: +65 5383122
Fax: +65 5383022

Kim Eng Futures Pte Ltd
5 Shenton Way
#13–00 UIC Building
Singapore 068808
Tel: +65 2209090
Fax: +65 2258746

Lehman Brothers Pte Ltd
5 Temasek Boulevard
#11–01 Suntec City Tower
Singapore 038985
Tel: +65 4336330
Fax: +65 4336180

Merrill Lynch Futures (S) Pte Ltd
16 Collyer Quay
#11–00 Hitachi Tower
Singapore 049318
Tel: +65 4372625
Fax: +65 4372643

J P Morgan Futures Inc
6 Shenton Way
#32–08 DBS Building, Tower Two
Singapore 068809
Tel: +65 3269722
Fax: +65 3269987

Natwest Futures Asia Pte Ltd
50 Raffles Place
8th Floor Shell Tower
Singapore 048623
Tel: +65 5301000
Fax: +65 5313133

The Nikko Futures (Singapore) Pte Ltd
6 Battery Road, #28–01
Singapore 049909
Tel: +65 2233390
Fax: +65 2249457

Nomura Futures (Singapore) Pte Ltd
6 Battery Road, #39–01
Singapore 049909
Tel: +65 4201811
Fax: +65 4201888

OCBC Bullion & Futures Ltd
65 Chulia Street
#12–07/08 OCBC Centre
Singapore 049513
Tel: +65 5301233
Fax: +65 5340009

OUB Bullion & Futures Ltd
1 Raffles Place, 15th Floor OUB Centre
Singapore 048616
Tel: +65 5338686
Fax: +65 5332360

Ong First Chicago Futures Pte Ltd
76 Shenton Way
#10–00 Ong Building
Singapore 079119
Tel: +65 2239477
Fax: +65 2239890

Phillip Futures Pte Ltd
95 South Bridge Road
#11–17 Pidemco Centre
Singapore 058717
Tel: +65 5351155
Fax: +65 5330593

Prudential-Bache Futures Asia Pacific Ltd
50 Raffles Place
28th Floor Shell Tower
Singapore 048623
Tel: +65 5383383
Fax: +65 5385585

Refco (Singapore) Pte Ltd
6 Shenton Way
#11–02 Treasury Building
Singapore 068811
Tel: +65 2253628
Fax: +65 2257373

Rothschild Bullion & Financial Futures Pte Ltd
20 Cecil Street
#09–00 The Exchange
Singapore 049705
Tel: +65 5358311
Fax: +65 5358713

Sassoon Financial Futures Pte Ltd
1 Raffles Place
#55–01 OUB Centre
Singapore 048616
Tel: +65 5341966
Fax: +65 5330086

Standard Chartered Futures (S) Pte Ltd
6 Battery Road, #09–30/04
Singapore 049909
Tel: +65 2277113
Fax: +65 2253122

Sun Hung Kai Bullion & Futures Pte Ltd
24 Raffles Place
#20–04 Clifford Centre
Singapore 048621
Tel: +65 5350688
Fax: +65 5381612

TLB Bullion & Futures Pte Ltd
63 Market Street
#09–06/10 Tat Lee Bank Building
Singapore 048942
Tel: +65 5356811
Fax: +65 5324218

UOB Bullion & Futures Ltd
80 Raffles Place
#05–00 UOB Plaza
Singapore 048624
Tel: +65 5339898
Fax: +65 5383990

Wardley Broking Services Pte Ltd
21 Collyer Quay
#17–01 HongKong Bank Building
Singapore 049320
Tel: +65 2254007
Fax: +65 2244395

Yamaichi Futures Pte Ltd
138 Robinson Road
#20–01/21–01 Hong Leong Centre
Singapore 068906
Tel: +65 2250688
Fax: +65 2279360

Non-Clearing Members

Asahi Financial Futures (Singapore) Pte Ltd
50 Raffles Place
#25–01/06 Shell Tower
Singapore 048623
Tel: +65 5354822
Fax: +65 5331462

BNP Futures (Singapore) Pte Ltd
20 Collyer Quay
#04–00 Tung Centre
Singapore 049319
Tel: +65 2240211
Fax: +65 2243459

BOC Futures (S) Pte Ltd
4 Battery Road
#10–00 Bank of China Building
Singapore 049908
Tel: +65 5352411
Fax: +65 5384517

DKB Futures (Singapore) Pte Ltd
1 Raffles Place
#47–00 OUB Centre
Singapore 048616
Tel: +65 5332626
Fax: +65 5332190

DMT Futures (Asia) Pte Ltd
9 Temasek Boulevard
#19–03 Suntec Tower Two
Singapore 038989
Tel: +65 3379119/3372078
Fax: +65 3371138/3373832

Diamond Futures (Singapore) Pte Ltd
20 Collyer Quay
#12–01 Tung Centre
Singapore 049319
Tel: +65 2205666
Fax: +65 2254739

FCT Singapore (Pte) Ltd
15 Phillip Street
#07–00 Tan Ean Kiam Building
Singapore 048694
Tel: +65 5383103/5332064
Fax: +65 5389378

GNI (Singapore) Pte Ltd
20 Raffles Place
#10–07 Ocean Towers
Singapore 048620
Tel: +65 5367812
Fax: +65 5367813

LTCB Futures (Singapore) Pte Ltd
80 Raffles Place
#27–01 UOB Plaza 1
Singapore 048624
Tel: +65 5359633
Fax: +65 5326048

Morgan Grenfell Asia Futures Pte Ltd
20 Raffles Place
#20–01 Ocean Towers
Singapore 048620
Tel: +65 5332828
Fax: +65 5382673

Morgan Stanley Futures (Singapore) Pte Ltd
80 Raffles Place
#42–01 UOB Plaza 1
Singapore 048624
Tel: +65 4396900
Fax: +65 4396969

NJI Futures Pte Ltd
16 Collyer Quay
#13–01 Hitachi Tower
Singapore 049318
Tel: +65 5383400
Fax: +65 5384100

Nations-CRT Asia, Inc
80 Raffles Place
#30–01 UOB Plaza 2
Singapore 048624
Tel: +65 2302200
Fax: +65 2302201

Orix Commodities Singapore Pte Ltd
331 North Bridge Road
#16–04/05 Odeon Towers
Singapore 188720
Tel: +65 3391976
Fax: +65 3391981

Peregrine Futures (Singapore) Pte Ltd
1 Temasek Avenue
#33–01 Millenia Tower
Singapore 039192
Tel: +65 5352818/5359289
Fax: +65 5339698

Phibro Trading Pte Ltd
101 Thomson Road
#16–03 United Square
Singapore 307591
Tel: +65 2506088
Fax: +65 2506124

Sakura Financial Futures (Singapore) Pte Ltd
16 Raffles Quay
#35–01 Hong Leong Building
Singapore 048581
Tel: +65 3217250
Fax: +65 2250962

Sanwa Futures (Singapore) Pte Ltd
6 Raffles Quay
#24–01 John Hancock Tower
Singapore 048580
Tel: +65 5383878
Fax: +65 5384636

SBC Warburg Asia Ltd
c/o Swiss Bank Corporation Singapore
5 Temasek Boulevard
#18–00 Suntec City Tower
Singapore 038985
Tel: +65 4318000
Fax: +65 4318188

SIMBL Investments Pte Ltd
65 Chulia Street
#36–01 OCBC Centre
Singapore 049513
Tel: +65 5353411
Fax: +65 5343917

Smith Barney (Singapore) Pte Ltd
20 Collyer Quay
#18–00 Tung Centre
Singapore 049319
Tel: +65 5381233
Fax: +65 5383511

STB Financial Futures (Singapore) Pte Ltd
5 Shenton Way
#35–00 UIC Building
Singapore 068808
Tel: +65 2249055
Fax: +65 2242873

Sumitomo Financial Futures (Singapore) Pte Ltd
6 Shenton Way
#27–08 DBS Building, Tower Two
Singapore 068809
Tel: +65 2201611
Fax: +65 2262879

Takugin Financial Futures (Singapore) Pte Ltd
65 Chulia Street
#48–01 OCBC Centre
Singapore 049513
Tel: +65 5332155
Fax: +65 5354047

Tokai Financial Futures (Singapore) Pte Ltd
80 Raffles Place
#16–01 UOB Plaza 1
Singapore 048624
Tel: +65 5358222
Fax: +65 5325453

Tokyo Forex & Tullet (Futures) Pte Ltd
10 Anson Road
#16–11 International Plaza
Singapore 079903
Tel: +65 2248077
Fax: +65 2241021

UBS (Futures) Singapore Pte Ltd
80 Raffles Place
#36–00 UOB Plaza 1
Singapore 048624
Tel: +65 5382888
Fax: +65 5316300

Vickers Ballas Futures Pte Ltd
30 Raffles Place
#06–00 Caltex House
Singapore 048622
Tel: +65 5353677/5324633
Fax: +65 5341313

Wocom Commodities Pte Ltd
4 Shenton Way
#18–06/10 Shing Kwan House
Singapore 068807
Tel: +65 2255988
Fax: +65 2205748

YTB Financial Futures (Singapore) Pte Ltd
50 Raffles Place
#16–02 Shell Tower
Singapore 048623
Tel: +65 2237266
Fax: +65 2241613

Commercial Associate Members

BP Singapore Pte Ltd
BP House, 1 Pasir Panjang Road
Singapore 118479
Tel: +65 4756633
Fax: +65 2737897

Caltex Singapore Pte Ltd
30 Raffles Place
#25–00 Caltex House
Singapore 048622
Tel: +65 5333000
Fax: +65 4391791

Caltex Trading Pte Ltd
30 Raffles Place
#25–00 Caltex House
Singapore 048622
Tel: +65 5333000
Fax: +65 4391729

Hin Leong Trading (Pte) Ltd
1 Playfair Road
Singapore 367981
Tel: +65 2849134
Fax: +65 2882653

ITOCHU Petroleum Co (Singapore) Pte Ltd
16 Raffles Quay
#13–01 Hong Leong Building
Singapore 048581
Tel: +65 2255555
Fax: +65 2259809

Marubeni International Petroleum (S) Pte Ltd
16 Raffles Quay
#40–01A Hong Leong Building
Singapore 048581
Tel: +65 2240446
Fax: +65 2215458

Mitsui & Co Ltd
16 Raffles Quay
#17–00 Hong Leong Building
SIngapore 048581
Tel: +65 3213111
Fax: +65 2243458/7289

Mobil Sales & Supply Corp
18 Pioneer Road
Singapore 628498
Tel: +65 6606000
Fax: +65 2641693

Petro-Diamond Singapore (Pte) Ltd
51 Bras Basah Road
#06–02/03 Plaza By The Park
Singapore 189554
Tel: +65 3382000
Fax: +65 3388287

Shell Eastern Trading (Pte) Ltd
50 Raffles Place, 39th Floor Shell Tower
Singapore 048623
Tel: +65 2247777
Fax: +65 2240379

Singapore Petroleum Co Ltd
6 Shenton Way
#33–08 DBS Building, Tower Two
Singapore 068809
Tel: +65 2213166
Fax: +65 2213691

Yutaka Futures Pte Ltd
10 Anson Road
#27–06 International Plaza
Singapore 079903
Tel: +65 2262829
Fax: +65 2208179

South Africa

South African Futures Exchange

Members

(CM) Clearing member
(NCM) Non-clearing member
(BM) Broking member
(NBM) Non-broking member

ABSA Bank Ltd (CM, BM)
Tel: +27 11 330 3111
Fax: +27 11 330 3189

Alexander Paterson Faure Inc (NCM, BM)
Tel: +27 11 832 2586
Fax: +27 11 838 5648

Barnard Jacobs Mellet & Co (Pty) Ltd (NCM, BM)
Tel: +27 11 836 2511
Fax: +27 11 834 1085

Board of Executors Ltd (NCM, NBM)
Tel: +27 21 481 1000
Fax: +27 21 221346

BOE Natwest Securities Ltd (NCM, BM)
Tel: +27 11 836 5211
Fax: +27 11 834 3508

Boland Bank Ltd (NCM, BM)
Tel: +27 21 807 2911
Fax: +27 21 807 2808

Bretton Woods Futures (Pty) Ltd (NCM, NBM)
Tel: +27 21 419 8870
Fax: +27 21 217 780

CA Miller & Co Inc (NCM, BM)
Tel: +27 11 836 2075
Fax: +27 11 836 0365

Capital Securities Ltd (CM, NBM)
Tel: +27 21 509 2357
Fax: +27 21 509 3517

Coronation Asset Management (Pty) Ltd (NCM, BM)
Tel: +27 21 418 3670
Fax: +27 21 419 2330

De Witt Morgan & Co (NCM, BM)
Tel: +27 11 833 7920
Fax: +27 11 838 2301

Delta One Futures (Pty) Ltd (NCM, NBM)
Tel: +27 11 836 1601
Fax: +27 11 834 9197

District Securities Bank Ltd (NCM, BM)
Tel: +27 21 419 9020
Fax: +27 21 419 9030

Edey Rogers & Co (Pty) Ltd (NCM, BM)
Tel: +27 11 377 3000
Fax: +27 11 838 7653

Electra Investments SA (Pty) Ltd (CM, NBM)
Tel: +27 21 947 9111
Fax: +27 21 947 3373

Eskom (NCM, NBM)
Tel: +27 11 800 8111
Fax: +27 11 800 4499

Eskom Pension & Provident Fund (NCM, BM)
Tel: +27 11 709 7400
Fax: +27 11 709 7477

Fedsure Asset Management Co (Pty) Ltd (NCM, BM)
Tel: +27 11 332 6000
Fax: +27 11 332 6601

Fergusson Bros, Hall, Stewart & Co Inc (NCM, BM)
Tel: +27 11 833 5740
Fax: +27 11 834 2877

Financial Currency Brokers (Holdings) (Pty) Ltd (NCM, NBM)
Tel: +27 11 834 6941
Fax: +27 11 836 7052

Financial Instrument Clearing (Pty) Ltd (CM, NBM)
Tel: +27 11 371 9111
Fax: +27 11 371 6508

Firstcorp Merchants Bank Ltd (NCM, BM)
Tel: +27 11 371 8336
Fax: +27 11 371 8352

First Derivatives Joint Venture Partnership (NCM, BM)
Tel: +27 11 371 8174
Fax: +27 11 371 7018

First Financial Futures (Pty) Ltd (NCM, BM)
Tel: +27 11 444 5220
Fax: +27 11 444 5228

Fleming Martin Securities Ltd (NCM, BM)
Tel: +27 11 240 2400
Fax: +27 11 838 2344

Frankel Pollak (Pty) Ltd (NCM, BM)
Tel: +27 11 833 5640
Fax: +27 11 836 0402

Futureline (Pty) Ltd (NCM, BM)
Tel: +27 21 236375
Fax: +27 21 238321

Genbel SA Ltd (NCM, NBM)
Tel: +27 11 280 1000
Fax: +27 11 280 1096

G O'Flaherty & Co (NCM, BM)
Tel: +27 11 836 8367
Fax: +27 11 834 5639

Golding & Slabbert Inc (NCM, BM)
Tel: +27 11 836 7151
Fax: +27 11 836 4502

Huysamer, Stals Inc (NCM, BM)
Tel: +27 11 240 3500
Fax: +27 11 836 6743

Ing Baring Securities Southern Africa (Pty) Ltd (NCM, BM)
Tel: +27 11 492 2941
Fax: +27 11 492 1090

Investec Asset Management Ltd (NCM, BM)
Tel: +27 21 410 5100
Fax: +27 21 418 5825/6

Investec Bank Ltd (CM, NBM)
Tel: +27 11 498 2000
Fax: +27 11 498 2699

Investec Merchant Bank Ltd (NCM, BM)
Tel: +27 11 498 2000
Fax: +27 11 498 2699

Irish Menell Rosenberg (Pty) Ltd (NCM, BM)
Tel: +27 11 836 8141
Fax: +27 11 838 4202

Ivor Jones Roy & Co Inc (NCM, BM)
Tel: +27 11 377 2111
Fax: +27 11 377 2000

JCI Ltd (NCM, BM)
Tel: +27 11 272 9111
Fax: +27 11 834 6415

Kaplan & Stewart Inc (NCM, BM)
Tel: +27 11 833 7777
Fax: +27 11 836 0794

Liberty Asset Management Ltd (NCM, NBM)
Tel: +27 11 408 3913
Fax: +27 11 403 1777

Lowenthal & Co (NCM, BM)
Tel: +27 11 836 7431
Fax: +27 11 838 7232

Maize Board (NCM, NBM)
Tel: +27 12 325 2133
Fax: +27 12 325 2636

Martindale, Stacey, Trollip (Pty) Ltd (NCM, BM)
Tel: +27 11 838 2131
Fax: +27 11 838 1433

Mathison & Hollidge Inc (NCM, BM)
Tel: +27 11 833 6331
Fax: +27 11 836 8911

MPF Management Services (Pty) Ltd (NCM, BM)
Tel: +27 11 497 8000
Fax: +27 11 497 8010

Msele Corporate & Merchant Bank (NCM, BM)
(A division of Citizen Bank Ltd)
Tel: +27 11 447 6870
Fax: +27 11 447 5506

NBS Bank Ltd (NCM, NBM)
Tel: +27 31 364 1111
Fax: +27 31 364 2917

NDH Bank Ltd (NCM, BM)
Tel: +27 11 880 9510
Fax: +27 11 880 9549

Nedcor Bank Ltd (CM, NBM)
Tel: +27 11 630 7111
Fax: +27 11 630 7811

Nick Fredericksz, Britz & Co (NCM, BM)
Tel: +27 11 492 1510
Fax: +27 11 838 1304

Norwich Life SA Ltd (NCM, BM)
Tel: +27 21 658 2911
Fax: +27 21 658 2260

Peregrine Securities (Pty) Ltd (NCM, BM)
Tel: +27 11 463 7087
Fax: +27 11 463 3844

PLJ van Rensburg & Partners Inc (NCM, BM)
Tel: +27 11 836 0381
Fax: +27 11 836 9924

Portfolio Investment Network Holdings (NCM, BM)
Tel: +27 11 469 0091
Fax: +27 11 469 0064

Rand Merchant Bank Ltd (CM, BM)
Tel: +27 11 269 8000
Fax: +27 11 269 9598

RMB Asset Management (Pty) Ltd (NCM, BM)
Tel: +27 11 282 1555
Fax: +27 11 282 1440

RMB Securities Trading (Pty) Ltd (NCM, BM)
Tel: +27 11 838 2139
Fax: +27 11 833 3100

Rice Rinaldi Turner & Co (NCM, BM)
Tel: +27 11 836 2441
Fax: +27 11 836 1393

RF Cadiz & Co (Pty) Ltd (NCM, BM)
Tel: +27 21 683 2566
Fax: +27 21 683 2577

Ryan Anderson & Co (Pty) Ltd (NCM, BM)
Tel: +27 11 838 1058
Fax: +27 11 838 2742

Sage Capital Managers (NCM, BM)
Tel: +27 11 491 0911
Fax: +27 11 836 6935

SA International Money Brokers (Pty) Ltd
Tel: +27 11 833 5684
Fax: +27 11 834 4177

SA Mutual Life Assurance Society (NCM, BM)
Tel: +27 21 509 2357
Fax: +27 21 509 3517

SA National Life Assurance Co (NCM, BM)
Tel: +27 21 947 9111
Fax: +27 21 947 3373

SA Reserve Bank (NCM, NBM)
Tel: +27 12 313 3911
Fax: +27 12 313 3841

SBC Warburg (South Africa) (Pty) Ltd (NCM, BM)
Tel: +27 11 836 2601
Fax: +27 11 834 2772

Securities Investment Bank Ltd (NCM, BM)
Tel: +27 11 328 9000
Fax: +27 11 486 3218/9

Simpson McKie James Capel (Pty) Ltd (NCM, BM)
Tel: +27 11 377 4200
Fax: +27 11 838 7603

Smith Borkhum Hare (Pty) Ltd (NCM, BM)
Tel: +27 11 492 6000
Fax: +27 11 833 1967

SMK Securities (Pty) Ltd (NCM, BM)
Tel: +27 11 833 8110
Fax: +27 11 836 9118/9

Société Générale SA Ltd (NCM, BM)
Tel: +27 11 488 1400
Fax: +27 11 488 1401

Southern Life Association (NCM, BM)
Tel: +27 21 508 1166
Fax: +27 21 508 1144

Standard Corporate & Merchant Bank (CM, BM)
(A division of the Standard Bank of SA Ltd)
Tel: +27 11 636 9112
Fax: +27 11 636 6634

Syfrets Managed Assets Ltd (NCM, BM)
Tel: +27 21 488 2911
Fax: +27 21 488 2125

Thirty Four South Research & Trading (Pty) Ltd (NCM, BM)
Tel: +27 21 683 2293
Fax: +27 21 611233

Transnet (NCM, NBM)
Tel: +27 11 488 7512
Fax: +27 11 488 7552

UAL Merchant Bank Ltd (NCM, BM)
Tel: +27 11 630 6111
Fax: +27 11 836 4526

UAL Securities (Pty) Ltd (NCM, BM)
Tel: +27 11 838 8550
Fax: +27 11 838 7526

UBS Securities (Pty) Ltd (NCM, BM)
Tel: +27 11 838 3025
Fax: +27 11 838 3032

Vector Corporate Services (Pty) Ltd
Tel: +27 21 419 3992
Fax: +27 21 254822

SAFEX Agricultural Markets Division Members

Clearing Members

ABSA Bank Ltd
Tel: +27 11 336 7101
Fax: +27 11 350 5494

Financial Instruments Clearing (Pty) Ltd
Tel: +27 11 371 7380
Fax: +27 11 371 6508

Imex Agricultural Services Ltd
Tel: +27 31 427925
Fax: +27 31 426944

Investec Bank Ltd
Tel: +27 11 498 2601
Fax: +27 11 498 2699

Nedbank Ltd
Tel: +27 11 630 7111
Fax: +27 11 630 7523

Rand Merchant Bank Ltd
Tel: +27 11 883 3650
Fax: +27 11 783 0715

Securities Investment Bank Ltd
Tel: +27 11 328 9000
Fax: +27 11 486 3219

The Standard Bank of SA Ltd
Tel: +27 11 636 5841
Fax: +27 11 636 1275

Non-Clearing Members

Alberti Livestock (Pty) Ltd
Tel: +27 11 613 5846
Fax: +27 11 613 4110

Alexander Commodities (Pty) Ltd
Tel: +27 11 832 1586
Fax: +27 11 836 9534

Anderson Wilson & Partners Ltd
Tel: +27 11 491 4600
Fax: +27 11 838 3798

Andre-Genfood International Commodities (Pty) Ltd
Tel: +27 12 804 1718
Fax: +27 12 868290

Bell Ceres Vrugte (Edms) Beperk
Tel: +27 233 65603
Fax: +27 233 65750

BOE Natwest Securities
Tel: +27 11 836 5211
Fax: +27 11 838 2196

Boland Bank Beperk
Tel: +27 2211 72911
Fax: +27 2211 72813

Boner & Freemantle Inc
Tel: +27 11 838 3781
Fax: +27 11 834 8465

Brian Herman (Esq)
Tel: +27 21 927039
Fax: +27 21 927039

Coronation Specialised Funds (Pty) Ltd
Tel: +27 21 683 3829
Fax: +27 21 683 3892

Croplink (Private) Ltd
Tel: +27 9263 4 736881/7
Fax: +27 9263 4 736825

De Witt Morgan & Co
Tel: +27 11 838 2374
Fax: +27 11 838 1499

Die Johan Slaber Trust
Tel: +27 12 327 4413
Fax: +27 12 327 4412

District Securities Bank Ltd
Tel: +27 21 419 9020
Fax: +27 21 419 9030

Edey Rogers & Co Inc
Tel: +27 11 833 5530
Fax: +27 11 838 7653

Extatrade Commodities (Pty) Ltd
Tel: +27 11 804 5080
Fax: +27 11 804 4844

Farm Feed Services (Pty) Ltd
Tel: +27 11 955 2135
Fax: +27 11 955 1665

Farmwise Ltd
Tel: +27 11 613 8027
Fax: +27 11 613 2094

Financial Currency Brokers (Holdings) (Pty) Ltd
Tel: +27 11 838 6155
Fax: +27 11 836 7052

First National Bank of SA Ltd
Tel: +27 11 371 0544
Fax: +27 11 371 2357

Fleming Martin Securities Ltd
Tel: +27 11 240 2400
Fax: +27 11 836 4563

Foodcorp Bedrywe Beperk H/A Karoo-Ochse
Tel: +27 11 789 1224
Fax: +27 11 886 3387

Futureline (Pty) Ltd
Tel: +27 21 236385
Fax: +27 21 238321

Genbel Investments Ltd
Tel: +27 11 280 1000
Fax: +27 11 280 1093

Hobson & Louw
Tel: +27 41 486 1143
Fax: +27 41 486 1325

Hochfield Commodities (Pty) Ltd
Tel: +27 11 483 1920
Fax: +27 11 483 1919

Huysamer, Stals Inc
Tel: +27 11 836 7871
Fax: +27 11 834 2799

Independent Commodity Management (Pty) Ltd
Tel: +27 11 476 3255
Fax: +27 11 476 7104

Joseph Itzkin (Esq)
Tel: +27 21 438 5619
Fax: +27 21 438 2162

Koopkor Koöperatief Beperk
Tel: +27 12 328 3481
Fax: +27 12 328 3484

KWV van SA Beperk
Tel: +27 2211 73911
Fax: +27 2211 73000

Lesotho Milling Co (Pty) Ltd
Tel: +27 5192 4487/8
Fax: +27 5192 5038

Lowenthal & Co
Tel: +27 21 262370
Fax: +27 21 242147

Maize Board
Tel: +27 12 325 2133
Fax: +27 12 323 2636

Martin Birch
Tel: +27 21 488 2727
Fax: +27 21 488 2146

Martindale, Stacey, Trollip, Inc
Tel: +27 11 838 2131
Fax: +27 11 838 1433

Mechiel du Toit
Tel: +27 11 838 3781
Fax: +27 11 834 8465

Mitsui Market Agency (Pty) Ltd
Tel: +27 11 484 7250
Fax: +27 11 484 3324

Model Market Agency (Pty) Ltd
Tel: +27 31 465 1411
Fax: +27 31 465 1419

NBS Bank Ltd
Tel: +27 31 364 1111
Fax:+27 31 364 2917

NDH Bank Ltd
Tel: +27 11 880 9510
Fax: +27 11 880 9549

Omnia Fertilizers Ltd
Tel: +27 11 463 2883
Fax: +27 11 463 4435

Otterbea International (Pty) Ltd
Tel: +27 11 482 3222
Fax: +27 11 482 3324

PIN Holdings (Pty) Ltd
Tel: +27 11 442 9858
Fax: +27 11 442 8753

PLJ van Rensburg & Vennote Ing
Tel: +27 11 836 0381
Fax: +27 11 836 9924

Premier Food Industries Ltd
Tel: +27 11 491 2911
Fax: +27 11 491 4450

Ryan Anderson & Co (Pty) Ltd
Tel: +27 11 838 1058
Fax: +27 11 838 2742

SBC Warburg
Tel: +27 11 836 2601
Fax: +27 11 834 2772

SMK Securities
Tel: +27 11 833 8110
Fax: +27 11 824 2772

Sentraalwes (Koöperatief) Beperk
Tel: +27 18 464 2011
Fax: +27 18 464 1094

SIS Farming Group (Pty) Ltd
Tel: +27 132 462600
Fax: +27 132 462611

Sentraaloos (Koöperatief) Beperk
Tel: +27 58 303 5757
Fax: +27 58 303 5018

UAL Merchant Bank Ltd
Tel: +27 11 630 6111
Fax: +27 11 630 6338

Unie Graankoöperatie Beperk
Tel: +27 12 320 3782
Fax: +27 12 320 0409

Spain

FC&M

Members

Banca Catalana
Avenida Diagonal, 662
08034 Barcelona
Tel: +34 3 404 4000
Fax: +34 3 404 3738

Banco Bilbao-Vizcaya
Alcalá, 45, 6th Floor
28014 Madrid
Tel: +34 1 374 3030
Fax: +34 1 523 1051

Banco Central Hispanoamericano
Plaza de Canalejas, 1
28014 Madrid
Tel: +34 1 558 1111
Fax: +34 1 522 3453

Banco Español de Crédito, Banesto
Torre de Operaciones
Calle Mecena, 80, 6th Floor
28033 Madrid
Tel: +34 1 338 3191

Fax: +34 1 338 3241
Banco de Sabadell
Plaza de Cataluña, 1
08201 Sabadell
Tel: +34 3 728 9289
Fax: +34 3 725 5175

Banco Urquijo
Calle Principe de Vergara, 131
28002 Madrid
Tel: +34 1 337 2097
Fax: +34 1 337 2096

Banco de Valencia
Pintor Sorolla, 2
46002 Valencia
Tel: +34 6 398 4557/4553
Fax: +34 6 398 4536/4535

Caja de Ahorros del Mediterráneo
Avenida Oscar Esplá, 37
03007 Alicante
Tel: +34 6 590 6106
Fax: +34 6 590 6186

Caja Rural Alicante, Cooperativa de Crédito Valenciana
Avenida Doctor Gadea, 27
03003 Alicante
Tel: +34 6 512 5700/592 2520
Fax: +34 6 592 5174

Caja de Ahorros de Valencia, Castellón Y Alicante, Banacja
Calle Pintor Sorolla, 8
46002 Valencia
Tel: +34 6 387 5531
Fax: +34 6 352 7550

Caja Rural Credicoop
Calle Enmedio, 3
12001 Castellón
Tel: +34 64 203399
Fax: +34 64 212946

Caja Rural de Sevilla
Calle Murillo, 2
41001 Seville
Tel: +34 5 459 9100
Fax: +34 5 422 8160

Caja Rural de Torrent
Avenida del País Valencià, 3
46900 Torrent
Tel: +34 6 155 3054
Fax: +34 6 155 5952

Caja Rural Valencia
Paseo de la Alameda, 34
46023 Valencia
Tel: +34 6 387 0800
Fax: +34 6 337 4891

Deutsche Bank
Paseo de la Castellaba, 18
28046 Madrid
Tel: +34 1 578 3282
Fax: +34 1 435 8220

Fimat International Banque
Sucursal en España
Plaza de Colón, 2
Torre de Colón, 1st Floor, 18
28046 Madrid
Tel: +34 1 349 3435
Fax: +34 1 349 3402

Intermediarios Financieros
Calle Colón, 58, 1st Floor
46004 Valencia
Tel: +34 6 351 0625
Fax: +34 6 352 7039

Mercados y Gestion de Valores, AVB
Almagro, 21, 4th Floor
28010 Madrid
Tel: +34 1 347 0600
Fax: +34 1 347 0683

United Kingdom

International Petroleum Exchange

Floor Member Companies

Amerex Futures Ltd
1st Floor
Albemarle House
1 Albemarle Street
London W1X 3HF
Tel: +44 171 629 6668
Fax: +44 171 493 4406
Tx: +44 96673
Contact: M Cosgrove

Arcadia Petroleum Ltd
10 Stratton Street
London W1X 6AP
Tel: +44 171 4955717
Fax: +44 171 4950355
Contact: C Hurley

Bear, Stearns International Ltd
One Canada Square
London E14 5AD
Tel: +44 171 516 6000
Fax: +44 171 515 6030
Tx: +44 11424
Contact: P Heales

BP Oil International Ltd
1 Broadgate
London EC2M 2AP
Tel: +44 171 496 4000
Fax: +44 171 579 6102
Contact: D Katsis

BZW Futures, A Division of Barclays Bank Plc
2nd Floor
Murray House
1 Royal Mint Street
London EC3N 4HH
Tel: +44 171 623 2323
Fax: +44 171 248 0531
Contact: P E Fenner

Cannon Bridge Corp Ltd
Exchange House
Primrose Street
Broadgate
London EC2A 2EH
Tel: +44 171 628 6018
Fax: +44 171 374 2552
Contact: M Cohen

Cargill Investor Services Ltd
Cannon Bridge
Level 2
25 Dowgate Hill
London EC4R 2SL
Tel: +44 171 283 5272
Fax: +44 171 929 4885
Tx: +44 20153
Contact: S Kirby

Citifutures Ltd
Citibank House
336 Strand
London WC2R 1HB
Tel: +44 171 438 0405
Fax: +44 171 438 0462
Tx: +44 8956866
Contact: D Thompson

Credit Agricole Futures Snc
2nd Floor
162 Queen Victoria Street
London EC4V 4BS
Tel: +44 171 329 3232
Fax: +44 171 955 9520
Contact: S Price

Credit Lyonnais Rouse Ltd
Broadwalk House
5 Appold Street
London EC2A 2DA
Tel: +44 171 6380300
Fax: +44 171 6380369
Tx: +44 8950831
Contact: J Ward

DBMG Futures & Options Ltd
23 Great Winchester Street
London EC2P 2AX
Tel: +44 171 588 4545
Fax: +44 171 826 7005
Contact: P Lewis

Dean Witter International Ltd
1 Appold Street
6th Floor
Broadgate 5
London EC2A 2AA
Tel: +44 171 294 8500
Fax: +44 171 294 8846
Tx: +44 25380
Contact: M Thomas

Fimat Futures UK Ltd
Exchange House
Primrose Street
Broadgate
London EC2A 2EH
Tel: +44 171 628 6018
Fax: +44 171 628 5060
Tx: +44 11292
Contact: K Fitzgerald

Gerald Ltd
Europe House
World Trade Centre
London E1 9AA
Tel: +44 171 867 9400
Fax: +44 171 867 9402
Tx: +44 84377
Contact: D Over

GNI Ltd
4th Floor, Atrium Building
Cannon Bridge
25 Dowgate Hill
London EC4R 2GN
Tel: +44 171 337 3500
Fax: +44 171 337 3501
Tx: +44 84962
Contact: K Hull

Goldman Sachs International
Peterborough Court
133 Fleet Street
London EC4A 2BB
Tel: +44 171 774 1000
Fax: +44 171 774 1202
Contact: P Hole

Indosuez Carr Futures Inc
122 Leadenhall Street
London EC3V 4QH
Tel: +44 171 971 4240
Fax: +44 171 971 4210
Contact: A Chupin

ING Derivatives (London) Ltd
75 King William Street
London EC4N 7EE
Tel: +44 171 410 9944
Fax: +44 171 283 4321
Contact: H Cooper

Ixomex Ltd
49 Wigmore Street
London W1H 9LE
Tel: +44 171 935 4455
Fax: +44 171 935 4233
Tx: +44 21223
Contact: J Boxer

Lehman Brothers Inc
World Financial Centre
American Express Tower
7th Floor
New York, NY 10285
USA

One Broadgate
London EC2M 7HA
Tel: +44 171 601 0011
Fax: +44 171 260 2262
Tx: +44 88881
Contact: P Barrowcliff

Lloyds Bank Plc
Faryners House
25 Monument Street
London EC3R 8BQ
Tel: +44 171 283 1000
Fax: +44 171 623 7560
Tx: +44 13559
Contact: R Hawkins

ED & F Man International Ltd
Sugar Quay
Lower Thames Street
London EC3R 6DU
Tel: +44 171 285 3000
Fax: +44 171 621 0149
Tx: +44 84531
Contact: D Peterson

MeesPierson Derivatives Ltd
Camomile Court
23 Camomile Street
London EC3A 7PP
Tel: +44 171 444 8100
Fax: +44 171 920 9550
Contact: A Harris

MeesPierson ICS Ltd
Camomile Court
23 Camomile Street
London EC3A 7PP
Tel: +44 171 444 8800
Fax: +44 171 444 8888
Contact: S Grimwood

Merrill Lynch Pierce Fenner & Smith
(Brokers & Dealers Ltd)
Pellipar House
9 Cloak Lane
London EC4R 2RU
Tel: +44 171 867 6803
Fax: +44 171 867 6810
Contact: M Mills

JP Morgan Securities Ltd
60 Victoria Embankment
London EC4Y 0JP
Tel: +44 171 600 2300
Fax: +44 171 325 8267
Contact: K Sykes

Morgan Stanley International
25 Cabot Square
Canary Wharf
London E14 4QA
Tel: +44 171 425 7633
Fax: +44 171 425 7649
Contact: C Bryce

Nationsbank Europe Ltd
New Broad Street House
35 New Broad Street
London EC2M 1NH
Tel: +44 171 282 2206
Fax: +44 171 282 2201
Contact: D Goldman

PaineWebber International (UK) Ltd
1 Finsbury Avenue
London EC2M 2PA
Tel: +44 171 377 0055
Fax: +44 171 247 7189
Tx: +44 297361
Contact: J Weiland

Paribas Futures Ltd
33 Wigmore Street
London W1H 0BN
Tel: +44 171 895 4800/4810
Fax: +44 171 895 4808
Tx: +44 884108
Contact: T Knight

Phibro Energy Futures Ltd
Victoria Plaza
111 Buckingham Palace Road
London SW1W 0SL
Tel: +44 171 721 4555
Fax: +44 171 630 8286
Tx: +44 952963
Contact: R Plaisted

Prudential-Bache (Futures) Ltd
9 Devonshire Square
London EC2M 4HP
Tel: +44 171 283 9166
Fax: +44 171 626 6785
Tx: +44 883251
Contact: W Smit

PVM Oil Futures Ltd
Calder House
1 Dover Street
London W1X 3PJ
Tel: +44 171 355 4400
Fax: +44 171 499 8301
Contact: T Butler

Refco Overseas Ltd
Europe House
World Trade Centre
London E1 9AA
Tel: +44 171 488 3232
Fax: +44 171 480 7069
Tx: +44 87438
Contact: R Reinert

Rudolf Wolff & Co Ltd
2nd Floor, D Section
Plantation House
31–35 Fenchurch Street
London EC3M 3DX
Tel: +44 171 626 8765
Fax: +44 171 626 3939
Tx: +44 885034
Contact: W Harker

Saratoga Ltd
65–66 Queen Street
London EC4R 1EB
Tel: +44 171 329 0339
Fax: +44 171 329 8986
Contact: M David

Shell International Trading & Shipping Co Ltd
Shell-Mex House
Strand
London WC2R 0ZA
Tel: +44 171 546 5000
Fax: +44 171 546 7580
Tx: +44 919651
Contact: J N Lobb/OTF1

Skandinaviska Enskilda Banken
2–6 Cannon Street
London EC4M 6XX
Tel: +44 171 246 4000
Fax: +44 171 588 0929
Tx: +44 950281
Contact: S Martin

Smith Barney Europe, Ltd
10 Piccadilly
London W1V 9LA
Tel: +44 171 548 5600
Fax: +44 171 548 5599
Contact: P Gignoux

Societe Generale Options UK Ltd
Exchange House
Primrose Street
London EC2A 2HT
Tel: +44 171 762 4180
Fax: +44 171 638 7375
Contact: K Balinska-Jundzill

Spectron Futures Ltd
Liscartan House
127 Sloane Street
London SW1X 9BA
Tel: +44 171 823 6600
Tel: +44 171 823 4747
Contact: J Frestadius

Standard Chartered Bank
Mocatta House
4 Crosby Square
London EC3A 6AQ
Tel: +44 171 638 3636
Fax: +44 171 256 7750
Tx: +44 887419
Contact: N Dentoom

Sucden (UK) Ltd
5 London Bridge Street
London SE1 9SG
Tel: +44 171 940 9400
Fax: +44 171 940 9500
Tx: +44 883780
Contact: M Overlander

Swiss Finance Corp
33 Cavendish Square
London W1M 9HF
Tel: +44 171 412 0500/499 2844
Fax: +44 171 412 0026
Contact: H Barkhordar

Trafalgar Commodities Ltd
c/o Fordyce Curry & Co
St. Bartholomew Chambers
61 West Smithfield
London EC1A 9AE
Tel: +44 171 600 1676/283 6402
Fax: +44 171 600 1930
Contact: R Cole

Triland Metals Ltd
Bow Bells House
Bread Street
London EC4M 9BQ
Tel: +44 171 236 5551
Fax: +44 171 489 1104
Tx: +44 888677
Contact: E Watts

Trade Associate Member Companies

Conoco Ltd
Park Lane
116 Park Street
London W1Y 4NN
Tel: +44 171 408 6000
Fax: +44 171 408 6969

ICI Chemicals & Polymers Ltd
Crude Oil Feedstocks
S & T Department
PO Box 90
Wilton
Middlesbrough
Cleveland TS6 8JE
Tel: +44 642 454144
Fax: +44 642 433838

Mitsubishi Corp (UK) Ltd
Bow Bells House
Bread Street
Cheapside
London EC4M 9BQ
Tel: +44 171 822 0289
Fax: +44 171 822 0089
Tx: +44 888251

A/S Torvald Klaveness Commodities
Hofvaret 17
PO Box 182 Skoyen
0212 Oslo 2
Norway
Tel: +44 47 2 252600

London Clearing House

Members

IPE International Petroleum Exchange
LCE London Commodities Exchange
LCE merged with LIFFE in September 1996; see note on p.311 for details.
LIFFE London International Financial Futures & Options Exchange
LME London Metal Exchange

ABN Amro Securities (UK) Ltd (LIFFE)
199 Bishopsgate
London EC2M 3TY
Tel: +44 171 392 3000

ADM Investor Services Inc (LCE)
141 West Jackson Boulevard, Suite 1610A
Chicago
Illinois 60604
USA
Tel: +1 312 435 7000

AIB Capital Markets Plc (LIFFE)
Futures Administration
12 Old Jewry
London EC2R 8DP
Tel: +44 171 606 3070

AIG International Ltd (LME)
120 Leman Street
London E1 8EU
Tel: +44 171 709 2500

AMT (Futures) Ltd (LIFFE, LCE)
Adelaide House
London Bridge
London EC4R 9DT
Tel: +44 171 626 4521

Amalgamated Metal Trading Ltd (LME, LCE)
Ground Floor
Adelaide House
London Bridge
London EC4R 9DT
Tel: +44 626 4521

Amerex Futures Ltd (IPE)
1st Floor, Albemarle House
1 Albemarle Street
London W1X 3HF
Tel: +44 171 629 6668

Arcadia Petroleum Ltd (IPE)
10 Stratton Street
London W1X 6AP
Tel: +44 171 495 5717

Australia & New Zealand Banking Group Ltd (LIFFE)
Minerva House
Montague Close
London SE1 9DH
Tel: +44 171 378 2090

BA Futures Inc (LIFFE)
Bank of America House
1 Alie Street
London E1 8DE
Tel: +44 171 634 4491

BNP Capital Markets Ltd (LIFFE)
PO Box 506
8–13 King William Street
London EC4N 7DN
Tel: +44 171 548 9548

BP Oil International Ltd (IPE)
Britannic Tower
Moor Lane
London EC2A 2HE
Tel: +44 171 496 2651

BT Futures Corporation (LIFFE)
1 Appold Street
Broadgate
London EC2A 2HE
Tel: +44 171 982 2500

Banca Commerciale Italiana SpA (LIFFE)
42 Gresham Street
London EC2V 7LA
Tel: +44 171 776 2000

Banco Bilbao Vizcaya (LIFFE)
100 Cannon Street
London EC4N 6EH
Tel: +44 171 623 3060

Bank of America Illinois (LME)
Bank of America House
1 Alie Street
London E1 8DE
Tel: +44 171 634 4000

The Bank of Nova Scotia (LIFFE)
Scotia House
33 Finsbury Square
London EC2A 1BB
Tel: +44 171 638 5644

Bank of Scotland (TPT)
PO Box 30, Broad Street House
55 Old Broad Street
London EC2P 2HL
Tel: +44 171 601 6666

Bank of Tokyo Capital Markets Ltd (LIFFE)
Finsbury Circus House
12–15 Finsbury Circus
London EC2M 7BT
Tel: +44 171 628 8111

Bankers Trust International Plc (LME)
1 Appold Street
Broadgate
London EC2A 2HE
Tel: +44 171 982 2500

Banque Nationale de Paris Plc (LIFFE)
Administration Department
8–13 King William Street
London EC4P 4HS
Tel: +44 171 895 7070

Banque Paribas SA (LIFFE)
33 Wigmore Street
London W1H 0BN
Tel: +44 171 355 2000

Barclays Bank Plc (LIFFE, IPE, TPT)
2nd Floor, Murray House
1 Royal Mint Court
London EC3N 4HH
Tel: +44 171 623 2323

Barclays Metals Plc (LME)
6th Floor, 2 Minster Court
Mincing Lane
London EC3R 7BB
Tel: +44 171 283 6362

Bear Sterns International Ltd (LIFFE, IPE, LCE)
1 Canada Square
London E14 5AD
Tel: +44 171 516 6000

Billiton Metals Ltd (LME)
84 Fenchurch Street
London EC3M 4BY
Tel: +44 171 860 8250

Brandeis (Brokers) Ltd (LME)
4 Fore Street
London EC3M 4BY
Tel: +44 171 638 5877

Brody White (UK) Ltd (LME, LCE)
Devonshire House
146 Bishopsgate
London EC2M 4JX
Tel: +44 171 377 8050

CAGF London Ltd (LIFFE)
Cannon Centre
78 Cannon Street
London EC4P 4LN
Tel: +44 171 623 3646

Cadbury Ltd (LCE)
Confectionery – Finance Department
Bournville
Birmingham B30 2LU
Tel: +44 121 458 2000

Canadian Imperial Bank of Commerce (LIFFE)
Cottons Centre
Cottons Lane
London SE1 2QI
Tel: +44 171 234 6000

Cantor Fitzgerald International (LIFFE, TPT)
Park House
16 Finsbury Circus
London EC2M 7DJ
Tel: +44 171 617 7000

Cargill Investor Services Ltd (LIFFE, LCE, IPE, LME)
Cannon Bridge
Level 2, 25 Dowgate Hill
London EC4R 2SL
Tel: +44 171 283 5272

Cater Allen Futures Ltd (LIFFE)
20 Birchin Lane
London EC3V 9DJ
Tel: +44 171 623 2070

Charterhouse Bank Ltd (LIFFE)
1 Paternoster Row
St Pauls
London EC4M 7DH
Tel: +44 171 248 4000

Chase Investment Bank Ltd (LME)
Woolgate House
Coleman Street
London EC2P 2HD
Tel: +44 171 962 5000

Chase Manhattan Futures (UK) Ltd (LIFFE)
PO Box 16
Woolgate House
Coleman Street
London EC2P 2HD
Tel: +44 171 962 5000

Chemical Futures & Options Inc (LIFFE)
125 London Wall
London EC2Y 5AJ
Tel: +44 171 777 4419

Christiania Bank OG Kreditkasse (LIFFE)
Lloyds Chambers
1 Portsoken Street
London E1 8RU
Tel: +44 171 680 7000

Citifutures Ltd (LIFFE, IPE, TPT)
336 Strand
London WC2R 1HB
Tel: +44 171 438 0405

Commerzbank AG (LIFFE)
Commerzbank House
23 Austin Friars
London EC2N 2EN
Tel: +44 171 638 5895

Continaf BV (LCE)
Herengracht 214
1016 BS Amsterdam
PO Box 3779
1001 AN Amsterdam
The Netherlands
Tel: +31 20 524 0524

Credit Agricole Futures SNC (LIFFE, LCE, IPE)
2nd Floor, 162 Queen Victoria Street
London EC4V 4BS
Tel: +44 171 329 3232

Credit Lyonnais Rouse Ltd (LIFFE, LCE, IPE, LME)
2nd Floor, Broadwalk House
5 Appold Street
London EC2A 2DA
Tel: +44 171 374 6100

Credit Lyonnais Securities (LIFFE, TPT)
Broadwalk House
5 Appold Street
London EC2A 2DA
Tel: +44 171 588 4000

CS First Boston Ltd (LIFFE, TPT)
1 Cabot Square
London E14 4QJ
Tel: +44 171 516 1616

DBMG Futures & Options Ltd (LIFFE, LCE, IPE)
23 Great Winchester Street
London EC2P 2AX
Tel: +44 171 588 4545

DG Bank, Deutsche Genossenschaftsbank (LIFFE)
10 Aldersgate Street
London EC1A 4XX
Tel: +44 171 776 6000

DKB International Plc (LIFFE)
DKB House
24 King William Street
London EC4R 9DB
Tel: +44 171 929 7777

The Dai-Ichi Kangyo Bank Ltd (LIFFE)
DKB House
24 King William Street
London EC4R 9DB
Tel: +44 171 283 0929

Daiwa Bank (Capital Management) Plc (LIFFE)
6th Floor, 4 Broadgate
London EC2M 2AH
Tel: +44 171 623 1494

Daiwa Europe Ltd (LIFFE)
5 King William Street
London EC4N 7AX
Tel: +44 171 548 8080

Dean Witter International Ltd (LIFFE, LCE, IPE, LME)
1 Appold Street
6th Floor, Broadgate 5
London EC2A 2AA
Tel: +44 171 294 8500

Den Norske Bank AS (LIFFE)
20 St Dunstans Hill
London EC3R 8HY
Tel: + 44 171 621 1111

Deutsche Sharps Pixley Metals Ltd (LME)
6 Bishopsgate
London EC2P 2AT
Tel: +44 171 971 7000

Dresdner Bank AG (LIFFE)
125 Wood Street
London EC2V 7AQ
Tel: +44 171 606 7030

ED & F Man Cocoa Brokers Ltd (LCE)
Sugar Quay
Lower Thames Street
London EC3R 6DU
Tel: +44 171 285 3000

ED & F Man International Ltd (LIFFE, LCE, IPE, LME)
Sugar Quay
Lower Thames Street
London EC3R 6DU
Tel: +44 171 285 3000

FCT Group LLC (LIFFE)
Buckingham House
62–63 Queen Street
London EC4R 1AD
Tel: +44 171 334 4800

Fimat Futures UK Ltd (LIFFE, LCE, IPE, TPT)
Exchange House
Primrose Street
Broadgate
London EC2A 2EH
Tel: +44 171 628 6018

First Chicago Futures Inc (LIFFE)
First Chicago House
90 Long Acre
London WC2E 9RB
Tel: +44 171 240 7240

The Fuji Bank Ltd (LIFFE)
River Plate House
7–11 Finsbury Circus
London EC2M 7DH
Tel: +44 171 588 2211

Fuji International Finance Ltd (LIFFE)
River Plate House
7–11 Finsbury Circus
London EC2M 7NT
Tel: +44 171 256 8888

GH Financial Ltd (LIFFE)
111 Cannon Street
London EC4N 5AR
Tel: +44 171 929 0552

LIFFE Ltd (LIFFE, LCE, IPE, LME, TPT)
4th Floor, Atrium Building
Cannon Bridge
25 Dowgate Hill
London EC4R 2GN
Tel: +44 171 337 3500

GNI Wallace Ltd (LIFFE)
4th Floor, Atrium Building
Cannon Bridge
25 Dowgate Hill
London EC4R 2GN
Tel: +44 171 337 3500

Gerald Ltd (LIFFE, LCE, IPE, LME)
Europe House
World Trade Centre
St Katharine by The Tower
London E1 9AA
Tel: +44 171 867 9400

Glencore UK Ltd (LME)
49 Wigmore Street
London W1H 9LE
Tel: +44 171 935 4455

Goldenberg Hehmeyer & Co (LIFFE)
Cannon Centre
78 Cannon Street
London EC2M 7DJ
Tel: +44 171 626 8001

Goldman Sachs International (LIFFE, LCE, IPE, LME)
Peterborough Court
133 Fleet Street
London EC4A 2BB
Tel: +44 171 774 1000

Griffin Trading Co (LIFFE)
Cannon Centre
78 Cannon Street
London EC4N 6HH
Tel: +44 171 919 9199

Hambros Bank Ltd (LIFFE)
41 Tower Hill
London EC3N 4HA
Tel: +44 171 480 5000

Hambro Clearing Ltd (LIFFE)
Lloyds Court
1 Goodman's Yard
London E1 8AT
Tel: +44 171 488 1006

Helaba Financial Futures Ltd (LIFFE)
8 Moorgate
London EC2R 6DD
Tel: +44 171 334 4500

J Henry Schroder & Co Ltd (LIFFE)
120 Cheapside
London EC2V 6DS
Tel: +44 171 382 6000

Hoare Govett Securities Ltd (LIFFE)
4 Broadgate
London EC2M 7LE
Tel: +44 171 382 6000

Hunter Douglas NV (LME)
Postbus 560
3331 LR Zwijndrecht
The Netherlands
Tel: +31 78 121888

Hydro Aluminium AS (LME)
Post Boks 80
1321 Stabekk
Norway
Tel: +47 22 738100

IBJ International Plc (LIFFE)
Bracken House
1 Friday Street
London EC4M 9JA
Tel: +44 171 236 1090

Indosuez Carr Futures Inc (LIFFE, IPE)
8th Floor, 122 Leadenhall Street
London EC3V 4QH
Tel: +44 171 895 1334

Instinet UK Ltd (TPT)
Commodity Quay
East Smithfield
London E1 9UN
Tel: +44 171 702 4040

ING Derivatives (London) Ltd (LIFFE, LCE, IPE, LME)
75 King William Street
London EC4N 7EE
Tel: +44 171 410 9944

Internationale Nederlanden Bank NV (LIFFE)
60 Basinghall Street
London EC2V 5EQ
Tel: +44 171 865 6060

Ixomex Ltd (IPE, LCE)
49 Wigmore Street
London W1H 9LE
Tel: +44 171 935 4455

James Capel & Co Ltd (LIFFE)
Thames Exchange Building
10 Queen Street Place
London EC4R 1BL
Tel: +44 171 621 0011

Karintina Trading Pte Ltd (LCE)
4 Pont Street
London SW1X 9El
Tel: +44 171 823 2848

KAS-Associatie NV (TPT)
Suite 560, Salisbury House
London Wall
London EC2M 5NU
Tel: +44 171 528 8846

KAS Clearing London Ltd (LIFFE, TPT)
Suite 560, Salisbury House
London Wall
London EC2M 5NU
Tel: +44 171 588 6440

Kleinwort Benson Ltd (LIFFE, TPT)
PO Box 560, Fenchurch Street
London EC3P 3DB
Tel: +44 171 623 8000

Kredietbank NV (LIFFE)
Arenbergstraat 7
1000 Brussels
Belgium
Tel: +32 2 517 6202

The KYTE Group Ltd (LIFFE)
2nd Floor, Walbrook House
Walbrook
London EC4N 8LA
Tel: +44 171 390 7777

Lazmet Ltd (LME)
Trans-World House
82–100 City Road
London EC1Y 2BJ
Tel: +44 171 972 0380

Lehman Brothers Commodities Ltd
(LIFFE, LCE, IPE)
5th Floor, 1–2 Broadgate
London EC2M 7HA
Tel: +44 171 601 0011

Lloyds Bank Plc (LIFFE, IPE, TPT)
4th Floor, Faryners House
25 Monument Street
London EC3R 8BQ
Tel: +44 171 283 1000

Louis Dreyfus Trading Ltd (LCE)
162 Queen Victoria Street
London EC4V 4DB
Tel: +44 171 489 948

Macquarie Securities (UK) Ltd (LME)
9th Floor, Alban Gate
125 London Wall
London EC2Y 5AS
Tel: +44 171 776 7060

Mars UK Ltd (LCE)
Dundee Road
Slough
Berkshire SL1 4JX
Tel: +44 1753 550055

MHF Futures Ltd (LCE)
4 Ivory House
St Katharine by The Tower
London E1 9AT
Tel: +44 171 702 9443

MeesPierson ICS Ltd (LIFFE, LCE, IPE,
LME, TPT)
Camomile Court
23 Camomile Street
London EC3A 7PP
Tel: +44 171 444 8800

Merita Bank Ltd (LIFFE)
Kansillis House
19 Thomas More Street
London E1 9YW
Tel: +44 171 265 3333

Merrill Lynch Pierce Fenner & Smith
(LIFFE, LCE, IPE, LME)
(Brokers & Dealers Ltd)
Ropemaker Place
25 Ropemaker Street
London EC2Y 9LY
Tel: +44 171 628 1000

Metallgesellschaft Ltd (LME)
One America Square
17 Crosswall
London EC3N 2LB
Tel: +44 171 488 2244

Metdist Trading Ltd (LME)
80 Cannon Street
London EC4N 6EJ
Tel: +44 171 606 0463

Midland Bank Plc (LIFFE, TPT)
Financial Futures Ltd
10 Queens Street Place
London EC4R 1BE
Tel: +44 171 283 7071

The Mitsubishi Bank Ltd (LIFFE)
6 Broadgate
London EC2M 2SX
Tel: +44 171 638 2222

Mitsubishi Finance International Plc
(LIFFE)
6 Broadgate
London EC2M 2AA
Tel: +44 171 628 5555

Mitsubishi Trust International Ltd
(LIFFE)
24 Lombard Street
London EC3V 9AJ
Tel: +44 171 929 2866

Mitsui Bussan Commodities Ltd (LME)
20 Old Bailey
London EC4M 7QQ
Tel: +44 171 248 6133

The Mitsui Trust & Banking Co Ltd
(LIFFE)
5th Floor, 6 Broadgate
London EC2M 2TB
Tel: +44 171 638 0841

JP Morgan Securities Ltd (LIFFE, LME,
IPE, TPT)
1 Angel Court
London EC2R 7AE
Tel: +44 171 600 2300

Morgan Stanley & Co International Ltd
(LIFFE, LCE, IPE, LME, TPT)
25 Cabot Square
Çanary Wharf
London E14 4QA
Tel: +44 171 425 8000

Muirpace Ltd (LIFFE, LCE)
6 Lloyds Avenue
London EC3N 3NX
Tel: +44 171 702 9776

NationsBanc-CRT Energy (UK) Ltd (IPE)
New Broad Street House
35 New Broad Street
London EC2M 1NH
Tel: +44 171 282 2200

NatWest Futures Ltd (LIFFE)
135 Bishopsgate
London EC2M 3UR
Tel: +44 171 334 1000

NatWest Securities Ltd (LIFFE, TPT)
135 Bishopsgate
London EC2M 3XT
Tel: +44 171 375 5000

New Japan Securities Europe Ltd (LIFFE)
Bracken House
One Friday Street
London EC4M 9JA
Tel: +44 171 489 1111

Nikko Europe Plc (LIFFE)
55 Victoria Street
London SW1H 0EU
Tel: +44 171 799 2222

The Nippon Credit Bank Ltd (LIFFE)
London Branch
40 Basinghall Street
London EC2V 5DE
Tel: +44 171 638 6411

Nomura International Plc (LIFFE, TPT)
Nomura House
1 St Martin's le Grand
London EC1A 4NP
Tel: +44 171 521 2000

Norinchukin International Plc (LIFFE)
1st Floor, 4 Broadgate
London EC2M 2AE
Tel: +44 171 588 6593

Orebi & Cie (LCE)
79 bis, Rue de Paris
92100 Boulogne
France
Tel: +33 1 47 12 17 17

PVM Oil Futures Ltd (IPE)
1 Dover Street
London W1X 3PJ
Tel: +44 171 355 4400

Paine Webber International (UK) Ltd (LIFFE, LCE, IPE, LME)
1 Finsbury Avenue
London EC2M 2PA
Tel: +44 171 377 0055

Paribas Futures Ltd (IPE)
33 Wigmore Street
London W1H 0BN
Tel: +44 171 895 4810

Phiboro Futures Ltd (LCE, IPE, LME)
Victoria Plaza
Buckingham Palace Road
London SW1W 0SB
Tel: +44 171 721 4555

Prudential-Bache (Futures) Ltd (LIFFE, LCE, IPE, LME)
Ground Floor, 9 Devonshire Square
London EC2M 4HP
Tel: +44 171 283 9166

RBL Ltd (LCE)
Glen House
Stag Place
Victoria
London SW1E 5AQ
Tel: +44 171 630 8160

Refco Overseas Ltd (LIFFE, LCE, IPE, LME)
Europe House
World Trade Centre
London E1 9AA
Tel: +44 171 488 3232

Republic National Bank of New York (LIFFE)
30 Monument Street
London EC3R 8NB
Tel: +44 171 860 3000

Robert Fleming & Co Ltd (TPT)
25 Copthall Avenue
London EC2R 7DR
Tel: +44 171 638 5858

NM Rothschild & Sons Ltd (LIFFE, LME)
New Court
St Swithins Lane
London EC4P 4DU
Tel: +44 171 280 5000

Rowntree Mackintosh (Ingredients) Ltd (LCE)
Cocoa Purchasing Department
Wiggington Road
York YO1 1XY
Tel: +44 1904 604604

The Royal Bank of Scotland Plc (LIFFE, TPT)
Treasury and Capital Markets
Waterhouse Square
138–142 Holborn
London EC1N 2TH
Tel: +44 171 427 8000

Rudolf Wolff & Co Ltd (LIFFE, LCE, IPE, LME)
2nd Floor, D Section
Plantation House
31–35 Fenchurch Street
London EC3M 3DX
Tel: +44 171 626 8765

SGH Cocoa Ltd (LCE)
Europe House
World Trade Centre
London E1 9AA
Tel: +44 171 454 9875

The Sakura Bank Ltd (LIFFE)
Ground and 1st Floor
6 Broadgate
London EC2M 2RQ
Tel: +44 171 638 3131

Salomon Brothers International Ltd (LIFFE, TPT)
Derivatives Department
Victoria Plaza
111 Buckingham Palace Road
London SW1W 0SB
Tel: +44 171 721 2000

San Paolo Bank SpA (LIFFE)
Wren House
15 Carter Lane
London EC4V 5SP
Tel: +44 171 214 8000

The Sanwa Bank Ltd (LIFFE)
7th Floor, City Place House
55 Basinghall Street
London EC2V 5DL
Tel: +44 171 330 5000

Sanwa Futures LLC (LIFFE)
8th Floor, City Place House
55 Basinghall Street
London EC2V 5DU
Tel: +44 171 330 0300

Sanwa International Ltd (LIFFE)
City Place House
55 Basinghall Street
London EC2V 5DJ
Tel: +44 171 330 0300

Saratoga Ltd (LIFFE, IPE)
65–66 Queen Street
London EC4R 1EB
Tel: +44 171 329 0339

Saudi International Bank (LIFFE)
1 Knightsbridge
London SW1X 7XS
Tel: +44 171 259 3456

Shell International Trading & Shipping Co Ltd (IPE)
Shell Centre
York Road
London SE1 7NA
Tel: +44 171 934 1234

Skandinaviska Enskilda Banken (LIFFE, LCE, IPE)
Scandinavian House
2–6 Cannon Street
London EC4M 6XX
Tel: +44 171 236 6090

Smith Barney Europe Ltd (LIFFE, IPE)
10 Piccadilly
London W1V 9LA
Tel: +44 171 548 5555

Sogemin Metals Ltd (LME)
4th Floor, 98 Cannon Street
London EC4N 6EN
Tel: +44 171 410 4950

Spectron Futures Ltd (IPE)
Liscartan House
127 Sloane Street
London SW1X 9BA
Tel: +44 171 823 6600

Standard Bank London Ltd (LME)
Cannon Bridge House
25 Dowgate Hill
London EC4R 2SB
Tel: +44 171 815 3000
Standard Chartered Bank (LIFFE, IPE, LME)
22 Billiter Street
London EC3A 2BE
Tel: +44 171 280 7500

Sucden (UK) Ltd (LIFFE, LCE, IPE, LME)
5 London Bridge Street
London SE1 9SG
Tel: +44 171 940 9400
Sumitomo Finance International Plc (LIFFE)
Temple Court
11 Queen Victoria Street
London EC4N 4UQ
Tel: +44 171 842 3000

Sumitomo Trust International Plc (LIFFE)
155 Bishopsgate
London EC2M 3TS
Tel: +44 171 315 8000

Svenska Hendelsbanken (LIFFE)
Svenska House
3–5 Newgate Street
London EC1A 7DA
Tel: +44 171 329 4467

Swiss Bank Corporation (LIFFE, TPT)
Swiss Bank House
1 High Timber Street
London EC4V 3SB
Tel: +44 171 329 0329

Swiss Finance Corporation Ltd (IPE)
33 Cavendish Square
London W1N 9HF
Tel: +44 171 499 2840

Tardivat Futures Ltd (LCE)
Suite 6, Free Trade Wharf
350 The Highway
London E1 9DH
Tel: +44 171 265 8155

Tate & Lyle International (LCE)
(Division of Tate and Lyle Industries Ltd)
Dexter House
2 Royal Mint Court
London EC2N 4PE
Tel: +44 171 626 6525

Theobroma NV (LCE)
PO Box 12200
1100 AE Amsterdam
The Netherlands
Tel: +31 20 567 5911

The Tokai Bank Ltd (LIFFE)
1 Exchange Square
London EC2A 2EH
Tel: +44 171 496 8000

Tokai Bank Europe Plc (LIFFE)
107 Cheapside
London EC2V 6BR
Tel: +44 171 638 6030

Toyota Tsusho UK Ltd (LME)
6th Floor, UK House
180 Oxford Street
London W1N 0DT
Tel: +44 171 436 5680

Toyo Trust International Ltd (LIFFE)
36 Queen Street
London EC4R 1BN
Tel: +44 171 236 5272

Transoptions Finance SA (LIFFE)
1 College Hill
London EC4R 2AR
Tel: +44 171 329 1580

Triland Metals Ltd (LME, IPE)
Bow Bells House
Bread Street
London EC4M 9BQ
Tel: +44 171 248 0126

TRX Futures Ltd (LIFFE, LCE)
5th Floor, Michael House
35 Chiswell Street
London EC1Y 4SE
Tel: +44 171 628 9311

Tullett & Tokto (Futures & Traded Options) Ltd (LIFFE)
Cable House
54–62 New Broad Street
London EC2M 1JJ
Tel: +44 171 895 9595

UBS Futures & Options Ltd (LIFFE, LCE, LME, TPT)
100 Liverpool Street
London EC2M 2RH
Tel: +44 171 901 3333

Unidaf Trading Co Ltd (LCE)
3rd Floor, 6–7 St Mary at Hill
London EC3R 8EE
Tel: +44 171 623 1991

Union Cal Ltd (LIFFE)
162 Queen Victoria Street
London EC4V 4DB
Tel: +44 171 329 3333

Wako International (Europe) Ltd (LIFFE)
155 Bishopsgate
London EC2M 3YX
Tel: +44 171 374 6055

SG Warburg Futures & Options Ltd (LIFFE)
1st Floor, Finsbury Avenue
London EC2M 2PP
Tel: +44 171 606 1066

Warenhandelsgesellschaft 'Corinth' mbH (LCE)
Haus der Seefahrt
Hohe Brücke 1
20459 Hamburg
Germany
Tel: +49 40 370 9090

Westdeutsche Landesbank Girozentrale (LIFFE)
51 Moorgate
London EC2R 6AE
Tel: +44 171 638 6141

Westpac Banking Corporation (LIFFE)
Westpac House
75 King William Street
London EC4N 7HA
Tel: +44 171 621 7000

Yamiaichi International (Europe) Ltd (LIFFE)
Finsbury Court
111–117 Finsbury Pavement
London EC2A 1EQ
Tel: +44 171 330 8000

Yasuda Trust Europe Ltd (LIFFE)
1 Liverpool Street
London EC2M 7NH
Tel: +44 171 256 6188

London Commodity Exchange

LCE merged with LIFFE in September 1996; see note on p.311 for details.

Authorized Floor Members

AMT (Futures) Ltd
55 Bishopsgate
London
EC2N 3AH
Tel: +44 171 6264521
Fax: +44 171 2832441
(Sugar)

Brody White (UK) Ltd
Devonshire House
146 Bishopsgate
London
EC2M 4JX
Tel: +44 171 3778050
Fax: +44 171 2476470
(Cocoa; Coffee; OPT)

Credit Agricole Futures, SNC
2nd Floor
162 Queen Victoria Street
London
EC4B 4DB
Tel: +44 171 3293232
Fax: +44 171 3296329
(Cocoa; Coffee; OPT; Sugar)

Cannon Bridge Corp Ltd
Exchange House
Primrose Street
Broadgate
London
EC2A 2EH
Tel: +44 171 6286018
Fax: +44 171 6285060
(OPT)

Cargill Investor Services Ltd
Cannon Bridge, Level 2
25 Dowgate Hill
London
EC4R 2SL
Tel: +44 171 2835272
Fax: +44 171 9294885
(Biffex; Cocoa; Coffee; Grain; OPT; Potatoes; Sugar)

Credit Lyonnais Rouse Ltd
Broadwalk House
6 Appold Street
London
EC2A 2DA
Tel: +44 171 3746100
Fax: +44 171 6380369
(Cocoa; Coffee; OPT; Sugar)

DBMG Futures & Options Ltd
23 Great Winchester Street
London
EC2P 2AX
Tel: +44 171 5884545
Fax: +44 171 8266155
(Cocoa; Coffee; Sugar)

Dean Witter International Ltd
1 Appold Street
6th Floor
Broadgate 5
London
EC2A 2AA
Tel: +44 171 2948500
Fax: +44 171 9561247
(Cocoa)

E D & F Man International Ltd
Sugar Quay
Lower Thames Street
London
EC3R 6DU
Tel: +44 171 2853000
Fax: +44 171 6233203
(Biffex; Cocoa; Coffee; Grain; OPT; Potatoes; Sugar)

Fimat Futures UK Ltd
Exchange House
Primrose Street
Broadgate
London
EC2A 2EH
Tel: +44 171 6286018
Fax: +44 171 6285060
(Sugar)

GNI Wallace Ltd
4th Floor
Atrium Building, Cannon Bridge
25 Dowgate Hill
London
EC4R 2GN
Tel: +44 171 3373500
Fax: +44 171 3373501
(Cocoa; OPT)

GNI Ltd
4th Floor
Atrium Building, Cannon Bridge
Dowgate Hill
London
EC4R 2GN
Tel: +44 171 3373500
Fax: +44 171 3373501
(Biffex; Cocoa; Coffee; Grain; OPT; Potatoes; Sugar)

Goulandris Bros Ltd
34a Queen Anne's Gate
London
SW1H 9AB
Tel: +44 171 2225244
Fax: +44 171 2226817
(Biffex)

Goldman Sachs International
Peterborough Court
133 Fleet Street
London
EC4A 2BB
Tel: +44 171 7745173
Fax: +44 171 7741313
(Cocoa; Coffee; OPT; Sugar)

ING Derivatives (London) Ltd
75 King William Street
London
EC4N 7EE
Tel: +44 171 4109944
Fax: +44 171 2834321
(Cocoa; Coffee; OPT; Sugar)

J Aron & Co (UK)
Peterborough Court
133 Fleet Street
London
EC4A 2BB
Tel: +44 171 7742501
Fax: +44 171 7742500
(Cocoa; Coffee; OPT; Sugar)

MHF Futures Ltd
4 Ivory House
St Katharine by The Tower
London
E1 9AT
Tel: +44 171 7029443
Fax: +44 171 7029455
(Cocoa; Coffee)

Merrill Lynch Pierce Fenner & Smith
(Brokers & Dealers) Ltd
Ropemaker Place
25 Ropemaker Street
London
EC2Y 9LY
Tel: +44 171 6281000
Fax: +44 171 8672867
(Biffex; Cocoa; Coffee; OPT; Sugar)

MeesPierson Derivatives Ltd
Camomile Court
23 Camomile Street
London
EC3A 7PP
Tel: +44 171 4448100
Fax: +44 171 4448973
(Biffex; Cocoa; Coffee; Grain; OPT;
Potatoes; Sugar)

MeesPierson ICS Ltd
Camomile Court
23 Comomile Street
London
EC3A 7PP
Tel: +44 171 4448800
Fax: +44 171 4448888
(Biffex; Cocoa; Coffee; Grain; OPT;
Potatoes; Sugar)

Morgan Stanley & Co International Ltd
25 Cabot Square
Canary Wharf
London
E14 4QA
Tel: +44 171 4258000
Fax: +44 171 4258990
(Cocoa; Coffee; OPT; Sugar)

Reynolds Futures
Watts Hill
Westerham Road
Limpsfield
Surrey
RH8 0SW
Tel: +44 171 7020805
Fax: +44 171 7020803
(Cocoa; Coffee; OPT)

Orebi Futures Ltd
106 Sparrows Herne
Basildon
Essex
SS16 5EU
Tel: +44 171 4812199
Fax: +44 171 7024323
(Cocoa; Coffee; OPT)

Phibro Futures Ltd
Victoria Plaza
111 Buckingham Palace Road
London
SW1W 0SR
Tel: +44 171 7214555
Fax: +44 171 6300501
(Cocoa; OPT)

Phillip Alexander Securities & Futures Ltd
Veritas House
125 Finsbury Pavement
London
EC2A 1PA
Tel: +44 171 4179700
Fax: +44 171 4179707
(Cocoa; Coffee; Grain)

Prudential-Bache (Futures) Ltd
Ground Floor
9 Devonshire Square
London
EC2M 4HP
Tel: +44 171 2839166
Fax: +44 171 6266785
(Biffex; Cocoa; Coffee; Grain; OPT;
Sugar)

RBL Ltd
Commodity Futures Brokerage
Glen House
Stag Place
London
SW1E 5AQ
Tel: +44 171 6308160
Fax: +44 171 6308083
(Cocoa; Coffee; OPT)

Refco Overseas Ltd
5th Floor
Europe House
East Smithfield
London
E1 9AA
Tel: +44 171 4883232
Fax: +44 171 2853959
(Biffex; Cocoa; Coffee; Grain; OPT; Potatoes; Sugar)

Rudolf Wolff & Co Ltd
D Section
Plantation House
31–35 Fenchurch Street
London
EC3M 3DX
Tel: +44 171 6268765
Fax: +44 171 6263939
(Biffex; Cocoa; Coffee; OPT; Sugar)

Sucden (UK) Ltd
5 London Bridge Street
London
SE1 9SG
Tel: +44 171 9409400
Fax: +44 171 9409500
(Cocoa; Coffee; OPT; Sugar)

SFH Cocoa Ltd
Europe House
4th Floor
World Trade Centre
London
E1 9AA
Tel: +44 171 4549875
Fax: +44 171 4818160
(Cocoa; OPT)

TRX Futures Ltd
Michael House
Fifth Floor
35 Chiswell Street
London
EC1Y 4SE
Tel: +44 171 8806000
Fax: +44 171 8806050
(Cocoa; Coffee; OPT)

Tardival Futures Ltd
Suite No 6
Free Trade Wharf
350 The Highway
London
E1 9HU
Tel: +44 171 2658155
Fax: +44 171 2658042
(Cocoa; Coffee; OPT)

UBS Futures & Options Ltd
100 Liverpool Street
London
EC2M 2RH
Tel: +44 171 9011292
Fax: +44 171 9011500
(Coffee)

Unidaf Trading Co Ltd
6 St Mary at Hill
London
EC3R 8EE
Tel: +44 171 6231991
Fax: +44 171 2832593
(Cocoa; Coffee; OPT)

Exchange Associate Members

B D F Commodities Ltd
22 South Street
Rochford
Essex
SS4 1BJ
Tel: +44 1702 543456
Fax: +44 1702 543457
(Potatoes)

Berkeley Futures Ltd
38 Dover Street
London
W1X 3RB
Tel: +44 171 6291133
Fax: +44 171 4950022
(Potatoes)

Bear Stearns International Ltd
1 Canada Square
London
E14 5AD
Tel: +44 171 5166000
Fax: +44 171 5166030
(Coffee)

C Czarnikow Sugar Futures Ltd
24 Chiswell Street
London
EC1Y 4SG
Tel: +44 171 9726600
Fax: +44 171 9726699
(Sugar)

Dean Witter International Ltd
1 Appold Street
6th Floor
Broadgate 5
London
EC2A 2AA
Tel: +44 171 2948500
Fax: +44 171 9561247
(Biffex; Coffee; Sugar)

Gerald Ltd
Europe House
World Trade Centre
St Katharine By The Tower
London
E1 9AA
Tel: +44 171 8679400
Fax: +44 171 8679402
(Biffex; Cocoa; Coffee; Sugar)

Lehman Brothers Inc
3rd Floor
1 Broadgate
London
EC2M 7HA
Tel: +44 171 6010011
Fax: +44 171 2602933
(Sugar)

Merrill Lynch Pierce Fenner & Smith (Brokers & Dealers) Ltd
Ropemaker Place
25 Ropemaker Street
London
EC2Y 9LY
Tel: +44 171 6281000
Fax: +44 171 8672867
(Grain)

Mitsubishi Corporation (UK) Plc
Bow Bells House
Bread Street
Cheapside
London
EC4M 9BQ
Tel: +44 171 8220022
Fax: +44 171 2362415
(Cocoa; Coffee; Sugar)

Muirpace Ltd
6 Lloyds Avenue
London
EC3N 3NX
Tel: +44 171 7029776
Fax: +44 171 4806115
(Grain)

PaineWebber International (UK) Ltd
1 Finsbury Avenue
London
EC2M 2PA
Tel: +44 171 4222000
Fax: +44 171 2478923
(Cocoa; Coffee; Sugar)

Phibro Futures Ltd
Victoria Plaza
111 Buckingham Palace Road
London
SW1W 0SR
Tel: +44 171 7214555
Fax: +44 171 6300501
(Coffee)

Phillip Alexander Securities & Futures Ltd
Veritas House
125 Finsbury Pavement
London
EC2A 1PA
Tel: +44 171 4179700
Fax: +44 171 4179707
(Potatoes; Sugar)

Prudential-Bache (Futures) Ltd
Ground Floor
9 Devonshire Square
London
EC2M 4HP
Tel: +44 171 2839166
Fax: +44 171 6266785
(Potatoes)

Standard Chartered Bank
The Mocatta Group
Mocatta House
4 Crosby Square
London
EC3A 6AQ
Tel: +44 171 6385789
Fax: +44 171 2568200
(Cocoa; Coffee; Sugar)

Tomen (UK) Plc
13 Charles II Street
London
SW1Y 4QT
Tel: +44 171 3216643
Fax: +44 171 3216640
(Sugar)

London Metal Exchange

Ring Dealing Members

Amalgamated Metal Trading Ltd
55 Bishopsgate
London EC2N 3AH
Tel: +44 171 626 4521
Fax: +44 171 623 3982

Barclays Metals Ltd
6th Floor, 2 Minster Court
Mincing Lane
London EC3R 7BB
Tel: +44 171 283 6362
Fax: +44 171 621 5290

Billiton Metals Ltd
84 Fenchurch Street
London EC3M 4BY
Tel: +44 171 860 8250
Fax: +44 171 488 1986

Brandels (Brokers) Ltd
Salters' Hall
4 Fore Street
London EC2P 2NU
Tel: +44 171 638 5877
Fax: +44 171 638 3031

Brody White (UK) Ltd
Devonshire House
146 Bishopsgate
London EC2M 4JX
Tel: +44 171 377 8050
Fax: +44 171 247 6470

Credit Lyonnais Rouse Limited
Broadwalk House
5 Appold Street
London EC2A 2DA
Tel: +44 171 374 6100
Fax: +44 171 638 0886

Deutsche Sharps Pixley Metals Ltd
6–8 Bishopsgate
London EC2P 2AT
Tel: +44 171 971 7000
Fax: +44 171 971 7183

Gerald Ltd
Europe House
World Trade Centre
St Katharine by The Tower
London E1 9AA
Tel: +44 171 867 9400
Fax: +44 171 867 9402

Lehman Brothers Commodities Ltd
One Broadgate
London EC2M 7HA
Tel: +44 171 601 0011
Fax: +44 171 260 2999

Metallgesellschaft Ltd
One America Square
17 Crosswall
London EC3N 2LB
Tel: +44 171 488 2244
Fax: +44 171 702 9650

Metdist Trading Ltd
80 Cannon Street
London EC4N 6EJ
Tel: +44 171 606 0463
Fax: +44 171 606 6650

Refco Overseas Ltd
Europe House
World Trade Centre
London E1 9AA
Tel: +44 171 488 3232
Fax: +44 171 265 3959

Rudolf Wolff & Co Ltd
D Section, 2nd Floor
Plantation House
31–35 Fenchurch Street
London EC3M 3DX
Tel: +44 171 626 8765
Fax: +44 171 626 3939

Sogemin Metals Ltd
4th Floor
98 Cannon Street
London EC4N 6EN
Tel: +44 171 410 4950
Fax: +44 171 283 6788

Standard Chartered Bank
Mocatta House
4 Crosby Square
London EC3A 6AQ
Tel: +44 171 638 3636
Fax: +44 171 256 7750

Sucden (UK) Ltd
5 London Bridge Street
London SE1 9SG
Tel: +44 171 940 9400
Fax: +44 171 940 9500

Triland Metals Ltd
Bow Bells House
Bread Street
London EC4M 9BQ
Tel: +44 171 236 5551
Fax: +44 171 489 1104

Associate Broker Members

Charles Davis (Metal Brokers) Ltd
One America Square
17 Crosswall
London EC3N 2LB
Tel: +44 171 702 9735
Fax: +44 171 702 9650

Dean Witter Reynolds Inc
2 World Trade Center
62nd Floor, New York
NY 10048, USA
Tel: +1 212 392 2222
Fax: +1 212 392 4727

J Aron & Co (UK)
Peterborough Court
133 Fleet Street
London EC4A 2BB
Tel: +44 171 774 1000
Fax: +44 171 774 2020

Engelhard International Ltd
Engelhard House
8 Throgmorton Avenue
London EC2N 2DL
Tel: +44 171 588 4080
Fax: +44 171 628 5527

Lehman Brothers Inc
One Broadgate
London EC2M 7HA
Tel: +44 171 601 0011
Fax: +44 171 260 2999

MetChim Ltd
80 Cannon Street
London EC4N 6EJ
Tel: +44 171 606 0463
Fax: +44 171 606 6650

Smith Barney Europe Ltd
10 Piccadilly
London W1V 9LA
Tel: +44 171 548 5555
Fax: +44 171 548 5637

Associate Broker Clearing Members

AIG International Ltd
120 Leman Street
London E1 8EU
Tel: +44 171 709 2500
Fax: +44 171 709 2990

Bankers Trust International Plc
1 Appold Street
Broadgate
London EC2A 2HE
Tel: +44 171 982 2500
Fax: +44 171 982 2279

Cargill Investor Services Ltd
Cannon Bridge, Level 2
25 Dowgate Hill
London EC4R 2SL
Tel: +44 171 283 5272
Fax: +44 171 929 4885

Chase Investment Bank Ltd
Woolgate House
Coleman Street
London EC2P 2HD
Tel: +44 171 962 5213
Fax: +44 171 962 3019

Dean Witter International Ltd
1 Appold Street
6th Floor, Broadgate 5
London EC2A 2AA
Tel: +44 171 294 8500
Fax: +44 171 956 1247

ED & F Man International Ltd
Sugar Quay
Lower Thames Street
London EC3R 6DU
Tel: +44 171 285 3000
Fax: +44 171 621 0149

GNI Ltd
4th Floor, Atrium Bldg
Cannon Bridge, 25 Dowgate Hill
London EC4R 2GN
Tel: +44 171 337 3500
Fax: +44 171 337 3501

Goldman Sachs International
Peterborough Street
133 Fleet Street
London EC4A 2BB
Tel: +44 171 774 1000
Fax: +44 171 774 2020

ING Derivatives (London) Ltd
75 King William Street
London EC4N 7EE
Tel: +44 171 410 9944
Fax: +44 171 283 4321

Macquarie Securities (UK) Ltd
9th Floor, Alban Gate
125 London Wall
London EC2Y 5AS
Tel: +44 171 776 7060
Fax: +44 171 776 7061

MeesPierson ICS Ltd
Camomile Court
23 Camomile Street
London EC3A 7PP
Tel: +44 171 444 8000
Fax: +44 171 444 8888

Merrill Lynch Pierce Fenner & Smith
(Brokers & Dealers) Ltd
Ropemaker Place
25 Ropemaker Street
London EC2Y 9LY
Tel: +44 171 628 1000
Fax: +44 171 867 2867

Mitsui Bussan Commodities Ltd
20 Old Bailey
London EC4M 7QQ
Tel: +44 171 248 6133
Fax: +44 171 236 0435

JP Morgan Securities Ltd
POB 161
60 Victoria Embankment
London EC4Y 0JP
Tel: +44 171 600 2300
Fax: +44 171 325 8267

Morgan Stanley & Co Int Ltd
25 Cabot Square
Canary Wharf
London E14 4QA
Tel: +44 171 513 8000
Fax: +44 171 513 8990

NM Rothschild & Sons Ltd
New Court
St Swithin's Lane
London EC4P 4DU
Tel: +44 171 280 5000
Fax: +44 171 280 5139

PaineWebber Int (UK) Ltd
1 Finsbury Avenue
London EC2M 2PA
Tel: +44 171 377 0055
Fax: +44 171 247 6039

Phibro Futures Ltd
Victoria Plaza
111 Buckingham Palace Road
London SW1W 0SR
Tel: +44 171 721 4555
Fax: +44 171 488 3116

Prudential-Bache (Futures) Ltd
9 Devonshire Square
London EC2M 4HP
Tel: +44 171 283 9166
Fax: +44 171 548 4433

Standard Bank London Ltd
Cannon Bridge House
25 Dowgate Hill
London EC4R 2SB
Tel: +44 171 815 3000
Fax: +44 171 815 3099

UBS Futures & Options Ltd
100 Liverpool Street
London EC2M 2RH
Tel: +44 171 901 3333
Fax: +44 171 901 2345

Tea Brokers' Association of London

Members

Thompson, Lloyd & Ewart
Sir John Lyon House
5 High Timber Street
London EC4V 3LA
Tel: +44 171 236 3368
Fax: +44 171 248 3011

Wilson Smithett & Co
Sir John Lyon House
Upper Thames Street
London EC4V 3LS
Tel: +44 171 236 0611
Fax: +44 171 236 4976

United States of America

Mid America Commodity Exchange

Clearing Firms and Contacts

Cunningham Commodities, Inc
141 W Jackson – Ste #211A
Chicago, IL 60604
Tel: + 1312 9398958
Contact: Robert Westlund

Dorman Trading, LLC
141 W. Jackson – #2070
Chicago, IL 60604
Tel: + 1312 347070
(On and off the floor)
Contact: Robert Sheeren

Eagle Market Makers, Inc
141 W Jackson – #1531A
Chicago, IL 60604
Tel: + 1312 3418834
(On and off the floor)
Contact: Glen Levitas

E M Combs & Sons
141 W Jackson – Ste #3382
Chicago, IL 60604
Tel: +1312 9223900
(On the floor)
Contact: Earle Combs

First Options of Chicago, Inc/Lit
141 W Jackson – Ste #1320A
Chicago, IL 60604
Tel: +1312 4352127
(On the floor)
Contact: Bob Brennan

First Options of Chicago, Inc
141 W Jackson – Ste #1320A
Chicago, IL 60604
Tel: +1312 4354779
(On the floor)
Contact: Dawn Anderson

LFG, LLC
141 W Jackson – Ste #1260
Chicago, IL 60604
Tel: + 1312 4416025
(On and off the floor)
Contact: Charles Rondoni

Rosenthal Collins Group
216 W Jackson – Ste #200
Chicago, IL 60604
Tel: +1312 9845900
(On the floor)
Contact: George Recchia

Shatkin, Arbor, Karlov & Co
141 W Jackson – Ste #388
Chicago, IL 60604
Tel: +1312 3471708
(On and off the floor)
Contact: Jeanne Aleksiewicz

Singer/Wenger Trading Co
141 W Jackson – Ste #2120A
Chicago, IL 60604
Tel: +1312 9136100
(On the floor)
Contact: Sidney Kaz

USA Trading
289 S LaSalle – #300
Chicago, IL 60604
Tel: +1312 4352800
Contact: Bill Levinske

New York Mercantile Exchange

Clearing Members

(C) COMEX Division only
(I) Inactive Clearing Member
(N) NYMEX Division only

ADM Investor Services, Inc (C) (I)

AGE Commodity Clearing Corporation
AIG Clearing Corporation
Basis Clearing, Inc (N)
Bear, Stearns Securities Corp
Brighton Trading Corporation (N)
BUCC Trading Corporation (N)
Cargill Investor Services, Inc
Chase Manhattan Futures Corporation (N) (I)
Chicago Corporation, The
Citicorp Futures Corp
Credit Lyonnais Rouse (USA), Ltd (C)
Dalwa Securities America, Inc (N)
Dean Witter Reynolds, Inc
Deutsche Bank Futures Corp (C)
E D & F Man International Inc
FIMAT Futures USA, Inc
First Chicago Stone, Inc
First Options of Chicago, Inc
Geldermann, Inc
Gerald, Inc
Gerald Metals, Inc
Goldman Sachs & Co
Index Futures Group, Inc
Indosuez Carr Futures, Inc
ING (US) Securities Futures & Options Inc
J P Morgan Futures, Inc
Klein & Co Futures, Inc
Lehman Brothers, Inc
Lind-Waldock & Company
Linnco Futures Group, LLC
Marc Commodities Corporation (N)
MBF Clearing Corporation
Merrill Lynch Futures, Inc
M G London, Inc
Morgan Stanley & Co, Inc
NationsBanc – C R T Services, Inc (C=I)
PaineWebber, Inc
Paribas Futures, Inc (N)
Phibro Energy Clearing Inc
Pioneer Futures, Inc
Prudential Securities Inc
Rama International, Inc (N)
Rand Financial Services Inc
Redel Trading Co, Inc
Refco, Inc
Republic New York Securities Corp
Rosenthal Collins Group
Saul Stone & Co
SHB Commodities, Inc
Singer/Wenger Trading Co Inc
Smith Barney, Inc
Spear, Leeds & Kellogg
Standard Chartered Bank (C)
Sterling Commodities Corp
Term Commodities Inc (N)
Triland USA Inc
Warren Corporation, George E

COMEX Division

Non-Clearing Member Firms

*Option Member Firm

ABS Co
AIG International Inc
Asarco Inc
Atlantic Capital Co*
BT Futures Corp
Barclays Bank Plc
Billiton Stratcor Inc
Birch Brokerage Co of New York, Inc
Bruckmann Trading Group

Capital Management Execution Services
Cargill, Inc
Cerro Sales Corp
Chase Futures Corp
Chase Manhattan Bank, NA, The
Commodities Co U(USA) NV
Cooper, Neff & Associates
Credit Lyonnais Rouse, Ltd
Credit Suisse
Deutsche Bank AG
Dresdner Bank AG
DY DX Trading Corp
Engelhard Corp
GSA Clearing Corp
Glencore Ltd
Growth Management Capital Corp
Great Lakes Trading
H & M Trading Co*
Indosuez Carr Futures, Inc
Interactive Brokers, Inc
J. Aron & Co
J D Trading Corp
J G Trading Corp
KBIG
Kachel, Spiller & Co
Kottke Associates, Inc
Lehman Brothers Commercial Corp
LFG, LLC
MKS Finance S A
MTB Banking Corp
Mintz & Co
Mitsui & Co (USA), Inc
Monarch Brass & Copper Corp
Morgan Guaranty Trusts Co
NYAM Options Trading, Inc*
NationsBank of North Carolina, NA
Oppenheimer & Co, Inc
O'Reilly, Wm J, Inc
Pell Brothers Trading
Phibro Bullion Ltd
Phibro Division of Salomon Inc
Prime International Trading, Ltd
RAD & Co
Republic National Bank of New York
Republic Mase Inc
Richardson Greenshields Sec, Inc
Rudolf Wolff & Co, Inc
Sabin Capital Corp
Sabin Commodities, Inc
Sabin Metal Corp
Silgo Corporation
Societe Generale
Stockton Reinsurance Ltd
Sumitomo Corp, Futures, Inc
Sun Hung Kal Commodities Ltd
Swiss Bank Corp
Tradelink LLC
Trout Trading Fund, Ltd
Union Bank of Switzerland
William J O'Reilly, Inc
ZAHR Trading

NYMEX Division

Non-Clearing Member Firms

ADM Investor Services, Inc
AIG International, Inc
AIG Trading Corp
Amerada Hess Corp
Amoco Corp
Atlantic Capital Co
Atlantic Richfield Co

BP Oil Supply Company

Bankers Trust Company

Barclays Bank Plc

Basis Petroleum Inc

Bear Stearns NY Inc

Britannic Trading Ltd

CATEX Vitol Trading, LLC

Cargill, Inc

Cargill International SA

CENEX, Inc

Chevron, USA Inc

Coastal Holding Corp

Conoco, Inc

Cooper, Neff and Associates, LP

Credit Lyonnais SA

Degussa, AG

Energex, Ltd

Engelhard Corp

Enron Capital & Trade Resources Corp

EOTT Energy Operating Ltd Partnership

ERI Trading Co

First Continental Trading Inc

Glencore Ltd

Global Petroleum Corp

Greenwich Energy Partners

GSA Clearing Corp

Ixomex Ltd

J Aron & Co

Koch Fuels Inc

Kotte Associates, Inc

Lehman Brothers Commercial Corp

Louis Dreyfus Energy Corp

MFX Commodities

MG Refining and Marketing Inc

MIECO Inc

Mitusi & Co (USA), Inc

Mobil Oil Corporation

Mobil Trading, BV

Morgan Guaranty Trust Company of New York

Morgan Stanley Capital Group Inc

NationsBank of North Carolina, NA

Neste Oy

NGC Corp

Northville Industries Corp

Phibro Energy Division of Salomon, Inc

Phillips Petroleum Co

Statoil North America Inc

Sun Company, Inc (R&M)

Swiss Bank Corporation

Texaco Refining & Marketing Inc

Texport Oil Co

Tosco Corporation

Transworld Oil USA Inc

Transworld Oil Ltd

Tricentrol Oil Trading Inc

United Energy Inc

Valero Marketing & Supply Co

Vitol SA

ZAHR Trading

Please contact the membership department (*Tel:* +1 212 7483370) for information on becoming a member firm or clearing member.

Coffee, Sugar & Cocoa Exchange, Inc

Member Firms

AIG Trading Corporation

Amerop Sugar Corporation

Armenia Coffee Corporation

Atlantic (USA) Inc

Atlantic Capital Co

August Topfer & Co GmbH
Barretto Products Inc
C Czarnikow Sugar Inc
C E Bickford & Co Inc
C J Trading Associates
Cacao Barry Merchants Distribution Inc
California & Hawaiian Sugar Co
Cargill Inc
Cocoline Chocolate Co
Comfin Trading Ltd
Copia Trading Co Ltd
Credit Agricole Futures Inc
Czarnikow-Rionda Sugar Trading Inc
DeMarco Commodities Inc
Domino Sugar Corp
E D & F Man International Ltd
E D & F Man Cocoa Inc
E D & F Man Cocoa Canada Ltd
E D & F Man Sugar Inc
E D & F Man (Sugar) Ltd
Essex Trading Group Inc
Finagra USA Inc
General Cocoa Co Inc
Gerald Inc
Gill & Duffus SA
Glencore UK Ltd
Hershey Foods Corp
Hogan & Co Inc
Imperial Sugar Co
Itochu International Inc
J Aron & Co
Jean Lion & Cie
Kerry Foodstuffs Co Ltd
Kerry Trading Co Ltd
Kraft General Foods Inc
Lancom Ltd
Lantic Sugar Ltd
Lombard World Trade Inc
Louis Drefus Corp
M&M/Mars Inc
Marubeni America Corp
Mercon Coffee Corp
Mitsubishi International Corp
Mitsui & Co (USA) Inc
Mitsui & Co Ltd
Morgan Stanley Capital Group Inc
NYAM Options Trading NV Inc
Nabisco Brands Inc
Nestle Beverage Co
Nestle Foods Corp
Nichimen America Inc
Nissho-Iwai American Corp
Okura & Co Ltd
Pepsico Inc
Phibro Inc
Prime International Trading Ltd
Queensland Sugar Corporation
Redpath Industries Ltd
Republic New York Securities Corp
Richardson Greenshields Securities Inc
Rockrimmon Commodities LLC
Rothfos Corp
Savannah Foods & Industries, Inc
South African Sugar Association
Stockton Reinsurance Ltd
Sucden Kerry International
Sucden (UK) Ltd
Sumitomo Corp of America
System Trading Arbitrage & Research Inc (STAR)

Taiyo (USA) Inc

Tate & Lyle Industries Ltd

The Blommer Chocolate Co

Tokyo General USA Inc

Tomen America Inc

Toshoku America Inc

Tristao Trading Inc

Trout Trading Fund Ltd

US Cocoa Corp

Volcafe Ltd

Wilbur Chocolate Co

Zahr Trading

Clearing Members

ADM Investor Services Inc

AGE Commodity Clearing Corp

Alco Commodities Inc

Bear Stearns Securities Corp

C Czarnikow Sugar Futures Inc

Cargil Investor Services Inc

Citicorp Futures Corp

Dean Witter Reynolds Inc

ED&F Man International Futures Inc

Espo Commodities Inc

FIMAT Futures USA Inc

First Options of Chicago Inc

Gelderman Inc

Goldman Sachs & Co

Holco Commodities Inc

ING (US) Securities Futures & Options Inc

Index Futures Group Inc

Klein & Co Futures Inc

LFG, LLC

Lehman Brothers Inc

Lind-Waldock & Co

MA Clearing Inc

MBF Clearing Corp

Melroe Corp

Merrill Lynch Futures Inc

Morgan Stanley & Co Inc

PaineWebber Inc

Phibro Energy Clearing Inc

Pioneer Futures Inc

Prudential Securities Inc

Rand Financial Services Inc

Redal Trading Co Ltd

Refco Inc

Reinhardt & Merz Inc

Rosenthal Collins Group

SHB Commodities Inc

Saul Stone & Co

Singer/Wenger Trading Co

Smith Barney Inc

Spear, Leeds & Kellogg

Sterling Commodities Corp

Term Commodities Inc

The Chicago Corp

Appendices

Appendix 1: Glossary of Commodity Market Terms

Abandon: When an option holder/owner/taker elects not to exercise the option.

Actuals: Physical commodities, also commodies readily available. The commodity itself as opposed to a futures contract.

Afloats: Commodities on board, on route to destination.

Allowances: Discounts/premiums allowed for grades or locations of a commodity below/above those specified in a futures contract.

Arbitrage: Purchase of contract in one market while simultaneously selling the same amount in another to take advantage of price or currency differentials.

At-the-money: An option with an exercise price equal or near to the current underlying futures price.

Backwardation: When the spot or nearby prices are higher than those for future delivery months. Usually caused by delays in shipment thus creating shortages in available supplies.

Basis: The difference between a spot or cash price of a commodity and the futures price of same/related commodity.

Basis grade: The grade of a commodity used as the standard for a contract.

Basis quote: Offer/sale of cash commodity as a difference above or below a futures price.

Bear: Person expecting a decline in prices.

Bear covering: Buying back a speculative short position on a steady or rising market, against an original intention to wait for a market fall.

Bear market: A market in which prices are declining.

Best orders: These are buy or sell orders executed by the broker at what is considered to be the best price.

Beta/beta coefficient: The relationship between the risk of an individual stock or stock portfolio and the risk of the overall market, measures the volatility of said stock/portfolio relative to the overall market.

Bid: An offer to purchase at a specified price.

Board Order or Market if Touched (MIT) order: An order that becomes a market order when a particular price is reached. A sell MIT is placed above the market.

Borrowing: Purchase of a nearby delivery date and simultaneous sale of a forward date. Used mainly on the London Metal Exchange.

Break: A sudden steep price fall.

Broker: Establishes contact between buyer and seller, for a fee. In the US, floor dealing members of futures markets are frequently called brokers.

Brokerage: Fee charged by broker to execute a transaction, either a flat rate or a percentage.

Bull: Person expecting a rise in prices.

Bull market: A market in which prices are rising.

Buy in: To cover, offset or close out a short position.

Buying basis: Difference between cost of a cash commodity and a future sold as a hedge. See *selling basis*.

Buy on close: To buy at the end of a trading session at a price within the closing range.

Buy on opening: To buy at the beginning of a trading session at a price within the opening range.

Call: Period at opening and close of futures market in which price for each contract is established by auction.

Call option: An option that gives the holder the right to enter a long futures position at a specific price, and obligates the seller to enter a short futures position at a specific price, should the option be exercised.

C & F: Cost and freight.

Carrying: General term covering both *borrowing* and *lending*.

Carrying costs: Costs connected with warehouse storage, insurance, etc. Sometimes includes interest and estimated changes in weight.

Carryover: Supply (crop, and/or stocks) of a commodity surplus to that year/season's estimated demand and carried into the subsequent year/season as stocks.

Cash market: Market for the physical commodity.

Cash price: In the US the price of the physical commodity; on the London Metal Exchange the spot price.

Certificate of deposit: Private short-term debt issued by banks.

Certified stocks: Supplies rated as deliverable.

Charting/chartist: Use of charts in the technical analysis of futures markets to plot trends of price movements, average prices, volume and open interest.

CIF: Cost, insurance and freight (included in the price).

Clearances: Aggregate shipments of a commodity made by sea on a specified date.

Clearing: Procedure by which clearing house or association becomes buyer to each seller and seller to each buyer of a futures contract, thereby assuring performance on each contract and assuming responsibility for protecting the trading parties from financial loss.

Clearing house: An adjunct to a futures exchange through which transactions executed on the floor are settled using a process of matching purchases and sales. A clearing organization is also charged with the proper conduct of delivery procedures and the adequate financing of the entire operation.

Clearing member: Member of a Clearing house or association. All trades of a non-clearing member must be registered and eventually settled through a clearing member.

Close-out (washout) of a position: An offsetting transaction to liquidate a futures contract before maturity/expiry date, that is the sale of a contract to buy or the purchase of a contract to sell, as opposed to taking or making delivery of the commodity or making financial settlement on a market where cash-settlement is available.

Closing price: The price (or range) that recorded in the final moments of a day's trade.

Commission: The one time fee charged by a broker to a customer when a position is liquidated either by offset or delivery.

Commission house: A company which trades on behalf of clients for a commission. The commission house only handles clients' business and does not trade on its own account.

Commodity boom bonds: Issued by a country's government or central bank to local commodity exporters when prices are booming and denominated in foreign, rather than local, currency. These are force savings in foreign currency to protect the country's economy from the effects of a sudden influx of foreign exchange.

Commodity Futures Trading Commission (CFTC): A US regulatory agency which exercises control over US commodity futures market trading.

Commodity Price Index: Index, or average, of commodity price movements.

Commodity swap: Counterparties exchange cash flows based on a commodity price on at least one side of the transaction.

Contango: A situation where prices are higher in the forward delivery months than in the nearby delivery month. Opposite of *backwardation*. Normally in evidence when supplies are adequate or in surplus. The contango reflects either wholly or in part the costs of holding and financing.

Contract: An agreement to buy or sell a specified amount of a particular commodity. The contract details show the amount and grade of the product and the date on which the contract will mature and become deliverable, if not previously liquidated.

Contract grades: That which is deliverable on a futures contract. Basic contract grade is the one deliverable at par. There may be more than one basic grade.

Contract month(s): The month(s) in which futures contracts may be satisfied by making or accepting a delivery.

Contract unit: Amount of a commodity designated in a given futures contract.

Contract weights: Deliverable weights of contract as shown on warehouse receipts.

Corner: Securing sufficient control of a commodity to manipulate its price. In the extreme situation obtaining contracts requiring delivery of more commodities than are available for delivery.

Correlation coefficient: A statistical measurement between the price of a stock and the overall market. The correlation coefficient is as an R value ranging from zero to no correlation to 1.0 for perfect correlation. Negative correlation is the measurement of a commodity/group of commodity prices counter to the prevailing trend in equity or bond markets.

Cover: The balancing of an open position by buying or selling in the market.

Cross-rate: In foreign exchange, price of one currency in terms of another, in the market of a third country; e.g. London dollar cross-rate may be price of one dollar in terms of French franc on the London market.

Current delivery month: Futures contract month which matures and becomes deliverable during the current month.

Current yield: Annual interest on a bond divided by its current market price.

Day order/trading: Order valid throughout trading hours during day on which it is placed.

Day trading: Establishing and liquidating the same position or positions within one day's trading.

Dealer option: A put or call on a physical commodity not originating on or subject to the rules of an exchange (the obligation for performance rests with the writer of the option).

Deck: Orders held in the hands of a floor broker.

Declaration date: Last date (specified on the contract) on which a buyer has the right to exercise an option. Failure to declare by such date results in automatic expiry.

Default: Failure to perform on a futures contract as required by exchange rules e.g. failure to meet a margin call or to make a delivery).

Deferred delivery/futures: Distant months in which futures trading takes place sometimes called forward months.

Delivery: There are three types of delivery: 'current' – delivery during the present month; 'nearby' – delivery during the nearest active month; 'distant' – delivery in a month further off.

Delivery date: Date on which the commodity must be delivered to fulfil the terms of the contract.

Delivery points: Locations designated by futures exchanges to which the commodity may be physically delivered.

Delivery price: Price fixed by clearing house at which futures deliveries are invoiced. Also price at which a commodities futures contract is settled when deliveries are made.

Deposit: Sum of money required by the broker from his client, usually 10 per cent of the value of the contract, to justify opening of a futures position.

Depository or warehouse receipt: Document issued by a bank, warehouse or other depository indicating ownership of a stored commodity. For some commodities deliverable against futures contracts, transfer of ownership of a this type of receipt may effect contract delivery.

Derivative: A contract whose value is based on an underlying commodity or financial instrument, standardized exchange-traded futures and options as well as OTC options, swaps and other customized instruments.

Differentials: Premiums paid for grades better than basic grade or discounts allowed for grades below basic grade.

Discretionary account: Arrangement by which a holder of an account gives written power of attorney to another party, often his broker, to buy and sell without prior approval of the holder.

Double option: An option which gives the buyer or person taking the option the right either to buy from or sell to the seller of the option or the person who gives it, at the *basis price*.

Easing (or softening): A slow decline in prices.

Econometrics: Use of statistical/mathematical methods to plot the development of a commodity market.

Elasticity: Measurement of the interaction of supply, demand and price. A commodity is elastic in demand when consumption is altered by a change in price.

Equity: Residual value of a futures trading account if liquidated at current prices.

Exercise: To elect to buy or sell taking advantage of the right conferred by an options contract.

Exercise (strike) price: The price at which a buyer of a call option or seller of a put option can purchase or sell a commodity during the term of the option contract.

Expiration date: The last day that an option may be exercised.

Ex-pit transaction: Trades executed for technical purposes in location other than regular exchange trading pit or ring.

Ex-store: The price of a commodity held in warehouse.

Ex-silo, ex-tank: The price of a commodity held at production point (e.g. grain/soyabeans and oil respectively).

FAQ: Fair average quality.

FAS: Free alongside (delivery term/price at point of sale).

FOB: Free on board.

FOT: Free on truck (delivery term/price at point of sale).

Feed ratio: Ratio between cost of feed and value of livestock (e.g. corn/hog ratio), indicators followed by grain and livestock futures markets.

Fill or kill order: Order demanding immediate execution or cancellation.

Financial instruments: Currency, securities and 'basket' indices of these.

First notice day: First day on which notices of intention to deliver actual commodities against futures market positions can be received (varies between commodities and exchanges).

Forward: In the future (e.g. forward futures months).

Forward market: Informal, non-exchange trading of a commodity for delivery at a future date.

Forward purchase or sale: Trades conducted for deferred deliveries.

Forward shipment: Contract covering cash commodities for shipment at later specified date.

Fundamental analysis: Study of underlying factors affecting supply and demand of a commodity.

Futures: A term used to designate all contracts covering the purchase and sale of physical commodities or financial instruments for future delivery on a commodity exchange.

Good Till Cancelled order (GTC): Order which is valid at any time during market hours until executed or cancelled by the client.

Grading certificates: Formal paper setting forth quality of a commodity as determined by inspectors or graders.

Grantor: The maker, issuer or writer of an option contract.

Hardening: When price of a commodity is gradually stabilizing or slowly advancing.

Hedge: The purchase or sale of a futures contract as a temporary substitute for a transaction to be made at a later date. Usually it involves opposite positions in the cash market and the futures market at the same time.

Initial margin: Customers' funds put up as security for a guarantee of contract fulfilment when a futures market position is established.

In-the-money: A situation where the market price of a futures contract is higher than the exercise price of a call, or lower than the exercise price of a put.

Inflation loving note: See *structured note*.

Job lot: Unit of trading smaller than the regular contract unit.

Kerb trading: Unofficial trading when the market has closed. The term 'kerb' dates from the time when dealers continued trading on the kerb outside the exchanges after they had closed.

Last notice day: Final day on which notices of intent to deliver against a futures contract may be issued.

Last trading day: The final day under an exchange's rules during which trading may take place in a particular delivery futures month. Positions which have not been closed by the last trading day must be fulfilled by making or taking delivery of the physical commodities or financial instruments.

Lending: Sale of a nearby delivery date coupled with the simultaneous purchase of a more distant date (LME term).

Life of contract: Period between a contract month commencing quotation and expiring/maturing on a futures market.

Limit order: An order given to a broker by a customer which has restrictions upon its execution. The customer specifies a price and the order can only be executed if the market reaches or betters that price.

Limit price: Largest permitted price fluctuation in a futures contract during a trading session, as fixed by the contract market's rules. Also known as 'maximum price fluctuation'.

Liquid (or deep) market: One in which trading is sufficient to allow buying and selling without undue price disturbance.

Liquidation: Any transaction that offsets or closes out a long or short position. See *buy in*.

Locals: Small, private individual traders on US exchanges, whose activities provide liquidity.

Long: An open purchased futures contract. Buying forward on the market.

Long hedge: The purchase of a futures contract in ancticipation of actual purchases in the cash market.

Long the basis: Buying a spot commodity and hedging with a sale of futures.

Lot: On futures exchanges, the unit of trading.

Maintenance margin: A sum, usually smaller than, but part of, the original margin, which must be maintained on deposit at all times. If a customer's equity in any futures position drops to, or under, the maintenance margin level, the broker must issue a *margin call* for the amount of money required to restore the customer's equity in the account to the original margin level.

Margin: A cash amount of funds that must be deposited with the broker for each futures contract as a guarantee of fulfilment of the contract. Also called *security deposit*.

Margin call: A commodity broker's request to a client for additional funds to secure the original deposits.

Mark to market: The daily adjustment of an account to reflect profits and losses.

Maturity: Period within which a futures contract can be settled by delivery of the actual commodity.

Minimum price fluctuation: Set by the rules of the exchange, this is the minimum unit by which the price of a commodity can fluctuate per trade.

Nearby delivery: The nearest active month of delivery on a futures market.

Net position: Difference between open long contracts and open short contracts held in any one commodity.

Nominal price: Price quotations on futures period in which no actual trading took place.

Notice day: A day on which notices of intent to deliver pertaining to a specified delivery month may be issued.

Notice of delivery: Notification by the clearing house of intention to deliver a commodity.

Offer: Indicates a willingness to sell a futures contract at a given price.

Offset: Liquidation of a long or short position by the opposite transaction: the sale offsets a long position; the purchase offsets a short position.

Open contracts: Contracts which have been bought or sold without the transaction being completed by subsequent sale or purchase, or by making or taking actual delivery of the commodity.

Open interest: Number of open futures contracts – unliquidated purchases or sales.

Open (GTC) order: One that remains in force until customer cancels or until the futures contract expires (GTC, 'good till cancelled').

Open outcry: Trading conducted by calling out *bids* and *offers* across a *ring* or a *pit* and having them accepted.

Opening price (or range): Recorded during the period designated by the exchange as the official opening.

Option: An option is a method of trading a futures market with a predetermined maximum risk. For the payment of a premium, the buyer may purchase the right to buy or sell a commodity or financial instrument at a specified price within a specified time limit, regardless of the price of that commodity at the time.

Original margin: The margin needed to cover a specific new position.

OTC, 'over the counter': Unofficial, non-exchange-traded options, swaps, etc.

Out-of-the-money: A situation where the market price of a futures contract is below the exercise price of a call, or above the exercise price of a put.

Pit: Place where futures are traded on the floor of the commodity exchange. Also known as *ring*.

Point: Minimum price unit in which a commodity price is quoted.

Position trader: Someone who takes long or short position in futures markets in consequence of an opinion that prices are about to advance or decline.

Premium: The excess of one futures contract price over that of another or over the cash market price.

Put option: Gives the buyer (or taker) of the option, in exchange for the premium which he pays, the right to decide at a later date whether or not to sell to the seller (or grantor) at the price (*basis* or striking price) agreed at the tme the premium was paid. The right may be exercised at any point from the purchase of the option up to the *expiration date* (the date on which the option expires).

Pyramiding: Use of profits on existing futures positions as margins to raise the size of the position (normally in successively smaller increments).

Rally: An upward movement of prices following a decline. Also known as a 'recovery'.

Resting order: Order to buy at a price below or sell above the prevailing market held by a floor broker. May be either day orders or open orders.

Ring: Space on trading floor where futures are traded. Also known as the *pit*.

Roll over: Shifting of one month in a straddle into another future month while holding the other contract month. Or lifting a near futures position and re-establishing it in a more deferred delivery month.

Round turn: A completed transaction involving both a purchase and a liquidating sale or a sale followed by a covering purchase.

Scale-down (or up): To purchase or sell on a declining (or advancing) market at regular intervals.

Scalper: One who trades for small gains. This trader normally establishes and liquidates a position quickly, usually within the same day.

Security deposit – initial: A cash amount of funds that must be deposited with the broker for each contract as a guarantee of fulfilment of the futures contract. It is not considered as part payment or purchase.

Sellers' option: Seller's right to select within the contract limits, quality of commodity, time and place of delivery.

Selling basis: Term meaning that the buying basis is increased to include costs and profits.

Short: One who has sold a futures contract to establish a market position and who has not yet closed out this position through an offsetting purchase; the opposite of a *long*.

Short covering: Purchasing to offset a short position.

Short hedge: The sale of a futures contract(s) to eliminate or lessen the possible decline in value of ownership of an approximately equal amount of the actual physical commodity or financial instrument.

Spot: Term denoting immediate delivery for cash as distinct from future delivery.

Spot limit order: Goes into force when a price is traded but can only be filled at the stop limit price or better.

Spot month: The first month in which delivery can take place and for which a quotation is made on the futures market.

Spread: Refers to a simultaneous purchase and sale of futures contracts for the same commodity or instrument for delivery in different months or in different but related markets.

Squeeze: Pressure on a delivery date which results in the price of that date becoming firmer in relation to other dates.

Stop loss order: An order which can be fulfilled only when the price has reached the level specified by the client. As soon as the price has been traded, the order is executed at the next obtainable price. There is no guarantee that the order will be executed at the level specified in the original order.

Straddle: The simultaneous buying and selling of the same commodity on the same market.

Strike price: See *exercise price*.

Structured note: Sometimes called an 'inflation loving note' these are designed like bonds, but mix commodity performers like gold, oil or natural gas with conventional portfolios containing equities or bonds to suit the individual customer's requirements.

Swap: A contract to exchange a flow of periodic payments with a counterparty.

Switch: Offsetting a position in one delivery month and simultaneously initiating a similar position in another delivery month (of the same commodity). When used by hedgers, this corresponds to 'rolling forward'.

Taker: The buyer of an option contract.

Technical analysis: Plotting future market trends by analysing patterns of price change, rates of change and changes in volume of trade and open interest, including charting.

Technical position: When a market is considered 'oversold' or 'overbought' its technical position can be considered technically strong or weak respectively.

Tender: To offer for delivery against futures.

Tenderable grades and staples: These are grades and staples deliverable to settle a futures contract.

Terminal market: Usually synonymous with commodity exchange or futures market, especially in the UK. Also used to signify principals' market as opposed to brokers' market.

Tick: Refers to a change in price, either up or down.

Traded options: Standardized options traded on an exchange.

Trading limit: Maximum and minimum price fluctuation allowed on an exchange contract in any one day. (Limits may sometimes be extended under exceptional circumstances).

Transferable notice: A notice signifying the intention to make actual delivery. This is given by the seller of a futures contract, usually specifying a day about one week hence.

Variation margin: Payment required upon a margin call.

Volume: The number of transactions in a futures contract made during a specified period of time.

Warehouse receipt: A receipt for a commodity given by a licensed or authorized warehouseman and issued as a tender on futures contracts.

Warrant: Certificate of physical deposit, giving title to the commodity, usually in an exchange-approved warehouse.

Wet barrels: Oil trading term signifying delivery of a product rather than the transfer of a tanker receipt.

Writer: The issuer, grantor or maker of an option contract.

Appendix 2: World Time Zones

Standard Times at Noon Greenwich Mean Time

Accra	12.00	Damascus	14.00	Ottawa	07.00
Adelaide	21.30	Darwin	21.30	Panama	07.00
Algiers	13.00	Delhi	17.30	Paris	13.00
Amman	14.00	Djakarta	20.00	Peking	20.00
Amsterdam	13.00	Dublin	12.00	Perth	20.00
Ankara	14.00	Gibraltar	13.00	Prague	13.00
Athens	14.00	Helsinki	14.00	Quebec	07.00
Auckland	24.00	Hobart	22.00	Rangoon	18.30
Baghdad	15.00	Hong Kong	20.00	Rawalpindi	17.00
Bangkok	19.00	Istanbul	14.00	Reykjavik	12.00
Beirut	14.00	Jerusalem	14.00	Rio de Janeiro	09.00
Belgrade	13.00	Karachi	17.00	Rome	13.00
Berlin	13.00	Kuala Lumpur	20.00	San Francisco	04.00
Berne	13.00	Lagos	13.00	Santiago	08.00
Bombay	17.30	Leningrad	15.00	Sofia	14.00
Bonn	13.00	Lima	07.00	Singapore	19.30
Brisbane	22.00	Lisbon	13.00	Stockholm	13.00
Brussels	13.00	Luxemburg	13.00	Sydney	22.00
Bucharest	14.00	Madras	17.30	Tehran	15.30
Budapest	13.00	Madrid	13.00	Tokyo	21.00
Buenos Aires	09.00	Melbourne	22.00	Toronto	07.00
Cairo	14.00	Mexico City	06.00	Tunis	13.00
Calcutta	17.30	Montevideo	08.30	Vancouver	04.00
Canberra	22.00	Moscow	15.00	Vienna	13.00
Cape Town	14.00	Nairobi	15.00	Warsaw	13.00
Caracas	08.00	New York	07.00	Washington	07.00
Chicago	06.00	Nicosia	14.00	Wellington	24.00
Copenhagen	13.00	Oslo	13.00	Winnipeg	06.00

Note to World Time Zones map
The earth turns one complete revolution in 24 hours. The surface of the earth is divided into 24 time zones, each of 15° longitude or 1 hour of time. In 24 hours it turns through 360°. The times shown are the standard times on land and sea when it is 12.00 hours on the Greenwich Meridian.

World Time Zones

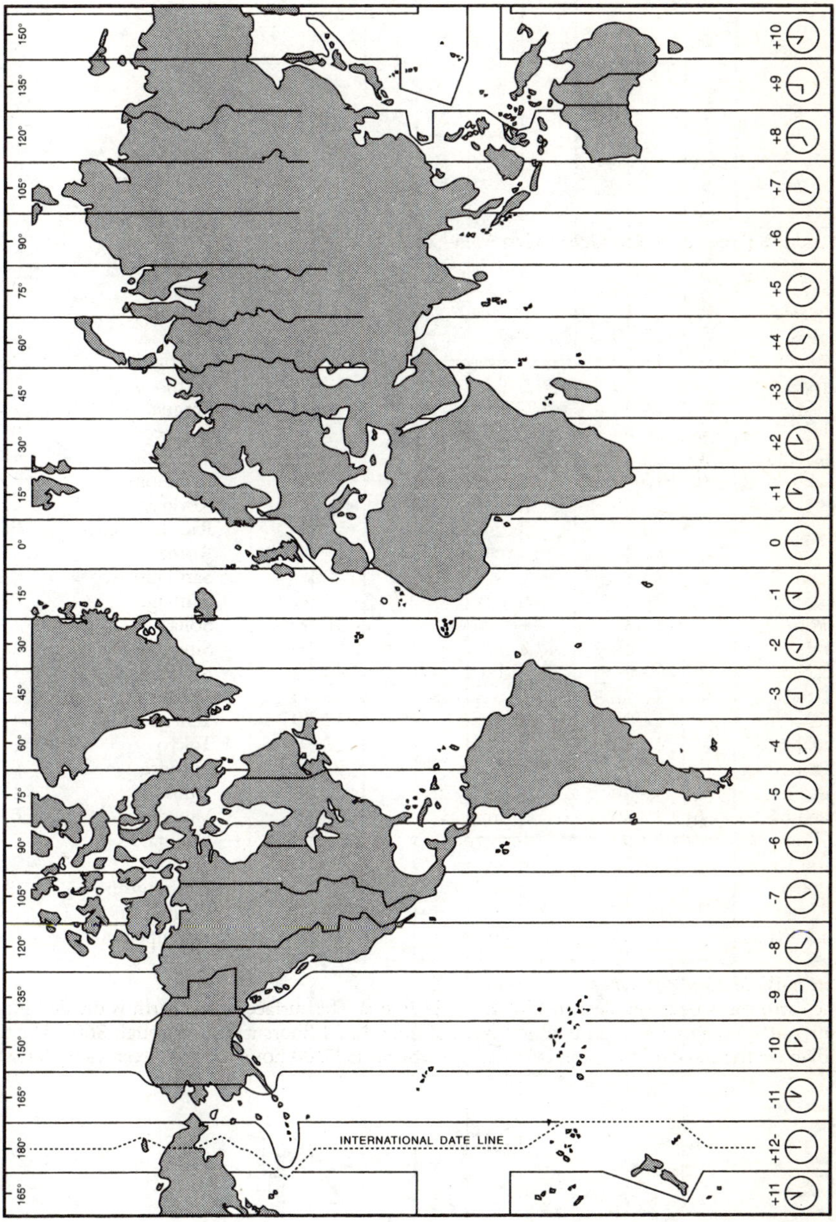

Appendix 3: Conversion Tables

Mass	Long tons	Metric tons	Short tons	Pikuls	Kilograms	Pounds	Ounces troy	Pennyweights	Grains
Long ton		1.016	1.120	16.8	1,016	2,240			
Metric ton	0.984		1.102	16.535	1,000	2,204.5			
Short ton	0.893	0.907		15.00	907	2,000			
Pikul	0.0595	0.0605	0.067		60.48	133.33			
Kilogram	0.00098	0.0001	0.0011	0.0165		2.2045	32.150	642.83	15,431.5
Pound	0.0004	0.0004	0.0005	0.0075	0.4536		14.583	291.6	7,000
Ounce troy					0.03112	0.0686		20.00	480.0
Pennyweight					0.00015				24.00

Area	Hectares	Acres	Square Kilometres	Square Miles	Square Metres	Square Feet
Hectare	—	2.471	0.01	0.004	10,000	—
Acre	0.405	—	0.004	0.0015	4,046.86	—
Square Kilometre	100.0	247.1	—	0.386	—	—
Square Mile	259.0	640.0	2.590	—	—	—
Square Metre	10,000	4,046.86	—	—	—	10,764
Square Foot	—	—	—	—	0.093	—

Volume	Barrels	Imperial Gallons	US Gallons	Kilolitres	Cubic Feet	Cubic Metres
Barrel	—	34.973	42	0.159	5.614	0.1589
Imperial Gallon	0.028	—	1.201	0.004	0.1605	0.0045
US Gallon	0.0238	0.833	—	0.003	0.134	0.0037
Kilolitre	6.289	219.97	264.17	—	—	—
Cubic Foot	0.178	6.2288	7.4805	—	—	0.028
Cubic Metre	6.289	219.97	264.17	—	35.315	—

Appendix 4: US Dollar Exchange Rates

Figure 1 Monthly average exchange rates for US dollar/sterling

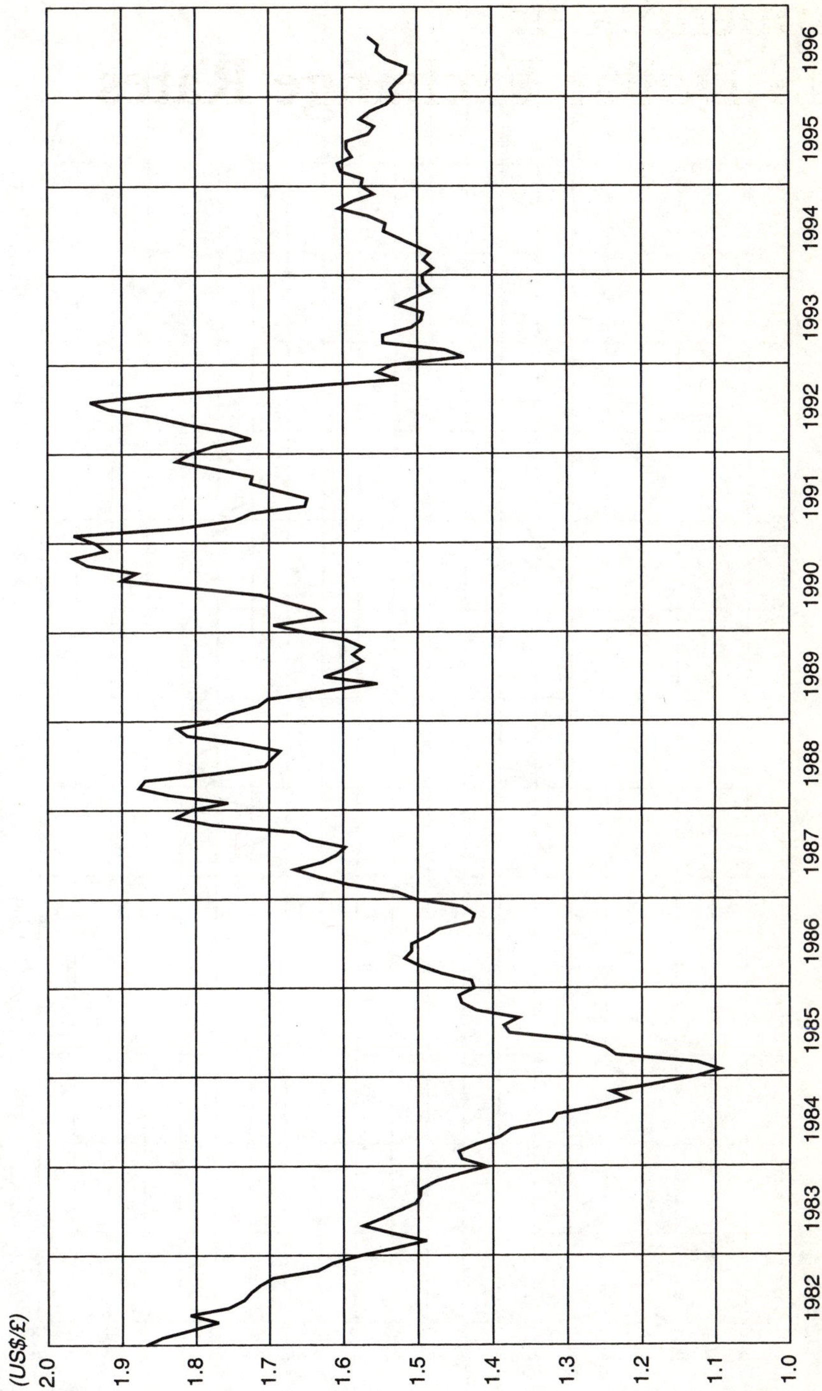

Source: Barclays Bank plc

Figure 2 Monthly average exchange rates for US dollar/yen

(YEN/US$)

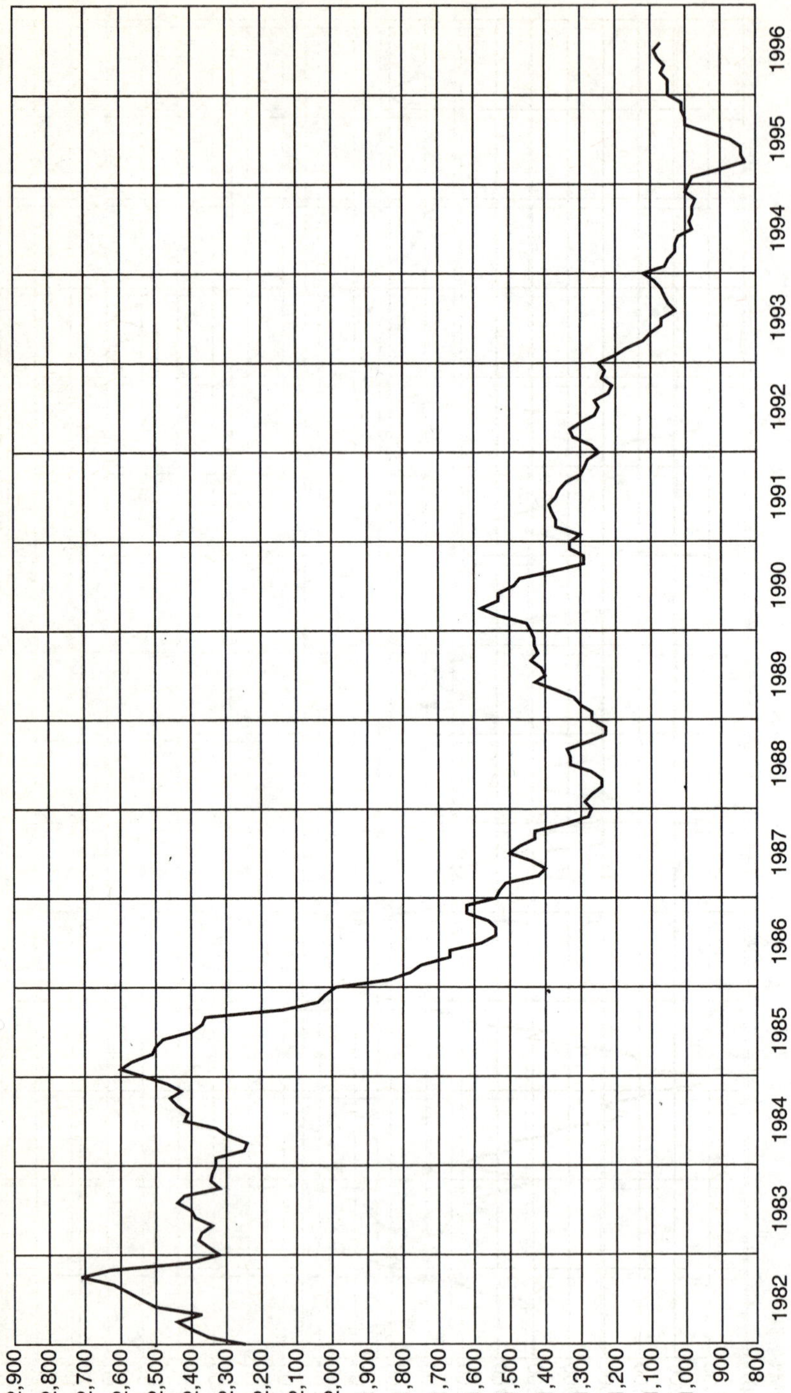

Source: Barclays Bank plc

Figure 3 Monthly average exchange rates for US dollar/deutschmark

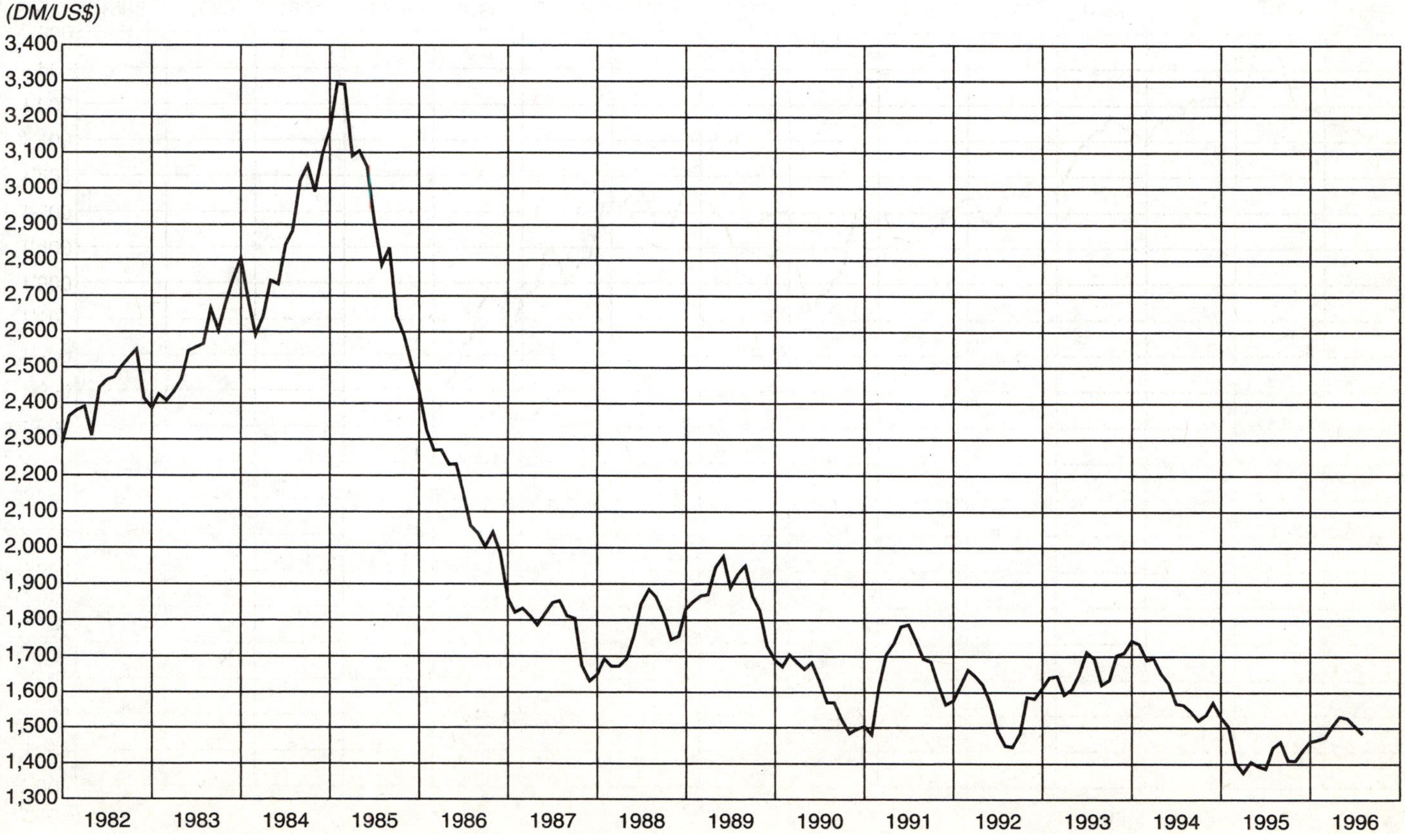

Source: Barclays Bank plc

Index

(Note: Individual commodities from Part 3 are not included.)